C#: A Programmer's Introduction

Introduction

Deitel™ Developer Series

Deitel™ Books, Cyber Classrooms, Complete Tra
published by

DEITEL™ *Developer* Series

C#: A Programmer's Introduction

C# for Experienced Programmers

Java™ Web Services for Experienced Programmers

Visual Basic® .NET for Experienced Programmers

Visual C++® .NET: A Managed Code Approach
   For Experienced Programmers

Web Services: A Technical Introduction

Java 2 Micro Edition for Experienced Programmers (Spring 2003)

Java 2 Enterprise Edition for Experienced Programmers (Spring 2003)

ASP .NET and Web Services with Visual Basic® .NET for Experienced
   Programmers (Fall 2002)

ASP .NET and Web Services with C# for Experienced Programmers
   (Spring 2003)

How to Program Series

Advanced Java™ 2 Platform How to
   Program

C How to Program, 3/E

C++ How to Program, 3/E

C# How to Program

e-Business and e-Commerce How to
   Program

Internet and World Wide Web How to
   Program, 2/E

Java™ How to Program, 4/E

Perl How to Program

Python How to Program

Visual Basic® 6 How to Program

Visual Basic® .NET How to
   Program, 2/E

Wireless Internet & Mobile Business
   How to Program

XML How to Program

.NET How to Program Series

C# How to Program
Visual Basic® .NET How to Program, 2/E

Visual Studio® Series

C# How to Program
Visual Basic® .NET How to Program, 2/E
Getting Started with Microsoft® Visual
   C++™ 6 with an Introduction to
   MFC
Visual Basic® 6 How to Program

For Managers Series

e-Business and e-Commerce for
   Managers

Coming Soon

e-books and e-whitepapers
Premium CourseCompass, WebCT and
   Blackboard Multimedia Cyber
   Classroom versions

Multimedia Cyber Classroom and *Web-Based Training* Series

(For information regarding Deitel™ Web-based training visit **www.ptgtraining.com**)

C++ Multimedia Cyber Classroom, 3/E

C# Multimedia Cyber Classroom

e-Business and e-Commerce Multimedia Cyber Classroom

Internet and World Wide Web Multimedia Cyber Classroom, 2/E

Java™ 2 Multimedia Cyber Classroom, 4/E

Perl Multimedia Cyber Classroom

Python Multimedia Cyber Classroom

Visual Basic® 6 Multimedia Cyber Classroom

Visual Basic® .NET Multimedia Cyber Classroom, 2/E

Wireless Internet & Mobile Business Programming Multimedia Cyber Classroom

XML Multimedia Cyber Classroom

The Complete Training Course Series

The Complete C++ Training Course, 3/E

The Complete C# Training Course

The Complete e-Business and e-Commerce Programming Training Course

The Complete Internet and World Wide Web Programming Training Course, 2/E

The Complete Java™ 2 Training Course, 4/E

The Complete Perl Training Course

The Complete Python Training Course

The Complete Visual Basic® 6 Training Course

The Complete Visual Basic® .NET Training Course, 2/E

The Complete Wireless Internet & Mobile Business Programming Training Course

The Complete XML Programming Training Course

To communicate with the authors, send e-mail to:

deitel@deitel.com

For information on corporate on-site seminars and public seminars offered by Deitel & Associates, Inc. worldwide, visit:

www.deitel.com

For continuing updates on Prentice Hall and Deitel publications visit:

www.deitel.com,
www.prenhall.com/deitel or
www.InformIT.com/deitel

To follow the Deitel publishing program, please register at

www.deitel.com/newsletter/subscribe.html

for the *DEITEL™ BUZZ ONLINE* e-mail newsletter.

C#: A Programmer's Introduction

Deitel™ Developer Series

H. M. Deitel
Deitel & Associates, Inc.

P. J. Deitel
Deitel & Associates, Inc.

J. A. Listfield

T. R. Nieto
Deitel & Associates, Inc.

C. H. Yaeger
Deitel & Associates, Inc.

M. Zlatkina

PRENTICE HALL, Upper Saddle River, New Jersey 07458

Library of Congress Cataloging-in-Publication Data

On file

Acquisitions Editor: *Karen McLean*
Project Manager: *Mike Ruel*
Executive Managing Editor: *Vince O'Brien*
Formatters: *Chirag Thakkar, John Lovell*
Director of Creative Services: *Paul Belfanti*
Art Editor: *Xiaohong Zhu*
Creative Director: *Carole Anson*
Design Technical Support: *John Christiana*
Chapter Opener and Cover Designers: *Dr. Harvey M. Deitel, Laura Treibick and Tamara L. Newnam*
Manufacturing Manager: *Trudy Pisciotti*
Manufacturing Buyer: *Lisa McDowell*
Marketing Manager: *Kate Hargett*
Marketing Assistant: *Corrine Mitchell*

© 2003 Pearson Education, Inc.
Upper Saddle River, New Jersey 07458

Printed in the United States of America

Cover photo: *Golden Gate Bridge* from Diaphor Agency/Index Stock Imagery, Inc.

10 9 8 7 6 5 4 3 2 1

ISBN 0-13-046132-6

Pearson Education Ltd., *London*
Pearson Education Australia Pty. Ltd., *Sydney*
Pearson Education Singapore, Pte. Ltd.
Pearson Education North Asia Ltd., *Hong Kong*
Pearson Education Canada, Inc., *Toronto*
Pearson Educacion de Mexico, S.A. de C.V.
Pearson Education–Japan, *Tokyo*
Pearson Education Malaysia, Pte. Ltd.
Pearson Education, Inc., *Upper Saddle River, New Jersey*

To Mark Taub, Editor-in-Chief of Computer Publications at PH/PTR:

With sincere appreciation for your efforts in creating and sponsoring the Deitel™ Developer Series.
It is a privilege to work with you.
Thank you for believing in us. Thank you for being our friend.

Harvey and Paul Deitel

To Gahiji Marshall:

For being my best friend through the years.

Jeff

In loving memory of Grandma Foster.

Tem R. Nieto

To my Nana:

For all the good times we have had together. Your wonderful spirit has always brought a smile to my face.

Cheryl

To my mother and role model:

Thank you for your unending strength and courage.

Love, Marina

Trademarks

Microsoft® Visual Studio® .NET are either registered trademarks or trademarks of Microsoft Corporation in the United States and/or other countries.

Adobe® Photoshop® Elements are either registered trademarks or trademarks of Adobe Systems Incorporated in the United States and/or other countries.

Java and all Java-based marks are trademarks or registered trademarks of Sun Microsystems, Inc. in the United States and other countries. Prentice Hall is independent of Sun Microsystems, Inc.

Openwave, the Openwave logo, Openwave SDK, Openwave SDK Universal Edition, Openwave SDKWAP Edition are trademarks of Openwave Systems Inc. All rights reserved.

Contents

Illustrations

5   Control Structures: Part 2   111

6   Methods   146

9   Object-Oriented Programming: Inheritance   292

10   Exception Handling   329

Preface

Live in fragments no longer. Only connect.
Edward Morgan Forster

We wove a web in childhood,
A web of sunny air.
Charlotte Brontë

Welcome to C# and the world of Windows, Internet and World-Wide-Web programming with Visual Studio .NET and the .NET platform! This book is the first in the new *Deitel™ Developer Series*, which presents leading-edge computing technologies to software developers and IT professionals.

C# (pronounced "C-sharp") was developed by Microsoft expressly for its .NET platform. C# provides the features that are most important to programmers, such as object-oriented programming, graphics, graphical-user-interface (GUI) components, exception handling, multithreading, multimedia (audio, images, animation and video), file processing, prepackaged data structures, database processing, Internet and World-Wide-Web-based multi-tier application development, networking, Web services and distributed computing. The language is appropriate for implementing Internet- and World-Wide-Web-based applications that integrate seamlessly with Windows-based applications.

The .NET platform offers powerful capabilities for software development and deployment, including language and platform independence. For example, developers writing code in any (or several) of the .NET languages (such as C#, Visual Basic .NET and Visual C++ .NET) can contribute components to the same software product. In addition to providing language independence, .NET extends program portability by enabling .NET applications to reside on, and communicate across, multiple platforms. This facilitates the creation and use of *Web services*, which are applications that expose functionality to clients via the Internet.

The .NET platform enables Web-based applications to be distributed to consumer-electronic devices, such as wireless phones and personal digital assistants (PDAs), as well as to desktop computers. The capabilities that Microsoft has incorporated into the .NET platform increase programmer productivity and decrease development time.

Who Should Read This Book

Deitel & Associates, Inc. has several C# publications, intended for various audiences. We provide information on **www.deitel.com**, here and inside this book's back cover to help you determine which publication is best for you.

Our first C# book, *C# How to Program*, was published as part of our *How to Program Series*, for college and university students. It provides a comprehensive treatment of C# and includes learning aids and extensive ancillary support. *C# How to Program* assumes that the reader has little or no programming experience. Early chapters focus on fundamental programming principles. The book builds on this to create increasingly complex and sophisticated programs that demonstrate how to use C# to create graphical user interfaces, networking applications, multithreaded applications, Web-based applications and more. We encourage professors and professionals to consider the *C# Complete Training Course*. This package includes *C# How to Program* as well as the *C# Multimedia Cyber Classroom*, an interactive multimedia CD-ROM that provides extensive e-Learning features. The *C# Complete Training Course* and *C# Multimedia Cyber Classroom* are discussed in detail later in this Preface.

This book, *C#: A Programmer's Introduction*, is part of the new *Deitel™ Developer Series*, intended for professional software developers—from novices through experienced programmers. *C#: A Programmer's Introduction* is a part of the *A Programmer's Introduction* subseries, which is designed for programmers with little (or no) programming experience. The book begins with C# programming fundamentals. The core of *C#: A Programmer's Introduction* emphasizes achieving program clarity through the proven techniques of *structured programming*, *object-based programming*, *object-oriented programming (OOP)* and *event-driven programming*. The book provides a rigorous introduction to programming principles in general and to C# fundamentals, in particular. It continues with brief introductions to upper-level topics such as ASP .NET, ADO .NET and Web services. Unlike the *How to Program Series* books, the *Deitel™ Developer Series* books do not include the extensive pedagogic features and ancillary support materials required for academic courses.

Our third C# publication, *C# for Experienced Programmers*, is also part of the *Deitel™ Developer Series*. This publication is a part of the *For Experienced Programmers* subseries, designed for the experienced software developer who wants a deep treatment of a new technology with minimal, if any, introductory material. *C# for Experienced Programmers* delves deeply into the more sophisticated topics that are introduced briefly in *C#: A Programmer's Introduction*. There is considerable overlap between these books.

A fourth publication, ASP .NET with C# for Experienced Programmers, is forthcoming. This book was originally titled *Advanced C# for Experienced Programmers*.

Each of our C# books presents many complete, working C# programs and depicts their inputs and outputs in actual screen shots of running programs. This is our signature *LIVE-CODE™ approach*—we present all concepts in the context of complete working programs. Each book's source code is available free for download at **www.deitel.com**.

Please examine both the *Deitel*™ *Developer Series* professional books and the *How to Program Series* textbooks to determine which best suits your needs. *C#: A Programmer's Introduction* and *C# for Experienced Programmers* are both derived from *C# How to Program*. Depending on your particular needs, you should purchase either one or both of these *Deitel*™ *Developer Series* books, or *C# How to Program*.

The C# books in the *Deitel*™ *Developer Series* were written after the first edition of *C# How to Program*. We added to each of these *Deitel*™ *Developer Series* books a chapter on the new Microsoft Mobile Internet Toolkit for our readers who wish to develop wireless Internet applications for cell phones, pagers and PDAs. This material will be added to the second edition of *C# How to Program*.

For a detailed listing of Deitel™ products and services, please see the "advertorial" pages at the back of this book and visit **www.deitel.com**. Readers may also want to register for our new *Deitel*™ *Buzz Online* e-mail newsletter (**www.deitel.net/news-letter/subscribe.html**), which provides information about our publications, company announcements, links to informative technical articles, programming tips, teaching tips, challenges and anecdotes.

As you proceed, if you would like to communicate with us, please send an e-mail to **deitel@deitel.com**—we always respond promptly. Please check our Web sites, **www.deitel.com**, **www.prenhall.com/deitel** and **www.InformIT.com/deitel** for frequent updates, errata, FAQs, etc. When sending an e-mail, please include the book's title and edition number. We sincerely hope that you enjoy learning C# with our publications.

Features of *C#: A Programmer's Introduction*

This edition contains many features, including:

- *Syntax Highlighting.* This book uses five-way syntax highlighting to emphasize C# programming elements in a manner similar to that of Visual Studio .NET. Our syntax-highlighting conventions are as follows:

```
comments
keywords
literal values
errors and ASP .NET directives
text, class, method and variable names
```

- *"Code Washing."* This is our term for the process we use to format the book's programs so that they have a carefully commented, open layout. The code is grouped into small, well-documented pieces. This greatly improves code readability—an especially important goal for us, considering that this book contains approximately 11,550 lines of code in 152 complete LIVE-CODE™ programs.

- *Web Forms, Web Controls and ASP .NET.* The .NET platform enables developers to create robust, scalable Web-based applications. Microsoft's .NET server-side technology, Active Server Pages (ASP) .NET, allows programmers to build Web documents that respond to client requests. To enable interactive Web pages, server-side programs process information users input into HTML forms. ASP .NET is a significant departure from ASP 3.0, allowing developers to program Web-based applications using .NET's powerful object-oriented languages such as C# and Visual Basic .NET, rather than using only scripting languages. ASP .NET also provides enhanced visual programming capabilities, similar to those used in building Windows forms for desktop programs. Programmers can create Web pages visually, by dragging and dropping Web controls onto Web forms. Chapter 17, ASP .NET, Web Forms and Web Controls, introduces these powerful technologies.

- *Web Services and ASP .NET.* Microsoft's .NET strategy embraces the Internet and Web as integral to software development and deployment. Web services technology enables information sharing, e-commerce and other interactions using standard Internet protocols and technologies, such as Hypertext Transfer Protocol (HTTP), Extensible Markup Language (XML) and Simple Object Access Protocol (SOAP). Web services enable programmers to package application functionality in a manner that turns the Web into a library of reusable software components. In Chapter 19, ASP .NET and Web Services, we present a Web service that allows users to manipulate "huge integers"—integers too large to be contained in C#'s built-in data types. In this example, a user enters two huge integers and presses buttons to invoke Web services that add, subtract and compare the two integers. We also present information related to Web services in Appendix K, Crystal Reports® for Visual Studio .NET, which discusses a popular reporting program for database-intensive applications. Crystal Reports, which is integrated into Visual Studio .NET, provides the ability to expose a report as a Web service. The appendix provides introductory information and directs readers to a walk-through of this process on the Crystal Decisions Web site, **www.crystalde-cisions.com/netzone**.

- *Object-Oriented Programming.* Object-oriented programming is the most widely employed technique for developing robust, reusable software. This text offers a rich treatment of C#'s object-oriented programming features. Chapter 8, Object-Based Programming, introduces how to create classes and objects. These concepts are extended in Chapter 9, Object-Oriented Programming: Inheritance, which discusses how programmers can create powerful new classes quickly by "absorbing" the capabilities of existing classes.

- *XML.* Use of Extensible Markup Language (XML) is exploding in the software-development industry, in the e-business and e-commerce communities, and is pervasive throughout the .NET platform. Because XML is a platform-independent technology for describing data and for creating markup languages, XML's data portability integrates well with C#-based portable applications and services. Chapter 18, Extensible Markup Language (XML), introduces XML. In this chapter, we present XML markup and discuss the Document Object Model (DOM™), which is used to manipulate XML documents programmatically.

- *Multithreading.* Computers enable programmers to perform many tasks in parallel (i.e., concurrently), such as printing documents, downloading files from a network and surfing the Web. Multithreading is the technology through which programmers can develop applications that perform concurrent tasks. Historically, a computer has contained a single, expensive processor, which its operating system would share among all applications. Today, processors are becoming increasingly inexpensive, making it possible to build affordable computers with many processors working in parallel—such computers are called multiprocessors. Multithreading is effective on both single-processor and multiprocessor systems. .NET's multithreading capabilities make the platform and its related technologies better prepared to handle today's sophisticated multimedia-intensive, database-intensive, network-based, multiprocessor-based, distributed applications. Chapter 12, Multithreading, introduces this powerful capability.

- *ADO .NET.* Databases store vast amounts of information that individuals and organizations must access to conduct business. As an evolution of Microsoft's ActiveX Data Objects (ADO) technology, ADO .NET represents a new approach for building applications that interact with databases. ADO .NET uses XML and an enhanced object model to provide developers with the tools they need to access and manipulate databases for large-scale, extensible, mission-critical multi-tier applications. Chapter 16, Database, SQL and ADO .NET, introduces the capabilities of ADO .NET and the Structured Query Language (SQL) to manipulate databases.

- *Wireless Development.* By some estimates, about a billion people worldwide are using mobile devices, such as wireless phones and PDAs, and this number is increasing rapidly. To simplify the creation of Web content for mobile devices, Microsoft provides the Mobile Internet Toolkit (MIT). The MIT, which is built on ASP .NET, allows wireless content to be created using Visual Studio .NET's object-oriented languages. One program can be created that will be compatible with a variety of devices and able to display different content based on the type of device (e.g., a wireless phone versus a PDA). Chapter 23, Mobile Internet Toolkit, introduces wireless Web application development.

- *Visual Studio .NET Debugger.* Debuggers help programmers find and correct logic errors in program code. In Appendix D, Visual Studio .NET Debugger, we explain how to use key debugger features, such as setting "breakpoints" and "watches," stepping into and out of methods, and examining the method call stack.

- *Career Opportunities.* Appendix C, Career Opportunities, introduces career services available on the Internet. We explore online career services from both the employer's and employee's perspectives. We list many Web sites where you can submit applications, search for jobs and review applicants. We also review services that build recruiting pages directly into e-businesses. One of our reviewers told us that he had used the Internet as a primary tool in a recent job search, and that this appendix would have helped him dramatically expand his search.

- *Unicode*®. As computer systems evolved worldwide, computer vendors developed numeric representations of character sets and special symbols for the local languages spoken in different countries. In some cases, different representations were developed for the same languages. Such disparate character sets hindered communication among computer systems. C# supports the *Unicode Standard* (maintained by a non-profit organization called the *Unicode Consortium*), which maintains a single character set that specifies unique numeric values for characters and special symbols in most of the world's languages. Appendix F, Unicode®, discusses the standard, overviews the Unicode Consortium Web site, **www.unicode.org** and presents a C# application that displays "Welcome to Unicode!" in several languages.

- *Accessibility.* Although the World Wide Web has become an important part of many people's lives, the medium currently presents many challenges to people with disabilities. Individuals with hearing and visual impairments, in particular, have difficulty accessing multimedia-rich Web sites. In an attempt to improve this situation, the World Wide Web Consortium (W3C) launched the Web Accessibility Initiative (WAI), which provides guidelines for making Web sites accessible to people with disabilities. Chapter 22, Accessibility, describes these guidelines and highlights various products and services designed to improve the Web-browsing experiences of individuals with disabilities. For example, the chapter introduces VoiceXML™ and CallXML—two XML-based technologies for increasing the accessibility of Web-based content for people with visual impairments.

Pedagogic Approach

C#: A Programmer's Introduction contains a rich collection of examples that have been tested on Windows 2000 and Windows XP. The book concentrates on the principles of good software engineering and stresses program clarity. We are educators who teach edge-of-the-practice topics in industry classrooms worldwide. We avoid arcane terminology and syntax specifications in favor of teaching by example. The text emphasizes good pedagogy.

We use fonts to distinguish between Visual Studio .NET's Integrated Development Environment (IDE) features (such as menu names and menu items) and other elements that appear in the IDE. Our convention is to emphasize IDE features in a sans-serif bold Helvetica font (e.g., **Project** menu) and to emphasize program text in a serif bold Courier font (e.g., **bool x = true;**).

LIVE-CODE™ Teaching Approach

C#: A Programmer's Introduction is loaded with numerous LIVE-CODE™ examples. This style exemplifies the way we teach and write about programming and is the focus of our multimedia *Cyber Classrooms* and Web-based training courses as well. Each new concept is presented in the context of a complete, working example that is followed by one or more windows showing the program's input/output dialog. We call this method of teaching and writing the *LIVE-CODE™ Approach*. *We use programming languages to teach programming languages.* Reading the examples in the text is much like entering and running them on a computer. Readers have the option of downloading all of the book's code examples from **www.deitel.com**, under the **Downloads/Resources** link. Other links provide errata and answers to frequently asked questions.

World Wide Web Access

All of the source code for the program examples in *C#: A Programmer's Introduction* (and our other publications) is available on the Internet as downloads from the following Web sites:

```
www.deitel.com
www.prenhall.com/deitel
```

Registration is quick and easy and these downloads are free. We suggest downloading all the examples, then running each program as you read the corresponding portion of the book. Make changes to the examples and immediately see the effects of those changes—this is a great way to improve your programming skills. Any instructions for running the examples assumes that the user is running Windows 2000 or Windows XP and is using Microsoft's Internet Information Services (IIS). Additional setup instructions for IIS and other software can be found at our Web sites along with the examples. [*Note:* This is copyrighted material. Feel free to use it as you study, but you may not republish any portion of it in any form without explicit permission from Prentice Hall and the authors.]

Visual Studio .NET belongs to a family of products that are available for purchase and download from Microsoft. Visual Studio .NET, which includes C#, comes in four different editions—Academic, Professional, Enterprise Developer and Enterprise Architect. Visual Studio .NET Academic contains Visual Studio .NET Professional's features in addition to features designed for students and professors (e.g., an Assignment Manager that documents assignment submission, Application Publishing Tools that aid in the notification of assignments, code samples and more).

Microsoft also offers stand-alone products (Visual C# .NET Standard, Visual C++ .NET Standard and Visual Basic .NET Standard) for various .NET-languages. Each product provides an integrated development environment (similar to Visual Studio .NET) and a compiler. Visit **msdn.microsoft.com/vstudio/howtobuy** for descriptions and ordering information.

Objectives

Each chapter begins with objectives that inform readers of what to expect and give them an opportunity, after reading the chapter, to determine whether they have met the intended goals. The objectives serve as confidence builders and as a source of positive reinforcement.

Quotations

The chapter objectives are followed by sets of quotations. Some are humorous, some are philosophical and some offer interesting insights. We have found that readers enjoy relating the quotations to the chapter material. Many of the quotations are worth a "second look" *after* you read each chapter.

Outline

The chapter outline enables readers to approach the material in top-down fashion. Along with the chapter objectives, the outline helps users anticipate topics and set a comfortable and effective learning pace.

Approximately 11,550 Lines of Code in 152 Example Programs (with Program Outputs)

We present C# features in the context of complete, working C# programs. The programs range in size from just a few lines of code to substantial examples containing hundreds of lines of code. All examples are available as downloads from our Web site, **www.deitel.com**.

456 Illustrations/Figures

An abundance of charts, line drawings and program outputs is included. The discussion of control structures, for example, features carefully drawn flowcharts. [*Note:* We do not teach flowcharting as a program-development tool, but we do use a brief, flowchart-oriented presentation to explain the precise operation of each C# control structure.]

353 Programming Tips

We have included programming tips to help readers focus on important aspects of program development. We highlight hundreds of these tips in the form of *Good Programming Practices*, *Common Programming Errors*, *Testing and Debugging Tips, Performance Tips, Portability Tips, Software Engineering Observations* and *Look-and-Feel Observations*. These tips and practices represent the best the authors have gleaned from many decades of programming and teaching experience. One of our customers—a mathematics major—told us that she feels this approach is like the highlighting of axioms, theorems and corollaries in mathematics books; it provides a foundation on which to build good software.

72 Good Programming Practices

Good Programming Practices *are tips that call attention to techniques that will help developers produce programs that are clearer, more understandable and more maintainable.*

113 Common Programming Errors

Developers learning a language tend to make certain kinds of errors frequently. Pointing out these Common Programming Errors *reduces the likelihood that readers will make the same mistakes.*

38 Testing and Debugging Tips

When we first designed this "tip type," we thought the tips would contain suggestions strictly for exposing bugs and removing them from programs. In fact, many of the tips describe aspects of C# that prevent "bugs" from getting into programs in the first place, thus simplifying the testing and debugging processes.

29 Performance Tips

Developers like to "turbo charge" their programs. We have included 29 Performance Tips *that highlight opportunities for improving program performance—making programs run faster or minimizing the amount of memory that they occupy.*

11 Portability Tips

We include Portability Tips *to help developers write portable code and to provide insights on how C# achieves its high degree of portability.*

76 Software Engineering Observations

The object-oriented programming paradigm necessitates a complete rethinking of the way we build software systems. C# is an effective language for achieving good software engineering. The Software Engineering Observations *highlight architectural and design issues that affect the construction of software systems, especially large-scale systems.*

14 Look-and-Feel Observations

We provide Look-and-Feel Observations *to highlight graphical-user-interface conventions. These observations help developers design attractive, user-friendly graphical user interfaces that conform to industry norms.*

Summary

Each chapter ends with a summary that helps readers review and reinforce key concepts.

Approximately 3,485 Index Entries (with approximately 5,004 Page References)
We have included an extensive Index. This resource enables readers to search for any term or concept by keyword. The Index is especially useful to practicing programmers who use the book as a reference.

"Double Indexing" of All C# LIVE-CODE™ Examples
C#: A Programmer's Introduction has 152 LIVE-CODE™ examples, which we have "double indexed." For every C# source-code program in the book, we took the file name with the **.cs** extension, such as **ShowColors.cs**, and indexed it both alphabetically (in this case, under "S") and as a subindex item under "Examples." This makes it easier to find examples using particular features.

C# Multimedia Cyber Classroom and The Complete C# Training Course

We have prepared an interactive, CD-ROM-based, software version of *C# How to Program*, called the *C# Multimedia Cyber Classroom*. This resource, ideal for corporate training and college courses, is loaded with interactive e-learning features. The *Cyber Classroom* is packaged with the *C# How to Program* textbook at a discount in *The Complete C# Training Course*. If you already have that book and would like to purchase the *C# Multimedia Cyber Classroom* separately, please visit **www.InformIT.com/cyber-classrooms**. The ISBN number for the *C# Multimedia Cyber Classroom* is 0-13-064587-7. Many Deitel™ *Cyber Classrooms* are available in CD-ROM and Web-based training formats.

The CD-ROM provides an introduction in which the authors overview the *Cyber Classroom*'s features. The textbook's 152 LIVE-CODE™ example C# programs truly "come alive" in the *Cyber Classroom*. If you are viewing a program and want to execute it, you simply click the lightning-bolt icon, and the program will run. You immediately will see—and hear, when working with audio-based multimedia programs—the program's output. Click the audio icon, and one of the authors will discuss the program and "walk you through" the code.

The *Cyber Classroom* also provides navigational aids, including extensive hyperlinking. The *Cyber Classroom* is browser based, so it remembers sections that you have visited recently and allows you to move forward or backward among those sections. The thousands of index entries are hyperlinked to their text occurrences. Furthermore, when you key in a term using the "find" feature, the *Cyber Classroom* will locate occurrences of that term throughout the text. The Table of Contents entries are "hot," so clicking a chapter name takes you immediately to that chapter.

Readers like the fact that solutions to approximately half the exercises in *C# How to Program* are included with the *Cyber Classroom*. Studying and running these extra programs is a great way for readers to enhance their learning experience.

Professionals and student users of our *Cyber Classrooms* tell us that they like the interactivity and that the *Cyber Classroom* is an effective reference due to its extensive hyperlinking and other navigational features. We received an e-mail from a reader who said he lives "in the boonies" and cannot attend a live course at a university, so the *Cyber Classroom* provided an ideal solution to his educational needs.

Professors tell us that their students enjoy using the *Cyber Classroom* and spend more time on the courses and master more of the material than in textbook-only courses. For a complete list of the available and forthcoming *Cyber Classrooms* and *Complete Training Courses*, see the *Deitel™ Series* page at the beginning of this book, the product listing and ordering information at the end of this book or visit **www.deitel.com**, **www.prenhall.com/deitel** or **www.InformIT.com/deitel**.

Deitel e-Learning Initiatives

e-Books and Support for Wireless Devices

Wireless devices will play an enormous role in the future of the Internet. Given recent bandwidth enhancements and the emergence of 2.5 and 3G wireless technologies, it is projected that, within two years, more people will access the Internet through wireless devices than through desktop computers. Deitel & Associates, Inc., is committed to wireless accessibility and has recently published *Wireless Internet & Mobile Business How to Program*. To fulfill the needs of a wide range of customers, we are developing our content in traditional print formats and in new electronic formats, such as e-books, so that readers can access content virtually anytime, anywhere. Visit **www.deitel.com** for periodic updates on all Deitel technology initiatives.

e-Matter

Deitel & Associates, Inc., is partnering with Prentice Hall's parent company, Pearson PLC, and its information technology Web site, **InformIT.com**, to launch the Deitel e-Matter series at **www.InformIT.com/deitel** in Fall 2002. The Deitel e-Matter series will provide professionals with an additional source of information on specific programming topics at modest prices. e-Matter consists of stand-alone sections taken from published texts, forthcoming texts or pieces written during the Deitel research-and-development process. Developing e-Matter based on pre-publication manuscripts allows us to offer significant amounts of the material well before our books are published.

Course Management Systems: WebCT, Blackboard, CourseCompass and Premium CourseCompass

We are working with Prentice Hall to integrate our *How to Program Series* courseware into four Course Management Systems: WebCT, Blackboard™, CourseCompass and Premium CourseCompass. These enable instructors to create, manage and use sophisticated Web-based educational programs. Course Management Systems feature course customization (such as posting contact information, policies, syllabi, announcements, assignments, grades, performance evaluations and progress tracking), class and student management tools, a grade book, reporting tools, communication tools (such as chat rooms), a whiteboard, document sharing, bulletin boards and more. Instructors can use these products to communicate with their students, create online quizzes and exams from questions directly linked to the text and efficiently grade and track test results. For more information about these upcoming products, visit **www.prenhall.com/cms**. For demonstrations of existing WebCT, Blackboard and CourseCompass course materials, visit **cms.prenhall.com/webct**, **cms.prenhall.com/blackboard** and **cms.prenhall.com/coursecompass**, respectively.

Deitel and InformIT Newsletters

Deitel Column in the InformIT Newsletters

Deitel & Associates, Inc., contributes articles to the free *InformIT* weekly e-mail newsletter, subscribed to by more than 750,000 IT professionals worldwide. For registration information, visit **www.InformIT.com** and click the **MyInformIT** tab.

Deitel™ Buzz Online Newsletter

Our own free newsletter, the *Deitel™ Buzz Online*, includes commentary on industry trends and developments, links to articles and resources from our published books and upcoming publications, product-release schedules, challenges, anecdotes and more. For registration information, visit **www.deitel.com/newsletter/subscribe.html**.

The Deitel™ Developer Series

Deitel & Associates, Inc., is making a major commitment to .NET programming through the launch of our *Deitel™ Developer Series*. *C#: A Programmer's Introduction*, *C# for Experienced Programmers*, *Visual Basic .NET for Experienced Programmers* and *Visual C++ .NET for Experienced Programmers* are the first .NET books in this new series. These will be followed by several advanced books, beginning with *ASP .NET with Visual Basic .NET for Experienced Programmers* and *ASP .NET with C# for Experienced Programmers*.

The *Deitel™ Developer Series* is divided into three subseries. The *A Technical Introduction* subseries provides IT managers and developers with detailed overviews of emerging technologies. The *A Programmer's Introduction* subseries is designed to teach the fundamentals of new languages and software technologies to developers from the ground up. These books discuss programming fundamentals, followed by brief introductions to more sophisticated topics. Finally, the *For Experienced Programmers* subseries is designed for seasoned developers seeking to learn new programming languages and technologies without the encumbrance of introductory material. The books in this subseries move quickly to in-depth coverage of the intermediate features of the programming languages and software technologies being covered.

ASP .NET with C# for Experienced Programmers

Our forthcoming publication *ASP .NET with C# for Experienced Programmers* (available in 2003) is geared toward experienced .NET developers. This new book will cover enterprise-level Web-programming topics, including: Creating multi-tier, database intensive ASP .NET applications using ADO .NET and XML; constructing custom Web controls and developing Web services. This book also will include configuration and security topics. Updates on the status of this publication are posted at **www.deitel.com**. Before reading this book you should be familiar with C# at the level of either *C# How to Program* or *C# for Experienced Programmers*.

Acknowledgments

One of the great pleasures of writing a book is acknowledging the efforts of many people whose names may not appear on the cover, but whose hard work, cooperation, friendship and understanding were crucial to the production of the book. Because this publication has been derived from *C# How to Program*, we would like to acknowledge those who have helped us with both publications.

Many other people at Deitel & Associates, Inc., devoted long hours to this project. Below is a list of our full-time employees who contributed to this publication:

Sean E. Santry
Matthew R. Kowalewski
Jonathan Gadzik
Kyle Lomelí
Lauren Trees
Rashmi Jayaprakash
Laura Treibick
Betsy DuWaldt
Barbara Deitel
Abbey Deitel

We would also like to thank the participants in the Deitel & Associates, Inc., College Internship Program who contributed to this publication.[1]

Jeffrey Hamm (Northeastern)
Kalid Azad (Princeton)
Christopher Cassa (Massachusetts Institute of Technology)
David Tuttle (Harvard)
Thiago Lucas da Silva (Northeastern)
Ori Schwartz (Boston University)
Elizabeth Rockett (Princeton)
Barbara Strauss (Brandeis)
Christina Carney (Framingham State)
Brian Foster (Northeastern)
Mike Preshman (Northeastern)

We are fortunate to have been able to work with the talented and dedicated team of publishing professionals at Prentice Hall. We especially appreciate the extraordinary efforts of our editors, Petra Recter and Karen McLean of Prentice Hall and PH/PTR, respectively and Michael Ruel, who managed the extraordinary review processes for our *Deitel™ Developer Series* C# publications. We would also like to thank Mark L. Taub, Editor-in-Chief for computer publications at PH/PTR, for conceptualizing the *Deitel™ Developer Series*. He provided the necessary environment and resources to help us generate

---

1. The *Deitel & Associates, Inc. College Internship Program* offers a limited number of salaried positions to Boston-area college students majoring in Computer Science, Information Technology, Marketing, Management and English. Students work at our corporate headquarters in Maynard, Massachusetts full-time in the summers and (for those attending college in the Boston area) part-time during the academic year. We also offer full-time internship positions for students interested in taking a semester off from school to gain industry experience. Regular full-time positions are available to college graduates. For more information about this competitive program, please contact Abbey Deitel at **deitel@deitel.com** and visit **www.deitel.com**.

the many books in this series. A special note of appreciation goes to Marcia Horton, Editor-in-Chief of Engineering and Computer Science at Prentice Hall. Marcia has been our mentor and our friend for 18 years at Prentice Hall. She is responsible for all aspects of Deitel publications at all Pearson divisions including Prentice Hall, PH/PTR and Pearson International.

Laura Treibick, the Director of Multimedia at Deitel & Associates, Inc., designed the cover. Tamara Newnam (**smart_art@earthlink.net**) carried the cover through to completion, and produced the art work for our programming-tip icons.

We wish to acknowledge the efforts of our first- and second-round reviewers. Adhering to a tight time schedule, these reviewers scrutinized the text and the programs, providing countless suggestions for improving the accuracy and completeness of the presentation. We sincerely appreciate the time these people took from their busy professional schedules to help us ensure the quality, accuracy and timeliness of this book.

Merged reviewer list from *C# How to Program* and *C#: A Programmer's Introduction*:

Hussein Abuthuraya (Microsoft)
Lars Bergstrom (Microsoft)
Indira Dhingra (Microsoft)
Eric Gunnerson (Microsoft)
Peter Hallam (Microsoft)
Habib Hegdarian (Microsoft)
Anson Horton (Microsoft)
Latha Lakshminarayanan (Microsoft)
Kerry Loynd (Microsoft)
Tom McDade (Microsoft)
Syed Mehdi (Microsoft)
Shanku Niyogi (Microsoft)
Cosmin Radu (Microsoft)
Paul Randal (Microsoft)
Ratta Rakshminarayana (Microsoft)
Imtiaz Syed (Microsoft)
Ed Thornburg (Microsoft)
Richard Van Fossen (Microsoft)
Dharmesh Chauhan (Microsoft Consultant, Singapore)
Rishabh Agarwal (Delteq Systems Pte. Ltd.)
José Antonio González Seco (Sadiel S.A.)
Paul Bohman (WebAIM)
Alex Bondarev (SureFire Commerce, Inc.)
Ron Braithwaite (Nutriware)
Filip Bulovic (Objectronics PTY Ltd.)
Mark Burhop (University of Cincinnati)
Carl Burnham (Southpoint)
Matt Butler (Oakscape Inc.)
Andrew Chau (Rich Solutions, Inc.)
Shyam Chebrolu (SAIC Broadway & Seymour Group)
Kunal Cheda (**DotNetExtreme.com**)

Edmund Chou (MIT Student, **www.devhood.com** project, Microsoft Intern)

James Chegwidden (Tarrant County College)

Vijay Cinnakonda (University of Toledo)

Michael Colynuck (Sierra Systems)

Jay Cook (Canon Development Americas)

Jeff Cowan (Magenic Technologies)

Robert Dombroski (AccessOnTime)

Shaun Eagan (Eagan Consulting)

Brian Erwin (Extreme Logic)

Hamilton Fong (Montag & Caldwell, Inc.)

Gnanavel Gnana Arun Ganesh (Arun Microsystems)

Sam Gentile (Consultant)

Sam Gill (San Francisco State University)

John Godel (TJX)

David Haglin (Minnesota State University in Mankato)

James Huddleston (IBM)

Jeff Isom (WebAIM)

Rex Jaeschke (Consultant)

Amit Kalani (MobiCast)

Priti Kalani (Consultant)

Bryan Keller (**csharphelp.com**)

Patrick Lam (EdgeNet Communications)

Yi-Fung Lin (MIT Student, **www.devhood.com** project, Microsoft Intern)

Maxim Loukianov (SoloMio Corporation)

Gaurav Mantro (EDS PLM Solutions)

Jaimon Mathew (Osprey Software Technology)

Robert Meagher (Compuware NuMega Lab)

Arun Nair (iSpan Technologies)

Saurabh Nandu (**Mastercsharp.com**)

Simon North (Synopsys)

Jibin Pan (**csharpcorner.com**)

Graham Parker (VBUG)

Bryan Plaster (Valtech)

Chris Rausch (Sheridan Press)

Debbie Reid (Santa Fe Community College)

Bryn Rhodes (Softwise, Inc.)

Craig Schofding (C.A.S. Training)

Rahul Sharma (Maxutil Software)

Devan Shepherd (XMaLpha Technologies)

Srinivasa Sivakumar (Equity Office)

David Talbot (Reallinx, Inc.)

Satish Talim (Pune-Csharp)

Pavel Tsekov (Consultant)

John Varghese (UBS Warburg)

Peter Weng (MIT Student, **www.devhood.com** project, Microsoft Intern)

Jesse Wilkins (Metalinear Media)

Warren Wiltsie (Fairleigh Dickinson University/Seton Hall University)
Phil Wright (Crownwood Consulting Ltd.)
Norimasa Yoshida (MIT Graduate Student)

We would sincerely appreciate your comments, criticisms, corrections and suggestions for improving the book. Please address all correspondence to:

deitel@deitel.com

We will respond promptly.

Well, that's it for now. Welcome to the exciting world of C# programming. We hope you enjoy this introductory look at Microsoft's premier .NET language. Good luck!

Dr. Harvey M. Deitel
Paul J. Deitel
Jeff Listfield
Tem R. Nieto
Cheryl H. Yaeger
Marina Zlatkina

About the Authors

Dr. Harvey M. Deitel, Chairman and Chief Strategy Officer of Deitel & Associates, Inc., has 41 years experience in the computing field, including extensive industry and academic experience. Dr. Deitel earned B.S. and M.S. degrees from the Massachusetts Institute of Technology and a Ph.D. from Boston University. He worked on the pioneering virtual-memory operating-systems projects at IBM and MIT that developed techniques now widely implemented in systems such as Unix, Linux™ and Windows XP. He has 20 years of college teaching experience, including earning tenure and serving as the Chairman of the Computer Science Department at Boston College before founding Deitel & Associates, Inc., with his son, Paul J. Deitel. He is the author or co-author of several dozen books and multimedia packages and is writing many more. With translations published in Japanese, Russian, Spanish, Traditional Chinese, Simplified Chinese, Korean, French, Polish, Italian, Portuguese and Greek, Dr. Deitel's texts have earned international recognition. Dr. Deitel has delivered professional seminars to major corporations, and to government organizations and various branches of the military.

Paul J. Deitel, CEO and Chief Technical Officer of Deitel & Associates, Inc., is a graduate of the Massachusetts Institute of Technology's Sloan School of Management, where he studied Information Technology. Through Deitel & Associates, Inc., he has delivered Java, C, C++ and Internet and World Wide Web programming courses to industry clients including Compaq, Sun Microsystems, White Sands Missile Range, Rogue Wave Software, Boeing, Dell, Stratus, Fidelity, Cambridge Technology Partners, Open Environment Corporation, One Wave, Hyperion Software, Lucent Technologies, Adra Systems, Entergy, CableData Systems, NASA at the Kennedy Space Center, the National Severe Storms Laboratory, IBM and many other organizations. He has lectured on C++ and Java for the Boston Chapter of the Association for Computing Machinery and has taught satellite-based Java courses through a cooperative venture of Deitel & Associates, Inc., Prentice Hall and the Technology Education Network. He and his father, Dr. Harvey M. Deitel, are the world's best-selling programming language textbook authors.

Tem R. Nieto, Director of Product Development of Deitel & Associates, Inc., is a graduate of the Massachusetts Institute of Technology, where he studied engineering and computing. Through Deitel & Associates, Inc., he has delivered courses for industry clients including Sun Microsystems, Compaq, EMC, Stratus, Fidelity, NASDAQ, Art Technology, Progress Software, Toys "R" Us, Operational Support Facility of the National Oceanographic and Atmospheric Administration, Jet Propulsion Laboratory, Nynex, Motorola, Federal Reserve Bank of Chicago, Banyan, Schlumberger, University of Notre Dame, NASA, Hewlett-Packard, various military installations and many others. He has co-authored numerous books and multimedia packages with the Deitels and has contributed to virtually every Deitel & Associates, Inc., publication.

Cheryl H. Yaeger, Director of Microsoft Software Publications with Deitel & Associates, Inc., graduated from Boston University in three years with a bachelor's degree in Computer Science. Cheryl has co-authored various Deitel & Associates publications, including *C# How to Program, C#: A Programmer's Introduction, C# for Experienced Programmers* and *Visual Basic .NET for Experienced Programmers* as well as contributed to other Deitel publications including *Perl How to Program, Wireless Internet & Mobile Business How to Program, Internet and World Wide Web How to Program, Second Edition* and *Visual Basic .NET How to Program, Second Edition.*

Marina Zlatkina graduated from Brandeis University in three years with degrees in Computer Science and Mathematics, and in her fourth year earned a Master of Arts in Computer Science. During her Brandeis career, she conducted research in databases and has been a teaching assistant. Marina co-authored *C# How to Program, C#: A Programmer's Introduction* and *C# for Experienced Programmers*, and contributed to another Deitel publication, *e-Business & e-Commerce for Managers.*

Jeff A. Listfield is a Computer Science graduate of Harvard College. His coursework included classes in computer graphics, networks and computational theory and he has programming experience in C, C++, Java, Perl and Lisp. Jeff has co-authored *C# How to Program, C#: A Programmer's Introduction* and *C# for Experienced Programmers*, and contributed to *Perl How to Program.*

About Deitel & Associates, Inc.

Deitel & Associates, Inc., is an internationally recognized corporate instructor-led training and content-creation organization specializing in Internet/World Wide Web software technology, e-business/e-commerce software technology, object technology and computer programming languages education. The company provides courses in Internet and World Wide Web programming, wireless Internet programming, Web services (in both Java and .NET languages), object technology, and major programming languages and platforms, such as Visual Basic .NET, C#, Visual C++ .NET, Java, Advanced Java, C, C++, XML, Perl, Python, ASP .NET, ADO .NET and more. Deitel & Associates, Inc., was founded by Dr. Harvey M. Deitel and Paul J. Deitel, the world's leading programming-language textbook authors. The company's clients include many of the largest computer companies, government agencies, branches of the military and business organizations. Through its 25-year publishing partnership with Prentice Hall, Deitel & Associates, Inc., publishes leading-edge programming textbooks, professional books, interactive CD-ROM-based multimedia *Cyber Classrooms*, *Complete Training Courses*, e-books, e-matter, Web-based training courses and course management systems e-content. Deitel & Associates, Inc., and the authors can be reached via e-mail at:

deitel@deitel.com

To learn more about Deitel & Associates, Inc., its publications and its worldwide corporate on-site curriculum, see the last few pages of this book or visit:

www.deitel.com

Individuals wishing to purchase Deitel books, *Cyber Classrooms*, *Complete Training Courses* and Web-based training courses can do so through bookstores, online booksellers and:

www.deitel.com
www.prenhall.com/deitel
www.InformIT.com/deitel
www.InformIT.com/cyberclassrooms

Bulk orders by corporations and academic institutions should be placed directly with Prentice Hall. See the last few pages of this book for worldwide ordering details. To follow the Deitel publishing program, please register at

www.deitel.com/newsletter/subscribe.html.

The World Wide Web Consortium (W3C)

W3C® Deitel & Associates, Inc., is a member of the *World Wide Web Consortium*
MEMBER *(W3C)*. The W3C was founded in 1994 "to develop common protocols for the evolution of the World Wide Web." As a W3C member, Deitel & Associates, Inc., holds a seat on the W3C Advisory Committee (the company's representative is our CEO and Chief Technology Officer, Paul Deitel). Advisory Committee members help provide "strategic direction" to the W3C through meetings held around the world. Member organizations also help develop standards recommendations for Web technologies (such as XHTML, XML and many others) through participation in W3C activities and groups. Membership in the W3C is intended for companies and large organizations. To obtain information on becoming a member of the W3C visit **www.w3.org/Consortium/Prospectus/Joining**.

Introduction to .NET and C#

Objectives

- To learn the history of the Internet and the World Wide Web.
- To become familiar with the World Wide Web Consortium (W3C).
- To learn what the Extensible Markup Language (XML) is and why it is an important technology.
- To understand the impact of object technology on software development.
- To understand the Microsoft® .NET initiative.
- To preview the remaining chapters of the book.

Things are always at their best in their beginning.
Blaise Pascal

High thoughts must have high language.
Aristophanes

Our life is frittered away by detail...Simplify, simplify.
Henry David Thoreau

Before beginning, plan carefully....
Marcus Tullius Cicero

Look with favor upon a bold beginning.
Virgil

I think I'm beginning to learn something about it.
Auguste Renoir

Outline

1.1 Introduction

Welcome to C#! We have worked hard to provide programmers with the most accurate and complete information regarding the C# language and the .NET platform. We hope that this book will provide an informative, entertaining and challenging learning experience for you. In this chapter, we present the history of the Internet and World Wide Web and introduce Microsoft's .NET initiative. The chapter concludes by touring the remainder of the book.

1.2 History of the Internet and World Wide Web

In the late 1960s, at a conference at the University of Illinois Urbana-Champaign, ARPA—the Advanced Research Projects Agency of the Department of Defense—rolled out the blueprints for networking the main computer systems of approximately a dozen ARPA-funded universities and research institutions. The computers were to be connected with communications lines operating at a then-stunning 56 Kbps (1 Kbps is equal to 1,024 bits per second), at a time when most people (of the few who had access to networking technologies) were connecting over telephone lines to computers at a rate of 110 bits per second. Researchers at Harvard talked about communicating with the Univac 1108 "supercomputer," which was located across the country at the University of Utah, to handle calculations related to their computer graphics research. Many other intriguing possibilities were discussed. Academic research was about to take a giant leap forward. Shortly after this conference, ARPA proceeded to implement what quickly became called the *ARPAnet*, the grandparent of today's *Internet*.

Things worked out differently from the original plan. Although the ARPAnet did enable researchers to network their computers, its chief benefit proved to be the capability for quick and easy communication via what came to be known as *electronic mail* (*e-mail*). This is true even on today's Internet, with e-mail, instant messaging and file transfer facilitating communications among hundreds of millions of people worldwide.

The network was designed to operate without centralized control. This meant that if a portion of the network should fail, the remaining working portions would still be able to route data packets from senders to receivers over alternative paths.

The protocol (i.e., set of rules) for communicating over the ARPAnet became known as the *Transmission Control Protocol (TCP)*. TCP ensured that messages were routed properly from sender to receiver and that those messages arrived intact.

In parallel with the early evolution of the Internet, organizations worldwide were implementing their own networks to facilitate both intra-organization (i.e., within the organization) and inter-organization (i.e., between organizations) communication. A huge variety of networking hardware and software appeared. One challenge was to enable these diverse products to communicate with each other. ARPA accomplished this by developing the *Internet Protocol (IP),* which created a true "network of networks," the current architecture of the Internet. The combined set of protocols is now commonly called *TCP/IP*.

Initially, use of the Internet was limited to universities and research institutions; later, the military adopted the technology. Eventually, the government decided to allow access to the Internet for commercial purposes. When this decision was made, there was resentment among the research and military communities—it was felt that response times would become poor as "the Net" became saturated with so many users.

In fact, the opposite has occurred. Businesses rapidly realized that, by making effective use of the Internet, they could refine their operations and offer new and better services to their clients. Companies started spending vast amounts of money to develop and enhance their Internet presence. This generated fierce competition among communications carriers and hardware and software suppliers to meet the increased infrastructure demand. The result is that *bandwidth* (i.e., the information-carrying capacity of communications lines) on the Internet has increased tremendously, while hardware costs have plummeted. The Internet has played a significant role in the economic growth that many industrialized nations experienced over the last decade.

The *World Wide Web* allows computer users to locate and view multimedia-based documents (i.e., documents with text, graphics, animations, audios or videos) on almost any subject. Even though the Internet was developed more than three decades ago, the introduction of the World Wide Web (WWW) was a relatively recent event. In 1989, Tim Berners-Lee of CERN (the European Organization for Nuclear Research) began to develop a technology for sharing information via hyperlinked text documents. Basing the new language on the well-established *Standard Generalized Markup Language (SGML)*—a standard for business data interchange—Berners-Lee called his invention the *HyperText Markup Language (HTML)*. He also wrote communication protocols to form the backbone of his new hypertext information system, which he referred to as the World Wide Web.

Surely historians will list the Internet and the World Wide Web among the most important and profound creations of humankind. In the past, most computer applications ran on "stand-alone" computers (computers that were not connected to one another). Today's applications can be written to communicate among the world's hundreds of millions of computers. The Internet and World Wide Web merge computing and communications technologies, expediting and simplifying our work. They make information instantly and conveniently accessible to large numbers of people. They enable individuals and small businesses to achieve worldwide exposure. They are changing the way we do business and conduct our personal lives.

1.3 World Wide Web Consortium (W3C)

In October 1994, Tim Berners-Lee founded an organization, called the *World Wide Web Consortium (W3C)*, that is devoted to developing nonproprietary, interoperable technologies for the World Wide Web. One of the W3C's primary goals is to make the Web universally accessible—regardless of its users' disabilities, languages or cultures.

The W3C is also a standardization organization and is comprised of three *hosts*—the Massachusetts Institute of Technology (MIT), France's INRIA (Institut National de Recherche en Informatique et Automatique) and Keio University of Japan—and over 400 members, including Deitel & Associates, Inc. Members provide the primary financing for the W3C and help provide the strategic direction of the Consortium. To learn more about the W3C, visit **www.w3.org**.

Web technologies standardized by the W3C are called *Recommendations*. Current W3C Recommendations include *Extensible HyperText Markup Language (XHTML™)* for marking up content for the Web, *Cascading Style Sheets (CSS™)* for describing how content is formatted and the *Extensible Markup Language (XML)* for creating markup languages. Recommendations are not actual software products, but documents that specify the role, syntax and rules of a technology. Before becoming a W3C Recommendation, a document passes through three major phases: *Working Draft*, which, as its name implies, specifies an evolving draft; *Candidate Recommendation,* a stable version of the document that industry can begin to implement; and *Proposed Recommendation*, a Candidate Recommendation that is considered mature (i.e., has been implemented and tested over a period of time) and is ready to be considered for W3C Recommendation status. For detailed information about the W3C Recommendation track, see "6.2 The W3C Recommendation track" at

```
www.w3.org/Consortium/Process/Process-19991111/
process.html#RecsCR
```

1.4 Extensible Markup Language (XML)

As the popularity of the Web exploded, HTML's limitations became apparent. HTML's lack of *extensibility* (the ability to change or add features) frustrated developers, and its ambiguous definition allowed erroneous HTML to proliferate. In response to these problems, the W3C added limited extensibility to HTML. This was, however, only a temporary solution—the need for a standardized, fully extensible and structurally strict language was apparent. As a result, XML was developed by the W3C. XML combines the power and extensibility of its parent language, Standard Generalized Markup Language (SGML), with the simplicity that the Web community demands.

Data independence, the separation of content from its presentation, is an essential characteristic of XML. Since an XML document describes data, any application conceivably can process an XML document. Recognizing this, software developers are integrating XML into their applications to improve Web functionality and interoperability. XML's flexibility and power make it perfect for the middle tier of client/server systems, which must interact with a wide variety of clients. Much of the processing that was once limited to server computers now can be performed by client computers, because XML's semantic and structural information enables it to be manipulated by any application that can process text. This reduces server loads and network traffic, resulting in a faster, more efficient Web.

XML is not limited to Web applications. Increasingly, XML is being employed in databases—the structure of an XML document enables it to be integrated easily with database applications. As applications become more Web enabled, it seems likely that XML will become the universal technology for data representation. All applications employing XML will be able to communicate, provided that they could understand each other's XML markup, or *vocabulary*.

Simple Object Access Protocol (SOAP) is a technology for the distribution of objects (marked up as XML) over the Internet. Developed initially by Microsoft and DevelopMentor, SOAP is a W3C Working Draft that provides a framework for expressing application semantics, encoding data and packaging data. Microsoft .NET (discussed in Sections 1.6 and 1.7) uses XML and SOAP to mark up and transfer data over the Internet. XML and SOAP are at the core of .NET—they allow software components to interoperate (i.e., communicate easily with one another). SOAP is supported by many platforms, because of its foundations in XML and HTTP. We discuss XML in Chapter 18, Extensible Markup Language (XML), and SOAP in Chapter 19, ASP .NET and Web Services.

1.5 Key Software Trend: Object Technology

What are objects, and why are they special? Object technology is a packaging scheme that facilitates the creation of meaningful software units. These units are large and focused on particular application areas. There are date objects, time objects, paycheck objects, invoice objects, audio objects, video objects, file objects, record objects and so on. In fact, almost any noun can be represented as a software object. Objects have *properties* (i.e., *attributes*, such as color, size and weight) and perform *actions* (i.e., *behaviors*, such as moving, sleeping or drawing). Classes represent groups of related objects. For example, all cars belong to the "car" class, even though individual cars vary in make, model, color and options packages. A class specifies the general format of its objects; the properties and actions available to an object depend on its class.

We live in a world of objects. Just look around you—there are cars, planes, people, animals, buildings, traffic lights, elevators and so on. Before object-oriented languages appeared, *procedural programming languages* (such as Fortran, Pascal, BASIC and C) focused on actions (verbs) rather than things or objects (nouns). We live in a world of objects, but earlier programming languages forced individuals to program primarily with verbs. This paradigm shift made program writing a bit awkward. However, with the advent of popular object-oriented languages, such as C++, Java and C#, programmers can program in an object-oriented manner that reflects the way in which they perceive the world. This process, which seems more natural than procedural programming, has resulted in significant productivity gains.

One of the key problems with procedural programming is that the program units created do not mirror real-world entities effectively and therefore are difficult to reuse. Programmers often write and rewrite similar software for various projects. This wastes precious time and money as programmers repeatedly "reinvent the wheel." With object technology, properly designed software entities (called objects) can be reused on future projects. Using libraries of reusable componentry can reduce the amount of effort required to implement certain kinds of systems (as compared to the effort that would be required to reinvent these capabilities in new projects). C# programmers use the .NET Framework Class Library (known commonly as the FCL), which is introduced in Section 1.8.

Some organizations report that software reusability is not, in fact, the key benefit of object-oriented programming. Rather, they indicate that object-oriented programming tends to produce software that is more understandable because it is better organized and has fewer maintenance requirements. As much as 80 percent of software costs are not associated with the original efforts to develop the software, but instead are related to the continued evolution and maintenance of that software throughout its lifetime. Object orientation allows programmers to abstract the details of software and focus on the "big picture." Rather than worrying about minute details, the programmer can focus on the behaviors and interactions of objects. A roadmap that showed every tree, house and driveway would be difficult, if not impossible, to read. When such details are removed and only the essential information (roads) remains, the map becomes easier to understand. In the same way, a program that is divided into objects is easy to understand, modify and update because it hides much of the detail. It is clear that object-oriented programming will be the key programming methodology for at least the next decade.

Software Engineering Observation 1.1

Use a building-block approach to create programs. By using existing pieces in new projects, programmers avoid reinventing the wheel. This is called software reuse, *and it is central to object-oriented programming.*

[*Note*: We will include many of these *Software Engineering Observations* throughout the book to explain concepts that affect and improve the overall architecture and quality of a software system and, particularly, of large software systems. We also will highlight *Good Programming Practices* (practices that can help programmers write programs that are clearer, more understandable, more maintainable and easier to test and debug), *Common Programming Errors* (problems we highlight to ensure that programmers avoid the most common errors), *Performance Tips* (techniques that will help programmers write programs that run faster and use less memory), *Portability Tips* (techniques that will help programmers write programs that can run, with little or no modification, on a variety of computers), *Testing and Debugging Tips* (techniques that will help programmers remove bugs from their programs and, more importantly, write bug-free programs in the first place) and *Look-and-Feel Observations* (techniques that will help programmers design the "look and feel" of their graphical user interfaces for appearance and ease of use). Many of these techniques and practices are only guidelines; you will, no doubt, develop your own preferred programming style.]

The advantage of writing your own code is that you will know exactly how it works. The code will be yours to examine, modify and improve. The disadvantage is the time and effort that goes into designing, developing and testing new code.

Performance Tip 1.1

Reusing proven code components instead of writing your own versions can improve program performance, because these components normally are written to perform efficiently.

Software Engineering Observation 1.2

Extensive class libraries of reusable software components are available over the Internet and the World Wide Web; many are offered free of charge.

1.6 Introduction to Microsoft .NET

In June 2000, Microsoft announced its *.NET* (pronounced "dot-net") *initiative*. The *.NET platform* is one that provides significant enhancements to earlier developer platforms. .NET offers a new software-development model that allows applications created in disparate programming languages to communicate with each other. The platform also allows developers to create Web-based applications that can be distributed to a great variety of devices (even wireless phones) and to desktop computers.

Microsoft's .NET initiative is a broad new vision for embracing the Internet and the Web in the development, engineering and use of software. One key aspect of the .NET strategy is its independence from a specific language or platform. Rather than requiring programmers to use a single programming language, developers can create a .NET application by using any combination of .NET-compatible languages (Fig. 1.1). Programmers can contribute to the same software project, writing code in the .NET languages (such as C#, Visual C++ .NET, Visual Basic .NET and many others) in which they are most proficient. Part of the initiative includes Microsoft's *Active Server Pages (ASP) .NET* technology, which allows programmers to create applications for the Web. With ASP .NET, developers can create Web-based, database-intensive applications quickly by harnessing the power of .NET's object-oriented languages. Developers can use ASP .NET to develop powerful and robust Web applications, taking advantage of ASP .NET's optimizations for performance, testing and security.

A key component of the .NET architecture is *Web services*, which are applications that expose (i.e., make available) functionality to clients via the Internet. Clients and other applications can use these Web services as reusable building blocks. One example of a Web service is Dollar Rent a Car's reservation system, known as Quick Keys.[1] Dollar wanted to expose the functionality of its mainframe-based system, so that other companies could provide customers with the ability to make rental-car reservations. Dollar could have created individual, proprietary solutions for its business partners. To expose its functionality in a reusable way, Dollar implemented its solution using Web services. The results have been phenomenal. By creating a Web service, airlines and hotels can use Dollar's reservation system to reserve cars for their clients. Dollar's business partners do not need to use the same platform as Dollar uses, nor do they need to understand how the reservation system is implemented. Reimplementing its application as a Web service has provided Dollar with millions of dollars of additional revenue, as well as thousands of new customers.

Programming Languages	
APL	Oberon
C#	Oz

Fig. 1.1   .NET Languages (table information from Microsoft Web site, `www.microsoft.com`). (Part 1 of 2.)

---

1. Microsoft Corporation, "Dollar Rent A Car Breathes New Life Into Legacy Systems Using .NET Connected Software," 15 March 2002 **`<www.microsoft.com/business/casestudies/b2c/dollarrentacar.asp>`**.

Programming Languages (Cont.)	
COBOL	Pascal
Component Pascal	Perl
Curriculum	Python
Eiffel	RPG
Fortran	Scheme
Haskell	Smalltalk
J#	Standard ML
JScript .NET	Visual Basic .NET
Mercury	Visual C++ .NET

Fig. 1.1   .NET Languages (table information from Microsoft Web site, **www.microsoft.com**). (Part 2 of 2.)

Web services extend the concept of software reuse by allowing programmers to concentrate on their specialties without having to implement every component of every application. Instead, companies can buy Web services and devote their time and energy to developing their products. Visual programming (discussed in Chapter 2) has become popular, because it enables programmers to create applications easily, using such prepackaged components as buttons, textboxes and labels. Similarly, programmers may create an application using Web services for databases, security, authentication, data storage and language translation without having to know the internal details of those components.

When companies link their products via Web services, a new user experience emerges. For example, a single application could manage bill payments, tax refunds, loans and investments, using Web services from various companies. An online merchant could buy Web services for online credit-card payments, user authentication, network security and inventory databases to create an e-commerce Web site.

The keys to this interaction are XML and SOAP, which enable Web services to communicate. XML gives meaning to data, and SOAP is the protocol that allows Web services to communicate easily with one another. XML and SOAP act as the "glue" that combines various Web services to form applications.

Universal data access is another essential .NET concept. If two copies of a file exist (such as on a personal and a company computer), the oldest version must be updated constantly—this is called file *synchronization*. If the files are different, they are *unsynchronized*, a situation that could lead to errors. With .NET, data can reside in one central location rather than on separate systems. Any Internet-connected device can access the data (under tight control, of course), which would then be formatted appropriately for use or display on the accessing device. Thus, the same document could be seen and edited on a desktop PC, a PDA, a wireless phone or other device. Users would not need to synchronize the information, because it would be fully up-to-date in a central location.

.NET is an immense undertaking. We discuss various aspects of .NET throughout this book. Additional information is available at **www.microsoft.com/net**.

1.7 C#

The *C#* (pronounced "C-Sharp") programming language, developed at Microsoft by a team led by Anders Hejlsberg and Scott Wiltamuth, was designed specifically for the .NET platform as a language that would enable programmers to migrate to .NET. This migration is easy for a large base of programmers because C# has roots in C, C++ and Java, adapting the best features of each and adding new features of its own. The C# Language Specification is available for download at **msdn.microsoft.com/vstudio/techinfo/articles/upgrade/Csharpdownload.asp**.

C# is an event-driven, fully object-oriented, visual programming language in which programs are created using an *Integrated Development Environment* (*IDE*). With the IDE, a programmer can create, run, test and debug C# programs conveniently, thereby reducing the time it takes to produce a working program to a fraction of the time it would have taken without using the IDE. The process of creating an application rapidly using an IDE is referred to as *Rapid Application Development (RAD)*.

1.8 .NET Framework and the Common Language Runtime

The *.NET Framework* is at the heart of .NET. This framework manages and executes applications, contains a class library (called the *Framework Class Library* or *FCL*), enforces security and provides many other programming capabilities. The details of the .NET Framework are found in the *Common Language Specification* (*CLS*), which contains information about the storage of objects and so on. The CLS has been submitted for standardization to ECMA (the European Computer Manufacturers Association). This allows independent software vendors to create the .NET Framework for other platforms. The .NET Framework exists only for the Windows platform, but is being developed for other platforms, as well, such as Microsoft's *Shared Source CLI* (*Common Language Infrastructure*). The Shared Source CLI is an archive of source code that provides a subset of the Microsoft .NET Framework for both Windows XP and the FreeBSD[2] operating systems.[3] For more information in the Shared Source CLI, visit **msdn.microsoft.com/library/default.asp?url=/library/en-us/dndotnet/html/msshar-sourcecli.asp**.

The *Common Language Runtime (CLR)* is another central part of the .NET Framework—it executes C# programs. Programs are compiled into machine-specific instructions in two steps. First, the program is compiled into *Microsoft Intermediate Language (MSIL)*, which defines instructions for the CLR. Code converted into MSIL from other languages and sources is woven together by the CLR. Then, another compiler in the CLR compiles the MSIL into machine code (for a particular platform), creating a single application.

Why bother having the extra step of converting from C# to MSIL, instead of compiling directly into machine language? The key reasons are portability between operating sys-

---

2. The FreeBSD project provides a freely available and open-source UNIX-like operating system that is based on UC Berkeley's *Berkeley System Distribution* (*BSD*). For more information on BSD, visit **www.freebsd.org**.
3. Microsoft Corporation, "The Microsoft Shared Source CLI Implementation," March 2002 **<msdn.microsoft.com/library/en-us/Dndotnet/html/msshasource-cli.asp>**.

tems, interoperability between languages and execution-management features such as memory management and security.

If the .NET Framework exists (and is installed) for a platform, that platform can run any .NET program. The ability of a program to run (without modification) across multiple platforms is known as *platform independence*. Code written once can be used on another machine without modification, saving both time and money. In addition, software can target a wider audience—previously, companies had to decide whether converting (some-times called *porting*) their programs to different platforms was worth the cost. With .NET, porting is simplified.

The .NET Framework also provides a high level of *language interoperability*. Pro-grams written in different languages are all compiled into MSIL—the different parts can be combined to create a single, unified program. MSIL allows the .NET Framework to be *lan-guage independent*, because MSIL is not tied to a particular programming language. Any language that can be compiled into MSIL is called a *.NET-compliant language*.

Language interoperability offers many benefits to software companies. C#, Visual Basic .NET and Visual C++ .NET developers, for example, can work side-by-side on the same project without having to learn another programming language—all their code is compiled into MSIL and linked together to form one program. In addition, the .NET Frame-work can package preexisting components (i.e., components created using tools that pre-date .NET) and .NET components to work together. This allows companies to reuse the code that they have spent years developing and integrate it with the .NET code that they write. Integration is crucial, because companies cannot migrate easily to .NET unless they can stay productive, using their existing developers and software.

Another benefit of the .NET Framework is the CLR's execution-management features. The CLR manages memory, security and other features, relieving the programmer of these responsibilities. With languages like C++, programmers must manage their own memory. This leads to problems if programmers request memory and never release it—programs could consume all available memory, which would prevent applications from running. By managing the program's memory, the .NET Framework allows programmers to concen-trate on program logic.

The .NET Framework also provides programmers with a huge library of reusable classes. This library, called the Framework Class Library (FCL), can be used by any .NET language.

This book explains how to develop .NET software with C# and the FCL. Steve Ballmer, Microsoft's CEO, stated in May 2001 that Microsoft was "betting the company" on .NET. Such a dramatic commitment surely indicates a bright future for C# and its com-munity of developers.

1.9 Tour of the Book

In this section, we tour the chapters and appendices of *C#: A Programmer's Introduction*. Several of the chapters contain an Internet and Web Resources section that lists additional sources of C# information.

Chapter 1—Introduction to .NET and C#
The first chapter presented the history of the Internet, World Wide Web and various tech-nologies (such as XML and SOAP) that have led to advances in how computers are used.

We then introduced the Microsoft .NET initiative and the C# programming language, including Web services. We explore the impact of .NET on software development and software reusability. The chapter concludes by touring the remainder of the book.

Chapter 2—Introduction to the Visual Studio® .NET IDE

Chapter 2 introduces Visual Studio .NET, an *integrated development environment* (*IDE*) that allows programmers to create C# programs. Visual Studio .NET enables *visual programming*, in which *controls* (such as buttons and text boxes) are "dragged" and "dropped" into place, rather than added by writing code and typing it in. Visual programming increases software-development productivity by eliminating many tedious programming tasks. For example, a graphical user interface (GUI's) properties (information such as size and color) can be modified through the Visual Studio .NET environment, allowing changes to be made quickly and causing the results to appear immediately on the screen. Rather than having to guess how the GUI will appear while writing a program, programmers view the GUI exactly as it will appear when the finished program runs. Visual Studio .NET also contains advanced tools for debugging, documenting and writing code. The chapter presents features of Visual Studio .NET, including its key windows and shows how to compile and run programs. We provide an example of the capabilities of Visual Studio .NET by using it to create a simple Windows application without typing a single line of code.

Chapter 3—Introduction to C# Programming

This chapter introduces readers to our LIVE-CODE™ approach. Every concept is presented in the context of a complete working C# program and is followed by one or more screen shots showing actual inputs and outputs as the program executes. Our first program prints a line of text—we carefully discuss each line of code. Our next program prints text to a **Message-Box**, a small message dialog defined by the FCL. This example demonstrates using FCL classes programmatically. We then discuss how a program inputs data from its users and how to write arithmetic expressions. The last example demonstrates using the equality and relational operators to compare two numbers entered by the user.

Chapter 4—Control Structures: Part 1

This chapter introduces the principles of structured programming, a set of techniques that will help the reader develop clear, understandable and maintainable programs. The first part of this chapter presents program-development and problem-solving techniques. The chapter demonstrates how to transform a written specification to a program by using such techniques as *pseudocode* and *top-down*, *stepwise refinement*. We then progress through the entire process, from developing a problem statement into a working C# program. We build on information presented in the previous chapter to create programs that are interactive (i.e., they change their behavior to suit user-supplied inputs). The chapter then introduces the use of control structures that affect the sequence in which statements are executed. We discuss the three forms of program control—sequence, selection and repetition—focusing on the **if/else** and **while** control structures. Flowcharts (i.e., graphical representations that show the order in which actions are executed) appear throughout the chapter, reinforcing and augmenting the explanations. The chapter concludes with a program walkthrough that expands upon the program created in Chapter 2. Readers combine their programming skills with the visual programming skills introduced earlier to create programs that are both visual and interactive.

Chapter 5—Control Structures: Part 2

Chapter 5 introduces more complex control structures and the logical operators. It uses flowcharts to illustrate the flow of control through each control structure, including the **for**, **do/while** and **switch** structures. We explain the **break** and **continue** statements and the logical operators. Examples include calculating compound interest and printing the distribution of grades on an exam (with some simple error checking). The chapter concludes with a structured programming summary.

Chapter 6—Methods

A *method* allows the programmer to create a block of code that can be called upon from various points in a program. Larger programs can be divided into interacting classes, each consisting of methods—this is sometimes called the "divide and conquer" strategy. Programs are divided into simple components that interact in straightforward ways. We discuss how to create our own methods that can take inputs, perform calculations and return outputs. We examine the FCL's **Math** class, which contains methods for performing complex calculations (e.g., trigonometric and logarithmic calculations). *Recursive* methods (methods that call themselves) and method overloading, which allows multiple methods to have the same name, are introduced. We demonstrate overloading by creating two **Square** methods that each take an integer (i.e., whole number) and a floating-point number (i.e., a number with a decimal point), respectively. To conclude the chapter, we create a graphical simulation of the "craps" dice game, using the random-number generation techniques presented in the chapter.

Chapter 7—Arrays

Chapter 7 introduces arrays, our first data structure. Data structures are crucial to storing, sorting, searching and manipulating large amounts of information. *Arrays* are groups of related data items that allow the programmer to access any element directly. Rather than creating 100 separate variables that are all related in some way, the programmer instead can create an array of 100 elements and access these elements by their location in the array. We discuss how to declare and allocate arrays, and we build on the techniques of the previous chapter by passing arrays to methods. Chapters 4 and 5 provide essential background for the discussion of arrays, because repetition structures are used to iterate through elements in the array. The combination of these concepts helps the reader create highly structured and well-organized programs. We then demonstrate how to sort and search arrays. We discuss multidimensional arrays (both rectangular and jagged), which can be used to store tables of data. We introduce the **foreach** structure, which can be used to iterate through arrays.

Chapter 8—Object-Based Programming

Chapter 8 serves as our introduction to the powerful concepts of objects and *classes* (i.e., programmer-defined types). As mentioned in Chapter 1, object technology has led to considerable improvements in software development, allowing programmers to create reusable software components. Objects allow programs to be organized in natural and intuitive ways. This chapter presents the fundamentals of object-based programming, such as encapsulation, data abstraction and abstract data types (ADTs). These techniques hide the details of components so that the programmer can concentrate on the "big picture." We create a **Time** class, which displays the time in standard and universal formats. We show how to create reusable software components with assemblies, namespaces and Dynamic Link Library (DLL) files. The reader will learn how to create classes and namespaces. We discuss properties and the **readonly** and **const** keywords.

Chapter 9—Object-Oriented Programming: Inheritance
In this chapter, we discuss inheritance—a form of software reusability in which classes (called *derived classes*) are created by absorbing attributes and methods of existing classes (called *base classes*). The inherited class (i.e., the derived class) can contain additional attributes and methods. We show how finding the commonality between classes of objects can reduce the amount of work it takes to build large software systems. These proven techniques help programmers create and maintain software systems. A detailed case study demonstrates software reuse and good programming techniques by finding the commonality among a three-level inheritance hierarchy: The **Point**, **Circle** and **Cylinder** classes. We discuss the software engineering benefits of object-oriented programming. Crucial object-oriented programming concepts, such as creating and extending classes, are presented in this chapter.

Chapter 10—Exception Handling
Exception handling is one of the most important topics in C# from the standpoint of building mission-critical and business-critical applications. People can enter incorrect data, data can be corrupted and clients can try to access records that do not exist or are restricted. A simple division-by-zero error may cause a calculator program to crash, but what if such an error occurs in the navigation system of an airplane while it is in flight? In some cases, the results of program failure could be disastrous. Programmers need to know how to recognize the errors (*exceptions*) that could occur in software components and handle those exceptions effectively, allowing programs to deal with problems and continue executing instead of "crashing." Programmers who construct software systems from reusable components built by other programmers must deal with the exceptions that those components may "throw." This chapter covers the details of C# exception handling, the termination model of exception handling, throwing and catching exceptions, and FCL class **Exception**.

Chapter 11—Graphical User Interface Concepts
Chapter 11 explains how to add sophisticated GUIs to programs. By using the techniques of rapid application development (RAD), programmers can create GUIs from reusable components, rather than explicitly programming every detail. The Visual Studio .NET IDE makes developing GUIs even easier by allowing the programmer to position components in a window through so-called visual programming. We discuss how to construct user interfaces with *Windows Forms controls* such as labels, buttons, textboxes and picture boxes. We also introduce *events*, which are messages sent by a program to signal to an object or a set of objects that an action has occurred. Events most commonly are used to signal user interactions with GUI controls, but also can signal internal actions in a program. We overview event handling and discuss how to handle events specific to controls, the keyboard and the mouse. Tips are included throughout the chapter to help the programmer create visually appealing, well-organized and consistent GUIs. The last section of this chapter introduces visual inheritance, which enables programmers to combine the GUI concepts presented in this chapter with the object-oriented concepts presented in Chapter 9 to create user interfaces that can be used and extended by other programmers.

Chapter 12—Multithreading

Users have come to expect much from applications. Users want to download files from the Internet, listen to music, print documents and browse the Web—all at the same time! To do this, programmers need a feature called *multithreading*, which allows applications to perform multiple activities concurrently. The .NET Framework includes built-in capabilities to enable multithreaded applications, while shielding programmers from complex details. The .NET languages are better equipped to deal with more sophisticated multimedia, network-based and multiprocessor-based applications than those languages that do not have multithreading features. This chapter introduces the FCL's threading classes and covers threads, thread life-cycles, time-slicing, scheduling and priorities. This chapter lays the foundation for creating the multithreaded programs that clients demand.

Chapter 13—Strings and Characters

In this chapter, we discuss the processing of words, sentences, characters and groups of characters. In C#, **string**s (groups of characters) are objects. This is yet another benefit of C#'s emphasis on object-oriented programming. Objects of type **string** contain methods that can copy, search, extract substrings and concatenate strings with one another. We introduce class **StringBuilder**, which defines string-like objects that can be modified after initialization. As an interesting example of strings, we create a card shuffling-and-dealing simulation.

Chapter 14—Graphics

In this chapter, we discuss *GDI+* (an extension of the *Graphics Device Interface—GDI*), the Windows service that provides the graphical features used by .NET applications. The extensive graphical capabilities of GDI+ can make programs more visual and fun to create and use. We discuss C#'s treatment of graphics objects and color control. We also discuss how to draw lines, rectangles and ovals. The chapter also demonstrates how to use various pens and brushes to create color effects, and introduces techniques for turning text-only applications into exciting, aesthetically pleasing programs that even novice programmers can write with ease.

Chapter 15—Files and Streams

Imagine a program that could not save data to a file. Once the program is closed, all the work performed in the program is lost forever. For this reason, this chapter is one of the most important for programmers who will be developing commercial applications. We introduce FCL classes for file inputting and outputting data. A detailed example demonstrates these concepts by allowing the user to read and write bank account information to and from files. We introduce the FCL classes and methods that help perform input and output conveniently—they demonstrate the power of object-oriented programming and reusable classes. This chapter lays the groundwork for the material presented in Chapter 20, Networking: Streams-Based Sockets.

Chapter 16—Database, SQL and ADO .NET

Data storage and access are integral to creating powerful software applications. This chapter discusses .NET support for database manipulation. Today's most popular database systems are relational databases. In this chapter, we introduce the Structured Query Language (SQL) for performing queries on relational databases. We introduce *ActiveX Data Objects* ADO .NET—an extension of ADO that enables .NET applications to access and manipulate databases. We show the reader how to create database connections, using tools provided in Visual Studio .NET, and how to use some of the classes in namespace **System.Data** to query a database.

Chapter 17—ASP .NET, Web Forms and Web Controls

Previous chapters demonstrated how to create applications that execute locally on the user's computer. In this chapter and Chapter 19, we discuss how to create Web-based applications using *Active Server Pages (ASP) .NET*. This is a crucial aspect of .NET and of Microsoft's vision of how software should be developed and deployed on the Internet. ASP .NET is an integral technology for creating dynamic Web content marked up as HTML. (For readers who are unfamiliar with HTML, we provide a detailed introduction in Appendices G and H.) *Web Forms* provide GUIs for ASP .NET pages and can contain *Web controls*, such as labels, buttons and textboxes with which users interact. Like Windows Forms, Web Forms are designed using visual programming.

Chapter 18—Extensible Markup Language (XML)

The Extensible Markup Language (XML) derives from SGML (Standard Generalized Markup Language), which became an industry standard in 1986. Although SGML is employed in publishing applications worldwide, it has not been incorporated into the mainstream programming community because of its sheer size and complexity. XML is an effort to make SGML-like technology available to a much broader community. XML, created by the World Wide Web Consortium (W3C), is used for describing data in a portable format. XML differs in concept from markup languages such as HTML, which describes how information is rendered in a browser. XML is a technology for creating markup languages for virtually any type of information. Document authors use XML to create entirely new markup languages to describe specific types of data, including mathematical formulas, chemical molecular structures, music, recipes and much more. Markup languages created with XML include XHTML (Extensible HyperText Markup Language, for Web content), MathML (for mathematics), VoiceXML™ (for speech), SMIL™ (Synchronized Multimedia Integration Language, for multimedia presentations), CML (Chemical Markup Language, for chemistry) and XBRL (Extensible Business Reporting Language, for financial data exchange). The extensibility of XML has made it one of the most important technologies in industry today and is being integrated into almost every field. Companies and individuals constantly are finding new and innovative uses for XML. In this chapter, we present examples that illustrate the basics of marking up data as XML.

Chapter 19—ASP .NET and Web Services

Chapter 19 continues our discussion of ASP .NET. In this chapter, we introduce *Web services*, which are programs that "expose" services (i.e., methods) to clients over the Internet, intranets and extranets. Web services offer increased software reusability by allowing services on disparate platforms to interact with each other seamlessly. This chapter presents an interesting example of a Web service that manipulates huge integers (up to 100 digits).

Chapter 20—Networking: Streams-Based Sockets

Chapter 20 introduces the fundamental techniques of streams-based networking. We demonstrate how streams-based *sockets* allow programmers to hide many networking details. With sockets, networking is as simple as if the programmer were reading from and writing to a file. The example provided in this chapter demonstrates using streams-based sockets to communicate between two C# programs.

Chapter 21—FCL Collections

This chapter discusses the prebuilt collection classes in the .NET Framework Class Library. These collections classes store sets, or collections, of data and provide functionality that allow the developer to sort, insert, delete and retrieve data items. Different collections classes store data in different ways. This chapter focuses on classes **Array**, **ArrayList**, **Stack** and **Hashtable**, discussing the details of each.

Chapter 22—Accessibility

The World Wide Web presents challenges to individuals with disabilities. Multimedia-rich Web sites are difficult for text readers and other programs to interpret; thus, users with hearing and visual impairments may have difficulty browsing such sites. To help rectify this situation, the World Wide Web Consortium (W3C) launched the *Web Accessibility Initiative (WAI)*, which provides guidelines for making Web sites accessible to people with disabilities. This chapter provides a description of these guidelines, such as the use of the **headers** element to make tables more accessible to page readers, the **alt** attribute of the **img** element to describe images and the combination of XHTML and Cascading Style Sheets (CSS), to ensure that a page can be viewed on almost any type of display or reader. We illustrate key accessibility features of Visual Studio .NET, Internet Explorer and Windows 2000. We also introduce *VoiceXML™* and *CallXML*, two technologies for increasing the accessibility of Web-based content. VoiceXML helps people with visual impairments to access Web content via speech synthesis and speech recognition. CallXML allows users with visual impairments to access Web-based content through a telephone.

Chapter 23—Mobile Internet Toolkit

The demand for wireless applications is growing rapidly. By 2003, the number of people browsing the Web from wireless devices will exceed the number browsing from desktop computers. The *Mobile Internet Toolkit* (MIT) extends Visual Studio .NET by providing a set of FCL classes for creating mobile applications. We introduce Mobile Web controls and Mobile Web Forms that can be used to create ASP .NET applications that target a wide range of mobile devices.

Appendix A—Operator Precedence Chart

This appendix lists C# operators and their precedence.

Appendix B—Number Systems

This appendix explains the binary, octal, decimal and hexadecimal number systems. It also reviews the conversion of numbers among these bases and illustrates mathematical operations in each base.

Appendix C—Career Opportunities

This appendix provides career resources for C# programmers.

Appendix D—Visual Studio .NET Debugger

This appendix introduces the Visual Studio .NET debugger for locating logic errors in programs. Key features of this appendix include setting breakpoints, stepping through programs line-by-line and "watching" variable values.

Appendix E—ASCII Character Set

This appendix contains a table of the 128 ASCII (American Standard Code for Information Interchange) alphanumeric symbols and their corresponding integer values.

Appendix F—Unicode®

This appendix introduces the Unicode Standard, an encoding scheme that assigns unique numeric values to the characters of most of the world's languages. We include a Windows application that uses Unicode encoding to print welcome messages in several languages.

Appendices G and H—Introduction to HyperText Markup Language 4: 1 & 2

These appendices provide an introduction to HTML—a markup language for describing the elements of a Web page so that a browser, such as Microsoft's Internet Explorer, can render that page. The reader should be familiar with these appendices before studying Chapter 17, ASP .NET, Web Forms and Web Controls. No C# programming is presented in these appendices. Some key topics covered in Appendix G include incorporating text and images in an HTML document, linking to other HTML documents on the Web, incorporating special characters (such as copyright and trademark symbols) into an HTML document and separating parts of an HTML document with horizontal lines (called *horizontal rules*). In Appendix H, we discuss more substantial HTML elements and features. We demonstrate how to present information in lists and tables. We discuss how to collect information from users browsing a site. We explain how to use internal linking and image maps to make Web pages easier to navigate. We also discuss how to use frames to display multiple documents in the browser window.

Appendix I—HTML Special Characters

This appendix provides many commonly used HTML special characters, called *character entity references*.

Appendix J—HTML Colors

This appendix lists commonly used HTML color names and their corresponding hexadecimal values.

Appendix K—Crystal Reports

Visual Studio .NET integrates a special edition of *Crystal Reports*®—a Windows-based report generator. This appendix presents the resources that *Crystal Decisions*, the company that produces Crystal Reports, offers on its Web site and overviews Crystal Report's unique functionality and features in Visual Studio .NET.

1.10 Summary

In the late 1960s, at a conference at the University of Illinois Urbana-Champaign, ARPA— the Advanced Research Projects Agency of the Department of Defense—rolled out the blueprints for networking the main computer systems of approximately a dozen ARPA-funded universities and research institutions. Shortly after this conference, ARPA proceeded to implement the ARPAnet, the grandparent of today's Internet.

Although the ARPAnet did enable researchers to network their computers, its chief benefit proved to be the capability for quick and easy communication via what came to be known as electronic mail (e-mail). This is true even on today's Internet, with e-mail, instant messaging and file transfer facilitating communications among hundreds of millions of people worldwide.

The protocol (i.e., set of rules) for communicating over the ARPAnet became known as the Transmission Control Protocol (TCP). TCP ensured that messages were routed properly from sender to receiver and that those messages arrived intact. ARPA developed the Internet Protocol (IP), which created a true "network of networks," the current architecture of the Internet. The combined set of protocols is now commonly called TCP/IP.

The World Wide Web allows computer users to locate and view multimedia-based documents (i.e., documents with text, graphics, animations, audios or videos) on almost any subject. In 1989, Tim Berners-Lee of CERN (the European Organization for Nuclear Research) began to develop a technology for sharing information via hyperlinked text documents. Berners-Lee called his invention the HyperText Markup Language (HTML). He also wrote communication protocols to form the backbone of his new hypertext information system, which he referred to as the World Wide Web.

In October 1994, Tim Berners-Lee founded an organization, called the World Wide Web Consortium (W3C), that is devoted to developing nonproprietary, interoperable technologies for the World Wide Web. One of the W3C's primary goals is to make the Web universally accessible—regardless of disabilities, language or culture.

The Extensible Markup Language (XML) combines the power and extensibility of its parent language, Standard Generalized Markup Language, with the simplicity that the Web community demands. Data independence, the separation of content from its presentation, is an essential characteristic of XML. Because an XML document describes data, any application conceivably can process an XML document. XML's flexibility and power make it perfect for client/server systems, which must interact with a wide variety of clients.

Simple Object Access Protocol (SOAP) is a technology for the distribution of objects (marked up as XML) over the Internet. Developed initially by Microsoft and Develop-Mentor, SOAP is a W3C Working Draft that provides a framework for expressing application semantics, encoding data and packaging data. Microsoft .NET uses XML and SOAP to mark up and transfer data over the Internet. XML and SOAP are at the core of .NET—they allow software components to communicate easily with one another.

Object technology is a packaging scheme that facilitates the creation of meaningful software units. Objects have properties (i.e., attributes, such as color, size and weight) and perform actions (i.e., behaviors, such as moving, sleeping or drawing). Classes represent groups of related objects.

With the advent of popular object-oriented languages, such as C++, Java and C#, programmers can program in an object-oriented manner that reflects the way in which they perceive the world. This process, which seems more natural than procedural programming, has resulted in significant productivity gains.

With object technology, properly designed software entities (called objects) can be reused on future projects. Using libraries of reusable componentry can reduce the amount of effort required to implement certain kinds of systems (as compared to the effort that would be required to reinvent these capabilities in new projects). C# programmers use the .NET Framework Class Library (known commonly as the FCL).

In June 2000, Microsoft announced its .NET initiative. The .NET platform is one that provides significant enhancements to earlier developer platforms. .NET offers a new software-development model that allows applications created in disparate programming languages to communicate with each other. The platform also allows developers to create Web-based applications that can be distributed to a great variety of devices (even wireless phones) and to desktop computers.

One key aspect of the .NET strategy is its independence from a specific language or platform. Rather than requiring programmers to use a single programming language, developers can create a .NET application by using any combination of .NET-compatible languages. Programmers can contribute to the same software project, writing code in the .NET languages in which they are most proficient. Part of the initiative includes Microsoft's Active Server Pages (ASP) .NET technology, which allows programmers to create applications for the Web.

A key component of the .NET architecture is Web services, which are applications that expose functionality to clients via the Internet. Clients and other applications can use these Web services as reusable building blocks.

Universal data access is another essential .NET concept. With .NET, data can reside in one central location rather than on separate systems. Any Internet-connected device can access the data (under tight control, of course), which would then be formatted appropriately for use or display on the accessing device.

C# is an event-driven, fully object-oriented, visual programming language in which programs are created using an Integrated Development Environment (IDE). With the IDE, a programmer can create, run, test and debug C# programs conveniently, thereby reducing the time it takes to produce a working program to a fraction of the time it would have taken without using the IDE.

The .NET Framework is at the heart of .NET. This framework manages and executes applications, contains the FCL, enforces security, and provides many other programming capabilities. The details of the .NET Framework are found in the Common Language Specification (CLS), which contains information about the storage of data types, objects and so on.

The Common Language Runtime (CLR) is another central part of the .NET Framework—it executes C# programs. Programs are compiled into machine-specific instructions in two steps. First, the program is compiled into Microsoft Intermediate Language (MSIL), which defines instructions for the CLR. Code converted into MSIL from other .NET languages and sources is woven together by the CLR. Then, another compiler in the CLR compiles the MSIL into machine code (for a particular platform), creating a single application.

1.11 Internet and World Wide Web Resources

www.deitel.com
This is the official Deitel & Associates, Inc. Web site. Here you will find updates, corrections, downloads and additional resources for all Deitel publications. In addition, this site provides information about Deitel & Associates, Inc., downloads and resources related to our publications, information on international translations, and much more.

www.deitel.com/newsletter/subscribe.html
You can register here to receive the *DEITEL™ BUZZ ONLINE* e-mail newsletter. This free monthly newsletter updates readers on our publishing program, instructor-led corporate training courses, hottest industry trends and topics, and much more. The newsletter is available in full-color HTML and plain-text formats.

www.prenhall.com/deitel
This is Prentice Hall's Web site for Deitel publications, which contains information about our products and publications, downloads, Deitel curriculum, and author information.

www.InformIT.com/deitel

This is the Deitel & Associates, Inc. page on Pearson's InformIT Web site (Pearson owns our publisher Prentice Hall.) InformIT is a comprehensive resource for IT professionals providing articles, electronic publications and other resources for today's hottest information technologies. The Deitel kiosk at **InformIT.com** provides two or three free articles per week and for-purchase electronic publications. All Deitel publications can be purchased at this site.

www.w3.org

The World Wide Web Consortium (W3C) is an organization that develops and recommends technologies for the Internet and World Wide Web. This site includes links to W3C technologies, news, mission statements and frequently asked questions (FAQs). Deitel and Associates, Inc. is a member of the W3C.

www.netvalley.com/intval.html

This site presents the history of the Internet and the World Wide Web.

www.microsoft.com

The Microsoft Corporation Web site provides information and technical resources for all Microsoft products, including .NET, enterprise software and the Windows operating system.

www.microsoft.com/net

The .NET home page provides downloads, news and events, certification information, and subscription information.

Introduction to the
Visual Studio .NET IDE

Objectives

- To become familiar with the Visual Studio .NET Integrated development environment (IDE).
- To be able to use the commands contained in the IDE's menus and toolbars.
- To understand the various kinds of windows in Visual Studio .NET.
- To be able to use the features provided by the toolbar.
- To understand Visual Studio .NET's help features.
- To be able to create, compile and execute a simple C# program.

Seeing is believing.
Proverb

Form ever follows function.
Louis Henri Sullivan

Intelligence... is the faculty of making artificial objects, especially tools to make tools.
Henri-Louis Bergson

2.1 Introduction

Visual Studio .NET is Microsoft's integrated development environment (IDE) for creating, documenting, running and debugging programs written in a variety of .NET programming languages. Visual Studio .NET also offers editing tools for manipulating several types of files. Visual Studio .NET is a powerful and sophisticated tool for creating business-critical and mission-critical applications. In this chapter, we provide an overview of the Visual Studio .NET features needed to create a simple C# program. We introduce additional IDE features throughout the book.

2.2 Visual Studio .NET Integrated Development Environment (IDE) Overview

When Visual Studio .NET is executed for the first time, the **Start Page** is displayed (Fig. 2.1). This page contains helpful links, which appear on the left side of the **Start Page**. Users can click the name of a section (such as **Get Started**) to browse its contents. We refer to single-clicking with the left mouse button as *selecting* or *clicking* and to clicking twice with the left mouse button as *double-clicking*. [*Note*: The user should be aware that there are slight differences in the way Visual Studio .NET appears based on the version being used.]

Figure 2.1 displays the **Start Page** when the **Get Started** link is selected. The **Get Started** section contains links to recently opened projects. The most recently opened projects appear on this list (such as **WindowsApplication1** in Fig. 2.1), along with their modification dates. Alternately, the user can select **Recent Projects** from the **File** menu. The first time Visual Studio .NET is loaded, this section will be empty. Notice the two *buttons* on the page: **Open Project** and **New Project**. A button is a raised, rectangular area that performs an action when clicked.

Let us briefly describe the other **Start Page** links,[1] shown in Fig. 2.1. The **What's New** section displays new features and updates for Visual Studio .NET, including down-

---

1. Note that, for many of the links provided by the **Start Page**, an Internet connection is required.

loads for code samples and new programming tools. The **Online Community** section includes ways to contact other software developers, using newsgroups, Web pages and other online resources. The **Headlines** section provides a way to browse news, articles and how-to guides. Use the **Search Online** section to browse through the *MSDN (Microsoft Developer Network)* online library. The MSDN site includes numerous articles, downloads and tutorials for a variety of technologies. The **Downloads** section allows the user to obtain updates and code samples. The **XML Web Services** page provides programmers with information about *Web services*, which are reusable pieces of software available on the Internet. We discuss this technology in Chapter 19, ASP .NET and Web Services. **Web Hosting** provides information for developers who wish to post their software (such as Web services) online for public use. The **My Profile** page allows users to customize Visual Studio .NET, such as setting keyboard and window layout preferences. Users also can customize Visual Studio .NET by selecting **Options...** or **Customize...** from the **Tools** menu. [*Note*: From this point forward, we use the > character to indicate the selection of a menu command. For example, we use the notation **Tools > Options...** and **Tools > Customize...** to indicate the selection of the **Options...** and **Customize...** commands, respectively.] Visual Studio .NET can even browse the Web—the Internet Explorer Web browser is part of the IDE. To access a Web page, type its address into the location bar (see Fig. 2.1) and press the *Enter* key. Several other windows appear in the IDE in addition to the **Start Page**. We discuss these windows in the following sections.

To create a new C# program, click the **New Project** button in the **Get Started** section. This action displays the *dialog* in Fig. 2.2. Visual Studio .NET organizes programs into *projects* and *solutions*. A project is a group of related files, such as C# code, images and documentation. A solution is a group of projects that represent a complete application, or a set of related applications. Each project in the solution may perform a different task. In this chapter, we create a single-project solution.

Visual Studio .NET allows us to create projects in a variety of programming languages. This book focuses on C#, so select the **Visual C# Projects** folder in the **New Project** dialog (Fig. 2.2). There are a variety of project types from which to choose, several of which are used throughout this book. In this case, create a *Windows application*. Windows applications are programs that execute inside the Windows operating system, like Microsoft Word, Internet Explorer and Visual Studio .NET. Typically, such programs contain *controls*—graphical elements, such as buttons and labels—with which the user interacts.

By default, Visual Studio .NET assigns the name **WindowsApplication1** to the project and to the solution (Fig. 2.2). The default location for storing related files is the folder where the last project was created. The first time Visual Studio .NET executes, the default folder is the **Visual Studio Projects** folder in the **My Documents** folder. The user can change both the name and the location of the folder in which to save the project. After selecting a name and location for the project, click **OK** in the **New Project** dialog. The IDE will then change its appearance, as shown in Fig. 2.3.

In this figure, the large gray box to the left represents the window for our application. This rectangle is called the *form*. We discuss how to add controls to the form later in this chapter. The form and controls are the *graphical user interface (GUI)* of the program. They are the graphical components through which the user interacts with the program. Users enter data (*inputs*) into the program by entering information from the keyboard and by clicking the mouse buttons. The program displays instructions and other information (*outputs*) for users to read in the GUI.

Navigation buttons   Location bar

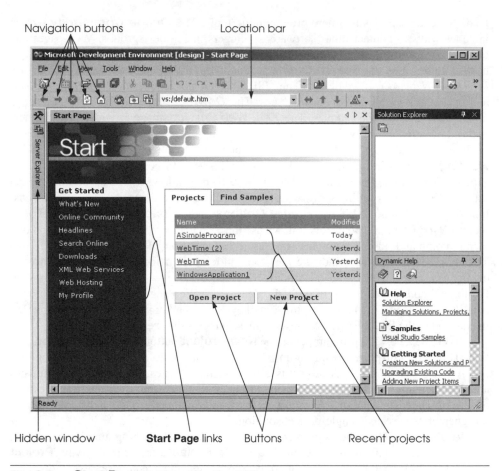

Hidden window   **Start Page** links   Buttons   Recent projects

Fig. 2.1   Start Page in Visual Studio .NET.

Notice how a tab appears for each open document (Fig. 2.3). In our case, the documents are the **Start Page** and **Form1.cs [Design]**. To view a tabbed document, click the tab with the name of the document you wish to view. Tabbing saves space and allows easy access to multiple documents.

The top of the IDE window (the *title bar* in Fig. 2.3) displays **WindowsApplication1 - Microsoft Visual C# .NET [design] - Form1.cs [Design]**. This title provides the name of the project (**WindowsApplication1**), the programming language (**Microsoft Visual C# .NET**), the *mode of the IDE* (**design** mode), the file being viewed (**Form1.cs**) and the mode of the file being viewed (**Design** mode). The file name **Form1.cs** is the default for Windows applications. We discuss the various modes in Section 2.6.

2.3 Menu Bar and Toolbar

Commands for managing the IDE and for developing, maintaining and executing programs are contained in the menus. Figure 2.4 shows the menus displayed on the menu bar. Menus contain groups of related commands that, when selected, cause the IDE to perform various actions (e.g., open a window). For example, new projects can be created by selecting **File >**

New > Project... from the menu bar. The menus shown in Fig. 2.4 are summarized in Fig. 2.5. Visual Studio .NET provides different modes for the user. One of these modes is the design mode, which will be discussed in Section 2.6. Certain menu items appear only in specific IDE modes.

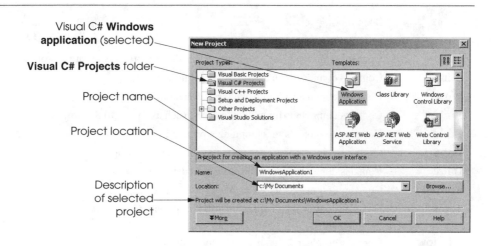

Fig. 2.2   New Project dialog.

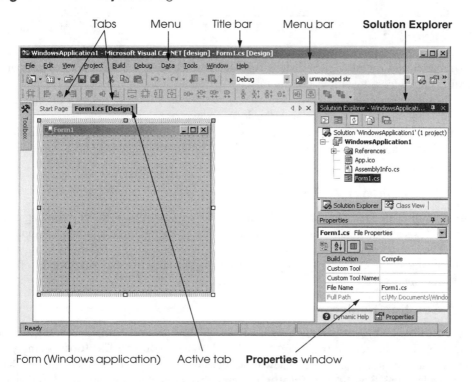

Fig. 2.3   Visual Studio .NET environment after a new project has been created.

File   Edit   View   Project   Build   Debug   Data   Format   Tools   Window   Help

Fig. 2.4   Visual Studio .NET menu bar.

Menu	Description
File	Contains commands for opening projects, closing projects, printing projects, etc.
Edit	Contains commands such as cut, paste, find, undo, etc.
View	Contains commands for displaying IDE windows and toolbars.
Project	Contains commands for adding features, such as forms, to the project.
Build	Contains commands for compiling a program.
Debug	Contains commands for debugging and executing a program.
Data	Contains commands for interacting with databases.
Format	Contains commands for arranging a form's controls.
Tools	Contains commands for additional IDE tools and options for customizing the environment.
Window	Contains commands for arranging and displaying windows.
Help	Contains commands for getting help.

Fig. 2.5   Visual Studio .NET menu summary.

Rather than having to navigate the menus for certain commonly used commands, the programmer can access the commands from the *toolbar* (Fig. 2.6). The toolbar contains pictures called *icons* that represent commands. To execute a command, click its icon. Click the *down arrow* beside an icon to display related options. Figure 2.6 shows the standard (default) toolbar and an icon that uses the down arrow.

Holding the mouse pointer over an icon on the toolbar highlights that icon and displays a description called a *tool tip* (Fig. 2.7). Tool tips help users understand the purposes of unfamiliar icons.

2.4 Visual Studio .NET Windows

Visual Studio .NET provides users with windows for exploring files and customizing controls. In this section, we discuss the windows that are essential for developing C# applications. These windows can be accessed using the toolbar icons below the menu bar and on the right edge of the toolbar (Fig. 2.8), or by selecting the name of the desired window from the **View** menu.

2.4.1 Solution Explorer

The **Solution Explorer** window (Fig. 2.9) lists all the files in the solution. When Visual Studio .NET is first loaded (right portion of Fig. 2.9), the **Solution Explorer** is empty—there are no files to display. After a new project has been created or an existing project has been loaded, the **Solution Explorer** displays that project's contents (left portion of Fig. 2.9).

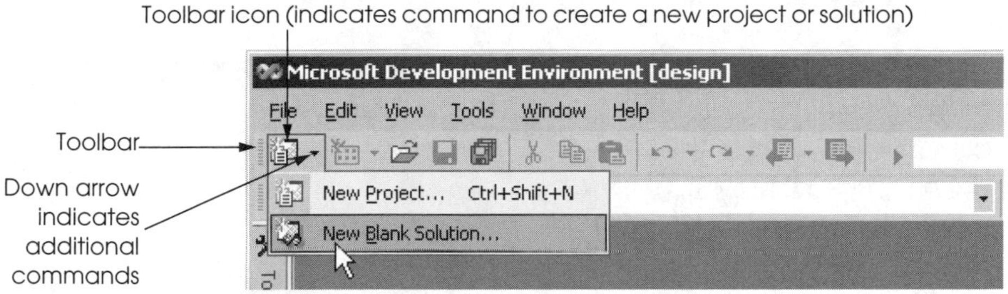

Toolbar icon (indicates command to create a new project or solution)

Fig. 2.6   Visual Studio .NET toolbar.

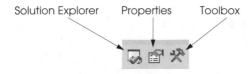

Fig. 2.7   Tool tip demonstration.

Solution Explorer   Properties   Toolbox

Fig. 2.8   Toolbar icons for various Visual Studio .NET windows.

The *startup project* of the solution is the project that runs when the solution is executed. It appears in bold text in the **Solution Explorer**. For our single-project solution, the startup project, **WindowsApplication1**, is the only project. The C# file is **Form1.cs**; it contains the program's code. We discuss the other files and folders later in the book.

The plus and minus boxes to the left of the **Solution Explorer** elements expand and collapse the tree, respectively (similar to those in Windows Explorer). Click a plus box to display more options; click a minus box to collapse a tree that already is expanded. Users also can expand or collapse a tree by double-clicking the name of the folder. Many other Visual Studio .NET windows also use the plus/minus convention.

The **Solution Explorer** contains a toolbar. One icon on the toolbar reloads the files in the solution (refreshes), and another icon displays all files in the solution (including hidden ones, or files located in the project's directory but that are not generally viewed as part of the project). The number of icons in the toolbar changes depending on the type of file selected. We discuss these icons later in the book.

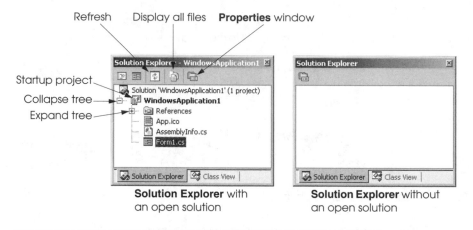

Fig. 2.9   Solution Explorer window.

2.4.2 Toolbox

The **Toolbox** (Fig. 2.10) contains reusable software components (or controls) that can be used to customize applications. Using *visual programming*, programmers can "drag and drop" controls onto a form instead of writing code themselves. Just as people do not need to know how to build an engine to drive a car, programmers do not need to build a control to use it. This allows them to concentrate on the big picture, rather than the complex details of every control. The wide variety of tools available to programmers is a powerful feature of C#. We demonstrate the power of the controls in the **Toolbox** when we create our own C# program visually later in the chapter.

The **Toolbox** contains groups of related components (e.g., **Data**, **Components**, **Windows Forms**) located toward the top of the **Toolbox** (Fig. 2.10). Expand the members of a group by clicking the name of the group. Users can scroll through the individual items by using the black scroll arrows on the right side of the **Toolbox**.

Selecting an item enables the programmer to add that item to their application. They can either double-click the item to add it to their application, or select the item (by clicking it once) and then use the mouse pointer to drag the item onto their application. The first item in the group is not a control—it is the mouse pointer (the selected item in Fig. 2.10). Clicking this icon allows the user to deselect the current control in the **Toolbox**, thus restoring the normal uses of the mouse pointer. Note that there are no tool tips, because the **Toolbox** icons already are labeled with the names of the controls. In later chapters, we discuss many of these controls.

Initially, the **Toolbox** may be hidden, with a **Toolbox** tab showing on the side of the IDE (Fig. 2.11). Moving the mouse pointer over a window name opens this window. Moving the mouse pointer outside the window causes the window to disappear. This feature is known as *auto hide*. To "pin down" the **Toolbox** (i.e., disable auto hide), click the *pin icon* in the upper-right corner of the window (see Fig. 2.11). If the window is not hidden (i.e., auto hide is disabled), the pin icon will appear to be standing up. To enable auto hide (if it has been disabled), click the pin icon again. Notice that when auto hide is enabled, the pin icon appears on its side, as is shown in Fig. 2.11.

2.4.3 Properties Window

The **Properties** window (Fig. 2.12) allows manipulation of the *properties* for a form or control. Properties specify information about a control, such as its size, color and position. Each control has its own set of properties. The bottom of the **Properties** window contains a description of the selected property.

The left column of the **Properties** window shows the properties of the control (a form in Fig. 2.12). The right column displays their current values. Icons on the toolbar sort the properties either alphabetically (by clicking the **Alphabetic** *icon*) or categorically (by clicking the **Categorized** *icon*), meaning that the properties are organized into groups based on their purpose. Users can scroll through the list of properties by *dragging* the scrollbar up or down (i.e., holding down the left mouse button while the mouse cursor is over the scrollbar, moving the mouse up or down and releasing the mouse button). The **Event** *icon* allows the control or form to respond to certain user actions. We discuss events in Chapter 11, Graphical User Interface Concepts. We show how to set individual properties later in this chapter and throughout the book.

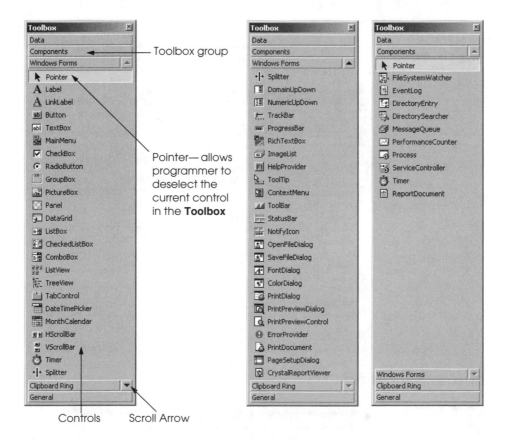

Fig. 2.10   Toolbox window.

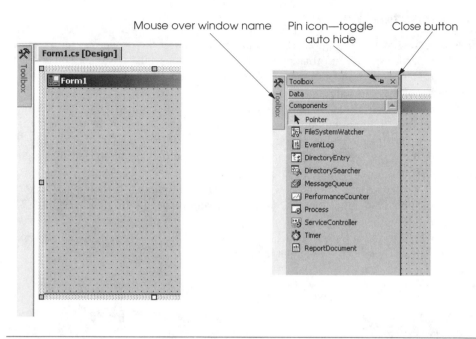

Fig. 2.11   Demonstrating window auto-hide.

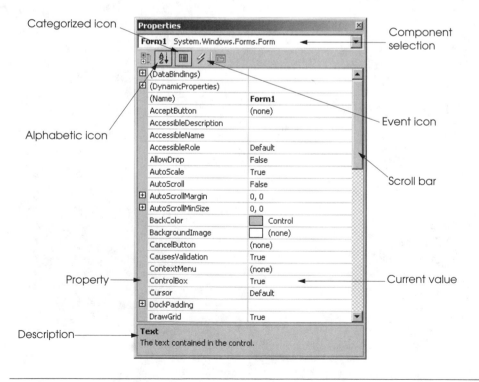

Fig. 2.12   **Properties** window.

The **Properties** window also is important to visual programming. Controls are usually customized after they are created from the **Toolbox**. The **Properties** window allows programmers to modify controls visually (i.e, without writing code). This setup has a number of benefits. First, the programmer can see which properties are available for modification and what the possible values are; the programmer does not have to look up or remember what settings a particular property can have. Second, the window displays a brief description of each property, allowing the programmer to understand each property's purpose. Third, a property's value can be set quickly using the window; only a single click is required, and no code need be written. All these features are designed to help software developers program without performing many repetitive tasks.

At the top of the **Properties** window is a drop-down list, or a control containing a down arrow, which when clicked displays a list of options. This drop-down list is called the *component selection*. This list shows the current component that is being altered. The programmer can use the list to choose which component to edit. For example, if a GUI contains several buttons, the programmer can select the name of a specific button to configure.

2.5 Using Help

Visual Studio .NET has an extensive help mechanism. The **Help** *menu* contains a variety of options. The **Contents** *menu item* displays a categorized table of contents. Menu item **Index** displays an alphabetical index that users can browse. The **Search** feature allows users to find particular help articles based on a few search words. In each case, a subset of available topics, or filter, can narrow the search to articles related only to C#.

Dynamic help (Fig. 2.13) provides a list of articles based on the current content (i.e., the items around the location of the mouse cursor). To open dynamic help (if it is not already open), select the **Help** menu's **Dynamic Help** command. Once you click an object to display in Visual Studio .NET, relevant help articles will appear in the **Dynamic Help** window. The window lists relevant help entries, samples and "Getting Started" information, in addition to providing a toolbar for the regular help features. Dynamic help is an excellent way to get information about the features of Visual Studio .NET. Note that **Dynamic Help** may slow down Visual Studio .NET.

Performance Tip 2.1

If you experience slow response times from Visual Studio, you can disable (i.e., close) **Dynamic Help** *by clicking the* **x** *in the upper-right corner of the window.*

In addition to dynamic help, Visual Studio .NET provides *context-sensitive help*. Context-sensitive help is similar to dynamic help, except that context-sensitive help immediately brings up a relevant help article rather than presenting a list. To use context-sensitive help, select an item and press the *F1* key. Help can appear either *internally* or *externally*. With external help, a relevant article immediately pops up in a separate window, outside the IDE. With internal help, a help article appears as a tabbed window inside Visual Studio .NET. The help options can be set from the **My Profile** section of the **Start Page**. Dynamic help and context-sensitive help are explained in the context of C# code later in the book.

2.6 Simple Program: Displaying Text and an Image

In this section, we create a program that displays the text "**Welcome to C#!**" and an image of the cover art from our book, *C# How to Program*. The program consists of a single form that uses a label to display text and a picture box to display an image. Figure 2.14 shows the program as it executes. The example here (as well as the image file used in the example) is available on our Web Site (**www.deitel.com**) under the **Downloads/Resources** link.

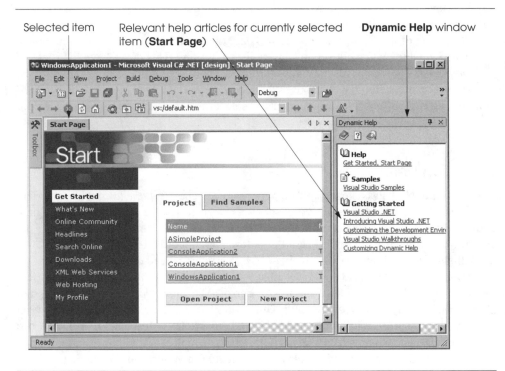

Selected item   Relevant help articles for currently selected   **Dynamic Help** window
                       item (**Start Page**)

Fig. 2.13   Dynamic Help window.

Fig. 2.14   Simple program as it executes.

We do not write a single line of program code. Instead, we use the techniques of visual programming. Various programmer *gestures* (such as using the mouse for pointing, clicking, dragging and dropping) provide Visual Studio .NET with sufficient information for it to generate all or a major portion of the program code. Later in this chapter, we begin our discussion of writing program code. Throughout the book, we produce increasingly substantial and more powerful programs. C# programming usually involves a combination of writing a portion of the program code and having Visual Studio .NET generate the remaining code.

To create, run and terminate this first program, perform the following steps:

1. *Create the new project.* If a project is already open, close it by selecting **File > Close Solution** from the menu. A dialog asking whether to save the current solution may appear, to keep any unsaved changes, save the solution. Create a new Windows application for our program. Open Visual Studio .NET, and select **File > New > Project... > Visual C# Projects > Windows Application** (Fig. 2.15). Name the project **ASimpleProject**, and select a directory in which to save the project. To do this, click the **Browse...** button, which opens a **Project Location** dialog (Fig. 2.16). Navigate through the directories, find one in which to place the project and select **OK**. This selection returns us to the **New Project** dialog; the selected folder appears in the **Location** text field. When you are satisfied with the location of the project, click **OK**. Visual Studio .NET will load the new solution, and a form labeled **Form1** will appear. We have already seen an example of this in Fig. 2.3.

2. *Set the form's title bar.* First, set the text that appears in the title bar. This text is determined by the form's **Text** property (Fig. 2.17). If the form's **Properties** window is not open, click the **Properties** icon in the toolbar or select the **View** menu's **Properties Window** command. Use the mouse to select the form; the **Properties** window shows information about the currently selected item. In the window, click in the box to the right of the **Text** property's box. To set a value for the **Text** property, type the value in the box. In this case, type **A Simple Program**, as in Fig. 2.17. When you have finished, press the *Enter* key to update the form's title bar in the design area.

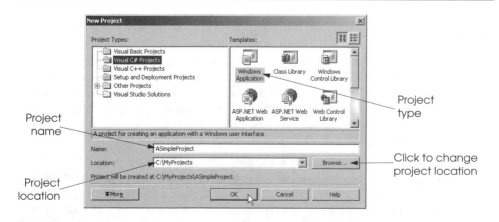

Fig. 2.15   Creating a new Windows application.

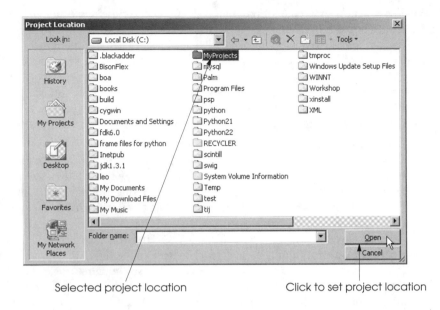

Selected project location   Click to set project location

Fig. 2.16 Setting the project location.

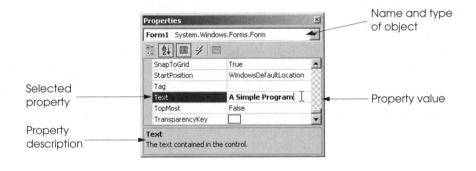

Name and type of object

Selected property

Property description

Property value

Fig. 2.17 Setting the form's **Text** property.

3. *Resize the form.* Click and drag one of the form's enabled *sizing handles* (the small squares around the form shown in Fig. 2.18) to change the size of the form. Enabled sizing handles are white. The mouse cursor changes appearance when it is over an enabled sizing handle. Disabled sizing handles are gray. The grid on the background of the form is used to align controls and does not appear when the program executes.

4. *Change the form's background color.* The **BackColor** property specifies a form's or control's background color. Clicking **BackColor** in the **Properties** window causes a down-arrow button to appear next to the property value (Fig. 2.19). When clicked, the down arrow drops down to display other options. (The options vary, depending on the property.) In this case, it displays the tabs **System** (the default), **Web** and **Custom**. Click the **Custom** tab to display the

palette (a selection box of colors). Select the box that represents yellow. The palette will disappear, and the form's background color will change to yellow.

5. *Add a label control to the form.* Double-click the label control in the **Toolbox**. This action creates a label with sizing handles in the upper-left corner of the form (Fig. 2.20). Double-clicking any **Toolbox** control places it on the form. Alternatively, programmers can "drag" controls from the **Toolbox** to the form. Labels display text; our label displays `label1` by default. Notice that our label is the same color as the form's background color. The form's background color is also the default background color of controls added to the form.

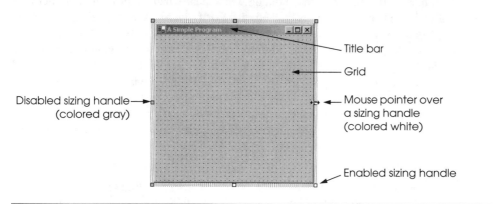

Fig. 2.18   Form with sizing handles.

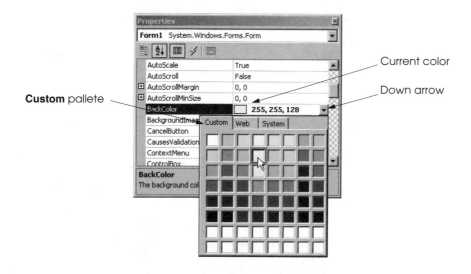

Fig. 2.19   Changing property **BackColor**.

6. *Set the label's text.* Select the label so that its properties appear in the **Properties** window. The label's **Text** property determines the text (if any) that the label displays. The form and label each have their own **Text** property. Forms and controls can have the same types of properties without conflict. We will see that many controls have property names in common. Set the **Text** property of the label to **Welcome to C#!** (Fig. 2.21). Resize the label (using the sizing handles) if the text does not fit. Move the label to the top center of the form by dragging it or using the arrow keys. Alternatively, you can move the label by selecting **Format > Center In Form > Horizontally** from the menu bar.

7. *Set the label's font size, and align the label's text.* Clicking the **Font** property value causes an *ellipsis* button (...) to appear next to the value, as in Fig. 2.22. The ellipsis button indicates that a dialog will appear when the programmer clicks the button. When the button is clicked, the **Font** *window* shown in Fig. 2.23 is displayed. Users can select the font name (**Microsoft Sans Serif**, **Arial**, etc.), font style (**Regular**, **Bold**, etc.) and font size (**8**, **10**, etc.) in this window. The text in the **Sample** *area* displays the selected font. Under the **Size** category, select **24** and click **OK**. If the text does not fit on a single line, it will wrap to the next line. Resize the label if it is not large enough to hold the text. Next, select the label's **TextAlign** property, which determines how the text is aligned within the label. A three-by-three grid of alignment choices is displayed, corresponding to where the text appears in the label (Fig. 2.24). Select the top-center grid item, so that the text will appear at the top center of the label.

8. *Add a picture box to the form.* The picture-box control displays images. This step is similar to Step 5. Find the picture box in the toolbox, and add it to the form. Move it underneath the label, by either dragging it or using the arrow keys (Fig. 2.25).

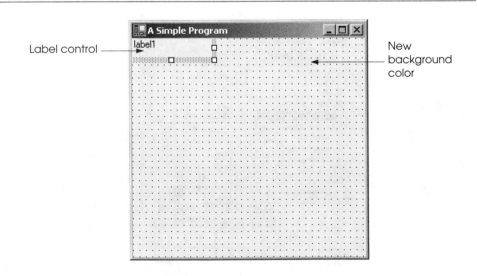

Fig. 2.20   Adding a new label to the form.

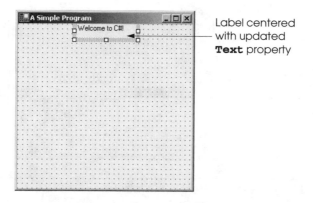

Label centered
with updated
Text property

Fig. 2.21   Label in position with its **Text** property set.

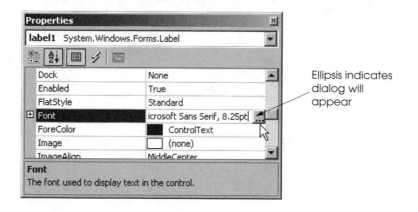

Ellipsis indicates
dialog will
appear

Fig. 2.22   **Properties** window displaying the label's properties.

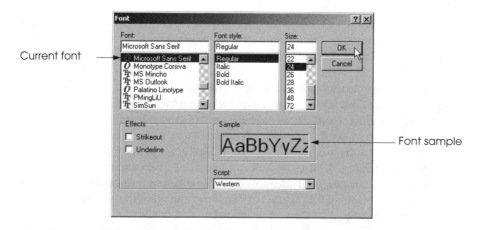

Current font

Font sample

Fig. 2.23   **Font** window for selecting fonts, styles and sizes.

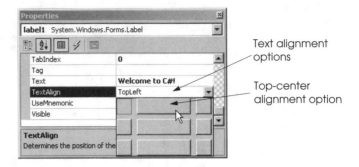

Text alignment options

Top-center alignment option

Fig. 2.24   Centering the text in the label.

Updated label

New picture box

Fig. 2.25   Inserting and aligning the picture box.

9. *Insert an image.* Click the picture box to load its properties in the **Properties** window, and find the *Image* property. The **Image** property shows a preview of the current picture. No picture has been assigned, so the **Image** property displays **(none)** (Fig. 2.26). Click the ellipsis button to display an **Open** dialog (Fig. 2.27). Browse for a picture to insert, and press *Enter* key. The proper formats of an image include PNG (Portable Networks Graphic), GIF (Graphic Interchange Format) and JPEG (Joint Photographic Experts Group). Each of these file formats is widely supported on the Internet. To create a new picture, it is necessary to use image-editing software, such as Jasc Paint Shop Pro, Adobe Photoshop Elements or Microsoft Paint. We use the picture **ASimpleProgramImage.png**, which is located with this example on our Web site (**www.deitel.com**). After the image has been inserted, the picture box displays as much of the picture as it can (depending on size) and the **Image** property shows a small preview. To display the entire image, resize the picture box by dragging the picture box's handles (Fig. 2.28).

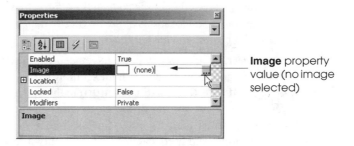

Fig. 2.26 **Image** property of the picture box.

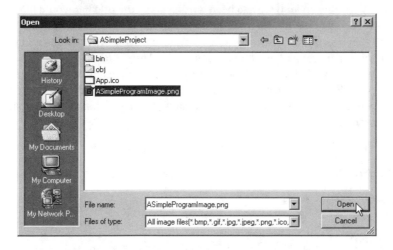

Fig. 2.27 Selecting an image for the picture box.

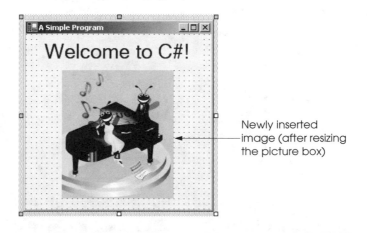

Fig. 2.28 Picture box after the image has been inserted.

10. *Save the project*. Select **File > Save All** to save the entire solution. To save an individual file, select it in the **Solution Explorer**, and select **File > Save**. The

created program stores the source code in the C# file **Form1.cs**. The project file contains the names and locations of all the files in the project. Choosing **Save All** saves both the project and the C# file.

11. *Run the project.* Prior to this step, we have been working in the IDE *design mode* (i.e., the program being created is not executing). This mode is indicated by the text **Microsoft Visual C# .NET [design]** in the title bar. While in design mode, programmers have access to all the environment windows (i.e., **Toolbox** and **Properties**), menus, toolbars and so forth. While in *run mode*, however, the program is executing, and users can interact with only a few IDE features. Features that are not available are disabled or grayed out. The text **Form1.cs [Design]** in the title bar means that we are designing the form visually, rather than programming it using code. If we had been writing code, the title bar would have contained only the text **Form1.cs**. To execute or run our program, we first need to compile it, which is accomplished by clicking the **Build Solution** *option* in the **Build** *menu* (or press the key combination *Ctrl + Shift + B*). The program can then be executed by clicking the **Start** button (the blue triangle), selecting the **Debug** menu's **Start** command or pressing the *F5* key. Figure 2.29 shows the IDE in run mode. Note that the IDE title bar displays **[run]** and that many toolbar icons are disabled.

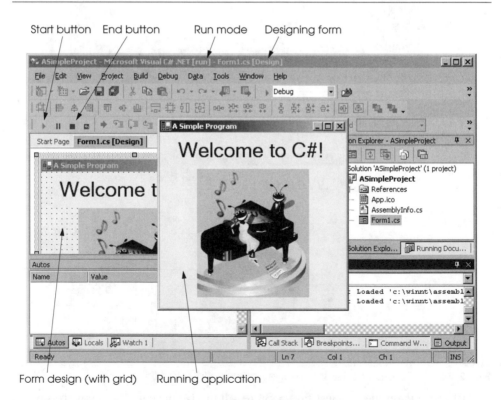

Fig. 2.29 IDE in run mode, with the running application in the foreground.

12. *Terminating execution.* To terminate the program, click the running application's **Close** button (the **x** in the top right corner). Alternatively, click the **End** button (the blue square) in the toolbar or enter *Shift + F5*. Either action stops program execution and puts the IDE into design mode.

Software Engineering Observation 2.1

Visual programming can be simpler and faster than writing code.

Software Engineering Observation 2.2

Most programs require more than visual programming. In such programs, some code must be written by the programmer. Examples include applications that employ event handlers (used to respond to the user's actions), databases, security, networking, text editing, graphics and multimedia.

2.7 Summary

Visual Studio .NET is Microsoft's integrated development environment (IDE) for creating, documenting, running and debugging programs. When Visual Studio .NET is loaded for the first time, the **Start Page** is displayed. This page contains helpful links, such as recent projects, online newsgroups, downloads and user profile settings. The **Get Started** section contains links to recent files. The **My Profile** page allows users to customize Visual Studio .NET.

Programs in Visual Studio .NET are organized into projects and solutions. A project is a group of related files. A solution is a group of projects that are combined to solve a developer's problem.

Windows applications are programs that execute inside the Windows OS, like Microsoft Word, Internet Explorer and Visual Studio .NET. They contain controls—reusable graphical elements, such as buttons and labels—which the user uses to interact with the application. The form is what the users interact with and view when programs run. The form and its controls constitute the graphical user interface (GUI) of the program. Controls are the graphical components with which the user interacts. Users enter data (inputs) into the program by entering information from the keyboard and clicking the mouse buttons. The program displays instructions and other information (outputs) for users to read in the GUI.

The title bar displays the name of the project, the programming language, the mode of the IDE, the file being viewed and the mode of the file being viewed. Visual Studio .NET displays multiple files simultaneously via tabbed windows. To view a tabbed document, click the tab with the name of the document. Tabbing saves space and allows easy access to multiple documents. Visual Studio .NET also provides several commands within menus. These commands, when selected, cause the IDE to perform some action. The different commands are grouped logically into the various menus. Many of the more commonly used menu commands also are provided in Visual Studio .NET's toolbar. The toolbar contains several icons representing commands that will execute when the corresponding icon is clicked. Click the down arrow beside an icon to display other available options.

The **Solution Explorer** lists all the files in a solution. The plus and minus boxes to the left of the project and solution names expand and collapse the tree, respectively. The **Toolbox** contains controls that customize forms. By using visual programming, programmers can "drag and drop" controls onto the form instead of writing the code themselves. The **Properties** window displays the properties for a form or control. Properties are information about a control, such as size, color and position. Each type of control has its own set of properties. The **Properties** window allows programmers to modify controls visually, without writing code.

The **Help** menu contains a variety of options. The **Contents** menu item displays a categorized table of contents. Menu item **Index** displays an alphabetical index that can be browsed. The **Search** feature allows users to find particular help articles, based on a few search words. For each option of the **Help** menu, a filter can be used to narrow the search to articles relating only to C#. Dynamic help provides a list of articles, based on the current content (i.e., the location of the mouse cursor). Context-sensitive help is similar to dynamic help, except that context-sensitive help immediately brings up a relevant help article. To use context-sensitive help, select an item and press the *F1* key.

C# programming usually involves a combination of writing a portion of the program code and having Visual Studio .NET generate the remaining code.

3

Introduction to C# Programming

Objectives

- To be able to write simple C# programs.
- To be able to use input and output statements.
- To become familiar with primitive data types.
- To understand basic memory concepts.
- To be able to use arithmetic operators.
- To understand the precedence of arithmetic operators.
- To be able to write decision-making statements.
- To be able to use relational and equality operators.

Comment is free, but facts are sacred.
C. P. Scott

The creditor hath a better memory than the debtor.
James Howell

When faced with a decision, I always ask, "What would be the most fun?"
Peggy Walker

Equality, in a social sense, may be divided into that of condition and that of rights.
James Fenimore Cooper

3.1 Introduction

This chapter introduces C# programming and presents examples that illustrate several important features of the language. Examples are analyzed one line at a time. In this chapter, we create *console applications*—applications that contain predominantly text output. There are several types of projects that we can create in C#; the console application is one of the basic types. Text output in a console application is displayed in a *command window* (also called a *console window*). On Microsoft Windows 95/98, the console window is the **MS-DOS prompt**. On Microsoft Windows NT/2000/XP, the console window is called the **command prompt**. With C#, a program can be created with multiple types of output (windows, dialogs and so forth). These programs are called *Windows applications* and provide graphical user interfaces. We showed an example of a Windows application in Chapter 2, when we printed a message on a form. These types of applications will be discussed in greater detail, beginning with Chapter 4, Control Structures: Part 1 and Chapter 5, Control Structures: Part 2. In these chapters, we also provide a detailed treatment of *program development* and *program control* in C#.

3.2 Simple Program: Printing a Line of Text

C# uses some notations that might appear strange to nonprogrammers. We begin by considering a simple program that displays a line of text. The program and its output are shown in Fig. 3.1. The program is followed by an output window that displays the program's results. When you execute this program, the output will appear in a console window.

```
1   // Fig. 3.1: Welcome1.cs
2   // A first program in C#.
3
4   using System;
5
6   class Welcome1
7   {
8      static void Main( string[] args )
9      {
10         Console.WriteLine( "Welcome to C# Programming!" );
11      }
12   }
```

Fig. 3.1   Our first program in C#. (Part 1 of 2.)

```
Welcome to C# Programming!
```

Fig. 3.1   Our first program in C#. (Part 2 of 2.)

This program illustrates several important features of C#. All programs we present in this book will include line numbers for the reader's convenience; these line numbers are not part of the C# programs. Line 10 in Fig. 3.1 does the "real work" of the program, displaying the phrase **Welcome to C# Programming!** on the screen.

Line 1 begins with **//**, indicating that the remainder of the line is a *comment*. Programmers insert comments to *document* and improve the readability of their code. Comments also help other people read and understand your programs. This comment simply indicates the figure number and file name for this program. We begin each program in this book in this manner. In this case, we have named the file **Welcome1.cs**. A comment that begins with **//** is called a *single-line comment*, because the comment terminates at the end of the line.

There is also a syntax for writing *multiple-line comments*. A multiple-line comment, such as

```
/* This is a multiple-line
   comment. It can be
   split over many lines */
```

begins with *delimiter* **/*** and ends with *delimiter* ***/**. All text between these delimiters is treated as a comment and is ignored by the compiler. In the Visual Studio .NET IDE, all comment text appears in green. Comments of the form **//** and **/* ... */** are ignored by the compiler; therefore, they do not cause the computer to perform any action when the program executes.

Common Programming Error 3.1

Forgetting one of the delimiters of a multiple-line comment is a syntax error. A syntax error is caused when the compiler cannot recognize a statement. The compiler normally issues an error message to help the programmer locate and fix the incorrect statement. Syntax errors are violations of the language rules. Syntax errors are also called compile errors, compile-time errors *or* compilation errors *because they are detected during the compilation phase. A program cannot compile or execute until all the syntax errors are corrected.*

Software Engineering Observation 3.1

Visual Studio will often catch syntax errors as you are creating the program, even before the program is compiled. Look out for red jagged lines that appear directly below a syntax error.

C# uses the same syntax as the C programming language for multiple-line comments (**/*...*/**) and the same syntax as C++ for single-line comments (**//**). C# programmers generally use C++-style single-line comments, instead of C-style comments. Throughout this book, we use mostly C++-style single-line comments.

Good Programming Practice 3.1

Every program should begin with one or more comments that describe the program's purpose.

Line 4 (known as a ***using*** *directive*) is added to our code by the Visual Studio IDE and declares that the program uses features in the ***System*** *namespace*. A *namespace* groups various C# features into related categories. One of the great strengths of C# is that C# programmers can use the rich set of namespaces provided by the .NET framework. These namespaces contain code that programmers can reuse, rather than "reinventing the wheel." This makes programming easier and faster. The namespaces that are defined in the .NET Framework contain preexisting code known as the *.NET Framework Class Library*. An example of one of the features in namespace **System** is **Console**, which we discuss momentarily. The various features are organized into namespaces that enable programmers to locate them easily. We discuss many namespaces and their features throughout the book.

Line 5 is a blank line. Programmers often use blank lines and space characters throughout a program to make the program easier to read. Collectively, blank lines, space characters, newline characters and tab characters are known as *whitespace* (space characters and tabs are known specifically as *whitespace characters*). *Newline characters* characters are "special characters" that indicate when to position the output cursor at the beginning of the next line in the console window to continue output. The compiler ignores blank lines, tabs and extra spaces that separate language elements. Several conventions for using whitespace characters are discussed in this and subsequent chapters.

Good Programming Practice 3.2

Use blank lines, space characters and tab characters in a program to enhance program readability.

Lines 6–12 define our first *class* (these lines collectively are called a *class definition*). C# programs consist of pieces called classes, which are logical groupings of members (e.g., *methods*) that simplify program organization. These methods (which are like functions in procedural programming languages) perform tasks and return information when the tasks are completed. A C# program consists of classes and methods created by the programmer and of preexisting classes found in the Framework Class Library. Throughout this book, we demonstrate how to use both techniques in programs. Every program in C# consists of at least one class definition that the programmer defines. These classes are known as *programmer-defined classes*. In Chapter 8, Object-Based Programming, we discuss programs that contain multiple programmer-defined classes. The ***class*** *keyword* begins a class definition in C# and is followed immediately by the *class name* (**Welcome1**, in this example). Keywords (or *reserved words*) are reserved for use by C# and always consist of lowercase letters. (A complete table of C# keywords is presented in the next chapter.) By convention, each word in a class name begins with an uppercase letter and has an uppercase letter to begin each additional word in the class name (e.g., **SampleClassName**). The name of the class is known as an *identifier*, which is a series of characters consisting of letters, digits, underscores (_) and "at" symbols (**@**). Identifiers cannot begin with a digit and cannot contain spaces. Examples of valid identifiers are **Welcome1**, **_value**, **m_inputField1** and **button7**. The name **7button** is not a valid identifier because it begins with a digit, and the name **input field** is not a valid identifier because it contains a space. The "at" character (**@**) can be used only as the first character in an identifier. C# is *case sensitive*—uppercase and lowercase letters are considered different letters, so **a1** and **A1** are different identifiers.

Common Programming Error 3.2

*C# is case sensitive. Not using the proper case for an identifier, e.g., writing **Total** when the identifier is **total**, is a compiler error.*

Good Programming Practice 3.3

Always begin a class name with an uppercase first letter. This practice makes class names easier to identify.

The *left brace* (**{**) in line 7 begins the *body of the class definition*. The corresponding *right brace* (**}**) in line 12 ends the class definition. Notice that lines 8–11 in the body of the class are indented. This is one of the spacing conventions mentioned earlier. Indentation improves program readability. We define each spacing convention as a *Good Programming Practice*.

Common Programming Error 3.3

If braces do not occur in matching pairs, a syntax error occurs.

Good Programming Practice 3.4

*When typing an opening left brace (**{**) in a program, immediately type the closing right brace (**}**) then reposition the cursor between the braces to begin typing the body. This practice helps prevent missing braces. Readers may notice that, when they type the closing brace, Visual Studio .NET makes both braces bold (as well as the first line of the class definition). This is helpful in the creation of more complex programs that involve multiple sets of opening and closing braces.*

Good Programming Practice 3.5

*Indent the entire body of each class definition one "level" of indentation between the left brace (**{**) and the right brace (**}**) that delimit the class body. This emphasizes the structure of the class definition and helps make the class definition easier to read. Visual Studio .NET provides indentation in several places as programmers enter code.*

Line 8 is present in all C# console and Windows applications. These applications begin executing at **Main**, which is known as the *entry point* of the program. The parentheses after **Main** indicate that **Main** is a program building block, called a method. C# class definitions normally contain one or more methods and C# applications contain one or more classes. For a C# console or Windows application, exactly one of those methods must be called **Main**, and it must be defined as shown on line 8; otherwise, the program is not executable. Normally, a console applications's **Main** method is defined as shown on line 8. Methods are explained in detail in Chapter 6, Methods. For now, simply mimic **Main**'s first line in each C# application.

The left brace (**{**) in line 9 begins the *body of the method definition* (the code which will be executed as a part of our program). A corresponding right brace (**}**) terminates the method definition's body (line 11). Notice that the line in the body of the method is indented between these braces (as a matter of good style).

Good Programming Practice 3.6

*Indent the entire body of each method definition one "level" of indentation between the left brace (**{**) and the right brace (**}**) that define the method body. This makes the structure of the method stand out, improving the method definition's readability.*

Line 10 instructs the computer to perform an *action,* namely, to print the series of characters contained between the double quotation marks. Characters delimited in this manner are called *strings, character strings* or *string literals.* We refer to characters between double quotation marks generically as strings. Whitespace characters in strings are significant—the compiler does not ignore these characters when they appear in strings.

The **Console** *class* enables programs to output information to the computer's *standard output,* normally the screen. Class **Console** provides methods that allow C# programs to display strings and other types of information in the Windows command prompt.

Method **Console.WriteLine** *displays* (or *prints*) a line of text in the console window. When **Console.WriteLine** completes its task, it positions the *output cursor* (the location where the next character will be displayed) at the beginning of the next line in the console window. (This is similar to pressing the *Enter* key when typing in a text editor—the cursor is repositioned at the beginning of the next line in the file.)

The entire line, including **Console.WriteLine**, its *argument* in the parentheses (**"Welcome to C# Programming!"**) and the *semicolon* (**;**), is called a *statement.* Every statement must end with a semicolon (known as the *statement terminator*). When this statement executes, it displays the message **Welcome to C# Programming!** in the console window (Fig. 3.1).

In C# statements we normally precede each class name with its namespace name and a period. For example, line 10 would normally be

```
System.Console.WriteLine( "Welcome to C# Programming!" );
```

for the program to run correctly. The **using** directive on line 4 eliminates the need to specify explicitly the namespace **System** when using classes in that namespace. This can save time and confusion for programmers.

Common Programming Error 3.4
Omitting the semicolon at the end of a statement is a syntax error.

Testing and Debugging Tip 3.1
When the compiler reports a syntax error, the error might not be on the line indicated by the error message. First, check the line where the error was reported. If that line does not contain syntax errors, check the lines that precede the one reported.

Now that we have presented this program to you, let us explain step-by-step how to create and run it in Visual Studio.

1. *Create the console application.* Go to the **File** menu and choose **New,** then **Project....** A dialog will appear. In the left pane, choose **Visual C# Projects;** from the right pane, choose **Console Application.** It is possible to specify other information about the project in the bottom portion of this dialog (i.e., the name and location of the project). After entering all the necessary information, click **OK** to create the project. The project is created, and the code window is opened for editing. The new application is shown in Fig. 3.2. Note that this is the same way we created our application in Chapter 2, except that now we have chosen a console application, instead of a Windows application.

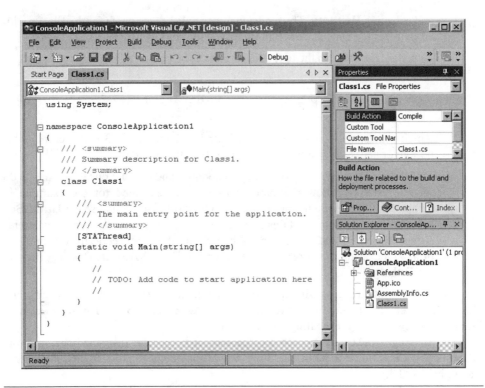

Fig. 3.2   Visual Studio .NET-generated console application.

This application can be built (compiled) and executed, but will not do anything until we add more code (this is done in Step 3). Let us briefly look at the code generated for us by the IDE.

Notice that this code contains features that we have not yet discussed. We have done this for both display and clarity reasons—at this point in the book, this code is neither required nor relevant to the discussion of this program. Much of the extra code that the IDE provides is used either for documentation or to help create graphical user interfaces. One of the things that the reader will no doubt notice is that we do not show the lines directly above and below the class definition. These lines are used to create namespaces, a topic that will be discussed in Chapter 8, Object-Based Programming. [*Note*: Several times early in this text, we ask the reader to mimic certain C# features that we introduce. We do this especially when it is not yet important to know all the details of a feature to use that feature in C#. Programmers often learn how to program by mimicking what other programmers have done. For each detail, we ask the reader to mimic, we indicate where the full discussion will be presented later in the text.] The code for all examples in the book is included for the reader on our Web site **www.deitel.com** under the **Downloads/Resources** link.

2. *Change the name of the program file.* For the programs in this book, we usually change the name of the code file. By default, the file is named **Class1.cs**. This can be changed by right-clicking the name of the file in the **Solution Explorer**

and selecting **Rename**. The reader can then enter a new name for the file, provided that this file ends in **.cs** (the file extension for C# code files).

3. *Complete the code.* In the text editor, replace the comment

```
//
// TODO: Add code to start application here
//
```

which is located within method **Main** with line 10 from Fig. 3.1 (this comment is no longer necessary, for we are adding code to the program).

4. *Run the program.* We are now ready to compile and execute our program. To do this, we simply follow the same steps that we executed for the example in Chapter 2. To compile the program, go to the **Build** menu and select **Build Solution**. If the program contains no syntax errors, the preceding command creates a new file called **Welcome1.exe**, containing the MSIL code for our application.[1] To execute this program, choose option **Start Without Debugging**[2] in the **Debug** menu.

Program execution begins with method **Main**, which is the entry point to the program. Next, the statement at line 10 of **Main** displays **Welcome to C# Programming!** Figure 3.3 shows result of executing the program.

The message **Welcome to C# Programming!** can be displayed via multiple method calls. Class **Welcome2** of Fig. 3.4 uses two statements to produce the same output shown in Fig. 3.3.

Lines 10–11 of Fig. 3.4 display one line in the console window. The first statement calls **Console** method **Write** to display a string. Unlike **WriteLine**, **Write** does not position the output cursor at the beginning of the next line in the console window after displaying its string, rather the next character displayed in the console window appears immediately after the last character displayed with **Write**. Thus, when line 11 executes, the first character displayed ("**C**") appears immediately after the last character displayed with **Write** (i.e., the space character after the word **"to"** in line 10). Each **Write** or **WriteLine** statement resumes displaying characters from where the last **Write** or **WriteLine** stopped.

Fig. 3.3   Execution of the **Welcome1** program.

---

1. For information on MSIL, Microsoft's Intermediate Language, please see Section 1.8.
2. Selecting **Debug > Start Without Debugging** causes the command window to prompt the user to press a key after the program terminates, allowing the user to observe the program's output. In contrast, if we run this program using **Debug > Start**, as we did for the Windows application in Chapter 2, a command window opens, the program displays the message **Welcome to C# Programming!**, then the command window closes immediately.

```
1   // Fig. 3.4: Welcome2.cs
2   // Printing a line with multiple statements.
3
4   using System;
5
6   class Welcome2
7   {
8      static void Main( string[] args )
9      {
10        Console.Write( "Welcome to " );
11        Console.WriteLine( "C# Programming!" );
12     }
13  }
```

```
Welcome to C# Programming!
```

Fig. 3.4   Printing on one line with separate statements.

A single statement can display multiple lines by using newline characters. Recall that these characters indicate when to position the output cursor at the beginning of the next line in the console window to continue output. Figure 3.5 demonstrates using newline characters.

Line 10 produces four separate lines of text in the console window. Normally, the characters in a string are displayed exactly as they appear between the double quotes. However, notice that the two characters "****" and "**n**" do not appear on the screen. The *backslash* (****) is called an *escape character*. It indicates that a "special" character is to be output. When a backslash is encountered in a string of characters, the next character is combined with the backslash to form an *escape sequence*. This escape sequence **\n** is the *newline character*. It causes the *cursor* (i.e., the current screen position indicator) to move to the beginning of the next line in the console window. Some common escape sequences are listed in Fig. 3.6.

```
1   // Fig. 3.5: Welcome3.cs
2   // Printing multiple lines with a single statement.
3
4   using System;
5
6   class Welcome3
7   {
8      static void Main( string[] args )
9      {
10        Console.WriteLine( "Welcome\nto\nC#\nProgramming!" );
11     }
12  }
```

```
Welcome
to
C#
Programming!
```

Fig. 3.5   Printing on multiple lines with a single statement.

Escape sequence	Description
\n	Newline. Position the screen cursor to the beginning of the next line.
\t	Horizontal tab. Move the screen cursor to the next tab stop.
\r	Carriage return. Position the screen cursor to the beginning of the current line; do not advance to the next line. Any characters output after the carriage return overwrite the previous characters output on that line.
\\	Backslash. Used to print a backslash character.
\"	Double quote. Used to print a double quote (") character.

Fig. 3.6   Some common escape sequences.

Although the first several programs display output in the command prompt, most C# applications use windows or *dialogs* to display output. As mentioned earlier, dialogs are windows that typically display important messages to the user of an application. The .NET Framework Class Library includes class **MessageBox** for creating dialogs. Class **MessageBox** is defined in namespace **System.Windows.Forms**. The program in Fig. 3.7 displays the same string as Fig. 3.5 in a message dialog using class **MessageBox**.

```
1   // Fig. 3.7: Welcome4.cs
2   // Printing multiple lines in a dialog Box.
3
4   using System;
5   using System.Windows.Forms;
6
7   class Welcome4
8   {
9      static void Main( string[] args )
10     {
11        MessageBox.Show( "Welcome\nto\nC#\nprogramming!" );
12     }
13  }
```

Fig. 3.7   Displaying multiple lines in a dialog.

Many compiled classes in C# (including **MessageBox**) need to be referenced, or specified as a part of the project, before they can be used in a program. Depending on the type of application we create, classes may be compiled into files with a **.exe** (*executable*) extension, a **.dll** (or *dynamic link library*) extension or one of several other extensions. Such files are called *assemblies* and are the packaging units for code in C#. [Note: Assemblies can be comprised of many files of several different types.] Namespaces group related *classes* together; the assembly is a package containing the Microsoft Intermediate Language (MSIL) code that a project has been compiled into, plus any other information that is needed for these classes. The assembly that we need to reference can be found in the Visual Studio .NET documentation (also called the MSDN Documentation) for the class we wish to use. The easiest way to access this information is to go to the **Help** menu in Visual Studio, and choose **Index**. The reader can then type in the name of the class to access the documentation. Class **MessageBox** is located in assembly **System.Windows.Forms.dll**. As mentioned previously, we must add a reference to this assembly to use class **MessageBox** in our program. Let us discuss an example of adding a reference to **System.Windows.Forms** within the IDE.

Common Programming Error 3.5

*Including a namespace with the **using** directive, but not adding a reference to the proper assembly, results in a compiler error.*

To begin, make sure you have an application open. Select the **Add Reference...** option from the **Project** menu, or right click the **References** folder in the **Solution Explorer** and select **Add Reference...** from the popup menu that appears. This opens the **Add Reference** dialog (Fig. 3.8). Double click **System.Windows.Forms.dll** to add this file to the **Selected Components** list at the bottom of the dialog, then click **OK**. Notice that **System.Windows.Forms** now appears in the **References** folder of the **Solution Explorer** (Fig. 3.8).

After referencing the appropriate assembly and providing a **using** directive for the corresponding namespace (line 5), we can use the classes in that namespace (such as **MessageBox**).

The reader may notice that we did not add any references to our previous programs. Visual Studio adds a few common references when a project is created. Also, by default, some assemblies do not require references. Class **Console**, for instance, is located in the assembly **mscorlib.dll**, but a reference to this assembly is not required to use it.

The **System.Windows.Forms** namespace contains many classes that help C# programmers define graphical user interfaces (GUIs) for their applications. *GUI components* (e.g., buttons) facilitate both data entry by the user and the formatting or presenting of data outputs to the user. For example, Fig. 3.9 is an Internet Explorer window with a bar containing menus (**File**, **Edit**, **View** etc.). Below the menu bar there is a set of buttons, each with a defined task in Internet Explorer. Below the buttons there is a *text field* in which the user can type the location of a Web site to visit. To the left of the text field is a *label* that indicates the purpose of the text field. The menus, buttons, text fields and labels are part of Internet Explorer's GUI. They enable users to interact with Internet Explorer. C# contains classes that create the GUI components described here. Other classes that create GUI components are described in Chapter 11, Graphical User Interface Concepts.

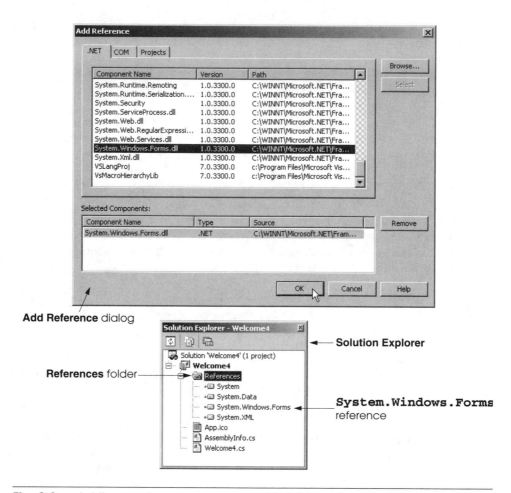

Fig. 3.8   Adding a reference to an assembly in Visual Studio .NET.

In **Main** (Fig. 3.7), line 11 calls method **Show** of class **MessageBox**. This method takes a string as an argument and displays it to the user in a message dialog. Method **Show** is called a *static method*. Such methods are always called by using their class name (in this case, **MessageBox**) followed by the *dot operator* (**.**) and the method name (in this case, **Show**). We discuss static methods in Chapter 8, Object-Based Programming.

Line 11 displays the dialog box shown in Fig. 3.10. The dialog includes an **OK** button that allows the user to *dismiss (close)* the dialog. Positioning the *mouse cursor* (also called the *mouse pointer*) over the **OK** button and clicking the mouse dismisses the dialog.

C# allows large statements to be split over many lines. For example, we could have split the statement on line 11 into the following two lines:

```
MessageBox.Show(
    "Welcome\nto\nC#\nprogramming!" );
```

All statements end with a semicolon (**;**), so the compiler recognizes that these two lines represent only one statement. However, you cannot split a statement in the middle of an identifier (e.g., the class name) or a string.

Label   Button   Menu   Text field   Menu bar

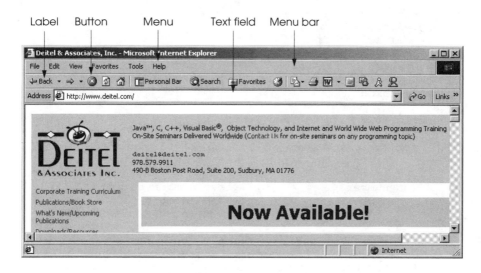

Fig. 3.9   Internet Explorer's GUI.

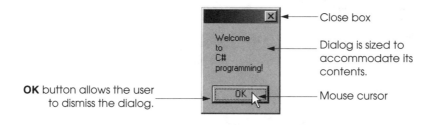

Close box

Dialog is sized to accommodate its contents.

OK button allows the user to dismiss the dialog.

Mouse cursor

Fig. 3.10   Dialog displayed by calling **MessageBox.Show**.

 Common Programming Error 3.6

Splitting a statement in the middle of an identifier or a string is a syntax error.

The user can close the dialog by clicking the **OK** button or the close box. Once this occurs, the program terminates, because the **Main** method terminates.

3.3 Another Simple Program: Adding Integers

Our next application (Fig. 3.11) inputs two integers (whole numbers) typed by a user at the keyboard, computes the sum of these values and displays the result. As the user types each integer and presses the *Enter* key, the integer is read into the program and added to the total. Lines 1–2 are single-line comments stating the figure number, file name and purpose of the program.

As stated previously, every C# program consists of at least one class definition. Line 6 begins the definition of class **Addition**. Lines 7–37 define the body of the class. Recall that all class definitions start with an opening left brace (**{**) and end with a closing right brace (**}**).

```
1    // Fig. 3.11: Addition.cs
2    // An addition program.
3
4    using System;
5
6    class Addition
7    {
8       static void Main( string[] args )
9       {
10         string firstNumber,      // first string entered by user
11                secondNumber;     // second string entered by user
12
13         int number1,             // first number to add
14             number2,             // second number to add
15             sum;                 // sum of number1 and number2
16
17         // prompt for and read first number from user as string
18         Console.Write( "Please enter the first integer: " );
19         firstNumber = Console.ReadLine();
20
21         // read second number from user as string
22         Console.Write( "\nPlease enter the second integer: " );
23         secondNumber = Console.ReadLine();
24
25         // convert numbers from type string to type int
26         number1 = Int32.Parse( firstNumber );
27         number2 = Int32.Parse( secondNumber );
28
29         // add numbers
30         sum = number1 + number2;
31
32         // display results
33         Console.WriteLine( "\nThe sum is {0}.", sum );
34
35      } // end method Main
36
37   } // end class Addition
```

```
Please enter the first integer: 45

Please enter the second integer: 72

The sum is 117.
```

Fig. 3.11   Addition program that adds two values entered by the user.

The program begins execution with method **Main** on line 8. The left brace (line 9) begins **Main**'s body and the corresponding right brace (line 35) terminates **Main**'s body.

Lines 10–11 are a *declaration*. The words **firstNumber** and **secondNumber** are the names of *variables*. A variable is a location in the computer's memory where a value can be stored for use by a program. All variables must be declared with a name and a data type before they can be used in a program. This declaration specifies that the variables **firstNumber** and **secondNumber** are data of type *string*, which means that these variables store strings of characters. There are certain data types already defined in the .NET Framework, known as *built-in data types* or *primitive data types*. Types such as **string**, **int**, **double** and **char** are examples of primitive data types. Primitive type names are keywords. The 15 primitive types are summarized in Chapter 6, Methods.

A variable name can be any valid identifier. Declarations end with a semicolon (**;**) and can be split over several lines for readability with each variable in the declaration separated by a comma (i.e., a *comma-separated list* of variable names). Several variables of the same type may be declared in one or in multiple declarations. We could have written two declarations, one for each variable, but the preceding declaration is more concise. Notice the single-line comments at the end of each line. This is a common syntax used by programmers to indicate the purpose of each variable in the program.

Good Programming Practice 3.7

Choosing meaningful variable names helps a program to be "self-documenting" (i.e., easier to understand simply by reading it, rather than having to read manuals or use excessive comments).

Good Programming Practice 3.8

*By convention, variable-name identifiers begin with a lowercase letter. As with class names, every word in the name after the first word should begin with a capital letter. For example, identifier **firstNumber** has a capital **N** in its second word, **Number**.*

Good Programming Practice 3.9

Some programmers prefer to declare each variable on a separate line. This format allows for easy insertion of a comment that describes each variable.

Lines 13–15 declare that variables **number1**, **number2** and **sum** are of data type *int*, which means that these variables will hold *integer* values (i.e., whole numbers such as −11, 7, 0 and 31914). In contrast, the data types **float** and **double** specify real numbers (i.e., floating-point numbers with decimal points, such as 3.4, 0.0 and −11.19) and variables of type **char** specify character data. A **char** variable may hold only a single lowercase letter, a single uppercase letter, a single digit or a single character, such as **x**, **$**, **7**, ***** and escape sequences (like as the newline character **\n**). Oftentimes in programs, characters are denoted in single quotes, such as **'x'**, **'$'**, **'7'**, **'*'** and **'\n'**, to differentiate between a value and a variable name. C# is also capable of representing all Unicode® characters. *Unicode®* is an extensive international *character set* (collection of characters) that enables the programmer to display letters in different languages, mathematical symbols and much more. For more information on this topic, see Appendix F, Unicode®.

Lines 18–19 prompt the user to input an integer and read from the user a **string** representing the first of the two integers that the program will add. The message on line 18 is called a *prompt*, because it directs the user to take a specific action. Method *ReadLine* (line 19) causes the program to pause and wait for user input. The user inputs characters from the keyboard, then presses the *Enter* key to return the string to the program. Unfortunately, the .NET Framework does not provide a simple input dialog. For this reason, the examples in these early chapters receive user input through the command prompt.

Technically, the user can send anything to the program as input. For this program, if the user types a noninteger value, a *run-time logic error* (an error that has its effect at execution time) occurs. Chapter 10, Exception Handling, discusses how to make your programs more robust by handling such errors.

When the user enters a number and presses *Enter*, the program assigns the string representation of this number to variable **firstNumber** (line 19) with the *assignment operator =*. The statement is read as, "**firstNumber** *gets* the value returned by method **ReadLine**." The **=** operator is a *binary operator*, because it has two *operands*—**first-Number**, and the result of applying method **Console.ReadLine**. The entire statement is an *assignment statement*, because it assigns a value to a variable. In an assignment statement, first the right side of the assignment is evaluated, then the result is assigned to the variable on the left side of the assignment. So, line 19 executes method **ReadLine**, then assigns the string value to **firstNumber**.

Good Programming Practice 3.10

Place spaces on either side of a binary operator. This makes the operator stand out and makes the program more readable.

Lines 22–23 prompt the user to enter a second integer and read from the user a string representing the value. Lines 26–27 convert the two strings input by the user to **int** values that can be used in a calculation. Method ***Int32.Parse*** (a static method of class **Int32**) converts its **string** argument to an integer. Class **Int32** is part of the **System** namespace. Line 26 assigns the integer that **Int32.Parse** returns to variable **number1**. Any subsequent references to **number1** in the program use this integer value. Line 27 assigns the integer that **Int32.Parse** returns to variable **number2**. Any subsequent references to **number2** in the program use this integer value. You can eliminate the need for **string** variables **firstNumber** and **secondNumber** by combining the input and conversion operations as follows:

```
int number1;
number1 = Int32.Parse( Console.ReadLine() );
```

In C#, users input data as **string**s. We convert these strings to perform integer arithmetic. Arithmetic operations, as we will discuss in Section 3.5, do not work with **string**s the same way operations work with integers. To add numbers and get the proper sum, we must convert the strings to integers. The preceding statements do not make use of the **string** variable (**firstNumber**). This variable is required only to store the **string** temporarily until the program converts it. Reading the **string** and converting it on one line makes the variable unnecessary.

The assignment statement on line 30 calculates the sum of the variables **number1** and **number2** and assigns the result to variable **sum** by using the assignment operator **=**. The statement is read as, "**sum** *gets* the value of **number1** plus **number2**." Most calculations are performed in assignment statements.

After performing the calculation, line 33 displays the result of the addition. In this example, we want to output the value in a variable using method **WriteLine**. Let us discuss how this is done.

The *comma-separated* arguments to **Console.WriteLine**

```
"\nThe sum is {0}.", sum
```

use **{0}** to indicate a placeholder for a variable's value. If we assume that **sum** contains the value **117**, the expression evaluates as follows: Method **WriteLine** encounters a number in curly braces, **{0}**, known as a *format* (sometimes known as a *format string*). This indicates that the variable found after the string in the list of arguments (in this case, **sum**) will be evaluated and incorporated into our string, in place of the format. The resulting string will be "**The sum is 117.**" Similarly, in the statement

```
Console.WriteLine(
    "The numbers entered are {0} and {1}", number1, number2 );
```

the value of **number1** would replace **{0}** (because it is the first variable) and the value of **number2** would replace **{1}** (because it is the second variable). The resulting string would be **"The numbers entered are 45 and 72"**. More formats can be used (**{2}**, **{3}** etc.) if there are more variables to display in the string.

Good Programming Practice 3.11

Place a space after each comma in a method's argument list to make programs more readable.

Some programmers find it difficult, when reading or writing a program, to match the left and right braces (**{** and **}**) that delimit the body of a class or method definition. For this reason, some programmers include a single-line comment after each closing right brace that ends a method or class definition, as we do in lines 35 and 37.

Good Programming Practice 3.12

Follow the closing right brace (**}** *) of the body of a method or class definition with a single-line comment. This comment should indicate the method or class that the right brace terminates.*

3.4 Memory Concepts

Variable names, such as **number1**, **number2** and **sum**, actually correspond to *locations* in the computer's memory. Every variable has a *name,* a *type,* a *size* and a *value.*

In the addition program in Fig. 3.11, the statement (line 26)

```
number1 = Int32.Parse( firstNumber );
```

converts to an **int** the string that the user entered. This **int** is placed into a memory location to which the name **number1** has been assigned by the compiler. Suppose the user enters the string **45** as the value for **firstNumber**. The program converts **firstNumber** to an **int**, and the computer places the integer value **45** into location **number1**, as shown in Fig. 3.12.

When a value is placed in a memory location, this value replaces the previous value in that location. The previous value is lost (or destroyed).

---

number1 | 45 |

Fig. 3.12   Memory location showing name and value of variable **number1**.

When the statement (line 27)

```
number2 = Int32.Parse( secondNumber );
```

executes, suppose the user types **72** as the value for **secondNumber**. The program converts **secondNumber** to an **int**, the computer places the integer value **72** into location **number2** and memory appears as shown in Fig. 3.13.

Once the program has obtained values for **number1** and **number2**, it adds these values and places their total into variable **sum**. The statement

```
sum = number1 + number2;
```

performs the addition and replaces (i.e., destroys) **sum**'s previous value. After calculating the **sum**, memory appears as shown in Fig. 3.14. Note that the values of **number1** and **number2** appear exactly as they did before the calculation of **sum**. These values were used, but not destroyed, as the computer performed the calculation. Thus, when a value is read from a memory location, the process is *nondestructive*.

3.5 Arithmetic

Most programs perform arithmetic calculations. Figure 3.15 summarizes the *arithmetic operators*. Note the use of various special symbols not used in algebra. The *asterisk* (*****) indicates multiplication, and the *percent sign* (**%**) represents the *modulus operator*, which is discussed shortly. The arithmetic operators in Fig. 3.15 are binary operators, because they each require two operands. For example, the expression **sum + value** contains the binary operator **+** and the two operands **sum** and **value**.

number1	45
number2	72

Fig. 3.13 Memory locations after values for variables **number1** and **number2** have been input.

number1	45
number2	72
sumOfNumbers	117

Fig. 3.14 Memory locations after a calculation.

C# operation	Arithmetic operator	Algebraic expression	C# expression
Addition	+	$f + 7$	f + 7
Subtraction	–	$p - c$	p - c
Multiplication	*	bm	b * m
Division	/	$x / y \ \text{or} \ \dfrac{x}{y} \ \text{or} \ x \div y$	x / y
Modulus	%	$r \bmod s$	r % s

Fig. 3.15 Arithmetic operators.

Integer division contains two **int** operands. The result of this computation is an integer quotient; for example, the expression **7 / 4** evaluates to **1** and the expression **17 / 5** evaluates to **3**. Note that any fractional part in integer division simply is discarded (i.e., truncated)—no rounding occurs. C# provides the modulus operator, **%**, which yields the remainder after integer division. The expression **x % y** yields the remainder after **x** is divided by **y**. Thus, **7 % 4** yields **3** and **17 % 5** yields **2**. This operator is used most commonly with integer operands, but also can be used with other arithmetic types. There is no arithmetic operator for exponentiation in C#. (Chapter 6, Methods, discusses how to perform exponentiation in C#.)

Arithmetic expressions in C# must be written in *straight-line form* to facilitate entering programs into a computer. Thus, expressions such as "**a** divided by **b**" must be written as **a / b** so that all constants, variables and operators appear in a straight line. The following algebraic notation generally is not acceptable to compilers:

$$\frac{a}{b}$$

C# expressions can use parentheses in the same manner as in algebraic expressions. For example, to multiply **a** times the quantity **b + c**, we write

    a * (b + c)

C# applies the operators in arithmetic expressions in a precise sequence, determined by the following *rules of operator precedence,* which are generally the same as those followed in algebra:

1. Operators in expressions contained within pairs of parentheses are evaluated first. Thus, *parentheses may be used to force the order of evaluation to occur in any sequence desired by the programmer.* Parentheses are at the highest level of precedence. With *nested* (or *embedded*) parentheses, the operators in the innermost pair of parentheses are applied first.

2. Multiplication, division and modulus operations are applied next. If an expression contains several multiplication, division and modulus operations, operators are

applied from left to right. Multiplication, division and modulus are said to have the same level of precedence.

3. Addition and subtraction operations are applied last. If an expression contains several addition and subtraction operations, operators are applied from left to right. Addition and subtraction have the same level of precedence.

The rules of operator precedence enable C# to apply operators in the correct order. When we say operators are applied from left to right, we are referring to the *associativity* of the operators. If there are multiple operators, each with the same precedence, the associativity determines the order in which the operators are applied. We will see that some operators associate from right to left. Figure 3.16 summarizes the rules of operator precedence. This table will expand as we introduce additional C# operators in subsequent chapters. See Appendix A for a complete operator-precedence chart.

Notice in the chart that we make note of nested parentheses. Not all expressions with several pairs of parentheses contain nested parentheses. For example, the expression

```
a * ( b + c ) + c * ( d + e )
```

has multiple sets of parentheses, but not nested parentheses. Rather, these parentheses are said to be "on the same level."

Let us consider several expressions in light of the rules of operator precedence. Each example lists an algebraic expression and its C# equivalent.

The following is an example of an arithmetic mean (average) of five terms:

$$\text{Algebra: } m = \frac{a + b + c + d + e}{5}$$

```
C#: m = ( a + b + c + d + e ) / 5;
```

The parentheses are required because division has higher precedence than addition. The entire quantity (a + b + c + d + e) is to be divided by 5. If the parentheses are erroneously omitted, we obtain a + b + c + d + e / 5, which evaluates as

Operator(s)	Operation	Order of evaluation (precedence)
( )	Parentheses	Evaluated first. If the parentheses are nested, the expression in the innermost pair is evaluated first. If there are several pairs of parentheses "on the same level" (i.e., not nested), they are evaluated left to right.
*, / or %	Multiplication Division Modulus	Evaluated second. If there are several such operators, they are evaluated left to right.
+ or -	Addition Subtraction	Evaluated last. If there are several such operators, they are evaluated left to right.

Fig. 3.16 Precedence of arithmetic operators.

$$a + b + c + d + \frac{e}{5}$$

The following is the equation of a straight line:

Algebra: $y = mx + b$

C#:   `y = m * x + b;`

No parentheses are required. The multiplication occurs first because multiplication has a higher precedence than addition. The assignment occurs last because it has a lower precedence than multiplication and division.

The following example contains modulus (**%**), multiplication, division, addition and subtraction operations:

Algebra: $z = pr\%q + w/x - y$

C#:

The circled numbers under the statement indicate the order in which C# applies the operators. The multiplication, modulus and division operators evaluate first in left-to-right order (i.e., they associate from left to right). The addition and subtraction evaluate next. These also are applied from left to right.

To develop a better understanding of the rules of operator precedence, consider how a second-degree polynomial ($y = ax^2 + bx + c$) evaluates:

The circled numbers under the statement indicate the order in which C# applies the operators. There is no arithmetic operator for exponentiation in C#; x^2 is represented as **x * x**. The .NET Framework Class Library provides method **Math.Pow** for exponentiation (see Chapter 6, Methods).

Suppose **a, b, c** and **x** are initialized as follows: **a = 2, b = 3, c = 7** and **x = 5**. Figure 3.17 illustrates the order of evaluation of the operators.

As in algebra, it is acceptable to place unnecessary parentheses in an expression to make the expression easier to read. Unnecessary parentheses are also called *redundant parentheses*. For example, the preceding assignment statement might be parenthesized as

`y = ( a * x * x ) + ( b * x ) + c;`

 Good Programming Practice 3.13

Using parentheses for more complex arithmetic expressions, even when the parentheses are not necessary can make the arithmetic expressions easier to read.

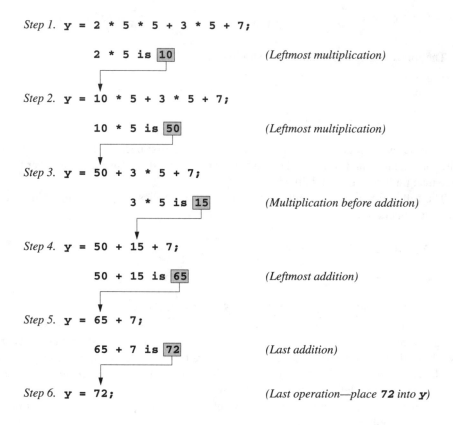

Step 1. **y = 2 * 5 * 5 + 3 * 5 + 7;**

          2 * 5 is **10**   *(Leftmost multiplication)*

Step 2. **y = 10 * 5 + 3 * 5 + 7;**

          10 * 5 is **50**   *(Leftmost multiplication)*

Step 3. **y = 50 + 3 * 5 + 7;**

          3 * 5 is **15**   *(Multiplication before addition)*

Step 4. **y = 50 + 15 + 7;**

          50 + 15 is **65**   *(Leftmost addition)*

Step 5. **y = 65 + 7;**

          65 + 7 is **72**   *(Last addition)*

Step 6. **y = 72;**   *(Last operation—place **72** into **y**)*

Fig. 3.17   Order in which a second-degree polynomial is evaluated.

3.6 Decision Making: Equality and Relational Operators

This section introduces C#'s **if** structure, which allows a program to make a decision based on the truth or falsity of some *condition*. If the condition is met (i.e., the condition is *true*), the statement in the body of the **if** structure executes. If the condition is not met (i.e., the condition is *false*), the body statement does not execute. Conditions in **if** structures can be formed by using the *equality operators* and *relational operators,* summarized in Fig. 3.18. The relational operators all have the same level of precedence and associate from left to right. The equality operators both have the same level of precedence, which is lower than the precedence of the relational operators. The equality operators also associate from left to right.

The next example uses six **if** statements to compare two numbers input into a program by the user. If the condition in any of these **if** statements is true, the assignment statement associated with that **if** executes. The user inputs values that the program converts to integers and stores in variables **number1** and **number2**. The program compares the numbers and displays the results of the comparison in the command prompt. The program and sample outputs are shown in Fig. 3.19.

Standard algebraic equality operator or relational operator	C# equality or relational operator	Example of C# condition	Meaning of C# condition
Equality operators			
=	==	x == y	x is equal to y
≠	!=	x != y	x is not equal to y
Relational operators			
>	>	x > y	x is greater than y
<	<	x < y	x is less than y
≥	>=	x >= y	x is greater than or equal to y
≤	<=	x <= y	x is less than or equal to y

Fig. 3.18 Equality and relational operators.

Common Programming Error 3.7

It is a syntax error if the operators **==**, **!=**, **>=** *and* **<=** *contain spaces between their symbols (as in* **= =**, **! =**, **> =**, **< =**).

Common Programming Error 3.8

Reversing the operators **!=**, **>=** *and* **<=** *(as in* **=!**, **=>** *and* **=<**) *is a syntax error.*

Common Programming Error 3.9

Confusing the equality operator **==** *with the assignment operator* **=** *is a logic error. The equality operator should be read "is equal to," and the assignment operator should be read "gets" or "gets the value of." Some people prefer to read the equality operator as "double equals" or "equals equals."*

```
1   // Fig. 3.19: Comparison.cs
2   // Using if statements, relational operators and equality
3   // operators.
4
5   using System;
6
7   class Comparison
8   {
9      static void Main( string[] args )
10     {
11        int number1,        // first number to compare
12           number2;         // second number to compare
13
14        // read in first number from user
15        Console.Write( "Please enter first integer: " );
16        number1 = Int32.Parse( Console.ReadLine() );
```

Fig. 3.19 Using equality and relational operators. (Part 1 of 2.)

```
17
18          // read in second number from user
19          Console.Write( "\nPlease enter second integer: " );
20          number2 = Int32.Parse( Console.ReadLine() );
21
22          if ( number1 == number2 )
23             Console.WriteLine( number1 + " == " + number2 );
24
25          if ( number1 != number2 )
26             Console.WriteLine( number1 + " != " + number2 );
27
28          if ( number1 < number2 )
29             Console.WriteLine( number1 + " < " + number2 );
30
31          if ( number1 > number2 )
32             Console.WriteLine( number1 + " > " +  number2 );
33
34          if ( number1 <= number2 )
35             Console.WriteLine( number1 + " <= " + number2 );
36
37          if ( number1 >= number2 )
38             Console.WriteLine( number1 + " >= " + number2 );
39
40       } // end method Main
41
42    } // end class Comparison
```

```
Please enter first integer: 2000

Please enter second integer: 1000
2000 != 1000
2000 > 1000
2000 >= 1000
```

```
Please enter first integer: 1000

Please enter second integer: 2000
1000 != 2000
1000 < 2000
1000 <= 2000
```

```
Please enter first integer: 1000

Please enter second integer: 1000
1000 == 1000
1000 <= 1000
1000 >= 1000
```

Fig. 3.19 Using equality and relational operators. (Part 2 of 2.)

The definition of class **Comparison** begins on line 7, and the **Main** method begins on line 9. Lines 11–12 declare the variables used in method **Main**. Note that there are two variables of type **int**. Remember that variables of the same type may be declared in one declaration or in multiple declarations. Also recall that, if more than one variable is placed in one declaration (lines 11–12), those variables are separated by commas (**,**). The comment at the end of each line indicates the purpose of each variable in the program.

Line 16 reads in the first number from the user. Line 20 reads in the second number from the user. These values are stored in variables **number1** and **number2**, respectively. Recall that arithmetic operators cannot be used with strings. Relational and equality operators also cannot be used with strings. Therefore, the two input strings must be converted to integers.

Lines 16 and 20 both get an input, convert the input to type **int** and assign the values to the appropriate variable in one step. Notice that this step can be combined with the variable declaration and placed on one line with the statement

```
int number1 = Int32.Parse( Console.ReadLine() );
```

which declares the variable, reads a string from the user, converts the string to an integer and stores the integer in the variable.

The **if** structure in lines 22–23 compares the values of the variables **number1** and **number2** for equality. If the values are equal, the program outputs the value of **number1 + " == " + number2**. Notice that this expression uses the operator **+** to "add" (or combine) numbers and strings. This version of the **+** operator is used for *string* con-catenation. Concatenation is the process that enables a **string** and a value of another data type (including another **string**) to be combined to form a new **string**.

If **number1** contains the value **1000** and **number2** contains the value **1000**, the expression evaluates as follows: C# determines that the operands of the **+** operator are of different types and that one of them is a **string** (both **number1** and **number2** are **int**s, but **" == "** is a **string**). Next, **number1** and **number2** are converted to a **string** and concatenated with **" == "**. At this point, the **string**, namely **"1000 == 1000"**, is sent to method **Console.WriteLine** to be output. As the program proceeds through the **if** structures, more **string**s will be output by these **Console.WriteLine** statements. For example, given the value **1000** for **number1** and **number2**, the **if** conditions at lines 34 (**<=**) and 37 (**>=**) will also be true. Thus, the output displayed will be

```
1000 == 1000
1000 <= 1000
1000 >= 1000
```

The third output window of Fig. 3.19 demonstrates this case.

Common Programming Error 3.10

*Confusing the **+** operator used for string concatenation with the **+** operator used for addition can lead to strange results. For example, assuming integer variable **y** has the value **5**, the expression **"y + 2 = " + y + 2** results in the string **"y + 2 = 52"**, not **"y + 2 = 7"**. First the value of **y** (**5**) is concatenated with the string **"y + 2 = "**, then the value **2** is concatenated with the new, larger string **"y + 2 = 5"**. The expression **"y + 2 = " + (y + 2)** would produce the desired result.*

Common Programming Error 3.11

*Replacing operator == in the condition of an **if** structure, such as **if (x == 1)**, with operator =, as in **if (x = 1)**, is a syntax error.*

Notice the indentation in the **if** statements throughout the program. Such indentation enhances program readability.

Good Programming Practice 3.14

*Indent the statement in the body of an **if** structure to make the body of the structure stand out and to enhance program readability.*

Good Programming Practice 3.15

Place only one statement per line in a program. This enhances program readability.

Common Programming Error 3.12

*Forgetting the left and right parentheses for the condition in an **if** structure is a syntax error. The parentheses are required.*

There is no semicolon (;) at the end of the first line of each **if** structure in Fig. 3.19. Such a semicolon would result in a logic error at execution time. For example,

```
if ( number1 == number2 );
   Console.WriteLine( number1 + " == " + number2 );
```

would actually be treated by C# as

```
if ( number1 == number2 )
   ;

Console.WriteLine( number1 + " == " + number2 );
```

where the semicolon on the line by itself—called the *empty statement*—is the statement to execute if the condition is true. When the empty statement executes, no task is performed. The program continues with the **Console.WriteLine** statement, which executes regardless of whether the condition is true or false; this is, of course, incorrect.

Common Programming Error 3.13

*Placing a semicolon immediately after the right parenthesis of the condition in an **if** structure is normally a logic error. The semicolon causes the body of the **if** structure to be empty, so the **if** structure performs no action, regardless of whether its condition is true. Worse, the intended body statement of the **if** structure becomes a statement in sequence with the **if** structure and always executes.*

Notice the use of spacing in Fig. 3.19. Remember that the compiler normally ignores whitespace characters, such as tabs, newlines and spaces. Statements may be split over several lines and may be spaced according to the programmer's preferences without affecting the meaning of a program. It is incorrect to split identifiers and string literals. Ideally, statements should be kept small, but it is not always possible to do so.

The chart in Fig. 3.20 shows the precedence of the operators introduced in this chapter. The operators are displayed from top to bottom in decreasing order of precedence. Notice that all these operators, with the exception of the assignment operator =, associate from left to right. Addition is left associative, so an expression such as **x + y + z** is evaluated as if it were written $(x + y) + z$. The assignment operator = associates from right to left, so an expression such as $x = y = 0$ is evaluated as if it were written $x = (y = 0)$. The latter expression, $x = (y = 0)$, first assigns the value 0 to variable y and then assigns the result of that assignment, 0, to x; this is a concise way to assign the same value to several variables.

Good Programming Practice 3.16

A lengthy statement may be spread over several lines. If a single statement must be split across lines, choose breaking points that make sense, such as after a comma in a comma-separated list or after an operator in a lengthy expression. If a statement is split across two or more lines, indent all subsequent lines with one level of indentation to show clearly that the continuation line(s) is (are) part of the same statement.

Good Programming Practice 3.17

Refer to the operator-precedence chart when writing expressions containing many operators. Confirm that the operators in the expression are performed in the expected order. If you are uncertain about the order of evaluation in a complex expression, use parentheses to force the order, as you would do in an algebraic expression. Remember that some operators, such as assignment (=), associate from right to left rather than from left to right.

In this chapter, we introduced important features of C#, including displaying data on the screen, inputting data from the keyboard, performing calculations and making decisions. The next chapter demonstrates many similar techniques, as we reintroduce C# Windows applications (applications that provide a graphical user interface). We also introduce *structured programming* and familiarize the reader further with indentation techniques. We study how to specify and vary the order in which statements execute—this order is called *flow of control.*

3.7 Summary

A console application is an application that predominantly displays text output in a command window (also called a console window). On Microsoft Windows 95/98, the console window is the **MS-DOS prompt**. On Microsoft Windows NT/2000/XP, the console window is called the **command prompt**.

Programmers insert comments to document programs and improve program readability. The compiler ignores all text between the delimiters of the comment.

Operators	Associativity	Type
( )	left to right	parentheses
* / %	left to right	multiplicative
+ -	left to right	additive
< <= > >=	left to right	relational
== !=	left to right	equality
=	right to left	assignment

Fig. 3.20   Precedence and associativity of operators discussed in this chapter.

Classes consist of pieces (called methods) that perform tasks and return information (or program control) when they complete their tasks. Each piece that is needed to form a C# program can be defined by programmers. Classes defined by the programmer are known as programmer-defined, or user-defined, classes. C# applications contain one or more classes. By convention, all class names in C# begin with an uppercase letter and have an uppercase letter as the first letter of every word in the class name. One of the classes in every C# application must contain method **Main**.

Every statement in a C# program must end with a semicolon (the statement terminator). Omitting the semicolon at the end of a statement is a syntax error.

C# has a version of the **+** operator for string concatenation that enables a string and a value of another data type (including another string) to be concatenated; the result of this operation is a new (and normally longer) string. String contents always must be delimited with double quotes.

Class **MessageBox** allows programmers to display a dialog containing information. Class **MessageBox** is defined in namespace **System.Windows.Forms**. Namespaces group various C# features into related categories, providing programmers with the ability to identify them quickly. The predefined namespaces in C# contain classes that are collectively referred to as the .NET Framework Class Library.

Depending on the type of application created, classes may be compiled into files with an **.exe** (executable) extension, a **.dll** (dynamic link library) extension or one of several other extensions. This type of file is called an assembly, the packaging unit for code in C#.

A variable is a location in memory where a value can be stored for use by a program. All variables must be declared with a name and data type before they can be used in a program. A variable name can be any valid identifier. Several variables of the same type may be declared in either one declaration or separate declarations. Variable names actually correspond to locations in the computer's memory. Every variable has a name, a type, a size and a value. Every variable declared in a method must be initialized (i.e., given a value) before it can be used in an expression, or else a syntax error will occur.

C# applies the operators in arithmetic expressions in a precise sequence determined by the rules of operator precedence. As in algebra, it is acceptable to place unnecessary (redundant) parentheses in an expression to make the expression clearer.

The **if** structure allows a program to make a decision based on the truth or falsity of some condition. If the condition is met (i.e., the condition is true), the statement in the body of the **if** structure executes. If the condition is not met (i.e., the condition is false), the body statement does not execute. Conditions in **if** structures can be formed by using equality operators and relational operators.

Control Structures:
Part 1

Objectives

- To understand basic problem-solving techniques of programming.
- To develop algorithms through the process of top-down, stepwise refinement.
- To use the **if** and **if/else** selection structures to choose among alternative actions.
- To use the **while** repetition structure to execute statements in a program repeatedly.
- To understand counter-controlled repetition and sentinel-controlled repetition.
- To use the increment, decrement and assignment operators.

Let's all move one place on.
Lewis Carroll

The wheel is come full circle.
William Shakespeare

How many apples fell on Newton's head before he took the hint?
Robert Frost

Outline

4.1 Introduction

Before writing a program to solve a problem, it is essential to have a thorough understanding of the problem and a carefully planned approach. When writing a program, it is equally essential to understand the types of building blocks that are available and to employ proven program construction principles. In this chapter and the next, we present the theory and principles of structured programming. The techniques you will learn are applicable to most high-level languages, including C#. When we study object-based programming in more depth in Chapter 8, we will see that control structures are helpful in building and manipulating objects. The control structures discussed in this chapter will enable you to build these objects in a quick and easy manner.

4.2 Algorithms

Any computing problem can be solved by executing a series of actions in a specific order. A *procedure* for solving a problem in terms of

1. the *actions* to be executed and

2. the *order* in which these actions are to be executed

is called an *algorithm*. The example that follows demonstrates the importance of correctly specifying the order in which the actions are to be executed.

Consider the "rise-and-shine algorithm" followed by one junior executive for getting out of bed and going to work: (1) get out of bed, (2) take off pajamas, (3) take a shower, (4) get dressed, (5) eat breakfast, (6) carpool to work. This routine gets the executive to work well-prepared to make critical decisions.

Suppose that the same steps are performed in a slightly different order: (1) get out of bed, (2) take off pajamas, (3) get dressed, (4) take a shower, (5) eat breakfast, (6) carpool to work. In this case, our executive shows up for work soaking wet.

The importance of correctly specifying the order in which actions appear applies to computer programs, as well. *Program control* refers to the task of ordering a program's statements correctly. In this chapter, we begin to investigate the program control capabilities of C#.

4.3 Pseudocode

Pseudocode is an artificial and informal language that helps programmers develop algorithms. The pseudocode we present is particularly useful for developing algorithms that will be converted to structured portions of C# programs. Pseudocode is similar to everyday English; it is convenient and user-friendly, and it is not an actual computer programming language.

Pseudocode is not executed on computers. Rather, pseudocode helps the programmer "think out" a program before attempting to write it in a programming language, such as C#. In this chapter, we provide several examples of pseudocode algorithms.

Software Engineering Observation 4.1

Pseudocode helps the programmer conceptualize a program during the program design process. The pseudocode may then be converted to C#.

The style of pseudocode that we present consists solely of characters, thus programmers may type pseudocode conveniently using an editor program. Programmers can convert carefully prepared pseudocode programs to corresponding C# programs easily. In many cases, this conversion takes place simply by replacing pseudocode statements with their C# equivalents.

Pseudocode normally describes only executable statements—the actions that are performed when the pseudocode is converted to C# and executed. Declarations are not executable statements. For example, the declaration

```
int i;
```

informs the compiler of the type of variable **i** and instructs the compiler to reserve space in memory for this variable. This declaration does not cause any action, such as input, output or a calculation, to occur when the program executes. Some programmers choose to list variables and their purposes at the beginning of a pseudocode program.

4.4 Control Structures

Normally, statements in a program execute one after the other in the order in which they appear in the program. This is called *sequential execution*. Various C# statements enable the programmer to specify that the next statement to execute may not be the next one in sequence. A *transfer of control* occurs when a statement other than the next one in the program executes.

During the 1960s, it became clear that the indiscriminate use of transfers of control was causing difficulty for software development groups. The problem was the ***goto*** *statement,* which, in some programming languages, allows the programmer to specify a transfer of control to one of a wide range of possible destinations in a program. This caused programs to become quite unstructured and hard to follow. The notion of *structured programming* became almost synonymous with "***goto*** elimination."

The research of Bohm and Jacopini[1] demonstrated that all programs with **goto** statements could be written without them. The challenge of the era for programmers was to shift their styles to "**goto**-less programming." It was not until the 1970s that programmers started taking structured programming seriously. The results were impressive, as software development groups reported reduced development times, more frequent on-time delivery of systems and more frequent within-budget completion of software projects. The key to these successes was that structured programs were clearer, easier to debug and modify and more likely to be bug-free in the first place.

Bohm and Jacopini's work demonstrated that all programs could be written in terms of only three *control structures*, namely, the *sequence structure*, the *selection structure* and the *repetition structure*. The sequence structure is built into C#. Unless directed otherwise, the computer executes C# statements one after the other in the order in which they appear in a program. The *flowchart* segment of Fig. 4.1 illustrates a typical sequence structure in which two calculations are performed in order.

A flowchart is a graphical representation of an algorithm or of a portion of an algorithm. Flowcharts contain certain special-purpose symbols, such as rectangles, diamonds, ovals and small circles. These symbols are connected by arrows called *flowlines,* which indicate the order in which the actions of the algorithm execute. This order is known as the flow of control.

Like pseudocode, flowcharts often are useful for developing and representing algorithms, although pseudocode is preferred by many programmers. Flowcharts show clearly how control structures operate; that is all we use them for in this text. The reader should compare carefully the pseudocode and flowchart representations of each control structure.

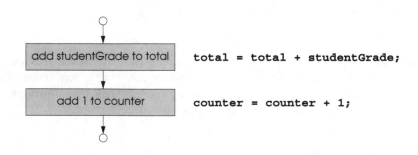

Fig. 4.1   Flowcharting C#'s sequence structure.

1. Bohm, C., and G. Jacopini, "Flow Diagrams, Turing Machines, and Languages with Only Two Formation Rules," *Communications of the ACM*, Vol. 9, No. 5, May 1966, pp. 336–371.

Consider the flowchart segment for the sequence structure in Fig. 4.1. We use the *rectangle symbol*, also called the *action symbol,* to indicate any type of action, including a calculation or an input/output operation. The flowlines in the figure indicate the order in which the actions are to be performed—first, **studentGrade** is to be added to **total**, then **1** is to be added to **counter**. We can have as many actions as we want in a sequence structure. Anywhere in a sequence that a single action may be placed, several actions may also be placed.

When drawing a flowchart that represents a complete algorithm, an *oval symbol* containing the word "Begin" is the first symbol used; an oval symbol containing the word "End" indicates where the algorithm ends. When drawing only a portion of an algorithm, as in Fig. 4.1, the oval symbols are omitted in favor of using *small circle symbols,* also called *connector symbols*.

Perhaps the most important flowcharting symbol is the *diamond symbol*, also called the *decision symbol,* which indicates that a decision is to be made. We discuss the diamond symbol in Section 4.5.

C# provides three types of selection structures, which we discuss in this chapter and the next. The **if** selection structure performs (selects) an action if a condition is true or skips the action if the condition is false. The **if/else** selection structure performs an action if a condition is true and performs a different action if the condition is false. The **switch** selection structure, discussed in Chapter 5, Control Structures: Part 2, performs one of many actions, depending on the value of an expression.

The **if** structure is called a *single-selection structure* because it selects or ignores a single action (or a single group of actions). The **if/else** structure is called a *double-selection structure* because it selects between two different actions (or groups of actions). The **switch** structure is called a *multiple-selection structure* because it selects among many different actions (or groups of actions).

C# provides four repetition structures—**while**, **do/while**, **for** and **foreach** (**while** is covered in this chapter, **do/while** and **for** are covered in Chapter 5, Control Structures: Part 2, and **foreach** is covered in Chapter 7, Arrays). Each of the words **if**, **else**, **switch**, **while**, **do**, **for** and **foreach** are C# keywords. Figure 4.2 lists the complete set of C# keywords. We discuss the vast majority of C#'s keywords throughout this book.

C# Keywords				
abstract	as	base	bool	break
byte	case	catch	char	checked
class	const	continue	decimal	default
delegate	do	double	else	enum
event	explicit	extern	false	finally
fixed	float	for	foreach	goto
if	implicit	in	int	interface

Fig. 4.2   C# keywords. (Part 1 of 2.)

C# Keywords				
internal	is	lock	long	namespace
new	null	object	operator	out
override	params	private	protected	public
readonly	ref	return	sbyte	sealed
short	sizeof	stackalloc	static	string
struct	switch	this	throw	true
try	typeof	uint	ulong	unchecked
unsafe	ushort	using	virtual	void
volatile	while			

Fig. 4.2   C# keywords. (Part 2 of 2.)

C# has only eight control structures—sequence, three types of selection and four types of repetition. Each program is formed by combining as many of each type of control structure as is necessary. As with the sequence structure in Fig. 4.1, each control structure is flowcharted with two small circle symbols, one at the entry point to the control structure and one at the exit point.

Single-entry/single-exit control structures make it easy to build programs—the control structures are attached to one another by connecting the exit point of one control structure to the entry point of the next. This is similar to the stacking of building blocks; thus, we call it *control-structure stacking*. There is only one other way control structures may be connected, and that is through *control-structure nesting*, where one control structure can be placed inside another. Thus, algorithms in C# programs are constructed from only eight different types of control structures combined in only two ways.

4.5 `if` Selection Structure

In a program, a selection structure chooses among alternative courses of action. For example, suppose that the passing grade on an examination is 60 (out of 100). Then the pseudocode statement

> *If student's grade is greater than or equal to 60*
> > *Print "Passed"*

determines if the condition "student's grade is greater than or equal to 60" is true or false. If the condition is true, then *Passed* is printed, and the next pseudocode statement in order is "performed." (Remember that pseudocode is not a real programming language.) If the condition is false, the print statement is ignored, and the next pseudocode statement in order is performed. Note that the second line of this selection structure is indented. Such indentation is optional, but it is highly recommended because it emphasizes the inherent structure of structured programs. The preceding pseudocode *If* statement may be written in C# as

```
if ( studentGrade >= 60 )
   Console.WriteLine( "Passed" );
```

Notice that the C# code corresponds closely to the pseudocode, demonstrating how pseudocode can be useful as a program development tool. The statement in the body of the **if** structure outputs the character string **"Passed"** in the console window.

The flowchart in Fig. 4.3 illustrates the single-selection **if** structure. This flowchart contains the most important flowcharting symbol—the decision (or diamond) symbol, which indicates that a decision is to be made. The decision symbol contains a condition, that can be either **true** or **false**. The decision symbol has two flowlines emerging from it. One indicates the direction to be taken when the condition in the symbol is true; the other indicates the direction to be taken when the condition is false. A decision can be made on any expression that evaluates to a value of C#'s **bool** type (i.e., any expression that evaluates to **true** or **false**).

Note that the **if** structure, too, is a single-entry/single-exit structure. The flowcharts for the remaining control structures also contain (aside from small circle symbols and flowlines) only rectangle symbols, to indicate the actions to be performed, and diamond symbols, to indicate decisions to be made. This is the *action/decision model of programming* we have been emphasizing.

We can envision eight bins, each containing control structures for only one of the eight types. The control structures in each bin are empty; nothing is written in the rectangles or diamonds. The programmer's task is to assemble a program using as many control structures as the algorithm demands, combining those control structures in only two possible ways (stacking or nesting), then filling in the actions and decisions in a manner appropriate for the algorithm. We will discuss the variety of ways in which actions and decisions may be written.

4.6 if/else Selection Structure

The **if** selection structure performs an indicated action only when the condition evaluates to true; otherwise, the action is skipped. The **if/else** selection structure allows the programmer to specify different actions to perform when the condition is true and when the condition is false. For example, the pseudocode statement

> *If student's grade is greater than or equal to 60*
> > *Print "Passed"*
> *Else*
> > *Print "Failed"*

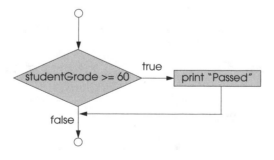

Fig. 4.3   Flowcharting a single-selection **if** structure.

prints *Passed* if the student's grade is greater than or equal to 60, and prints *Failed* if the student's grade is less than 60. In either case, after printing occurs, the next pseudocode statement in sequence is "performed."

The preceding pseudocode *If/Else* structure may be written in C# as

```
if ( studentGrade >= 60 )
    Console.WriteLine( "Passed" );
else
    Console.WriteLine( "Failed" );
```

Good Programming Practice 4.1

*Indent both body statements of an **if/else** structure.*

Note that the body of the **else** statement also is indented. The indentation convention you choose should be applied carefully throughout your programs. It is difficult to read programs that do not use uniform spacing conventions.

The flowchart in Fig. 4.4 illustrates the flow of control in the **if/else** structure. Note that (besides small circles and arrows) the only symbols in the flowchart are rectangles (for actions) and a diamond (for a decision). We continue to emphasize this action/decision model of computing.

The *conditional operator (?:)* is related closely to the **if/else** structure. The **?:** is C#'s only *ternary operator*—it takes three operands. The operands and the **?:** form a *conditional expression*. The first operand is a *condition* (i.e., an expression that evaluates to a **bool** value), the second is the value for the conditional expression if the condition evaluates to **true** and the third is the value for the conditional expression if the condition evaluates to **false**. For example, the output statement

```
Console.WriteLine( studentGrade >= 60 ? "Passed" : "Failed" );
```

contains a conditional expression that evaluates to the string **"Passed"** if the condition **studentGrade >= 60** is true and evaluates to the string **"Failed"** if the condition is false.

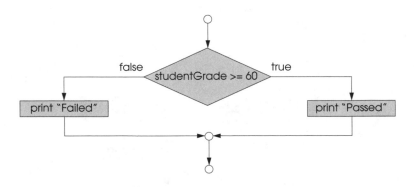

Fig. 4.4   Flowcharting a double-selection **if/else** structure.

The statement with the conditional operator performs in the same manner as the preceding **if/else** statement. The precedence of the conditional operator is low, so the entire conditional expression normally is placed in parentheses. Conditional operators can be used in some situations where **if/else** statements cannot, such as the argument to the **WriteLine** method shown earlier.

Nested if/else structures can test for multiple cases by placing **if/else** structures inside other **if/else** structures. For example, the following pseudocode statement will print **A** for exam grades greater than or equal to 90, **B** for grades in the range 80–89, **C** for grades in the range 70–79, **D** for grades in the range 60–69 and **F** for all other grades:

> *If student's grade is greater than or equal to 90*
> > *Print "A"*
>
> *Else*
> > *If student's grade is greater than or equal to 80*
> > > *Print "B"*
> >
> > *Else*
> > > *If student's grade is greater than or equal to 70*
> > > > *Print "C"*
> > >
> > > *Else*
> > > > *If student's grade is greater than or equal to 60*
> > > > > *Print "D"*
> > > >
> > > > *Else*
> > > > > *Print "F"*

This pseudocode may be written in C# as

```
if ( studentGrade >= 90 )
   Console.WriteLine( "A" );
else
   if ( studentGrade >= 80 )
      Console.WriteLine( "B" );
   else
      if ( studentGrade >= 70 )
         Console.WriteLine( "C" );
      else
         if ( studentGrade >= 60 )
            Console.WriteLine( "D" );
         else
            Console.WriteLine( "F" );
```

If **studentGrade** is greater than or equal to 90, the first four conditions are true, but only the **Console.WriteLine** statement after the first test executes. After that particular **Console.WriteLine** executes, the program skips the **else** part of the "outer" **if/else** structure.

Good Programming Practice 4.2

If there are several levels of indentation, each level should be indented the same additional amount of space.

Most C# programmers prefer to write the preceding **if** structure as

```
if ( studentGrade >= 90 )
   Console.WriteLine( "A" );
else if ( studentGrade >= 80 )
   Console.WriteLine( "B" );
else if ( studentGrade >= 70 )
   Console.WriteLine( "C" );
else if ( studentGrade >= 60 )
   Console.WriteLine( "D" );
else
   Console.WriteLine( "F" );
```

Both forms are equivalent. The latter form is popular because it avoids the deep indentation of the code. Such indentation often leaves little room on a line, forcing lines to be split and decreasing program readability.

The C# compiler always associates an **else** with the previous **if**, unless told to do otherwise by the placement of braces (**{ }**). This is referred to as the *dangling-else problem*. For example,

```
if ( x > 5 )
   if ( y > 5 )
      Console.WriteLine( "x and y are > 5" );
else
   Console.WriteLine( "x is <= 5" );
```

appears to indicate that if **x** is greater than **5**, the **if** structure in its body determines if **y** is also greater than **5**. If so, the string **"x and y are > 5"** is output. Otherwise, it *appears* that if **x** is not greater than **5**, the **else** part of the **if/else** structure outputs the string **"x is <= 5"**.

 Testing and Debugging Tip 4.1

The reader can use Visual Studio to indent code properly. In order to check indentation, the reader should highlight the relevant code and press Ctrl-K *followed immediately by* Ctrl-F.

However, the preceding nested **if** structure does not execute as its indentation implies. The compiler actually interprets the structure as

```
if ( x > 5 )
   if ( y > 5 )
      Console.WriteLine( "x and y are > 5" );
   else
      Console.WriteLine( "x is <= 5" );
```

in which the body of the first **if** structure is an **if/else** structure. This structure tests if **x** is greater than **5**. If so, execution continues by testing if **y** is also greater than **5**. If the second condition is true, the proper string—**"x and y are > 5"**—is displayed. However, if the second condition is false, the string **"x is <= 5"** is displayed, even though we know **x** is greater than **5**.

To force the preceding nested **if** structure to execute as it was originally intended, the structure must be written as follows:

```
if ( x > 5 )
{
   if ( y > 5 )
      Console.WriteLine( "x and y are > 5" );
}
else
   Console.WriteLine( "x is <= 5" );
```

The braces (**{ }**) indicate to the compiler that the second **if** structure is in the body of the first **if** structure and that the **else** is matched with the first **if** structure.

The **if** selection structure normally expects only one statement in its body. To include several statements in the body of an **if**, enclose these statements in braces (**{** and **}**). A set of statements contained in a pair of braces is called a *block*.

Software Engineering Observation 4.2

A block can be placed anywhere in a program at which a single statement can be placed.

The following example includes a block in the **else** part of an **if/else** structure:

```
if ( studentGrade >= 60 )
   Console.WriteLine( "Passed" );
else
{
   Console.WriteLine( "Failed" );
   Console.WriteLine( "You must take this course again." );
}
```

In this case, if **studentGrade** is less than 60, the program executes both statements in the body of the **else** and prints

```
Failed
You must take this course again.
```

Notice the braces surrounding the two statements in the **else** clause. These braces are important. Without the braces, the statement

```
Console.WriteLine( "You must take this course again." );
```

would be outside the body of the **else** and would execute regardless of whether the grade is less than 60.

Common Programming Error 4.1

Forgetting one of the braces that delimit a block can lead to syntax errors. Forgetting both of the braces that delimit a block can lead to syntax and/or logic errors.

Syntax errors, such as when one brace in a block is left out of the program, are caught by the compiler. A *logic error*, such as the error caused when both braces in a block are left out of the program, has its effect at execution time. A *fatal logic error* causes a program to fail and terminate prematurely. A *nonfatal logic error* allows a program to continue executing, but the program produces incorrect results.

Software Engineering Observation 4.3

*Just as a block can be placed anywhere a single statement can be placed, it is also possible to have an empty statement, which is represented by placing a semicolon (**;**) where a statement normally would be.*

Common Programming Error 4.2

*Placing a semicolon after the condition in an **if** structure leads to a logic error in single-selection **if** structures and a syntax error in double-selection **if** structures (if the **if** clause contains a nonempty body statement).*

Good Programming Practice 4.3

Some programmers prefer to type the beginning and ending braces of blocks before typing the individual statements within the braces. This practice helps avoid omitting one or both of the braces.

In this section, we introduced the notion of a block. A block may contain declarations. The declarations in a block commonly are placed first in the block before any action statements, but declarations may be intermixed with action statements.

4.7 `while` Repetition Structure

A *repetition structure* allows the programmer to specify that an action is to be repeated while a condition remains true. The pseudocode statement

> *While there are more items on my shopping list*
> *Purchase next item and cross it off my list*

describes the repetition that occurs during a shopping trip. The condition, "there are more items on my shopping list" may be true or false. If it is true, then the action, "Purchase next item and cross it off my list" is performed. This action executes repeatedly while the condition remains true. The statement(s) contained in the *while* repetition structure constitute the body of the *while*. The *while* structure body may be a single statement or a block. Eventually, the condition becomes false (when the last item on the shopping list has been purchased and crossed off the list). At this point, the repetition terminates, and the first statement after the repetition structure executes.

As an example of a **while** structure, consider a program segment designed to find the first power of 2 larger than 1000. Suppose **int** variable **product** contains the value 2. When the following **while** structure finishes executing, **product** contains the result:

```
int product = 2;

while ( product <= 1000 )
    product = 2 * product;
```

The flowchart in Fig. 4.5 illustrates the flow of control of the preceding **while** repetition structure. Once again, note that (besides small circles and arrows) the flowchart contains only a rectangle symbol and a diamond symbol.

Common Programming Error 4.3

*Not providing in the body of a **while** structure an action that eventually causes the condition to become false is a logic error. Normally, such a repetition structure will never terminate, which is an error called an "infinite loop."*

Common Programming Error 4.4

*Beginning the keyword **while** with an uppercase W, as in **While**, is a syntax error. Remember that C# is a case-sensitive language. All of C#'s keywords—**while**, **if**, **else**, etc.—contain only lowercase letters.*

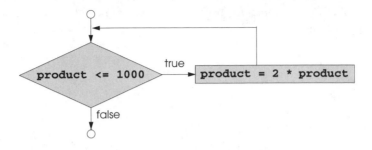

Fig. 4.5   Flowcharting the **while** repetition structure.

 Testing and Debugging Tip 4.2

Visual Studio .NET will not color a keyword properly unless that keyword is spelled correctly and with the correct case.

Imagine, again, a deep bin of empty **while** structures that may be stacked and nested with other control structures to form a structured implementation of an algorithm's flow of control. The empty rectangles and diamonds are filled with appropriate actions and decisions. The flowchart clearly shows the repetition. The flowline emerging from the rectangle indicates that program control continues with the decision, which is tested during each iteration of the loop until the decision eventually becomes false. At this point, the **while** structure terminates, and control passes to the next statement following the **while** structure in the program.

When the **while** structure begins executing, **product** is 2. Variable **product** is repeatedly multiplied by 2, taking on the values 4, 8, 16, 32, 64, 128, 256, 512 and 1024, successively. When **product** becomes 1024, the condition **product <= 1000** in the **while** structure becomes **false**. This terminates the repetition with 1024 as **product**'s final value. Execution continues with the next statement after the **while**. [*Note*: If a **while** structure's condition is initially **false**, the body statement(s) will never be executed.]

4.8 Formulating Algorithms: Case Study 1 (Counter-Controlled Repetition)

To illustrate how algorithms are developed, we solve several variations of a class-averaging problem. Consider the following problem statement:

> *A class of ten students took a quiz. The grades (integers in the range 0 to 100)*
> *for this quiz are available to you. Determine the class average on the quiz.*

The class average is equal to the sum of the grades divided by the number of students. The algorithm for solving this problem on a computer must input each of the grades, perform the averaging calculation and display the result.

Let us use pseudocode to list the actions to execute and to specify the order of execution. We use *counter-controlled repetition* to input the grades one at a time. This technique uses a variable called a *counter* to control the number of times a set of statements will execute. In this example, repetition terminates when the counter exceeds 10. This section presents a pseudocode algorithm (Fig. 4.6) and the corresponding program (Fig. 4.7). In

Section 4.9, we show how to develop a pseudocode algorithm. Counter-controlled repetition is also called *definite repetition* because the number of repetitions is known before the loop begins executing.

Set total to zero
Set grade counter to one

While grade counter is less than or equal to ten
    Input the next grade
    Add the grade into the total
    Add one to the grade counter

Set the class average to the total divided by ten
Print the class average

Fig. 4.6   Pseudocode algorithm that uses counter-controlled repetition to solve the class-average problem.

```
1   // Fig. 4.7: Average1.cs
2   // Class average with counter-controlled repetition.
3
4   using System;
5
6   class Average1
7   {
8      static void Main( string[] args )
9      {
10        int total,            // sum of grades
11            gradeCounter,     // number of grades entered
12            gradeValue,       // grade value
13            average;          // average of all grades
14
15        // initialization phase
16        total = 0;            // clear total
17        gradeCounter = 1;     // prepare to loop
18
19        // processing phase
20        while ( gradeCounter <= 10 )   // loop 10 times
21        {
22           // prompt for input and read grade from user
23           Console.Write( "Enter integer grade: " );
24
25           // read input and convert to integer
26           gradeValue = Int32.Parse( Console.ReadLine() );
27
28           // add gradeValue to total
29           total = total + gradeValue;
30
```

Fig. 4.7   Class average program with counter-controlled repetition. (Part 1 of 2.)

```
31              // add 1 to gradeCounter
32              gradeCounter = gradeCounter + 1;
33          }
34
35          // termination phase
36          average = total / 10;   // integer division
37
38          // display average of exam grades
39          Console.WriteLine( "\nClass average is {0}", average );
40
41      } // end Main
42
43  } // end class Average1
```

```
Enter integer grade: 100
Enter integer grade: 88
Enter integer grade: 93
Enter integer grade: 55
Enter integer grade: 68
Enter integer grade: 77
Enter integer grade: 83
Enter integer grade: 95
Enter integer grade: 73
Enter integer grade: 62

Class average is 79
```

Fig. 4.7 Class average program with counter-controlled repetition. (Part 2 of 2.)

Note the references in the algorithm (Fig. 4.6) to a total and a counter. The pseudocode variable *total* accumulates the sum of a series of values. A counter is a variable that counts—in this case, that counts the number of grades entered. Variables that store totals normally should be initialized to zero before being used in a program; otherwise, the sum would include the previous value stored in the total's memory location.

Testing and Debugging Tip 4.3

Initialize counters and totals.

Line 6 begins the definition of class **Average1**. Remember that an application class definition must contain a **Main** method (lines 8–41) to begin execution of the application.

Lines 10–13 declare variables **total**, **gradeCounter**, **gradeValue** and **average** to be of type **int**. Variable **gradeValue** will store the value the user inputs after the value is converted from a **string** to an **int**.

Good Programming Practice 4.4

Always place a blank line between a declaration and executable statements. This makes the declarations stand out in a program and contributes to program clarity.

Lines 16–17 are assignment statements that initialize **total** to **0** and **grade-Counter** to **1**. Variables **total** and **gradeCounter** are initialized before they are used in a calculation. Recall that using uninitialized variables in calculations results in compilation errors.

Line 20 indicates that the **while** structure should continue as long as the value of **gradeCounter** is less than or equal to 10. Lines 23 and 26 correspond to the pseudocode statement *"Input the next grade."* The statement on line 23 displays the prompt "**Enter integer grade:**" on the screen. The statement on line 26 reads the information entered by the user, converts it to an **int** and stores the value in **gradeValue**. Next, line 29 updates the **total** with the new **gradeValue** by adding **gradeValue** to the previous value of **total** and assigning the result to **total**.

The program is now ready to increment the variable **gradeCounter** to indicate that a grade has been processed. Line 32 adds **1** to **gradeCounter**, so the condition in the **while** structure eventually will become false and terminate the loop. Line 36 assigns the results of the average calculation to variable **average**. Line 39 displays a message containing the string **"Class average is "** followed by the value of variable **average**.

The averaging calculation produces an integer result. Actually, the sum of the grade-point values in this example is 794, which, when divided by 10, yields 79.4. Such numbers with a decimal point are called floating-point numbers; we discuss floating-point numbers in the next section.

4.9 Formulating Algorithms with Top-Down, Stepwise Refinement: Case Study 2 (Sentinel-Controlled Repetition)

Let us generalize the class-average problem. Consider the following problem:

> *Develop a class-averaging program that processes an arbitrary number of grades each time the program executes.*

In the first class-average example, the number of grades (10) was known in advance. In this example, no indication is given of how many grades are to be input. The program must process an arbitrary number of grades. How can the program determine when to stop the input of grades? How will it know when to calculate and print the class average?

One way to solve this problem is to use a special value called a *sentinel value* (also called a *signal value*, a *dummy value* or a *flag value*) to indicate "end of data entry." The user inputs all grades and then types the sentinel value to indicate that the last grade has been entered. Sentinel-controlled repetition often is called *indefinite repetition* because the number of repetitions is not known before the loop begins executing.

The sentinel value cannot be confused with an acceptable input value. Grades on a quiz are normally nonnegative integers, thus –1 is an acceptable sentinel value for this problem. A run of the class-average program might process a stream of inputs such as 95, 96, 75, 74, 89 and –1. The program would then compute and print the class average for the grades 95, 96, 75, 74 and 89. The sentinel value, –1, should not enter into the averaging calculation.

Common Programming Error 4.5

Choosing a sentinel value that is also a legitimate data value results in a logic error and may prevent a sentinel-controlled loop from terminating properly, a problem known as an infinite loop.

We approach the class-average program with *top-down, stepwise refinement*, a technique essential to the development of well-structured algorithms. We begin with a pseudocode representation of the *top:*

Determine the class average for the quiz

The top is a single statement that conveys the overall function of the program. As such, the top is a complete representation of a program. Unfortunately, the top rarely conveys a sufficient amount of detail from which to write the C# algorithm. Therefore, we conduct the refinement process. We divide the top into a series of smaller tasks and list these in the order in which they must be performed. This results in the following *first refinement*:

Initialize variables
Input, sum up and count the quiz grades
Calculate and print the class average

Here, only the sequence structure has been used—the steps listed are to be executed in order, one after the other.

Software Engineering Observation 4.4

Each refinement, including the top, is a complete specification of the algorithm; only the level of detail in each refinement varies.

To proceed to the next level of refinement (i.e., the *second refinement*), we commit to specific variables. We need a running total of the numbers, a count of how many numbers have been processed, a variable to receive the value of each grade and a variable to hold the calculated average. The pseudocode statement

Initialize variables

may be refined as follows:

Initialize total to zero
Initialize counter to zero

Notice that only the variables *total* and *counter* are initialized before they are used; the variables *average* and *grade* (for the calculated average and the user input, respectively) need not be initialized because their values are determined as they are calculated or input.

The pseudocode statement

Input, sum up and count the quiz grades

requires a repetition structure (i.e., a loop) that successively inputs each grade. We do not know how many grades are to be processed, thus we use sentinel-controlled repetition. The user types in legitimate grades one at a time. After the last legitimate grade is typed, the user types the sentinel value. The program tests for the sentinel value after each grade is input and terminates the loop when the user enters the sentinel value. The second refinement of the preceding pseudocode statement is then

Input the first grade (possibly the sentinel)

While the user has not as yet entered the sentinel
    Add this grade into the running total
    Add one to the grade counter
    Input the next grade (possibly the sentinel)

We do not use braces around the pseudocode that forms the body of the *while* structure. We simply indent the pseudocode under the *while* to show that it belongs to the *while* structure.

Note that a value is input both before reaching the loop and at the end of the loop's body. As we enter the loop, the value input before the loop is tested to determine whether it is the sentinel. If so, the loop terminates; otherwise, the body of the loop executes. The body processes the grade, then inputs the next grade. Then, the new grade is tested at the top of the loop to determine if that grade is the sentinel.

The pseudocode statement

> *Calculate and print the class average*

may be refined as follows:

> *If the counter is not equal to zero*
> > *Set the average to the total divided by the counter*
> > *Print the average*
> *Else*
> > *Print "No grades were entered"*

We test for the possibility of division by zero—a logic error that, if undetected, causes the program to produce invalid output. The complete second refinement of the pseudocode algorithm for the class-average problem is shown in Fig. 4.8.

Testing and Debugging Tip 4.4

When performing division by an expression whose value could be zero, explicitly test for this case and handle it appropriately in your program, possibly printing an error message.

Good Programming Practice 4.5

Include blank lines in pseudocode programs for increased readability. The blank lines separate pseudocode control structures and the program's phases.

Initialize total to zero
Initialize counter to zero

Input the first grade (possibly the sentinel)

While the user has not as yet entered the sentinel
> *Add this grade into the running total*
> *Add one to the grade counter*
> *Input the next grade (possibly the sentinel)*

If the counter is not equal to zero
> *Set the average to the total divided by the counter*
> *Print the average*
Else
> *Print "No grades were entered"*

Fig. 4.8   Pseudocode algorithm that uses sentinel-controlled repetition to solve the class-average problem.

Software Engineering Observation 4.5

Many algorithms can be divided logically into three phases—an initialization phase that initializes the program variables, a processing phase that inputs data values and adjusts program variables accordingly and a termination phase that calculates and prints the results.

The pseudocode algorithm in Fig. 4.8 solves the more general class-averaging problem. This algorithm was developed after only two levels of refinement. Sometimes more levels are necessary.

Software Engineering Observation 4.6

The programmer terminates the top-down, stepwise refinement process when the pseudocode algorithm is specified in sufficient detail for the programmer to convert the pseudocode to a C# program. Implementing the C# program then normally occurs in a straightforward manner.

The C# program for this pseudocode is shown in Fig. 4.9. Notice from the output that each grade entered is an integer, although the averaging calculation is likely to produce a number with a decimal point. The type **int** cannot represent real numbers, so this program uses data type **double** to handle floating-point numbers.

The program also introduces the *cast operator* (line 44) to handle the type conversion for the averaging calculation. These features are explained in detail in our discussion of Fig. 4.9.

```
1   // Fig. 4.9: Average2.cs
2   // Class average with sentinel-controlled repetition.
3
4   using System;
5
6   class Average2
7   {
8      static void Main( string[] args )
9      {
10        int total,          // sum of grades
11            gradeCounter,    // number of grades entered
12            gradeValue;      // grade value
13
14        double average;      // average of all grades
15
16        // initialization phase
17        total = 0;           // clear total
18        gradeCounter = 0;    // prepare to loop
19
20        // processing phase
21        // prompt for input and convert to integer
22        Console.Write( "Enter Integer Grade, -1 to Quit: " );
23        gradeValue = Int32.Parse( Console.ReadLine() );
24
25        // loop until a -1 is entered by user
26        while ( gradeValue != -1 )
27        {
28           // add gradeValue to total
29           total = total + gradeValue;
```

Fig. 4.9   Class-average program with sentinel-controlled repetition. (Part 1 of 2.)

```
30
31              // add 1 to gradeCounter
32              gradeCounter = gradeCounter + 1;
33
34              // prompt for input and read grade from user
35              // convert grade from string to integer
36              Console.Write( "Enter Integer Grade, -1 to Quit: " );
37              gradeValue = Int32.Parse( Console.ReadLine() );
38
39          } // end while
40
41          // termination phase
42          if ( gradeCounter != 0 )
43          {
44              average = ( double ) total / gradeCounter;
45
46              // display average of exam grades
47              Console.WriteLine( "\nClass average is {0}", average );
48
49          }
50          else
51          {
52              Console.WriteLine( "No grades were entered." );
53          }
54
55      } // end method Main
56
57  } // end class Average2
```

```
Enter Integer Grade, -1 to Quit: 97
Enter Integer Grade, -1 to Quit: 88
Enter Integer Grade, -1 to Quit: 72
Enter Integer Grade, -1 to Quit: -1

Class average is 85.6666666666667
```

Fig. 4.9   Class-average program with sentinel-controlled repetition. (Part 2 of 2.)

In this example, we examine how control structures may be stacked on top of one another, in sequence. The **while** structure (lines 26–39) is followed immediately by an **if/else** structure (lines 42–53). Much of the code in this program is identical to the code in Fig. 4.7, so we concentrate on the new features in this example.

Line 14 declares variable **average** to be of type **double**. This change allows us to store the result of the class-average calculation as a floating-point number. Line 18 initializes **gradeCounter** to **0** because no grades have been input yet—recall that this program uses sentinel-controlled repetition. To keep an accurate record of the number of grades entered, variable **gradeCounter** is incremented only when a valid grade value is input.

Notice the differences between sentinel-controlled repetition and the counter-controlled repetition of Fig. 4.7. In counter-controlled repetition, we read a value from the user during each pass of the **while** structure for the specified number of iterations. In sentinel-controlled repetition, we read one value (line 23) before the program reaches the **while** structure. This value is used to determine if the program's flow of control should enter the body of the **while** structure. If the **while** structure condition is false (i.e., the user has entered the sentinel value), the body of the **while** structure does not execute (i.e., no grades were entered). If, on the other hand, the condition is true, the body begins execution, and the value input by the user is processed (added to the **total**). Then, the next value is input from the user before the end of the **while** structure's body. When program control reaches the closing right brace (**}**) of the body (line 39), execution continues with the next test of the **while** structure condition. The new value input by the user determines if the **while** structure's body should execute again. Notice that the next value is input from the user immediately before the **while** structure condition is evaluated (line 37). This allows the program to determine whether the value just input by the user is the sentinel value *before* the program processes that value as a valid grade. If the value is the sentinel value, the **while** structure terminates, and the value is not added to the **total**.

Notice the block that composes the **while** loop in Fig. 4.9. Without the braces, the last three statements in the body of the loop would be outside the loop, causing the computer to interpret the code incorrectly, as follows:

```
while ( gradeValue != -1 )

   // add gradeValue to total
   total = total + gradeValue;

// add 1 to gradeCounter
gradeCounter = gradeCounter + 1;

// prompt for input and read grade from user
Console.Write( "Enter Integer Grade, -1 to Quit: " );
gradeValue = Int32.Parse( Console.ReadLine() );
```

An infinite loop occurs in the program if the user fails to input the sentinel **-1** as the input value at line 23 (before the **while** structure).

Common Programming Error 4.6

Omitting the curly braces that delimit a block in a repetition structure can lead to logic errors, such as infinite loops.

Good Programming Practice 4.6

In a sentinel-controlled loop, the prompts requesting data entry should remind the user of the sentinel value.

Averages do not always evaluate to integer values. Often, an average is a value such as 3.333 or 2.7, that contains a fractional part. These values are floating-point numbers and usually are represented by the data type **double**. We declare the variable **average** as type **double** to capture the fractional result of our calculation. However, the result of the calculation **total / gradeCounter** is an integer because **total** and **grade-Counter** are both integer variables. Dividing two integers results in *integer division*, in which any fractional part of the calculation is *truncated* and the result is a whole number. The calculation is performed first, thus the fractional part is lost before the result is assigned to **average**. To produce a floating-point calculation with integer values, we must create temporary values that are floating-point numbers for the calculation. C# provides the *unary* *cast operator* to create this temporary value. Line 44 uses the cast operator **(double)** to create a temporary floating-point copy of its operand—**total**. Using a cast operator in this manner is called *explicit conversion*. The value stored in **total** is still an integer. The calculation now consists of a floating-point value (the temporary **double** version of **total**) divided by the integer **gradeCounter**. Note that the cast does not modify the value stored in memory for **total**. Rather it creates a temporary value that is used only for this calculation.

Common Programming Error 4.7

Assuming that integer division rounds (rather than truncates) can lead to incorrect results.

C# can evaluate only arithmetic expressions in which the data types of the operands are identical. To ensure that the operands are of the same type, C# performs *implicit conversion* (also called *promotion*) on selected operands. Through implicit conversion, in an expression containing the data types **int** and **double**, **int** operands are *promoted* to **double**. In our example, the temporary **double** version of **total** is divided by the **int** **gradeCounter**. Therefore, a temporary version of **gradeCounter** is promoted to **double**, the calculation is performed and the result of the floating-point division is assigned to **average**.

Cast operators are available for most data types. The cast operator is known as a *unary operator* (i.e., an operator that takes only one operand) and is formed by placing parentheses around a data type name. In Chapter 3, Introduction to C# Programming, we studied the binary arithmetic operators. C# also supports unary versions of the plus (**+**) and minus (**-**) operators, so the programmer can write expressions like **-7** or **+5**. Cast operators associate from right to left and have the same precedence as other unary operators, such as unary **+** and unary **-**. This precedence is one level higher than that of the *multiplicative operators* *****, **/** and **%** and one level lower than that of parentheses. (See the operator precedence chart in Appendix A.) In our precedence charts, we indicate the cast operator with the notation *(type)* to show that any type name can form a cast operator.

Common Programming Error 4.8

Using floating-point numbers in a manner that assumes that they are precisely represented real numbers can lead to incorrect results. Real numbers are represented only approximately by computers.

Good Programming Practice 4.7

Do not compare floating-point values for equality or inequality. Rather, test that the absolute value of the difference between two floating-point numbers is less than a specified small value.

Despite the fact that floating-point numbers are not always "100% precise," they have numerous applications. For example, when we speak of a "normal" body temperature of 98.6, we do not need to be precise to a large number of digits. When we view the temperature on a thermometer and read it as 98.6, it may actually be 98.5999473210643. Calling such a number simply 98.6 is fine for most applications.

Floating-point numbers also develop through division. When we divide 10 by 3, the result is 3.3333333..., with the sequence of 3s repeating infinitely. The computer allocates only a fixed amount of space to hold such a value, so the stored floating-point value can be only an approximation.

Line 47 displays the value of **average**. We specify average as the second argument to **WriteLine**. Method **WriteLine** will convert this argument to a **string** and display its value.

4.10 Formulating Algorithms with Top-Down, Stepwise Refinement: Case Study 3 (Nested Control Structures)

Let us work through another complete problem. We will again formulate the algorithm using pseudocode and top-down, stepwise refinement; we will write a corresponding C# program.

Consider the following problem statement:

> *A college offers a course that prepares students for the state licensing exam for real estate brokers. Last year, several of the students who completed this course took the licensing examination. The college wants to know how well its students did on the exam. You have been asked to write a program to summarize the results. You have been given a list of the 10 students. Next to each name is written a 1 if the student passed the exam and a 2 if the student failed the exam.*

> *Your program should analyze the results of the exam as follows:*

> 1. *Input each test result (i.e., a 1 or a 2). Display the message "Enter result" on the screen each time the program requests another test result.*

> 2. *Count the number of test results of each type.*

> 3. *Display a summary of the test results, indicating the number of students who passed and the number of students who failed the exam.*

> 4. *If more than 8 students passed the exam, print the message "Raise tuition."*

After reading the problem statement carefully, we make the following observations about the problem:

1. The program must process test results for 10 students. A counter-controlled loop will be used.

2. Each test result is a number—either a 1 or a 2. Each time the program reads a test result, the program must determine if the number is a 1 or a 2. If the number is either a 1 or a 2, the loop counter is incremented by 1. Otherwise, the loop counter is not incremented and the value input is ignored.

3. Two counters keep track of the exam results—one to count the number of students who passed the exam and one to count the number of students who failed.

4. After the program processes all the results, it must decide if more than eight students passed the exam.

Let us proceed with top-down, stepwise refinement. We begin with a pseudocode representation of the top:

> *Analyze exam results and decide if tuition should be raised*

Once again, it is important to emphasize that the top is a complete representation of the program, but several refinements are likely to be needed before the pseudocode can be evolved naturally into a C# program. Our first refinement is

> *Initialize variables*
> *Input the ten exam grades and count passes and failures*
> *Print a summary of the exam results and decide if tuition should be raised*

Even though we have a complete representation of the entire program, further refinement is necessary. We must commit to specific variables. Counters are needed to record the passes and failures. A counter controls the looping process and a variable stores the user input. The pseudocode statement

> *Initialize variables*

may be refined as follows:

> *Initialize passes to zero*
> *Initialize failures to zero*
> *Initialize student to one*

Only the counters for the number of passes, number of failures and number of students are initialized. The pseudocode statement

> *Input the ten quiz grades and count passes and failures*

requires a loop that successively inputs the result of each exam. Here, it is known in advance that there are precisely ten exam results, so counter-controlled repetition is appropriate. Inside the loop (i.e., *nested* within the loop) a double-selection structure determines whether each exam result is a pass or a failure, and the structure increments the appropriate counter accordingly. The refinement of the preceding pseudocode statement is

> *While student counter is less than or equal to ten*
>   *Input the next exam result*
>
>   *If the student passed*
>   *Add one to passes*
>   *Add one to student counter*
>
>   *Else If the student failed*
>   *Add one to failures*
>   *Add one to student counter*

Notice the use of blank lines to offset the *If/Else* control structure to improve program readability. The pseudocode statement

> *Print a summary of the exam results and decide if tuition should be raised*

may be refined as follows:

> *Print the number of passes*
> *Print the number of failures*
>
> *If more than eight students passed*
>   *Print "Raise tuition"*

The complete second refinement appears in Fig. 4.10. Notice that blank lines also set off the *While* structure for program readability.

The pseudocode now is refined sufficiently for conversion to C#. The C# program and sample executions are shown in Fig. 4.11.

Lines 10–13 declare the variables used in **Main** to process the examination results. We have taken advantage of a C# feature that incorporates variable initialization into declarations (**passes** is assigned **0**, **failures** is assigned **0** and **student** is assigned **1**). Programs that contain repetition may require initialization at the beginning of each repetition; such initialization normally occurs in assignment statements. Notice the use of the nested **if/else** structure (lines 21–31) in the **while** structure's body. Also, notice the new statement at line 35 that uses **Console.WriteLine** to output a blank line.

Software Engineering Observation 4.7

The most difficult part of solving a problem on a computer is developing the algorithm for the solution. Once a correct algorithm has been specified, the process of producing a working C# program from the algorithm is normally straightforward.

Software Engineering Observation 4.8

Many experienced programmers write programs without ever using program development tools like pseudocode. These programmers feel that their ultimate goal is to solve the problem on a computer, and that writing pseudocode merely delays the production of final output. Although this may work for simple and familiar problems, it can lead to serious problems on large, complex projects.

Initialize passes to zero
Initialize failures to zero
Initialize student to one

While student counter is less than or equal to ten
    Input the next exam result

    If the student passed
        Add one to passes
        Add one to student counter

    Else If the student failed
        Add one to failures
        Add one to student counter

Print the number of passes
Print the number of failures

If more than eight students passed
    Print "Raise tuition"

Fig. 4.10   Pseudocode for examination-results problem.

```
1   // Fig. 4.11: Analysis.cs
2   // Analysis of Examination Results.
3
4   using System;
5
6   class Analysis
7   {
8      static void Main( string[] args )
9      {
10        int passes = 0,           // number of passes
11            failures = 0,         // number of failures
12            student = 1,          // student counter
13            result;               // one exam result
14
15        // process 10 students; counter-controlled loop
16        while ( student <= 10 )
17        {
18           Console.Write( "Enter result (1=pass, 2=fail): " );
19           result = Int32.Parse( Console.ReadLine() );
20
21           if ( result == 1 )
22           {
23              passes = passes + 1;
24              student = student + 1;
25           }
26
27           else if ( result == 2 )
28           {
29              failures = failures + 1;
30              student = student + 1;
31           }
32        }
33
34        // termination phase
35        Console.WriteLine();
36        Console.WriteLine( "Passed: " + passes );
37        Console.WriteLine( "Failed: " + failures );
38
39        if ( passes > 8 )
40           Console.WriteLine( "Raise Tuition\n" );
41
42     } // end of method Main
43
44  } // end of class Analysis
```

```
Enter result (1=pass, 2=fail): 1
Enter result (1=pass, 2=fail): 2
Enter result (1=pass, 2=fail): 1
Enter result (1=pass, 2=fail): 1
Enter result (1=pass, 2=fail): 1
Enter result (1=pass, 2=fail): 1
```

Continued at the top of the next page

Fig. 4.11   C# program for examination-results problem. (Part 1 of 2.)

Continued from the previous page

```
Enter result (1=pass, 2=fail): 1
Enter result (1=pass, 2=fail): 1
Enter result (1=pass, 2=fail): 1
Enter result (1=pass, 2=fail): 1

Passed: 9
Failed: 1
Raise Tuition
```

```
Enter result (1=pass, 2=fail): 1
Enter result (1=pass, 2=fail): 2
Enter result (1=pass, 2=fail): 2
Enter result (1=pass, 2=fail): 2
Enter result (1=pass, 2=fail): 2
Enter result (1=pass, 2=fail): 2
Enter result (1=pass, 2=fail): 1
Enter result (1=pass, 2=fail): 1
Enter result (1=pass, 2=fail): 1
Enter result (1=pass, 2=fail): 1

Passed: 5
Failed: 5
```

Fig. 4.11   C# program for examination-results problem. (Part 2 of 2.)

4.11 Assignment Operators

C# provides several assignment operators for abbreviating assignment expressions. For example, the statement

    c = c + 3;

can be abbreviated with the *addition assignment operator* **+=** as

    c += 3;

The **+=** operator adds the value of the expression on the right of the operator to the value of the variable on the left of the operator and stores the result in the variable on the left of the operator. Any statement of the form

    variable = *variable operator expression;*

where *operator* is one of the binary operators **+**, **-**, *****, **/** or **%** (or others we will discuss later in the book), can be written in the form

    variable operator= *expression;*

Figure 4.12 includes the arithmetic assignment operators, sample expressions using these operators and explanations.

Common Programming Error 4.9

Placing a space character between the symbols that compose an arithmetic assignment operator is a syntax error.

Assignment operator	Sample expression	Explanation	Assigns
Assume: `int c = 3, d = 5, e = 4, f = 6, g = 12;`			
`+=`	`c += 7`	`c = c + 7`	10 to `c`
`-=`	`d -= 4`	`d = d - 4`	1 to `d`
`*=`	`e *= 5`	`e = e * 5`	20 to `e`
`/=`	`f /= 3`	`f = f / 3`	2 to `f`
`%=`	`g %= 9`	`g = g % 9`	3 to `g`

Fig. 4.12   Arithmetic assignment operators.

4.12 Increment and Decrement Operators

C# provides the unary *increment operator*, **++**, and the unary *decrement operator*, **--**, which are summarized in Fig. 4.13. A program can increment the value of a variable called **c** by 1 using the increment operator, **++**, rather than the expression **c = c + 1** or **c += 1**. If an increment or decrement operator is placed before a variable, it is referred to as the *preincrement* or *predecrement operator*, respectively. If an increment or decrement operator is placed after a variable, it is referred to as the *postincrement* or *postdecrement operator*, respectively.

Preincrementing (or predecrementing) a variable causes the variable to be incremented (or decremented) by 1, and then the new value of the variable is used in the expression in which it appears. Postincrementing (or postdecrementing) the variable causes the current value of the variable to be used in the expression in which it appears, and then the variable value is incremented (or decremented) by 1.

The application in Fig. 4.14 demonstrates the difference between the preincrementing version and the postincrementing version of the **++** increment operator. Postincrementing the variable **c** causes it to be incremented after it is used in the **Console.WriteLine** method call (line 14). Preincrementing the variable **c** causes it to be incremented before it is used in the **Console.WriteLine** method call (line 21).

Operator	Called	Sample expression	Explanation
`++`	preincrement	`++a`	Increment **a** by 1, then use the new value of **a** in the expression in which **a** resides.
`++`	postincrement	`a++`	Use the current value of **a** in the expression in which **a** resides, then increment **a** by 1.
`--`	predecrement	`--b`	Decrement **b** by 1, then use the new value of **b** in the expression in which **b** resides.
`--`	postdecrement	`b--`	Use the current value of **b** in the expression in which **b** resides, then decrement **b** by 1.

Fig. 4.13   increment and decrement operators.

```
1   // Fig. 4.14: Increment.cs
2   // Preincrementing and postincrementing
3
4   using System;
5
6   class Increment
7   {
8      static void Main( string[] args )
9      {
10        int c;
11
12        c = 5;
13        Console.WriteLine( c );     // print 5
14        Console.WriteLine( c++ );   // print 5 then postincrement
15        Console.WriteLine( c );     // print 6
16
17        Console.WriteLine();        // skip a line
18
19        c = 5;
20        Console.WriteLine( c );     // print 5
21        Console.WriteLine( ++c );   // preincrement then print 6
22        Console.WriteLine( c );     // print 6
23
24     } // end of method Main
25
26  } // end of class Increment
```

```
5
5
6

5
6
6
```

Fig. 4.14   The difference between preincrementing and postincrementing.

The program displays the value of **c** before and after the **++** operator is used. The decrement operator (**--**) works similarly.

Good Programming Practice 4.8

For readability, unary operators should be placed next to their operands, with no intervening spaces.

Line 17,

```
Console.WriteLine();        // skip a line
```

uses **Console.WriteLine** to output a blank line. If **Console.WriteLine** receives no arguments, it simply outputs a newline character.

The arithmetic assignment operators and the increment and decrement operators can be used to simplify program statements. For example, the three assignment statements in Fig. 4.11 (lines 22, 25 and 27)

```
passes = passes + 1;
failures = failures + 1;
student = student + 1;
```

can be written more concisely with assignment operators as

```
passes += 1;
failures += 1;
student += 1;
```

with preincrement operators as

```
++passes;
++failures;
++student;
```

or with postincrement operators as

```
passes++;
failures++;
student++;
```

It is important to note here that when incrementing or decrementing a variable in an expression or statement by itself, the preincrement and postincrement forms have the same effect, and the predecrement and postdecrement forms have the same effect. It is only when a variable appears in the context of a larger expression that preincrementing and postincrementing the variable have different effects (and similarly for predecrementing and postdecrementing).

Common Programming Error 4.10

Attempting to use the increment or decrement operator on an expression other than a variable reference *is a syntax error. A* variable reference *is a variable or expression that can appear on the left side of an assignment operation. For example, writing* **++(x + 1)** *is a syntax error, because* **(x + 1)** *is not a* variable reference.[2]

The chart in Fig. 4.15 shows the precedence and associativity of the operators introduced to this point. The operators are shown top to bottom in decreasing order of precedence. The second column describes the associativity of the operators at each level of precedence. Notice that the conditional operator (**?:**), the unary operators increment (**++**), decrement (**--**), plus (**+**), minus (**-**), cast and the assignment operators (**=, +=, -=, *=, /= and %=**) associate from right to left. All other operators in the operator precedence chart of Fig. 4.15 associate from left to right. The third column names the groups of operators.

Operators	Associativity	Type
()	left to right	parentheses
++ --	right to left	unary postfix

Fig. 4.15 Precedence and associativity of the operators discussed so far in this book. (Part 1 of 2.)

---

2. The term *variable reference* is equivalent to the term *lvalue* ("left value"), which is popular among C and C++ programmers.

Operators	Associativity	Type
++ -- + - (*type*)	right to left	unary prefix
* / %	left to right	multiplicative
+ -	left to right	additive
< <= > >=	left to right	relational
== !=	left to right	equality
? :	right to left	conditional
= += -= *= /= %=	right to left	assignment

Fig. 4.15   Precedence and associativity of the operators discussed so far in this book. (Part 2 of 2.)

4.13 Introduction to Windows Application Programming

Today, users demand software with rich graphical user interfaces (GUIs) that allow them to click buttons, select items from menus and much more. In this chapter and the previous, we created console applications. However, most C# programs used in industry are Windows applications with GUIs.

In Chapter 2, Introduction to the Visual Studio .NET IDE, we introduced the concept of visual programming, which allows programmers to create GUIs without writing any programming code. In this section, we combine visual programming with the conventional programming techniques introduced in this chapter and the previous chapter. Through this combination, we can enhance considerably the Windows application introduced in Chapter 2.

Load the project **ASimpleProject** from Chapter 2 into the IDE. To identify easily the form and its controls in the program code, change the **Name** properties of the form, label and picture box to **ASimpleProgram, welcomeLabel** and **bugPictureBox**, respectively. [Note: This property may appear as **(Name)** in the **Properties** window.] To change a GUI component's properties, select (click) the component in the design window, then locate the property in the **Properties** window. Click the box to the right of the property name to input a new value, and press the *Enter* key once the new value has been entered.

With visual programming, the IDE generates the program code that creates the GUI. This code contains instructions for the creation of the form and every control on it. Unlike a console application, a Windows application's program code is not displayed initially in the editor window. Once the program's project (e.g., **ASimpleProgram**) is opened in the IDE, the program code can be viewed by selecting **View > Code**. Figure 4.16 shows the code editor displaying the program code.

Every Windows application consists of at least one class that *inherits* from class **Form** (which represents a form) in the .NET Framework Class Library's **System.Windows.Forms** namespace. The keyword **class** begins a class definition and is followed immediately by the class name (**ASimpleProgram**). Recall that the form's name is set using the **Name** property. A colon (**:**) indicates that the class **ASimpleProgram** inherits existing pieces from another class. The class from which **ASimpleProgram** inherits—

here, **System.Windows.Forms.Form**—appears to the right of the colon. In this inheritance relationship, **Form** is called the *base class* (or *superclass*), and **ASimpleProgram** is called the *derived class* (or *subclass*). With inheritance **ASimpleProgram**'s class definition has the *attributes* (data) and *behaviors* (methods) of class **Form**. We discuss the significance of the keyword **public** in Chapter 8. [*Note*: Changing a control's name in the **Properties** window may not change all occurrences of the control's name in the code. The reader should search the code and replace names that were not changed by the IDE. For example, the original form name (and class name) was **Form1**. Search the code for **Form1** and change any remaining instances to **ASimpleProgram**.]

A key benefit of inheriting from class **Form** is that someone else has previously defined "what it means to be a form." The Windows operating system expects every window (e.g., form) to have certain attributes and behaviors. However, because class **Form** already provides those capabilities, programmers do not need to "reinvent the wheel" by defining all those capabilities themselves. In fact, class **Form** has hundreds of methods! In our programs up to this point, we have used only one method (i.e., **Main**), so you can imagine how much work went into creating class **Form**. The use of the colon to extend from class **Form** enables programmers to create forms quickly.

In the editor window (Fig. 4.16), notice that portions of text are enclosed in small rectangles with small plus boxes to their left. The plus box indicates that this section of code is *collapsed*. Although collapsed code is not visible, it is still part of the program. Code collapsing allows programmers to hide code in the editor, so that they can focus on smaller (and perhaps more important) code segments. Clicking the plus box expands the code (i.e., displays the entire segment of code). A small minus box to the left of expanded code can be clicked in order to collapse that portion of code. If the programmer wishes to briefly view collapsed code, they can place the cursor over the rectangle for that portion of code. Doing so will display the code in a small window.

The appearance of collapsed code differs depending on the nature of the code. Figure 4.16 demonstrates that collapsed comments appear as **/**/** within a rectangle, while collapsed statements appear as an ellipses (**...**) within a rectangle. Finally, *regions* of code can be created in a C# program. A region is a portion of code specified between the text **#region** and **#endregion**. These tags specify the text that appears in the rectangle when the code is collapsed. One such region is shown at the bottom of Fig. 4.16, containing the text **Windows Form Designer generated code**. The description in the rectangle indicates that the collapsed code was created by the *Windows Form Designer* (i.e., the part of the IDE that creates the code for the GUI). This collapsed code contains the code created by the IDE for the form and its controls, as well as code that enables the program to run. We will describe how this region was created shortly.

Upon initial inspection, the *expanded code* (Fig. 4.17) looks complex. This code is created by the IDE and normally is not edited by the programmer. Such code is present in every Windows application. Allowing the IDE to create this code saves the programmer considerable development time. If the IDE did not provide the code, the programmer would have to write it, and that would require a considerable amount of time. The vast majority of the code shown has not been introduced yet, so you are not expected to understand how it works. However, certain programming constructs, such as comments and control structures, should be familiar. As you continue to study C#, especially in Chapters 8–11, the purpose of this code will become clearer.

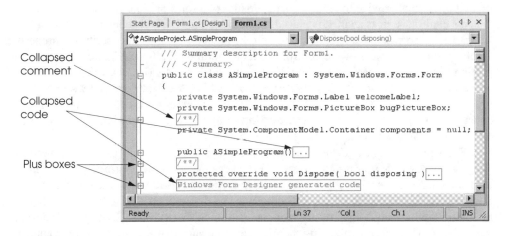

Fig. 4.16   IDE showing program code for Fig. 2.14.

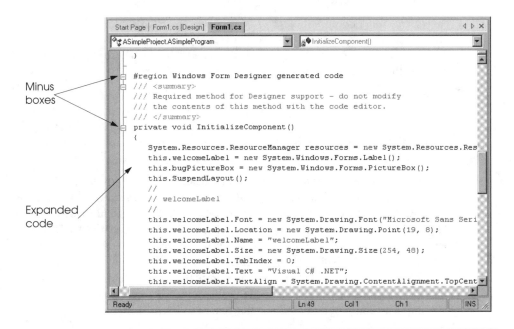

Fig. 4.17   Windows Form Designer generated code when expanded.

Towards the top of Fig. 4.17 we see the text **#region**. This text indicates the beginning of a collapsible region of code. After **#region** we see the text that will be displayed when the region is collapsed. This region ends when the text **#endregion** is encountered, after the end of method **InitializeComponent**.

When we created this application in Chapter 2, we used the **Properties** window to set properties for the form, label and picture box. Once a property was set, the form or control was updated immediately. Forms and controls contain a set of *default properties*, which are displayed initially in the **Properties** window when a form or control is selected. These default properties provide the initial characteristics of a form or control when it is created. When a control, such as a label, is placed on the form, the IDE adds code to the class (e.g., **ASimpleProgram**) that creates the control and sets some of the control's property values, such as the name of the control and its location on the form. Figure 4.18 shows a portion of the code generated by the IDE for setting the label's (i.e., **welcomeLabel**'s) properties. These include the label's **Font**, **Location**, **Name**, **Text** and **TextAlign** properties. Recall from Chapter 2 that we explicitly set values for the label's **Name**, **Text** and **TextAlign** properties in the **Properties** window. Other properties, such as **Location** are set only when the label is placed on the form.

The values assigned to the properties are based on the values in the **Properties** window. We now demonstrate how the IDE updates the Windows Form Designer generated code it generates when a property value in the **Properties** window changes. During this process, we must switch between code view and design view. To switch views, select the corresponding tabs—**Form1.cs*** for code view and **Form1.cs* [Design]** for design view. [*Note*: The asterisk following the file name indicates that the file has been changed, and therefore needs to be saved.] Alternatively, the programmer can select **View > Code** or **View > Designer**. Perform the following steps:

1. *Modify the label control's **Text** property using the **Properties** window.* Recall that properties can be changed in design view by clicking a form or control to select it, then modifying the appropriate property in the **Properties** window. Change the **Text** property of the label to "**Deitel**" (Fig. 4.19).

2. *Examine the changes in the code view.* Switch to code view (**View > Code**) and examine the code. Notice that the label's **Text** property is now assigned the text that we entered in the **Properties** window (Fig. 4.20). When a property is changed in design mode, the Windows Form Designer updates the appropriate line of code in the class to reflect the new value.

3. *Modifying a property value in code view.* In the code view editor, locate the three lines of comments indicating the initialization for **welcomeLabel** and change the **string** assigned to **this.welcomeLabel.Text** from "**Deitel**" to "**Visual C# .NET**" (Fig. 4.21). Now, switch to design mode (**View > Designer**). The label now displays the updated text, and the **Properties** window for **welcomeLabel** displays the new **Text** value (Fig. 4.22). [*Note*: Property values should not be set using the techniques presented in this step. Here, we modify the property value in the IDE generated code only as a demonstration of the relationship between program code and the Windows Form Designer.]

4. *Change the label's **Text** property at runtime.* In the previous steps, we set properties at design time. Often, however, it is necessary to modify a property while a program is running. For example, to display the result of a calculation, a label's text can be assigned a **string** containing the result. In console applications, such code is located in **Main**. In Windows applications, we must create a method that executes when the form is loaded into memory during program execution. Like **Main**, this method is invoked when the program is run. Double-clicking the form in design view adds a method named **ASimpleProgram_Load** to the class (Fig. 4.23). The cursor is placed in the body of the **ASimpleProgram_Load** method definition. Notice that **ASimpleProgram_Load** is not part of the Windows Form De-

signer generated code. Add the statement **welcomeLabel.Text = "C#";** in the body of the method definition (Fig. 4.23). In C#, properties are accessed by placing the property name (i.e., **Text**) after the object name (i.e., **welcomeLabel**), separated by a dot operator. This syntax is similar to that used when accessing object methods. Notice that the *IntelliSense* feature displays the **Text** property in the member list after the class name and dot operator have been typed (Fig. 4.24). In Chapter 8, Object-Based Programming, we discuss how programmers can create their own properties.

Property initializations   Click here for   Click here for
for **welcomeLabel**   design view   code view

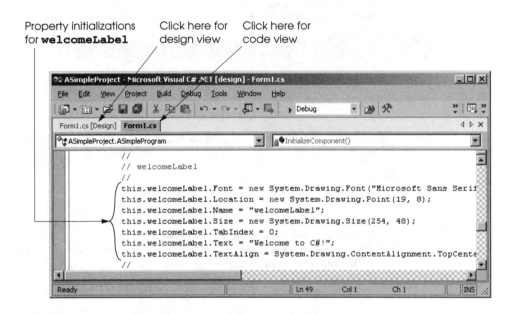

Fig. 4.18   Code generated by the IDE for **welcomeLabel**.

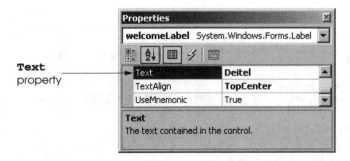

Text
property

Fig. 4.19   Using the **Properties** window to set a property value.

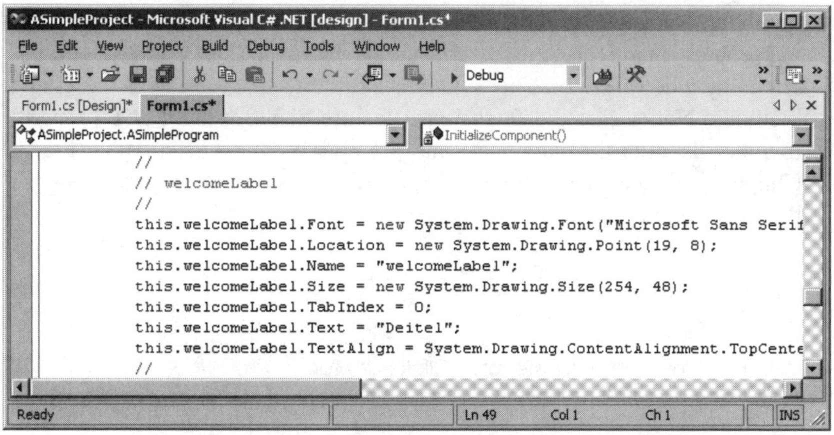

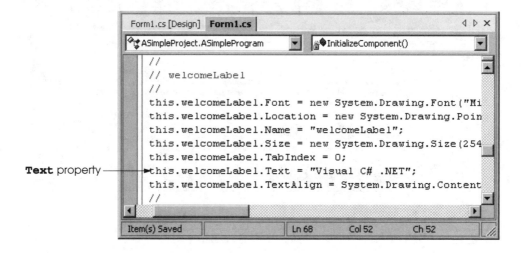

Fig. 4.20 Windows Form Designer generated code reflecting new property values.

Fig. 4.21 Changing a property in the code view editor.

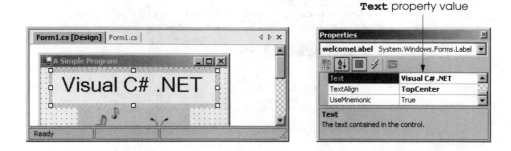

Fig. 4.22 New **Text** property value reflected in design mode.

`ASimpleProgram_Load` method

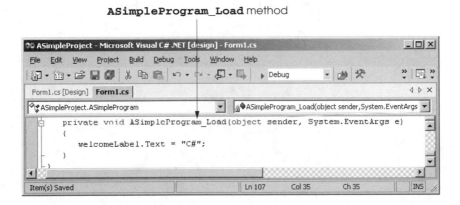

Fig. 4.23 Method `ASimpleProgram_Load`.

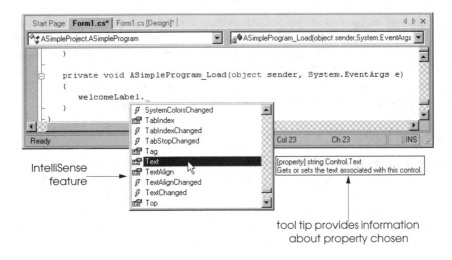

IntelliSense feature

tool tip provides information about property chosen

Fig. 4.24 IntelliSense feature of Visual Studio .NET.

5. *Examine the results of the* `ASimpleProgram_Load` *method.* Notice that the text in the label looks the same in **Design** mode as it did in Fig. 4.22. Note also that the property window still displays the value "**Visual C# .NET**" as the label's **Text** property and that the IDE-generated code has not changed either. Select **Build > Build** and then **Debug > Start** to run the program. Once the form is displayed, the text in the label reflects the property assignment in `ASimpleProgram_Load` (Fig. 4.25).

6. *Terminate program execution.* Click the close button to terminate program execution. Once again, notice that both the label and the label's **Text** property contain the text **Visual C# .NET**. The IDE-generated code also contains the text **Visual C# .NET**, which is assigned to the label's **Text** property.

Fig. 4.25   Result of changing a property value at runtime.

This chapter has discussed how to compose programs from control structures that contain actions and decisions. In Chapter 6, Methods, we introduce another program-structuring unit, called the *method*. We discuss how to compose large programs by combining methods that are composed of control structures. We also discuss how methods promote software reusability. In Chapter 8, Object-Based Programming, we discuss in more detail another C# program-structuring unit, called the *class*. We then create objects from classes and proceed with our treatment of object-oriented programming—the key focus of this book.

4.14 Summary

Executing a series of actions in a specific order can solve many computing problems. A procedure for solving a problem in terms of the actions to execute and the order in which the actions execute is called an algorithm. Program control specifies the order in which statements execute in a computer program.

Pseudocode is an artificial and informal language that helps programmers develop algorithms and "think out" a program during the program design process. C# code corresponds closely to pseudocode. This property makes pseudocode a useful program development tool.

Normally, statements in a program execute one after the other in the order in which they appear. This process is called sequential execution. The sequence structure is built into C#. Various C# statements enable the programmer to specify that the next statement to execute may be other than the next one in sequence. This event is called transfer of control.

A flowchart is a graphical representation of an algorithm or of a portion of an algorithm. Flowcharts are drawn using symbols, such as rectangles, diamonds, ovals and small circles; these symbols are connected by arrows called flowlines, which indicate the order in which the algorithm's actions execute. Small circles indicate the single entry point and exit point of each structure. Control-structure flowcharts contain (besides small circle symbols and flowlines) only rectangle symbols, which indicate the actions to be performed, and diamond symbols, which indicate decisions to be made. This system is the action/decision model of programming.

Single-entry/single-exit control structures make it easy to build programs. The control structures are attached to one another by connecting the exit point of one control structure to the entry point of the next. This technique is called control-structure stacking. There is only one other way in which control structures may be connected—through control-structure nesting, where one control structure can be placed inside another.

Every program is formed by combining as many of each type of C#'s eight control structures as is appropriate for the algorithm the program implements. Algorithms in C# programs are constructed from only eight different types of control structures combined in only two ways.

A single-selection structure is a structure that selects or ignores a single action. A double-selection structure is a structure that selects between two actions. A multiple-selection structure is a structure that selects among many actions.

The **if** selection structure performs (selects) an action if a condition is true or skips the action if the condition is false. The **if/else** selection structure performs an action if a condition is **true** and performs a different action if the condition is **false**.

The ternary conditional operator (**? :**) is closely related to the **if/else** structure. The operands and the **? :** character sequence form a conditional expression. The first operand is a condition that evaluates to a **bool** value, the second is the value for the conditional expression if the condition evaluates to **true** and the third is the value for the conditional expression if the condition evaluates to **false**.

A repetition structure repeats an action (or set of actions) while some condition remains true. The simplest repetition structure in C# is the **while** structure. The general format of a **while** structure is

```
while ( expression )
{
    statement;
}
```

where *expression* defines the condition that will be evaluated and *statement* represents the statement that will execute repeatedly while the condition remains true. This statement can be replaced with a set of several statements. Eventually, the condition in a **while** structure will become false. At this point, the repetition terminates, and the first statement after the repetition structure executes.

Counter-controlled repetition is used to input data values one at a time for a specified number of times. This technique uses a variable called a *counter* to control the number of times a set of statements will execute. Counter-controlled repetition often is called definite repetition, because the number of repetitions is known before the loop begins executing.

Sentinel-controlled repetition is often called indefinite repetition, because the number of repetitions is not known before the loop begins executing. The sentinel value (also called the signal value, dummy value or flag value) determines when to terminate a repetition structure.

We address programming problems with the top-down, stepwise refinement approach—a technique that is essential to the development of well-structured algorithms. The top is a single statement that conveys the overall function of the program. As such, the top is a complete representation of a program. We divide the top into a series of smaller tasks and list the tasks in the order in which they must be performed. Each refinement, including the top itself, is a complete specification of the algorithm; only the level of detail in each refinement varies. The programmer terminates the top-down, stepwise refinement process when the pseudocode algorithm is specified in sufficient detail for the programmer to convert the pseudocode to a C# program.

Many algorithms can be divided logically into three phases—an initialization phase that initializes the program variables, a processing phase that inputs data values and adjusts program variables accordingly, and a termination phase that calculates and prints the results.

With visual programming, the IDE generates the program code that creates the GUI. This code contains instructions for the creation of the form and every control on it. When a control's properties are modified in the IDE's **Properties** window, the code is updated accordingly. Unlike with a console application, a Windows application's program code is not displayed initially in the editor window. Once the program's project is opened in the IDE, the program code can be viewed by selecting **View > Code**.

Every Windows application consists of at least one class that inherits from class **Form** (which represents a form) in the FCL's **System.Windows.Forms** namespace. A key benefit of inheriting from class **Form** is that someone else has previously defined "what it means to be a form." Programmers specify that they want to inherit from an existing class by placing a colon (**:**) after the name of the inheriting class and specifying the name of the class that is being inherited from to the right of the colon.

Control Structures:
Part 2

Objectives

- To be able to use the **for** and **do/while** repetition
  structures to execute statements in a program
  repeatedly.
- To understand multiple selection with the **switch**
  selection structure.
- To be able to use the **break** and **continue**
  program-control statements.
- To be able to use the logical operators.

Who can control his fate?
William Shakespeare

The used key is always bright.
Benjamin Franklin

Man is a tool-making animal.
Benjamin Franklin

*Intelligence ... is the faculty of making artificial objects,
especially tools to make tools.*
Henri Bergson

5.1 Introduction

Chapter 4 began our introduction to the types of building blocks that are available for problem solving and used those building blocks to implement proven program-construction principles. In this chapter, we continue our presentation of the theory and principles of structured programming by introducing C#'s remaining control structures. As in Chapter 4, the C# techniques you learn here are applicable to most high-level languages. When we begin our formal treatment of object-based programming in C# in Chapter 8, we will see that the control structures we study in this chapter and in Chapter 4 are helpful in building and manipulating objects.

5.2 Essentials of Counter-Controlled Repetition

In the last chapter, we introduced the concept of counter-controlled repetition. In this section, we formalize the elements needed in counter-controlled repetition, namely:

1. The *name* of a *control variable* (or loop counter), used to determine whether the loop continues.

2. The *initial value* of the control variable.

3. The *increment* (or *decrement*) by which the control variable is modified each time through the loop (also known as *each iteration of the loop*).

4. The condition that tests for the *final value* of the control variable (i.e., whether looping should continue).

To see the four elements of counter-controlled repetition, consider the simple program in Fig. 5.1, which displays the digits 1–5.

The declaration (line 10)

```
int counter = 1;
```

names the control variable (**counter**), declares it to be an integer, reserves space for it in memory and sets it to an *initial value* of **1**. This statement is a declaration that includes an

```
1   // Fig. 5.1: WhileCounter.cs
2   // Counter-controlled repetition.
3
4   using System;
5
6   class WhileCounter
7   {
8      static void Main( string[] args )
9      {
10         int counter = 1;           // initialization
11
12         while ( counter <= 5 )     // repetition condition
13         {
14            Console.WriteLine( counter );
15            counter++;              // increment
16
17         } // end while
18
19      } // end method Main
20
21   } // end class WhileCounter
```

```
1
2
3
4
5
```

Fig. 5.1   Counter-controlled repetition with **while** structure.

initialization. The declaration and initialization of **counter** could also have been accomplished with the declaration and statement

```
int counter;   // declare counter
counter = 1;   // initialize counter to 1
```

The declaration is not executable, but the assignment statement is. We use both approaches to initialization throughout this book.

Lines 12–17 define the **while** structure. During each iteration of the loop, line 14 displays the current value of **counter**, and line 15 *increments* the control variable by **1** upon each iteration of the loop. The loop-continuation condition in the **while** structure tests whether the value of the control variable is less than or equal to **5** (the *final value* for which the condition is true). The body of this **while** is performed even when the control variable is **5**. The loop terminates when the control variable exceeds **5** (i.e., **counter** becomes **6**).

The program in Fig. 5.1 can be made more concise by initializing **counter** to **0** and replacing the **while** structure with

```
while ( ++counter <= 5 )   // repetition condition
   Console.WriteLine( counter );
```

This code saves a statement and eliminates the need for braces around the loop's body, because the incrementing occurs directly in the **while** condition before the condition is tested (remember that the precedence of **++** is higher than **<=**).

Good Programming Practice 5.1

Control counting loops with integer values.

Good Programming Practice 5.2

Place a blank line before and after each major control structure to make it stand out in the program.

Good Programming Practice 5.3

Vertical spacing above and below control structures, and indentation of the bodies of control structures within the control structure headers, gives programs a two-dimensional appearance that enhances readability.

5.3 `for` Repetition Structure

The **for** repetition structure handles the details of counter-controlled repetition. To illustrate the power of **for**, let us rewrite the program in Fig. 5.1. The result is displayed in Fig. 5.2.

Method **Main** (lines 8–14) operates as follows: When the **for** structure (line 12) begins executing, the program initializes the control variable **counter** to **1** (the first two elements of counter-controlled repetition—control variable *name* and *initial value*). Next, the program tests the loop-continuation condition, **counter <= 5**. The initial value of **counter** is **1**, thus the condition is true, so line 13 outputs the **counter**'s value. Then, the program increments variable **counter** in the expression **counter++**, and the loop begins again with the loop-continuation test. The control variable is now equal to **2**. This value does not exceed the final value, so the program performs the body statement again (i.e., performs the next iteration of the loop). This process continues until the control variable **counter** becomes **6**, causing the loop-continuation test to fail and repetition to terminate. The program continues by performing the first statement after the **for** structure. (In this case, method **Main** terminates because the program reaches the end of **Main**'s body.)

```
1   // Fig. 5.2: ForCounter.cs
2   // Counter-controlled repetition with the for structure.
3
4   using System;
5
6   class ForCounter
7   {
8      static void Main( string[] args )
9      {
10         // initialization, repetition condition and incrementing
11         // are all included in the for structure
12         for ( int counter = 1; counter <= 5; counter++ )
13            Console.WriteLine( counter );
14      }
15   }
```

Fig. 5.2   Counter-controlled repetition with the **for** structure. (Part 1 of 2.)

```
1
2
3
4
5
```

Fig. 5.2   Counter-controlled repetition with the **for** structure. (Part 2 of 2.)

Figure 5.3 takes a closer look at the **for** structure in Fig. 5.2. The first line of the **for** structure (including the keyword **for** and everything in parentheses after **for**) sometimes is called the *for structure header*. Notice that the **for** structure specifies each of the items needed for counter-controlled repetition with a control variable. If there is more than one statement in the body of the **for**, braces (**{** and **}**) are required to define the loop's body.

Figure 5.2 uses the loop-continuation condition **counter <= 5**. If the programmer incorrectly writes **counter < 5**, the loop executes only four times. This common logic error is called an *off-by-one error*.

Common Programming Error 5.1

*Using an incorrect relational operator or using an incorrect final value for a loop counter in the condition of a **while**, **for** or **do/while** structure (introduced in Section 5.6) can cause an off-by-one error.*

Common Programming Error 5.2

Floating-point values may be approximate, so controlling counting loops with floating-point variables can result in imprecise counter values and inaccurate tests for termination.

Testing and Debugging Tip 5.1

*Using the final value in the condition of a **while** or **for** structure and using the **<=** relational operator will help avoid off-by-one errors. For a loop used to print the values from 1 to 10, for example, the loop-continuation condition should be **counter <= 10**, rather than **counter < 10** (which is an off-by-one error) or **counter < 11** (which also works). This approach is commonly known as* one-based counting. *When we study arrays in Chapter 7, Arrays, we will see when programmers prefer* zero-based counting, *in which to count 10 times through a loop,* **counter** *is initialized to zero and the loop-continuation test is* **counter < 10**.

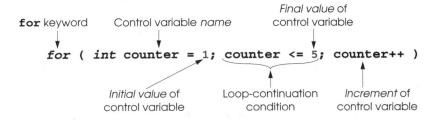

Fig. 5.3   Components of a typical **for** header.

The general format of the **for** structure is

> **for** (*expression1*; *expression2*; *expression3*)
>   *statement*;

where *expression1* names the loop's control variable and provides its initial value, *expression2* is the loop-continuation condition (containing the control variable's final value) and *expression3* increments or decrements the control variable. In most cases, the **for** structure can be represented with an equivalent **while** structure, with *expression1*, *expression2* and *expression3* placed as follows:

> *expression1*;
>
> **while** (*expression2*)
> {
>   *statement*;
>   *expression3*;
> }

In Section 5.7, we discuss an exception to this rule.

In C#, programmers may declare the control variable in *expression1* of the **for** structure header (i.e., the control variable's type is specified before the variable name), rather than earlier in the code. When this occurs, the control variable can be used only in the body of the **for** structure (i.e., the name of the control variable will be unknown outside the **for** structure). Such a restriction on the use of a control variable name defines the variable's *scope*, where that variable can be used in a program. Scope is discussed in detail in Chapter 6, Methods.

Common Programming Error 5.3

*When a control variable is declared in the initialization section of a **for** structure header, using that control variable after the **for** structure's body is a compiler error.*

Sometimes, *expression1* and *expression3* in a **for** structure are comma-separated lists of expressions that enable the programmer to use multiple initialization expressions and/or multiple increment or decrement expressions. For example, there may be several control variables in a single **for** structure that must be initialized and incremented or decremented.

Good Programming Practice 5.4

*Place only expressions involving control variables in the initialization and increment or decrement sections of a **for** structure. Manipulations of other variables should appear either before the loop (if they execute only once, like initialization statements) or in the loop body (if they execute once per iteration of the loop, like incrementing or decrementing statements).*

The three expressions in the **for** structure are optional. If *expression2* is omitted, C# assumes that the loop-continuation condition is always true, thus creating an infinite loop. A programmer might omit *expression1* if the program initializes the control variable before the loop. *Expression3* might be omitted if statements in the body of the **for** calculate the increment or decrement, or if no increment or decrement is necessary. The increment (or decrement) expression in the **for** structure acts as if it were a standalone statement at the end of the **for** body. Therefore, the expressions

```
counter = counter + 1
counter += 1
++counter
counter++
```

are equivalent when used in *expression3*. Some programmers prefer the form
counter++, because the control variable increment occurs after the loop body executes.
For this reason, the postincrementing (or postdecrementing) form in which the variable is
incremented after it is used seems more natural. Because the variable being either incremented or decremented does not appear in a larger expression, preincrementing and postincrementing the variable have the same effect. The two semicolons in the **for** structure are
required.

Common Programming Error 5.4

*Using commas in a **for** structure header instead of the two required semicolons is a syntax
error.*

Common Programming Error 5.5

*Placing a semicolon immediately to the right of a **for** structure header's right parenthesis
makes the body of that **for** structure an empty statement. This is normally a logic error.*

The initialization, loop-continuation condition and increment or decrement portions of
a **for** structure can contain arithmetic expressions. For example, assume that **x = 2** and **y
= 10**. If **x** and **y** are not modified in the loop body, the statement

```
for ( int j = x; j <= 4 * x * y; j += y / x )
```

is equivalent to the statement

```
for ( int j = 2; j <= 80; j += 5 )
```

The "increment" of a **for** structure may be negative, in which case it is really a decrement and the loop actually counts downward.

If the loop-continuation condition in the **for** structure is initially false, the body of the
for structure does not execute. Instead, execution proceeds with the statement that follows
the **for** structure.

The control variable frequently is printed or used in calculations in the body of a **for**
structure, but it does not have to be. Often the control variable simply controls repetition
and is not mentioned in the body of the **for** structure.

Testing and Debugging Tip 5.2

*Avoid changing the value of the control variable in the body of a **for** loop, to avoid subtle
errors.*

The **for** structure flowchart is similar to that of the **while** structure. For example,
the flowchart of the **for** structure in Fig. 5.2 appears in Fig. 5.4. This flowchart clarifies
that the initialization occurs only once, and that incrementing occurs each time *after* the
body statement is performed. Note that (besides small circles and flowlines) the flowchart
contains only rectangle symbols and a diamond symbol. The rectangles and diamonds are
filled with actions and decisions appropriate to the algorithm.

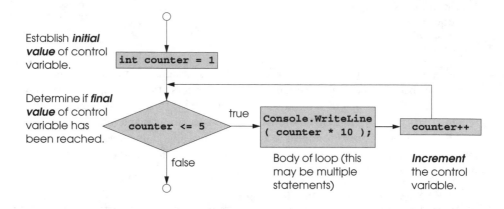

Fig. 5.4   Flowcharting a typical **for** repetition structure.

5.4 Examples Using the **for** Structure

The following examples demonstrate methods of varying the control variable in a **for** structure. In each case, we write the appropriate **for** header. Note the change in the relational operator for loops that decrement the control variable.

a)   Vary the control variable from **1** to **100** in increments of **1**.

    for (int i = 1; i <= 100; i++)

b)   Vary the control variable from **100** to **1** in increments of **–1** (decrements of **1**).

    for (int i = 100; i >= 1; i--)

c)   Vary the control variable from **7** to **77** in steps of **7**.

    for (int i = 7; i <= 77; i += 7)

d)   Vary the control variable from **20** to **2** in steps of **–2**.

    for (int i = 20; i >= 2; i -= 2)

e)   Vary the control variable over the sequence of the following values: **2, 5, 8, 11, 14, 17, 20**.

    for (int j = 2; j <= 20; j += 3)

f)   Vary the control variable over the sequence of the following values: **99, 88, 77, 66, 55, 44, 33, 22, 11, 0**.

    for (int j = 99; j >= 0; j -= 11)

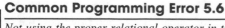

Common Programming Error 5.6

Not using the proper relational operator in the loop-continuation condition of a loop that counts downward (e.g., using **i <= 1** *in a loop counting down to 1) is usually a logic error that will yield incorrect results when the program runs.*

The next two sample programs demonstrate simple applications of the **for** repetition structure. The program in Fig. 5.5 uses the **for** structure to sum all the even integers from **2** to **100**, then displays the result in a **MessageBox**. Remember that to use **MessageBox**, you must add a reference to **System.Windows.Forms.dll** to your project, as explained in Chapter 3 (Section 3.2).

C# allows several methods in a class to be defined with the same name. Programmers often use this technique, known as *method overloading*, to define several methods that perform similar actions, but take a different set of arguments. One example of this is method **MessageBox.Show**. In the past, we have provided only one argument to this method—a **string** to be displayed in a message dialog. Figure 5.5 uses a version of method **MessageBox.Show** (lines 16–19) that takes four arguments. The dialog in the output of Fig. 5.5 illustrates the four arguments. The first argument is the message to display. The second argument is the string to display in the dialog's title bar. The third argument is a value indicating which button(s) to display. The fourth argument indicates which icon to display to the left of the message. Figures 5.6 and 5.7 provide a listing of the **MessageBoxButtons** and **MessageBoxIcon** choices. Information about other versions of method **MessageBox.Show** can be found via the MSDN documentation provided with Visual Studio .NET. We discuss method overloading in more detail in Chapter 6, Methods.

```
1   // Fig. 5.5: Sum.cs
2   // Summation with the for structure.
3
4   using System;
5   using System.Windows.Forms;
6
7   class Sum
8   {
9      static void Main( string[] args )
10     {
11        int sum = 0;
12
13        for ( int number = 2; number <= 100; number += 2 )
14           sum += number;
15
16        MessageBox.Show( "The sum is " + sum,
17           "Sum Even Integers from 2 to 100",
18           MessageBoxButtons.OK,
19           MessageBoxIcon.Information );
20
21     } // end method Main
22  } // end class Sum
```

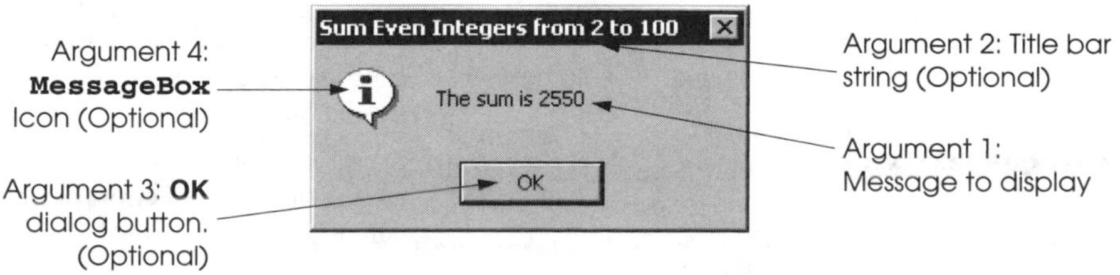

Argument 4: **MessageBox** Icon (Optional)

Argument 3: **OK** dialog button. (Optional)

Argument 2: Title bar string (Optional)

Argument 1: Message to display

Fig. 5.5   Summation using **for**.

MessageBox Buttons	Description
MessageBoxButtons.OK	Specifies that the dialog should include an **OK** button.
MessageBoxButtons.OKCancel	Specifies that the dialog should include **OK** and **Cancel** buttons. Warns the user about some condition and allows the user to either continue or cancel an operation.
MessageBoxButtons.YesNo	Specifies that the dialog should contain **Yes** and **No** buttons. Used to ask the user a question.
MessageBoxButtons.YesNoCancel	Specifies that the dialog should contain **Yes**, **No** and **Cancel** buttons. Typically used to ask the user a question but still allows the user to cancel the operation.
MessageBoxButtons.RetryCancel	Specifies that the dialog should contain **Retry** and **Cancel** buttons. Typically used to inform a user about a failed operation and allow the user to retry or cancel the operation.
MessageBoxButtons.AbortRetryIgnore	Specifies that the dialog should contain **Abort, Retry** and **Ignore** buttons. Typically used to inform the user that one of a series of operations has failed and allow the user to abort the series of operations, retry the failed operation or ignore the failed operation and continue.

Fig. 5.6   Buttons for message dialogs.

MessageBox Icons	Icon	Description
MessageBoxIcon.Exclamation		Specifies an exclamation point icon. Typically used to caution the user against potential problems.
MessageBoxIcon.Information		Specifies that the dialog contains an informational message for the user.
MessageBoxIcon.Question		Specifies a question mark icon. Typically used in dialogs that ask the user a question.
MessageBoxIcon.Error		Specifies a dialog with an ∞ in a red circle. Alerts user of errors or important messages.

Fig. 5.7   Icons for message dialogs.

The body of the **for** structure in Fig. 5.5 actually could be merged into the rightmost portion of the **for** header by using a *comma* as follows:

```
for ( int number = 2; number <= 100;
      sum += number, number += 2 )
  ; // empty statement
```

Similarly, the initialization **sum = 0** could be merged into the initialization section of the **for** structure. Statements that precede a **for** and statements in the body of a **for** often can be merged into the **for** header. However, such merging often decreases the readability of the program.

Good Programming Practice 5.5

Limit the size of control structure headers to a single line if possible.

The next example uses a **for** structure to compute compound interest. Consider the following problem statement:

> *A person invests $1000.00 in a savings account yielding 5% interest. Assuming that all interest is left on deposit, calculate and print the amount of money in the account at the end of each year for 10 years. To determine these amounts, use the following formula:*
>
> $$a = p\,(1 + r)^{\,n}$$
>
> *where*
>
> > p is the original amount invested (i.e., the principal)
> > r is the annual interest rate
> > n is the number of years
> > a is the amount on deposit at the end of the nth year.

This problem involves a loop that performs the indicated calculation for each of the 10 years that the money remains on deposit. A solution is the program shown in Fig. 5.8.

Line 11 in method **Main** declares two *decimal* variables—**amount** and **principal**—and initializes **principal** to **1000.00**. The type **decimal** is a primitive data type used for monetary calculations. C# treats such constants as the **1000.00** in Fig. 5.8 as type **double**. Similarly, C# treats whole number constants, like 7 and –22, as having type **int**. Values of type **double** cannot be converted implicitly to type **decimal**, so we use a cast operator to convert the **double** value **1000.00** to type **decimal**. It also is possible to specify that a constant is of type **decimal** by appending the letter **m** to the constant, as in **1000.0m**. Line 12 declares **double** variable **rate**, which we initialize to **.05**.

The **for** structure executes its body 10 times, varying control variable **year** from **1** to **10** in increments of **1**. Note that **year** represents n in the problem statement. C# does not have an exponentiation operator, so we use **static** method **Pow** in class **Math** for this purpose. **Math.Pow(x, y)** calculates the value of **x** raised to the **y**th power. Method **Math.Pow** takes two arguments of type **double** and returns a **double** value. Lines 18–19 perform the calculation from the problem statement

$$a = p\,(1 + r)^{\,n}$$

where a is **amount**, p is **principal**, r is **rate** and n is **year**.

```
1   // Fig. 5.8: Interest.cs
2   // Calculating compound interest.
3
4   using System;
5   using System.Windows.Forms;
6
7   class Interest
8   {
9      static void Main( string[] args )
10     {
11        decimal amount, principal = ( decimal ) 1000.00;
12        double rate = .05;
13
14        string output = "Year\tAmount on deposit\n";
15
16        for ( int year = 1; year <= 10; year++ )
17        {
18           amount = principal *
19              ( decimal ) Math.Pow( 1.0 + rate, year );
20
21           output += year + "\t" +
22              String.Format( "{0:C}", amount ) + "\n";
23        }
24
25        MessageBox.Show( output, "Compound Interest",
26           MessageBoxButtons.OK, MessageBoxIcon.Information );
27
28     } // end method Main
29
30  } // end class Interest
```

Fig. 5.8   Calculating compound interest with **for**.

Lines 21–22 append additional text to the end of the string **output**. The text includes the current **year** value, a tab character to position to the second column, the result of the method call **String.Format("{0:C}", amount)** and a newline character to position to the next line. The call to method **String.Format** converts **amount** to a **string** and formats this **string** so that it will display with two decimal places. [*Note*:

Method **Format** uses .NET's string formatting codes to represent numeric and monetary values according to the user's *localization settings*.[1] For example, in the United States, dollars are represented as **$634,307.08** but Malaysian ringgits are represented as **R634.307,08**.] The first argument to method **String.Format** is the format string, while the second argument specifies the value to be formatted. Notice that format strings begin with an opening curly brace (**{**) and end with a closing curly brace (**}**). Within the braces are two values separated by a colon (**:**). The first value is a number indicating which argument is to be formatted, where 0 represents the first argument found after the format string, 1 represents the second argument, and so on. In this example we have specified 0, indicating that we wish to format the first argument after our format string (variable **amount**). The letter **C**, found after the colon, specifies the formatting of the argument, and is referred to as the *formatting code* or *format specifier*. In this case, we are using formatting code **C** (for "currency"), which indicates that the string should be displayed as a monetary amount with two digits after the decimal point. There are several other formatting codes, which can be found in the MSDN documentation. Figure 5.9 demonstrates the *numeric formatting codes*, the formatting codes used for string representations of numeric values.

The variables **amount** and **principal** were declared to be of type **decimal** because the program deals with fractional parts of dollars. In such cases, programs need a type that allows decimal points in its values. Variable **rate** is of type **double** because it is used in the calculation **1.0 + rate**, which appears as a **double** argument to the **Pow** method of class **Math**. Note that the calculation **1.0 + rate** appears in the body of the **for** statement. The calculation produces the same result each time through the loop, so repeating the calculation is unnecessary.

Performance Tip 5.1

Avoid placing expressions with values that do not change inside a loop. Such expressions should be evaluated once before the loop. Most good compilers will do this automatically with a process that compilers perform called optimization.

Format Code	Description
C or **c**	Formats the string as currency. Precedes the number with an appropriate currency symbol (**$** in the US). Separates digits with an appropriate separator character (comma in the US) and sets the number of decimal places to two by default.
D or **d**	Formats the string as a decimal.
N or **n**	Formats the string with commas and two decimal places.

Fig. 5.9   Numeric formatting codes. (Part 1 of 2.)

---

1. Localization is the customization of software (e.g., an operating system) to display information using the customs and languages of a geographical region. Localization settings can be customized through the **Start Menu** by selecting **Control Panel > Regional and Language Options > Regional Options** in Windows XP, and by selecting **Control Panel > Regional Options** in Windows 2000.

Format Code	Description
E or **e**	Formats the number using scientific notation with a default of six decimal places (e.g., the value 27,900,000 becomes 2.790000E+007).
F or **f**	Formats the string with a fixed number of decimal places (two by default).
G or **g**	Formats string as decimal using **E** or **F** format code, uses most compact result.
P or **p**	Formats string as a percentage. By default, value is multiplied by 100 and appended by a percent sign.
R or **r**	Ensures that value converted to string can be converted back without loss of precision or data.
X or **x**	Formats the string as hexadecimal.

Fig. 5.9   Numeric formatting codes. (Part 2 of 2.)

5.5 `switch` Multiple-Selection Structure

The previous chapter discussed the **if** single-selection and the **if/else** double-selection structures. Occasionally, an algorithm contains a series of decisions in which the algorithm tests a variable or expression separately for each *constant integral expression* or *constant string expression* the variable or expression may assume. A constant integral expression is any expression involving character and integer constants that evaluates to an integer value (e.g., values of type **int** or **char**). A constant string expression is any expression composed of string literals that always results in the same **string**. The algorithm then takes different actions based on those values. C# provides the ***switch*** *multiple-selection structure* to handle such decision making.

In the next example (Fig. 5.10), let us assume that a class of 10 students took an exam and that each student received a letter grade of A, B, C, D or F. The program will input the letter grades and summarize the results by using **switch** to count the number of each different letter grade that students earned on an exam. Line 10 declares variable **grade** as type **char**. This variable stores the user's input for each letter grade. Lines 11–15 define counter variables that the program uses to count each letter grade. Line 17 begins a **for** structure that loops 10 times. At each iteration, line 19 prompts the user for the next grade, and line 20 invokes **Char** method **Parse** to read the user input as a **char**. Nested in the body of the **for** structure is a **switch** structure (lines 22–55) that processes the letter grades. The **switch** structure consists of a series of *case labels* and an optional ***default*** *case*.

When the flow of control reaches the **switch** structure (line 22), the program evaluates the *controlling expression* (**grade** in this example) in the parentheses following keyword **switch**. The value of this expression is compared with each **case** label until a match occurs. Assume the user entered the letter **B** as the grade. **B** is compared to each **case** in the **switch**, until a match occurs at line 29 (**case 'B':**). When this happens, the statements for that **case** execute. For the letter **B**, lines 31–32 increment the number of **B** grades stored in variable **bCount**, and the **switch** structure exits immediately with the ***break*** *statement*. The **break** statement causes program control to proceed with the first statement after the **switch** structure. In this case, we reach the end of the **for** struc-

ture's body, so control flows to the control-variable increment expression in the **for** structure header. Then the counter variable in the **for** structure is incremented, and the loop-
continuation condition is evaluated to determine whether another iteration of the loop is
necessary.

```
1   // Fig. 5.10: SwitchTest.cs
2   // Counting letter grades.
3
4   using System;
5
6   class SwitchTest
7   {
8      static void Main( string[] args )
9      {
10        char grade;        // one grade
11        int aCount = 0,    // number of As
12            bCount = 0,    // number of Bs
13            cCount = 0,    // number of Cs
14            dCount = 0,    // number of Ds
15            fCount = 0;    // number of Fs
16
17        for ( int i = 1; i <= 10; i++ )
18        {
19           Console.Write( "Enter a letter grade: " );
20           grade = Char.Parse( Console.ReadLine() );
21
22           switch ( grade )
23           {
24              case 'A':    // grade is uppercase A
25              case 'a':    // or lowercase a
26                 ++aCount;
27                 break;
28
29              case 'B':    // grade is uppercase B
30              case 'b':    // or lowercase b
31                 ++bCount;
32                 break;
33
34              case 'C':    // grade is uppercase C
35              case 'c':    // or lowercase c
36                 ++cCount;
37                 break;
38
39              case 'D':    // grade is uppercase D
40              case 'd':    // or lowercase d
41                 ++dCount;
42                 break;
43
44              case 'F':    // grade is uppercase F
45              case 'f':    // or lowercase f
46                 ++fCount;
47                 break;
```

Fig. 5.10   **switch** multiple-selection structure. (Part 1 of 2.)

```
48
49                 default:       // processes all other characters
50                     Console.WriteLine(
51                         "Incorrect letter grade entered." +
52                         "\nGrade not added to totals." );
53                     break;
54
55             } // end switch
56
57         } // end for
58
59         Console.WriteLine(
60             "\nTotals for each letter grade are:\nA: {0}" +
61             "\nB: {1}\nC: {2}\nD: {3}\nF: {4}", aCount, bCount,
62             cCount, dCount, fCount );
63
64     } // end method Main
65
66 } // end class SwitchTest
```

```
Enter a letter grade: a
Enter a letter grade: A
Enter a letter grade: c
Enter a letter grade: F
Enter a letter grade: z
Incorrect letter grade entered.
Grade not added to totals.
Enter a letter grade: D
Enter a letter grade: d
Enter a letter grade: B
Enter a letter grade: a
Enter a letter grade: C

Totals for each letter grade are:
A: 3
B: 1
C: 2
D: 2
F: 1
```

Fig. 5.10 **switch** multiple-selection structure. (Part 2 of 2.)

Good Programming Practice 5.6

*Indent the body statements of each **case** in a **switch** structure.*

If no match occurs between the controlling expression's value and any **case** label, the **default** case (line 49) executes. Lines 50–52 display an error message. Note that the **default** case is optional in the **switch** structure. If the controlling expression does not match a **case** and there is no **default** case, program control proceeds to the next statement after the **switch** structure. Note that only the statements for one **case** can be executed in a **switch** statement; Once those statements have been executed, the **break** statement for the current **case** will be reached, causing immediate exit from the structure.

Each **case** can contain one action, multiple actions or no actions at all. A **case** with no statements is considered an *empty case*, and can omit the **break** statement. The **break** statement is required for each **case** (including the **default** case) that contains statements. The last **case** in a **switch** structure cannot be an empty **case**. If the controlling expression matches an empty **case**, the statements in the next non-empty case will be executed. This behavior is known as *fall through*. This provides the programmer with a way to specify that certain statements are to be executed for several **case**s. Figure 5.10 demonstrates fall through. For instance, lines 26–27 execute when the grade entered is either **'A'** or **'a'**, and lines 31–32 execute when the grade entered is either **'B'** or **'b'**.

Common Programming Error 5.7

*Not including a **break** statement at the end of each **case** in a **switch** is a syntax error. The exception to this rule is the empty **case**.*

Common Programming Error 5.8

*Be sure to check all possible values when creating **case**s to confirm that no two **case**s in a **switch** statement are for the same integral value. If the values are the same, a compile-time error will occur.*

Finally, it is important to notice that the **switch** structure is different from other structures in that braces are not required around multiple actions in a **case** of a **switch**. The general **switch** structure (using a **break** in each **case**) is flowcharted in Fig. 5.11.

Again, note that (besides small circles and flowlines) the flowchart contains only rectangle and diamond symbols. The programmer fills the rectangles and diamonds with actions and decisions appropriate to the algorithm. Although nested control structures are common, it is rare to find nested **switch** structures in a program.

Good Programming Practice 5.7

*Provide a **default** case in every **switch** structure. Cases not explicitly tested in a **switch** that lacks a **default** case are ignored. Including a **default** case focuses the programmer on processing exceptional conditions. There are situations, however, in which no **default** processing is required.*

Good Programming Practice 5.8

*Although the **case**s in a **switch** structure can occur in any order, it is considered a good programming practice to place the **default** case last.*

When using the **switch** structure, remember that all cases in a particular **switch** structure must be either integral values or strings. A *character constant* is represented as a specific character in single quotes (such as **'A'**). An integer constant is simply an integer value. The expression after each **case** can also be a *constant*—a variable that contains a value that does not change throughout the entire program. Such a variable is declared with keyword **const** (discussed in Chapter 7, Arrays).

5.6 do/while Repetition Structure

The *do/while* repetition structure is similar to the **while** structure. In the **while** structure, the test of the loop-continuation condition occurs at the beginning of the loop, before the body of the loop executes. The **do/while** structure tests the loop-continuation condition *after* the loop body executes; therefore, *the loop body always executes at least once.* When a **do/while** structure terminates, execution continues with the statement after the **while** clause. The program in Fig. 5.12 uses a **do/while** structure to output the values 1–5.

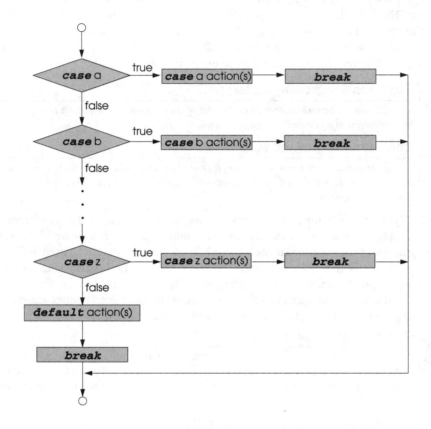

Fig. 5.11   Flowcharting the **switch** multiple-selection structure.

```
1    // Fig. 5.12: DoWhileLoop.cs
2    // The do/while repetition structure.
3
4    using System;
5
6    class DoWhileLoop
7    {
8       static void Main( string[] args )
9       {
10          int counter = 1;
11
```

Fig. 5.12   do/while repetition structure. (Part 1 of 2.)

```
12          do
13          {
14              Console.WriteLine( counter );
15              counter++;
16          } while ( counter <= 5 );
17
18      } // end method Main
19
20  } // end class DoWhileLoop
```

```
1
2
3
4
5
```

Fig. 5.12 **do/while** repetition structure. (Part 2 of 2.)

Lines 12–16 demonstrate the **do/while** structure. When program execution reaches this **do/while** structure, the program executes lines 14–15, which display the value of **counter** (at this point, **1**) and increment **counter** by **1**. Then, the program evaluates the condition on line 16. At this point, variable **counter** is **2**, which is less than or equal to **5**, so the **do/while** structure's body executes again. The fifth time the structure executes, line 14 outputs the value **5** and line 15 increments **counter** to **6**. Then the condition on line 16 evaluates to false and the **do/while** structure exits.

The **do/while** flowchart (Fig. 5.13) makes it clear that the loop-continuation condition does not execute until the body executes at least once. The flowchart contains only a rectangle and a diamond. The programmer fills the rectangle and diamond with actions and decisions appropriate to the algorithm.

Note that it is not necessary to use braces in the **do/while** structure if there is only one statement in the body. However, the braces normally are included to avoid confusion between the **while** and **do/while** structures. For example,

```
while ( condition )
```

typically is the header to a **while** structure. A **do/while** with no braces around the single statement body appears as

```
do
    statement;
while ( condition );
```

which can be confusing. The last line—**while(** *condition* **);**—might be misinterpreted by the reader as a **while** structure containing an empty statement (the semicolon by itself). Thus, the **do/while** with one statement often is written as follows to avoid confusion:

```
do
{
    statement;
} while ( condition );
```

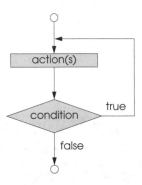

Fig. 5.13   Flowcharting the **do/while** repetition structure.

Good Programming Practice 5.9

*Some programmers always include braces in a **do/while** structure, even when the braces are unnecessary. This helps eliminate ambiguity between a **while** structure and a **do/while** structure that contains only one statement.*

Common Programming Error 5.9

*Infinite loops occur when the loop-continuation condition in a **while**, **for** or **do/while** structure never becomes false. To prevent this, make sure there is no semicolon immediately after the header of a **while** or **for** structure or after the word **do** in a **do/while** statement. In a counter-controlled loop, make sure the control variable is incremented (or decremented) in the body of the loop. In a sentinel-controlled loop, make sure the sentinel value eventually is input.*

5.7 Statements `break` and `continue`

The **break** and **continue** statements alter the flow of control. The **break** statement, when executed in a **while**, **for**, **do/while** or **switch** structure, causes immediate exit from that structure. Execution continues with the first statement that follows the structure. Common uses of the **break** statement are to exit prematurely from a loop or to exit a **switch** structure (as in Fig. 5.10). Figure 5.14 demonstrates the **break** statement in a **for** repetition structure.

When the **if** structure in line 16 detects that **count** is **5**, **break** is executed. This terminates the **for** structure and the program proceeds to line 24 (immediately after the **for**). Notice that if we had defined variable **count** in our **for** structure, it would be inaccessible here. The string-concatenation statement produces the string that is displayed in the message dialog in lines 26–27. The loop executes its body only four times.

```
1   // Fig. 5.14: BreakTest.cs
2   // Using the break statement in a for structure.
```

Fig. 5.14   **break** statement in a **for** structure. (Part 1 of 2.)

```
3
4    using System;
5    using System.Windows.Forms;
6
7    class BreakTest
8    {
9       static void Main( string[] args )
10      {
11         string output = "";
12         int count;
13
14         for ( count = 1; count <= 10; count++ )
15         {
16            if ( count == 5 )
17               break;                // skip remaining code in loop
18                                     // if count == 5
19
20            output += count + " ";
21
22         } // end for loop
23
24         output += "\nBroke out of loop at count = " + count;
25
26         MessageBox.Show( output, "Demonstrating the break statement",
27            MessageBoxButtons.OK, MessageBoxIcon.Information );
28
29      } // end method Main
30
31   } // end class BreakTest
```

Fig. 5.14 **break** statement in a **for** structure. (Part 2 of 2.)

The **continue** statement, when executed in a **while**, **for** or **do/while** structure, skips the remaining statements in the body of that structure and proceeds with the next iteration of the loop. In **while** and **do/while** structures, the loop-continuation condition evaluates immediately after **continue** executes. In a **for** structure, the increment/decrement expression executes, then the loop-continuation test evaluates.

We have stated that the **while** structure can replace the **for** structure in most cases. One exception occurs when the increment/decrement expression in the **while** structure follows the **continue** statement. In this case, the increment/decrement does not execute before the repetition-continuation condition is tested, and the **while** does not execute in the same manner as the **for**.

Figure 5.15 uses the **continue** statement in a **for** structure to skip the string-concatenation statement on line 19 when the **if** structure (line 15) determines that the value of

count is **5**. When the **continue** statement executes, program control continues with the increment of the control variable in the **for** structure.

Good Programming Practice 5.10

*Some programmers believe that **break** and **continue** violate structured programming. The effects of these statements can be achieved by structured programming techniques, so these programmers avoid **break** and **continue**.*

Performance Tip 5.2

*When used properly, the **break** and **continue** statements perform faster than their corresponding structured techniques.*

```csharp
1   // Fig. 5.15: ContinueTest.cs
2   // Using the continue statement in a for structure.
3
4   using System;
5   using System.Windows.Forms;
6
7   class ContinueTest
8   {
9      static void Main( string[] args )
10     {
11        string output = "";
12
13        for ( int count = 1; count <= 10; count++ )
14        {
15           if ( count == 5 )
16              continue;          // skip remaining code in loop
17                                 // only if count == 5
18
19           output += count + " ";
20        }
21
22        output += "\nUsed continue to skip printing 5";
23
24        MessageBox.Show( output, "Using the continue statement",
25           MessageBoxButtons.OK, MessageBoxIcon.Information );
26
27     } // end method Main
28
29  } // end class ContinueTest
```

Fig. 5.15 **continue** statement in a **for** structure.

Software Engineering Observation 5.1

There is a debate between achieving quality software engineering and achieving the best per-forming software. Often, one of these goals is achieved at the expense of the other. For all but the most performance-intensive situations, apply the following "rule of thumb": First, make your code simple and correct; then make it fast and small, but only if necessary.

5.8 Logical and Conditional Operators

So far, we have studied only *simple conditions,* such as **count <= 10**, **total > 1000** and **number != sentinelValue**. These conditions were expressed in terms of the re-lational operators **>**, **<**, **>=** and **<=** and the equality operators **==** and **!=**. Each decision tested one condition. To test multiple conditions in the process of making a decision, we performed these tests in separate statements or in nested **if** or **if/else** structures.

C# provides several *logical and conditional operators* that may be used to form com-plex conditions by combining simple conditions. The operators are **&&** (*conditional AND*), **&** (*logical AND*), **||** (*conditional OR*), **|** (*logical OR*), **^** (*logical exclusive OR or logical XOR*) and **!** (*logical NOT,* also called *logical negation*). We will consider examples using each of these operators.

Common Programming Error 5.10

*Placing a space between the characters of **&&** or **||** operator is a syntax error.*

Suppose we wish to ensure that two conditions are *both* true in a program before we choose a certain path of execution. In this case, we can use the conditional **&&** operator as follows:

```
if ( gender == 1 && age >= 65 )
    ++seniorFemales;
```

This **if** statement contains two simple conditions. The condition **gender == 1** might be evaluated to determine whether a person is female. The condition **age >= 65** is evaluated to determine whether a person is a senior citizen. The two simple conditions are evaluated first, because the precedences of **==** and **>=** are both higher than the precedence of **&&**. The **if** statement then considers the combined condition

```
gender == 1 && age >= 65
```

This condition is true *if and only if* both the simple conditions are true. Finally, if this com-bined condition is true, the body statement increments the count of **seniorFemales** by **1**. If either or both of the simple conditions are false, the program skips the incrementing and proceeds to the statement that follows the **if** structure. The preceding combined con-dition can be made more readable by adding redundant parentheses:

```
( gender == 1 ) && ( age >= 65 )
```

The table in Fig. 5.16 summarizes the **&&** operator. The table shows all four possible combinations of false and true values for *expression1* and *expression2*. Such tables often are called *truth tables*. C# evaluates to true or false expressions that include relational oper-ators, equality operators, logical operators and/or conditional operators.

expression1	expression2	expression1 && expression2
false	false	false
false	true	false
true	false	false
true	true	true

Fig. 5.16 Truth table for the **&&** (conditional AND) operator.

Now let us consider the **||** (conditional OR) operator. Suppose we wish to ensure that either *or* both of two conditions are true before we choose a certain path of execution. We use the **||** operator in the following program segment:

```
if ( semesterAverage >= 90 || finalExam >= 90 )
    Console.WriteLine( "Student grade is A" );
```

which also contains two simple conditions. The condition **semesterAverage >= 90** determines whether the student deserves an "A" in the course because of a solid performance throughout the semester. The condition **finalExam >= 90** determines whether the student deserves an "A" in the course because of an outstanding performance on the final exam. The **if** statement then considers the combined condition

```
semesterAverage >= 90 || finalExam >= 90
```

and awards the student an "A" if either or both of the simple conditions are true. Note that the message "**Student grade is A**" prints unless *both* of the simple conditions are false. Figure 5.17 is a truth table for the conditional OR operator (**||**).

The **&&** operator has a higher precedence than the **||** operator. Both operators associate from left to right. An expression containing **&&** or **||** operators is evaluated only until truth or falsity is known. Thus, evaluation of the expression

```
gender == 1 && age >= 65
```

stops immediately if **gender** is not equal to **1** (i.e., if one condition is **false**, the entire expression is **false**) and continue if **gender** is equal to **1** (i.e., the entire expression could still be **true** if the condition **age >= 65** is **true**). This performance feature for the evaluation of conditional AND and conditional OR expressions is called *short-circuit evaluation*.

expression1	expression2	expression1 || expression2
false	false	false
false	true	true
true	false	true
true	true	true

Fig. 5.17 Truth table for the **||** (conditional OR) operator.

Performance Tip 5.3

*In expressions using operator **&&**, if the separate conditions are independent of one another, make the condition most likely to be false the leftmost condition. In expressions using operator **||**, make the condition most likely to be true the leftmost condition. This use of short-circuit evaluation can reduce a program's execution time.*

The *logical AND* (**&**) and *logical OR* (**|**) operators are similar to the conditional AND and conditional OR operators, with one exception—the logical operators always evaluate both of their operands (i.e., there is no short-circuit evaluation). Therefore, the expression

```
gender == 1 & age >= 65
```

evaluates **age >= 65**, regardless of whether **gender** is equal to **1**. This is useful if the right operand of the logical AND or logical OR operator includes a needed *side effect*—a modification of a variable's value. For example, the expression

```
birthday == true & Console.WriteLine( age )
```

guarantees that variable **age** is printed in the preceding expression, regardless of whether the overall expression is true or false. Likewise, if we want the condition in the right operand to be the result of a mathematical operation, and we want the operation to execute in any case, then we can use the **|** operator.

Common Programming Error 5.11

Avoid expressions with side effects in conditions. The side effects might look clever, but they often cause subtle errors and can be confusing to other people reading or maintaining your code.

A condition containing the *logical exclusive OR* (**^**) operator (sometimes known as the *logical XOR* operator) is true *if and only if one of its operands results in a true value and one results in a false value*. If both operands are true or both are false, the result of the entire condition is false. Figure 5.18 is a truth table for the logical exclusive OR operator (**^**). This operator evaluates both of its operands (i.e., there is no short-circuit evaluation).

C# provides the **!** (logical negation) operator to enable a programmer to "reverse" the meaning of a condition. Unlike the logical operators **&&**, **&**, **||**, **|** and **^**, which combine two conditions (binary operators), the logical negation operator has only a single condition as an operand (unary operator). The logical negation operator is placed before a condition to choose a path of execution if the original condition (without the logical negation operator) is false. This is demonstrated by the following program segment:

```
if ( ! ( grade == sentinelValue ) )
    Console.WriteLine( "The next grade is " + grade );
```

The parentheses around the condition **grade == sentinelValue** are needed because the logical negation operator has a higher precedence than the equality operator. Figure 5.19 is a truth table for the logical negation operator.

In most cases, the programmer can avoid using logical negation by expressing the condition differently with relational or equality operators. For example, the preceding statement may also be written as follows:

```
if ( grade != sentinelValue )
   Console.WriteLine( "The next grade is " + grade );
```

This flexibility can help a programmer express a condition more naturally.

The console application in Fig. 5.20 demonstrates all the conditional and logical operators by displaying their truth tables in a label.

expression1	expression2	expression1 ^ expression2
false	false	false
false	true	true
true	false	true
true	true	false

Fig. 5.18   Truth table for the logical exclusive OR (^) operator.

expression	! expression
false	true
true	false

Fig. 5.19   Truth table for operator ! (logical NOT).

```
1   // Fig. 5.20: LogicalOperators.cs
2   // Demonstrating the logical operators.
3
4   using System;
5
6   class LogicalOperators
7   {
8      // main entry point for application
9      static void Main( string[] args )
10     {
11        // testing the conditional AND operator (&&)
12        Console.WriteLine( "Conditional AND (&&)" +
13           "\nfalse && false: " + ( false && false ) +
14           "\nfalse && true:  " + ( false && true ) +
15           "\ntrue && false:  " + ( true && false ) +
16           "\ntrue && true:   " + ( true && true ) );
17
18        // testing the conditional OR operator (||)
19        Console.WriteLine( "\nConditional OR (||)" +
20           "\nfalse || false: " + ( false || false ) +
21           "\nfalse || true:  " + ( false || true ) +
```

Fig. 5.20   Conditional and logical operators. (Part 1 of 3.)

```
22              "\ntrue || false:  " + ( true || false ) +
23              "\ntrue || true:   " + ( true || true ) );
24
25          // testing the logical AND operator (&)
26          Console.WriteLine( "\nLogical AND (&)" +
27              "\nfalse & false: " + ( false & false ) +
28              "\nfalse & true:  " + ( false & true ) +
29              "\ntrue & false:  " + ( true & false ) +
30              "\ntrue & true:   " + ( true & true ) );
31
32          // testing the logical OR operator (|)
33          Console.WriteLine( "\nLogical OR (|)" +
34              "\nfalse | false: " + ( false | false ) +
35              "\nfalse | true:  " + ( false | true ) +
36              "\ntrue | false:  " + ( true | false ) +
37              "\ntrue | true:   " + ( true | true ) );
38
39          // testing the logical exclusive OR operator (^)
40          Console.WriteLine( "\nLogical exclusive OR (^)" +
41              "\nfalse ^ false: " + ( false ^ false ) +
42              "\nfalse ^ true:  " + ( false ^ true ) +
43              "\ntrue ^ false:  " + ( true ^ false ) +
44              "\ntrue ^ true:   " + ( true ^ true ) );
45
46          // testing the logical NOT operator (!)
47          Console.WriteLine( "\nLogical NOT (!)" +
48              "\n!false: " + ( !false ) +
49              "\n!true:  " + ( !true ) );
50
51      } // end method Main
52
53  } // end class LogicalOperators
```

```
Conditional AND (&&)
false && false: False
false && true:  False
true && false:  False
true && true:   True

Conditional OR (||)
false || false: False
false || true:  True
true  || false: True
true  || true:  True

Logical AND (&)
false & false: False
false & true:  False
true & false:  False
true & true:   True
```

Continued at the top of the next page

Fig. 5.20 Conditional and logical operators. (Part 2 of 3.)

Continued from the previous page

```
Logical OR (|)
false | false: False
false | true:  True
true  | false: True
true  | true:  True

Logical exclusive OR (^)
false ^ false: False
false ^ true:  True
true  ^ false: True
true  ^ true:  False

Logical NOT (!)
!false: True
!true:  False
```

Fig. 5.20   Conditional and logical operators. (Part 3 of 3.)

On line 6, we begin class **LogicalOperators**. Method **Main** (lines 9–51) contains the code for this program. Lines 12–16 demonstrate the **&&** operator; lines 26–30 demonstrate the **&** operator. The remainder of **Main** demonstrates the **||**, **|**, **^** and **!** operators.

When a **bool** value is concatenated to a **string**, C# converts that **bool** value to its string representation, which will be either **"False"** or **"True"**.

Figure 5.21 shows the precedence and associativity of the C# operators introduced to this point. The operators are shown from top to bottom in decreasing order of precedence.

5.9 Structured-Programming Summary

Just as architects design buildings by employing the collective wisdom of their profession, so should programmers design programs. Our field is younger than architecture is, and our collective wisdom is considerably sparser. We have learned that structured programming produces programs that are easier to understand, test, debug, modify and prove correct in a mathematical sense than unstructured programs.

Figure 5.22 summarizes C#'s control structures. Small circles in the figure indicate the single entry point and the single exit point of each structure. Connecting individual flowchart symbols arbitrarily can lead to unstructured programs. Therefore, the programming profession has chosen to combine flowchart symbols to form only a limited set of control structures and to build structured programs by combining control structures in only two simple ways.

For simplicity, only single-entry/single-exit control structures are used—there is only one way to enter and only one way to exit each control structure. To connect control structures in sequence to form structured programs, the exit point of one control structure is connected to the entry point of the next control structure (i.e., the control structures are simply placed one after another in a program). We call this process "control-structure stacking." The rules for forming structured programs also allow control structures to be nested. Figure 5.23 contains the rules for forming properly structured programs. The rules assume that the rectangle flowchart symbol can indicate any action, including input/ output.

Operators	Associativity	Type
( )	left to right	parentheses
++ --	right to left	unary postfix
++ -- + - ! (*type*)	right to left	unary prefix
* / %	left to right	multiplicative
+ -	left to right	additive
< <= > >=	left to right	relational
== !=	left to right	equality
&	left to right	logical AND
^	left to right	logical exclusive OR (XOR)
|	left to right	logical inclusive OR
&&	left to right	conditional AND
||	left to right	conditional OR
? :	right to left	conditional
= += -= *= /= %=	right to left	assignment

Fig. 5.21   Precedence and associativity of the operators discussed so far.

Applying the rules of Fig. 5.23 always results in a structured flowchart with a neat, building-block appearance. For example, repeatedly applying rule 2 to the simplest flowchart results in a structured flowchart that contains many rectangles in sequence (Fig. 5.25). Notice that rule 2 generates a stack of control structures; therefore, we call rule 2 the *stacking rule*.

Rule 3 is the *nesting rule*. Repeatedly applying rule 3 to the simplest flowchart results in a flowchart with neatly nested control structures. For example, in Fig. 5.26, the rectangle in the simplest flowchart first is replaced with a double-selection (**if/else**) structure. Then rule 3 is applied again to both rectangles in the double-selection structure, replacing each of the rectangles with a double-selection structure. The dashed boxes around each of the double-selection structures represent the rectangles that were replaced with these structures.

Good Programming Practice 5.11

Too many levels of nesting can make a program difficult to understand. As a general rule, try to avoid using more than three levels of nesting.

Rule 4 generates larger, more involved and deeply-nested structures. The flowcharts that emerge from applying the rules in Fig. 5.23 constitute the set of all possible structured flowcharts and the set of all possible structured programs.The structured approach has the advantage of using only eight simple single-entry/single-exit pieces and allowing us to assemble them in only two simple ways. Figure 5.27 shows the kinds of correctly stacked building blocks that emerge from applying rule 2 and the kinds of correctly nested building blocks that emerge from applying rule 3. The figure also shows the kind of overlapped building blocks that cannot occur in structured flowcharts (as a result of avoiding **goto** statements).

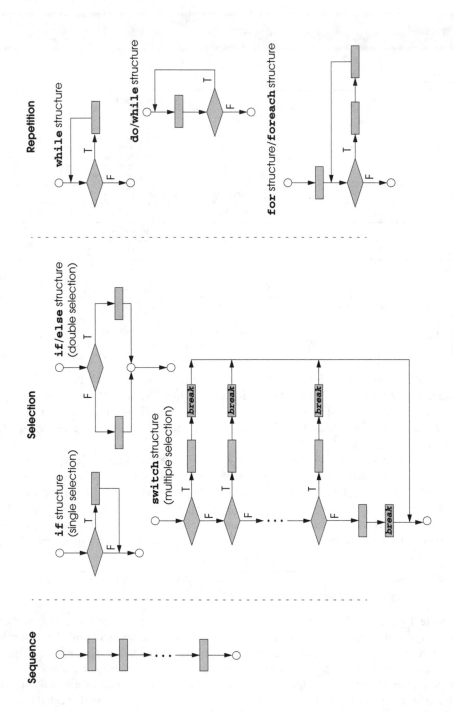

Fig. 5.22   C#'s single-entry/single-exit sequence, selection and repetition structures.

Rules for Forming Structured Programs

1) Begin with the "simplest flowchart" (Fig. 5.24).

2) Any rectangle (action) can be replaced by two rectangles (actions) in sequence.

3) Any rectangle (action) can be replaced by any control structure (sequence, **if**, **if/else**, **switch**, **while**, **do/while**, **for** or **foreach**, as we will see in Chapter 7, Arrays).

4) Rules 2 and 3 may be applied as often as you like and in any order.

Fig. 5.23   Rules for forming structured programs.

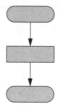

Fig. 5.24   Simplest flowchart.

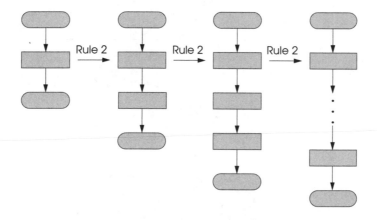

Fig. 5.25   Repeatedly applying rule 2 of Fig. 5.23 to the simplest flowchart.

If the rules in Fig. 5.23 are followed, an unstructured flowchart (such as that in Fig. 5.28) cannot be created. If you are uncertain about whether a particular flowchart is structured, apply the rules in Fig. 5.23 in reverse to try to reduce the flowchart to the simplest flowchart. If the flowchart can be reduced to the simplest flowchart, the original flowchart is structured; otherwise, it is not.

In summary, structured programming promotes simplicity. Bohm and Jacopini have found that only three forms of control are necessary:

- Sequence
- Selection
- Repetition

Sequence is trivial. Selection is implemented in one of three ways:

- **if** structure (single selection)
- **if/else** structure (double selection)
- **switch** structure (multiple selection)

In fact, it is straightforward to prove that the **if** structure is sufficient to provide any form of selection. Everything that can be done with the **if/else** and **switch** structures can be implemented by combining **if** structures (although perhaps not as elegantly).

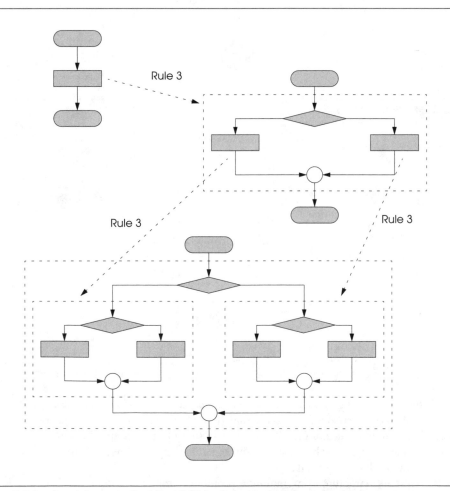

Fig. 5.26 Applying rule 3 of Fig. 5.23 to the simplest flowchart.

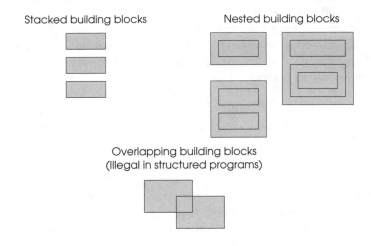

Fig. 5.27   Stacked, nested and overlapped building blocks.

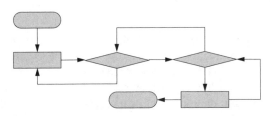

Fig. 5.28   Unstructured flowchart.

Repetition is implemented in one of four ways:

- **while** structure
- **do/while** structure
- **for** structure
- **foreach** structure (discussed in Chapter 7)

It is straightforward to prove that the **while** structure is sufficient to provide any form of repetition. Everything that can be done with the **do/while**, **for** and **foreach** structures can be done with the **while** structure (although perhaps not as elegantly).

Combining these results illustrates that any form of control ever needed in a C# program can be expressed in terms of

- sequence
- **if** structure (selection)
- **while** structure (repetition)

These control structures can be combined in only two ways—stacking and nesting. Indeed, structured programming promotes simplicity.

In this chapter, we have discussed how to compose programs from control structures that contain actions and decisions. In Chapter 6, Methods, we introduce another program-structuring unit, called the *method*. We discuss how to compose large programs by combining methods that are composed of control structures. We also discuss how methods promote software reusability. In Chapter 8, Object-Based Programming, we discuss in more detail another C# program-structuring unit, called the *class*. We then create objects from classes and proceed with our treatment of object-oriented programming—the key focus of this book.

5.10 Summary

Counter-controlled repetition requires the name of a control variable (or loop counter), the initial value of the control variable, the increment (or decrement) by which the control variable is modified each time through the loop and the condition that tests for the final value of the control variable (i.e., whether looping should continue).

The general format of the **for** structure is

> **for** (*expression1*; *expression2*; *expression3*)
>   *statement*;

where *expression1* names the loop's control variable and provides its initial value, *expression2* is the loop-continuation condition (containing the control variable's final value) and *expression3* increments the control variable.

The three expressions in the **for** structure are optional. The two semicolons in the **for** structure are required. If the loop-continuation condition is initially false, the body of the **for** structure does not execute.

The **switch** multiple-selection structure consists of a series of **case** labels and an optional **default** case. Each label (**case** or **default**) contains statements to be executed if that label is selected. A **break** is required in every **case** of a **switch** structure, except for empty **case**s. Listing **case** labels together (as in **case 'C': case 'c':**, with no statements between the **case**s) causes the same set of actions to be performed for each of the **case**s. When using the **switch** structure, remember that the expression after each **case** must be a constant integral expression (i.e., any combination of character and integer constants that evaluates to a constant integer value).

The **do/while** structure tests the loop-continuation condition after the body of the loop executes; therefore, the body of the loop always executes at least once.

The **break** statement, when executed in a **while**, **for**, **do/while** or **switch** structure, causes immediate exit from that structure. Execution continues with the first statement after the structure. The **continue** statement, when executed in a **while**, **for** or **do/while** structure, skips the remaining statements in the body of that structure and proceeds with the next iteration of the loop.

C# uses conditional and logical operators to form complex conditions by combining simple ones. The conditional and logical operators are **&&** (conditional AND), **&** (logical AND), **||** (conditional OR), **|** (logical inclusive OR), **^** (logical exclusive OR) and **!** (logical NOT, also called logical negation). The conditional **&&** operator ensures that two conditions are both **true** before a path of execution is chosen. The logical | | operator ensures that at least one of two conditions is **true** before a certain path of execution is chosen. A condition containing the boolean logical exclusive OR (^) operator is true if and only if one of its operands is true and the other is false. The **!** (logical negation) operator "reverses" the meaning of a condition.

Connecting individual flowchart symbols arbitrarily can lead to unstructured programs. The rules for forming structured programs enable the programmer to create flowcharts that are always structured, with neatly nested control structures. The rules instruct the programmer to begin with the simplest flowchart and subsequently replace any action with a set of actions or control structures. Notice that following these rules permits the programmer to combine control structures in only two simple ways—stacking and nesting.

Bohm and Jacopini have found that only three forms of control are necessary—sequence, selection and repetition. Selection is implemented with one of three control structures—**if**, **if/else** and **switch**. The **if** structure is sufficient to provide any form of selection. Repetition is implemented with one of four control structures—**while, do/ while, for** and **foreach**. The **while** structure is sufficient to provide any form of repetition.

6

Methods

Objectives

- To construct programs modularly from methods.
- To introduce the common math methods available in the Framework Class Library.
- To be able to create new methods.
- To understand the mechanisms for passing information between methods.
- To introduce simulation techniques that use random number generation.
- To understand how the visibility of identifiers is limited to specific regions of programs.
- To understand how to write and use methods that call themselves.

Form ever follows function.
Louis Henri Sullivan

E pluribus unum.
(One composed of many.)
Virgil

O! call back yesterday, bid time return.
William Shakespeare

Call me Ishmael.
Herman Melville

When you call me that, smile.
Owen Wister

Outline

6.1 Introduction

Most computer programs that solve real problems are much larger than the programs presented in the first few chapters of this text. Experience has shown that the best way to develop and maintain a large program is to construct it from small, simple pieces. This technique is known as *divide and conquer.* In the previous chapters, we called various methods to perform specific tasks. We also defined our own **Main** methods, specifying the actions to occur in our program. This chapter investigates methods in depth, describing many key features of the C# language that facilitate the design, implementation, operation and maintenance of large programs.

6.2 Methods in C#

C# programs are written by combining new methods and classes that the programmer writes with "prepackaged" methods and classes available in the *.NET Framework Class Library (FCL)*. In this chapter, we concentrate on methods. We discuss classes in detail in Chapter 8, Object-Based Programming.

The FCL provides a rich collection of classes and methods for performing common mathematical calculations, string manipulations, character manipulations, input/output operations, error checking and many other useful operations. This set of preexisting code makes the programmer's job easier by providing many of the capabilities programmers need. The FCL methods are part of the .NET Framework, which includes FCL classes **Console** and **MessageBox** used in earlier examples.

Software Engineering Observation 6.1

Familiarize yourself with the rich collection of classes and methods in the FCL.

Software Engineering Observation 6.2

When possible, use .NET Framework classes and methods instead of writing new classes and methods. This reduces both program development time and errors.

The programmer can write methods to define specific tasks that may be used at many points in a program. Such methods are known as *programmer-defined* (or *user-defined*) *methods*. The actual statements defining the method are written only once and are hidden from other methods.

A method is *invoked* (i.e., made to perform its designated task) by a *method call*. The method call specifies the name of the method and may provide information (as *arguments*) that the called method requires to perform its task. When the method call completes, the method either returns a result to the *calling method* (or *caller*) or simply returns control to the calling method. A common analogy for this is the hierarchical form of management. A boss (the calling method or caller) asks a worker (the *called method*) to perform a task and report back (i.e., *return*) the results after completing the task. The boss method does not know *how* the worker method performs its designated tasks. The worker may also call other worker methods, and the boss will be unaware of these calls. We will see how this "hiding" of implementation details promotes good software engineering. Figure 6.1 shows a **Boss** method communicating with worker methods **Worker1**, **Worker2** and **Worker3** in a hierarchical manner. Note that **Worker1** acts as a "boss" method to **Worker4** and **Worker5** in this particular example.

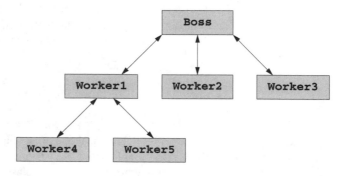

Fig. 6.1   Hierarchical boss method/worker method relationship.

6.3 **Math** Class Methods

Math class methods allow the programmer to perform certain common mathematical cal-culations. We use various **Math** class methods to introduce the concept of methods in gen-eral. Throughout the book, we discuss many other methods from the classes of the Framework Class Library.

Methods are called by writing the name of the method, followed by a left parenthesis, the *argument* (or a comma-separated list of arguments) of the method and a right paren-thesis. The parentheses may be empty, if the called method needs no arguments. For example, a programmer wishing to calculate and print the square root of **900.0** might write

```
Console.WriteLine( Math.Sqrt( 900.0 ) );
```

When this statement executes, the method **Math.Sqrt** calculates the square root of the number in parentheses (**900.0**). The number **900.0** is the argument to the **Math.Sqrt** method. The **Math.Sqrt** method takes an argument of type **double** and returns a result of type **double**. The preceding statement uses the result of method **Math.Sqrt** as the argument to method **Console.WriteLine** and displays **30.0**. Note that all **Math** class methods must be invoked by preceding the method name with the class name **Math** and a dot (**.**) operator (also called the member access operator).

Software Engineering Observation 6.3

*It is not necessary to add an assembly reference to use the **Math** class methods in a program. Class **Math** is located in namespace **System**, which is available to every program.*

Common Programming Error 6.1

*Forgetting to invoke a **Math** class method by preceding the method name with the class name **Math** and a dot operator (**.**) results in a syntax error.*

Method arguments may be constants, variables or expressions. If **c1 = 13.0, d = 3.0** and **f = 4.0**, then the statement

```
Console.WriteLine( Math.Sqrt( c1 + d * f ) );
```

calculates and displays the square root of **13.0 + 3.0 * 4.0 = 25.0**, which is **5.0**.

Figure 6.2 summarizes some **Math** class methods. In this figure, the variables **x** and **y** are of type **double**; however, many of the methods provide versions that take values of other data types as arguments. The **Math** class also defines two commonly used mathematical con-stants—**Math.PI** (3.14159265358979323846) and **Math.E** (2.7182818284590452354). The constant **Math.PI** of class **Math** is the ratio of a circle's circumference to its diameter. The constant **Math.E** is the base value for natural logarithms (calculated with the **Math.Log** method).

6.4 Methods

Methods allow programmers to modularize programs. Variables declared in method defi-nitions are *local variables*—only the method that defines them knows they exist. Most methods have a list of *parameters* that enable method calls to communicate information be-tween methods. A method's parameters are also local variables to that method and are not visible in any other methods.

Method	Description	Example
Abs(x)	absolute value of *x*	**Abs(23.7)** is **23.7** **Abs(0)** is **0** **Abs(-23.7)** is **23.7**
Ceiling(x)	rounds *x* to the smallest integer not less than *x*	**Ceiling(9.2)** is **10.0** **Ceiling(-9.8)** is **-9.0**
Cos(x)	trigonometric cosine of *x* (*x* in radians)	**Cos(0.0)** is **1.0**
Exp(x)	exponential method e^x	**Exp(1.0)** is approximately **2.7182818284590451** **Exp(2.0)** is approximately **7.3890560989306504**
Floor(x)	rounds *x* to the largest integer not greater than *x*	**Floor(9.2)** is **9.0** **Floor(-9.8)** is **-10.0**
Log(x)	natural logarithm of *x* (base *e*)	**Log(2.7182818284590451)** is approximately **1.0** **Log(7.3890560989306504)** is approximately **2.0**
Max(x, y)	larger value of *x* and *y* (also has versions for **float**, **int** and **long** values)	**Max(2.3, 12.7)** is **12.7** **Max(-2.3, -12.7)** is **-2.3**
Min(x, y)	smaller value of *x* and *y* (also has versions for **float**, **int** and **long** values)	**Min(2.3, 12.7)** is **2.3** **Min(-2.3, -12.7)** is **-12.7**
Pow(x, y)	*x* raised to power *y* (x^y)	**Pow(2.0, 7.0)** is **128.0** **Pow(9.0, .5)** is **3.0**
Sin(x)	trigonometric sine of *x* (*x* in radians)	**Sin(0.0)** is **0.0**
Sqrt(x)	square root of *x*	**Sqrt(900.0)** is **30.0** **Sqrt(9.0)** is **3.0**
Tan(x)	trigonometric tangent of *x* (*x* in radians)	**Tan(0.0)** is **0.0**

Fig. 6.2   Commonly used **Math** class methods.

There are several motivations for modularizing a program with methods. The divide-and-conquer approach makes program development more manageable. Another motivation is *software reusability*—using existing methods (and classes) as building blocks to create new programs. With proper method naming and definition, we can create programs from standardized methods, rather than building customized code. For example, we did not have to define how to convert **string**s to integers—The .NET Framework Class Library already defines such methods for us (**Int32.Parse**). A third motivation is to avoid repeating code in a program. Packaging code as a method allows that code to be executed from several locations in a program—we simply have to call that method.

Good Programming Practice 6.1

Make good use of modularity to increase the clarity and organization of your program. This will not only help others understand your program, but it also will aid in program development, testing and debugging.

Software Engineering Observation 6.4

To promote reusability, each method should perform a single, well-defined task, and the name of the method should express that task effectively.

Software Engineering Observation 6.5

If you cannot choose a concise name that expresses what the method does, it is possible that your method is attempting to perform too many diverse tasks. Usually it is best to break such a method into several smaller methods.

6.5 Method Definitions

The programs presented up to this point each contained at least one method definition (such as **Main**) that called existing FCL methods to accomplish the program's tasks. We now consider how to write customized methods.

Consider the Windows application in Fig. 6.3, which uses a method called **Square** to calculate the squares of the integers from 1 to 10. Notice the comment on line 15

```
// Visual Studio .NET generated code
```

Throughout the book we will use this comment to denote code that we are not displaying in the chapter. In all cases, this represents code created by the IDE. Most of this code initializes properties of GUI components. The examples in all chapters of the book are included in their entirety and can be downloaded from **www.deitel.com** via the **Downloads/ Resources** link, then compiled and executed to produce the same results we show in our screen shots. The next example (Fig. 6.4) displays all the code. However, you do not need to understand all the code at this point in the book. Chapter 11, Graphical User Interface Concepts, presents an example in which we discuss all the code in detail.

```
1    // Fig. 6.3: SquareInt.cs
2    // Demonstrates a programmer-defined Square method.
3    using System;
4    using System.Drawing;
5    using System.Collections;
6    using System.ComponentModel;
7    using System.Windows.Forms;
8    using System.Data;
9
10   public class SquareInt : System.Windows.Forms.Form
11   {
12       private System.Windows.Forms.Button calculateButton;
13       private System.Windows.Forms.Label outputLabel;
14
```

Fig. 6.3   Using programmer-defined method **Square**. (Part 1 of 2.)

```
15      // Visual Studio .NET generated code
16
17      [STAThread]
18      static void Main()
19      {
20          Application.Run( new SquareInt() );
21      }
22
23      // Square method definition
24      int Square( int y )
25      {
26          return y * y; // return square of y
27
28      } // end method Square
29
30      private void calculateButton_Click( object sender,
31          System.EventArgs e )
32      {
33          outputLabel.Text = "";
34
35          // loop 10 times
36          for ( int counter = 1; counter <= 10; counter++ )
37          {
38              // calculate square of counter and store in result
39              int result = Square( counter );
40
41              // append result to outputLabel
42              outputLabel.Text += "The square of " + counter +
43                  " is " + result + "\n";
44          }
45
46      } // end method calculateButton_Click
47
48  } // end of class SquareInt
```

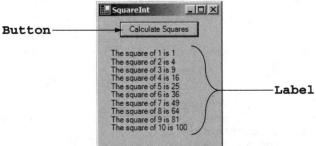

Fig. 6.3   Using programmer-defined method **Square**. (Part 2 of 2.)

Until now, our programs have used methods of class **Console** to obtain user input from the command prompt. These programs output their results either to the command prompt or in **MessageBox**es. Although these are valid ways to receive input from a user and display output, they are fairly limited in their capabilities—the command prompt can obtain only one value at a time from the user, and a message dialog can display only one message. It is much more common for programs to read multiple inputs simultaneously (e.g., when the user enters name and address information) or to display many pieces of data at once (such as the squares of the first ten integers in this example). To introduce more elaborate user interfaces, the program in Fig. 6.3 illustrates two graphical user interface concepts—attaching multiple GUI components to an application and *event handling*.

To create the graphical user interface for this program, drag the appropriate components (a **Button** and a **Label**) from the **Toolbox** onto the **Form** in the Windows Form Designer. We demonstrated how to do this in Section 2.6. The label is used to display the results of calculating the first ten squares. The program invokes a special method, known as an *event handler*, when the user clicks the **Calculate Squares** button. An event handler is a method that performs some action in response to an *event*. Events occur when certain actions take place in a graphical user interface, such as when the user clicks a button. Using GUI component objects and events together allows programmers to create applications that interact with users in more sophisticated ways than we have seen previously. In Visual Studio .NET's Windows Form Designer, double clicking a GUI component object causes Visual Studio .NET to generate an empty event handler method. The event handler method's name defaults to the GUI component's name, followed by an underscore and the name of the event. In this example, the event handler is named **calculateButton_Click** (lines 30–46), and is therefore the event handler method for **calculateButton**'s *Click* event. The **Click** event is the event that occurs when the user clicks this button.

The programmer can fill in the event handler method with code that performs an appropriate task when that event occurs. Fill **calculateButton_Click** with the code shown on lines 33–44. This event handler begins by assigning the empty string (**""**) to **output-Label**'s **Text** property on line 33. This action ensures that the output does not scroll off the form if the user presses the **Calculate Squares** button more than once. Lines 36–44 repeatedly invoke method **Square** (lines 24–28) to calculate the squares of the integers from 1 to 10. Line 39 invokes the **Square** method and passes the variable **counter** as an argument.

As in some of our previous Windows applications, we create a label called **output-Label** to display the program's output. Every label contains a **string** property called **Text**, which can be accessed using the dot operator (**.**). We append the results of the square calculations to this label's **Text** property.

Line 39 declares **int** variable **result** to store the result of each square calculation. Lines 36–44 contain a **for** repetition structure in which each iteration of the loop calculates the **Square** of the current value of control variable **counter** and stores the value in **result**. Lines 42–43 concatenate each result to the **Text** property of **outputLabel**. At the end of the loop, the **Label** contains the results of squaring the values from 1 to 10.

The program invokes method **Square** on line 39. The parentheses, **()**, after **Square** represent the *method-call operator*, which has high precedence. At this point, the program makes a copy of the value of **counter** (the argument to the method call), and program control transfers to method **Square** (defined at lines 24–28). Method **Square** receives the copy of the value of **counter** in the *parameter* **y**. Then, **Square** calculates **y * y** (line 26). Method **Square** uses a ***return*** statement to return the result of the calculation to the statement that invoked **Square** (located in line 39). Line 39 then assigns the returned value to variable **result**. Lines 42–43 concatenate **"The square of"**, the value of **counter**, **" is "**, the value of **result** and a newline character to the end of **outputLabel**'s **Text** property. The **for** repetition structure repeats this process 10 times.

The definition of method **Square** (line 24) shows (inside the parentheses) that **Square** expects an integer parameter **y**. Parameter **y** is the variable that holds the value passed to **Square** as an argument. The parameter name provides access to the argument value, so that code in the method body can use that value. Keyword **int**, which precedes the method name, indicates that method **Square** returns an integer result. The **return** statement in **Square** (line 26) passes the result of the calculation **y * y** back to the calling statement (line 39). Note that the entire method definition appears inside the braces of class **SquareInt**. All methods must be defined inside a class definition.

Good Programming Practice 6.2

Place a blank line between adjacent method definitions to separate the methods and enhance program readability.

Common Programming Error 6.2

Defining a method outside the braces of a class definition is a syntax error.

The format of a method definition is

```
return-value-type  method-name ( parameter-list )
{
   declarations and statements
}
```

The first line is sometimes known as the *method header*. The *method-name* is any valid identifier. The *return-value-type* is the data type of the result that the method returns to its caller. The *return-value-type* **void** indicates that a method does not return a value. Methods can return at most one value.

Common Programming Error 6.3

Omitting the return-value-type *in a method definition is a compilation error. If a method does not return a value, the method's* return-value-type *must be* **void***.*

Common Programming Error 6.4

Forgetting to return a value from a method that is supposed to return a value is a compilation error. If a return-value-type *other than* **void** *is specified, the method must contain a* **return** *statement that returns a value.*

Common Programming Error 6.5

Returning a value from a method whose return type has been declared **void** *is a compilation error.*

The *parameter-list* is a comma-separated list in which the method declares each parameter's type and name. The method call must specify one argument for each parameter in the method definition and the arguments must appear in the same order as the parameters in the method definition. The arguments also must be compatible with the parameter's type. For example, a parameter of type **double** could receive values of 7.35, 22 or –.03546, but not **"hello"** because a **string** cannot be implicitly converted into a **double**. If a method does not receive any values, the parameter list is empty (i.e., the method name is followed by an empty pair of parentheses). Each parameter in a method's parameter list must have a data type; otherwise, a syntax error occurs.

Common Programming Error 6.6

Declaring method parameters of the same type as **float x, y** *instead of* **float x, float y** *is a syntax error, because a type is required for each parameter in the parameter list.*

Common Programming Error 6.7

Placing a semicolon after the right parenthesis enclosing the parameter list of a method definition is a syntax error.

Common Programming Error 6.8

Redefining a method parameter in the method's body is a compilation error.

Common Programming Error 6.9

Passing to a method an argument that is not compatible with the corresponding parameter's type is a syntax error. If the argument is not of the same type as its corresponding parameter's type, the argument's type must be one that can be implicitly converted to the type of the corresponding parameter.

The declarations and statements within braces form the *method body*. The method body is also referred to as a block. As discussed previously, a block is a set of declarations and statements enclosed in curly braces. Variables can be declared in any block, and blocks can be nested.

Common Programming Error 6.10

Defining a method inside another method is a syntax error (i.e., methods cannot be nested).

Good Programming Practice 6.3

Choosing meaningful method names and parameter names makes programs more readable and helps avoid excessive use of comments.

Software Engineering Observation 6.6

As a rule of thumb, a method should be no longer than one page. Better yet, a method should be no longer than half a page. Regardless of how long a method is, it should perform one task well. Small methods promote software reusability.

Testing and Debugging Tip 6.1

Small methods are easier to test, debug and understand than large methods.

Software Engineering Observation 6.7

A method requiring a large number of parameters may be performing too many tasks. Consider dividing the method into smaller methods that perform separate tasks. As a rule of thumb, the method header should fit on one line (if possible).

Software Engineering Observation 6.8

The number, type and order of arguments in a method call must exactly match those of the parameters in the corresponding method header.

There are three ways to return control to the point at which a method was invoked. If the method does not return a result (i.e., the method has a **void** return type), control returns when the program reaches the method-ending right brace or when the statement

```
return;
```

executes. If the method does return a result, the statement

```
return expression;
```

returns the value of *expression* to the caller. When a **return** statement executes, control returns immediately to the point at which the method was invoked.

Notice the syntax that invokes method **Square** in Fig. 6.3—we use the method name, followed by the arguments to the method in parentheses. Methods in a class definition are allowed to invoke all other methods in the same class definition by using this syntax (an exception to this is discussed in Chapter 8, Object-Based Programming). We now have seen three ways to call a method with arguments—a method name by itself (as shown with **Square(x)**), a reference to an object followed by the dot (**.**) operator and the method name (such as **string1.CompareTo(string2)**) and a class name followed by a method name (such as **Math.Sqrt(9.0)**). The last syntax is for calling the *static methods* of a class—we discuss this in detail in Chapter 8, Object-Based Programming.

The application in our next example (Fig. 6.4) uses programmer-defined method **Maximum** to determine and return the largest of three floating-point values that the user inputs through the program's graphical user interface. Note that in this example, we show all of the code that the Windows Form Designer generates. Throughout the rest of the book, we omit portions of the generated code that are not relevant to our discussions. In such programs, we place a comment that indicates where the Visual Studio .NET generated code appears in the original source file.

The graphical user interface for this program consists of three **TextBox**es in which the user can enter floating-point numbers, a **Button** for calculating the maximum, **Label**s for each **TextBox** and a **Label** for displaying the maximum value. Lines 31–182 contain the Visual Studio .NET generated code for constructing this graphical user interface. Lines 31–42 define a special type of method called a *constructor*. Programs invoke constructors to create objects. The constructor performs tasks necessary for preparing an object for use in a program. We discuss constructors in detail in Chapter 8. In the case of Windows applications, the constructor invokes method **InitializeComponent** to create the program's graphical user interface (line 36). Method **InitializeComponent** (lines 64–181) configures and arranges the program's graphical user interface component objects, such as its **Label**s, **Button**s and **TextBox**es.

```
1   // Fig. 6.4: MaximumValue.cs
2   // Finding the maximum of three double values.
3   using System;
4   using System.Drawing;
5   using System.Collections;
6   using System.ComponentModel;
```

Fig. 6.4   Programmer-defined **Maximum** method. (Part 1 of 6.)

```
 7   using System.Windows.Forms;
 8   using System.Data;
 9
10   namespace MaximumValue
11   {
12       /// <summary>
13       /// Summary description for Form1.
14       /// </summary>
15       public class MaximumValue : System.Windows.Forms.Form
16       {
17           private System.Windows.Forms.Label firstNumberLabel;
18           private System.Windows.Forms.Label secondNumberLabel;
19           private System.Windows.Forms.Label thirdNumberLabel;
20           private System.Windows.Forms.Label maximumLabel;
21           private System.Windows.Forms.TextBox firstNumberTextBox;
22           private System.Windows.Forms.TextBox secondNumberTextBox;
23           private System.Windows.Forms.TextBox thirdNumberTextBox;
24           private System.Windows.Forms.Button calculateButton;
25
26           /// <summary>
27           /// Required designer variable.
28           /// </summary>
29           private System.ComponentModel.Container components = null;
30
31           public MaximumValue()
32           {
33               //
34               // Required for Windows Form Designer support
35               //
36               InitializeComponent();
37
38               //
39               // TODO: Add any constructor code after
40               //       InitializeComponent call
41               //
42           }
43
44           /// <summary>
45           /// Clean up any resources being used.
46           /// </summary>
47           protected override void Dispose( bool disposing )
48           {
49               if( disposing )
50               {
51                   if (components != null)
52                   {
53                       components.Dispose();
54                   }
55               }
56               base.Dispose( disposing );
57           }
58
59           #region Windows Form Designer generated code
```

Fig. 6.4   Programmer-defined **Maximum** method. (Part 2 of 6.)

```
60          /// <summary>
61          /// Required method for Designer support - do not modify
62          /// the contents of this method with the code editor.
63          /// </summary>
64          private void InitializeComponent()
65          {
66             this.calculateButton =
67                new System.Windows.Forms.Button();
68             this.secondNumberTextBox =
69                new System.Windows.Forms.TextBox();
70             this.thirdNumberTextBox =
71                new System.Windows.Forms.TextBox();
72             this.firstNumberLabel =
73                new System.Windows.Forms.Label();
74             this.secondNumberLabel =
75                new System.Windows.Forms.Label();
76             this.thirdNumberLabel =
77                new System.Windows.Forms.Label();
78             this.maximumLabel = new System.Windows.Forms.Label();
79             this.firstNumberTextBox =
80                new System.Windows.Forms.TextBox();
81             this.SuspendLayout();
82             //
83             // calculateButton
84             //
85             this.calculateButton.Location =
86                new System.Drawing.Point(24, 120);
87             this.calculateButton.Name = "calculateButton";
88             this.calculateButton.Size =
89                new System.Drawing.Size(112, 23);
90             this.calculateButton.TabIndex = 0;
91             this.calculateButton.Text = "Calculate Maximum";
92             this.calculateButton.Click +=
93                new System.EventHandler(this.calculateButton_Click);
94             //
95             // secondNumberTextBox
96             //
97             this.secondNumberTextBox.Location =
98                new System.Drawing.Point(176, 49);
99             this.secondNumberTextBox.Name = "secondNumberTextBox";
100            this.secondNumberTextBox.TabIndex = 2;
101            this.secondNumberTextBox.Text = "";
102            //
103            // thirdNumberTextBox
104            //
105            this.thirdNumberTextBox.Location =
106               new System.Drawing.Point(176, 81);
107            this.thirdNumberTextBox.Name = "thirdNumberTextBox";
108            this.thirdNumberTextBox.TabIndex = 3;
109            this.thirdNumberTextBox.Text = "";
110            //
111            // firstNumberLabel
112            //
```

Fig. 6.4   Programmer-defined **Maximum** method. (Part 3 of 6.)

```
113            this.firstNumberLabel.Location =
114               new System.Drawing.Point(8, 16);
115            this.firstNumberLabel.Name = "firstNumberLabel";
116            this.firstNumberLabel.Size =
117               new System.Drawing.Size(136, 23);
118            this.firstNumberLabel.TabIndex = 4;
119            this.firstNumberLabel.Text =
120               "First Floating-Point Value:";
121            //
122            // secondNumberLabel
123            //
124            this.secondNumberLabel.Location =
125               new System.Drawing.Point(8, 48);
126            this.secondNumberLabel.Name = "secondNumberLabel";
127            this.secondNumberLabel.Size =
128               new System.Drawing.Size(152, 23);
129            this.secondNumberLabel.TabIndex = 5;
130            this.secondNumberLabel.Text =
131               "Second Floating-Point Value:";
132            //
133            // thirdNumberLabel
134            //
135            this.thirdNumberLabel.Location =
136               new System.Drawing.Point(8, 80);
137            this.thirdNumberLabel.Name = "thirdNumberLabel";
138            this.thirdNumberLabel.Size =
139               new System.Drawing.Size(144, 23);
140            this.thirdNumberLabel.TabIndex = 6;
141            this.thirdNumberLabel.Text =
142               "Third Floating-Point Value:";
143            //
144            // maximumLabel
145            //
146            this.maximumLabel.Location =
147               new System.Drawing.Point(176, 120);
148            this.maximumLabel.Name = "maximumLabel";
149            this.maximumLabel.Size =
150               new System.Drawing.Size(100, 80);
151            this.maximumLabel.TabIndex = 7;
152            //
153            // firstNumberTextBox
154            //
155            this.firstNumberTextBox.Location =
156               new System.Drawing.Point(176, 16);
157            this.firstNumberTextBox.Name = "firstNumberTextBox";
158            this.firstNumberTextBox.TabIndex = 1;
159            this.firstNumberTextBox.Text = "";
160            //
161            // MaximumValue
162            //
163            this.AutoScaleBaseSize = new System.Drawing.Size(5, 13);
164            this.ClientSize = new System.Drawing.Size(292, 205);
165            this.Controls.AddRange(
```

Fig. 6.4   Programmer-defined **Maximum** method. (Part 4 of 6.)

```
166                  new System.Windows.Forms.Control[] {
167                      this.firstNumberTextBox,
168                      this.maximumLabel,
169                      this.thirdNumberLabel,
170                      this.secondNumberLabel,
171                      this.firstNumberLabel,
172                      this.thirdNumberTextBox,
173                      this.secondNumberTextBox,
174                      this.calculateButton
175                  }
176              );
177              this.Name = "MaximumValue";
178              this.Text = "MaximumValue";
179              this.ResumeLayout(false);
180
181          }
182      #endregion
183
184      /// <summary>
185      /// The main entry point for the application.
186      /// </summary>
187      [STAThread]
188      static void Main()
189      {
190          Application.Run(new MaximumValue());
191      }
192
193      // Method Maximum uses method Math.Max to determine the
194      // maximum value among the three double arguments
195      double Maximum( double x, double y, double z )
196      {
197          return Math.Max( x, Math.Max( y, z ) );
198      }
199
200      // get the floating-point values that the user entered and
201      // invoke method Maximum to determine the maximum value
202      private void calculateButton_Click( object sender,
203          System.EventArgs e )
204      {
205          // get inputted values and convert strings to doubles
206          double number1 =
207              Double.Parse( firstNumberTextBox.Text );
208
209          double number2 =
210              Double.Parse( secondNumberTextBox.Text );
211
212          double number3 =
213              Double.Parse( thirdNumberTextBox.Text );
214
215          // invoke method Maximum to determine the largest value
216          double maximum = Maximum( number1, number2, number3 );
217
```

Fig. 6.4   Programmer-defined **Maximum** method. (Part 5 of 6.)

```
218              // display maximum value
219              maximumLabel.Text = "maximum is: " + maximum;
220
221          }   // end method calculateButton_Click
222
223      }  // end class MaximumValue
224
225  }  // end namespace MaximumValue
```

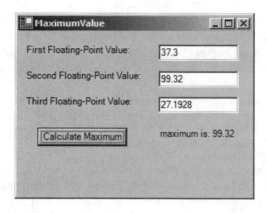

Fig. 6.4   Programmer-defined **Maximum** method. (Part 6 of 6.)

When the user closes a program's window, the system invokes method **Dispose** (lines 47–57) to "clean up" resources used by the Window.

To create the graphical user interface for this program, drag the appropriate components from the **Toolbox** onto the **Form** in the Windows Form Designer. Arrange the components as shown in the screen capture of Fig. 6.4 and set the **Text** properties for the **Label**s and **Button**. Then, double click the **Calculate Maximum** button to add an empty event handler. Fill in this empty event handler with the code shown on lines 202–221. Lines 206–213 invoke **Double** method **Parse** on the **Text** property of each **TextBox** to retrieve the values that the user entered. Line 216 then invokes our **Maximum** method to determine which value is the largest. Method **Maximum** provides the largest number as its return value, which line 216 stores in **double** variable **maximum**. Line 219 appends the **maximum** value to the **maximumLabel**'s **Text** property to display the result to the user.

Now let us examine the implementation of method **Maximum** (lines 195–198). The first line indicates that the method returns a **double** floating-point value, that the method's name is **Maximum** and that the method takes three **double** parameters (**x**, **y** and **z**). The statement in the body of the method (line 197) returns the largest of the three floating-point values using two calls to method **Math.Max**. First, method **Math.Max** is invoked and passed the values of variables **y** and **z** to determine the larger of these two values. Next, the value of variable **x** and the result of the first call to **Math.Max** are passed to method **Math.Max**. Finally, the result of the second call to **Math.Max** is returned to the caller.

6.6 Argument Promotion

Another important feature of method definitions is the *coercion of arguments* (i.e., forcing arguments to the appropriate type to pass to a method). This process commonly is referred to as implicit conversion (discussed briefly in Chapter 4, Control Structures: Part 1), in that a copy of the variable's value is converted to a different type without an explicit cast. Explicit conversion (also introduced in Chapter 4, Control Structures: Part 1) occurs when an explicit cast specifies that conversion is to occur. Such conversions also can be done with class **Convert** in namespace **System**. C# supports both widening and narrowing conversions—*widening conversion* occurs when a type is converted to other types (usually types that can hold more data) without losing data, and a *narrowing conversion* occurs when data may be lost through a conversion (usually to types that hold a smaller amount of data). Figure 6.5 provides size information for the various built-in types of C#, and Fig. 6.6 shows the allowable implicit conversions.

For example, the **Math** class method **Sqrt** can be called with an integer argument, even though the method is defined in class **Math** to receive a **double** argument. The statement

```
Console.WriteLine( Math.Sqrt( 4 ) );
```

correctly evaluates **Math.Sqrt(4)** and displays the value **2**. C# implicitly converts the **int** value **4** to the **double** value **4.0** before passing the value to **Math.Sqrt**. In many cases, C# applies implicit conversions to argument values that do not correspond precisely to the parameter types in the method definition. In some cases, attempting these conversions leads to compilation errors because C# uses conversion rules to determine when a widening conversion can occur. In our previous **Math.Sqrt** example, C# converts an **int** to a **double** without changing its value. However, converting a **double** to an **int** truncates the fractional part of the **double** value. Converting large integer types to small integer types (e.g., **long** to **int**) also can result in changed values. Such narrowing conversions can lose data; C# does not allow narrowing conversions without an explicit cast operation.

Type	Size in bits	Values	Standard
bool	8	*true* or *false*	
char	16	`'\u0000'` to `'\uFFFF'`	(Unicode character set)
byte	8	0 to 255	(unsigned)
sbyte	8	−128 to +127	
short	16	−32,768 to +32,767	
ushort	16	0 to 65,535	(unsigned)
int	32	−2,147,483,648 to 2,147,483,647	
uint	32	0 to 4,294,967,295	(unsigned)
long	64	−9,223,372,036,854,775,808 to +9,223,372,036,854,775,807	
ulong	64	0 to 18,446,744,073,709,551,615	(unsigned)

Fig. 6.5   C# built-in data types. (Part 1 of 2.)

Type	Size in bits	Values	Standard
decimal	128	1.0×10^{-28} to 7.9×10^{28}	
float	32	$\pm 1.5 \infty 10^{-45}$ to $\pm 3.4 \infty 10^{38}$	(IEEE 754 floating point)
double	64	$\pm 5.0 \infty 10^{-324}$ to $\pm 1.7 \infty 10^{308}$	(IEEE 754 floating point)
object			
string			(Unicode character set)

Fig. 6.5   C# built-in data types. (Part 2 of 2.)

Type	Can be Converted to Type(s)
bool	*object*
byte	*decimal*, *double*, *float*, *int*, *uint*, *long*, *ulong*, *short*, *ushort* or *object*
sbyte	*decimal*, *double*, *float*, *int*, *long*, *short* or *object*
char	*decimal*, *double*, *float*, *int*, *uint*, *long*, *ulong*, *ushort* or *object*
decimal	*object*
double	*object*
float	*double* or *object*
int	*decimal*, *double*, *float*, *long* or *object*
uint	*decimal*, *double*, *float*, *long*, *ulong* or *object*
long	*decimal*, *double*, *float* or *object*
ulong	*decimal*, *double*, *float* or *object*
short	*decimal*, *double*, *float*, *int*, *long* or *object*
ushort	*decimal*, *double*, *float*, *int*, *uint*, *long*, *ulong* or *object*

Fig. 6.6   Allowed implicit conversions.

The conversion rules apply to expressions containing values of two or more data types (also referred to as *mixed-type expressions*) and to primitive data-type values passed as arguments to methods. C# converts the type of each value in a mixed-type expression to the "highest" type in the expression. C# creates a temporary copy of each value and uses it in the expression—the original values remain unchanged. A method argument's type can be promoted to any "higher" type. Figure 6.6 can be used to determine the highest type in an expression. For each type in the left column, the corresponding types in the right column are considered to be of a higher type. For instance, types **decimal**, **double**, **float**, **long** and **object** are higher than type **int**.

Converting values to lower types can result in data loss. In cases where information could be lost through conversion, the compiler requires the programmer to use a cast to force the conversion to occur. For example, to invoke our **Square** method, which takes an integer parameter (Fig. 6.3) with the **double** variable **y**, the method call would be written as

```
int result = Square( ( int ) y );
```

This statement explicitly casts (converts) a copy of the value of **y** to an integer for use in method **Square**. Thus, if **y**'s value is **4.5**, method **Square** returns **16**, not **20.25**.

Common Programming Error 6.11

*When performing a narrowing conversion (e.g., **double** to **int**), converting a primitive-data-type value to another primitive data type may result in loss of data.*

6.7 C# Namespaces

As we have seen, C# contains many predefined classes that are grouped into namespaces. Collectively we refer to this preexisting code as the Framework Class Library. The actual code for the classes is located in **.dll** files called assemblies.

Throughout the text, **using** statements specify the namespaces we use in each program. For example, a program includes the statement

```
using System;
```

to tell the compiler that we are using the **System** namespace. This **using** statement allows us to write **Console.WriteLine** rather than **System.Console.WriteLine** throughout the program. To use a class in a particular namespace, we must add a reference to the appropriate assembly (demonstrated in Section 3.2). Assembly references for namespace **System** are added automatically—other assemblies must be added explicitly.

We use a large number of the FCL classes in this book. Figure 6.7 lists a subset of the many namespaces in the FCL and provides a brief description of each. We use classes from these and other namespaces throughout the book.

Namespace	Description
System	Contains essential classes and data types (such as *int*, *double*, *char*, etc.). Implicitly referenced by all C# programs.
System.Data	Contains classes that form ADO .NET, used for database access and manipulation.
System.Drawing	Contains classes used for drawing and graphics.
System.IO	Contains classes for the input and output of data, such as with files.
System.Threading	Contains classes for multithreading, used to specify that multiple actions can occur concurrently.
System.Windows.Forms	Contains classes used to create graphical user interfaces.
System.Xml	Contains classes used to process XML data.

Fig. 6.7   Namespaces in the Framework Class Library.

The set of namespaces available in the FCL is quite large (at the time of this book's publication, there were approximately 100 namespaces including hundreds of classes). In addition to the namespaces summarized in Fig. 6.7, the FCL includes namespaces for complex graphics, advanced graphical user interfaces, printing, advanced networking, security, multimedia, accessibility (for people with disabilities) and many more. For an overview of the namespaces in the FCL, look up "Class Library" in the help index.

6.8 Value Types and Reference Types

In the next section, we will discuss passing arguments to methods by value and by reference. To understand this, we first need to make a distinction between data types that are *value types* and data types that are *reference types*. A variable of a value type contains data of that type. A variable of a reference type, in contrast, contains the address of the location in memory where the data for that variable is stored. Value types normally represent single pieces of data, such as **int** or **bool** values. Reference types, however, refer to objects, which can contain many individual pieces of data. We discuss objects in detail in Chapters 8 and 9 (Object-Based Programming, and Object-Oriented Programming: Inheritance).

C# includes built-in value types and reference types. The built-in value types are the *integral types* (**sbyte**, **byte**, **char**, **short**, **ushort**, **int**, **uint**, **long** and **ulong**), the *floating-point types* (**float** and **double**) and the types **decimal** and **bool**. The built-in reference types are **string** and **object**. Programmers can create new value types and reference types; the reference types include classes (Chapter 8) and delegates (Chapter 11).

The table in Fig. 6.5 lists the primitive data types; these are often used as building blocks for more complicated types. C#, like its predecessor languages C and C++, C# requires all variables to have a type before they can be used in a program. For this reason, C# is referred to as a *strongly typed language*.

In C and C++ programs, programmers frequently must write separate program versions to support different computer platforms because the primitive data types are not guaranteed to be identical from computer to computer. For example, an **int** value on one computer might occupy 16 bits (2 bytes) of memory, whereas an **int** value on another computer might occupy 32 bits (4 bytes) of memory. In C#, **int** values are always 32 bits (4 bytes).

Portability Tip 6.1

Primitive data types in C# are portable across all platforms that support C#.

Each data type in the table is listed with its size in bits (there are 8 bits to a byte) and its range of values. The designers of C# wanted code to be portable; therefore, they chose to use internationally recognized standards for both character formats (Unicode®) and floating-point numbers (IEEE 754). Unicode® is discussed more in Appendix F.

6.9 Passing Arguments: Pass-by-Value vs. Pass-by-Reference

Two ways to pass arguments to methods in many programming languages are *pass-by-value* and *pass-by-reference*. When an argument is passed by value, the called method receives a *copy* of the argument's value.

When an argument is passed using pass-by-reference, the caller gives the method the ability to access and modify the caller's original data directly. Pass-by-reference can improve performance because it eliminates the overhead of copying large data items such as objects; however, pass-by-reference can weaken security because the called method can modify the caller's data.

Testing and Debugging Tip 6.2

With pass-by-value, changes to the called method's copy do not affect the original variable's value. This prevents some possible side effects that hinder the development of correct and reliable software systems.

Software Engineering Observation 6.9

*When returning information from a method via a **return** statement, value-type variables always are returned by value (i.e., a copy is returned), and reference-type variables are always returned by reference (i.e., a reference to the object is returned).*

To pass an object reference into a method, simply specify the reference name in the method call. Then, in the method body, reference the object using the parameter name. This refers to the original object in memory, which allows the called method to access the original object in the caller directly.

In Section 6.8, we discussed the difference between value types and reference types. At this point, the reader can understand one of the major differences between the two data types—value-type variables are passed to methods by value, whereas reference-type variables are passed to methods by reference. What if the programmer would like to pass a value type by reference? To do this, C# provides the ***ref*** and ***out*** *keywords*. The **ref** keyword specifies that a value-type argument should be passed by reference, which enables the called method to modify the original variable. This keyword is used for variables that already have been initialized. The **out** keyword specifies an output parameter, which is an argument to which the called method will assign a value. Normally, when a method receives an uninitialized value, the compiler generates an error. Preceding the parameter with keyword **out** specifies that the called method will initialize the variable and prevents the compiler from generating an error message for the uninitialized variable. Figure 6.8 demonstrates using the **ref** and **out** keywords to manipulate integer values.[1]

```
1    // Fig. 6.8: RefOutTest.cs
2    // Demonstrating ref and out parameters.
3
4    using System;
5    using System.Drawing;
6    using System.Collections;
7    using System.ComponentModel;
8    using System.Windows.Forms;
9    using System.Data;
10
11   public class RefOutTest : System.Windows.Forms.Form
12   {
13       private System.Windows.Forms.Button showOutputButton;
14       private System.Windows.Forms.Label outputLabel;
```

Fig. 6.8   Demonstrating **ref** and **out** parameters. (Part 1 of 3.)

---

1. In Chapter 7 we discuss passing reference-type arguments by value and by reference.

```
15
16        // Visual Studio .NET generated code
17
18        // main entry point for the application
19        [STAThread]
20        static void Main()
21        {
22            Application.Run( new RefOutTest() );
23        }
24
25        // x passed in by value and method cannot modify
26        // original variable's value
27        void Square( int x )
28        {
29            x = x * x;
30
31            outputLabel.Text +=
32                "Value of variable within Square, " +
33                "after calculation: " + x + "\n";
34        }
35
36        // x passed in by reference and method modifies
37        // original variable's value
38        void SquareRef( ref int x )
39        {
40            x = x * x;
41
42            outputLabel.Text +=
43                "Value of variable within SquareRef, " +
44                "after calculation: " + x + "\n";
45        }
46
47        // x passed in as out parameter and method initializes
48        // and modifies original variable's value
49        void SquareOut( out int x )
50        {
51            x = 6;       // initialize
52            x = x * x;   // modify
53
54            outputLabel.Text +=
55                "Value of variable within SquareOut, " +
56                "after calculation: " + x + "\n";
57        }
58
59        private void showOutputButton_Click(
60            object sender, System.EventArgs e )
61        {
62            int y = 5; // create new int and initialize to 5
63            int z;       // declare z, but do not initialize it
64
65            // display original value of y
66            outputLabel.Text =
67                "Value of y before calling SquareRef: " + y + "\n";
```

Fig. 6.8   Demonstrating **ref** and **out** parameters. (Part 2 of 3.)

```
68
69              // use ref keyword to pass y by reference
70              SquareRef( ref y );
71              outputLabel.Text +=
72                 "Value of y after exiting SquareRef: " + y + "\n";
73
74              // display original value of z
75              outputLabel.Text +=
76                 "\nValue of z before calling SquareOut: " +
77                 "uninitialized\n";
78
79              // z not yet initialized; must use
80              // out keyword to pass z by reference
81              SquareOut( out z );
82              outputLabel.Text +=
83                 "Value of z after exiting SquareOut: " + z + "\n";
84
85              outputLabel.Text +=
86                 "_____\n\n";
87
88              // display value of y
89              outputLabel.Text +=
90                 "Value of y before calling Square: " + y + "\n";
91
92              // pass y by value
93              Square( y );
94              outputLabel.Text +=
95                 "Value of y after exiting Square: " + y + "\n";
96
97              // display value of z
98              outputLabel.Text +=
99                 "\nValue of z before calling Square: " + z + "\n";
100
101             // pass z by value
102             Square( z );
103             outputLabel.Text +=
104                "Value of z after exiting Square: " + z + "\n";
105
106      } // end method showOutputButton_Click
107
108 } // end class RefOutTest
```

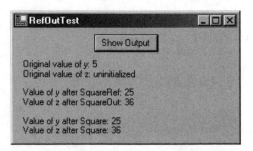

Fig. 6.8   Demonstrating **ref** and **out** parameters. (Part 3 of 3.)

This program contains three methods to calculate the square of an integer. Method **Square**, defined on lines 27–34, multiplies its argument by itself and assigns that new value to **x**. The original value passed is a value-type integer, and is therefore unchanged after the method executes. Method **SquareRef**, defined on lines 38–45, performs the same action. **SquareRef** receives its argument as a **ref int**, specifying that **x** is an integer that is passed by reference to the method. As a result, the assignment on line 40 modifies the original argument's value in the caller, rather than a copy of that value. Method **SquareOut** (defined on lines 49–57) also calculates the square of an integer, but initializes **x** to **6** on line 51. **SquareOut** receives its argument as an **out int**, which indicates that **x** is an integer variable that is to be passed by reference, and that may be passed to the method in an uninitialized state.

Method **showOutputButton_Click** (lines 59–106) is an event handler that invokes methods **SquareRef**, **SquareOut** and **Square** when the user clicks the **Show Output** button. This method begins by initializing **y** to **5** and declaring (but not initializing) **z**. Lines 70 and 81 call methods **SquareRef** and **SquareOut**. Notice the syntax used for passing **y** and **z**—in each case, we precede the argument either with **ref** or with **out**, as specified in the method header. If the proper keyword is left out, a syntax error occurs. Notice that **y** has been changed to **25** and **z** has been set to **36**. On lines 93 and 102 we call method **Square**, passing values **y (25)** and **z (36)**. Arguments **y** and **z** both are passed by value—only copies of their values are passed to the method. As a result, the values of **y** and **z** remain **25** and **36** after the method call. The output displays the values of **y** and **z** before, during and after each method call.

Common Programming Error 6.12

*The **ref** and **out** arguments in a method call must match those specified in the method definition; otherwise, a syntax error occurs.*

Software Engineering Observation 6.10

By default, C# does not allow the programmer to choose whether to pass each argument by value or by reference. Value-type variables are passed by value. Objects are not passed to methods; rather, references to objects are passed to methods. The references themselves are passed by value. When a method receives a reference to an object, the method can manipulate the object directly, but the reference value cannot be changed (e.g., to refer to a new object).

6.10 Random-Number Generation

We now take a brief and hopefully entertaining diversion into a popular programming application—simulation and game playing. In this section and the next, we develop a nicely structured game-playing program that includes multiple methods. The program uses most of the control structures we have studied to this point and also introduces several new concepts.

There is something in the air of a gambling casino that invigorates every type of person—from the high rollers at the plush mahogany-and-felt craps tables to the quarter poppers at the one-armed bandits. It is the *element of chance,* the possibility that luck will convert a pocketful of money into a mountain of wealth. The element of chance can be introduced into computer applications with the ***Random*** class (located in namespace **System**).

Consider the following statements:

```
Random randomObject = new Random();
int randomNumber = randomObject.Next();
```

The **Next** method generates a positive **int** value between zero and the constant **Int32.MaxValue** (the value 2,147,483,647). If **Next** produces values at random, every value in this range has an equal *chance* (or *probability*) of being chosen when **Next** is called. Note that values returned by **Next** are actually *pseudo-random numbers*—a sequence of values produced by a complex mathematical calculation. A *seed* value is required in this mathematical calculation. When we create our **Random** object, we use the current time of day as the seed. A particular seed value always produces the same series of random numbers. Programmers commonly use the current time of day as a seed value, since it changes each second and, therefore produces different random-number sequences each time the program executes.

The range of values produced directly by **Next** often is different from the range of values required in a particular application. For example, a program that simulates coin-tossing might require only 0 for "heads" and 1 for "tails." A program that simulates rolling a six-sided die would require random integers in the range 1–6. A video-game program that randomly predicts the next type of spaceship (out of four possibilities) that will fly across the horizon might require random integers in the range 1–4.

The one-argument version of method **Next** returns values in the range from 0 up to (but not including) the value of that argument. For example,

```
randomValue = randomObject.Next( 6 );
```

produces values from 0–5, inclusive. This is called *scaling*, because the range of values produced has been scaled down from over two billion to only six. The number 6 is the *scaling factor*. The two-argument version of method **Next** allows us to *shift* and scale the range of numbers. For example, we can use method **Next** as follows

```
randomValue = randomObject.Next( 1, 7 );
```

to produce integers in the range from 1–6, inclusive. In this case, we have shifted the numbers to produce a range from 1 up to (but not including) 7.

The Windows application of Fig. 6.9 simulates 20 rolls of a six-sided die and shows the integer value of each roll. The dice-rolling simulation begins when the user clicks the **Show Ouput** button, which invokes the **showOutputButton_Click** event handler (lines 24–44). The **for** loop on lines 32–43 repeatedly invokes method **Next** of class **Random** to simulate rolling the die. Lines 37–38 append the value rolled to **outputLabel**'s **Text** property. After every five rolls, line 42 appends a newline character to make the output more readable.

```
1   // Fig. 6.9: RandomInt.cs
2   // Generating random integer values.
3   using System;
4   using System.Drawing;
5   using System.Collections;
6   using System.ComponentModel;
7   using System.Windows.Forms;
8   using System.Data;
9
```

Fig. 6.9   Random integers in the range 1–6. (Part 1 of 2.)

```
10   public class RandomInt : System.Windows.Forms.Form
11   {
12      private System.Windows.Forms.Button showOutputButton;
13      private System.Windows.Forms.Label outputLabel;
14
15      // Visual Studio .NET generated code
16
17      // the main entry point for the application
18      [STAThread]
19      static void Main()
20      {
21         Application.Run( new RandomInt() );
22      }
23
24      private void showOutputButton_Click( object sender,
25         System.EventArgs e )
26      {
27         Random randomInteger = new Random();
28
29         outputLabel.Text = "";
30
31         // loop 20 times
32         for ( int counter = 1; counter <= 20; counter++ )
33         {
34            // pick random integer between 1 and 6
35            int nextValue = randomInteger.Next( 1, 7 );
36
37            outputLabel.Text +=
38               nextValue + "    "; // append value to output
39
40            // add newline after every 5 values
41            if ( counter % 5 == 0 )
42               outputLabel.Text += "\n";
43         }
44      }
45   }
```

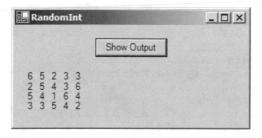

Fig. 6.9   Random integers in the range 1–6. (Part 2 of 2.)

The Windows application of Fig. 6.10 simulates rolls of four dice. The program enables the user to click a button that "rolls" four dice at a time and displays an image of each die in the window. The next example (Fig. 6.11) uses many of this example's features to demonstrate that the numbers generated by **Next** occur with approximately equal likelihood.

Method **DisplayDie** (lines 39–47) invokes **Random** method **Next** to simulate a roll of a die (line 41) and loads an image that corresponds to the value rolled (lines 44–46). Line 44 uses class **Label**'s **Image** property to display the die. Notice that we specify which image will be displayed by invoking method *FromFile* of class **Image**, which specifies the location of the file on disk that contains the image. Each click of the button displays four images that represent the four new values of the dice. Note that the user must click **roll-Button** at least once to display the dice. **Directory** method **GetCurrentDirectory** (line 45) returns the path of the folder in which the program is executing. If you run the program from Visual Studio .NET, this will be the **bin\Debug** directory in the project's directory. The die images must be in this folder for the example to operate properly. These images are placed in the proper folders with the book's examples.

```csharp
1    // Fig. 6.10: RollDie.cs
2    // Using random number generation to simulate dice rolling.
3    using System;
4    using System.Drawing;
5    using System.Collections;
6    using System.ComponentModel;
7    using System.Windows.Forms;
8    using System.Data;
9    using System.IO;    // enables reading data from files
10
11   public class RollDie : System.Windows.Forms.Form
12   {
13      private System.Windows.Forms.Button rollButton;
14
15      private System.Windows.Forms.Label dieLabel2;
16      private System.Windows.Forms.Label dieLabel1;
17      private System.Windows.Forms.Label dieLabel3;
18      private System.Windows.Forms.Label dieLabel4;
19
20      private Random randomNumber = new Random();
21
22      // Visual Studio .NET generated code
23
24      // method called when rollButton clicked,
25      // passes labels to another method
26      protected void rollButton_Click(
27         object sender, System.EventArgs e )
28      {
29         // pass the labels to a method that will
30         // randomly assign a face to each die
31         DisplayDie( dieLabel1 );
32         DisplayDie( dieLabel2 );
33         DisplayDie( dieLabel3 );
34         DisplayDie( dieLabel4 );
35
36      } // end rollButton_Click
37
```

Fig. 6.10   Rolling dice in a Windows application (Part 1 of 2.).

```
38         // determines image to be displayed by current die
39         public void DisplayDie( Label dieLabel )
40         {
41            int face = randomNumber.Next( 1, 7 );
42
43            // displays image specified by filename
44            dieLabel.Image = Image.FromFile(
45               Directory.GetCurrentDirectory() +
46               "\\images\\die" + face + ".png" );
47         }
48
49         // main entry point for application
50         [STAThread]
51         static void Main()
52         {
53            Application.Run( new RollDie() );
54         }
55
56   } // end class RollDie
```

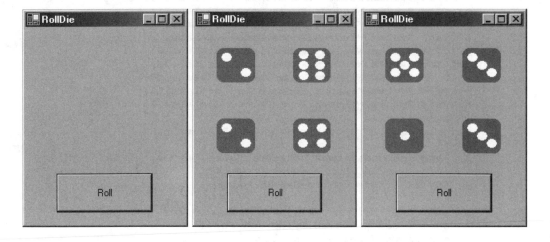

Fig. 6.10   Rolling dice in a Windows application (Part 2 of 2.).

To show that class **Random** produces numbers with approximately equal likelihood, let us modify the program in Fig. 6.10 to keep some simple statistics. The Windows application of Fig. 6.11 provides a **Roll** button for rolling the dice and a **TextBox** that displays the frequencies for each value rolled. The program output shows the results of clicking **Roll** 10 times.

When the user clicks the **Roll** button, the program invokes the **rollButton_Click** event handler on lines 38–73. This event handler invokes method **DisplayDie** for each of the 12 dice that the program simulates (lines 43–54). Lines 56–71 then calculate the frequencies for each die and displays the results by appending the information to **display-TextBox**'s **Text** property. Method **displayDie** (lines 76–113) simulates a die roll (line 78), loads the appropriate **Image** and increments the frequency count for the rolled value.

```
1   // Fig. 6.11: RollDie2.cs
2   // Rolling 12 dice with frequency chart.
3   using System;
4   using System.Drawing;
5   using System.Collections;
6   using System.ComponentModel;
7   using System.Windows.Forms;
8   using System.Data;
9   using System.IO;
10
11  public class RollDie2 : System.Windows.Forms.Form
12  {
13     private System.Windows.Forms.Button rollButton;
14
15     private System.Windows.Forms.RichTextBox displayTextBox;
16
17     private System.Windows.Forms.Label dieLabel1;
18     private System.Windows.Forms.Label dieLabel2;
19     private System.Windows.Forms.Label dieLabel3;
20     private System.Windows.Forms.Label dieLabel4;
21     private System.Windows.Forms.Label dieLabel5;
22     private System.Windows.Forms.Label dieLabel6;
23     private System.Windows.Forms.Label dieLabel7;
24     private System.Windows.Forms.Label dieLabel8;
25     private System.Windows.Forms.Label dieLabel9;
26     private System.Windows.Forms.Label dieLabel10;
27     private System.Windows.Forms.Label dieLabel11;
28     private System.Windows.Forms.Label dieLabel12;
29
30     private Random randomNumber = new Random();
31
32     private int ones, twos, threes, fours, fives, sixes;
33
34     // Visual Studio .NET generated code
35
36     // simulates roll by calling DisplayDie for
37     // each label and displaying the results
38     protected void rollButton_Click(
39        object sender, System.EventArgs e )
40     {
41        // pass the labels to a method that will
42        // randomly assign a face to each die
43        DisplayDie( dieLabel1 );
44        DisplayDie( dieLabel2 );
45        DisplayDie( dieLabel3 );
46        DisplayDie( dieLabel4 );
47        DisplayDie( dieLabel5 );
48        DisplayDie( dieLabel6 );
49        DisplayDie( dieLabel7 );
50        DisplayDie( dieLabel8 );
51        DisplayDie( dieLabel9 );
52        DisplayDie( dieLabel10 );
```

Fig. 6.11   Simulating rolling 12 six-sided dice. (Part 1 of 3.)

```
53          DisplayDie( dieLabel11 );
54          DisplayDie( dieLabel12 );
55
56          double total = ones + twos + threes + fours + fives + sixes;
57
58          // display the current frequency values
59          displayTextBox.Text = "Face\t\tFrequency\tPercent\n1\t\t" +
60             ones + "\t\t" +
61             String.Format( "{0:F2}", ones / total * 100 ) +
62             "%\n2\t\t" + twos + "\t\t" +
63             String.Format( "{0:F2}", twos / total * 100 ) +
64             "%\n3\t\t" + threes + "\t\t" +
65             String.Format( "{0:F2}", threes / total * 100 ) +
66             "%\n4\t\t" + fours + "\t\t" +
67             String.Format( "{0:F2}", fours / total * 100 ) +
68             "%\n5\t\t" + fives + "\t\t" +
69             String.Format( "{0:F2}", fives / total * 100 ) +
70             "%\n6\t\t" + sixes + "\t\t" +
71             String.Format( "{0:F2}", sixes / total * 100 ) + "%";
72
73       } // end rollButton_Click
74
75       // display the current die, and modify frequency values
76       public void DisplayDie( Label dieLabel )
77       {
78          int face = randomNumber.Next( 1, 7 );
79
80          dieLabel.Image = Image.FromFile(
81             Directory.GetCurrentDirectory() +
82             "\\images\\die" + face + ".png" );
83
84          // add one to frequency of current face
85          switch ( face )
86          {
87             case 1:
88                ones++;
89                break;
90
91             case 2:
92                twos++;
93                break;
94
95             case 3:
96                threes++;
97                break;
98
99             case 4:
100                fours++;
101                break;
102
103             case 5:
104                fives++;
105                break;
```

Fig. 6.11 Simulating rolling 12 six-sided dice. (Part 2 of 3.)

```
106
107              case 6:
108                  sixes++;
109                  break;
110
111          } // end switch
112
113      } // end DisplayDie
114
115      // main entry point for the application
116      [STAThread]
117      static void Main()
118      {
119          Application.Run( new RollDie2() );
120      }
121
122  } // end of class RollDie2
```

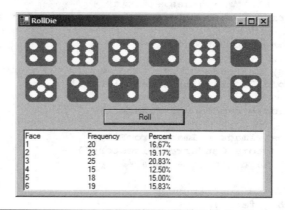

Fig. 6.11   Simulating rolling 12 six-sided dice. (Part 3 of 3.)

As the program output demonstrates, over a large number of die rolls, each of the possible faces from 1 through 6 appears with approximately equal likelihood (i.e., about one-sixth of the time). After studying arrays in Chapter 7, Arrays, we will show how to replace the entire **switch** structure in this program with a single-line statement.

6.11 Example: Game of Chance

One of the most popular games of chance is a dice game known as "craps," played in casinos and back alleys throughout the world. The rules of the game are straightforward:

> *A player rolls two dice. Each die has six faces. Each face contains 1, 2, 3, 4, 5 or 6 spots. After the dice have come to rest, the sum of the spots on the two upward faces is calculated. If the sum is 7 or 11 on the first throw, the player wins. If the sum is 2, 3 or 12 on the first throw (called "craps"), the player loses (i.e., the "house" wins). If the sum is 4, 5, 6, 8, 9 or 10 on the first throw, that sum becomes the player's "point." To win, players must continue rolling the dice until they "make their point" (i.e., roll their point value). The player loses by rolling a 7 before making the point.*

Figure 6.12 simulates the game of craps with a simple graphical user interface.

Notice that the player rolls two dice on each roll. When executing the application, clicking the **Play** button begins the game and makes the first roll. The form displays the results of each roll. The screen captures show the execution of several games.

```
1    // Fig. 6.12: CrapsGame.cs
2    // Simulating the game of Craps.
3    using System;
4    using System.Drawing;
5    using System.Collections;
6    using System.ComponentModel;
7    using System.Windows.Forms;
8    using System.Data;
9    using System.IO;
10
11   public class CrapsGame : System.Windows.Forms.Form
12   {
13      private System.Windows.Forms.Button rollButton;
14      private System.Windows.Forms.Button playButton;
15
16      int myPoint; // player's point value
17      private System.Windows.Forms.PictureBox pointFirstDieImage;
18      private System.Windows.Forms.Label statusLabel;
19      private System.Windows.Forms.PictureBox firstDieImage;
20      private System.Windows.Forms.PictureBox pointSecondDieImage;
21      private System.Windows.Forms.PictureBox secondDieImage;
22      private System.Windows.Forms.GroupBox pointGroupBox;
23      int myDie1; // value of first die
24      int myDie2; // value of second die
25
26      public enum DiceNames
27      {
28         SNAKE_EYES = 2,
29         TREY = 3,
30         YO_LEVEN = 11,
31         BOX_CARS = 12,
32      }
33
34      // Visual Studio .NET generated code
35
36      // simulate next roll and result of that roll
37      protected void rollButton_Click(
38         object sender, System.EventArgs e )
39      {
40         int sum = rollDice();
41
42         if ( sum == myPoint )
43         {
44            statusLabel.Text = "You Win!!!";
45            rollButton.Enabled = false;
46            playButton.Enabled = true;
47         }
```

Fig. 6.12   Program to simulate the game of craps. (Part 1 of 4.)

```
48            else
49              if ( sum == 7 )
50              {
51                  statusLabel.Text = "Sorry. You lose.";
52                  rollButton.Enabled = false;
53                  playButton.Enabled = true;
54              }
55
56      } // end rollButton_Click
57
58      // simulate first roll and result of that roll
59      protected void playButton_Click(
60          object sender, System.EventArgs e )
61      {
62          pointGroupBox.Text = "Point";
63          statusLabel.Text = "";
64          pointFirstDieImage.Image = null;
65          pointSecondDieImage.Image = null;
66
67          myPoint = 0;
68          int sum = rollDice();
69
70          switch ( sum )
71          {
72              case 7:
73              case ( int ) DiceNames.YO_LEVEN:
74                  rollButton.Enabled = false;  // disable Roll button
75                  statusLabel.Text = "You Win!!!";
76                  break;
77
78              case ( int ) DiceNames.SNAKE_EYES:
79              case ( int ) DiceNames.TREY:
80              case ( int ) DiceNames.BOX_CARS:
81                  rollButton.Enabled = false;
82                  statusLabel.Text = "Sorry. You lose.";
83                  break;
84
85              default:
86                  myPoint = sum;
87                  pointGroupBox.Text = "Point is " + sum;
88                  statusLabel.Text = "Roll Again";
89                  displayDie( pointFirstDieImage, myDie1 );
90                  displayDie( pointSecondDieImage, myDie2 );
91                  playButton.Enabled = false;
92                  rollButton.Enabled = true;
93                  break;
94
95          } // end switch
96
97      } // end playButton_Click
98
```

Fig. 6.12 Program to simulate the game of craps. (Part 2 of 4.)

```
99      // display an image for the specified face
100     private void DisplayDie( PictureBox dieImage, int face )
101     {
102         dieImage.Image = Image.FromFile(
103             Directory.GetCurrentDirectory() +
104             "\\images\\die" + face + ".png" );
105     }
106
107     // simulates rolling two dice
108     private int RollDice()
109     {
110         int die1, die2, dieSum;
111         Random randomNumber = new Random();
112
113         die1 = randomNumber.Next( 1, 7 );
114         die2 = randomNumber.Next( 1, 7 );
115
116         displayDie( firstDieImage, die1 );
117         displayDie( secondDieImage, die2 );
118
119         myDie1 = die1;
120         myDie2 = die2;
121         dieSum = die1 + die2;
122         return dieSum;
123
124     } // end method rollDice
125
126     // main entry point for application
127     [STAThread]
128     static void Main()
129     {
130         Application.Run( new CrapsGame() );
131     }
132
133 } // end class CrapsGame
```

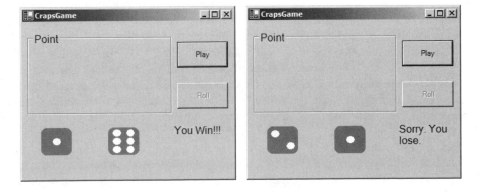

Fig. 6.12 Program to simulate the game of craps. (Part 3 of 4.)

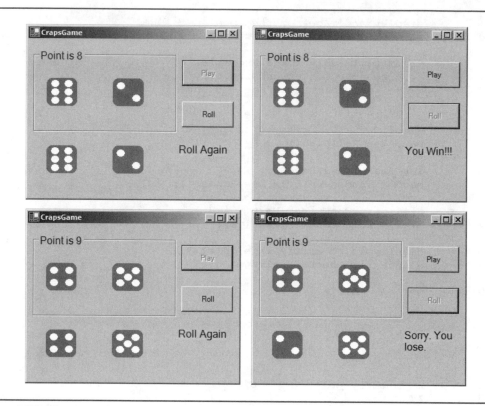

Fig. 6.12 Program to simulate the game of craps. (Part 4 of 4.)

Before its method definitions, the program includes several declarations, including an *enumeration* on lines 26–32. An enumeration is a value type that contains a set of constant values and is created using the keyword **enum**. This enumeration is a convenient way of referring to constant values used throughout the program. We have used the identifiers **SNAKE_EYES**, **TREY**, **YO_LEVEN** and **BOX_CARS**, to represent significant values in craps. Using these identifiers makes the program more readable. Additionally, if we need to change one of these values, we can modify the enumeration instead of changing the values where they are used throughout the program.

This example introduces a new GUI component called a **GroupBox**, used in this example to display the user's point. A **GroupBox** is a container for other components and helps group components logically. Within the **GroupBox**, we add two **PictureBox**es to display our dice images. These are added, as with other components, by clicking **PictureBox** in the **ToolBox** and dragging this component within the borders of the **GroupBox**.

The **playButton_Click** event handler begins the game. Line 68 invokes method **RollDice** (defined on lines 108–124), which rolls the dice, displays the dice and returns their sum. Lines 70–95 use a **switch** structure to determine whether the player won, lost or established a point value. If the player won by rolling a 7 or 11, line 74 disables **RollButton** to prevent the player from rolling the dice again. Line 75 displays a message to indicate that the user won. If the player lost by rolling **SNAKE_EYES**, **TREY** or **BOX_CARS** (i.e., 2, 3 or 12), line 82 displays a message to indicate that the user lost. Otherwise, the default case (lines 85–93) sets the player's point, displays the dice in **pointGroupBox**, enables **RollButton** and disables **playButton**. Notice that for many of the **case**s, we cast the enumeration values to type **int**. Although each enumeration value is assigned an integer value on lines 26–32, each value is considered to be of **enum** type **DiceNames**, and therefore must be cast to **int** for use in the **switch** structure, which requires constant integral expressions.

The **rollButton_Click** event handler's task is to roll the dice and determine if the player won by making the point value or lost by rolling 7. Line 40 calls method **Roll-Dice**. Lines 42–54 in method **rollButton_Click** analyze the roll. Depending on the value of the roll, the buttons **rollButton** and **playButton** will become either disabled or enabled. This is done by setting the **Enabled** property to **true** or **false**.

6.12 Duration of Variables

The attributes of variables include name, type, size and value. Each variable in a program has additional attributes, including *duration* and *scope*.

A variable's duration (also called its *lifetime*) is the period during which the variable exists in memory. Some variables exist briefly, some are created and destroyed repeatedly and others exist for the entire execution of a program.

A variable's *scope* is where the variable's identifier (i.e., name) can be referenced in a program. Some variables can be referenced throughout a program, while others can be referenced from limited portions of a program. This section discusses the duration of variables. Section 6.13 discusses the scope of identifiers.

Local variables in a method (i.e., parameters and variables declared in the method body) have *automatic duration*. Automatic duration variables are created when program control reaches their declaration; that is, they exist while the block in which they are declared is active, and they are destroyed when that block is exited. For the remainder of the book, we refer to variables of automatic duration as automatic variables, or local variables.

The instance variables of a class are initialized by the compiler if the programmer does not provide initial values. Variables of most primitive data types are initialized to zero, **bool** variables are initialized to **false** and references are initialized to **null**. Unlike instance variables of a class, automatic variables must be initialized by the programmer before they can be used.

Common Programming Error 6.13

Automatic variables must be initialized before their values are used in a method; otherwise, the compiler issues an error message.

Variables of *static duration* exist from the time at which the class that defines them is loaded into memory. These variables then last until the program terminates. Their storage is allocated and initialized when their classes are loaded into memory. Static-duration variable names exist when their classes are loaded into memory, but this does not mean that these identifiers necessarily can be used throughout the program—their scopes may be limited as we will see in the next section.

6.13 Scope Rules

The *scope* (sometimes called *declaration space*) of an identifier for a variable, reference or method is the portion of the program in which the identifier can be accessed. A local variable declared in a block can be used only in that block or in blocks nested within that block. We define the possible scopes for an identifier as *class scope* and *block scope*.

Members of a class have class scope and are visible in what is known as the *declaration space of a class*. Class scope begins at the opening left brace ({) of the class definition and terminates at the closing right brace (}). Class scope enables methods of a class to access all members defined in that class. In Chapter 8, Object-Based Programming, we see that **static** members are an exception to this rule. In a sense, all instance variables and methods of a class are *global* to the methods of the class in which they are defined (i.e., the methods can modify the instance variables directly and invoke other methods of the class).

Identifiers declared inside a block have block scope (*local-variable declaration space*). Block scope begins at the identifier's declaration and ends at the block's terminating right brace (}). Local variables of a method have block scope, as do method parameters, which are local variables of the method. Any block may contain variable declarations. When blocks are nested in a method's body, and a variable declared in an outer block has the same name as a variable declared in an inner block, an error is generated. On the other hand, if a local variable in a method has the same name as an instance variable, the value in the calling method (main program) is "hidden" until the method terminates execution. In Chapter 8, Object-Based Programming, we discuss how to access such "hidden" instance variables. The reader should note that block scope also applies to methods and **for** structures. With **for** structures, any variable declared in the initialization portion of the **for** header will be in scope only within that **for** structure.

> ### Testing and Debugging Tip 6.3
> *Avoid local-variable names that hide instance-variable names.*

The program in Fig. 6.13 demonstrates scoping issues with instance variables and local variables. Instance variable **x** (line 15) is initialized to **1**. This instance variable is hidden in any block (or method) that declares a local variable named **x**. The **showOutputButton_Click** event handler (lines 47–63) declares a local variable **x** and initializes it to **5** (line 50). Lines 52–53 display the value of this local variable to show that instance variable **x** (with value 1) is "hidden" in method **showOutputButton_Click**.

The program defines two other methods—**MethodA** and **MethodB**—that take no arguments and return nothing. The program calls each method twice from method **Scoping**. **MethodA** defines local variable **x** (line 21) and initializes it to **25**. Each call to **MethodA** displays the variable's value in **outputLabel**, increments the variable and displays it again before exiting the method. Each call to **MethodA** recreates automatic variable **x** and initializes it to **25**. Method **MethodB** does not declare any variables. Therefore, when it refers to variable **x**, the instance variable **x** is used. Each call to **MethodB** displays the instance variable in **outputLabel**, multiplies it by **10** (line 40) and displays it again before exiting the method. The next time method **MethodB** is called, the instance variable begins with its modified value, **10**. After the calls to **MethodA** and **MethodB**, the program again displays the local variable **x** in method **showOutputButton_Click** to show that none of the method calls modified this specific variable **x**, as the methods all referred to variables in other scopes.

```
1   // Fig. 6.13: Scoping.cs
2   // Demonstrating scope of local and instance variables.
3   using System;
4   using System.Drawing;
5   using System.Collections;
6   using System.ComponentModel;
7   using System.Windows.Forms;
8   using System.Data;
9
10  public class Scoping : System.Windows.Forms.Form
11  {
12     private System.Windows.Forms.Label outputLabel;
13     private System.Windows.Forms.Button showOutputButton;
14
15     public int x = 1; // instance variable
16
17     // Visual Studio .NET generated code
18
19     public void MethodA()
20     {
21        int x = 25;     // initialized each time a is called
22
23        outputLabel.Text = outputLabel.Text +
24           "\n\nlocal x in MethodA is " + x +
25           " after entering MethodA";
26
27        ++x; // increment local variable x
28
29        outputLabel.Text = outputLabel.Text +
30           "\nlocal x in MethodA is " + x +
31           " before exiting MethodA";
32     }
33
34     public void MethodB()
35     {
36        outputLabel.Text = outputLabel.Text +
37           "\n\ninstance variable x is " + x +
38           " on entering MethodB";
39
40        x *= 10;
41
42        outputLabel.Text = outputLabel.Text +
43           "\ninstance varable x is " + x +
44           " on exiting MethodB";
45     }
46
47     private void showOutputButton_Click( object sender,
48        System.EventArgs e )
49     {
50        int x = 5; // local x in method showOutputButton_Click
51
52        outputLabel.Text =
53           "local x in method showOutputButton_Click is " + x;
```

Fig. 6.13 Scoping. (Part 1 of 2.)

```
54
55          MethodA();    // MethodA has automatic local x;
56          MethodB();    // MethodB uses instance variable x
57          MethodA();    // MethodA creates new automatic local x
58          MethodB();    // instance variable x retains its value
59
60          outputLabel.Text = outputLabel.Text + "\n\n" +
61             "local x in method showOutputButton_Click is " + x;
62
63       }  // end method showOutputButton_Click
64
65       // main entry point for the application
66       [STAThread]
67       static void Main()
68       {
69          Application.Run( new Scoping() );
70       }
71
72    } // end of class Scoping
```

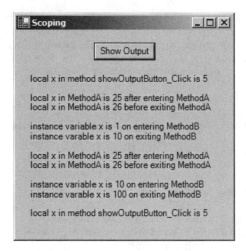

Fig. 6.13　Scoping. (Part 2 of 2.)

6.14 Recursion

The programs we have discussed generally are structured as methods that call one another in a hierarchical manner. For some problems, it is useful to have a method actually call itself. A *recursive method* is a method that calls itself either directly or indirectly through another method. Recursion is an important topic discussed at length in upper-level computer science courses. In this section and the next, we present two simple examples of recursion. We consider recursion conceptually first, then examine several programs containing recursive methods.

Recursive problem-solving approaches have a number of elements in common. A recursive method is called to solve a problem. The method actually knows how to solve only the simplest case(s), or *base case(s)*. If the method is called with a base case, the method returns a result. If the method is called with a more complex problem, the method divides the problem into two conceptual pieces—a piece that the method knows how to perform (base case) and a piece that the method does not know how to perform. To make recursion feasible, the latter piece must resemble the original problem, but be a slightly simpler or smaller version of it. The method invokes (calls) a fresh copy of itself to work on the smaller problem—this is referred to as a *recursive call*, or a *recursion step*. The recursion step also normally includes the keyword **return**, because its result will be combined with the portion of the problem that the method knew how to solve. Such a combination will form a result that will be passed back to the original caller.

The recursion step executes while the original call to the method is still "open" (i.e., it has not finished executing). The recursion step can result in many more recursive calls, as the method divides each new subproblem into two conceptual pieces. Each time the method calls itself with a slightly simpler version of the original problem, the sequence of smaller and smaller problems must converge on the base case, so the recursion can eventually terminate. At that point, the method recognizes the base case and returns a result to the previous copy of the method. A sequence of returns ensues up the line until the original method call returns the final result to the caller. As an example of these concepts, let us write a recursive program to perform a popular mathematical calculation.

The factorial of a nonnegative integer *n,* written *n!* (and pronounced "*n* factorial"), is the product

$$n \cdot (n - 1) \cdot (n - 2) \cdot \ldots \cdot 1$$

with 1! equal to 1, and 0! defined as 1. For example, 5! is the product $5 \cdot 4 \cdot 3 \cdot 2 \cdot 1$, which is equal to 120.

The factorial of an integer **number** greater than or equal to 0 can be calculated *iteratively* (nonrecursively) using **for** as follows:

```
factorial = 1;

for ( int counter = number; counter >= 1; counter-- )
    factorial *= counter;
```

We arrive at a recursive definition of the factorial method with the following relationship:

$$n! = n \cdot (n - 1)!$$

For example, 5! is clearly equal to 5 * 4!, as shown by the following:

$$5! = 5 \cdot 4 \cdot 3 \cdot 2 \cdot 1$$
$$5! = 5 \cdot (4 \cdot 3 \cdot 2 \cdot 1)$$
$$5! = 5 \cdot (4!)$$

A recursive evaluation of 5! would proceed as in Fig. 6.14. Figure 6.14a shows how the succession of recursive calls proceeds until 1! is evaluated to be 1, which terminates the recursion. Each rectangle represents a method call. Figure 6.14 shows the values returned from each recursive call to its caller until the final value is calculated and returned.

Figure 6.15 uses recursion to calculate and print the factorials of the integers 0–10. The recursive method **Factorial** (lines 17–24) first determines whether its terminating condition is **true** (i.e., **number** is less than or equal to **1**). If **number** is less than or equal to **1**, **factorial** returns **1**, no further recursion is necessary and the method

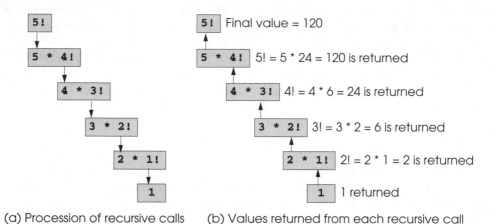

(a) Procession of recursive calls   (b) Values returned from each recursive call

Fig. 6.14   Recursive evaluation of 5!.

returns. If **number** is greater than 1, line 23 expresses the problem as the product of **number** and a recursive call to **Factorial**, evaluating the factorial of **number - 1**. Note that **Factorial(number - 1)** is a slightly simpler problem than the original calculation **Factorial(number)**.

```
1   // Fig. 6.15: FactorialTest.cs
2   // Calculating factorials with recursion.
3   using System;
4   using System.Drawing;
5   using System.Collections;
6   using System.ComponentModel;
7   using System.Windows.Forms;
8   using System.Data;
9
10  public class FactorialTest : System.Windows.Forms.Form
11  {
12     private System.Windows.Forms.Button showFactorialsButton;
13     private System.Windows.Forms.Label outputLabel;
14
15     // Visual Studio .NET generated code
16
17     public long Factorial( long number )
18     {
19        if ( number <= 1 )        // base case
20           return 1;
21
22        else
23           return number * Factorial( number - 1 );
24     }
25
```

Fig. 6.15   Calculating factorials with a recursive method. (Part 1 of 2.)

```
26      // main entry point for application
27      [STAThread]
28      static void Main()
29      {
30         Application.Run( new FactorialTest());
31      }
32
33      private void showFactorialsButton_Click( object sender,
34         System.EventArgs e )
35      {
36         outputLabel.Text = "";
37
38         for ( long i = 0; i <= 10; i++ )
39            outputLabel.Text += i + "! = " +
40               Factorial( i ) + "\n";
41      }
42
43   } // end class FactorialTest
```

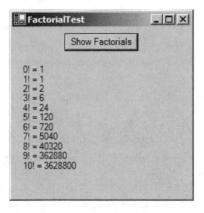

Fig. 6.15 Calculating factorials with a recursive method. (Part 2 of 2.)

Method **Factorial** receives a parameter of type **long** and returns a result of type **long**. As seen in Fig. 6.15, factorial values become large quickly. We choose data type **long** so the program can calculate factorials greater than 20!. Unfortunately, the **Factorial** method produces large values so quickly, even **long** does not help us print many more factorial values before the size of even the **long** variable is exceeded.

Factorials of larger numbers require the program to use **float** and **double** variables. This points to a weakness in most programming languages, namely, that the languages are not easily extended to handle the unique requirements of various applications. As we will see in our treatment of object-oriented programming beginning in Chapter 8, C# is an extensible language—programmers with unique requirements can extend the language with new data types (called classes). A programmer could create a **HugeInteger** class, for example, that would enable a program to calculate the factorials of arbitrarily large numbers.

 Common Programming Error 6.14

Forgetting to return a value from a recursive method can result in syntax and/or logic errors.

Common Programming Error 6.15

Omitting the base case or writing the recursion step so that it does not converge on the base case will cause infinite recursion, eventually exhausting memory. Infinite recursion is analogous to the problem of an infinite loop in an iterative (nonrecursive) solution.

6.15 Example Using Recursion: The Fibonacci Series

The Fibonacci series

$$0, 1, 1, 2, 3, 5, 8, 13, 21, \ldots$$

begins with 0 and 1 and has the property that each subsequent Fibonacci number is the sum of the previous two Fibonacci numbers.

The series occurs in nature and, in particular, describes a form of spiral. The ratio of successive Fibonacci numbers converges on a constant value of 1.618.... This number, too, repeatedly occurs in nature and has been called the *golden ratio* or the *golden mean*. Humans tend to find the golden mean aesthetically pleasing. Architects often design windows, rooms and buildings whose length and width are in the ratio of the golden mean. Postcards often are designed with a golden mean width-to-height ratio.

The recursive definition of the Fibonacci series is as follows:

Fibonacci(0) = 0
Fibonacci(1) = 1
Fibonacci(n) = *Fibonacci*(n – 1) + *Fibonacci*(n – 2)

Note that there are two base cases for the Fibonacci calculation—*fibonacci(0)* evaluates to 0, and *fibonacci(1)* evaluates to 1. The application in Fig. 6.16 calculates the ith Fibonacci number recursively using method **Fibonacci**. The user enters an integer in the text box, indicating the ith Fibonacci number to calculate, and clicks the **calculateButton** (which displays the text **Calculate Fibonacci**). Method **calculateButton_Click** (lines 22–29) executes in response to the user interface event and calls recursive method **Fibonacci** to calculate the specified Fibonacci number. In Fig. 6.16, the screen captures show the results of calculating several Fibonacci numbers.

```
1   // Fig. 6.16: FibonacciTest.cs
2   // Recursive fibonacci method.
3   using System;
4   using System.Drawing;
5   using System.Collections;
6   using System.ComponentModel;
7   using System.Windows.Forms;
8   using System.Data;
9
10  public class FibonacciTest : System.Windows.Forms.Form
11  {
12      private System.Windows.Forms.Button calculateButton;
13
14      private System.Windows.Forms.TextBox inputTextBox;
```

Fig. 6.16   Recursively generating Fibonacci numbers. (Part 1 of 2.)

```
15
16        private System.Windows.Forms.Label displayLabel;
17        private System.Windows.Forms.Label promptLabel;
18
19        // Visual Studio .NET generated code
20
21        // call Fibonacci and display results
22        protected void calculateButton_Click(
23            object sender, System.EventArgs e )
24        {
25            int number = Convert.ToInt32( inputTextBox.Text );
26            int fibonacciNumber = Fibonacci( number );
27            displayLabel.Text =
28                "Fibonacci Value is " + fibonacciNumber;
29        }
30
31        // calculates Fibonacci number
32        public int Fibonacci( int number )
33        {
34            if ( number == 0 || number == 1 )
35                return number;
36            else
37                return Fibonacci( number - 1 ) + Fibonacci( number - 2 );
38        }
39
40        // main entry point for application
41        [STAThread]
42        static void Main()
43        {
44            Application.Run( new FibonacciTest() );
45        }
46
47    } // end class FibonacciTest
```

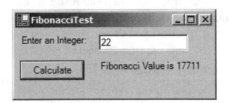

Fig. 6.16 Recursively generating Fibonacci numbers. (Part 2 of 2.)

The call to **Fibonacci** (line 26) from **calculateButton_Click** is not a recursive call, but all subsequent calls to **Fibonacci** from line 37 are recursive. Each time **Fibonacci** is invoked, it immediately tests for the base case—**number** equal to **0** or **1** (line 34). If this is true, **Fibonacci** returns **number** (*fibonacci(0)* is **0** and *fibonacci(1)* is **1**). Interestingly, if **number** is greater than **1**, the recursion step generates *two* recursive calls (line 37), each of which is for a slightly simpler problem than the original call to **Fibonacci**. Figure 6.17 shows how method **Fibonacci** would evaluate **Fibonacci(3)**.

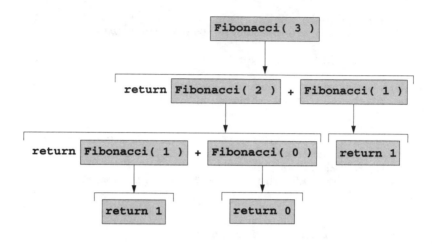

Fig. 6.17 Set of recursive calls to method **Fibonacci**.

This figure raises some issues about the order in which C# compilers will evaluate operands. Figure 6.17 shows that, during the evaluation of **Fibonacci(3)**, two recursive calls will be made—**Fibonacci(2)** and **Fibonacci(1)**. In what order will these calls be made? Most programmers assume the operands will be evaluated from left to right; in C# this is indeed true.

The C and C++ languages (on which many of C#'s features are based) do not specify the order in which the operands of most operators (including **+**) are evaluated. Therefore, in those languages, the programmer can make no assumption about the order in which these calls execute. The calls could, in fact, execute **Fibonacci(2)**, then **Fibonacci(1)**, or they could execute in the reverse order (**Fibonacci(1)**, then **Fibonacci(2)**). In this program and in most other programs, the final result would be the same. However, in some programs, the evaluation of an operand could have *side effects* that would affect the expression's final result. C# specifies that the order of evaluation of the operands is from left to right. Thus, the method calls are first **Fibonacci(2)**, then **Fibonacci(1)**.

 Good Programming Practice 6.4

Do not write expressions that depend on the order of evaluation of the operator's operands. Doing so often results in programs that are difficult to read, debug, modify and maintain.

A word of caution about using a recursive program to generate Fibonacci numbers: each invocation of the **Fibonacci** method that does not match one of the base cases (i.e., 0 or 1) results in two recursive calls to the **Fibonacci** method. This quickly results in many method invocations. Calculating the Fibonacci value of 20 using the program in Fig. 6.16 requires 21,891 calls to the **Fibonacci** method; calculating the Fibonacci value of 30 requires 2,692,537 calls to the **Fibonacci** method.

As the programmer tries larger values, each consecutive Fibonacci number that the program is asked to calculate results in a substantial increase in the number of calls to the **Fibonacci** method and hence in calculation time. For example, the Fibonacci value 31 requires 4,356,617 calls, and the Fibonacci value of 32 requires 7,049,155 calls. As you can see, the number of calls to Fibonacci increases quickly—1,664,080 additional calls between the Fibonacci values of 30 and 31, and 2,692,538 additional calls between the Fibonacci values of 31 and 32. This difference in number of calls made between the Fibonacci values of 31 and 32 is more than 1.5 times the difference for Fibonacci values of 30 and 31. Problems of this nature humble even the world's most powerful computers! In the field called *complexity theory*, computer scientists determine how hard algorithms work to do their jobs. Complexity issues are discussed in detail in the upper-level computer science curriculum course generally called "Algorithms."

Performance Tip 6.1

 Avoid Fibonacci-style recursive programs, which result in an exponential "explosion" of method calls.

6.16 Recursion vs. Iteration

In the previous sections, we studied two methods that can be implemented either recursively or iteratively. In this section, we compare the two approaches and discuss why the programmer might choose one approach over the other.

Both iteration and recursion are based on a control structure—iteration uses a repetition structure (such as **for**, **while** or **do/while**) and recursion uses a selection structure (such as **if**, **if/else** or **switch**). Both iteration and recursion involve repetition—iteration explicitly uses a repetition structure and recursion achieves repetition through repeated method calls. Iteration and recursion each involve a termination test—iteration terminates when the loop-continuation condition fails and recursion terminates when a base case is recognized. Iteration with counter-controlled repetition and recursion both gradually approach termination—iteration keeps modifying a counter until the counter assumes a value that makes the loop-continuation condition fail and recursion keeps producing simpler versions of the original problem until a base case is reached. Both iteration and recursion can execute infinitely—an infinite loop occurs with iteration if the loop-continuation test never becomes false and infinite recursion occurs if the recursion step does not reduce the problem in a manner that converges on a base case.

Recursion has disadvantages as well. It repeatedly invokes the mechanism, and consequently the overhead, of method calls. This can be costly in both processor time and memory space. Each recursive call creates another copy of the method (actually, only the method's variables); this can consume considerable memory. Iteration normally occurs within a method, so the overhead of repeated method calls and extra memory assignment is omitted. Why then would a programmer choose recursion?

Software Engineering Observation 6.11

Any problem that can be solved recursively also can be solved iteratively (nonrecursively). A recursive approach normally is chosen in preference to an iterative approach when the recursive approach more naturally mirrors the problem and results in a program that is easier to understand and debug. Recursive solutions also are chosen when iterative solutions are not apparent.

Performance Tip 6.2

 Avoid using recursion in performance situations. Recursive calls take time and consume additional memory.

Common Programming Error 6.16

Accidentally having a nonrecursive method call itself through another method can cause infinite recursion.

6.17 Method Overloading

C# enables several methods of the same name to be defined in the same class, as long as these methods have different sets of parameters (number of parameters, types of parameters or order of the parameters). This is called *method overloading*. When an overloaded method is called, the C# compiler selects the proper method by examining the number, types and order of the call's arguments. Method overloading commonly is used to create several methods with the same name that perform similar tasks, but on different data types. Figure 6.18 uses overloaded method **Square** to calculate the square of an **int** and a **double**.

The compiler distinguishes overloaded methods by their *signatures*. A method's signature is a combination of the method's name and parameter types. If the compiler looked only at method names during compilation, the code in Fig. 6.18 would be ambiguous—the compiler would not know how to distinguish the two **Square** methods. The compiler uses *overload resolution* to determine which method to call. This process first searches for all the methods that *can* be used in the context, based on the number and type of arguments that are present. It might seem that only one method would match, but recall that C# can convert variable values to other data types implicitly. Once all matching methods are found, the closest match is chosen. This match is based on a "best-fit" algorithm, which analyzes the implicit conversions that will take place.

Let us look at an example. In Fig. 6.18, the compiler might use the logical name "**Square** of **int**" for the **Square** method that specifies an **int** parameter (line 30) and "**Square** of **double**" for the **Square** method that specifies a **double** parameter (line 36). If a method **Foo**'s definition begins as

```
void Foo( int a, float b )
```

the compiler might use the logical name "**Foo** of **int** and **float**." If the parameters are specified as

```
void Foo( float a, int b )
```

the compiler might use the logical name "**Foo** of **float** and **int**." The order of the parameters is important to the compiler; it considers the preceding two **Foo** methods distinct.

```
1   // Fig. 6.18: MethodOverload.cs
2   // Using overloaded methods.
3   using System;
4   using System.Drawing;
5   using System.Collections;
6   using System.ComponentModel;
7   using System.Windows.Forms;
8   using System.Data;
9
```

Fig. 6.18 Using overloaded methods. (Part 1 of 2.)

```
10   public class MethodOverload : System.Windows.Forms.Form
11   {
12      private System.Windows.Forms.Button showOutputButton;
13      private System.Windows.Forms.Label outputLabel;
14
15      // Visual Studio .NET generated code
16
17      // first version, takes one integer
18      public int Square( int x )
19      {
20         return x * x;
21      }
22
23      // second version, takes one double
24      public double Square( double y )
25      {
26         return y * y;
27      }
28
29      // main entry point for application
30      [STAThread]
31      static void Main()
32      {
33         Application.Run( new MethodOverload() );
34      }
35
36      private void showOutputButton_Click( object sender,
37         System.EventArgs e )
38      {
39         // call both versions of Square
40         outputLabel.Text =
41            "The square of integer 7 is " + Square( 7 ) +
42            "\nThe square of double 7.5 is " + Square ( 7.5 );
43      }
44
45   } // end class MethodOverload
```

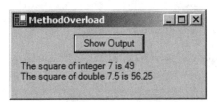

Fig. 6.18 Using overloaded methods. (Part 2 of 2.)

 Good Programming Practice 6.5

Overloading methods that perform closely related tasks can make programs more readable and understandable.

So far, the logical names of methods that have been used by the compiler have not mentioned the methods' return types. This is because method calls cannot be distinguished by return type. The program in Fig. 6.19 illustrates the syntax error that is generated when two methods have the same signature and different return types. Overloaded methods with different parameter lists can have different return types. Overloaded methods need not have the same number of parameters.

Common Programming Error 6.17

Creating overloaded methods with identical parameter lists and different return types is a syntax error.

6.18 Summary

The best way to develop and maintain a large program is to construct it from small pieces. This technique is called divide and conquer. Program pieces can be created with methods and classes. Programs are written by combining new methods and classes that the programmer writes with prepackaged methods and classes in the FCL and in various other method and class libraries. The FCL provides a rich collection of classes and methods for performing common mathematical calculations, string manipulations, character manipulations, input/output, error checking and other useful operations.

The programmer can write methods to define specific tasks that may be used at many points in a program. Such methods sometimes are referred to as programmer-defined methods. The actual statements defining the method are written only once and are hidden from other methods. Methods are called by writing the name of the method (sometimes preceded by the class name and a dot operator), followed by a left parenthesis, the method's argument (or a comma-separated list of arguments) and a right parenthesis. Packaging code as a method allows that code to be executed from several locations in a program when the method is called.

The format of a method definition is

```
return-value-type  method-name( parameter-list )
{
    declarations and statements
}
```

```
1   // Fig. 6.19: InvalidMethodOverload.cs
2   // Demonstrating incorrect method overloading.
3
4   public class InvalidMethodOverload
5   {
6      public int Square( double x )
7      {
8         return x * x;
9      }
10
11     // ERROR! Second Square method takes same number, order
12     // and types of arguments, but has different return type
13     public double Square( double y )
14     {
15        return y * y;
16     }
17  }
```

Fig. 6.19   Syntax error generated from overloaded methods with identical parameter lists and different return types. (Part 1 of 2.)

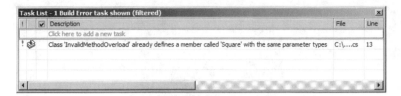

Fig. 6.19   Syntax error generated from overloaded methods with identical parameter lists and different return types. (Part 2 of 2.)

The first line of a method definition is sometimes called the method header. The attributes and modifiers in the method header specify information about the method. The method's *return-value-type* is the data type of the result that is returned from the method to the caller. Methods can return one value at most. The *parameter-list* is a comma-separated list containing the declarations of the parameters received by the called method. There must be one argument in the method call for each parameter in the method definition. The declarations and statements within the braces that follow the method header form the body of the method. The **return** statement passes the results of the method back to the calling method.

In many cases, an argument value that does not correspond precisely to the parameter types in the method definition is converted to the proper type before the method is called.

When an argument is passed by value, a copy of the argument's value is made and passed to the called method. With pass-by-reference, the caller enables the called method to access the caller's data directly and to modify those data if the called method chooses.

An event is a signal that is sent to a program when some action takes place, such as when the user clicks a button. The programmer writes the application to perform tasks when events occur. An event handler is a method that executes when an event occurs.

An identifier's duration (its lifetime) is the period during which the identifier exists in memory. Identifiers that represent local variables in a method (i.e., parameters and variables declared in the body of the method) have automatic duration. Automatic-duration variables are created when program control reaches the variable's declaration. They exist while the block in which they are declared is active, and they are destroyed when the block in which they are declared is exited. The scope (sometimes called a declaration space) of an identifier for a variable, reference or method is the portion of the program in which that identifier can be referenced.

A recursive method is a method that calls itself either directly, or indirectly through another method. A recursive method knows how to solve only the simplest case(s), or base case(s), of a problem. If the method is called with a base case, the method returns a result. If the method is called with a more complex problem, the method divides the problem into two conceptual pieces—a piece that the method knows how to solve (the base case) and a piece that the method does not know how to solve. To make recursion feasible, the portion of the problem that the method does not know how to solve must resemble the original problem, but be a slightly simpler or smaller version.

Several methods can have the same name, as long as the methods have different sets of parameters, in terms of the number of parameters, the types of the parameters or the order of the parameters. This technique is called method overloading. Method overloading commonly is used to create several methods with the same name that perform similar tasks, but on different data types.

7

Arrays

Objectives

- To introduce the array data structure.
- To understand how arrays store, sort and search lists and tables of values.
- To understand how to declare an array, initialize an array and refer to individual elements of an array.
- To be able to pass arrays to methods.
- To understand basic sorting techniques.
- To be able to declare and manipulate multiple-subscripted arrays.

With sobs and tears he sorted out
Those of the largest size ...
Lewis Carroll

Attempt the end, and never stand to doubt;
Nothing's so hard, but search will find it out.
Robert Herrick

Now go, write it before them in a table,
and note it in a book.
Isaiah 30:8

'Tis in my memory lock'd,
And you yourself shall keep the key of it.
William Shakespeare

7.1 Introduction

This chapter serves as an introduction to data structures. *Arrays* are data structures consisting of data items of the same type. Arrays are "static" entities, in that they remain the same size once they are created. We show how to create and access arrays, then use this knowledge to begin more complex array manipulations, including powerful searching and sorting techniques. We then demonstrate creating more sophisticated arrays that have multiple dimensions. Chapter 21, FCL Collections, introduces C#'s predefined data structures that enable the programmer to use existing data structures such as stacks (i.e., data structures that allow insertions and deletions only at one end), rather than having to "reinvent the wheel."

7.2 Arrays

An array is a group of contiguous memory locations that all have the same name and type. To refer to a particular location or element in the array, we specify the name of the array and the *position number* (a value that indicates a specific location within the array) of the element to which we refer.

Figure 7.1 shows an integer array called **c**. This array contains 12 *elements*. A program can refer to any element of an array by giving the name of the array followed by the position number of the element in square brackets (**[]**). The first element in every array is the *zeroth* *element.* Thus, the first element of array **c** is referred to as **c [0]**, the second element of array **c** is referred to as **c [1]**, the seventh element of array **c** is referred to as **c [6]** and so on. The *i*th element of array **c** is referred to as **c [i - 1]**. Array names follow the same conventions as other variable names, as discussed in Chapter 3, Introduction to C# Programming.

The position number in square brackets is more formally called a *subscript* (or an *index*). A subscript must be an integer or an integer expression. If a program uses an expression as a subscript, the program evaluates the expression first to determine the subscript. For example, if variable **a** is equal to **5** and variable **b** is equal to **6**, then the statement

```
c[ a + b ] += 2;
```

adds 2 to array element **c [11]**. Note that a subscripted array name is an *lvalue*—it can be used on the left side of an assignment to place a new value into an array element.

Let us examine array c in Fig. 7.1 more closely. The name of the array is **c**. Every array in C# "knows" its own length. The length of the array is determined by the expression:

```
c.Length
```

The array's 12 elements are referred to as **c [0]**, **c [1]**, **c [2]**, ..., **c [11]**. The *value* of **c [0]** is **-45**, the value of **c [1]** is **6**, the value of **c [2]** is **0**, the value of **c [7]** is **62** and the value of **c [11]** is **78**. To calculate the sum of the values contained in the first three elements of array **c** and to store the result in variable **sum**, we would write

```
sum = c[ 0 ] + c[ 1 ] + c[ 2 ];
```

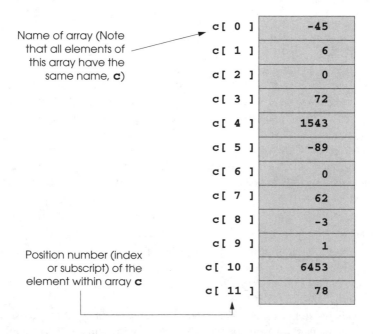

Fig. 7.1   A 12-element array.

To divide the value of the seventh element of array **c** by **2** and assign the result to the variable **x**, we would write

```
x = c[ 6 ] / 2;
```

Common Programming Error 7.1

It is important to note the difference between the "seventh element of the array" and "array element seven." Array subscripts begin at 0, thus the "seventh element of the array" has a subscript of 6, while "array element seven" has a subscript of 7 and is actually the eighth element of the array. This confusion is a source of "off-by-one" errors.

The brackets that enclose the subscript of an array are operators. Brackets have the same level of precedence as parentheses. The chart in Fig. 7.2 shows the precedence and associativity of the operators introduced to this point in the text. They are displayed top to bottom in decreasing order of precedence, with their associativity and type. The reader should note that the **++** and **--** operators in the first row represent the postincrement and postdecrement operators, while the **++** and **--** operators in the second row represent the preincrement and predecrement operators. Also, notice that in the first row the associativity is mixed. This is because the associativity of the postincrement and postdecrement operators is right to left, while the associativity for the other operators is left to right.

7.3 Declaring and Allocating Arrays

Arrays occupy space in memory. The programmer specifies the type of the elements and uses operator **new** to allocate dynamically the number of elements required by each array. Arrays are allocated with **new** because arrays are objects and all objects must be created with **new**. We will see an exception to this rule shortly.

Operators	Associativity	Type
() [] . ++ --	left to right	highest (unary postfix)
++ -- + - ! (*type*)	right to left	unary (unary prefix)
* / %	left to right	multiplicative
+ -	left to right	additive
< <= > >=	left to right	relational
== !=	left to right	equality
&	left to right	logical AND
^	left to right	logical exclusive OR
|	left to right	logical inclusive OR
&&	left to right	conditional AND
||	left to right	conditional OR
? :	right to left	conditional
= += -= *= /= %=	right to left	assignment

Fig. 7.2   Precedence and associativity of the operators discussed so far.

The declaration

```
int[] c = new int[ 12 ];
```

allocates 12 elements for integer array **c**. The preceding statement can also be performed in two steps as follows:

```
// declare array
int[] c;

// allocate space for array; set reference to that space
c = new int[ 12 ];
```

When arrays are allocated, the elements are initialized to zero for the numeric primitive-data-type variables, to **false** for **bool** variables and to **null** for reference types.

Common Programming Error 7.2

Unlike in C or C++, in C# the number of elements in the array is never specified in the square brackets after the array name. The declaration **int c[12];** *causes a syntax error.*

Memory may be reserved for several arrays with a single declaration. The following declaration reserves 100 elements for **string** array **b** and 27 elements for **string** array **x**:

```
string[] b = new string[ 100 ], x = new string[ 27 ];
```

Similarly, the following declaration reserves 10 elements for **array1** and 20 elements for **array2** (both of type **double**):

```
double[] array1 = new double[ 10 ],
         array2 = new double[ 20 ];
```

Arrays may be declared to contain any data types. In an array of value types, every element of the array contains one value of the declared type. For example, every element of an **int** array is an **int** value.

In an array of reference types, every element of the array is a reference to an object of the data type of the array. For example, every element of a **string** array is a reference to a **string**; each of these **string** references has the value **null** by default.

7.4 Examples Using Arrays

This section presents several examples using arrays that demonstrate declaring arrays, allocating arrays, initializing arrays and manipulating array elements in various ways. For simplicity, the examples in this section use arrays that contain elements of type **int**.

7.4.1 Allocating an Array and Initializing Its Elements

Figure 7.3 creates three integer arrays of 10 elements and displays those arrays in tabular format. The program demonstrates several techniques for declaring and initializing arrays.

Line 14 declares **x** as a reference to an array of integers. Each element in the array is of type **int**. The variable **x** is of type **int[]**, which denotes an array whose elements are of type **int**. Line 15 allocates the 10 elements of the array with **new** and assigns the array to reference **x**. Each element of this array has the default value 0.

Line 20 creates another **int** array and initializes each element using an *initializer list*. In this case, the number of elements in the initializer list determines the array's size. For example, line 20 creates a 10-element array with the indices **0–9** and the values **32, 27, 64**, and so on. Note that this declaration does not require the **new** operator to create the array object—the compiler allocates memory for the object when it encounters an array declaration that includes an initializer list.

```
1    // Fig. 7.3: InitArray.cs
2    // Different ways of initializing arrays.
3
4    using System;
5    using System.Windows.Forms;
6
7    class InitArray
8    {
9       // main entry point for application
10      static void Main( string[] args )
11      {
12         string output = "";
13
14         int[] x;             // declare reference to an array
15         x = new int[ 10 ];   // dynamically allocate array and set
16                              // default values
17
18         // initializer list specifies number of elements
19         // and value of each element
20         int[] y = { 32, 27, 64, 18, 95, 14, 90, 70, 60, 37 };
21
22         const int ARRAY_SIZE = 10; // named constant
23         int[] z;                   // reference to int array
24
25         // allocate array of ARRAY_SIZE (i.e., 10) elements
26         z = new int[ ARRAY_SIZE ];
27
28         // set the values in the array
29         for ( int i = 0; i < z.Length; i++ )
30            z[ i ] = 2 + 2 * i;
31
32         output += "Subscript\tArray x\tArray y\tArray z\n";
33
34         // output values for each array
35         for ( int i = 0; i < ARRAY_SIZE; i++ )
36            output += i + "\t" + x[ i ] + "\t" + y[ i ] +
37               "\t" + z[ i ] + "\n";
38
39         MessageBox.Show( output,
40            "Initializing an array of int values",
41            MessageBoxButtons.OK, MessageBoxIcon.Information );
42
43      } // end Main
44
45   } // end class InitArray
```

Fig. 7.3   Initializing element arrays in three different ways. (Part 1 of 2.)

Fig. 7.3   Initializing element arrays in three different ways. (Part 2 of 2.)

On line 22, we create constant integer **ARRAY_SIZE** using keyword **const**. A constant must be initialized in the same statement where it is declared and cannot be modified thereafter. If an attempt is made to modify a **const** variable after it is declared, the compiler issues a syntax error.

Constants also are called *named constants*. They often are used to make a program more readable and are usually denoted with variable names in all capital letters.

Common Programming Error 7.3

Assigning a value to a constant after the variable has been initialized is a compiler error.

On lines 23 and 26, we create integer array **z** of length 10 using the **ARRAY_SIZE** named constant. The **for** structure in lines 29–30 initializes each element in array **z**. The element values are generated by multiplying each successive value of the loop counter by **2** and adding **2** to the product. After this initialization, array **z** contains the even integers **2**, **4**, **6**, ..., **20**. The **for** structure in lines 35–37 uses the values in arrays **x**, **y** and **z** to build an output string, which will be displayed in a **MessageBox**. Zero-based counting (remember, array subscripts start at **0**) allows the loop to access every element of the array. The constant **ARRAY_SIZE** in the **for** structure condition (line 29) is the length of each of the arrays.

7.4.2 Totaling the Elements of an Array

Often, the elements of an array represent series of values to be used in calculations. For example, if the elements of an array represent the grades for an exam in a class, the professor may wish to total the elements of an array, then calculate the class average for the exam.

The application in Fig. 7.4 sums the values contained in the 10-element integer array **a** (declared, allocated and initialized on line 12). Line 16 in the body of the **for** loop performs the addition using the array element at position **i** during each loop iteration. Note that the values being supplied as initializers for array **a** normally would be read into the program. For example, in a Windows application, the user could enter the values through a **TextBox**, or the values could be read from a file on disk. (See Chapter 15, Files and Streams.)

```
1   // Fig. 7.4: SumArray.cs
2   // Computing the sum of the elements in an array.
```

Fig. 7.4   Computing the sum of the elements of an array. (Part 1 of 2.)

```
3
4    using System;
5    using System.Windows.Forms;
6
7    class SumArray
8    {
9       // main entry point for application
10      static void Main( string[] args )
11      {
12         int[] a = { 1, 2, 3, 4, 5, 6, 7, 8, 9, 10 };
13         int total = 0;
14
15         for ( int i = 0; i < a.Length; i++ )
16            total += a[ i ];
17
18         MessageBox.Show( "Total of array elements: " + total,
19            "Sum the elements of an array",
20            MessageBoxButtons.OK, MessageBoxIcon.Information );
21
22      } // end Main
23
24   } // end class SumArray
```

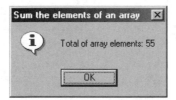

Fig. 7.4   Computing the sum of the elements of an array. (Part 2 of 2.)

7.4.3 Using Histograms to Display Array Data Graphically

Many programs present data to users in a graphical manner. For example, numeric values often are displayed as bars in a bar chart. In such a chart, longer bars represent larger numeric values. One simple way to display numeric data graphically is with a *histogram* that shows each numeric value as a bar of asterisks (*).

Our next application (Fig. 7.5) reads numbers from an array and graphs the information in the form of a bar chart, or histogram. The program displays each number followed by a bar consisting of a corresponding number of asterisks. The nested **for** loops (lines 18–24) append the bars to the **string** that will be displayed in the **MessageBox**. Note the loop continuation condition of the inner **for** structure on line 22 (**j <= n[i]**). Each time the program reaches the inner **for** structure, the loop counts from **1** to **n[i]**, using a value in array **n** to determine the final value of the control variable **j** and the number of asterisks to display.

```
1    // Fig. 7.5: Histogram.cs
2    // Using data to create a histogram.
```

Fig. 7.5   Program that prints histograms. (Part 1 of 2.)

```
3
4    using System;
5    using System.Windows.Forms;
6
7    class Histogram
8    {
9        // main entry point for application
10       static void Main( string[] args )
11       {
12           int[] n = { 19, 3, 15, 7, 11, 9, 13, 5, 17, 1 };
13           string output = "";
14
15           output += "Element\tvalue\tHistogram\n";
16
17           // build output
18           for ( int i = 0; i < n.Length; i++ )
19           {
20               output += "\n" + i + "\t" + n[ i ] + "\t";
21
22               for ( int j = 1; j <= n[ i ]; j++ ) // print a bar
23                   output += "*";
24           }
25
26           MessageBox.Show( output, "Histogram Printing Program",
27               MessageBoxButtons.OK, MessageBoxIcon.Information );
28
29       } // end Main
30
31   } // end class Histogram
```

Fig. 7.5   Program that prints histograms. (Part 2 of 2.)

7.4.4 Using the Elements of an Array as Counters

Sometimes programs use a series of counter variables to summarize data, such as the results of a survey. In Chapter 6, Methods, we used a series of counters in our dice-rolling program to track the number of occurrences of each side on a six-sided die as the program rolled 12 dice at a time. We also indicated that there is a more elegant method than that in Fig. 6.11 for writing the dice-rolling program. An array version of this application is shown in Fig. 7.6.

The program uses the seven-element array **frequency** to count the occurrences of each side of the die. Line 94, which uses the random **face** value as the subscript for array **frequency** to determine which element should be incremented during each iteration of the loop, replaces lines 85–111 of Fig. 6.11. The random number calculation on line 88 produces numbers 1–6 (the values for a six-sided die); thus, the **frequency** array must be large enough to allow subscript values of 1–6. The smallest number of elements required for an array to have these subscript values is seven elements (subscript values 0–6). In this program, we ignore element 0 of array **frequency**. Lines 75–80 replace lines 59–71 from Fig. 6.11. We can loop through array **frequency**; therefore, we do not have to enumerate each line of text to display in the **Label**, as we did in Fig. 6.11.

```
1   // Fig. 7.6: RollDie.cs
2   // Rolling 12 dice.
3
4   using System;
5   using System.Drawing;
6   using System.Collections;
7   using System.ComponentModel;
8   using System.Windows.Forms;
9   using System.Data;
10  using System.IO;
11
12  public class RollDie : System.Windows.Forms.Form
13  {
14     private System.Windows.Forms.Button rollButton;
15
16     private System.Windows.Forms.RichTextBox displayTextBox;
17
18     private System.Windows.Forms.Label dieLabel1;
19     private System.Windows.Forms.Label dieLabel2;
20     private System.Windows.Forms.Label dieLabel3;
21     private System.Windows.Forms.Label dieLabel4;
22     private System.Windows.Forms.Label dieLabel5;
23     private System.Windows.Forms.Label dieLabel6;
24     private System.Windows.Forms.Label dieLabel7;
25     private System.Windows.Forms.Label dieLabel8;
26     private System.Windows.Forms.Label dieLabel9;
27     private System.Windows.Forms.Label dieLabel10;
28     private System.Windows.Forms.Label dieLabel11;
29     private System.Windows.Forms.Label dieLabel12;
30
31     private System.ComponentModel.Container components = null;
32
33     Random randomNumber = new Random();
34     int[] frequency = new int[ 7 ];
35
36     public RollDie()
37     {
38        InitializeComponent();
39     }
40
```

Fig. 7.6   Using arrays to eliminate a **switch** structure. (Part 1 of 3.)

```
41     // Visual Studio .NET generated code
42
43     [STAThread]
44     static void Main()
45     {
46        Application.Run( new RollDie() );
47     }
48
49     private void rollButton_Click(
50        object sender, System.EventArgs e )
51     {
52        // pass the labels to a method that will
53        // randomly assign a face to each die
54        DisplayDie( dieLabel1 );
55        DisplayDie( dieLabel2 );
56        DisplayDie( dieLabel3 );
57        DisplayDie( dieLabel4 );
58        DisplayDie( dieLabel5 );
59        DisplayDie( dieLabel6 );
60        DisplayDie( dieLabel7 );
61        DisplayDie( dieLabel8 );
62        DisplayDie( dieLabel9 );
63        DisplayDie( dieLabel10 );
64        DisplayDie( dieLabel11 );
65        DisplayDie( dieLabel12 );
66
67        double total = 0;
68
69        for ( int i = 1; i < 7; i++ )
70           total += frequency[ i ];
71
72        displayTextBox.Text = "Face\tFrequency\tPercent\n";
73
74        // output frequency values
75        for ( int x = 1; x < frequency.Length; x++ )
76        {
77           displayTextBox.Text += x + "\t" +
78              frequency[ x ] + "\t\t" + String.Format( "{0:N}",
79              frequency[ x ] / total * 100 ) + "%\n";
80        }
81
82     } // end rollButton_Click
83
84     // simulates roll, display proper
85     // image and increment frequency
86     public void DisplayDie( Label dieLabel )
87     {
88        int face = randomNumber.Next( 1, 7 );
89
90        dieLabel.Image = Image.FromFile(
91           Directory.GetCurrentDirectory() +
92           "\\images\\die" + face + ".png" );
93
```

Fig. 7.6   Using arrays to eliminate a **switch** structure. (Part 2 of 3.)

```
94          frequency[ face ]++;
95       }
96
97    } // end class RollDie
```

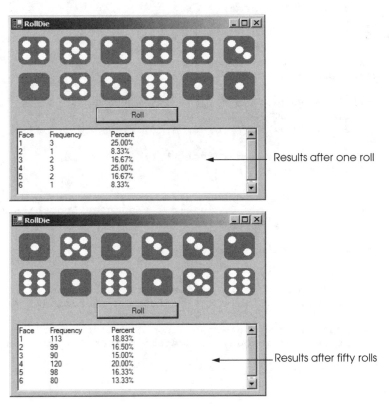

Results after one roll

Results after fifty rolls

Fig. 7.6   Using arrays to eliminate a **switch** structure. (Part 3 of 3.)

7.4.5 Using Arrays to Analyze Survey Results

Our next example uses arrays to summarize the results of data collected in a survey. Consider the following problem statement:

> *Forty students were asked to rate the quality of the food in the student cafeteria on a scale of 1 to 10, with 1 being awful and 10 being excellent. Place the 40 responses in an integer array and summarize the frequency for each rating.*

This is a typical array processing application (Fig. 7.7). We wish to summarize the number of responses of each type (i.e., 1–10). The array **responses** is a 40-element integer array of the students' responses to the survey. We use an 11-element array **frequency** to count the number of occurrences of each response. We ignore the first element, **frequency[0]**, because it is more logical to have a response of **1** increment **frequency[1]** than **frequency[0]**. We can use each response directly as a subscript on the **frequency** array. Each element of the array is used as a counter for one of the survey responses.

```csharp
1    // Fig. 7.7: StudentPoll.cs
2    // A student poll program.
3
4    using System;
5    using System.Windows.Forms;
6
7    class StudentPoll
8    {
9       // main entry point for application
10      static void Main( string[] args )
11      {
12         int[] responses = { 1, 2, 6, 4, 8, 5, 9, 7, 8, 10, 1,
13            6, 3, 8, 6, 10, 3, 8, 2, 7, 6, 5, 7, 6, 8, 6, 7,
14            5, 6, 6, 5, 6, 7, 5, 6, 4, 8, 6, 8, 10 };
15
16         int[] frequency = new int[ 11 ];
17         string output = "";
18
19         // increment the frequency for each response
20         for ( int answer = 0; answer < responses.Length; answer++ )
21            ++frequency[ responses[ answer ] ];
22
23         output += "Rating\tFrequency\n";
24
25         // output results
26         for ( int rating = 1; rating < frequency.Length; rating++ )
27            output += rating + "\t" + frequency[ rating ] + "\n";
28
29         MessageBox.Show( output, "Student poll program",
30            MessageBoxButtons.OK, MessageBoxIcon.Information );
31
32      } // end method Main
33
34   } // end class StudentPoll
```

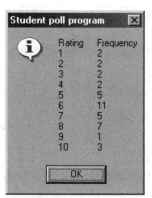

Fig. 7.7   Simple student-poll analysis program.

Good Programming Practice 7.1

Strive for program clarity. It is sometimes worthwhile to trade off the most efficient use of memory or processor time for writing clearer programs.

The **for** loop (lines 20–21) takes the responses from the array **response** one at a time and increments one of the 10 counters in the **frequency** array (**frequency[1]** to **frequency[10]**). The key statement in the loop is on line 21, which increments the appropriate counter in the **frequency** array, depending on the value of element **responses[answer]**.

Let us consider several iterations of the **for** loop. When counter **answer** is **0**, **responses[answer]** is the value of the first element of array **responses** (i.e., **1**). In this case, the program interprets **++frequency[responses[answer]];** as **++frequency[1];**, which increments array element one. In evaluating the expression, start with the value in the innermost set of square brackets (**answer**). Once you know the value of **answer**, plug that value into the expression and evaluate the next outer set of square brackets (**responses[answer]**). Use that value as the subscript for the **frequency** array to determine which counter to increment.

When **answer** is **1**, **responses[answer]** is the value of the second element of array **responses** (i.e., **2**), so the program interprets

```
++frequency[ responses[ answer ] ];
```

as **++frequency[2];**, which increments array element two (the third element of the array). When **answer** is **2**, **responses[answer]** is the value of the third element of array **responses** (i.e., **6**), so the program interprets

```
++frequency[ responses[ answer ] ];
```

as **++frequency[6];**, which increments array element six (the seventh element of the array) and so on. Note that, regardless of the number of responses processed in the survey, only an 11-element array is required (ignoring element zero) to summarize the results, because all the response values are between 1 and 10, and the subscript values for an 11-element array are 0–10. The results are correct, because the elements of the **frequency** array were initialized to zero when the array was allocated with **new**.

If the data contained invalid values, such as 13, the program would attempt to add **1** to **frequency[13]**. This is outside the bounds of the array. In the C and C++ programming languages, no checks are performed to prevent programs from reading data outside the bounds of arrays. At execution time, the program would "walk" past the end of the array to where element number 13 would be located and add 1 to whatever data are stored at that location in memory. This could potentially modify another variable in the program or even result in premature program termination. The .NET framework provides mechanisms to prevent accessing elements outside the bounds of arrays.

Testing and Debugging Tip 7.1

When a C# program executes, array element subscripts are checked for validity (i.e., all subscripts must be greater than or equal to 0 and less than the length of the array).

Testing and Debugging Tip 7.2

Exceptions indicate when errors occur in programs. Programmers can write code to recover from exceptions and continue program execution instead of terminating the program abnormally. When an invalid array reference occurs, C# generates an **IndexOutOfRange-Exception** *exception. We discuss exceptions in more detail in Chapter 10, Exception Handling.*

Common Programming Error 7.4

Referring to an element outside the array bounds is a logic error.

Testing and Debugging Tip 7.3

*When looping through an array, the array subscript never should go below 0 and should always be less than the total number of elements in the array (one less than the **Length** of the array). The loop-terminating condition should prevent accessing elements outside this range.*

Testing and Debugging Tip 7.4

Programs should validate the correctness of all input values to prevent erroneous information from affecting a program's calculations.

7.5 Passing Arrays to Methods

To pass an array argument to a method, specify the name of the array without using brackets. For example, if array **hourlyTemperatures** declared as

```
int[] hourlyTemperatures = new int[ 24 ];
```

the method call

```
ModifyArray( hourlyTemperatures );
```

passes array **hourlyTemperatures** to method **ModifyArray**. Every array object "knows" its own size (via the **Length** variable), so when we pass an array object into a method, we do not pass the size of the array as an additional argument.

Although entire arrays are passed by reference, individual array elements of primitive data types are passed by value, the same as simple variables are. (The objects referred to by individual elements of a nonprimitive-type array are passed by reference.) Such simple single pieces of data are sometimes called *scalars* or *scalar quantities*. To pass an array element to a method, use the subscripted name of the array element as an argument in the method call, i.e., the zeroth element of array **scores** is passed as **scores[0]**.

For a method to receive an array through a method call, the method's parameter list must specify that an array will be received. For example, the method header for method **ModifyArray** might be written as

```
public void ModifyArray( int[] b )
```

indicating that **ModifyArray** expects to receive an integer array in parameter **b**. Arrays are passed by reference; when the called method uses the array parameter name **b**, it refers to the actual array in the caller.

The application in Fig. 7.8 demonstrates the difference between passing an entire array and passing an array element.

The **for** loop on lines 32–33 appends the five elements of integer array **a** to the **Text** property of **outputLabel**. Line 33 invokes method **ModifyArray** and passes to it array **a**. Method **ModifyArray** multiplies each element by 2. To illustrate that array **a**'s elements were modified, the **for** loop on lines 41–42 appends the five elements of integer array **a** to the **Text** property of **outputLabel**. As the screen capture indicates, the elements of **a** are modified by **ModifyArray**.

```csharp
1    // Fig. 7.8: PassArray.cs
2    // Passing arrays and individual elements to methods.
3    using System;
4    using System.Drawing;
5    using System.Collections;
6    using System.ComponentModel;
7    using System.Windows.Forms;
8    using System.Data;
9
10   public class PassArray : System.Windows.Forms.Form
11   {
12      private System.Windows.Forms.Button showOutputButton;
13      private System.Windows.Forms.Label outputLabel;
14
15      // Visual Studio .NET generated code
16
17      [STAThread]
18      static void Main()
19      {
20         Application.Run( new PassArray() );
21      }
22
23      private void showOutputButton_Click( object sender,
24         System.EventArgs e )
25      {
26         int[] a = { 1, 2, 3, 4, 5 };
27
28         outputLabel.Text = "Effects of passing entire array " +
29            "call-by-reference:\n\nThe values of the original " +
30            "array are:\n\t";
31
32         for ( int i = 0; i < a.Length; i++ )
33            outputLabel.Text += "   " + a[ i ];
34
35         ModifyArray( a );    // array is passed by reference
36
37         outputLabel.Text +=
38            "\n\nThe values of the modified array are:\n\t";
39
40         // display elements of array a
41         for ( int i = 0; i < a.Length; i++ )
42            outputLabel.Text += "   " + a[ i ];
43
44         outputLabel.Text += "\n\nEffects of passing array " +
45            "element call-by-value:\n\na[ 3 ] before " +
46            "ModifyElement: " + a[ 3 ];
47
48         // array element passed call-by-value
49         ModifyElement( a[ 3 ] );
50
51         outputLabel.Text +=
52            "\na[ 3 ] after ModifyElement: " + a[ 3 ];
53      }
```

Fig. 7.8   Passing arrays and individual array elements to methods. (Part 1 of 2.)

```
54
55        // method modifies the array it receives,
56        // original will be modified
57        public void ModifyArray( int[] b )
58        {
59           for ( int j = 0; j < b.Length; j++ )
60              b[ j ] *= 2;
61        }
62
63        // method modifies the integer passed to it
64        // original will not be modified
65        public void ModifyElement( int e )
66        {
67           outputLabel.Text +=
68              "\nvalue received in ModifyElement: " + e;
69
70           e *= 2;
71
72           outputLabel.Text +=
73              "\nvalue calculated in ModifyElement: " + e;
74        }
75    }
```

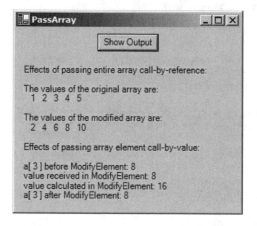

Fig. 7.8   Passing arrays and individual array elements to methods. (Part 2 of 2.)

To show the value of **a[3]** before the call to **ModifyElement**, lines 44–46 append the value of **a[3]** (and other information) to **outputLabel.Text**. Line 44 invokes method **ModifyElement** and passes **a[3]**. Remember that **a[3]** is a single **int** value in the array **a**. Also, remember that values of primitive types always are passed to methods by value. Therefore, a copy of **a[3]** is passed. Method **ModifyElement** multiplies its argument by 2 and stores the result in its parameter **e**. The parameter of **ModifyElement** is a local variable, so when the method terminates, the local variable is destroyed. Thus, when control is returned to **PassArray**, the unmodified value of **a[3]** is appended to the **outputLabel.Text** (line 51–52).

7.6 Passing Arrays by Value and by Reference

In C#, a variable that "stores" an object, such as an array, actually stores a reference to the object. The distinction between reference variables and primitive data type variables raises some subtle issues that programmers must understand to create secure, stable programs.

When a program passes an argument by value to a method, the called method receives a copy of that argument's value. Changes to the local copy do not affect the original variable that the program passed to the method. If the argument is of a reference type, the method makes a local copy of the reference itself, not a copy of the actual object to which the reference refers. The local copy of the reference still refers to the original object in the caller's memory. Thus, reference types are always passed by reference, which means that changes to those objects in called methods affect the original objects in memory.

Performance Tip 7.1

Passing arrays and other objects by reference makes sense for performance reasons. If arrays were passed by value, a copy of each element would be passed. For large, frequently passed arrays, this would waste time and would consume considerable storage for the copies of the arrays, causing poor performance.

C# also allows methods to pass references with keyword **ref**. This is a subtle capability, which, if misused, can lead to problems. For instance, when a reference-type object like an array is passed with **ref**, the called method actually gains control over the passed reference itself, allowing the called method to replace the original reference in the caller with a different object or even with **null**. Such behavior can lead to unpredictable effects, which can be disastrous in business-critical and mission-critical applications. The program in Fig. 7.9 demonstrates the subtle difference between passing a reference by value and passing a reference with keyword **ref**.

Lines 26 and 29 declare two integer array variables, **firstArray** and **firstArray-Copy** (we make the copy so we can determine whether reference **firstArray** gets overwritten). Line 26 initializes **firstArray** with the values **1**, **2** and **3**. The assignment statement on line 29 copies reference **firstArray** to variable **firstArrayCopy**, causing these variables to reference the same array object in memory. The **for** structure on lines 38–39 prints the contents of **firstArray** before it is passed to method **First-Double** (line 42) so we can verify that this array is passed by reference (i.e., the called method indeed changes the array's contents).

The **for** structure in method **FirstDouble** (lines 99–100) multiplies the values of all the elements in the array by **2**. Line 103 allocates a new array containing the values **11**, **12** and **13**; the reference for this array then is assigned to parameter **array** (in an attempt to overwrite reference **firstArray**—this, of course, will not happen, because the reference itself was passed by value). After method **FirstDouble** executes, the **for** structure on lines 48–49 prints the contents of **firstArray**, demonstrating that the values of the elements have been changed by the method (and confirming that in C# arrays are always passed by reference). The **if/else** structure on lines 52–57 compares references **firstArray** (which we just attempted to overwrite) and **firstArrayCopy**. The expression on line 40 evaluates to **true** if the operands to binary operator **==** indeed reference the same object. In this case, the object represented is the array allocated in line 26—not the array allocated in method **FirstDouble** (line 103).

```
1    // Fig. 7.9: ArrayReferenceTest.cs
2    // Testing the effects of passing array references
3    // by value and by reference.
4    using System;
5    using System.Drawing;
6    using System.Collections;
7    using System.ComponentModel;
8    using System.Windows.Forms;
9    using System.Data;
10
11   public class ArrayReferenceTest : System.Windows.Forms.Form
12   {
13      private System.Windows.Forms.Label outputLabel;
14      private System.Windows.Forms.Button showOutputButton;
15
16      [STAThread]
17      static void Main()
18      {
19         Application.Run( new ArrayReferenceTest() );
20      }
21
22      private void showOutputButton_Click( object sender,
23         System.EventArgs e )
24      {
25         // create and initialize firstArray
26         int[] firstArray = { 1, 2, 3 };
27
28         // copy firstArray reference (but not array itself)
29         int[] firstArrayCopy = firstArray;
30
31         outputLabel.Text =
32            "Test passing firstArray reference by value";
33
34         outputLabel.Text += "\n\nContents of firstArray " +
35            "before calling FirstDouble:\n\t";
36
37         // print contents of firstArray
38         for ( int i = 0; i < firstArray.Length; i++ )
39            outputLabel.Text += firstArray[ i ] + " ";
40
41         // pass reference firstArray by value to FirstDouble
42         FirstDouble( firstArray );
43
44         outputLabel.Text += "\n\nContents of firstArray after " +
45            "calling FirstDouble\n\t";
46
47         // print contents of firstArray
48         for ( int i = 0; i < firstArray.Length; i++ )
49            outputLabel.Text += firstArray[ i ] + " ";
50
```

Fig. 7.9   Passing an array reference by value and by reference. (Part 1 of 3.)

```
51          // test whether reference was changed by FirstDouble
52          if ( firstArray == firstArrayCopy )
53             outputLabel.Text +=
54                "\n\nThe references refer to the same array\n";
55          else
56             outputLabel.Text +=
57                "\n\nThe references refer to different arrays\n";
58
59          // create and initialize secondArray
60          int[] secondArray = { 1, 2, 3 };
61
62          // copy secondArray reference
63          int[] secondArrayCopy = secondArray;
64
65          outputLabel.Text += "\nTest passing secondArray " +
66             "reference by reference";
67
68          outputLabel.Text += "\n\nContents of secondArray " +
69             "before calling SecondDouble:\n\t";
70
71          // print contents of secondArray before method call
72          for ( int i = 0; i < secondArray.Length; i++ )
73             outputLabel.Text += secondArray[ i ] + " ";
74
75          SecondDouble( ref secondArray );
76
77          outputLabel.Text += "\n\nContents of secondArray " +
78             "after calling SecondDouble:\n\t";
79
80          // print contents of secondArray after method call
81          for ( int i = 0; i < secondArray.Length; i++ )
82             outputLabel.Text += secondArray[ i ] + " ";
83
84          // test whether reference was changed by SecondDouble
85          if ( secondArray == secondArrayCopy )
86             outputLabel.Text +=
87                "\n\nThe references refer to the same array\n";
88          else
89             outputLabel.Text +=
90                "\n\nThe references refer to different arrays\n";
91
92       } // end method showOutputButton_Click
93
94       // modify elements of array and attempt to modify
95       // reference
96       void FirstDouble( int[] array )
97       {
98          // double each element's value
99          for ( int i = 0; i < array.Length; i++ )
100            array[ i ] *= 2;
101
```

Fig. 7.9   Passing an array reference by value and by reference. (Part 2 of 3.)

```
102        // create new reference and assign it to array
103        array = new int[] { 11, 12, 13 };
104     }
105
106     // modify elements of array and change reference array
107     // to refer to a new array
108     void SecondDouble( ref int[] array )
109     {
110        // double each element's value
111        for ( int i = 0; i < array.Length; i++ )
112           array[ i ] *= 2;
113
114        // create new reference and assign it to array
115        array = new int[] { 11, 12, 13 };
116     }
117  }
```

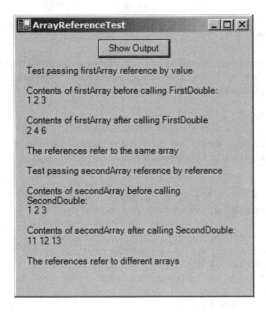

Fig. 7.9   Passing an array reference by value and by reference. (Part 3 of 3.)

Lines 60–90 perform similar tests, using array variables **secondArray** and **secondArrayCopy** and method **SecondDouble** (lines 108–116). Method **SecondDouble** performs the same operations as **FirstDouble**, but receives its array argument using keyword **ref**. In this case, the reference stored in **secondArray** after the method call is a reference to the array allocated on line 115 of **SecondDouble**, demonstrating that a reference passed with keyword **ref** can be modified by the called method so that the reference in the caller actually points to a different object, in this case an array allocated in method **SecondDouble**. The **if/else** structure in lines 85–90 demonstrates that **secondArray** and **secondArrayCopy** no longer refer to the same array.

Software Engineering Observation 7.1

When a method receives a reference-type object parameter by value, the object itself is not passed by value—the object still passes by reference. Rather, the object's reference is passed by value. This prevents a method from overwriting references passed to that method. In the vast majority of cases, protecting the caller's reference from modification is the desired behavior. In the rare situations where you truly want the called procedure to modify the caller's reference, pass the reference using keyword **ref***.*

Software Engineering Observation 7.2

*In C#, objects (including arrays) always pass by reference. So, a called method receiving a reference to an object can modify the caller's object via a non-***const*** reference parameter.*

7.7 Sorting Arrays

Sorting data (i.e., arranging the data into some particular order, such as ascending or descending) is one of the most important computing applications. A bank sorts all checks by account number so that it can prepare individual bank statements at the end of each month. Telephone companies sort their lists of accounts by last name, and within that, by first name to make it easy to find phone numbers. Virtually every organization must sort some data, and in many cases, massive amounts of it. Sorting data is an intriguing problem that has attracted some of the most intense research efforts in the computer science field. In this section, we discuss one of the simplest sorting schemes.

Performance Tip 7.2

Sometimes, the simplest algorithms perform poorly. Their virtue is that they are easy to write, test and debug. Complex algorithms sometimes are needed to realize maximum performance of a program.

Figure 7.10 sorts the values of the 10-element array **a** into ascending order. The technique we use is called the *bubble sort*, because smaller values gradually "bubble" their way to the top of the array (i.e., toward the first element) like air bubbles rising in water. The technique sometimes is called the *sinking sort*, because the larger values sink to the bottom of the array. Bubble sort uses nested loops to make several passes through the array. Each pass compares successive pairs of elements. If a pair is in increasing order (or the values are equal), the values remain in the same order. If a pair is in decreasing order, the bubble sort swaps the values in the array. The program contains methods **Main**, **BubbleSort** and **Swap**. Method **sortButton_Click** (lines 23–41) creates array **a**, invokes **BubbleSort** and displays output. Line 34 of **sortButton_Click** invokes method **BubbleSort** (lines 44–52) to sort array **a**. Line 51 in method **BubbleSort** calls method **Swap** (lines 55–62) to exchange two elements of the array.

```
1   // Fig. 7.10: BubbleSorter.cs
2   // Sorting an array's values into ascending order.
3   using System;
4   using System.Drawing;
5   using System.Collections;
```

Fig. 7.10   Sorting an array with bubble sort. (Part 1 of 3.)

```
6   using System.ComponentModel;
7   using System.Windows.Forms;
8   using System.Data;
9
10  public class BubbleSorter : System.Windows.Forms.Form
11  {
12     private System.Windows.Forms.Button sortButton;
13     private System.Windows.Forms.Label outputLabel;
14
15     // Visual Studio .NET generated code
16
17     [STAThread]
18     static void Main()
19     {
20        Application.Run( new BubbleSorter() );
21     }
22
23     private void sortButton_Click( object sender,
24           System.EventArgs e )
25     {
26        int[] a = { 2, 6, 4, 8, 10, 12, 89, 68, 45, 37 };
27
28        outputLabel.Text = "Data items in original order\n";
29
30        for ( int i = 0; i < a.Length; i++ )
31           outputLabel.Text += "   " + a[ i ];
32
33        // sort elements in array a
34        BubbleSort( a );
35
36        outputLabel.Text += "\n\nData items in ascending order\n";
37
38        for ( int i = 0; i < a.Length; i++ )
39           outputLabel.Text += "   " + a[ i ];
40
41     } // end method sortButton_Click
42
43     // sort the elements of an array with bubble sort
44     public void BubbleSort( int[] b )
45     {
46        for ( int pass = 1; pass < b.Length; pass++ ) // passes
47
48           for ( int i = 0; i < b.Length - 1; i++ )   // one pass
49
50              if ( b[ i ] > b[ i + 1 ] )         // one comparison
51                 Swap( b, i );                   // one swap
52     }
53
54     // swap two elements of an array
55     public void Swap( int[] c, int first )
56     {
57        int hold;       // temporary holding area for swap
58
```

Fig. 7.10   Sorting an array with bubble sort. (Part 2 of 3.)

```
59            hold = c[ first ];
60            c[ first ] = c[ first + 1 ];
61            c[ first + 1 ] = hold;
62        }
63    }
```

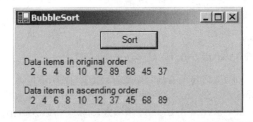

Fig. 7.10   Sorting an array with bubble sort. (Part 3 of 3.)

Method **BubbleSort** receives the array as parameter **b**. The nested **for** loop on lines
46–51 performs the sort. The outer loop controls the number of passes of the array. The inner
loop controls the comparisons and necessary swapping of the elements during each pass.

Method **BubbleSort** first compares **b[0]** to **b[1]**, then **b[1]** to **b[2]**, then
b[2] to **b[3]** and so on, until it completes the pass by comparing **b[8]** to **b[9]**.
Although there are 10 elements, the comparison loop performs only nine comparisons. As
a result of the way the successive comparisons are made, a large value may move down the
array (sink) many positions (and sometimes all the way to the bottom of the array) on a
single pass. However, a small value may move up (bubble) only one position. On the first
pass, the largest value is guaranteed to sink to the bottom element of the array, **b[9]**. On
the second pass, the second largest value is guaranteed to sink to **b[8]**. On the ninth pass,
the ninth largest value sinks to **b[1]**. This leaves the smallest value in **b[0]**, so only
nine passes are needed to sort a 10-element array.

If a comparison reveals that the two elements appear in descending order, **BubbleSort**
calls **Swap** to exchange the two elements so they will be in ascending order in the array.
Method **Swap** receives a reference to the array (which it calls **c**) and one integer representing
the subscript of the first element of the array to be exchanged. Three assignments on lines 59–
61 perform the exchange, where the extra variable **hold** temporarily stores one of the two
values being swapped. The swap cannot be performed with only the two assignments

```
c[ first ] = c[ first + 1 ];
c[ first + 1 ] = c[ first ];
```

If **c[first]** is **7** and **c[first + 1]** is **5**, after the first assignment, both elements of
the array contain **5** and the value **7** is lost—hence, the need for the extra variable **hold**.

The advantage of the bubble sort is that it is easy to program. However, the bubble sort
runs slowly, which becomes apparent when sorting large arrays. More advanced courses
(often titled "Data Structures" or "Algorithms" or "Computational Complexity") investigate sorting and searching in greater depth. Note that the .NET framework includes a built-
in array-sorting capability that implements a high-speed sort. To sort the array **a** in
Fig. 7.10, you can use the statement

```
Array.Sort( a );
```

7.8 Searching Arrays: Linear Search and Binary Search

Often, programmers work with large amounts of data stored in arrays. It might be necessary in this case to determine whether an array contains a value that matches a certain *key value*. The process of locating a particular element value in an array is called *searching*. In this section, we discuss two searching techniques—the simple *linear search* technique and the more efficient *binary search* technique.

7.8.1 Searching an Array with Linear Search

In the program in Fig. 7.11, method **LinearSearch** (defined on lines 44–54) uses a **for** structure containing an **if** structure to compare each element of an array with a *search key* (line 44). If the search key is found, the method returns the subscript value for the element to indicate the exact position of the search key in the array. If the search key is not found, the method returns **-1**. (The value **-1** is a good choice because it is not a valid subscript number.) If the elements of the array being searched are not in any particular order, it is just as likely that the value will be found in the first element as in the last. On average, the program will have to compare the search key with half the elements of the array. The program contains a 100-element array filled with the even integers from 0–198. The user types the search key in a **TextBox** (called **inputTextBox**) and clicks the **findButton** to start the search. [*Note*: The array is passed to **LinearSearch** even though the array is an instance variable of the class. This is done because an array normally is passed to a method of another class for searching.]

```
1   // Fig. 7.11: LinearSearcher.cs
2   // Demonstrating linear searching of an array.
3   using System;
4   using System.Drawing;
5   using System.Collections;
6   using System.ComponentModel;
7   using System.Windows.Forms;
8   using System.Data;
9
10  public class LinearSearcher : System.Windows.Forms.Form
11  {
12     private System.Windows.Forms.Button searchButton;
13     private System.Windows.Forms.TextBox inputTextBox;
14     private System.Windows.Forms.Label outputLabel;
15
16     int[] a = { 2, 4, 6, 8, 10, 12, 14, 16, 18, 20, 22, 24, 26,
17                 28, 30, 32, 34, 36, 38, 40, 42, 44, 46, 48, 50 };
18
19     // Visual Studio .NET generated code
20
21     [STAThread]
22     static void Main()
23     {
```

Fig. 7.11 Linear search of an array. (Part 1 of 2.)

```
24              Application.Run( new LinearSearcher() );
25        }
26
27        private void searchButton_Click( object sender,
28           System.EventArgs e )
29        {
30           int searchKey = Int32.Parse( inputTextBox.Text );
31
32           int subscriptIndex = LinearSearch( a, searchKey );
33
34           if ( subscriptIndex != -1 )
35              outputLabel.Text =
36                 "Found value in subscript " + subscriptIndex;
37
38           else
39              outputLabel.Text = "Value not found";
40
41        } // end method searchButton_Click
42
43        // search array for the specified key value
44        public int LinearSearch( int[] array, int key )
45        {
46           for ( int n = 0; n < array.Length; n++ )
47           {
48              if ( array[ n ] == key )
49                 return n;
50           }
51
52           return -1;
53
54        } // end method LinearSearch
55    }
```

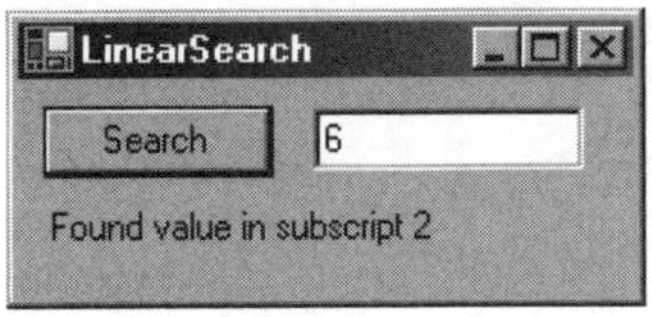

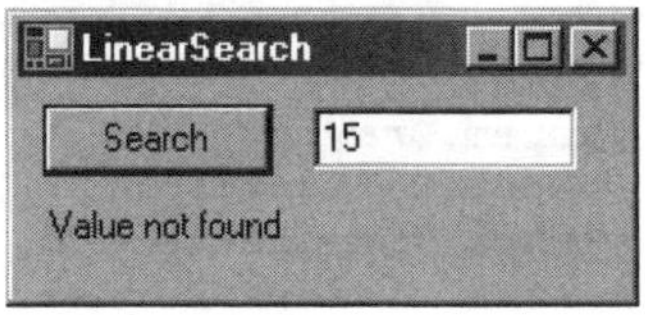

Fig. 7.11   Linear search of an array. (Part 2 of 2.)

7.8.2 Searching a Sorted Array with Binary Search

The linear search method works well for small or unsorted arrays. However, for large arrays, linear searching is inefficient. If the array is sorted, the high-speed *binary search* technique can be used. The binary search algorithm eliminates half of the elements in the array being searched after each comparison. The algorithm locates the middle array element and compares it with the search key. If they are equal, the search key has been found, and the subscript of that element is returned. Otherwise, the problem is reduced to searching half of the array. If the search key is less than the middle array element, the first half of the array is searched; otherwise, the second half of the array is searched. If the search key is not the middle element in the specified subarray (a piece of the original array), the algorithm is repeated in one quarter of the original array. The search continues until the search key is equal to the middle element of a subarray, or until the subarray consists of one element that is not equal to the search key (i.e., the search key is not found).

In a worst-case scenario, searching an array of 1024 elements will take only 10 comparisons by using a binary search. Repeatedly dividing 1024 by 2 (after each comparison we eliminate from consideration half the array) yields the values 512, 256, 128, 64, 32, 16, 8, 4, 2 and 1. The number 1024 (2^{10}) is divided by 2 only ten times to get the value 1. Dividing by 2 is equivalent to one comparison in the binary search algorithm. An array of 1,048,576 (2^{20}) elements takes a maximum of 20 comparisons to find the key. An array of one billion elements takes a maximum of 30 comparisons to find the key. This is a tremendous increase in performance over the linear search, which required comparing the search key with an average of half the elements in the array. For a one-billion-element array, the difference is between an average of 500 million comparisons and a maximum of 30 comparisons! The maximum number of comparisons needed for the binary search of any sorted array is the exponent of the first power of 2 greater than the number of elements in the array.

Figure 7.12 presents the iterative version of method **BinarySearch** (lines 59–85). The method receives two arguments—an integer array called **array** (the array to search) and an integer **key** (the search key). The array is passed to **BinarySearch** even though the array is an instance variable of the class. Once again, this is done because an array normally is passed to a method of another class for searching. Line 67 calculates the middle element of the array being searched by determining the number of elements in the array and dividing this value by 2. Recall that using the **/** operator with integers performs an integer division, which truncates the result. So, when there is an even number of elements in the array there is no "middle" element—the middle of our array is actually between two elements. When this occurs, the calculation on line 67 returns the smaller index of the two middle elements.

```
1   // Fig. 7.12: BinarySearchTest.cs
2   // Demonstrating a binary search of an array.
3
4   using System;
5   using System.Drawing;
6   using System.Collections;
7   using System.ComponentModel;
8   using System.Windows.Forms;
9   using System.Data;
10
11  public class BinarySearchTest : System.Windows.Forms.Form
12  {
13      private System.Windows.Forms.Label promptLabel;
14
15      private System.Windows.Forms.TextBox inputTextBox;
16
17      private System.Windows.Forms.Label resultLabel;
18      private System.Windows.Forms.Label displayLabel;
19      private System.Windows.Forms.Label outputLabel;
20
21      private System.Windows.Forms.Button findButton;
22
```

Fig. 7.12   Binary search of a sorted array. (Part 1 of 4.)

```
23        private System.ComponentModel.Container components = null;
24
25        int[] a = { 0, 2, 4, 6, 8, 10, 12, 14, 16,
26                    18, 20, 22, 24, 26, 28 };
27
28        // Visual Studio .NET generated code
29
30        // main entry point for application
31        [STAThread]
32        static void Main()
33        {
34           Application.Run( new BinarySearchTest() );
35        }
36
37        // searches for an element by calling
38        // BinarySearch and displaying results
39        private void findButton_Click( object sender,
40           System.EventArgs e )
41        {
42           int searchKey = Int32.Parse( inputTextBox.Text );
43
44           // initialize display string for the new search
45           outputLabel.Text = "Portions of array searched\n";
46
47           // perform the binary search
48           int subscript = BinarySearch( a, searchKey );
49
50           if ( subscript != -1 )
51              displayLabel.Text = "Found value in subscript " +
52                 subscript;
53           else
54              displayLabel.Text = "Value not found";
55
56        } // end findButton_Click
57
58        // searchs array for specified key
59        public int BinarySearch( int[] array, int key )
60        {
61           int low = 0;                    // low subscript
62           int high = array.Length - 1;   // high subscript
63           int middle;                     // middle subscript
64
65           while ( low <= high )
66           {
67              middle = ( low + high ) / 2;
68
69              // the following line displays the portion
70              // of the array currently being manipulated during
71              // each iteration of the binary search loop
72              BuildOutput( a, low, middle, high );
73
74              if ( key == array[ middle ] )    // match
75                 return middle;
```

Fig. 7.12 Binary search of a sorted array. (Part 2 of 4.)

```
76              else if ( key < array[ middle ] )
77                  high = middle - 1;    // search low end of array
78              else
79                  low = middle + 1;
80
81          } // end binary search
82
83          return -1;   // search key not found
84
85      } // end method BinarySearch
86
87      public void BuildOutput(
88          int[] array, int low, int mid, int high )
89      {
90          for ( int i = 0; i < array.Length; i++ )
91          {
92              if ( i < low || i > high )
93                  outputLabel.Text += "      ";
94
95              // mark middle element in output
96              else if ( i == mid )
97                  outputLabel.Text +=
98                      array[ i ].ToString( "00" ) + "* ";
99              else
100                 outputLabel.Text +=
101                     array[ i ].ToString( "00" ) + "   ";
102         }
103
104         outputLabel.Text += "\n";
105
106     } // end BuildOutput
107
108 } // end class BinarySearchTest
```

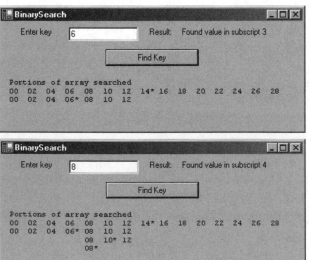

Fig. 7.12   Binary search of a sorted array. (Part 3 of 4.)

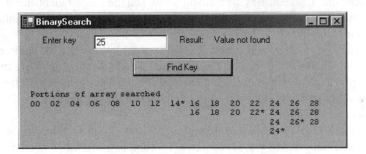

Fig. 7.12   Binary search of a sorted array. (Part 4 of 4.)

If **key** matches the **middle** element of a subarray (line 74), **BinarySearch** returns **middle** (the subscript of the current element), indicating that the value was found and the search is complete. If **key** does not match the **middle** element of a subarray, **Binary-Search** adjusts the **low** subscript or **high** subscript (both declared in the method) so that a smaller subarray can be searched. If **key** is less than the middle element (line 76), the **high** subscript is set to **middle - 1**, and the search continues on the elements from **low** to **middle - 1**. If **key** is greater than the middle element (line 78), the **low** subscript is set to **middle + 1**, and the search continues on the elements from **middle + 1** to **high**. These comparisons occur in the nested **if/else** structure on lines 74–79.

The program uses a 15-element array. The first power of 2 greater than the number of array elements is 16 (2^4)—so at most four comparisons are required to find the **key**. To illustrate this concept, method **BinarySearch** calls method **BuildOutput** (lines 87–106) to output each subarray during the binary search process. **BuildOutput** marks the middle element in each subarray with an asterisk (*****) to indicate the element with which the **key** is compared. Each search in this example results in a maximum of four lines of output—one per comparison. Note that the .NET framework includes a built-in array-searching capability that implements the binary-search algorithm. To search for the key 7 in the sorted array **a** in Fig. 7.12, you can use the statement

```
Array.BinarySearch( a, 7 );
```

7.9 Multiple-Subscripted Arrays

So far we have studied *single-subscripted* (or *one-dimensional*) arrays—i.e., those that contain single lists of values. In this section, we introduce *multiple-subscripted* (often called *multidimensional*) arrays. Such arrays require two or more subscripts to identify particular elements. There are two types of multiple-subscripted arrays—*rectangular* and *jagged*. Rectangular arrays often represent *tables* of values, while jagged arrays store arrays of arrays.

Arrays that require two subscripts to identify a particular element commonly are called *double-subscripted arrays*. We concentrate on double-subscripted arrays (often called *two-dimensional arrays*). Rectangular arrays with two subscripts often represent tables of values consisting of information arranged in *rows* and *columns*, where each row is the same size, and each column is the same size. An array with *m* rows and *n* columns is called an *m-by-n array*. To identify a particular table element, we must specify the two subscripts—

by convention, the first identifies the element's row and the second identifies the element's column. Figure 7.13 illustrates a double-subscripted rectangular array, **a**, containing three rows and four columns (i.e., a 3-by-4 array).

Every element in array **a** is identified in Fig. 7.13 by an element name of the form **a[i , j]**, in which **a** is the name of the array, and **i** and **j** are the subscripts that uniquely identify the row and column of each element in **a**. Notice that the names of the elements in the first row all have a first subscript of **0**; the names of the elements in the fourth column all have a second subscript of **3**.

Multiple-subscripted arrays can be initialized in declarations like single-subscripted arrays. A double-subscripted array **b** with two rows and two columns could be declared and initialized with

```
int[,] b = new int[ 2, 2 ];

b[ 0, 0 ] = 1;
b[ 0, 1 ] = 2;
b[ 1, 0 ] = 3;
b[ 1, 1 ] = 4;
```

or this can be written on one line using an *initializer list* as shown below:

```
int[,] b = { { 1, 2 }, { 3, 4 } };
```

The values are grouped by row in braces. Thus, **1** and **2** initialize **b[0 , 0]** and **b[0 , 1]**, and **3** and **4** initialize **b[1 , 0]** and **b[1 , 1]**. The compiler determines the number of rows by counting the number of sub-initializer lists (represented by sets of braces) in the main initializer list. The compiler determines the number of columns in each row by counting the number of initializer values in the sub-initializer list for that row. Method **GetLength** returns the length of a particular array dimension. In the preceding example, **b.GetLength(0)** returns the length of the zeroth dimension of **b**, which is **2**. The zeroth dimension of array **b** also can be thought of as row **0**.

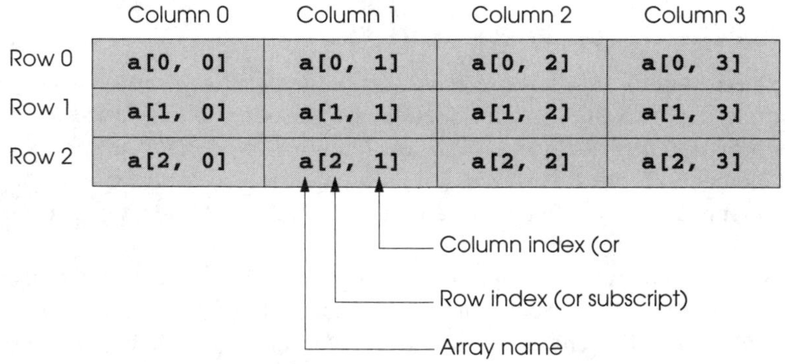

Fig. 7.13 Double-subscripted rectangular array with three rows and four columns.

We now demonstrate the creation of jagged arrays. Recall that jagged arrays are maintained as arrays of arrays. Unlike in rectangular arrays, the arrays that compose jagged arrays can be of different lengths. The declaration

```
int[][] c = new int[ 2 ][];   // allocate 2 rows (sub-arrays)

// allocate and initialize array for row 0
c[ 0 ] = new int[] { 1, 2, 3 };
// allocate and initialize array for row 1
c[ 1 ] = new int[] { 3, 4, 5 };
```

creates integer array **c** with row **0** (which is an array itself) containing three elements (**1**, **2** and **3**), and row **1** (another array) containing three elements (**3**, **4** and **5**). Each element of array **c** is an array itself, so jagged arrays can use property **Length** to determine the length of each sub-array, without the need for method **GetLength**. For the jagged array **c**, the size of the zeroth sub-array is **c[0].Length**, or **3**. To determine the number of sub-arrays in a jagged array, we can use the **Length** property with the jagged array itself, as in **c.Length** (which would evaluate to **2** in this example).

The application in Fig. 7.14 demonstrates the initialization of double-subscripted arrays in declarations and the use of nested **for** loops to traverse the arrays (i.e., to manipulate each array element).

```
1   // Fig. 7.14: TwoDimensionalArrays.cs
2   // Initializing two-dimensional arrays.
3   using System;
4   using System.Drawing;
5   using System.Collections;
6   using System.ComponentModel;
7   using System.Windows.Forms;
8   using System.Data;
9
10  public class TwoDimensionalArrays : System.Windows.Forms.Form
11  {
12     private System.Windows.Forms.Button showOutputButton;
13     private System.Windows.Forms.Label outputLabel;
14
15     // Visual Studio .NET generated code
16
17     [STAThread]
18     static void Main()
19     {
20        Application.Run( new TwoDimensionalArrays() );
21     }
22
23     private void showOutputButton_Click( object sender,
24        System.EventArgs e )
25     {
26        // declaration and initialization of rectangular array
27        int[,] array1 = new int[,] { { 1, 2, 3 }, { 4, 5, 6 } };
28
```

Fig. 7.14 Initializing multidimensional arrays. (Part 1 of 2.)

```
29              // declaration and initialization of jagged array
30              int[][] array2 = new int[ 3 ][];
31              array2[ 0 ] = new int[] { 1, 2 };
32              array2[ 1 ] = new int[] { 3 };
33              array2[ 2 ] = new int[] { 4, 5, 6 };
34
35              outputLabel.Text = "Values in array1 by row are\n";
36
37              // output values in array1
38              for ( int i = 0; i < array1.GetLength( 0 ); i++ )
39              {
40                  for ( int j = 0; j < array1.GetLength( 1 ); j++ )
41                      outputLabel.Text += array1[ i, j ] + "  ";
42
43                  outputLabel.Text += "\n";
44              }
45
46              outputLabel.Text += "\nValues in array2 by row are\n";
47
48              // output values in array2
49              for ( int i = 0; i < array2.Length; i++ )
50              {
51                  for ( int j = 0; j < array2[ i ].Length; j++ )
52                      outputLabel.Text += array2[ i ][ j ] + "  ";
53
54                  outputLabel.Text += "\n";
55              }
56
57          } // end method showOutputButton_Click
58
59      } // end class TwoDimensionalArrays
```

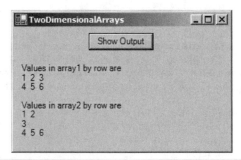

Fig. 7.14   Initializing multidimensional arrays. (Part 2 of 2.)

The declaration of **array1** (line 27) provides six initializers in two sublists. The first sublist initializes the first row of the array to the values 1, 2 and 3. The second sublist initializes the second row of the array to the values 4, 5 and 6. The declaration of **array2** (line 30) creates a jagged array of three arrays (specified by the **3** in the square brackets). Lines 31–33 initialize each subarray so that the first subarray contains the values 1 and 2, the second contains the value 3 and the last contains the values 4, 5 and 6.

The **for** structure on lines 38–44 appends the elements of **array1** to **string output**. Note the use of a nested **for** structure to output the rows of each double-subscripted array. In the nested **for** structures for **array1**, we use method **GetLength** to determine the number of elements in each dimension of the array. Line 38 determines the number of rows in the array by invoking **array1.GetLength(0)**, and line 40 determines the number of columns in the array by invoking **array1.GetLength(1)**. Arrays with additional dimensions would require more deeply nested **for** structures to process.

The nested **for** structures on lines 49–55 output the elements of jagged array **array2**. Recall that a jagged array is essentially an array that contains additional arrays as its elements. Line 49 uses the **Length** property of **array2** to determine the number of rows in the jagged array. Line 51 determines the **Length** of each subarray (i.e., row) with the expression **array2[i].Length**.

Many common array manipulations use **for** repetition structures. For the remainder of this section, we will focus on manipulations of jagged arrays. Imagine a jagged array **a**, which contains 3 rows, or arrays. The following **for** structure sets all the elements in the third row of array **a** to zero:

```
for ( int col = 0; col < a[ 2 ].Length; col++ )
    a[ 2 ][ col ] = 0;
```

We specified the *third* row; therefore, we know that the first subscript is always **2** (**0** is the first row and **1** is the second row). The **for** loop varies only the second subscript (i.e., the column subscript). Notice the use of **a[2].Length** in the **for** structure's conditional expression. Each row of **a** is an array itself, and therefore the program can access a typical array's properties, such as **Length**. This was demonstrated on line 51 of Fig. 7.14. Assuming that the length of array **a[2]** is **4**, the preceding **for** structure is equivalent to the assignment statements

```
a[ 2 ][ 0 ] = 0;
a[ 2 ][ 1 ] = 0;
a[ 2 ][ 2 ] = 0;
a[ 2 ][ 3 ] = 0;
```

The following nested **for** structure determines the total of all the elements in array **a**. We use **a.Length** in the conditional expression of the outer **for** structure to determine the number of rows in **a**, in this case, 3.

```
int total = 0;

for ( int row = 0; row < a.Length; row++ )

    for ( int col = 0; col < a[ row ].Length; col++ )
        total += a[ row ][ col ];
```

The **for** structure totals the elements of the array one row at a time. The outer **for** structure begins by setting the **row** subscript to **0**, so the elements of the first row may be totaled by the inner **for** structure. Then the outer **for** structure increments **row** to **1**, so the second row can be totaled. Finally, the outer **for** structure increments **row** to **2**, so the third row can be totaled. The result can be displayed when the nested **for** structure terminates.

The program in Fig. 7.15 performs several other array manipulations on 3-by-4 array **grades**. Each row of the array represents a student, and each column represents a grade on one of the four exams that the student took during the semester. The array manipulations are performed by four methods. Method **Minimum** (lines 64–76) determines the lowest grade of any student for the semester. Method **Maximum** (lines 79–91) determines the highest grade of any student for the semester. Method **Average** (lines 94–102) determines a particular student's semester average.

Methods **Minimum** and **Maximum** use array **grades** and the variables **students** (number of rows in the array) and **exams** (number of columns in the array). Each method loops through array **grades** by using nested **for** structures. Consider the nested **for** structure from method **Minimum** (lines 68–73). The outer **for** structure sets **i** (i.e., the row subscript) to **0** so the elements of the first row can be compared with variable **lowGrade** in the body of the inner **for** structure. The inner **for** structure loops through the four grades of a particular row and compares each grade with **lowGrade**. If a grade is less than **lowGrade**, then **lowGrade** is set to that grade. The outer **for** structure then increments the row subscript by **1**. The elements of the second row are compared with variable **lowGrade**. The outer **for** structure then increments the row subscript to **2**. The elements of the third row are compared with variable **lowGrade**. When execution of the nested structure is complete, **lowGrade** contains the smallest grade in the double-subscripted array. Method **Maximum** works similarly to method **Minimum**.

Method **Average** takes one argument—a single-subscripted array of test results for a particular student. When **Average** is called (line 59), the argument **grades[i]** specifies that a particular row of the double-subscripted array **grades** is to be passed to **Average**. For example, the argument **grades[1]** represents the four values (a single-subscripted array of grades) stored in the second row of the double-subscripted array **grades**. Remember that a jagged two-dimensional array is an array with elements that are single-subscripted arrays. Method **Average** calculates the sum of the array elements, divides the total by the number of test results and then returns the floating-point result cast as a **double** value (line 101).

```
1   // Fig. 7.15: DoubleArray.cs
2   // Manipulating a double-subscripted array.
3   using System;
4   using System.Drawing;
5   using System.Collections;
6   using System.ComponentModel;
7   using System.Windows.Forms;
8   using System.Data;
9
10  public class DoubleArray : System.Windows.Forms.Form
11  {
12     private System.Windows.Forms.Button showOutputButton;
13     private System.Windows.Forms.Label outputLabel;
14
15     int[][] grades;
16     int students, exams;
17
18     // Visual Studio .NET generated code
19
```

Fig. 7.15 Example using double-subscripted arrays. (Part 1 of 3.)

```
20        [STAThread]
21        static void Main()
22        {
23            Application.Run( new DoubleArray() );
24        }
25
26        private void showOutputButton_Click( object sender,
27            System.EventArgs e )
28
29        {
30            grades = new int[ 3 ][];
31            grades[ 0 ] =  new int[]{ 77, 68, 86, 73 };
32            grades[ 1 ] =  new int[]{ 96, 87, 89, 81 };
33            grades[ 2 ] =  new int[]{ 70, 90, 86, 81 };
34
35            students = grades.Length;       // number of students
36            exams = grades[ 0 ].Length;     // number of exams
37
38            // line up column headings
39            outputLabel.Text = "                    ";
40
41            // output the column headings
42            for ( int i = 0; i < exams; i++ )
43                outputLabel.Text += "[" + i + "]   ";
44
45            // output the rows
46            for ( int i = 0; i < students; i++ )
47            {
48                outputLabel.Text += "\ngrades[" + i + "]    ";
49
50                for ( int j = 0; j < exams; j++ )
51                    outputLabel.Text += grades[ i ][ j ] + "    ";
52            }
53
54            outputLabel.Text += "\n\nLowest grade: " + Minimum() +
55                "\nHighest grade: " + Maximum() + "\n";
56
57            for ( int i = 0; i < students; i++ )
58                outputLabel.Text += "\nAverage for student " + i + " is " +
59                    Average( grades[ i ] );
60
61        } // end method showOutputButton_Click
62
63        // find minimum grade in grades array
64        public int Minimum()
65        {
66            int lowGrade = 100;
67
68            for ( int i = 0; i < students; i++ )
69
70                for ( int j = 0; j < exams; j++ )
71
```

Fig. 7.15   Example using double-subscripted arrays. (Part 2 of 3.)

```
72                  if ( grades[ i ][ j ] < lowGrade )
73                     lowGrade = grades[ i ][ j ];
74
75            return lowGrade;
76         }
77
78         // find maximum grade in grades array
79         public int Maximum()
80         {
81            int highGrade = 0;
82
83            for ( int i = 0; i < students; i++ )
84
85               for ( int j = 0; j < exams; j++ )
86
87                  if ( grades[ i ][ j ] > highGrade )
88                     highGrade = grades[ i ][ j ];
89
90            return highGrade;
91         }
92
93         // determine average grade for a particular student
94         public double Average( int[] setOfGrades )
95         {
96            int total = 0;
97
98            for ( int i = 0; i < setOfGrades.Length; i++ )
99               total += setOfGrades[ i ];
100
101           return ( double ) total / setOfGrades.Length;
102        }
103
104   } // end class DoubleArray
```

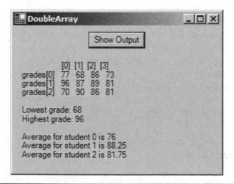

Fig. 7.15   Example using double-subscripted arrays. (Part 3 of 3.)

7.10 foreach Repetition Structure

C# provides the **foreach** repetition structure for iterating through values in data structures, such as arrays. When used with one-dimensional arrays, **foreach** behaves like a **for** structure that iterates through the range of indices from **0** to one less than the array's

Length. Instead of using the array name subscripted by a counter, **foreach** uses a variable to represent the value of each element. The program in Fig. 7.16 uses the **foreach** structure to determine the minimum value in a two-dimensional array of grades.

The header of the **foreach** structure (line 16) specifies a variable, **grade**, and an array, **gradeArray**. The **foreach** structure iterates through all elements in **grade-Array**, sequentially assigning each value to variable **grade**. Line 18 compares each value with variable **lowGrade**, and if the value is less than **lowGrade**, line 19 replaces **lowGrade** with the value.

For rectangular arrays, the repetition of the **foreach** structure begins with the element whose indices are all zero and subsequently iterates through all possible combinations of indices, incrementing the rightmost index first. When the rightmost index reaches its upper bound, it is reset to zero, and the index to the left of it is incremented by one. In this case, **grade** takes on the values as they are ordered in the initializer list in lines 11–12. When all the grades have been processed, **lowGrade** is displayed (line 22).

Although many array calculations are handled best with a counter, **foreach** is useful when the indices of the elements are not important. The **foreach** structure is particularly useful for looping through arrays of objects.

7.11 Summary

An array is a group of contiguous memory locations that all have the same name and type. To refer to a particular location or element in an array, specify the name of the array and the position number of the element within the array. The first element in every array is the zeroth element (i.e., element 0). The position number in square brackets is more formally called a subscript (or an index). This number must be an integer or an integer expression. To reference the ith element of a single-dimensional array, use i - 1 as the index. The brackets that enclose the subscript of an array are operators that have the same level of precedence as parentheses.

When arrays are allocated, the elements are initialized to zero for numeric primitive-data-type variables, to **false** for **bool** variables and to **null** for reference types. In an array of primitive data types, every element of the array contains one value of the declared data type of the array. In an array of a reference type, every element of the array is a reference to an object of the data type of the array. For example, every element of a **string** array is a reference to a **string**, and each reference has the value **null** by default.

```
1   // Fig. 7.16: UsingForEach.cs
2   // Demonstrating foreach structure.
3
4   using System;
5
6   class UsingForEach
7   {
8      // main entry point for the application
9      static void Main( string[] args )
10     {
11        int[,] gradeArray = { { 77, 68, 86, 73 },
12           { 98, 87, 89, 81 }, { 70, 90, 86, 81 } };
```

Fig. 7.16 Using **foreach** with an array. (Part 1 of 2.)

```
13
14          int lowGrade = 100;
15
16          foreach ( int grade in gradeArray )
17          {
18              if ( grade < lowGrade )
19                  lowGrade = grade;
20          }
21
22          Console.WriteLine( "The minimum grade is: " + lowGrade );
23      }
24  }
```

```
The minimum grade is: 68
```

Fig. 7.16 Using **foreach** with an array. (Part 2 of 2.)

The elements of single-dimensional and rectangular arrays can be allocated and initialized in the array declaration by following the declaration with an equal sign and a comma-separated initializer list enclosed in braces (**{** and **}**).

Unlike their predecessors C and C++, .NET-compliant languages provide mechanisms to prevent elements outside the bounds of an array from being accessed. When a reference is made to a nonexistent element of an array, an **IndexOutOfRangeException** occurs.

To pass an array argument to a method, specify the name of the array, without any brackets. Although entire arrays are passed by reference, individual array elements of primitive data types are passed by value, as are simple variables. To pass an array element to a method, use the subscripted name of the array element as an argument in the method call.

Sorting data (i.e., placing the data into a particular order, such as ascending or descending) is one of the most important computing applications. One technique used to sort data is the bubble sort. The chief virtue of the bubble sort is that it is easy to program. However, the bubble sort runs slowly, which becomes apparent when sorting large arrays.

The process of locating a particular element value in an array is called searching. The linear-search algorithm compares each value in an array with the value being searched for, until either the value is found or the entire array is traversed (i.e., the value does not exist in the array). The linear-search method works well for small or unsorted arrays. However, for large arrays, linear searching is inefficient. The binary-search algorithm compares the middle element in a sorted array with the value being searched for and uses the result of that comparison to eliminate one-half the elements in the array being searched. The maximum number of comparisons needed for the binary search of any sorted array is the exponent of the first power of two that is greater than the number of elements in the array.

There are two types of multiple-subscripted arrays—rectangular and jagged. In general, an array with *m* rows and *n* columns is referred to as an *m*-by-*n* array. Multiple-subscripted arrays can be initialized in declarations, as can single-subscripted arrays. The compiler determines the number of columns in each row by counting the number of initializer values in the subinitializer list for that row. Jagged arrays are maintained as arrays of arrays. Unlike rectangular arrays, rows in jagged arrays can be of different lengths.

When used with one-dimensional arrays, the **foreach** structure behaves like a **for** structure that iterates through the range of indices from **0** to the array's **Length**. For rectangular arrays, the repetition of the **foreach** structure begins with the element whose indices are all zero and subsequently iterates through all possible combinations of indices, incrementing the rightmost index first. When the rightmost index reaches its upper bound, it is reset to zero, and the index to the left of it is incremented by one.

Object-Based
Programming

Objectives
- To understand encapsulation and data hiding.
- To understand the concepts of data abstraction and abstract data types (ADTs).
- To be able to create, use and destroy objects.
- To be able to control access to object instance variables and methods.
- To be able to use properties to keep objects in consistent states.
- To understand the use of the **this** reference.
- To understand namespaces and assemblies.
- To be able to use the **Class View** and **Object Browser**.

My object all sublime
I shall achieve in time.
W. S. Gilbert

Is it a world to hide virtues in?
William Shakespeare

Your public servants serve you right.
Adlai Stevenson

Classes struggle, some classes triumph, others are eliminated.
Mao Zedong

This above all: to thine own self be true.
William Shakespeare

8.1 Introduction

In this chapter, we investigate object orientation in C#. Some readers might ask, why have we deferred this topic until now? There are several reasons. First, the objects we build in this chapter partially are composed of structured program pieces. To explain the organization of objects, we needed to establish a basis in structured programming with control structures. We also wanted to study methods in detail before introducing object orientation. Finally, we wanted to familiarize readers with arrays, which are C# objects.

In our discussions of object-oriented programs in Chapters 1–7, we introduced many basic concepts (i.e., "object think") and terminology (i.e., "object speak") that relate to C# object-oriented programming. We also discussed our program-development methodology: We analyzed typical problems that required programs to be built and determined what classes from the .NET Framework Class Library were needed to implement each program. We then selected appropriate instance variables and methods for each program and specified the manner in which an object of our class collaborated with objects from the .NET Framework classes to accomplish the program's overall goals.

Let us briefly review some key concepts and terminology of object orientation. Object orientation uses classes to *encapsulate* (i.e., wrap together) data (*attributes*) and methods (*behaviors*). Objects have the ability to hide their implementation from other objects (this principle is called *information hiding*). Although some objects can communicate with one another across well-defined *interfaces* (just like the driver's interface to a car includes a steering wheel, accelerator pedal, brake pedal and gear shift), objects are unaware of how other objects are implemented (just as the driver is unaware of how the steering, engine, brake and transmission mechanisms are implemented). Normally, implementation details are hidden within the objects themselves. Surely, it is possible to drive a car effectively without knowing the details of how engines, transmissions and exhaust systems work. Later, we will see why information hiding is so crucial to good software engineering.

In *procedural programming languages* (like C), programming tends to be *action oriented.* C# programming, however, is *object oriented.* In C, the unit of programming is the *function* (functions are called *methods* in C#). In C#, the unit of programming is the *class*. Objects eventually are *instantiated* (i.e., created) from these classes and functions are encapsulated within the "boundaries" of classes as methods.

C programmers concentrate on writing functions. They group actions that perform some task into a function and then group functions to form a program. Data are certainly important in C, but they exist primarily to support the actions that functions perform. The *verbs* in a system-requirements document describing the requirements for a new application help a C programmer determine the set of functions that will work together to implement the system.

By contrast, C# programmers concentrate on creating their own *user-defined types*, called *classes.* We also refer to classes as *programmer-defined types.* Each class contains both data and a set of methods that manipulate the data. The data components, or *data members*, of a class are called *member variables*, or *instance variables* (many C# programmers prefer the term *fields*).[1] Just as we call an instance of a built-in type—such as **int**—a *variable,* we call an instance of a user-defined type (i.e., a class) an *object*. In C#, attention is focused on classes, rather than on methods. The *nouns* in a system-requirements document help the C# programmer determine an initial set of classes with which to begin the design process. Programmers use these classes to instantiate objects that work together to implement the system.

This chapter explains how to create and use classes and objects, a subject known as *object-based programming (OBP).* Chapter 9 introduces *inheritance*—a key technology that enable *object-oriented programming (OOP).* Although we do not discuss inheritance in detail until Chapter 9, it is part of several class definitions in this chapter and has been used in several examples previously. For example, in the program of Section 4.13 (and several subsequent programs), we inherited a class from **System.Windows.Forms.Form** to create an application that executes in its own window.

Software Engineering Observation 8.1

All C# objects are passed by reference.

8.2 Implementing a Time Abstract Data Type with a Class

Classes in C# facilitate the creation of *abstract data types (ADT)*, which hide their implementation from clients (or users of the class object). A problem in procedural programming

---

1. We sometimes use industry-standard terminology, such as data members and instance members. rather than C# terms such as fields. For a listing of C#-specific terminology, please see the C# Language Specification, which can be downloaded from **msdn.microsoft.com/vstudio/ nextgen/technology/csharpdownload.asp**.

languages is that client code often is dependent on implementation details of the data used in the code. This dependency might necessitate rewriting the client code if the data implementation changes. ADTs eliminate this problem by providing implementation-independent *interfaces* to their clients. The creator of a class can change the internal implementation of that class without affecting the clients of that class.

Software Engineering Observation 8.2

It is important to write programs that are understandable and easy to maintain. Change is the rule, rather than the exception. Programmers should anticipate that their code will be modified. As we will see, classes facilitate program modifiability.

The following example (and subsequent examples) will require multiple class definitions in the same project. To add a class to a project, select **Add Class...** from the **Project** menu. In the **Add New Item** dialog box that appears, enter the new class name in the **Name** text box and click the **Open** button. Note that the file name (ending with the **.cs** file extension) appears in the **Solution Explorer** below the project name.

Our next example consists of classes **Time1** (Fig. 8.1) and **TimeTest1** (Fig. 8.2). Class **Time1** contains the time of day in 24-hour clock format. Class **TimeTest1** contains method **Main**, which creates an instance of class **Time1** and demonstrates the features of that class.

```
1   // Fig. 8.1: Time1.cs
2   // Class Time1 maintains time in 24-hour format.
3
4   using System;
5
6   // Time1 class definition
7   public class Time1 : Object
8   {
9      private int hour;      // 0-23
10     private int minute;    // 0-59
11     private int second;    // 0-59
12
13     // Time1 constructor initializes instance variables to
14     // zero to set default time to midnight
15     public Time1()
16     {
17        SetTime( 0, 0, 0 );
18     }
19
20     // Set new time value in 24-hour format. Perform validity
21     // checks on the data. Set invalid values to zero.
22     public void SetTime(
23        int hourValue, int minuteValue, int secondValue )
24     {
25        hour = ( hourValue >= 0 && hourValue < 24 ) ?
26           hourValue : 0;
27        minute = ( minuteValue >= 0 && minuteValue < 60 ) ?
28           minuteValue : 0;
```

Fig. 8.1   **Time1** abstract data type represents the time in 24-hour format. (Part 1 of 2.)

```
29            second = ( secondValue >= 0 && secondValue < 60 ) ?
30               secondValue : 0;
31
32      } // end method SetTime
33
34      // convert time to universal-time (24 hour) format string
35      public string ToUniversalString()
36      {
37         return String.Format(
38            "{0:D2}:{1:D2}:{2:D2}", hour, minute, second );
39      }
40
41      // convert time to standard-time (12 hour) format string
42      public string ToStandardString()
43      {
44         return String.Format( "{0}:{1:D2}:{2:D2} {3}",
45            ( ( hour == 12 || hour == 0 ) ? 12 : hour % 12 ),
46            minute, second, ( hour < 12 ? "AM" : "PM" ) );
47      }
48
49   } // end class Time1
```

Fig. 8.1   **Time1** abstract data type represents the time in 24-hour format. (Part 2 of 2.)

In Fig. 8.1, line 7 begins the **Time1** class definition, indicating that class **Time1** inherits from class *Object* (namespace **System**). C# programmers use *inheritance* to create classes from existing classes. In fact, every class in C# (except **Object**) inherits from an existing class definition. On line 7, the **:** followed by class name **Object** indicates that class **Time1** inherits existing pieces of class **Object**. If a new class definition does not specify a **:** and class name to the right of the new class name, the new class implicitly inherits from class **Object**. It is not necessary to understand inheritance to learn the concepts and programs in this chapter. We explore inheritance and class **Object** in detail in Chapter 9.

The opening left brace (**{**) at line 8 and closing right brace (**}**) at line 49 delineate the *body* of class **Time1**. Any information that we place in this body is said to be encapsulated (i.e., wrapped) in the class. For example, lines 9–11 of class **Time1** declare three **int** variables—**hour**, **minute** and **second**—that represent the time of day in *universal-time* format (*24-hour clock* format). Variables declared in a class definition, but not inside a method definition, are called *instance variables*—each instance (object) of the class contains its own separate copy of the class's instance variables.

Keywords *public* and *private* are *member access modifiers*. Instance variables or methods with member access modifier **public** are accessible wherever the program has a reference to a **Time1** object. However, instance variables or methods declared with member access modifier **private** are accessible only in that class definition. A class's **public** members and **private** members can be intermixed.

 Good Programming Practice 8.1

*Every instance variable or method definition should be preceded by a member access modifier. The default access modifier for class members is **private**.*

Lines 9–11 declare each of the three **int** instance variables—**hour, minute** and **second**—with member access modifier **private**, indicating that these instance variables of the class are accessible only to members of the class—this is known as *data hiding*. When an object of the class encapsulates such instance variables, only methods of that object's class can access the variables. Normally, instance variables are declared **private** and methods are declared **public**. However, it is possible to have **private** methods and **public** instance variables, as we will see later. Often, **private** methods are called *utility methods*, or *helper methods*, because they can be called only by other methods of that class. The purpose of utility methods is to support the operation of a class's other methods. Using **public** data in a class is an uncommon and dangerous programming practice. Providing such access to data members is unsafe—foreign code (i.e., code in other classes) could set **public** data members to invalid values, producing potentially disastrous results.

Good Programming Practice 8.2

We prefer to list instance variables of a class first, so that, when reading the code, programmers see the name and type of each instance variable before it is used in the methods of the class.

Good Programming Practice 8.3

*Even though **private** and **public** members can be intermixed, list all the **private** members of a class first in one group, then list all the **public** members in another group.*

Software Engineering Observation 8.3

*Declare all instance variables of a class as **private**. The architecture of accessing **private** data through **public** properties which first validate the data allows the developer to ensure that an object's data remains in a consistent state.*

Software Engineering Observation 8.4

*Make a class member **private** if there is no reason for that member to be accessed outside of the class definition.*

Classes often include *access methods* that can read or display data. Another common use for access methods is to test the truth of conditions—such methods often are called *predicate methods*. For example, we could design predicate method **IsEmpty** for a *container class*—a class capable of holding many objects, such as a linked list, a stack or a queue. (These data structures are discussed in detail in Chapter 21, FCL Collections.) **IsEmpty** would return **true** if the container is empty and **false** otherwise. A program might test **IsEmpty** before attempting to read another item from the container object. Similarly, a program might test another predicate method (e.g., **IsFull**) before attempting to insert an item into a container object.

Class **Time1** contains constructor **Time1** (lines 15–18) and methods **SetTime** (lines 22–32), **ToUniversalString** (lines 35–39) and **ToStandardString** (lines 42–47). These are the ***public*** methods (also called the ***public*** services or the ***public*** interface) of the class. *Clients* of class **Time1**, such as class **TimeTest1** (Fig. 8.2), use **Time1**'s **public** methods to manipulate the data stored in **Time1** objects or to cause class **Time1** to perform some service.

Lines 15–18 define the *constructor* of class **Time1**. A class's constructor initializes objects of that class. When a program creates an object of class **Time1** with operator **new**, the constructor automatically is called to initialize the object. Class **Time1**'s constructor calls method **SetTime** (lines 22–32) to initialize instance variables **hour, minute** and

second to **0** (representing midnight). Constructors can take arguments, but cannot return values. As we will see, a class can have overloaded constructors. An important difference between constructors and other methods is that constructors cannot specify a return type. Generally, constructors are declared **public**. Note that the constructor name must be the same as the class name.

Common Programming Error 8.1

Attempting to **return** *a value from a constructor is a syntax error.*

Method **SetTime** (lines 22–32) is a **public** method that receives three **int** parameters and uses them to set the time. A conditional expression tests each argument to determine whether the value is in a specified range. For example, the **hour** value must be greater than or equal to 0 and less than 24, because universal-time format represents hours as integers from 0 to 23. Similarly, both minute and second values must be greater than or equal to 0 and less than 60. Any values outside these ranges are invalid values and default to zero. Setting invalid values to zero ensures that a **Time1** object always contains valid data (because, in this example, zero is a valid value for **hour**, **minute** and **second**). When users supply invalid data to **SetTime**, the program might want to indicate that the time was invalid. In Chapter 10, we discuss exception handling, which can be used to indicate invalid initialization values.

Software Engineering Observation 8.5

Always define a class so that each of its instance variables always contains valid values.

Method **ToUniversalString** (lines 35–39) takes no arguments and returns a **string** in universal-time format, consisting of six digits—two for the hour, two for the minute and two for the second. For example, if the time were 1:30:07 PM, method **ToUniversalString** would return **13:30:07**. Lines 37–38 use **String** method **Format** to configure the universal time string. Line 37 passes to **Format** the *format string* **"{0:D2}:{1:D2}:{2:D2}"**, which contains several *format specifications* indicating that arguments **0**, **1** and **2** (the first three arguments after the format string argument) should each have the format **D2** (a two-digit base 10 decimal number format) for display purposes. The **D2** format specification causes single-digit values to appear as two digits with a leading **0** (e.g., **8** would be represented as **08**). The two colons that separate the curly braces **}** and **{** are the colons that separate the hour from the minute and the minute from the second in the resulting **string**.

Method **ToStandardString** (lines 42–47) takes no arguments and returns a **string** in standard-time format, consisting of the **hour**, **minute** and **second** values separated by colons and followed by an AM or a PM indicator (e.g., **1:27:06 PM**). Like method **ToUniversalString**, method **ToStandardString** uses **String** method **Format** to format the **minute** and **second** as two-digit values with leading zeros if necessary. Line 45 determines the value for **hour** in the **string**—if the **hour** is **0** or **12** (AM or PM), the **hour** appears as 12; otherwise, the **hour** appears as a value from 1–11.

After defining the class, we can use it as a type in declarations such as

```
Time1 sunset;  // reference to a Time1 object
```

The class name (**Time1**) is a type name. A class can yield many objects, just as a primitive data type, such as **int**, can yield many variables. Programmers can create class types as needed; this is one reason why C# is known as an *extensible language*.

Class **TimeTest1** (Fig. 8.2) uses an instance of class **Time1**. Method **Main** (lines 11–40) declares and initializes **Time1** instance **time** (line 13). When the object is instantiated, *operator* **new** allocates the memory in which the **Time1** object will be stored, then calls the **Time1** constructor (lines 15–18 of Fig. 8.1) to initialize the instance variables of the **Time1** object. As mentioned before, this constructor invokes method **SetTime** of class **Time1** to initialize each **private** instance variable to **0**. Operator **new** (line 13 of Fig. 8.2) then returns a reference to the newly created object; this reference is assigned to **time**.

Software Engineering Observation 8.6

*Note the relationship between operator **new** and the constructor of a class. When operator **new** creates an object of a class, that class's constructor is called to initialize the object's instance variables.*

```
1   // Fig. 8.2: TimeTest1.cs
2   // Demonstrating class Time1.
3
4   using System;
5   using System.Windows.Forms;
6
7   // TimeTest1 uses creates and uses a Time1 object
8   class TimeTest1
9   {
10      // main entry point for application
11      static void Main( string[] args )
12      {
13         Time1 time = new Time1();   // calls Time1 constructor
14         string output;
15
16         // assign string representation of time to output
17         output = "Initial universal time is: " +
18            time.ToUniversalString() +
19            "\nInitial standard time is: " +
20            time.ToStandardString();
21
22         // attempt valid time settings
23         time.SetTime( 13, 27, 6 );
24
25         // append new string representations of time to output
26         output += "\n\nUniversal time after SetTime is: " +
27            time.ToUniversalString() +
28            "\nStandard time after SetTime is: " +
29            time.ToStandardString();
30
31         // attempt invalid time settings
32         time.SetTime( 99, 99, 99 );
33
```

Fig. 8.2   Using an abstract data type. (Part 1 of 2.)

```
34          output += "\n\nAfter attempting invalid settings: " +
35              "\nUniversal time: " + time.ToUniversalString() +
36              "\nStandard time: " + time.ToStandardString();
37
38          MessageBox.Show( output, "Testing Class Time1" );
39
40      } // end method Main
41
42  } // end class TimeTest1
```

Fig. 8.2   Using an abstract data type. (Part 2 of 2.)

Note that the **TimeTest.cs** file does not use keyword **using** to import the namespace that contains class **Time1**. If a class is in the same namespace as the class that uses it, the **using** statement is not required. Every class in C# is part of a namespace. If a programmer does not specify a namespace for a class, the class is placed in the *default namespace*, which includes all compiled classes in the current directory that do not reside in a namespace. In Visual Studio, this current directory is the one in which the current project resides. We must specify **using** statements for classes from the .NET Framework, because they are defined outside the namespace of each new application we create. Note that **using** statements are not required if the program fully qualifies the name of each class by preceding the class name with its namespace name and a dot operator. For example, a program can invoke class **MessageBox**'s **Show** method as follows:

```
System.Windows.Forms.MessageBox.Show( "Your message here" );
```

However, such lengthy names can be cumbersome.

Line 14 declares **string** reference **output** to store the **string** containing the results, which later will be displayed in a **MessageBox**. Lines 17–20 assign to **output** the time in universal-time format (by invoking method **ToUniversalString** of the **Time1** object) and standard-time format (by invoking method **ToStandardString** of the **Time1** object). Note the syntax of the method call in each case—the reference **time** is followed by the member access operator (**.**) followed by the method name. The reference name specifies the object that will receive the method call.

Line 23 sets the time for the **Time1** object to which **time** refers by passing valid hour, minute and second arguments to **Time1** method **SetTime**. Lines 26–29 append to **output** the new time in both universal and standard formats to confirm that the time was set correctly.

To illustrate that method **SetTime** validates the values passed to it, line 32 passes invalid time arguments to method **SetTime**. Lines 34–36 append to **output** the new time in both formats. All three values passed to **SetTime** are invalid, so instance variables **hour**, **minute** and **second** are set to **0**. Line 38 displays a **MessageBox** with the results of our program. Notice in the last two lines of the output window that the time was indeed set to midnight when invalid arguments were passed to **SetTime**.

Time1 is our first example of a class that does not contain method **Main**. Thus, class **Time1** cannot be used to begin program execution. Class **TimeTest1** defines a **Main** method, so class **TimeTest1** can be used to begin program execution. A class containing method **Main** also is known as the *entry point* into the program.

Note that the program declares instance variables **hour**, **minute** and **second** as **private**. Such instance variables are not accessible outside the class in which they are defined. A class's clients should not be concerned with the data representation of that class. Clients of a class should be interested only in the services provided by that class. For example, the class could represent the time internally as the number of seconds that have elapsed since the previous midnight. Suppose the data representation changes. Clients still are able to use the same **public** methods and obtain the same results without being aware of the change in internal representation. In this sense, the implementation of a class is said to be *hidden* from its clients.

Software Engineering Observation 8.7

Information hiding promotes program modifiability and simplifies the client's perception of a class.

Software Engineering Observation 8.8

Clients of a class can (and should) use the class without knowing the internal details of how the class is implemented. If the class implementation changes (to improve performance, for example), but the class interface remains constant, the client's source code need not change. This makes it much easier to modify systems.

In this program, the **Time1** constructor initializes the instance variables to **0** (the universal time equivalent of 12 AM) to ensure that the object is created in a *consistent state*—i.e., all instance variables have valid values. The instance variables of a **Time1** object cannot store invalid values, because the constructor, which calls **SetTime**, is called to initialize the instance variables when the **Time1** object is created. Method **SetTime** scrutinizes subsequent attempts by a client to modify the instance variables.

Normally, the instance variables of a class are initialized in that class's constructor, but they also can be initialized when they are declared in the class body. If a programmer does not initialize instance variables explicitly, the compiler implicitly initializes them. When this occurs, the compiler sets primitive numeric variables to **0**, **bool** values to **false** and references to **null**.

Methods **ToUniversalString** and **ToStandardString** take no arguments, because, by default, these methods manipulate the instance variables of the particular **Time1** object on which they are invoked. This often makes method calls more concise than conventional function calls in procedural programming languages. It also reduces the likelihood of passing the wrong arguments, the wrong types of arguments or the wrong number of arguments.

Software Engineering Observation 8.9

The use of an object-oriented programming approach often simplifies method calls by reducing the number of parameters that must be passed. This benefit of object-oriented programming derives from the fact that encapsulation of instance variables and methods within an object gives the object's methods the right to access the object's instance variables.

Classes simplify programming, because the client need be concerned only with the **public** operations encapsulated in the object. Usually, such operations are designed to be client-oriented, rather than implementation-oriented. Clients are neither aware of, nor involved in, a class's implementation. Interfaces change less frequently than do implementations. When an implementation changes, implementation-dependent code must change accordingly. By hiding the implementation, we eliminate the possibility that other program parts will become dependent on the class-implementation details.

Often, programmers do not have to create classes "from scratch." Rather, they can derive classes from other classes that provide behaviors required by the new classes. Classes also can include references to objects of other classes as members. Such *software reuse* can greatly enhance programmer productivity. Chapter 9 discusses *inheritance*—the process by which new classes are derived from existing classes. Section 8.8 discusses *composition* (or *aggregation*), in which classes include as members references to objects of other classes.

8.3 Class Scope

In Section 6.13, we discussed method scope; now, we discuss class *scope*. A class's instance variables and methods belong to that class*'s* scope. Within a class's scope, class members are immediately accessible to all of that class's methods and can be referenced by name. Outside a class's scope, class members cannot be referenced directly by name. Those class members that are visible (such as **public** members) can be accessed only through a "handle" (i.e., members can be referenced via the format *referenceName.memberName*).

If a variable is defined in a method, only that method can access the variable (i.e., the variable is a local variable of that method). Such variables are said to have *block scope*. If a method defines a variable that has the same name as a variable with class scope (i.e., an instance variable), the method-scope variable hides the class-scope variable in that method's scope. A hidden instance variable can be accessed in a method by preceding its name with the keyword **this** and the dot operator, as in **this.hour**. We discuss keyword **this** in Section 8.9.

8.4 Controlling Access to Members

The member access modifiers **public** and **private** control access to a class's data and methods. (In Chapter 9, we introduce the additional access modifiers **protected** and **internal**.)

As previously stated, **public** methods present to the class's clients a view of the *services* that the class provides (i.e., the **public** interface of the class). Previously, we mentioned the merits of writing methods that perform only one task. If a method must execute other tasks to calculate its final result, these tasks should be performed by a helper method. A client does not need to call these helper methods, nor does it need to be concerned with how the class uses its helper methods. For these reasons, helper methods are declared as **private** members of a class.

Common Programming Error 8.2

*Attempting to access a **private** class member from outside that class is a compiler error.*

The application of Fig. 8.3 (which uses the **Time1** class from Fig. 8.1) demonstrates that **private** class members are not accessible outside the class. Lines 12–14 attempt to access the **private** instance variables **hour**, **minute** and **second** of the **Time1** object to which **time** refers. When this program is compiled, the compiler generates errors stating that the **private** members **hour**, **minute** and **second** are not accessible.

Access to **private** data should be controlled carefully by a class's methods. To allow clients to read the values of **private** data, the class can define a *property* that enables client code to access this **private** data safely. Properties, which we discuss in detail in Section 8.7, contain *accessor methods* that handle the details of modifying and returning data. A property definition can contain a ***get*** *accessor*, a ***set*** *accessor* or both. A ***get*** accessor enables a client to read a **private** data value; a ***set*** accessor enables the client to modify that value. Such modification would seem to violate the notion of **private** data. However, a ***set*** accessor can provide data-validation capabilities (such as range checking) to ensure that the value is set properly. A ***set*** accessor also can translate between the format of the data used in the interface and the format used in the underlying implementation. Similarly, a ***get*** accessor need not expose the data in "raw" format; rather, the ***get*** accessor can edit the data and limit the client's view of that data.

Software Engineering Observation 8.10

*Declaring the instance variables of a class as **private** and the methods and properties of the class as **public** facilitates debugging, because problems with data manipulations are localized to the class methods that manipulate that data.*

```
1   // Fig. 8.3: RestrictedAccess.cs
2   // Demonstrate compiler errors from attempt to access
3   // private class members.
4
5   class RestrictedAccess
6   {
7      // main entry point for application
8      static void Main( string[] args )
9      {
10         Time1 time = new Time1();
11
12         time.hour = 7;
13         time.minute = 15;
14         time.second = 30;
15      }
16
17   } // end class RestrictedAccess
```

Fig. 8.3   Accessing **private** class members from client code generates syntax errors. (Part 1 of 2.)

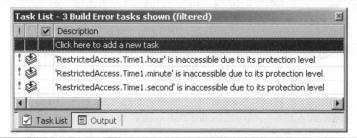

Fig. 8.3   Accessing **private** class members from client code generates syntax errors. (Part 2 of 2.)

Software Engineering Observation 8.11

*Class designers need not provide **set** or **get** accessors for each **private** data member; these capabilities should be provided only when doing so makes sense.*

8.5 Initializing Class Objects: Constructors

When a program creates an instance of a class, the program invokes the class's constructor to initialize the class's instance variables (data members). A class can contain overloaded constructors to provide multiple ways to initialize objects of that class. Instance variables can be initialized either by a constructor or when they are declared in the class body. Regardless of whether instance variables receive explicit initialization values, the instance variables always are initialized. In such cases, instance variables receive their default values (**0** for primitive numeric type variables, **false** for **bool** variables and **null** for references).

Software Engineering Observation 8.12

When appropriate, provide a constructor to ensure that every object is initialized with meaningful values.

When creating an object of a class, the programmer can provide *initializers* in parentheses to the right of the class name. These initializers are the arguments to the constructor. In general, declarations take the form:

> *ClassName objectReference* **= new** *ClassName* **(** *arguments* **) ;**

where *objectReference* is a reference of the appropriate data type, **new** indicates that an object is being created, *ClassName* indicates the type of the new object (and the name of the constructor being called) and *arguments* specifies a comma-separated list of the values used by the constructor to initialize the object. Figure 8.4 demonstrates using initializers and overloaded constructors.

Common Programming Error 8.3

*If a class has constructors, but none of the **public** constructors is a default constructor, and a program attempts to call a no-argument constructor to initialize an object of the class, a compilation error occurs. A constructor can be called with no arguments only if there are no constructors for the class (in which case the compiler-provided default constructor is called) or if the class defines a **public** no-argument constructor.*

If a class does not define any constructors, the compiler provides a *default (no-argument) constructor*. This compiler-provided default constructor contains no code (i.e., the constructor has an empty body) and takes no parameters. The programmer also can provide a default constructor, as we demonstrated in class **Time1** (Fig. 8.1). Programmer-provided default constructors can have code in their bodies.

8.6 Using Overloaded Constructors

Like methods, constructors of a class can be overloaded. The **Time1** constructor in Fig. 8.1 initialized **hour, minute** and **second** to **0** (i.e., 12 midnight in universal time) via a call to the class **SetTime** method. However, class **Time2** (Fig. 8.4) overloads the constructor to provide a variety of ways to initialize **Time2** objects. Each constructor calls **Time2** method **SetTime**, which ensures that the object begins in a consistent state by setting out-of-range values to zero. C# invokes the appropriate constructor by matching the number, types and order of the arguments specified in the constructor call with the number, types and order of the parameters specified in each constructor definition.

```
1   // Fig. 8.4: Time2.cs
2   // Class Time2 provides overloaded constructors.
3
4   using System;
5
6   // Time2 class definition
7   public class Time2
8   {
9      private int hour;     // 0-23
10     private int minute;   // 0-59
11     private int second;   // 0-59
12
13     // Time2 constructor initializes instance variables to
14     // zero to set default time to midnight
15     public Time2()
16     {
17        SetTime( 0, 0, 0 );
18     }
19
20     // Time2 constructor: hour supplied, minute and second
21     // defaulted to 0
22     public Time2( int hour )
23     {
24        SetTime( hour, 0, 0 );
25     }
26
27     // Time2 constructor: hour and minute supplied, second
28     // defaulted to 0
29     public Time2( int hour, int minute )
30     {
31        SetTime( hour, minute, 0 );
32     }
33
```

Fig. 8.4　Overloaded constructors provide flexible object-initialization options. (Part 1 of 2.)

```
34     // Time2 constructor: hour, minute and second supplied
35     public Time2( int hour, int minute, int second )
36     {
37        SetTime( hour, minute, second );
38     }
39
40     // Time2 constructor: initialize using another Time2 object
41     public Time2( Time2 time )
42     {
43        SetTime( time.hour, time.minute, time.second );
44     }
45
46     // Set new time value in 24-hour format. Perform validity
47     // checks on the data. Set invalid values to zero.
48     public void SetTime(
49        int hourValue, int minuteValue, int secondValue )
50     {
51        hour = ( hourValue >= 0 && hourValue < 24 ) ?
52           hourValue : 0;
53        minute = ( minuteValue >= 0 && minuteValue < 60 ) ?
54           minuteValue : 0;
55        second = ( secondValue >= 0 && secondValue < 60 ) ?
56           secondValue : 0;
57     }
58
59     // convert time to universal-time (24 hour) format string
60     public string ToUniversalString()
61     {
62        return String.Format(
63           "{0:D2}:{1:D2}:{2:D2}", hour, minute, second );
64     }
65
66     // convert time to standard-time (12 hour) format string
67     public string ToStandardString()
68     {
69        return String.Format( "{0}:{1:D2}:{2:D2} {3}",
70           ( ( hour == 12 || hour == 0 ) ? 12 : hour % 12 ),
71           minute, second, ( hour < 12 ? "AM" : "PM" ) );
72     }
73
74  } // end class Time2
```

Fig. 8.4   Overloaded constructors provide flexible object-initialization options. (Part 2 of 2.)

Because most of the code in class **Time2** is identical to that in class **Time1**, this discussion concentrates only on the overloaded constructors. Lines 15–18 define the no-argument constructor that sets the time to midnight. Lines 22–25 define a **Time2** constructor that receives a single **int** argument representing the **hour** and sets the time using the specified **hour** value and zero for the **minute** and **second**. Lines 29–32 define a **Time2** constructor that receives two **int** arguments representing the **hour** and **minute** and sets the time using those values and zero for the **second**. Lines 35–38 define a **Time2** constructor that receives three **int** arguments representing the **hour, minute** and **second** and uses those values to set the time. Lines 41–44 define a **Time2** constructor that receives a reference to another **Time2** object. When this last constructor is called, the values from the **Time2** argument are used to initialize the **hour**, **minute** and **second** values of the new **Time2** object. Even though class **Time2** declares **hour**, **minute** and **second** as **private** (lines 9–11), the **Time2** constructor can access these values in its **Time2** argument directly using the expressions **time.hour**, **time.minute** and **time.second**.

Software Engineering Observation 8.13

*When one object of a class has a reference to another object of the same class, the first object can access all the second object's data and methods (including those that are **private**).*

Notice that the second, third and fourth constructors (lines 22, 29 and 35) have some arguments in common and that those arguments are kept in the same order. For instance, the constructor that begins on line 29 has as its two arguments an integer representing the hour and an integer representing the minute. The constructor on line 35 has these same two arguments in the same order, followed by its last argument (an integer representing the second).

Good Programming Practice 8.4

When defining overloaded constructors, keep the order of arguments as similar as possible; this makes client programming easier.

Constructors do not specify return types; doing so results in syntax errors. Also, notice that each constructor receives a different number or different types of arguments. Even though only two of the constructors receive values for the **hour**, **minute** and **second**, each constructor calls **SetTime** with values for **hour**, **minute** and **second** and uses zeros for the missing values to satisfy **SetTime**'s requirement of three arguments.

Class **TimeTest2** (Fig. 8.5) starts the application that demonstrates the use of overloaded constructors (Fig. 8.4). Lines 15–20 create six **Time2** objects that invoke various constructors of the class. Line 15 invokes the no-argument constructor by placing an empty set of parentheses after the class name. Lines 16–20 invoke the **Time2** constructors that receive arguments. To invoke the appropriate constructor, pass the proper number, types and order of arguments (specified by the constructor's definition) to that constructor. For example, line 16 invokes the constructor that is defined in lines 22–25 of Fig. 8.4. Lines 22–47 invoke methods **ToUniversalString** and **ToStandardString** for each **Time2** object to demonstrate that the constructors initialize the objects correctly.

Each **Time2** constructor can be written to include a copy of the appropriate statements from method **SetTime**. This might be slightly more efficient, because it eliminates the extra call to **SetTime**. However, consider what would happen if the programmer were to change the representation of the time from three **int** values (requiring 12 bytes of memory) to a single **int** value representing the total number of seconds that have elapsed in the day (requiring 4 bytes of memory). Placing identical code in the **Time2** constructors and method **SetTime** makes such a change in the class definition more difficult, because every constructor's body would require modifications to manipulate the data as a single **int** rather than three **int**s. If the **Time2** constructors call **SetTime** directly, any changes to the implementation of **SetTime** must be made only once, in the body of **SetTime**. This reduces the likelihood of introducing a programming error when altering the implementation, because we make only one change in the class, rather than changing every constructor and method **SetTime**.

```
1   // Fig. 8.5: TimeTest2.cs
2   // Using overloaded constructors.
3
4   using System;
5   using System.Windows.Forms;
6
7   // TimeTest2 demonstrates constructors of class Time2
8   class TimeTest2
9   {
10      // main entry point for application
11      static void Main( string[] args )
12      {
13         Time2 time1, time2, time3, time4, time5, time6;
14
15         time1 = new Time2();                // 00:00:00
16         time2 = new Time2( 2 );             // 02:00:00
17         time3 = new Time2( 21, 34 );        // 21:34:00
18         time4 = new Time2( 12, 25, 42 );    // 12:25:42
19         time5 = new Time2( 27, 74, 99 );    // 00:00:00
20         time6 = new Time2( time4 );         // 12:25:42
21
22         String output = "Constructed with: " +
23            "\ntime1: all arguments defaulted" +
24            "\n\t" + time1.ToUniversalString() +
25            "\n\t" + time1.ToStandardString();
26
27         output += "\ntime2: hour specified; minute and " +
28            "second defaulted" +
29            "\n\t" + time2.ToUniversalString() +
30            "\n\t" + time2.ToStandardString();
31
32         output += "\ntime3: hour and minute specified; " +
33            "second defaulted" +
34            "\n\t" + time3.ToUniversalString() +
35            "\n\t" + time3.ToStandardString();
36
37         output += "\ntime4: hour, minute, and second specified" +
38            "\n\t" + time4.ToUniversalString() +
39            "\n\t" + time4.ToStandardString();
40
41         output += "\ntime5: all invalid values specified" +
42            "\n\t" + time5.ToUniversalString() +
43            "\n\t" + time5.ToStandardString();
44
45         output += "\ntime6: Time2 object time4 specified" +
46            "\n\t" + time6.ToUniversalString() +
47            "\n\t" + time6.ToStandardString();
48
49         MessageBox.Show( output,
50            "Demonstrating Overloaded Constructors" );
51
52      } // end method Main
53   } // end class TimeTest2
```

Fig. 8.5   Overloaded constructor demonstration. (Part 1 of 2.)

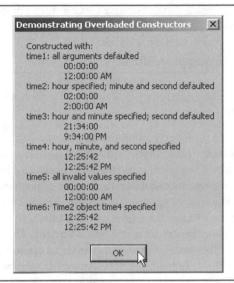

Fig. 8.5   Overloaded constructor demonstration. (Part 2 of 2.)

Software Engineering Observation 8.14

If a method of a class provides functionality required by a constructor (or other method) of the class, call that method from the constructor (or other method). This simplifies the maintenance of the code and reduces the likelihood of introducing errors into the code.

8.7 Properties

Methods of a class can manipulate that class's **private** instance variables. A typical manipulation might be the adjustment of a customer's bank balance—a **private** instance variable of a class **BankAccount**—by a **ComputeInterest** method.

Classes often provide **public** *properties* to allow clients to *set* (i.e., assign values to) or *get* (i.e., obtain the values of) **private** instance variables. For example, in Fig. 8.6, we create three properties—**Hour**, **Minute** and **Second**—which access variables **hour**, **minute** and **second**, respectively. Each property contains a *get accessor* (to retrieve the field value) and a *set accessor* (to modify the field value).

Providing **set** and **get** capabilities appears to be the same as making the instance variables **public**. However, this is another one of C#'s subtleties that makes the language so attractive from a software-engineering standpoint. If an instance variable is **public**, the instance variable can be read or written to by any method in the program. If an instance variable is **private**, a **public get** accessor seems to allow other methods to read the data at will. However, the **get** accessor can control the formatting and display of the data. Similarly, a **public set** accessor can scrutinize attempts to modify the instance variable's value, thus ensuring that the new value is appropriate for that data member. For example, an attempt to **set** the day of the month to 37 would be rejected, and an attempt to **set** a person's weight to a negative value would be rejected. So, **set** and **get** accessors can provide access to **private** data, but the implementation of these accessors controls what the client code can do to the data.

The declaration of instance variables as **private** does not guarantee their integrity. Programmers must provide validity checking—C# provides only the framework with which programmers can design better programs.

Testing and Debugging Tip 8.1

*Methods that set the values of **private** data should verify that the intended new values are valid; if they are not, the **set** accessors should place the **private** instance variables into an appropriate consistent state.*

The **set** accessors of a property cannot return values indicating a failed attempt to assign invalid data to objects of the class. Such return values could be useful to a client of a class when handling errors. The client could take appropriate actions if the objects occupy invalid states. Chapter 10 presents exception handling—a mechanism that can be used to indicate attempts to set an object's members to invalid values.

Figure 8.6 enhances our **Time** class, now called **Time3**, to include properties for the **private** instance variables **hour**, **minute** and **second**. The **set** accessors of these properties strictly control the setting of the instance variables to valid values. An attempt to set any instance variable to an incorrect value causes the instance variable to be set to zero (thus leaving the instance variable in a consistent state). Each **get** accessor returns the appropriate instance variable's value. This application also introduces enhanced GUI event-handling techniques, as we define a GUI (Fig. 8.7) that includes several buttons the user can click to manipulate the time stored in a **Time3** object.

```
1   // Fig. 8.6: Time3.cs
2   // Class Time2 provides overloaded constructors.
3
4   using System;
5
6   // Time3 class definition
7   public class Time3
8   {
9      private int hour;     // 0-23
10     private int minute;   // 0-59
11     private int second;   // 0-59
12
13     // Time3 constructor initializes instance variables to
14     // zero to set default time to midnight
15     public Time3()
16     {
17        SetTime( 0, 0, 0 );
18     }
19
20     // Time3 constructor: hour supplied, minute and second
21     // defaulted to 0
22     public Time3( int hour )
23     {
24        SetTime( hour, 0, 0 );
25     }
26
```

Fig. 8.6   Properties provide controlled access to an object's data. (Part 1 of 3.)

```
27      // Time3 constructor: hour and minute supplied, second
28      // defaulted to 0
29      public Time3( int hour, int minute )
30      {
31         SetTime( hour, minute, 0 );
32      }
33
34      // Time3 constructor: hour, minute and second supplied
35      public Time3( int hour, int minute, int second )
36      {
37         SetTime( hour, minute, second );
38      }
39
40      // Time3 constructor: initialize using another Time3 object
41      public Time3( Time3 time )
42      {
43         SetTime( time.Hour, time.Minute, time.Second );
44      }
45
46      // Set new time value in 24-hour format. Perform validity
47      // checks on the data. Set invalid values to zero.
48      public void SetTime(
49         int hourValue, int minuteValue, int secondValue )
50      {
51         Hour = hourValue;        // invoke Hour property set
52         Minute = minuteValue;    // invoke Minute property set
53         Second = secondValue;    // invoke Second property set
54      }
55
56      // property Hour
57      public int Hour
58      {
59         get
60         {
61            return hour;
62         }
63
64         set
65         {
66            hour = ( ( value >= 0 && value < 24 ) ? value : 0 );
67         }
68
69      } // end property Hour
70
71      // property Minute
72      public int Minute
73      {
74         get
75         {
76            return minute;
77         }
78
```

Fig. 8.6   Properties provide controlled access to an object's data. (Part 2 of 3.)

```
79        set
80        {
81            minute = ( ( value >= 0 && value < 60 ) ? value : 0 );
82        }
83
84    } // end property Minute
85
86    // property Second
87    public int Second
88    {
89        get
90        {
91            return second;
92        }
93
94        set
95        {
96            second = ( ( value >= 0 && value < 60 ) ? value : 0 );
97        }
98
99    } // end property Second
100
101    // convert time to universal-time (24 hour) format string
102    public string ToUniversalString()
103    {
104        return String.Format(
105            "{0:D2}:{1:D2}:{2:D2}", Hour, Minute, Second );
106    }
107
108    // convert time to standard-time (12 hour) format string
109    public string ToStandardString()
110    {
111        return String.Format( "{0}:{1:D2}:{2:D2} {3}",
112            ( ( Hour == 12 || Hour == 0 ) ? 12 : Hour % 12 ),
113            Minute, Second, ( Hour < 12 ? "AM" : "PM" ) );
114    }
115
116 } // end class Time3
```

Fig. 8.6   Properties provide controlled access to an object's data. (Part 3 of 3.)

Lines 57–69, 72–84 and 87–99 define **Time3** properties **Hour**, **Minute** and **Second**, respectively. Each property begins with a declaration line that includes the property's access modifier (**public**), type (**int**) and name (**Hour**, **Minute** or **Second**).

The body of each property contains **get** and **set** accessors, which are declared using the reserved words **get** and **set**. The **get** accessor declarations are on lines 59–62, 74–77 and 89–92. These accessors return the **hour**, **minute** and **second** instance variable values that objects request. The **set** accessors are declared on lines 64–67, 79–82 and 94–97. The body of each **set** accessor performs the same conditional statement that was previously performed by method **SetTime** to set the **hour**, **minute** or **second**.

Method **SetTime** (lines 48–54) now uses properties **Hour**, **Minute** and **Second** to ensure that instance variables **hour**, **minute** and **second** have valid values. After we define a property, we can use it in the same way that we use a variable. We assign values to properties using the **=** (assignment) operator. When this assignment occurs, the code in the **set** accessor for that property executes. The reserved word **value** represents the argument to the **set** accessor. Similarly, methods **ToUniversalString** (102–106) and **ToStandardString** (109–114) now use properties **Hour**, **Minute** and **Second** to obtain the values of instance variables **hour**, **minute** and **second**. Referencing the property executes the **get** accessor for that property.

When we use **set** and **get** accessor methods throughout the constructors and other methods of class **Time3**, we minimize the changes that we must make to the class definition in the event that we alter the data representation from **hour**, **minute** and **second** to another representation (such as total elapsed seconds in the day). When such changes are made, we must provide only new **set** and **get** accessor bodies. Using this technique also enables programmers to change the implementation of a class without affecting the clients of that class (as long as all the **public** methods of the class still are called in the same way).

Software Engineering Observation 8.15

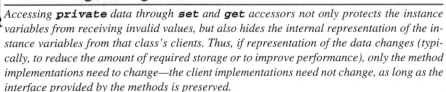

*Accessing **private** data through **set** and **get** accessors not only protects the instance variables from receiving invalid values, but also hides the internal representation of the instance variables from that class's clients. Thus, if representation of the data changes (typically, to reduce the amount of required storage or to improve performance), only the method implementations need to change—the client implementations need not change, as long as the interface provided by the methods is preserved.*

Class **TimeTest3** (Fig. 8.7) defines an application with a GUI for manipulating an object of class **Time3**. [*Note:* We do not show Visual Studio's *Windows Form Designer* generated code. Instead, line 45 provides a comment to indicate where the generated code appears in the source code file. You can download this code from our Web site (**www.deitel.com**), under the **Downloads/Resources** page.

Line 34 declares **Time3** reference **time**. Line 41 in the constructor creates an object of class **Time3** and assigns it to **time**. The GUI contains three text fields in which the user can input values for the **Time3** object's **hour**, **minute** and **second** variables, respectively. Next to each text field is a button the user can click to set the value of a particular **Time3** property. Lines 66–90 declare three event-handling methods for the buttons' **Click** events. Each event handler alters the values a **Time3** property (**Hour**, **Minute** or **Second**). The GUI also contains a button that enables the user to increment the **second** value by **1**. Using the **Time3** object's properties, method **addButton_Click** (lines 93–108) determines and sets the new time. For example, **23:59:59** becomes **00:00:00** when the user presses the button. Each modification of the time results in a call to **UpdateDisplay**, which uses the **Time3** properties to display the **hour**, **minute** and **second** values, and also displays the universal- and standard-time representations.

Properties are not limited to accessing **private** data—properties also can be used to calculate values associated with an object. One example of this would be a **student** object with a property representing the student's GPA (called **GPA**). Programmers can either provide code that calculates the student's GPA in the **get** accessor for this property, or they can simply return a **private** variable containing the GPA, called **gpa**. (The value in this variable will need to be calculated in some other way, such as using a **CalculateGPA** method.) The programmer can use either technique, but we recommend using a property that calculates the GPA. Remember that client code should not be required to tell the **student** object when to calculate the GPA. The client code simply should use the GPA property. The client should not be aware of the underlying implementation.

```
1    // Fig. 8.7: TimeTest3.cs
2    // Demonstrating Time3 properties Hour, Minute and Second.
3
4    using System;
5    using System.Drawing;
6    using System.Collections;
7    using System.ComponentModel;
8    using System.Windows.Forms;
9    using System.Data;
10
11   // TimeTest3 class definition
12   public class TimeTest3 : System.Windows.Forms.Form
13   {
14      private System.Windows.Forms.Label hourLabel;
15      private System.Windows.Forms.TextBox hourTextBox;
16      private System.Windows.Forms.Button hourButton;
17
18      private System.Windows.Forms.Label minuteLabel;
19      private System.Windows.Forms.TextBox minuteTextBox;
20      private System.Windows.Forms.Button minuteButton;
21
22      private System.Windows.Forms.Label secondLabel;
23      private System.Windows.Forms.TextBox secondTextBox;
24      private System.Windows.Forms.Button secondButton;
25
26      private System.Windows.Forms.Button addButton;
27
28      private System.Windows.Forms.Label displayLabel1;
29      private System.Windows.Forms.Label displayLabel2;
30
31      // required designer variable
32      private System.ComponentModel.Container components = null;
33
34      private Time3 time;
35
36      public TimeTest3()
37      {
38         // Required for Windows Form Designer support
39         InitializeComponent();
40
41         time = new Time3();
42         UpdateDisplay();
43      }
44
45      // Visual Studio .NET generated code
46
47      // main entry point for application
48      [STAThread]
49      static void Main()
50      {
```

Fig. 8.7   Properties demonstration for class **Time3**. (Part 1 of 4.)

```
 51            Application.Run( new TimeTest3() );
 52         }
 53
 54         // update display labels
 55         public void UpdateDisplay()
 56         {
 57            displayLabel1.Text = "Hour: " + time.Hour +
 58               "; Minute: " + time.Minute +
 59               "; Second: " + time.Second;
 60            displayLabel2.Text = "Standard time: " +
 61               time.ToStandardString() + "\nUniversal time: " +
 62               time.ToUniversalString();
 63         }
 64
 65         // set Hour property when hourButton pressed
 66         private void hourButton_Click(
 67            object sender, System.EventArgs e )
 68         {
 69            time.Hour = Int32.Parse( hourTextBox.Text );
 70            hourTextBox.Text = "";
 71            UpdateDisplay();
 72         }
 73
 74         // set Minute property when minuteButton pressed
 75         private void minuteButton_Click(
 76            object sender, System.EventArgs e )
 77         {
 78            time.Minute = Int32.Parse( minuteTextBox.Text );
 79            minuteTextBox.Text = "";
 80            UpdateDisplay();
 81         }
 82
 83         // set Second property when secondButton pressed
 84         private void secondButton_Click(
 85            object sender, System.EventArgs e )
 86         {
 87            time.Second = Int32.Parse( secondTextBox.Text );
 88            secondTextBox.Text = "";
 89            UpdateDisplay();
 90         }
 91
 92         // add one to Second when addButton pressed
 93         private void addButton_Click(
 94            object sender, System.EventArgs e )
 95         {
 96            time.Second = ( time.Second + 1 ) % 60;
 97
 98            if ( time.Second == 0 )
 99            {
100               time.Minute = ( time.Minute + 1 ) % 60;
101
102               if ( time.Minute == 0 )
103                  time.Hour = ( time.Hour + 1 ) % 24;
```

Fig. 8.7   Properties demonstration for class **Time3**. (Part 2 of 4.)

```
104          }
105
106          UpdateDisplay();
107
108     } // end method addButton_Click
109
110  } // end class TimeTest3
```

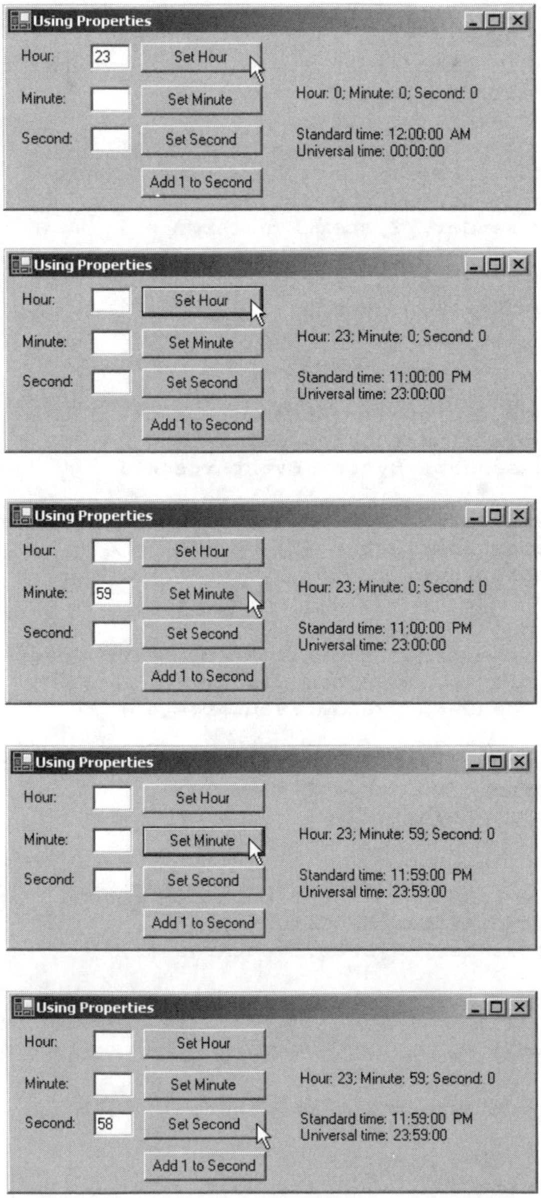

Fig. 8.7   Properties demonstration for class **Time3**. (Part 3 of 4.)

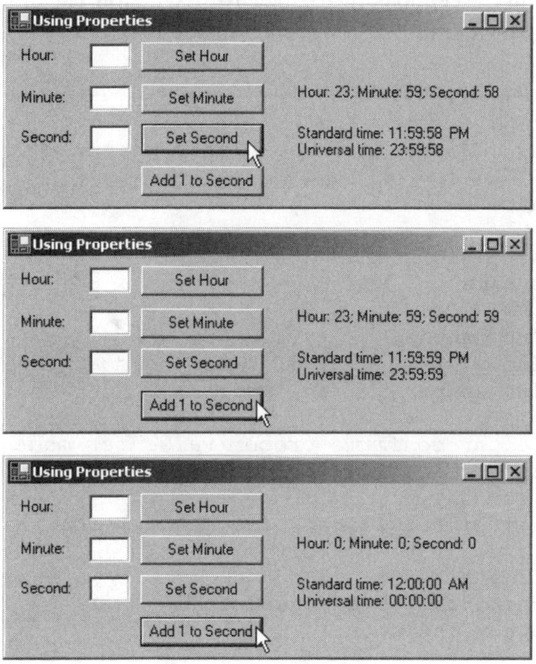

Fig. 8.7 Properties demonstration for class **Time3**. (Part 4 of 4.)

8.8 Composition: Objects References as Instance Variables of Other Classes

In many situations, referencing existing objects is more convenient than rewriting the objects' code for new classes in new projects. Suppose we were to implement an **Alarm-Clock** object that needs to know when to sound its alarm. Referencing an existing **Time** object (like those from earlier examples in this chapter) is easier than writing a new **Time** object. The use of references to objects of preexisting classes as members of new objects is called *composition* (or *aggregation*).

Software Engineering Observation 8.16

One form of software reuse is composition, in which a class has as members references to objects of other classes.

The application of Fig. 8.8, Fig. 8.9 and Fig. 8.10 demonstrates composition. The program contains three classes. Class **Date** (Fig. 8.8) encapsulates information relating to a specific date. Class **Employee** (Fig. 8.9) encapsulates the name of the employee and two **Date** objects representing the **Employee**'s birthday and hire date. Class **CompositionTest** (Fig. 8.10) creates an object of class **Employee** to demonstrate composition.

Class **Date** declares **int** instance variables **month**, **day** and **year** (lines 9–11). Lines 16–32 define the constructor, which receives values for **month**, **day** and **year** as arguments and assigns these values to the instance variables after ensuring that the values are in a consistent state. Note that lines 25–26 print an error message if the constructor receives an invalid month value. Ordinarily, rather than printing error messages, a constructor would "throw an exception." We discuss exceptions in Chapter 10, Exception Handling. Method **ToDateString** (lines 58–61) returns the string representation of a **Date**.

```
1   // Fig. 8.8: Date.cs
2   // Date class definition encapsulates month, day and year.
3
4   using System;
5
6   // Date class definition
7   public class Date
8   {
9      private int month;   // 1-12
10     private int day;     // 1-31 based on month
11     private int year;    // any year
12
13     // constructor confirms proper value for month;
14     // call method CheckDay to confirm proper
15     // value for day
16     public Date( int theMonth, int theDay, int theYear )
17     {
18        // validate month
19        if ( theMonth > 0 && theMonth <= 12 )
20           month = theMonth;
21
22        else
23        {
24           month = 1;
25           Console.WriteLine(
26              "Month {0} invalid. Set to month 1.", theMonth );
27        }
28
29        year = theYear;              // could validate year
30        day = CheckDay( theDay );    // validate day
31
32     } // end Date constructor
33
34     // utility method confirms proper day value
35     // based on month and year
36     private int CheckDay( int testDay )
37     {
38        int[] daysPerMonth =
39           { 0, 31, 28, 31, 30, 31, 30, 31, 31, 30, 31, 30, 31 };
40
41        // check if day in range for month
42        if ( testDay > 0 && testDay <= daysPerMonth[ month ] )
43           return testDay;
44
45        // check for leap year
46        if ( month == 2 && testDay == 29 &&
47           ( year % 400 == 0 ||
48              ( year % 4 == 0 && year % 100 != 0 ) ) )
49           return testDay;
```

Fig. 8.8   **Date** class encapsulates day, month and year information. (Part 1 of 2.)

```
50
51          Console.WriteLine(
52             "Day {0} invalid. Set to day 1.", testDay );
53
54          return 1;  // leave object in consistent state
55       }
56
57       // return date string as month/day/year
58       public string ToDateString()
59       {
60          return month + "/" + day + "/" + year;
61       }
62
63  }  // end class Date
```

Fig. 8.8   **Date** class encapsulates day, month and year information. (Part 2 of 2.)

Class **Employee** (Fig. 8.9) encapsulates information relating to an employee's birthday and hire date (lines 10–13) using instance variables **firstName**, **lastName**, **birthDate** and **hireDate**. Members' **birthDate** and **hireDate** are references to **Date** objects, each of which contains instance variables **month**, **day** and **year**. In this example, class **Employee** is *composed of* two references of type **string** and two references of class **Date**. The **Employee** constructor (lines 16–27) takes eight arguments (**first**, **last**, **birthMonth**, **birthDay**, **birthYear**, **hireMonth**, **hireDay** and **hireYear**). Line 24 passes arguments **birthMonth**, **birthDay** and **birth-Year** to the **Date** constructor to create the **birthDate** object. Similarly, line 25 passes arguments **hireMonth**, **hireDay** and **hireYear** to the **Date** constructor to create the **hireDate** object. Method **ToEmployeeString** (lines 30–35) returns a **string** containing the name of the **Employee** and the string representations of the **Employee**'s **birthDate** and **hireDate**.

Class **CompositionTest** (Fig. 8.10) runs the application with method **Main**. Lines 13–14 instantiate an **Employee** object and lines 16–17 display the string representation of the **Employee** to the user.

```
1   // Fig. 8.9: Employee.cs
2   // Employee class definition encapsulates employee's first name,
3   // last name, birth date and hire date.
4
5   using System;
6
7   // Employee class definition
8   public class Employee
9   {
10     private string firstName;
11     private string lastName;
12     private Date birthDate;   // reference to a Date object
13     private Date hireDate;    // reference to a Date object
14
```

Fig. 8.9   **Employee** class. (Part 1 of 2.)

```
15        // constructor initializes name, birth date and hire date
16        public Employee( string first, string last,
17           int birthMonth, int birthDay, int birthYear,
18           int hireMonth, int hireDay, int hireYear )
19        {
20           firstName = first;
21           lastName = last;
22
23           // create new Date objects
24           birthDate = new Date( birthMonth, birthDay, birthYear );
25           hireDate = new Date( hireMonth, hireDay, hireYear );
26
27        } // end Employee constructor
28
29        // convert Employee to String format
30        public string ToEmployeeString()
31        {
32           return lastName + ", " + firstName +
33              "  Hired: " + hireDate.ToDateString() +
34              "  Birthday: " + birthDate.ToDateString();
35        }
36
37     } // end class Employee
```

Fig. 8.9   **Employee** class. (Part 2 of 2.)

```
1     // Fig. 8.10: CompositionTest.cs
2     // Demonstrate an object with member object reference.
3
4     using System;
5     using System.Windows.Forms;
6
7     // Composition class definition
8     class CompositionTest
9     {
10       // main entry point for application
11       static void Main( string[] args )
12       {
13          Employee e =
14             new Employee( "Bob", "Jones", 7, 24, 1949, 3, 12, 1988 );
15
16          MessageBox.Show( e.ToEmployeeString(),
17             "Testing Class Employee" );
18
19       } // end method Main
20
21    } // end class CompositionTest
```

Fig. 8.10   Composition demonstration.

8.9 Using the `this` Reference

Every object can access a reference to itself, called the ***this*** *reference*. The **this** reference can refer implicitly to the instance variables, properties and methods of an object. Keyword **this** is commonly used within methods, where **this** is a reference to the object on which the method is performing operations. In the Windows application of Fig. 6.4, there are several uses of **this** in method **InitializeComponent**. The application uses the **this** keyword to reference the form that is being initialized. Every form has an **InitializeComponent** method, so the **this** reference provides us with an easy way to access the information in the current object. Additional examples of **this** appear in Chapter 11.

We now demonstrate implicit and explicit use of the **this** reference to display the **private** data of a **Time4** object. Class **Time4** (Fig. 8.11) defines three **private** instance variables—**hour**, **minute** and **second** (lines 9–11). The constructor (lines 14–19) receives three **int** arguments to initialize a **Time4** object. Note that, for this example, we have made the parameter names for the constructor (line 14) identical to the instance variable names for the class (lines 9–11). We did this to illustrate explicit use of the **this** reference. If a method contains a local variable with the same name as an instance variable of that class, that method will refer to the local variable, rather than to the instance variable (i.e., the local variable hides the instance variable in that method's scope). However, the method can use the **this** reference to refer to the hidden instance variables explicitly (lines 16–18).

Method **BuildString** (lines 22–27) returns a **string** created by a statement that uses the **this** reference explicitly and implicitly. Line 25 uses the **this** reference explicitly to call method **ToStandardString**, whereas line 26 uses the **this** reference implicitly to call the same method. Note that both lines perform the same task. Therefore, programmers usually do not use the **this** reference explicitly to reference methods within the current object.

```
1   // Fig. 8.11: Time4.cs
2   // Demonstrating the this reference.
3
4   using System;
5
6   // Time4 class definition
7   public class Time4
8   {
9      private int hour;      // 0-23
10     private int minute;    // 0-59
11     private int second;    // 0-59
12
13     // constructor
14     public Time4( int hour, int minute, int second )
15     {
16        this.hour = hour;
17        this.minute = minute;
18        this.second = second;
19     }
```

Fig. 8.11   **this** reference used implicitly and explicitly to enable an object to manipulate its own data and invoke its own methods. (Part 1 of 2.)

```
20
21      // create string using this and implicit references
22      public string BuildString()
23      {
24         return "this.ToStandardString(): " +
25            this.ToStandardString() +
26            "\nToStandardString(): " + ToStandardString();
27      }
28
29      // convert time to standard-time (12-hour) format string
30      public string ToStandardString()
31      {
32         return String.Format( "{0}:{1:D2}:{2:D2} {3}",
33            ( ( this.hour == 12 || this.hour == 0 ) ? 12 :
34            this.hour % 12 ), this.minute, this.second,
35            ( this.hour < 12 ? "AM" : "PM" ) );
36      }
37
38   } // end class Time4
```

Fig. 8.11   **this** reference used implicitly and explicitly to enable an object to manipulate its own data and invoke its own methods. (Part 2 of 2.)

Common Programming Error 8.4

*For a method in which a parameter (or local variable) has the same name as an instance variable, use reference **this** if you wish to access the instance variable; otherwise, the method parameter (or local variable) will be referenced.*

Testing and Debugging Tip 8.2

Avoid method-parameter names (or local variable names) that conflict with instance variable names to prevent subtle, hard-to-trace bugs.

Good Programming Practice 8.5

*The explicit use of the **this** reference can increase program clarity in some contexts where **this** is optional.*

Class **ThisTest** (Fig. 8.12) runs the application that demonstrates explicit use of the **this** reference. Line 13 instantiates an instance of class **Time4**. Lines 15–16 invoke method **BuildString** of the **Time4** object, then display the results to the user in a **MessageBox**.

The problem of parameters (or local variables) hiding instance variables can be solved by using properties. If we have a property **Hour** that accesses the **hour** instance variable, then we would not need to use **this.hour** to distinguish between a parameter (or local variable) **hour** and the instance variable **hour**—we would simply assign **hour** to **Hour**.

8.10 Garbage Collection

In previous examples, we have seen how a constructor initializes data in an object of a class after the object is created. Operator **new** allocates memory for the object, then calls that object's constructor. The constructor might acquire other system resources, such as network connections and databases or files. Objects must have a disciplined way to return memory and release resources when the program no longer uses those objects. Failure to release such resources causes *resource leaks*—potentially exhausting the pool of available resources that programs might need to continue executing.

Unlike C and C++, in which programmers must manage memory explicitly, C# performs memory management internally. The .NET Framework performs *garbage collection* of memory to return to the system memory that is no longer needed. When the *garbage collector* executes, it locates objects for which the application has no references. Such objects can be collected at that time or during a subsequent execution of the garbage collector. Therefore, the *memory leaks* that are common in such languages as C and C++, where memory is not reclaimed automatically, are rare in C#.

Allocation and deallocation of other resources, such as network connections, database connections and files, must be handled explicitly by the programmer. One technique employed to handle these resources (in conjunction with the garbage collector) is to define a *destructor* (sometimes known as a *finalizer*) that returns resources to the system. The garbage collector calls an object's destructor to perform *termination housekeeping* on that object just before the garbage collector reclaims the object's memory (called *finalization*).

Each class can contain only one destructor. The name of a destructor is formed by preceding the class name with a ~ character. For example, the destructor for class **Time** would be **~Time()**. Destructors do not receive arguments, so destructors cannot be overloaded. When the garbage collector is removing an object from memory, the garbage collector first invokes that object's destructor to clean up resources used by the class. However, we cannot determine exactly when the destructor is called, because we cannot determine exactly when garbage collection occurs. At program termination, any objects that have not been not garbage collected previously will receive destructor calls.

```csharp
1   // Fig. 8.12: ThisTest.cs
2   // Using the this reference.
3
4   using System;
5   using System.Windows.Forms;
6
7   // ThisTest class definition
8   class ThisTest
9   {
10     // main entry point for application
11     static void Main( string[] args )
12     {
13        Time4 time = new Time4( 12, 30, 19 );
14
15        MessageBox.Show( time.BuildString(),
16           "Demonstrating the \"this\" Reference" );
17     }
18  }
```

Demonstrating the "this" Reference

this.ToStandardString(): 12:30:19 PM
ToStandardString(): 12:30:19 PM

OK

Fig. 8.12 **this** reference demonstration.

8.11 `static` Class Members

Each object of a class has its own copy of all the instance variables of the class. However, in certain cases, all class objects should share only one copy of a particular variable. Such variables are called *static* variables. A program contains only one copy of each of a class's **static** variables in memory, no matter how many objects of the class have been instantiated. A **static** variable represents *class-wide information*—all class objects share the same **static** data item.

The declaration of a **static** member begins with the keyword **static**. A **static** variable can be initialized in its declaration by following the variable name with an **=** and an initial value. In cases where a **static** variable requires more complex initialization, programmers can define a *static* constructor to initialize only the **static** members. Such constructors are optional and must be declared with the **static** keyword, followed by the name of the class. **static** constructors are called before any **static** members are used and before any class objects are instantiated.

We now consider a video-game example to justify the need for **static** class-wide data. Suppose that we have a video game involving **Martian**s and other space creatures. Each **Martian** tends to be brave and willing to attack other space creatures when the **Martian** is aware that there are at least four other **Martian**s present. If there are fewer than five **Martian**s present, each **Martian** becomes cowardly. For this reason, each **Martian** must know the **martianCount**. We could endow class **Martian** with **martianCount** as instance data. However, if we were to do this, then every **Martian** would have a separate copy of the instance data, and, every time we create a **Martian**, we would have to update the instance variable **martianCount** in every **Martian**. The redundant copies waste space, and updating those copies is time-consuming. Instead, we declare **martianCount** to be **static** so that **martianCount** is class-wide data. Each **Martian** can see the **martianCount** as if it were instance data of that **Martian**, but C# maintains only one copy of the **static** variable **martianCount** to save space. This technique also saves time; because there is only one copy, we do not have to increment separate copies of **martianCount** for each **Martian** object.

Performance Tip 8.1

*When a single copy of the data will suffice, use **static** variables to save storage.*

Although **static** variables might seem like *global variables* (variables that can be referenced anywhere in a program) in other programming languages, **static** variables need not be globally accessible. **static** variables have class scope.

The **public static** data members of a class can be accessed through the class name using the dot operator (e.g., **Math.PI**). The **private static** members can be accessed only through methods or properties of the class. **static** members are available as soon as the class is loaded into memory at execution time and they exist for the duration of program execution, even when no objects of that class exist. To enable a program to access a **private static** member when no objects of the class exist, the class must provide a **public static** method or property.

A **static** method cannot access instance (non-**static**) members. Unlike instance methods, a **static** method has no **this** reference, because **static** variables and **static** methods exist independently of any class objects, even when there are no objects of that class.

Common Programming Error 8.5

*Using the **this** reference in a **static** method or **static** property is a compilation error.*

Common Programming Error 8.6

*A call to an instance method or an attempt to access an instance variable from a **static** method is a compilation error.*

Class **Employee** (Fig. 8.13) demonstrates a **public static** property that enables a program to obtain the value of a **private static** variable. The **static** variable **count** (line 11) is not initialized explicitly, so it receives the value zero by default. Class variable **count** maintains a count of the number of objects of class **Employee** that have been instantiated, including those objects that have already been marked for garbage collection, but have not yet been reclaimed by the garbage collector.

When objects of class **Employee** exist, **static** member **count** can be used in any method of an **Employee** object—in this example, the constructor (lines 14–23) increments **count**, and the destructor (lines 26–32) decrements **count**. If no objects of class **Employee** exist, the value of member **count** can be obtained through **static** property **Count** (lines 53–59); this also works when there are **Employee** objects in memory.

```
1    // Fig. 8.13: Employee.cs
2    // Employee class contains static data and a static method.
3
4    using System;
5
6    // Employee class definition
7    public class Employee
8    {
9       private string firstName;
10      private string lastName;
11      private static int count;   // Employee objects in memory
12
13      // constructor increments static Employee count
14      public Employee( string fName, string lName )
15      {
16         firstName = fName;
17         lastName = lName;
18
19         ++count;
20
21         Console.WriteLine( "Employee object constructor: " +
22            firstName + " " + lastName + "; count = " + Count );
23      }
24
25      // destructor decrements static Employee count
26      ~Employee()
27      {
28         --count;
29
```

Fig. 8.13   static members are accessible to all objects of a class. (Part 1 of 2.)

```
30              Console.WriteLine( "Employee object destructor: " +
31                 firstName + " " + lastName + "; count = " + Count );
32          }
33
34          // FirstName property
35          public string FirstName
36          {
37             get
38             {
39                return firstName;
40             }
41          }
42
43          // LastName property
44          public string LastName
45          {
46             get
47             {
48                return lastName;
49             }
50          }
51
52          // static Count property
53          public static int Count
54          {
55             get
56             {
57                return count;
58             }
59          }
60
61       } // end class Employee
```

Fig. 8.13   static members are accessible to all objects of a class. (Part 2 of 2.)

Class **StaticTest** (Fig. 8.14) runs the application that demonstrates the **static** members of class **Employee** (Fig. 8.13). Lines 12–13 use the **static** property **Count** of class **Employee** to obtain the current **count** value before the program creates **Employee** objects. Notice that the syntax used to access a **static** member is:

ClassName.*StaticMember*

On line 13, *ClassName* is **Employee** and *StaticMember* is **Count**. Recall that we used this syntax in prior examples to call the **static** methods of class **Math** (e.g., **Math.Pow**, **Math.Abs**, etc.) and other methods, such as **Int32.Parse** and **MessageBox.Show**.

Next, lines 16–17 instantiate two **Employee** objects and assign them to references **employee1** and **employee2**. Each call to the **Employee** constructor increments the **count** value by one. Lines 19–26 display the value of **Count** as well as the names of the two employees. Lines 30–31 set references **employee1** and **employee2** to **null**, so they no longer refer to the **Employee** objects. Because these were the only references in the program to the **Employee** objects, those objects can now be garbage collected.

The garbage collector is not invoked directly by the program. Either the garbage collector reclaims the memory for objects when the runtime determines garbage collection is appropriate, or the operating system recovers the memory when the program terminates. However, it is possible to request that the garbage collector attempt to collect available objects. Line 34 uses **public static** method *Collect* from class *GC* (namespace **System**) to make this request. The garbage collector is not guaranteed to collect all objects that are currently available for collection. If the garbage collector decides to collect objects, the garbage collector first invokes the destructor of each object. It is important to understand that the garbage collector executes as an independent entity called a *thread*. (Threads are discussed in Chapter 12, Multithreading.) It is possible for multiple threads to execute in parallel on a multiprocessor system or to share a processor on a single-processor system. Thus, a program could run in parallel with garbage collection. For this reason, we call **static** method *WaitForPendingFinalizers* of class **GC** (line 37), which forces the program to wait until the garbage collector invokes the destructors for all objects that are ready for collection and reclaims those objects. When the program reaches lines 41, we are assured that both destructor calls completed and that the value of **count** has been decremented accordingly.

```
1   // Fig. 8.14: StaticTest.cs
2   // Demonstrating static class members.
3
4   using System;
5
6   // StaticTest class definition
7   class StaticTest
8   {
9      // main entry point for application
10     static void Main( string[] args )
11     {
12        Console.WriteLine( "Employees before instantiation: " +
13           Employee.Count + "\n" );
14
15        // create two Employees
16        Employee employee1 = new Employee( "Susan", "Baker" );
17        Employee employee2 = new Employee( "Bob", "Jones" );
18
19        Console.WriteLine( "\nEmployees after instantiation: " +
20           "Employee.Count = " + Employee.Count + "\n" );
21
22        // display the Employees
23        Console.WriteLine( "Employee 1: " +
24           employee1.FirstName + " " + employee1.LastName +
25           "\nEmployee 2: " + employee2.FirstName +
26           " " + employee2.LastName + "\n" );
27
28        // remove references to objects to indicate that
29        // objects can be garbage collected
30        employee1 = null;
31        employee2 = null;
32
33        // force garbage collection
34        System.GC.Collect();
```

Fig. 8.14 **static** member demonstration. (Part 1 of 2.)

```
35
36          // wait until collection completes
37          System.GC.WaitForPendingFinalizers();
38
39          Console.WriteLine(
40             "\nEmployees after garbage collection: " +
41             Employee.Count );
42      }
43  }
```

```
Employees before instantiation: 0

Employee object constructor: Susan Baker; count = 1
Employee object constructor: Bob Jones; count = 2

Employees after instantiation: Employee.Count = 2

Employee 1: Susan Baker
Employee 2: Bob Jones

Employee object destructor: Bob Jones; count = 1
Employee object destructor: Susan Baker; count = 0

Employees after garbage collection: 0
```

Fig. 8.14   **static** member demonstration. (Part 2 of 2.)

In this example, the output shows that the destructor was called for each **Employee**, which decrements the **count** value by two (once per **Employee** being collected). Lines 39–41 use property **Count** to obtain the value of **count** after invoking the garbage collector. If the objects had not been collected, the **count** would be greater than zero.

Toward the end of the output, notice that the **Employee** object for **Bob Jones** was finalized before the **Employee** object for **Susan Baker**. However, the output of this program on your system could differ. The garbage collector is not guaranteed to collect objects in a specific order.

8.12 const and readonly Members

C# allows programmers to create *constants* whose values cannot change during program execution.

Testing and Debugging Tip 8.3

If a variable should never change, make it a constant. This helps eliminate errors that might occur if the value of the variable were to change.

To create a constant data member of a class, declare that member using either the **const** or **readonly** keyword. Data members declared as **const** implicitly are **static** and must be initialized in their declaration. Data members declared as **readonly** can be initialized in their declaration or in their class's constructor. Neither **const** nor **readonly** values can be modified once they are initialized, except that **readonly** variables can be assigned values in several constructors (only one of which will be called when an object is initialized).

Common Programming Error 8.7

*Declaring a class data member as **const** but failing to initialize it in that class's declaration is a syntax error.*

Common Programming Error 8.8

*Assigning a value to a **const** variable after that variable is initialized is a compilation error.*

Common Programming Error 8.9

*The declaration of a **const** member as **static** is a syntax error, because a **const** member implicitly is **static**.*

Common Programming Error 8.10

*Declaring a class data member as **readonly** and attempting to use it before it is initialized is a logic error.*

Members that are declared as **const** must be assigned values at compile time. Therefore, **const** members can be initialized only with other constant values, such as integers, string literals, characters and other **const** members. Constant members with values that cannot be determined at compile time must be declared with keyword **readonly**. We mentioned previously that a **readonly** member can be assigned a value only once, either when it is declared or within the constructor of the class. When initializing a **static readonly** member in a constructor, a **static** constructor must be used.

Figure 8.15 demonstrates constants. The program consists of two classes—class **Constants** (lines 8–22) defines two constants, and class **UsingConstAndReadonly** (lines 25–43) demonstrates the constants in class **Constants**.

Line 11 in class **Constants** creates constant **PI** using keyword **const** and initializes **PI** with the **double** value **3.14159**—an approximation of π that the program uses to calculate the circumferences of circles. Note that we could have used the predefined constant **PI** of class **Math** (**Math.PI**) as the value, but we wanted to demonstrate how to define a **const** variable explicitly. The compiler must be able to determine a **const** variable's value at compile time; otherwise, a compilation error will occur. For example, if line 11 initialized **PI** with the expression:

```
Double.Parse( "3.14159" )
```

the compiler would generate an error. Although the expression uses **string** literal **"3.14159"** (a constant value) as an argument, the compiler cannot evaluate the method call **Double.Parse** at compile time.

```
1  // Fig. 8.15: UsingConstAndReadOnly.cs
2  // Demonstrating constant values with const and readonly.
3
4  using System;
5  using System.Windows.Forms;
6
```

Fig. 8.15 **const** and **readonly** class member demonstration. (Part 1 of 2.)

```
7    // Constants class definition
8    public class Constants
9    {
10       // create constant PI
11       public const double PI = 3.14159;
12
13       // radius is a constant
14       // that is uninitialized
15       public readonly int radius;
16
17       public Constants( int radiusValue )
18       {
19          radius = radiusValue;
20       }
21
22    } // end class Constants
23
24    // UsingConstAndReadOnly class definition
25    public class UsingConstAndReadonly
26    {
27       // method Main creates Constants
28       // object and displays its values
29       static void Main( string[] args )
30       {
31          Random random = new Random();
32
33          Constants constantValues =
34             new Constants( random.Next( 1, 20 ) );
35
36          MessageBox.Show( "Radius = " + constantValues.radius +
37             "\nCircumference = " +
38             2 * Constants.PI * constantValues.radius,
39             "Circumference" );
40
41       } // end method Main
42
43    } // end class UsingConstAndReadOnly
```

Fig. 8.15 **const** and **readonly** class member demonstration. (Part 2 of 2.)

Variables declared **readonly** can be initialized at execution time. Line 15 declares **readonly** variable **radius**, but does not initialize it. The **Constants** constructor (lines 17–20) receives an **int** value and assigns it to **radius** when the program creates a **Constants** object. Note that radius also can be initialized with a more complex expression, such as a method call that returns an **int**.

Class **UsingConstAndReadonly** (lines 25–43) uses the **const** and **readonly** variables of class **Constants**. Lines 33–34 use a **Random** object to generate a random

int between **1** and **20** (using method **Next** of class **Random**) that corresponds to a circle's **radius**, then pass that value to the **Constants** constructor to initialize the **readonly** variable **radius**. Lines 36–39 output the radius and circumference of a circle in a **MessageBox**. Line 36 uses **Constants**'s reference **contantValues** to access **readonly** variable **radius**. Line 38 computes the circle's circumference using **const** variable **Constants.PI** and **readonly** variable **radius**. Note that we use **static** syntax to access **const** variable **PI**, because **const** variables implicitly are **static**.

8.13 Indexers

Sometimes a class encapsulates data that a program can manipulate as a list of elements. Such a class can define special properties called *indexers* that allow array-style indexed access to lists of elements. With "conventional" C# arrays, the subscript number must be an integer value. A benefit of indexers is that the programmer can define both integer subscripts and non-integer subscripts. For example, a programmer could allow client code to manipulate data using **string**s as subscripts that represent the data items' names or descriptions. When manipulating "conventional" C# array elements, the array subscript operator always returns the same data type—i.e., the type of the array. Indexers are more flexible—they can return any data type, even one that is different from the type of the data in the list of elements.

Although an indexer's subscript operator is used like an array-subscript operator, indexers are defined as properties in a class. Unlike normal properties, for which the programmer can choose an appropriate property name, indexers must be defined with keyword **this**. Indexers have the general form:

```
accessModifier returnType this[ IndexType1 name1, IndexType2 name2, ... ]
{
    get
    {
        // use name1, name2, ... here to get data
    }

    set
    {
        // use name1, name2, ... here to set data
    }
}
```

The *IndexType* parameters specified in the brackets (**[]**) are accessible to the **get** and **set** accessors. These accessors define how to use the index (or indices) to select or modify the appropriate data member. As with properties, **get** must **return** a value of type *returnType* and **set** can use the **value** keyword to reference the value that should be assigned to the data member.

Common Programming Error 8.11

Declaring indexers as **static** *is a syntax error.*

The program of Fig. 8.16 contains two classes—class **Box** (lines 14–74) represents a box with a length, a width and a height, and class **IndexerTest** (lines 77–177) demonstrates class **Box**'s indexers.

The **private** data members of class **Box** are **string** array **names** (line 16), which contains the names (i.e., **"length"**, **"width"** and **"height"**) for the dimensions of a **Box**, and **double** array **dimensions** (line 17), which contains the size of each dimension. Each element in array **names** corresponds to an element in array **dimensions** (e.g., **dimensions[2]** contains the height of the **Box**).

Box defines two indexers (lines 28–42 and lines 45–72) that each **return** a **double** value representing the size of the dimension specified by the indexer's parameter. Indexers can be overloaded like methods. The first indexer uses an **int** subscript to manipulate an element in the **dimensions** array. The second indexer uses a **string** subscript representing the name of the dimension to manipulate an element in the **dimensions** array. Each indexer returns **-1.0** if its **get** accessor encounters an invalid subscript. Each indexer's **set** accessor assigns **value** to the appropriate element of **dimensions** only if the index is valid. Normally, the programmer would have an indexer throw an exception if an indexer received an invalid index. We discuss how to throw exceptions in Chapter 10, Exception Handling.

```
1   // Fig. 8.16: IndexerTest.cs
2   // Indexers provide access to an object's members via a
3   // subscript operator.
4
5   using System;
6   using System.Drawing;
7   using System.Collections;
8   using System.ComponentModel;
9   using System.Windows.Forms;
10  using System.Data;
11
12  // Box class definition represents a box with length,
13  // width and height dimensions
14  public class Box
15  {
16     private string[] names = { "length", "width", "height" };
17     private double[] dimensions = new double[ 3 ];
18
19     // constructor
20     public Box( double length, double width, double height )
21     {
22        dimensions[ 0 ] = length;
23        dimensions[ 1 ] = width;
24        dimensions[ 2 ] = height;
25     }
26
27     // access dimensions by integer index number
28     public double this[ int index ]
29     {
30        get
31        {
32           return ( index < 0 || index >= dimensions.Length ) ?
33              -1.0 : dimensions[ index ];
34        }
```

Fig. 8.16 Indexers provide subscripted access to an object's members. (Part 1 of 5.)

```
35
36          set
37          {
38              if ( index >= 0 && index < dimensions.Length )
39                  dimensions[ index ] = value;
40          }
41
42      } // end numeric indexer
43
44      // access dimensions by their string names
45      public double this[ string name ]
46      {
47          get
48          {
49              // locate element to get
50              int i = 0;
51
52              while ( i < names.Length &&
53                  name.ToLower() != names[ i ] )
54                  i++;
55
56              return ( i == names.Length ) ? -1.0 : dimensions[ i ];
57          }
58
59          set
60          {
61              // locate element to set
62              int i = 0;
63
64              while ( i < names.Length &&
65                  name.ToLower() != names[ i ] )
66                  i++;
67
68              if ( i != names.Length )
69                  dimensions[ i ] = value;
70          }
71
72      } // end indexer
73
74  } // end class Box
75
76  // Class IndexerTest
77  public class IndexerTest : System.Windows.Forms.Form
78  {
79      private System.Windows.Forms.Label indexLabel;
80      private System.Windows.Forms.Label nameLabel;
81
82      private System.Windows.Forms.TextBox indexTextBox;
83      private System.Windows.Forms.TextBox valueTextBox;
84
85      private System.Windows.Forms.Button nameSetButton;
86      private System.Windows.Forms.Button nameGetButton;
87
```

Fig. 8.16   Indexers provide subscripted access to an object's members. (Part 2 of 5.)

```
88        private System.Windows.Forms.Button intSetButton;
89        private System.Windows.Forms.Button intGetButton;
90
91        private System.Windows.Forms.TextBox resultTextBox;
92
93        // required designer variable
94        private System.ComponentModel.Container components = null;
95
96        private Box box;
97
98        // constructor
99        public IndexerTest()
100       {
101          // required for Windows Form Designer support
102          InitializeComponent();
103
104          // create block
105          box = new Box( 0.0, 0.0, 0.0 );
106       }
107
108       // Visual Studio .NET generated code
109
110       // main entry point for application
111       [STAThread]
112       static void Main()
113       {
114          Application.Run( new IndexerTest() );
115       }
116
117       // display value at specified index number
118       private void ShowValueAtIndex( string prefix, int index )
119       {
120          resultTextBox.Text =
121             prefix + "box[ " + index + " ] = " + box[ index ];
122       }
123
124       // display value with specified name
125       private void ShowValueAtIndex( string prefix, string name )
126       {
127          resultTextBox.Text =
128             prefix + "box[ " + name + " ] = " + box[ name ];
129       }
130
131       // clear indexTextBox and valueTextBox
132       private void ClearTextBoxes()
133       {
134          indexTextBox.Text = "";
135          valueTextBox.Text = "";
136       }
137
```

Fig. 8.16   Indexers provide subscripted access to an object's members. (Part 3 of 5.)

```
138     // get value at specified index
139     private void intGetButton_Click(
140        object sender, System.EventArgs e )
141     {
142        ShowValueAtIndex(
143           "get: ", Int32.Parse( indexTextBox.Text ) );
144        ClearTextBoxes();
145     }
146
147     // set value at specified index
148     private void intSetButton_Click(
149        object sender, System.EventArgs e )
150     {
151        int index = Int32.Parse( indexTextBox.Text );
152        box[ index ] = Double.Parse( valueTextBox.Text );
153
154        ShowValueAtIndex( "set: ", index );
155        ClearTextBoxes();
156     }
157
158     // get value with specified name
159     private void nameGetButton_Click(
160        object sender, System.EventArgs e )
161     {
162        ShowValueAtIndex( "get: ", indexTextBox.Text );
163        ClearTextBoxes();
164     }
165
166     // set value with specified name
167     private void nameSetButton_Click(
168        object sender, System.EventArgs e )
169     {
170        box[ indexTextBox.Text ] =
171           Double.Parse( valueTextBox.Text );
172
173        ShowValueAtIndex( "set: ", indexTextBox.Text );
174        ClearTextBoxes();
175     }
176
177  } // end class IndexerTest
```

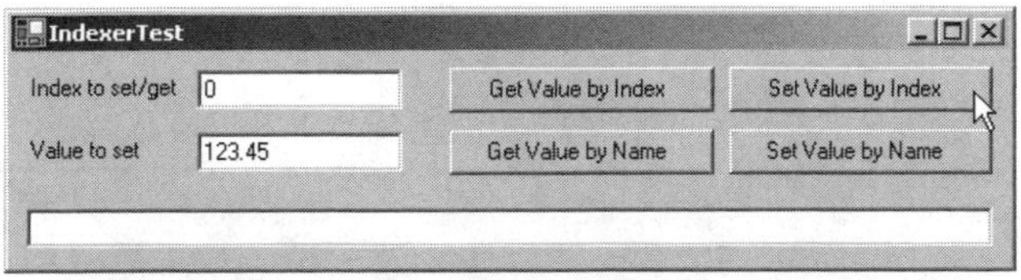

Before setting value
by index number

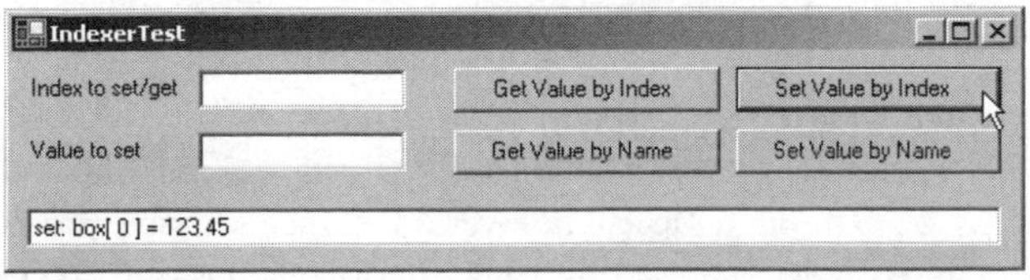

After setting value
by index number

Fig. 8.16 Indexers provide subscripted access to an object's members. (Part 4 of 5.)

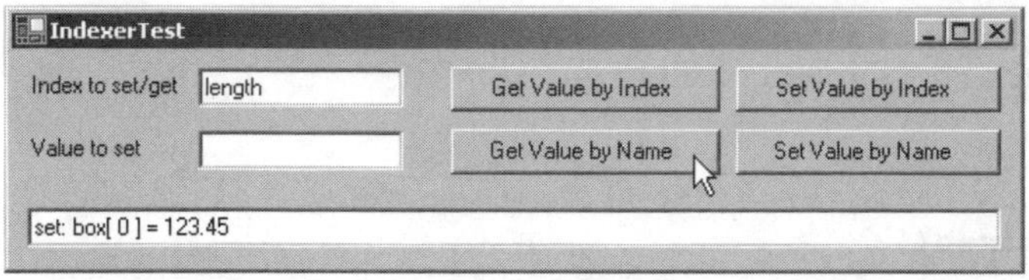

Before getting value by dimension name

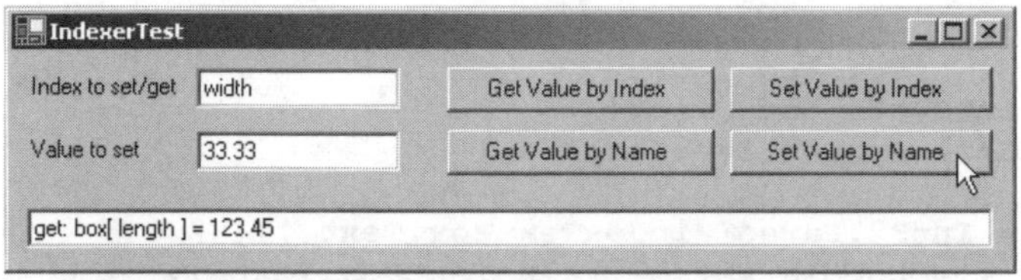

Before setting value by dimension name

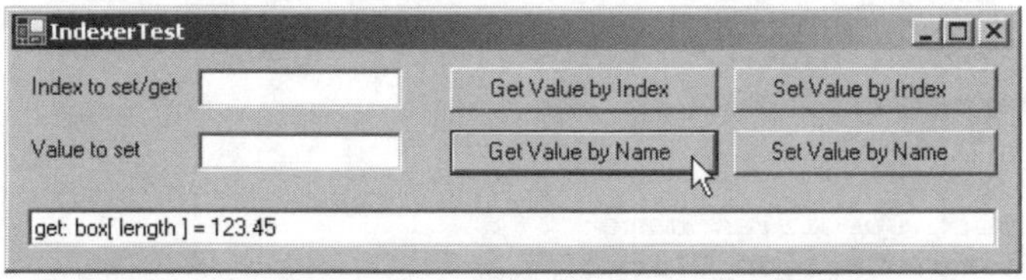

After getting value by dimension name

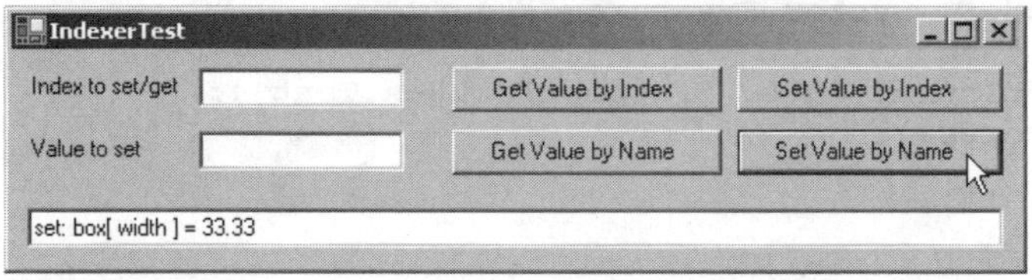

After setting value by dimension name

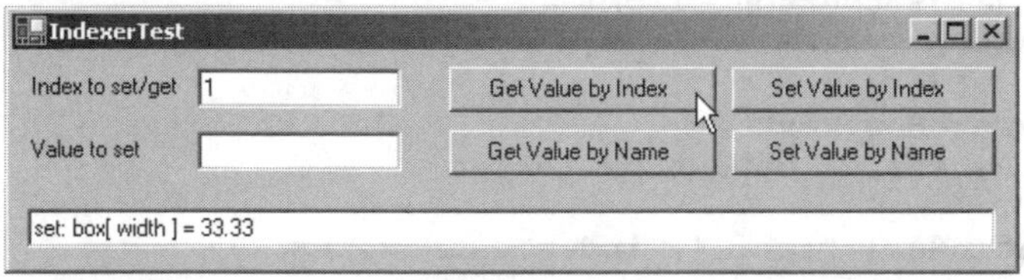

Before getting value by index number

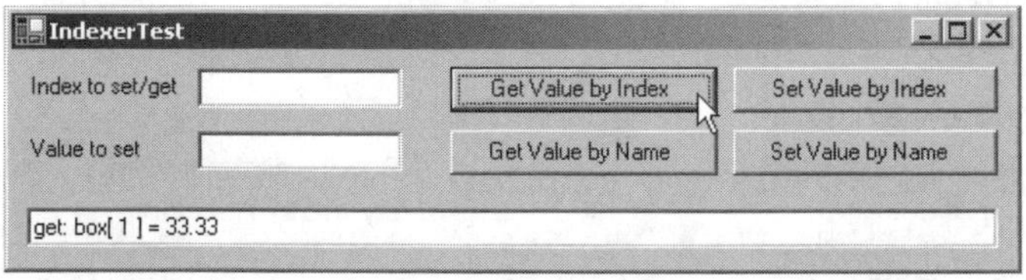

After getting value by index number

Fig. 8.16 Indexers provide subscripted access to an object's members. (Part 5 of 5.)

Notice that the **string** indexer uses a **while** structure to search for a matching **string** in the **names** array (lines 64–66). If a match is found, the indexer manipulates the corresponding element in array **dimensions** (line 69).

Class **IndexerTest** is a **System.Windows.Forms.Form** that manipulates the **private** data members of class **Box** through **Box**'s indexers. Instance variable **box** is declared at line 96 and initialized in the constructor at line 105 with dimensions of **0.0**. The event handler for button **Get Value by Index** (lines 139–145) invokes method **ShowVal-**

ueAtIndex (lines 118–122) to retrieve the value at the index number specified in **index-TextBox**. The event handler for button **Set Value by Index** (lines 148–156) assigns the value in **valueTextBox** to the location specified in **indexTextBox**. The event handler for button **Get Value by Name** (159–164) invokes the overloaded method **ShowValue-AtIndex** (lines 125–129) to retrieve the value with the name specified in **valueTextBox**. The event handler for button **Set Value by Name** (lines 167–175) assigns the value in **valueTextBox** to the location with the name specified in **indexTextBox**.

8.14 Data Abstraction and Information Hiding

As we pointed out at the beginning of this chapter, classes normally hide the details of their implementation from their clients. This is called *information hiding.* As an example of information hiding, let us consider a data structure called a *stack.*

Readers can think of a stack as analogous to a pile of dishes. When a dish is placed on the pile, it is always placed at the top (referred to as *pushing* the dish onto the stack). Similarly, when a dish is removed from the pile, it is always removed from the top (referred to as *popping* the dish off the stack). Stacks are known as *last-in, first-out (LIFO) data structures*—the last item pushed (inserted) on the stack is the first item popped (removed) from the stack.

Stacks can be implemented with arrays and with other data structures, such as linked lists. (We discuss stacks and linked lists in Chapter 21, FCL Collections.) A client of a stack class need not be concerned with the stack's implementation. The client knows only that when data items are placed in the stack, these items will be recalled in last-in, first-out order. The client cares about *what* functionality a stack offers, but not about *how* that functionality is implemented. This concept is referred to as *data abstraction.* Although programmers might know the details of a class's implementation, they should not write code that depends on these details. This enables a particular class (such as one that implements a stack and its operations, *push* and *pop*) to be replaced with another version without affecting the rest of the system. As long as the **public** services of the class do not change (i.e., every method still has the same name, return type and parameter list in the new class definition), the rest of the system is not affected.

Most programming languages emphasize actions. In these languages, data exist to support the actions that programs must take. Data are "less interesting" than actions. Data are "crude." Only a few built-in data types exist, and it is difficult for programmers to create their own data types. C# and the object-oriented style of programming elevate the importance of data. The primary activities of object-oriented programming in C# is the creation of data types (i.e., classes) and the expression of the interactions among objects of those data types. To create languages that emphasize data, the programming-languages community needed to formalize some notions about data. The formalization we consider here is the notion of *abstract data types (ADTs).* ADTs receive as much attention today as structured programming did decades earlier. ADTs, however, do not replace structured programming. Rather, they provide an additional formalization to improve the program-development process.

Consider built-in type **int**, which most people would associate with an integer in mathematics. Rather, an **int** is an abstract representation of an integer. Unlike mathematical integers, computer **int**s are fixed in size. For example, type **int** in .NET is limited approximately to the range –2 billion to +2 billion. If the result of a calculation falls outside this range, an error occurs, and the computer responds in some machine-dependent manner. It might, for example, "quietly" produce an incorrect result. Mathematical integers do not have this problem. Therefore, the notion of a computer **int** is only an approximation of the notion of a real-world integer. The same is true of **float** and other built-in types.

We have taken the notion of **int** for granted until this point, but we now consider it from a new perspective. Types like **int**, **float**, **char** and others are all examples of abstract data types. These types are representations of real-world notions to some satisfactory level of precision within a computer system.

An ADT actually captures two notions: A *data representation* and the *operations* that can be performed on that data. For example, in C#, an **int** contains an integer value (data) and provides addition, subtraction, multiplication, division and modulus operations; however, division by zero is undefined. C# programmers use classes to implement abstract data types.

 Software Engineering Observation 8.17

Programmers can create types through the use of the class mechanism. These new types can be designed so that they are as convenient to use as the built-in types. This marks C# as an extensible language. Although the language is easy to extend via new types, the programmer cannot alter the base language itself.

Another abstract data type we discuss is a *queue*, which is similar to a "waiting line." Computer systems use many queues internally. A queue offers well-understood behavior to its clients: Clients place items in a queue one at a time via an *enqueue* operation, then get those items back one at a time via a *dequeue* operation. A queue returns items in *first-in, first-out (FIFO)* order, which means that the first item inserted in a queue is the first item removed. Conceptually, a queue can become infinitely long, but real queues are finite.

The queue hides an internal data representation that keeps track of the items currently waiting in line, and it offers a set of operations to its clients (*enqueue* and *dequeue*). The clients are not concerned about the implementation of the queue—clients simply depend upon the queue to operate "as advertised." When a client enqueues an item, the queue should accept that item and place it in some kind of internal FIFO data structure. Similarly, when the client wants the next item from the front of the queue, the queue should remove the item from its internal representation and deliver the item in FIFO order (i.e., the item that has been in the queue the longest should be the next one returned by the next dequeue operation).

The queue ADT guarantees the integrity of its internal data structure. Clients cannot manipulate this data structure directly—only the queue ADT has access to its internal data. Clients are able to perform only allowable operations on the data representation; the ADT rejects operations that its public interface does not provide.

8.15 Software Reusability

C# programmers concentrate both on crafting new classes and on reusing classes from the Framework Class Library (FCL), which contains thousands of predefined classes. Developers construct software by combining programmer-defined classes with well-defined, carefully tested, well-documented, portable and widely available FCL classes. This kind of software reusability speeds the development of powerful, high-quality software. *Rapid applications development (RAD)* is of great interest today.

The FCL allows C# programmers to achieve software reusability across platforms that support .NET and rapid applications development. C# programmers focus on the high-level programming issues and leave the low-level implementation details to classes in the FCL. For example, a C# programmer who writes a graphics program does not need to know the details of every .NET-platform graphics capability. Instead, C# programmers concentrate on learning and using the FCL's graphics classes.

The FCL enables C# developers to build applications faster by reusing preexisting, extensively tested classes. In addition to reducing development time, FCL classes also improve programmers' abilities to debug and maintain applications, because proven software components are being used. For programmers to take advantage of the FCL's classes, they must familiarize themselves with the FCL's rich set of capabilities.

Software reuse is not limited to Windows-application development. The FCL also includes classes for creating *Web services*, which are applications packaged as services that clients can access via the Internet. Any C# application is a potential Web service, so C# programmers can reuse existing applications as building blocks to form larger, more sophisticated Web-enabled applications.

Many people believe that Web services represent the next phase in the evolution of software development, in which the Web provides a library of functionality from which developers can build applications in a platform-independent manner. As Microsoft's premier .NET language, C# provides all the features necessary for creating scalable, robust Web services. We formally introduce Web Services in Chapter 19, ASP .NET and Web Services.

8.16 Namespaces and Assemblies

As we have seen in almost every example in the text, classes from preexisting libraries, such as the .NET Framework, must be imported into a C# program by adding a reference to the appropriate libraries (a process we demonstrated in Section 3.2). Remember that each class in the Framework Class Library belongs to a specific namespace. The preexisting code in the FCL facilitates software reuse.

Programmers should concentrate on making the software components they create reusable. However, doing so often results in *naming collisions*. For example, two classes defined by different programmers can have the same name. If a program needs both of those classes, the program must have a way to distinguish between the two classes in the code.

Common Programming Error 8.12

Attempting to compile code that contains naming collisions will generate compilation errors.

Namespaces help minimize this problem by providing a convention for *unique class names*. No two classes in a given namespace can have the same name, but different namespaces can contain classes of the same name. With hundreds of thousands of people writing C# programs, there is a good chance the names that one programmer chooses to describe classes will conflict with the names that other programmers choose for their classes.

We begin our discussion of reusing existing class definitions in Fig. 8.17, which provides the code for class **Time3** (originally defined in Fig. 8.6). When reusing class definitions between programs, programmers create class libraries that can be imported for use in a program via a **using** statement. Only **public** classes can be reused from class libraries. Non-**public** classes can be used only by other classes in the same assembly.

The only difference between class **Time3** in this example and the version in Fig. 8.6 is that we show the **namespace**, i.e., **TimeLibrary**, in which **Time3** is defined. Each class library is defined in a **namespace** that contains all the classes in the library. We will demonstrate momentarily how to package class **Time3** into **TimeLibrary.dll**—the *dynamic link library* that we create for reuse in other programs. Programs can load dynamic link libraries at execution time to access common functionality that can be shared among many programs. A dynamic link library represents an assembly. When a project uses a class library, the project must contain a reference to the assembly that defines the class library.

```
1   // Fig. 8.17: TimeLibrary.cs
2   // Placing class Time3 in an assembly for reuse.
3
4   using System;
5
6   namespace TimeLibrary   // specifies namespace for class Time3
7   {
8      // Time3 class definition
9      public class Time3
10     {
11        private int hour;     // 0-23
12        private int minute;   // 0-59
13        private int second;   // 0-59
14
15        // Time3 constructor initializes instance variables to
16        // zero to set default time to midnight
17        public Time3()
18        {
19           SetTime( 0, 0, 0 );
20        }
21
22        // Time3 constructor: hour supplied, minute and second
23        // defaulted to 0
24        public Time3( int hour )
25        {
26           SetTime( hour, 0, 0 );
27        }
28
29        // Time3 constructor: hour and minute supplied, second
30        // defaulted to 0
31        public Time3( int hour, int minute )
32        {
33           SetTime( hour, minute, 0 );
34        }
35
36        // Time3 constructor: hour, minute and second supplied
37        public Time3( int hour, int minute, int second )
38        {
39           SetTime( hour, minute, second );
40        }
41
```

Fig. 8.17   Assembly **TimeLibrary** contains class **Time3**. (Part 1 of 3.)

```
42        // Time3 constructor: initialize using another Time3 object
43        public Time3( Time3 time )
44        {
45            SetTime( time.Hour, time.Minute, time.Second );
46        }
47
48        // Set new time value in 24-hour format. Perform validity
49        // checks on the data. Set invalid values to zero.
50        public void SetTime(
51            int hourValue, int minuteValue, int secondValue )
52        {
53            Hour = hourValue;
54            Minute = minuteValue;
55            Second = secondValue;
56        }
57
58        // property Hour
59        public int Hour
60        {
61            get
62            {
63                return hour;
64            }
65
66            set
67            {
68                hour = ( ( value >= 0 && value < 24 ) ? value : 0 );
69            }
70
71        } // end property Hour
72
73        // property Minute
74        public int Minute
75        {
76            get
77            {
78                return minute;
79            }
80
81            set
82            {
83                minute = ( ( value >= 0 && value < 60 ) ? value : 0 );
84            }
85
86        } // end property Minute
87
88        // property Second
89        public int Second
90        {
91            get
92            {
93                return second;
94            }
```

Fig. 8.17   Assembly **TimeLibrary** contains class **Time3**. (Part 2 of 3.)

```
 95
 96            set
 97            {
 98                second = ( ( value >= 0 && value < 60 ) ? value : 0 );
 99            }
100
101         } // end property Second
102
103         // convert time to universal-time (24 hour) format string
104         public string ToUniversalString()
105         {
106            return String.Format(
107                "{0:D2}:{1:D2}:{2:D2}", Hour, Minute, Second );
108         }
109
110         // convert time to standard-time (12 hour) format string
111         public string ToStandardString()
112         {
113            return String.Format( "{0}:{1:D2}:{2:D2} {3}",
114                ( ( Hour == 12 || Hour == 0 ) ? 12 : Hour % 12 ),
115                Minute, Second, ( Hour < 12 ? "AM" : "PM" ) );
116         }
117
118     } // end class Time3
119 }
```

Fig. 8.17   Assembly **TimeLibrary** contains class **Time3**. (Part 3 of 3.)

We now describe, step-by-step, how to create the class library **TimeLibrary** containing class **Time3**:

1. *Create a class library project.* From the **File** menu, choose option **New**, followed by **Project…**. In the **New Project** dialog, ensure that **C# Projects** is selected in the **Project Types** section and click **Class Library**. Name the project **TimeLibrary** and choose the directory in which you would like to store the project. A simple class library will be created, as shown in Fig. 8.18. There are two important points to note about the generated code. The first is that the class does not contain a **Main** method. This indicates that the class in the class library cannot be used to begin the execution of an application. This class is designed to be used by other programs. Also notice that **Class1** is created as a **public** class. If another project uses this library, only the library's **public** classes are accessible. We created class **Time3** as **public** for this purpose (line 9 of Fig. 8.17) by renaming the class **Class1** (created by Visual Studio as part of the project) to **Time3**. In the **Solution Explorer**, we also renamed the **Class1.cs** file as **Time3.cs**.

2. *Add the code for class Time3.* Delete the code for the **Class1** constructor. Then, copy the remainder of the **Time3** code (lines 11–116) from Fig. 8.17 (you can find this file in the examples that can be downloaded from our Web site) and paste the code in the body of the class definition shown in Fig. 8.18.

3. *Compile the code.* From the **Build** menu, choose option **Build Solution**. The code should compile successfully. Remember that this code cannot be executed—

there is no entry point into the program. In fact, if you try running the program by selecting the **Debug** menu and choosing **Start**, Visual Studio .NET displays an error message.

Compiling the project creates an assembly (a dynamic link library) that represents the new class library. This assembly can be found in the **bin\Debug** directory of the project. By default, the assembly name will include the namespace name. (In this case, the name will be **TimeLibrary.dll**.) The assembly file contains class **Time3**, which other projects can use. Assembly files, which have file extensions **.dll** and **.exe**, are integral to C#. The Windows operating system uses executable files (**.exe**) to run applications, whereas it uses library files (**.dll**, or *dynamic link library*) to represent code libraries that can be loaded dynamically by many applications and shared among those applications.

Next, we define a console application project containing class **AssemblyTest** (Fig. 8.19), which uses class **Time3** in assembly **TimeLibrary.dll** to create a **Time3** object and display its standard and universal string formats.

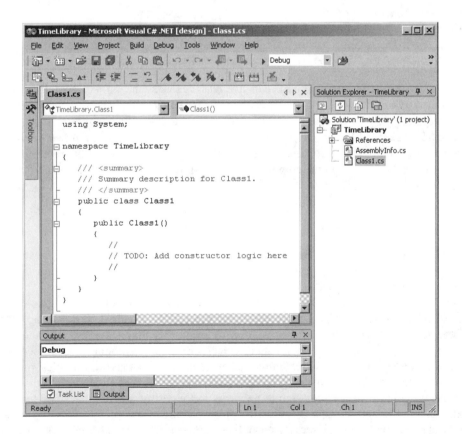

Fig. 8.18 Simple Class Library.

```
1   // Fig. 8.19: AssemblyTest.cs
2   // Using class Time3 from assembly TimeLibrary.
3
4   using System;
5   using TimeLibrary;
6
7   // AssemblyTest class definition
8   class AssemblyTest
9   {
10      // main entry point for application
11      static void Main( string[] args )
12      {
13         Time3 time = new Time3( 13, 27, 6 );
14
15         Console.WriteLine(
16            "Standard time: {0}\nUniversal time: {1}\n",
17            time.ToStandardString(), time.ToUniversalString() );
18      }
19   }
```

```
Standard time: 1:27:06 PM
Universal time: 13:27:06
```

Fig. 8.19 Assembly **TimeLibrary** used from class **AssemblyTest**.

Before class **AssemblyTest** can use class **Time3**, the project containing class **AssemblyTest** must have a reference to the **TimeLibrary** assembly. To add the reference, select **Add Reference** from the **Project** menu. Using the **Browse** button, select **TimeLibrary.dll** (located in the **bin\Debug** directory of the **TimeLibrary** project), then click **OK** to add the resource to the project. After adding the reference, use keyword **using** to inform the compiler that we will use classes from namespace **Time-Library** (line 5 in Fig. 8.19).

8.17 Class View and Object Browser

Now that we have introduced key concepts of object-based programming, we present two features that Visual Studio provides to facilitate the design of object-oriented applications—*Class View* and *Object Browser*.

The **Class View** displays the variables and methods for all classes in a project. To access this feature, select **Class View** from the **View** menu. Figure 8.20 shows the **Class View** for the **TimeTest1** project of Fig. 8.1 and Fig. 8.2 (class **Time1** and class **TimeTest1**). The view follows a hierarchical structure, positioning the project name (**TimeTest1**) as the root and including a series of nodes (e.g., classes, variables, methods etc.). If a plus sign (**+**) appears to the left of a node, that node can be expanded to show other nodes. By contrast, if a minus sign (**–**) appears to the left of a node, that node has been expanded (and can be collapsed). According to the **Class View**, project **TimeTest** contains class **Time1** and class **TimeTest1** as *children*. Class **Time1** contains methods **SetTime**, **Time1**, **ToStandardString** and **ToUniversalString** (indicated by purple boxes) and instance variables **hour**, **minute** and **second** (indicated by blue

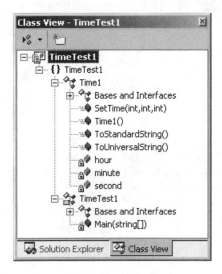

Fig. 8.20　Class View of class **Time1** (Fig. 8.1) and class **TimeTest** (Fig. 8.2).

boxes). The lock icons, placed to the left of the blue-box icons for the instance variables, specify that the variables are **private**. Class **TimeTest1** contains method **Main**. Note that both class **Time1** and class **TimeTest1** contain the **Bases and Interfaces** node. If you expand this node, you will see class **Object** in each case, because each class inherits from class **System.Object** (discussed in Chapter 9).

　Visual Studio's **Object Browser** lists all classes included in this project. Developers use the **Object Browser** to learn about the functionality provided by a specific class. To open the **Object Browser**, right click any built-in .NET class or method in the code editor and select **Go To Definition**. Figure 8.21 depicts the **Object Browser** when the user right clicks the class name **Object** in the code editor. Note that the **Object Browser** lists all methods provided by class **Object** in the **Members of 'Object'** window—this window offers developers "instant access" to information regarding the functionality of various objects. Note also that the **Object Browser** lists in the **Objects** window all classes in the FCL. The **Object Browser** can be a quick mechanism to learn about a class or method of a class. Remember that you can view the complete description of a class or method in the online documentation available through the **Help** menu in Visual Studio.

　This chapter is the first of two chapters that cover the fundamentals of object-based and object-oriented programming. In this chapter, we discussed how to create proper class definitions, how to control access to class members and several features commonly used to craft valuable classes for reuse by other programmers. Chapter 9, focuses on *inheritance*. In that chapter, you will learn how to build classes that inherit data and functionality from existing class definitions. You also will learn other C# features that are specific to the inheritance relationship between classes.

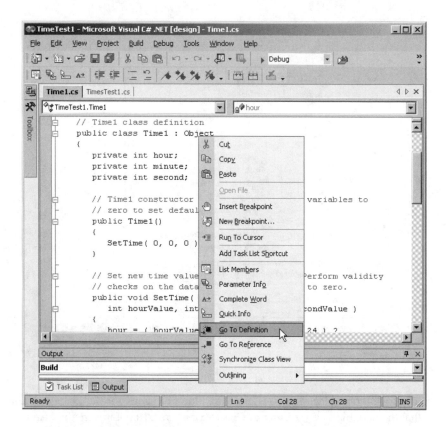

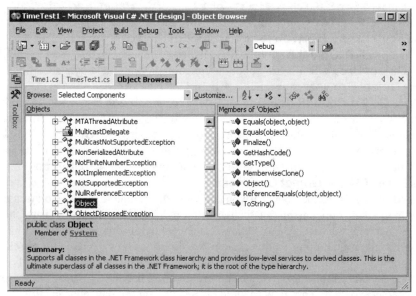

Fig. 8.21   Object Browser when user selects **Object** from **Time1.cs**.

8.18 Summary

Non-**static** instance variables and methods that are declared with member access modifier **public** are accessible wherever the program has a reference to an object of the class in which the **public** members are defined. Instance variables and methods that are declared with member access modifier **private** are accessible only to methods of the class in which the **private** members are defined.

A class's constructor is called when an object of that class is instantiated. Constructors initialize an object's instance variables and can be overloaded. If no constructors are defined for a class, a default constructor is provided by the compiler. The default constructor takes no parameters and has an empty body.

To allow clients to manipulate the values of **private** data, the class can provide a property definition. Property definitions contain accessor methods that handle the details of modifying and returning data. A property definition can contain a **set** accessor, a **get** accessor or both. A **get** accessor enables the client to read the field's value, and the **set** accessor enables the client to modify the field's value.

A class also can define indexers to provide subscripted access to the data in an object of that class. Each indexer can define a **get** and **set** accessor.

The .NET Framework performs automatic garbage collection. Every class in C# can have a destructor that returns resources to the system. The destructor for an object is guaranteed to be called to perform termination housekeeping on the object just before the garbage collector reclaims the memory for the object.

Each class in the .NET Framework belongs to a specific namespace (or library) that contains a group of related classes. Programmers can create their own namespaces to avoid naming collisions with identifiers in other programmer-defined libraries.

Object-Oriented Programming: Inheritance

Objectives

- To understand inheritance and software reusability.
- To understand the concepts of base classes and derived classes.
- To understand member access modifier **protected** and **internal**.
- To be able to use the **base** reference to access base-class members
- To understand the use of constructors and destructors in base classes and derived classes.
- To present a case study that demonstrates the mechanics of inheritance.

Say not you know another entirely, till you have divided an inheritance with him.
Johann Kasper Lavater

This method is to define as the number of a class the class of all classes similar to the given class.
Bertrand Russell

Good as it is to inherit a library, it is better to collect one.
Augustine Birrell

Outline

9.1 Introduction

In this chapter, we begin our discussion of object-oriented programming (OOP) by introducing one of its main features—*inheritance*. Inheritance is a form of software reusability in which classes are created by absorbing an existing class's data and behaviors and embellishing them with new capabilities. Software reusability saves time during program development. It also encourages the reuse of proven and debugged high-quality software, which increases the likelihood that a system will be implemented effectively.

When creating a class, instead of writing completely new instance variables and methods, the programmer can designate that the new class should *inherit* the class variables, properties and methods of another class. The previously defined class is called the *base class*, and the new class is referred to as the *derived class.* (Other programming languages, such as Java, refer to the base class as the *superclass*, and the derived class as the *subclass*.) Once created, each derived class can become the base class for future derived classes. A derived class, to which unique class variables, properties and methods normally are added, is often larger than its base class. Therefore, a derived class is more specific than its base class and represents a more specialized group of objects. Typically, the derived class contains the behaviors of its base class and additional behaviors. The *direct base class* is the base class from which the derived class explicitly inherits. An *indirect base class* is inherited from two or more levels up the *class hierarchy*. In the case of *single inheritance,* a class is derived from one base class. C#, unlike C++, does not support *multiple inheritance* (which occurs when a class is derived from more than one direct base class).

Every object of a derived class is also an object of that derived class's base class. However, base-class objects are not objects of their derived classes. For example, all cars are vehicles, but not all vehicles are cars. As we continue our study of object-oriented programming, we take advantage of this relationship to perform some interesting manipulations.

Experience in building software systems indicates that significant amounts of code deal with closely related special cases. When programmers are preoccupied with special cases, the details can obscure the "big picture." With object-oriented programming, programmers focus on the commonalities among objects in the system, rather than on the special cases. This process is called *abstraction*.

We distinguish between the *"is-a" relationship* and the *"has-a" relationship*. "Is-a" represents inheritance. In an "is-a" relationship, an object of a derived class also can be treated as an object of its base class. For example, a car *is a* vehicle. By contrast, "has-a" stands for composition (composition is discussed in Chapter 8). In a "has-a" relationship, a class object contains one or more object references as members. For example, a car *has a* steering wheel.

Derived-class methods might require access to their base-class instance variables, properties and methods. A derived class can access the non-**private** members of its base class. Base-class members that should not be accessible to properties or methods of a class derived from that base class via inheritance are declared **private** in the base class. A derived class can effect state changes in **private** base-class members, but only through non-**private** methods and properties provided in the base class and inherited into the derived class.

Software Engineering Observation 9.1

*Properties and methods of a derived class cannot directly access **private** members of their base class.*

Software Engineering Observation 9.2

*Hiding **private** members helps programmers test, debug and correctly modify systems. If a derived class could access its base class's **private** members, classes that inherit from that derived class could access that data as well. This would propagate access to what should be **private** data, and the benefits of information hiding would be lost.*

One problem with inheritance is that a derived class can inherit properties and methods it does not need or should not have. It is the class designer's responsibility to ensure that the capabilities provided by a class are appropriate for future derived classes. Even when a base-class property or method is appropriate for a derived class, that derived class often requires the property or method to perform its task in a manner specific to the derived class. In such cases, the base-class property or method can be *overridden* (redefined) in the derived class with an appropriate implementation.

New classes can inherit from abundant *class libraries*. Organizations develop their own class libraries and can take advantage of other libraries available worldwide. Someday, the vast majority of new software likely will be constructed from *standardized reusable components*, as most hardware is constructed today. This will facilitate the development of more powerful and abundant software.

9.2 Base Classes and Derived Classes

Often, an object of one class "is an" object of another class, as well. For example, a rectangle *is a* quadrilateral (as are squares, parallelograms and trapezoids). Thus, class **Rectangle** can be said to *inherit* from class **Quadrilateral**. In this context, class **Quadrilateral** is a base class, and class **Rectangle** is a derived class. A rectangle *is a* specific type of quadrilateral, but it is incorrect to claim that a quadrilateral *is a* rectangle—the quadrilateral could be a parallelogram or some other type of **Quadrilateral**. Figure 9.1 lists several simple examples of base classes and derived classes.

Base class	Derived classes
Student	GraduateStudent
	UndergraduateStudent
Shape	Circle
	Triangle
	Rectangle
Loan	CarLoan
	HomeImprovementLoan
	MortgageLoan
Employee	FacultyMember
	StaffMember
Account	CheckingAccount
	SavingsAccount

Fig. 9.1   Inheritance examples.

Every derived-class object "is an" object of its base class, and one base class can have many derived classes; therefore, the set of objects represented by a base class typically is larger than the set of objects represented by any of its derived classes. For example, the base class **Vehicle** represents all vehicles, including cars, trucks, boats, bicycles and so on. By contrast, derived-class **Car** represents only a small subset of all **Vehicle**s.

Inheritance relationships form tree-like hierarchical structures. A class exists in a hierarchical relationship with its derived classes. Although classes can exist independently, once they are employed in inheritance arrangements, they become affiliated with other classes. A class becomes either a base class, supplying data and behaviors to other classes, or a derived class, inheriting its data and behaviors from other classes.

Let us develop a simple inheritance hierarchy. A university community has thousands of members. These members consist of employees, students and alumni. Employees are either faculty members or staff members. Faculty members are either administrators (such as deans and department chairpersons) or teachers. This organizational structure yields the inheritance hierarchy, depicted in Fig. 9.2. Note that the inheritance hierarchy could contain many other classes. For example, students can be graduate or undergraduate students. Undergraduate students can be freshmen, sophomores, juniors and seniors. Each arrow in the hierarchy represents an "is-a" relationship. For example, as we follow the arrows in this class hierarchy, we can state, "an **Employee** *is a* **CommunityMember**" and "a **Teacher** *is a* **Faculty** member." **CommunityMember** is the *direct base class* of **Employee**, **Student** and **Alumnus**. In addition, **CommunityMember** is an *indirect base class* of all the other classes in the hierarchy diagram.

Starting from the bottom of the diagram, the reader can follow the arrows and apply the *is-a* relationship to the topmost base class. For example, an **Administrator** *is a* **Faculty** member, *is an* **Employee** and *is a* **CommunityMember**. In C#, an **Administrator** also *is an* **Object**, because all classes in C# have **Object** as either a direct or indirect base class. Thus, all classes in C# are connected via a hierarchical relationship in which they share the eight methods defined by class **Object**. We discuss some of these methods inherited from **Object** throughout the text.

Another inheritance hierarchy is the **Shape** hierarchy of Fig. 9.3. To specify that class **TwoDimensionalShape** is derived from (or inherits from) class **Shape**, class **TwoDimensionalShape** could be defined in C# as follows:

> *class* **TwoDimensionalShape : Shape**

In Chapter 8, we briefly discussed *has-a* relationships, in which classes have as members references to objects of other classes. Such relationships create classes by *composition* of existing classes. For example, given the classes **Employee**, **BirthDate** and **TelephoneNumber**, it is improper to say that an **Employee** *is a* **BirthDate** or that an **Employee** *is a* **TelephoneNumber**. However, it is appropriate to say that an **Employee** *has a* **BirthDate** and that an **Employee** *has a* **TelephoneNumber**.

With inheritance, **private** members of a base class are not accessible directly from that class's derived classes, but these **private** base-class members are still inherited. All other base-class members retain their original member access when they become members of the derived class (e.g., **public** members of the base class become **public** members of the derived class, and, as we will soon see, **protected** members of the base class become **protected** members of the derived class). Through these inherited base-class members, the derived class can manipulate **private** members of the base class (if these inherited members provide such functionality in the base class).

It is possible to treat base-class objects and derived-class objects similarly; their commonalities are expressed in the member variables, properties and methods of the base class. Objects of all classes derived from a common base class can be treated as objects of that base class.

Software Engineering Observation 9.3

Constructors never are inherited—they are specific to the class in which they are defined.

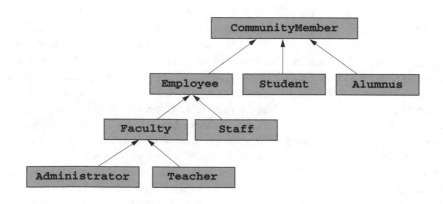

Fig. 9.2   Inheritance hierarchy for university **CommunityMember**s.

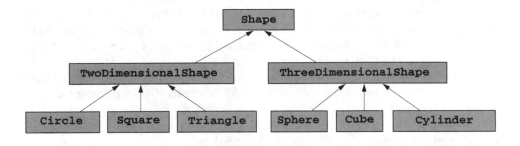

Fig. 9.3   Portion of a **Shape** class hierarchy.

9.3 `protected` and `internal` Members

Chapter 8 discussed **public** and **private** member access modifiers. A base class's non-**static public** members are accessible anywhere that the program has a reference to an object of that base class or one of its derived classes. A base class's **private** members are accessible only within the body of that base class. In this section, we introduce two additional member access modifiers, *protected* and *internal*.

Using **protected** access offers an intermediate level of protection between **public** and **private** access. A base class's **protected** members can be accessed only in that base class or in any classes derived from that base class.

Another intermediate level of access is known as **internal** access. A base class's **internal** members can be accessed only by objects declared in the same assembly. Note that an **internal** member is accessible in any part of the assembly in which that **internal** member is declared.

Derived-class methods normally can refer to **public**, **protected** and **internal** members of the base class simply by using the member names. When a derived-class method overrides a base-class member, the base-class member can be accessed from the derived class by preceding the base-class member name with keyword *base*, followed by the dot operator (**.**). We discuss keyword **base** in Section 9.4.

9.4 Relationship between Base Classes and Derived Classes

In this section, we use a point-circle hierarchy[1] to discuss the relationship between a base class and a derived class. We divide our discussion of the point-circle relationship into several parts. First, we create class **Point**, which directly inherits from class **System.Object** and contains as **private** data an *x-y* coordinate pair. Then, we create class **Circle**, which also directly inherits from class **System.Object** and contains as **private** data an *x-y* coordinate pair (representing the location of the center of the circle) and a radius. We do not use inheritance to create class **Circle**; rather, we construct the class by writing every line of code the class requires. Next, we create a separate **Circle2** class,

---

1. The point-circle relationship may seem unnatural when we discuss it in the context of a circle "is a" point. This example teaches what is sometimes called *structural inheritance*; the example focuses on the "mechanics" of inheritance and how a base class and a derived class relate to one another.

which directly inherits from class **Point** (i.e., class **Circle2** "is a" **Point** but also contains a radius) and attempts to use the **Point private** members—this results in compilation errors, because the derived class does not have access to the base-class's **private** data. We then show that if **Point**'s data is declared as **protected**, a **Circle3** class that inherits from class **Point** can access that data. Both the inherited and non-inherited **Circle** classes contain identical functionality, but we show how the inherited **Circle3** class is easier to create and manage. After discussing the merits of using **protected** data, we set the **Point** data back to **private** (to enforce good software engineering), then show how a separate **Circle4** class (which also inherits from class **Point**) can use **Point** methods to manipulate **Point**'s **private** data.

Let us first examine the **Point** (Fig. 9.4) class definition. The **public** services of class **Point** include two **Point** constructors (lines 13–24), properties **X** and **Y** (lines 27–54) and method **ToString** (lines 57–60). The instance variables **x** and **y** of **Point** are specified as **private** (line 10), so objects of other classes cannot access **x** and **y** directly. Technically, even if **Point**'s variables **x** and **y** were made **public**, **Point** can never maintain an inconsistent state, because the *x-y* coordinate plane is infinite in both directions, so **x** and **y** can hold any **int** value. In general, however, declaring data as **private**, while providing non-**private** properties to manipulate and perform validation checking on that data, enforces good software engineering.

We mentioned in Section 9.2 that constructors are not inherited. Therefore, class **Point** does not inherit class **Object**'s constructor. However, class **Point**'s constructors (lines 13–24) call class **Object**'s constructor implicitly. In fact, the first task of any derived-class constructor is to call its direct base class's constructor, either implicitly or explicitly. (The syntax for calling a base-class constructor is discussed later in this section.) If the code does not include an explicit call to the base-class constructor, an implicit call is made to the base class's default (no-argument) constructor. The comments in lines 15 and 21 indicate where the implicit calls to the base-class **Object**'s default constructor occur.

```
1   // Fig. 9.4: Point.cs
2   // Point class represents an x-y coordinate pair.
3
4   using System;
5
6   // Point class definition implicitly inherits from Object
7   public class Point
8   {
9      // point coordinates
10     private int x, y;
11
12     // default (no-argument) constructor
13     public Point()
14     {
15        // implicit call to Object constructor occurs here
16     }
17
18     // constructor
19     public Point( int xValue, int yValue )
20     {
```

Fig. 9.4 **Point** class represents an *x-y* coordinate pair. (Part 1 of 2.)

```
21          // implicit call to Object constructor occurs here
22          X = xValue;
23          Y = yValue;
24       }
25
26       // property X
27       public int X
28       {
29          get
30          {
31             return x;
32          }
33
34          set
35          {
36             x = value; // no need for validation
37          }
38
39       } // end property X
40
41       // property Y
42       public int Y
43       {
44          get
45          {
46             return y;
47          }
48
49          set
50          {
51             y = value; // no need for validation
52          }
53
54       } // end property Y
55
56       // return string representation of Point
57       public override string ToString()
58       {
59          return "[" + x + ", " + y + "]";
60       }
61
62    } // end class Point
```

Fig. 9.4　　**Point** class represents an *x-y* coordinate pair. (Part 2 of 2.)

Note that method **ToString** (lines 57–60) contains the keyword **override** in its declaration. Every class in C# (such as class **Point**) inherits either directly or indirectly from class **System.Object**, which is the root of the class hierarchy. As we mentioned previously, this means that every class inherits the eight methods defined by class **Object**. One of these methods is **ToString**, which returns a **string** containing the object's type preceded by its namespace—this method obtains an object's **string** representation and sometimes is called implicitly by the program (such as when an object is concatenated to a **string**). Method **ToString** of class **Point** *overrides* the original **ToString** from class **Object**—when invoked, method **ToString** of class **Point** returns a **string** containing an ordered pair of the values **x** and **y** (line 59), instead of returning a **string** containing the object's class and namespace. To override a base-class method definition, a derived class must specify that the derived-class method overrides the base-class method with keyword **override** in the method header.

Software Engineering Observation 9.4

*The C# compiler sets the base class of a derived class to **Object** when the program does not specify a base class explicitly.*

In C#, a base-class method must be declared **virtual** if that method is to be overridden in a derived class. Method **ToString** of class **Object** is, in fact, declared **virtual**, which enables derived class **Point** to override this method. To view the method header for **ToString**, select **Help > Index...**, and enter **Object.ToString method** (filtered by **.Net Framework SDK**) in the search text box. The page displayed contains a description of method **ToString**, which includes the following header:

> **public virtual string ToString();**

Keyword **virtual** allows programmers to specify those methods that a derived class can override—a method that has not been declared **virtual** cannot be overridden. We use this later in this section to enable certain methods in our base classes to be overridden.

Common Programming Error 9.1

*A derived class attempting to override (using keyword **override**) a method that has not been declared **virtual** is a syntax error.*

Class **PointTest** (Fig. 9.5) tests class **Point**. Line 14 instantiates an object of class **Point** and assigns **72** as the *x*-coordinate value and **115** as the *y*-coordinate value. Lines 17–18 use properties **X** and **Y** to retrieve these values, then append the values to **string output**. Lines 20–21 change the values of properties **X** and **Y** (implicitly invoking their **set** accessors), and line 24 calls **Point**'s **ToString** method implicitly to obtain the **Point**'s **string** representation.

```
1   // Fig. 9.5: PointTest.cs
2   // Testing class Point.
3
4   using System;
5   using System.Windows.Forms;
6
7   // PointTest class definition
8   class PointTest
9   {
10     // main entry point for application
11     static void Main( string[] args )
12     {
13        // instantiate Point object
14        Point point = new Point( 72, 115 );
15
```

Fig. 9.5   **PointTest** class demonstrates class **Point** functionality. (Part 1 of 2.)

```
16            // display point coordinates via X and Y properties
17            string output = "X coordinate is " + point.X +
18                "\n" + "Y coordinate is " + point.Y;
19
20            point.X = 10; // set x-coordinate via X property
21            point.Y = 10; // set y-coordinate via Y property
22
23            // display new point value
24            output += "\n\nThe new location of point is " + point;
25
26            MessageBox.Show( output, "Demonstrating Class Point" );
27
28         } // end method Main
29
30    } // end class PointTest
```

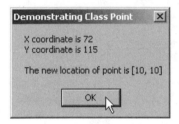

Fig. 9.5   PointTest class demonstrates class **Point** functionality. (Part 2 of 2.)

We now discuss the second part of our introduction to inheritance by creating and testing (a completely new) class **Circle** (Fig. 9.6), which directly inherits from class **System.Object** and represents an *x-y* coordinate pair (representing the center of the circle) and a radius. Lines 9–10 declare the instance variables **x, y** and **radius** as **private** data. The **public** services of class **Circle** include two **Circle** constructors (lines 13–25), properties **X, Y** and **Radius** (lines 28–71), methods **Diameter** (lines 74–77), **Circumference** (lines 80–83), **Area** (lines 86–89) and **ToString** (lines 92–96). These properties and methods encapsulate all necessary features (i.e., the "analytic geometry") of a circle; in the next section, we show how this encapsulation enables us to reuse and extend this class.

```
1    // Fig. 9.6: Circle.cs
2    // Circle class contains x-y coordinate pair and radius.
3
4    using System;
5
6    // Circle class definition implicitly inherits from Object
7    public class Circle
8    {
9       private int x, y;      // coordinates of Circle's center
10      private double radius; // Circle's radius
11
```

Fig. 9.6   Circle class contains an *x-y* coordinate and a radius. (Part 1 of 3.)

```
12      // default constructor
13      public Circle()
14      {
15          // implicit call to Object constructor occurs here
16      }
17
18      // constructor
19      public Circle( int xValue, int yValue, double radiusValue )
20      {
21          // implicit call to Object constructor occurs here
22          x = xValue;
23          y = yValue;
24          Radius = radiusValue;
25      }
26
27      // property X
28      public int X
29      {
30          get
31          {
32              return x;
33          }
34
35          set
36          {
37              x = value;   // no need for validation
38          }
39
40      } // end property X
41
42      // property Y
43      public int Y
44      {
45          get
46          {
47              return y;
48          }
49
50          set
51          {
52              y = value;   // no need for validation
53          }
54
55      } // end property Y
56
57      // property Radius
58      public double Radius
59      {
60          get
61          {
62              return radius;
63          }
64
```

Fig. 9.6   **Circle** class contains an x-y coordinate and a radius. (Part 2 of 3.)

```
65              set
66              {
67                  if ( value >= 0 )    // validation needed
68                      radius = value;
69              }
70
71          } // end property Radius
72
73          // calculate Circle diameter
74          public double Diameter()
75          {
76              return radius * 2;
77          }
78
79          // calculate Circle circumference
80          public double Circumference()
81          {
82              return Math.PI * Diameter();
83          }
84
85          // calculate Circle area
86          public double Area()
87          {
88              return Math.PI * Math.Pow( radius, 2 );
89          }
90
91          // return string representation of Circle
92          public override string ToString()
93          {
94              return "Center = [" + x + ", " + y + "]" +
95                  "; Radius = " + radius;
96          }
97
98      } // end class Circle
```

Fig. 9.6 **Circle** class contains an *x-y* coordinate and a radius. (Part 3 of 3.)

Class **CircleTest** (Fig. 9.7) tests class **Circle**. Line 14 instantiates an object of class **Circle**, assigning **37** as the *x*-coordinate value, **43** as the *y*-coordinate value and **2.5** as the radius value. Lines 17–19 use properties **X**, **Y** and **Radius** to retrieve these values, then concatenate the values to **string output**. Lines 22–24 use **Circle**'s **X**, **Y** and **Radius** properties to change the *x-y* coordinates and the radius, respectively. Property **Radius** ensures that member variable **radius** cannot be assigned a negative value. Line 28 calls **Circle**'s **ToString** method implicitly to obtain the **Circle**'s **string** representation, and lines 32–40 call **Circle**'s **Diameter**, **Circumference** and **Area** methods.

After writing all the code for class **Circle** (Fig. 9.6), we note that a major portion of the code in this class is similar, if not identical, to much of the code in class **Point**. For example, the declaration in **Circle** of **private** variables **x** and **y** and properties **X** and **Y** are identical to those of class **Point**. In addition, the class **Circle** constructors and method **ToString** are almost identical to those of class **Point**, except that they also supply **radius** information. The only other additions to class **Circle** are **private** member variable **radius**, property **Radius** and methods **Diameter**, **Circumference** and **Area**.

It appears that we literally copied code from class **Point**, pasted this code in the code from class **Circle**, then modified class **Circle** to include a radius. This "copy-and-paste" approach is often error-prone and time-consuming. Worse yet, it can result in many physical copies of the code existing throughout a system, creating a code-maintenance "nightmare." Is there a way to "absorb" the attributes and behaviors of one class in a way that makes them part of other classes without duplicating code?

```csharp
1   // Fig. 9.7: CircleTest.cs
2   // Testing class Circle.
3
4   using System;
5   using System.Windows.Forms;
6
7   // CircleTest class definition
8   class CircleTest
9   {
10      // main entry point for application.
11      static void Main( string[] args )
12      {
13         // instantiate Circle
14         Circle circle = new Circle( 37, 43, 2.5 );
15
16         // get Circle's initial x-y coordinates and radius
17         string output = "X coordinate is " + circle.X +
18            "\nY coordinate is " + circle.Y + "\nRadius is " +
19            circle.Radius;
20
21         // set Circle's x-y coordinates and radius to new values
22         circle.X = 2;
23         circle.Y = 2;
24         circle.Radius = 4.25;
25
26         // display Circle's string representation
27         output += "\n\nThe new location and radius of " +
28            "circle are \n" + circle + "\n";
29
30         // display Circle's diameter
31         output += "Diameter is " +
32            String.Format( "{0:F}", circle.Diameter() ) + "\n";
33
34         // display Circle's circumference
35         output += "Circumference is " +
36            String.Format( "{0:F}", circle.Circumference() ) + "\n";
37
38         // display Circle's area
39         output += "Area is " +
40            String.Format( "{0:F}", circle.Area() );
41
42         MessageBox.Show( output, "Demonstrating Class Circle" );
43
44      } // end method Main
```

Fig. 9.7   **CircleTest** demonstrates class **Circle** functionality. (Part 1 of 2.)

```
45
46   } // end class CircleTest
```

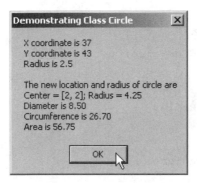

Fig. 9.7   `CircleTest` demonstrates class `Circle` functionality. (Part 2 of 2.)

In the next examples we answer that question, we use a more elegant class construction approach emphasizing the benefits of inheritance. Now, we create and test a class **Circle2** (Fig. 9.8) that inherits variables **x** and **y** and properties **X** and **Y** from class **Point** (Fig. 9.4). This class **Circle2** "is a" **Point** (because inheritance absorbs the capabilities of class **Point**), but also contains **radius** (line 9). The colon (**:**) symbol in the class declaration (line 7) indicates inheritance. As a derived class, **Circle2** inherits all the members of class **Point**, except for the constructors. Thus, the **public** services to **Circle2** include the two **Circle2** constructors (lines 12–24); the **public** methods inherited from class **Point**; property **Radius** (lines 27–40); and the **Circle2** methods **Diameter**, **Circumference**, **Area** and **ToString** (lines 43–65). We declare method **Area** as **virtual**, so that derived classes (such as class **Cylinder**, as we will see in Section 9.5) can override this method to provide a more appropriate implementation.

```
1    // Fig. 9.8: Circle2.cs
2    // Circle2 class that inherits from class Point.
3
4    using System;
5
6    // Circle2 class definition inherits from Point
7    class Circle2 : Point
8    {
9       private double radius; // Circle2's radius
10
11      // default constructor
12      public Circle2()
13      {
14         // implicit call to Point constructor occurs here
15      }
16
```

Fig. 9.8   `Circle2` class that inherits from class `Point`. (Part 1 of 3.)

```
17        // constructor
18        public Circle2( int xValue, int yValue, double radiusValue )
19        {
20           // implicit call to Point constructor occurs here
21           x = xValue;
22           y = yValue;
23           Radius = radiusValue;
24        }
25
26        // property Radius
27        public double Radius
28        {
29           get
30           {
31              return radius;
32           }
33
34           set
35           {
36              if ( value >= 0 )
37                 radius = value;
38           }
39
40        } // end property Radius
41
42        // calculate Circle diameter
43        public double Diameter()
44        {
45           return radius * 2;
46        }
47
48        // calculate Circle circumference
49        public double Circumference()
50        {
51           return Math.PI * Diameter();
52        }
53
54        // calculate Circle area
55        public virtual double area()
56        {
57           return Math.PI * Math.Pow( radius, 2 );
58        }
59
60        // return string representation Circle
61        public override string ToString()
62        {
63           return "Center = [" + x + ", " + y + "]" +
64              "; Radius = " + radius;
65        }
66
67  } // end class Circle2
```

Fig. 9.8   **Circle2** class that inherits from class **Point**. (Part 2 of 3.)

!	☑ Description	File	Line
	Click here to add a new task		
!	'Circle2.Point.x' is inaccessible due to its protection level	C:\...\Circle2.cs	23
!	'Circle2.Point.y' is inaccessible due to its protection level	C:\...\Circle2.cs	24
!	'Circle2.Point.x' is inaccessible due to its protection level	C:\...\Circle2.cs	65

Fig. 9.8   Circle2 class that inherits from class **Point**. (Part 3 of 3.)

Lines 14 and 20 in the **Circle2** constructors (lines 12–24) invoke the default **Point** constructor implicitly to initialize the base-class portion (variables **x** and **y**, inherited from class **Point**) of a **Circle2** object to **0**. However, because the parameterized constructor (lines 18–24) should set the x-y coordinate to a specific value, lines 21–22 attempt to assign argument values to **x** and **y** directly. Even though lines 21–22 attempt to set **x** and **y** values explicitly, line 20 first calls the **Point** default constructor to initialize these variables to their default values. The compiler generates syntax errors for lines 21 and 22 (and line 63, where **Circle2**'s method **ToString** attempts to use the values of **x** and **y** directly), because the derived class **Circle2** is not allowed to access the base class **Point**'s **private** members **x** and **y**. C# rigidly enforces restriction on accessing **private** data members, so that even a derived class (i.e., which is closely related to its base class) cannot access base-class **private** data.

To enable class **Circle2** to access **Point** member variables **x** and **y** directly, we can declare those variables as **protected**. As we discussed in Section 9.3, a base class's **protected** members can be accessed only in that base class or in any classes derived from that base class. Class **Point2** (Fig. 9.9) modifies class **Point** (Fig. 9.4) to declare variables **x** and **y** as **protected** (line 10) instead of **private**.

```
1   // Fig. 9.9: Point2.cs
2   // Point2 class contains an x-y coordinate pair as protected data.
3
4   using System;
5
6   // Point2 class definition implicitly inherits from Object
7   public class Point2
8   {
9      // point coordinate
10     protected int x, y;
11
12     // default constructor
13     public Point2()
14     {
15        // implicit call to Object constructor occurs here
16     }
17
```

Fig. 9.9   Point2 class represents an x-y coordinate pair as **protected** data. (Part 1 of 2.)

```
18       // constructor
19       public Point2( int xValue, int yValue )
20       {
21          // implicit call to Object constructor occurs here
22          X = xValue;
23          Y = yValue;
24       }
25
26       // property X
27       public int X
28       {
29          get
30          {
31             return x;
32          }
33
34          set
35          {
36             x = value; // no need for validation
37          }
38
39       } // end property X
40
41       // property Y
42       public int Y
43       {
44          get
45          {
46             return y;
47          }
48
49          set
50          {
51             y = value; // no need for validation
52          }
53
54       } // end property Y
55
56       // return string representation of Point2
57       public override string ToString()
58       {
59          return "[" + x + ", " + y + "]";
60       }
61
62    } // end class Point2
```

Fig. 9.9   **Point2** class represents an *x-y* coordinate pair as **protected** data. (Part 2 of 2.)

Class **Circle3** (Fig. 9.10) modifies class **Circle2** (Fig. 9.8) to inherit from class **Point2** rather than inheriting from class **Point**. Because class **Circle3** is a class derived from class **Point2**, class **Circle3** can access class **Point2**'s **protected** member variables **x** and **y** directly, and the compiler does not generate errors when compiling Fig. 9.10. This shows the special privileges that a derived class is granted to access

protected base-class data members. A derived class also can access **protected** methods in any of that derived class's base classes.

```csharp
1   // Fig. 9.10: Circle3.cs
2   // Circle2 class that inherits from class Point2.
3
4   using System;
5
6   // Circle3 class definition inherits from Point2
7   public class Circle3 : Point2
8   {
9      private double radius; // Circle's radius
10
11     // default constructor
12     public Circle3()
13     {
14        // implicit call to Point constructor occurs here
15     }
16
17     // constructor
18     public Circle3(
19        int xValue, int yValue, double radiusValue )
20     {
21        // implicit call to Point constructor occurs here
22        x = xValue;
23        y = yValue;
24        Radius = radiusValue;
25     }
26
27     // property Radius
28     public double Radius
29     {
30        get
31        {
32           return radius;
33        }
34
35        set
36        {
37           if ( value >= 0 )
38              radius = value;
39        }
40
41     } // end property Radius
42
43     // calculate Circle diameter
44     public double Diameter()
45     {
46        return radius * 2;
47     }
48
```

Fig. 9.10 Circle3 class that inherits from class **Point2**. (Part 1 of 2.)

```
49       // calculate circumference
50       public double Circumference()
51       {
52          return Math.PI * Diameter();
53       }
54
55       // calculate Circle area
56       public virtual double Area()
57       {
58          return Math.PI * Math.Pow( radius, 2 );
59       }
60
61       // return string representation of Circle3
62       public override string ToString()
63       {
64          return "Center = [" + x + ", " + y + "]" +
65             "; Radius = " + radius;
66       }
67
68    } // end class Circle3
```

Fig. 9.10   **Circle3** class that inherits from class **Point2**. (Part 2 of 2.)

Class **CircleTest3** (Fig. 9.11) performs identical tests on class **Circle3** as class **CircleTest** (Fig. 9.7) performed on class **Circle** (Fig. 9.6). Note that the outputs of the two programs are identical. We created class **Circle** without using inheritance and created class **Circle3** using inheritance; however, both classes provide the same functionality. However, observe that the code listing for class **Circle3**, which is 68 lines, is considerably shorter than the code listing for class **Circle**, which is 98 lines, because class **Circle3** absorbs part of its functionality from **Point2**, whereas class **Circle** does not. Also, there is now only one copy of the point functionality.

```
1    // Fig. 9.11: CircleTest3.cs
2    // Testing class Circle3.
3
4    using System;
5    using System.Windows.Forms;
6
7    // CircleTest3 class definition
8    class CircleTest3
9    {
10      // main entry point for application
11      static void Main( string[] args )
12      {
13         // instantiate Circle3
14         Circle3 circle = new Circle3( 37, 43, 2.5 );
15
16         // get Circle3's initial x-y coordinates and radius
17         string output = "X coordinate is " + circle.X + "\n" +
18            "Y coordinate is " + circle.Y + "\nRadius is " +
19            circle.Radius;
```

Fig. 9.11   **CircleTest3** demonstrates class **Circle3** functionality. (Part 1 of 2.)

```
20
21          // set Circle3's x-y coordinates and radius to new values
22          circle.X = 2;
23          circle.Y = 2;
24          circle.Radius = 4.25;
25
26          // display Circle3's string representation
27          output += "\n\n" +
28             "The new location and radius of circle are " +
29             "\n" + circle + "\n";
30
31          // display Circle3's Diameter
32          output += "Diameter is " +
33             String.Format( "{0:F}", circle.Diameter() ) + "\n";
34
35          // display Circle3's Circumference
36          output += "Circumference is " +
37             String.Format( "{0:F}", circle.Circumference() ) + "\n";
38
39          // display Circle3's Area
40          output += "Area is " +
41             String.Format( "{0:F}", circle.Area() );
42
43          MessageBox.Show( output, "Demonstrating Class Circle3" );
44
45       } // end method Main
46
47    } // end class CircleTest3
```

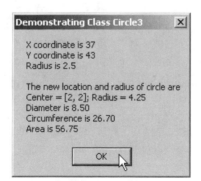

Fig. 9.11 `CircleTest3` demonstrates class `Circle3` functionality. (Part 2 of 2.)

In the previous example, we declared the base-class instance variables as **protected**, so that a derived class could modify their values directly. The use of **protected** variables allows for a slight increase in performance, because we avoid incurring the overhead of a method call to a property's **set** or **get** accessor. However, in most C# applications, in which user interaction comprises a large part of the execution time, the optimization offered through the use of **protected** variables is negligible.

Using **protected** instance variables creates two major problems. First, the derived-class object does not have to use a property to set the value of the base-class's **protected** data. Therefore, a derived-class object can easily assign an illegal value to the **protected** data, thus leaving the object in an inconsistent state. For example, if we were to declare **Circle3**'s variable **radius** as **protected**, a derived-class object (e.g., **Cylinder**), could then assign a negative value to **radius**. The second problem with using **protected** data is that derived-class methods are more likely to be written to depend on base-class implementation. In practice, derived classes should depend only on the base-class services (i.e., non-**private** methods and properties) and not on base-class implementation. With **protected** data in the base class, if the base-class implementation changes, we may need to modify all derived classes of that base class. For example, if for some reason we were to change the names of variables **x** and **y** to **xCoordinate** and **yCoordinate**, then we would have to do so for all occurrences in which a derived class references these base-class variables directly. In such a case, the software is said to be *fragile* or *brittle*. The programmer should be able to change the base-class implementation freely, while still providing the same services to derived classes. (Of course, if the base class services change, we must reimplement our derived classes, but good object-oriented design attempts to prevent this.)

Software Engineering Observation 9.5

*The most appropriate time to use the **protected** access modifier is when a base class should provide a service only to its derived classes (i.e., the base class should not provide the service to other clients).*

Software Engineering Observation 9.6

*Declaring base-class instance variables **private** (as opposed to declaring them **protected**) enables programmers to change base-class implementation without having to change derived-class implementation.*

Testing and Debugging Tip 9.1

*When possible, avoid including **protected** data in a base class. Rather, include non-**private** properties and methods that access **private** data, ensuring that the object maintains a consistent state.*

We reexamine our point-circle hierarchy example once more; this time, attempting to use the best software engineering. We use **Point3** (Fig. 9.12), which declares variables **x** and **y** as **private** and uses properties in method **ToString** to access these values. We show how derived class **Circle4** (Fig. 9.13) can invoke non-**private** base-class methods and properties to manipulate these variables.

```
1   // Fig. 9.12: Point3.cs
2   // Point3 class represents an x-y coordinate pair.
3
4   using System;
5
6   // Point3 class definition implicitly inherits from Object
7   public class Point3
8   {
9      // point coordinate
10     private int x, y;
11
```

Fig. 9.12   Point3 class uses properties to manipulate its **private** data. (Part 1 of 2.)

```
12      // default constructor
13      public Point3()
14      {
15         // implicit call to Object constructor occurs here
16      }
17
18      // constructor
19      public Point3( int xValue, int yValue )
20      {
21         // implicit call to Object constructor occurs here
22         X = xValue;    // use property X
23         Y = yValue;    // use property Y
24      }
25
26      // property X
27      public int X
28      {
29         get
30         {
31            return x;
32         }
33
34         set
35         {
36            x = value; // no need for validation
37         }
38
39      } // end property X
40
41      // property Y
42      public int Y
43      {
44         get
45         {
46            return y;
47         }
48
49         set
50         {
51            y = value; // no need for validation
52         }
53
54      } // end property Y
55
56      // return string representation of Point3
57      public override string ToString()
58      {
59         return "[" + X + ", " + Y + "]";
60      }
61
62   } // end class Point3
```

Fig. 9.12 **Point3** class uses properties to manipulate its **private** data. (Part 2 of 2.)

```
1   // Fig. 9.13: Circle4.cs
2   // Circle4 class that inherits from class Point3.
3
4   using System;
5
6   // Circle4 class definition inherits from Point3
7   public class Circle4 : Point3
8   {
9      private double radius;
10
11     // default constructor
12     public Circle4()
13     {
14        // implicit call to Point constructor occurs here
15     }
16
17     // constructor
18     public Circle4( int xValue, int yValue, double radiusValue )
19        : base( xValue, yValue )
20     {
21        Radius = radiusValue;
22     }
23
24     // property Radius
25     public double Radius
26     {
27        get
28        {
29           return radius;
30        }
31
32        set
33        {
34           if ( value >= 0 )      // validation needed
35              radius = value;
36        }
37
38     } // end property Radius
39
40     // calculate Circle diameter
41     public double Diameter()
42     {
43        return Radius * 2;       // use property Radius
44     }
45
46     // calculate Circle circumference
47     public double Circumference()
48     {
49        return Math.PI * Diameter();
50     }
51
```

Fig. 9.13 **Circle4** class that inherits from class **Point3**, which does not provide **protected** data. (Part 1 of 2.)

```
52        // calculate Circle area
53        public virtual double Area()
54        {
55            return Math.PI * Math.Pow( Radius, 2 );   // use property
56        }
57
58        // return string representation of Circle4
59        public override string ToString()
60        {
61            // use base reference to return Point string representation
62            return "Center= " + base.ToString() +
63                "; Radius = " + Radius;   // use property Radius
64        }
65
66   } // end class Circle4
```

Fig. 9.13 **Circle4** class that inherits from class **Point3**, which does not provide **protected** data. (Part 2 of 2.)

Software Engineering Observation 9.7

*When possible, use properties to alter and obtain the values of member variables, even if those values can be modified directly. A property's **set** accessor can prevent attempts to assign an inappropriate value to that member variable, and a property's **get** accessor can help control the presentation of the data to clients.*

Performance Tip 9.1

Using a property to access a variable's value is slightly slower than accessing the data directly. However, attempting to optimize programs by referencing data directly often is unnecessary, because the compiler optimizes the programs implicitly. [Today's so-called "optimizing compilers" are carefully designed to perform many optimizations implicitly, even if the programmer does not write what appears to be the most optimal code. A good rule is, "Do not second-guess the compiler."]

For the purpose of this example, to demonstrate both explicit and implicit calls to base-class constructors, we include a second constructor that calls the base-class constructor explicitly. Lines 18–22 declare the **Circle4** constructor that invokes the second **Point3** constructor explicitly (line 19) using the *base-class constructor-call syntax* (i.e., reference **base** followed by a set of parentheses containing the arguments to the base-class constructor). In this case, **xValue** and **yValue** are passed to initialize the **private** base-class members **x** and **y**. The colon symbol (**:**) followed by the **base** keyword accesses the base-class version of that method explicitly (line 19). By making this call, we can initialize **x** and **y** in the base class to specific values, rather than to **0**.

Common Programming Error 9.2

*It is a syntax error if a derived class uses **base** to call its base-class constructor with arguments that do not match exactly the number and types of parameters specified in one of the base-class constructor definitions.*

Class **Circle4**'s **ToString** method (line 59–64) overrides class **Point3**'s **ToString** method (lines 57–60 of Fig. 9.12). As we discussed earlier, overriding this method is possible, because method **ToString** of class **System.Object** (class

Point3's base class) is declared **virtual**. Method **ToString** of class **Circle4** displays the **private** instance variables **x** and **y** of class **Point3** by calling the base class's **ToString** method (in this case, **Point3**'s **ToString** method). The call is made in line 62 via the expression **base.ToString()** and causes the values of **x** and **y** to become part of the **Circle4**'s **string** representation. Using this approach is a good software engineering practice: Recall that if an object's method performs the actions needed by another object, the programmer should call that method rather than duplicating its code body. Duplicate code creates code-maintenance problems. By having **Circle4**'s **ToString** method use the formatting provided by **Point3**'s **ToString** method, we avoid duplicating code. Also, **Point3**'s **ToString** method performs part of the task of **Circle4**'s **ToString** method, so we call **Point3**'s **ToString** method from class **Circle4** with the expression **base.ToString()**.

Common Programming Error 9.3

*When a base-class method is overridden in a derived class, the derived-class version often calls the base-class version to do additional work. Failure to use the **base** reference when referencing the base class's method causes infinite recursion, because the derived-class method would then call itself.*

Common Programming Error 9.4

*The use of "chained" **base** references to refer to a member (a method, property or variable) several levels up the hierarchy (as in **base.base.mX**) is a syntax error.*

Software Engineering Observation 9.8

A redefinition in a derived class of a base-class method that uses a different signature than that of the base-class method is method overloading rather than method overriding.

Software Engineering Observation 9.9

*Although method **ToString** certainly could be overridden to perform arbitrary actions, the general understanding in the C# .NET community is that method **ToString** should be overridden to obtain an object's **string** representation.*

Class **CircleTest4** (Fig. 9.14) performs identical manipulations on class **Circle4** as did classes **CircleTest** (Fig. 9.7) and **CircleTest3** (Fig. 9.11). Note that the outputs of all three modules are identical. Therefore, although each "circle" class appears to behave identically, class **Circle4** is the most properly engineered. Using inheritance, we have efficiently and effectively constructed a well-engineered class.

```
1   // Fig. 9.14: CircleTest4.cs
2   // Testing class Circle4.
3
4   using System;
5   using System.Windows.Forms;
6
7   // CircleTest4 class definition
8   class CircleTest4
9   {
```

Fig. 9.14 CircleTest4 demonstrates class **Circle4** functionality. (Part 1 of 2.)

```
10        // main entry point for application
11        static void Main( string[] args )
12        {
13           // instantiate Circle4
14           Circle4 circle = new Circle4( 37, 43, 2.5 );
15
16           // get Circle4's initial x-y coordinates and radius
17           string output = "X coordinate is " + circle.X + "\n" +
18              "Y coordinate is " + circle.Y + "\n" +
19              "Radius is " + circle.Radius;
20
21           // set Circle4's x-y coordinates and radius to new values
22           circle.X = 2;
23           circle.Y = 2;
24           circle.Radius = 4.25;
25
26           // display Circle4's string representation
27           output += "\n\n" +
28              "The new location and radius of circle are " +
29              "\n" + circle + "\n";
30
31           // display Circle4's Diameter
32           output += "Diameter is " +
33              String.Format( "{0:F}", circle.Diameter() ) + "\n";
34
35           // display Circle4's Circumference
36           output += "Circumference is " +
37              String.Format( "{0:F}", circle.Circumference() ) + "\n";
38
39           // display Circle4's Area
40           output += "Area is " +
41              String.Format( "{0:F}", circle.Area() );
42
43           MessageBox.Show( output, "Demonstrating Class Circle4" );
44
45        } // end method Main
46
47     } // end class CircleTest4
```

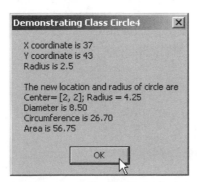

Fig. 9.14 **CircleTest4** demonstrates class **Circle4** functionality. (Part 2 of 2.)

9.5 Case Study: Three-Level Inheritance Hierarchy

Let us consider a more substantial inheritance example involving a three-level point-circle-cylinder hierarchy. In Section 9.4, we developed classes **Point3** (Fig. 9.12) and **Circle4** (Fig. 9.13). Now, we present an example in which we derive class **Cylinder** from class **Circle4**.

The first class that we use in our case study is class **Point3** (Fig. 9.12). We declared **Point3**'s instance variables as **private**. Class **Point3** also contains properties **X** and **Y** for accessing **x** and **y** and method **ToString** (which **Point3** overrides from class **Object**) for obtaining a **string** representation of the *x-y* coordinate pair.

We also created class **Circle4** (Fig. 9.13), which inherits from class **Point3**. Class **Circle4** contains the **Point3** functionality, in addition to providing property **Radius**, which ensures that the **radius** member variable cannot hold a negative value, and methods **Diameter**, **Circumference**, **Area** and **ToString**. Recall that method **Area** was declared **virtual** (line 53). As we discussed in Section 9.4, this keyword enables derived classes to override a base-class method. Derived classes of class **Circle4** (such as class **Cylinder**, which we introduce momentarily) can override these methods and provide specific implementations. A circle has an area that is calculated by the formula, πr^2, in which r represents the circle's radius. However, a cylinder has a surface area that is calculated by the formula, $(2\pi r^2) + (2\pi rh)$, in which r represents the cylinder's radius and h represents the cylinder's height. Therefore, class **Cylinder** must override method **Area** to include this calculation, so we declared class **Circle4**'s method **Area** as **virtual**.

Figure 9.15 presents class **Cylinder**, which inherits from class **Circle4** (line 7). Class **Cylinder**'s **public** services include the inherited **Circle4** methods **Diameter**, **Circumference**, **Area** and **ToString**; the inherited **Circle4** property **Radius**; the indirectly inherited **Point3** properties **X** and **Y**; the **Cylinder** constructor, property **Height** and method **Volume**. Method **Area** (lines 41–44) overrides method **Area** of class **Circle4**. Note that, if class **Cylinder** were to attempt to override **Circle4**'s methods **Diameter** and **Circumference**, syntax errors would occur, because class **Circle4** did not declare these methods **virtual**. Method **ToString** (lines 53–56) overrides method **ToString** of class **Circle4** to obtain a **string** representation for the cylinder. Class **Cylinder** also includes method **Volume** (lines 47–50) to calculate the cylinder's volume. Because we do not declare method **Volume** as **virtual**, no derived class of class **Cylinder** can override this method.

```
1   // Fig. 9.15: Cylinder.cs
2   // Cylinder class inherits from class Circle4.
3
4   using System;
5
6   // Cylinder class definition inherits from Circle4
7   public class Cylinder : Circle4
8   {
9      private double height;
10
```

Fig. 9.15 **Cylinder** class inherits from class **Circle4** and overrides method **Area**. (Part 1 of 2.)

```
11      // default constructor
12      public Cylinder()
13      {
14         // implicit call to Circle4 constructor occurs here
15      }
16
17      // four-argument constructor
18      public Cylinder( int xValue, int yValue, double radiusValue,
19         double heightValue ) : base( xValue, yValue, radiusValue )
20      {
21         Height = heightValue; // set Cylinder height
22      }
23
24      // property Height
25      public double Height
26      {
27         get
28         {
29            return height;
30         }
31
32         set
33         {
34            if ( value >= 0 ) // validate height
35               height = value;
36         }
37
38      } // end property Height
39
40      // override Circle4 method Area to calculate Cylinder area
41      public override double Area()
42      {
43         return 2 * base.Area() + base.Circumference() * Height;
44      }
45
46      // calculate Cylinder volume
47      public double Volume()
48      {
49         return base.Area() * Height;
50      }
51
52      // convert Cylinder to string
53      public override string ToString()
54      {
55         return base.ToString() + "; Height = " + Height;
56      }
57
58   } // end class Cylinder
```

Fig. 9.15 **Cylinder** class inherits from class **Circle4** and overrides method **Area**. (Part 2 of 2.)

Figure 9.16 is a **CylinderTest** application that tests the **Cylinder** class. Line 14 instantiates an object of class **Cylinder**. Lines 17–19 use properties **X**, **Y**, **Radius** and

Height to obtain information about the **Cylinder** object, because **CylinderTest** cannot reference the **private** data of class **Cylinder** directly. Lines 22–25 use properties **X**, **Y**, **Radius** and **Height** to reset the **Cylinder**'s *x-y* coordinates (we assume the cylinder's *x-y* coordinates specify its position on the *x-y* plane), radius and height. Class **Cylinder** can use class **Point3**'s **X** and **Y** properties, because class **Cylinder** inherits them indirectly from class **Point3**—Class **Cylinder** inherits properties **X** and **Y** directly from class **Circle4**, which inherited them directly from class **Point3**. Line 29 invokes method **ToString** implicitly to obtain the **string** representation of the **Cylinder** object. Lines 33–37 invoke methods **Diameter** and **Circumference** of the **Cylinder** object—because class **Cylinder** inherits these methods from class **Circle4** and cannot override them, these methods, exactly as listed in **Circle4**, are invoked. Lines 41–45 invoke methods **Area** and **Volume**.

Using the point-circle-cylinder example, we have shown the use and benefits of inheritance. We were able to develop classes **Circle4** and **Cylinder** using inheritance much faster than if we had developed these classes "from scratch." Inheritance avoids duplicating code and the associated code-maintenance problems.

```
1   // Fig. 9.16: CylinderTest.cs
2   // Tests class Cylinder.
3
4   using System;
5   using System.Windows.Forms;
6
7   // CylinderTest class definition
8   class CylinderTest
9   {
10     // main entry point for application
11     static void Main( string[] args )
12     {
13        // instantiate object of class Cylinder
14        Cylinder cylinder = new Cylinder(12, 23, 2.5, 5.7);
15
16        // properties get initial x-y coordinate, radius and height
17        string output = "X coordinate is " + cylinder.X + "\n" +
18           "Y coordinate is " + cylinder.Y + "\nRadius is " +
19           cylinder.Radius + "\n" + "Height is " + cylinder.Height;
20
21        // properties set new x-y coordinate, radius and height
22        cylinder.X = 2;
23        cylinder.Y = 2;
24        cylinder.Radius = 4.25;
25        cylinder.Height = 10;
26
27        // get new x-y coordinate and radius
28        output += "\n\nThe new location, radius and height of " +
29           "cylinder are\n" + cylinder + "\n\n";
30
31        // display Cylinder's Diameter
32        output += "Diameter is " +
33           String.Format( "{0:F}", cylinder.Diameter() ) + "\n";
```

Fig. 9.16 Testing class **Cylinder**. (Part 1 of 2.)

```
34
35          // display Cylinder's Circumference
36          output += "Circumference is " +
37             String.Format( "{0:F}", cylinder.Circumference() ) + "\n";
38
39          // display Cylinder's Area
40          output += "Area is " +
41             String.Format( "{0:F}", cylinder.Area() ) + "\n";
42
43          // display Cylinder's Volume
44          output += "Volume is " +
45             String.Format( "{0:F}", cylinder.Volume() );
46
47          MessageBox.Show( output, "Demonstrating Class Cylinder" );
48
49       } // end method Main
50
51    } // end class CylinderTest
```

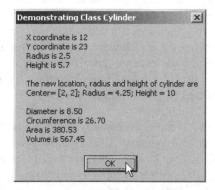

Fig. 9.16   Testing class **Cylinder**. (Part 2 of 2.)

9.6 Constructors and Destructors in Derived Classes

As we explained in the previous section, instantiating a derived-class object begins a chain of constructor calls in which the derived-class constructor, before performing its own tasks, invokes the base-class constructor either explicitly or implicitly. Similarly, if the base-class was derived from another class, the base-class constructor must invoke the constructor of the next class up in the hierarchy, and so on. The last constructor called in the chain is class **Object**'s constructor whose body actually finishes executing first—the original derived class's body finishes executing last. Each base-class constructor initializes the base-class instance variables that the derived-class object inherits. For example, consider the **Point3/Circle4** hierarchy from Fig. 9.12 and Fig. 9.13. When a program creates a **Circle4** object, one of the **Circle4** constructors is called. That constructor calls class **Point3**'s constructor, which in turn calls class **Object**'s constructor. When class **Object**'s constructor completes execution, it returns control to class **Point3**'s constructor, which initializes the *x-y* coordinates of **Circle4**. When class **Point3**'s constructor completes execution, it returns control to class **Circle4**'s constructor, which initializes the **Circle4**'s radius.

Software Engineering Observation 9.10

When a program creates a derived-class object, the derived-class constructor immediately calls the base-class constructor, the base-class constructor's body executes, then the derived-class constructor's body executes.

When the garbage collector removes a derived-class object from memory, the garbage collector calls that object's destructor. This begins a chain of destructor calls in which the derived-class destructor and the destructors of the direct and indirect base classes execute in the reverse order of the order in which the constructors executed. Executing the destructors should free all the resources the object acquired before the garbage collector reclaims the memory for that object. When the garbage collector calls a derived-class object's destructor, the destructor performs its task, then invokes the destructor of the base class. This process repeats until class **Object**'s destructor is called.

C# actually implements destructors using class **Object**'s *Finalize* method (one of the eight methods that every C# class inherits). When compiling a class definition that contains a destructor, the compiler translates a destructor definition into a **Finalize** method that performs the destructor's tasks, then invokes the base class **Finalize** method as the last statement in the derived-class **Finalize** method. As mentioned in Chapter 8, we cannot determine exactly when the destructor call will occur, because we cannot determine exactly when garbage collection occurs. However, by defining a destructor, we can specify code to execute before the garbage collector removes an object from memory.

Our next example revisits the point-circle hierarchy by defining class **Point4** (Fig. 9.17) and class **Circle5** (Fig. 9.18) that contain constructors *and* destructors, each of which prints a message when it runs.

Class **Point4** (Fig. 9.17) contains the features shown in Fig. 9.4. We modified the constructors (lines 13–17 and 20–26) to output a line of text when they are called and added a destructor (lines 29–32) that also outputs a line of text when it is called. Each output statement (lines 16, 25 and 31) adds reference **this** to the output string. This implicitly invokes the class's **ToString** method to obtain the **string** representation of **Point4**'s coordinates.

```
1   // Fig. 9.17: Point4.cs
2   // Point4 class represents an x-y coordinate pair.
3
4   using System;
5
6   // Point4 class definition
7   public class Point4
8   {
9      // point coordinate
10     private int x, y;
11
12     // default constructor
13     public Point4()
14     {
15        // implicit call to Object constructor occurs here
16        Console.WriteLine( "Point4 constructor: {0}", this );
17     }
```

Fig. 9.17   **Point4** base class contains constructors and finalizer. (Part 1 of 2.)

```
18
19     // constructor
20     public Point4( int xValue, int yValue )
21     {
22        // implicit call to Object constructor occurs here
23        X = xValue;
24        Y = yValue;
25        Console.WriteLine( "Point4 constructor: {0}", this );
26     }
27
28     // destructor
29     ~Point4()
30     {
31        Console.WriteLine( "Point4 destructor: {0}", this );
32     }
33
34     // property X
35     public int X
36     {
37        get
38        {
39           return x;
40        }
41
42        set
43        {
44           x = value; // no need for validation
45        }
46
47     } // end property X
48
49     // property Y
50     public int Y
51     {
52        get
53        {
54           return y;
55        }
56
57        set
58        {
59           y = value; // no need for validation
60        }
61
62     } // end property Y
63
64     // return string representation of Point4
65     public override string ToString()
66     {
67        return "[" + x + ", " + y + "]";
68     }
69
70  } // end class Point4
```

Fig. 9.17 **Point4** base class contains constructors and finalizer. (Part 2 of 2.)

Class **Circle5** (Fig. 9.18) contains the features in Fig. 9.13, and we modified the two constructors (lines 12–16 and 19–24) to output a line of text when they are called. We also added a destructor (lines 27–30) that also outputs a line of text when it is called. Each output statement (lines 15, 23 and 29) adds reference **this** to the output string. This implicitly invokes the **Circle5**'s **ToString** method to obtain the **string** representation of **Circle5**'s coordinates and radius.

Class **ConstructorAndFinalizer** (Fig. 9.19) demonstrates the order in which constructors and finalizers are called for objects of classes that are part of an inheritance class hierarchy. Method **Main** (lines 11–28) begins by instantiating an object of class **Circle5**, then assigns it to reference **circle1** (line 16). This invokes the **Circle5** constructor, which invokes the **Point4** constructor immediately. Then, the **Point4** constructor invokes the **Object** constructor. When the **Object** constructor (which does not print anything) returns control to the **Point4** constructor, the **Point4** constructor initializes the *x-y* coordinates, then outputs a **string** indicating that the **Point4** constructor was called. The output statement also calls method **ToString** implicitly (using reference **this**) to obtain the **string** representation of the object being constructed. Then, control returns to the **Circle5** constructor, which initializes the radius and outputs the **Circle5**'s *x-y* coordinates and radius by calling method **ToString** implicitly.

```
1   // Fig. 9.18: Circle5.cs
2   // Circle5 class that inherits from class Point4.
3
4   using System;
5
6   // Circle5 class definition inherits from Point4
7   public class Circle5 : Point4
8   {
9      private double radius;
10
11      // default constructor
12      public Circle5()
13      {
14         // implicit call to Point3 constructor occurs here
15         Console.WriteLine( "Circle5 constructor: {0}", this );
16      }
17
18      // constructor
19      public Circle5( int xValue, int yValue, double radiusValue )
20         : base( xValue, yValue )
21      {
22         Radius = radiusValue;
23         Console.WriteLine( "Circle5 constructor: {0}", this );
24      }
25
26      // destructor overrides version in class Point4
27      ~Circle5()
28      {
29         Console.WriteLine( "Circle5 destructor: {0}", this );
30      }
```

Fig. 9.18 **Circle5** class inherits from class **Point4** and overrides a finalizer method. (Part 1 of 2.)

```
31
32        // property Radius
33        public double Radius
34        {
35           get
36           {
37              return radius;
38           }
39
40           set
41           {
42              if ( value >= 0 )
43                 radius = value;
44           }
45
46        } // end property Radius
47
48        // calculate Circle5 diameter
49        public double Diameter()
50        {
51           return Radius * 2;
52        }
53
54        // calculate Circle5 circumference
55        public double Circumference()
56        {
57           return Math.PI * Diameter();
58        }
59
60        // calculate Circle5 area
61        public virtual double Area()
62        {
63           return Math.PI * Math.Pow( Radius, 2 );
64        }
65
66        // return string representation of Circle5
67        public override string ToString()
68        {
69           // use base reference to return Point3 string
70           return "Center = " + base.ToString() +
71              "; Radius = " + Radius;
72        }
73
74  } // end class Circle5
```

Fig. 9.18 **Circle5** class inherits from class **Point4** and overrides a finalizer method. (Part 2 of 2.)

Notice that the first two lines of the output from this program contain values for the *x*-*y* coordinates and the radius of **Circle5** object **circle1**. When constructing a **Circle5** object, the **this** reference used in the body of both the **Circle5** and **Point4** constructors refers to the **Circle5** object being constructed. When a program invokes method **ToString** on an object, the version of **ToString** that executes is always the version defined in that object's class. Because reference **this** refers to the current

Circle5 object being constructed, **Circle5**'s **ToString** method executes even when **ToString** is invoked from the body of class **Point4**'s constructor. [*Note*: This would not be the case if the **Point4** constructor were called to initialize an object that was actually a new **Point4** object.] When the **Point4** constructor invokes method **ToString** for the **Circle5** being constructed, the program displays **0** for the **radius** value, because the **Circle5** constructor's body has not yet initialized the **radius**. Remember that **0** is the default value of a **double** variable. The second line of output shows the proper **radius** value (**4.5**), because that line is output after the **radius** is initialized.

```csharp
1   // Fig. 9.19: ConstructorAndDestructor.cs
2   // Display order in which base-class and derived-class constructors
3   // and destructors are called.
4
5   using System;
6
7   // ConstructorAndDestructor class definition
8   class ConstructorAndDestructor
9   {
10      // main entry point for application.
11      static void Main( string[] args )
12      {
13         Circle5 circle1, circle2;
14
15         // instantiate objects
16         circle1 = new Circle5( 72, 29, 4.5 );
17         circle2 = new Circle5( 5, 5, 10 );
18
19         Console.WriteLine();
20
21         // mark objects for garbage collection
22         circle1 = null;
23         circle2 = null;
24
25         // inform garbage collector to execute
26         System.GC.Collect();
27
28      } // end method Main
29
30   } // end class ConstructorAndDestructor
```

```
Point4 constructor: Center = [72, 29]; Radius = 0
Circle5 constructor: Center = [72, 29]; Radius = 4.5
Point4 constructor: Center = [5, 5]; Radius = 0
Circle5 constructor: Center = [5, 5]; Radius = 10

Circle5 destructor: Center = [5, 5]; Radius = 10
Point4 destructor: Center = [5, 5]; Radius = 10
Circle5 destructor: Center = [72, 29]; Radius = 4.5
Point4 destructor: Center = [72, 29]; Radius = 4.5
```

Fig. 9.19 Order in which constructors and destructors are called.

Line 17 instantiates another object of class **Circle5**, then assigns it to reference **circle2**. Again, this begins the chain of constructor calls in which the **Circle5** constructor, the **Point4** constructor and the **Object** constructor are called. In the output, notice that the body of the **Point4** constructor executes before the body of the **Circle5** constructor. This demonstrates that objects are constructed "inside out" (i.e., the base-class constructor is called first).

Lines 22–23 set references **circle1** and **circle2** to **null**. This removes the only references to these **Circle5** objects in the program. Thus, the garbage collector can release the memory that these objects occupy. Remember that we cannot guarantee when the garbage collector will execute, nor can we guarantee that it will collect all available objects when it does execute. To demonstrate the destructor invocations for the two **Circle5** objects, line 26 invokes class **GC**'s method **Collect** to request the garbage collector to run. Notice that each **Circle5** object's destructor outputs information before calling class **Point4**'s destructor. Objects are destroyed "outside in" (i.e., the derived-class destructor completes its tasks before invoking the base-class destructor).

9.7 Software Engineering with Inheritance

In this section, we discuss the use of inheritance to customize existing software. When we use inheritance to create a new class from an existing one, the new class inherits the member variables, properties and methods of the existing class. We can customize the new class to meet our needs by including additional member variables, properties and methods, and by overriding base-class members.

Sometimes, it is difficult to appreciate the scope of problems faced by designers who work on large-scale software projects in industry. People experienced with such projects say that effective software reuse improves the software-development process. Object-oriented programming facilitates software reuse, thus shortening development times.

C# encourages software reuse by providing the .NET Framework Class Library (FCL), which delivers the maximum benefits of software reuse through inheritance. As interest in C# grows, interest in the FCL class libraries also increases. There is a worldwide commitment to the continued evolution of the FCL class libraries for a wide variety of applications. The FCL will grow as the .NET world grows explosively.

Software Engineering Observation 9.11

At the design stage in an object-oriented system, the designer often determines that certain classes are closely related. The designer should "factor out" common attributes and behaviors and place these in a base class. Then, use inheritance to form derived classes, endowing them with capabilities beyond those inherited from the base class.

Software Engineering Observation 9.12

The creation of a derived class does not affect its base class's source code. Inheritance preserves the integrity of a base class.

Software Engineering Observation 9.13

Just as designers of non-object-oriented systems should avoid proliferation of functions, designers of object-oriented systems should avoid proliferation of classes. Proliferation of classes creates management problems and can hinder software reusability, because it becomes difficult for a client to locate the most appropriate class of a huge class library. The alternative is to create fewer classes, in which each provides more substantial functionality, but such classes might provide too much functionality.

Performance Tip 9.2

If classes produced through inheritance are larger than they need to be (i.e., contain too much functionality), memory and processing resources might be wasted. Inherit from the class whose functionality is "closest" to what is needed.

Reading derived-class definitions can be confusing, because inherited members are not shown physically in the derived class, but nevertheless are present in the derived classes. A similar problem exists when documenting derived class members.

In this chapter, we introduced inheritance—the ability to create classes by absorbing an existing class's data members and behaviors and embellishing these with new capabilities. In Chapter 11, we introduce C#'s structured error handling capabilities—called exception handling.

9.8 Summary

Inheritance is the process by which one class "absorbs" the capabilities of an existing class. When a new class is created by inheriting from an existing class, the new class is called the derived class. The class from which the new class inherits is called the base class.

Because derived classes can include their own instance variables, properties and methods, derived classes are often larger than their base classes. A derived class is also more specific than its base class and represents a smaller group of objects.

Inheritance is an "is-a" relationship; that is, an object of a derived class also can be treated as an object of its base class. However, objects of a base class are not objects of that class's derived classes. Composition is a "has-a" relationship; that is, an object of a class has references to one or more objects of other classes as members.

A base class's non-**static public** members are accessible anywhere that the program has a reference to an object of the base class or to an object of one of the base class's derived classes. A base class's **private** members are accessible only within the definition of the base class. A base class's **protected** members have an intermediate level of protection between **public** and **private** access; the **protected** members can be accessed only in the base class or in any classes derived from the base class. A base class's **internal** members can be accessed only by objects in the same assembly.

When a base-class method is inappropriate for a derived class, that member can be overridden (redefined) in the derived class by using an appropriate implementation. When a method is overridden in a derived class and that method is called on a derived-class object, the derived-class version (not the base-class version) is called.

When an object of a derived class is instantiated, the base class's constructor is called immediately (either explicitly or implicitly) to do any necessary initialization of the base-class instance variables in the derived-class object (before the derived class's instance variable are initialized). Base-class constructors and destructors are not inherited by derived classes.

10

Exception Handling

Objectives

- To understand exceptions and error handling.
- To use **try** blocks to delimit code in which exceptions may occur.
- To **throw** exceptions.
- To use **catch** blocks to specify exception handlers.
- To use the **finally** block to release resources.
- To understand the C# exception-class hierarchy.
- To create programmer-defined exceptions.

It is common sense to take a method and try it. If it fails, admit it frankly and try another. But above all, try something.
Franklin Delano Roosevelt

O! throw away the worser part of it,
And live the purer with the other half.
William Shakespeare

If they're running and they don't look where they're going
I have to come out from somewhere and catch them.
Jerome David Salinger

And oftentimes excusing of a fault
Doth make the fault the worse by the excuse.
William Shakespeare

I never forget a face, but in your case I'll make an exception.
Groucho (Julius Henry) Marx

Outline

10.1 Introduction

In this chapter, we introduce *exception handling*. An *exception* is an indication of a problem that occurs during a program's execution. The name "exception" comes from the fact that although a problem can occur, the problem occurs infrequently—if the "rule" is that a statement normally executes correctly, then the "exception to the rule" is that a problem occurs. Exception handling enables programmers to create applications that can resolve (or handle) exceptions. In many cases, handling an exception allows a program to continue executing as if no problem was encountered. A more severe problem may prevent a program from continuing normal execution, instead requiring the program to notify the user of the problem, then terminate in a controlled manner. The features presented in this chapter enable programmers to write clear, robust and more *fault-tolerant programs*.

The style and details of exception handling in C# are based in part on the work of Andrew Koenig and Bjarne Stroustrup, as presented in their paper, "Exception Handling for C++ (revised)."[1] C#'s designers implemented an exception-handling mechanism similar to that used in C++, with Koenig's and Stroustrup's work as a model.

This chapter begins with an overview of exception-handling concepts, then demonstrates basic exception-handling techniques. The chapter continues with an overview of the exception-handling class hierarchy. Programs typically request and release resources (such as files on disk) during program execution. Often, these resources are in limited supply or can be used by only one program at a time. We demonstrate a part of the exception-handling mechanism that enables a program to use a resource, then guarantees that the program releases the resource for use by other programs. The chapter continues with an example that demonstrates several properties of class `System.Exception` (the base class of all exception classes), followed by an example that shows programmers how to create and use their own exception classes. The chapter concludes with a practical application of exception handling in which a program handles exceptions generated by arithmetic calculations that result in out-of-range values for a particular data type—a condition known as *arithmetic overflow*.

1. Koenig, A. and B. Stroustrup, "Exception Handling for C++ (revised)," *Proceedings of the Usenix C++ Conference*, 149-176, San Francisco, April 1990.

10.2 Exception Handling Overview

The logic of the program frequently tests conditions that determine how program execution proceeds. Consider the following pseudocode:

> *Perform a task*
>
> *If the preceding task did not execute correctly*
> > *Perform error processing*
>
> *Perform next task*
>
> *If the preceding task did not execute correctly*
> > *Perform error processing*
>
> *...*

In this pseudocode, we begin by performing a task. We then test whether that task executed correctly. If not, we perform error processing. Otherwise we start the entire process again and continue with the next task. Although this form of error handling logic works, intermixing the logic of the program with the error-handling logic can make the program difficult to read, modify, maintain and debug—especially in large applications. In fact, if many of the potential problems occur infrequently, intermixing program logic and error handling can degrade the performance of the program, because the program must test extra conditions to determine whether the next task can be performed.

Exception handling enables the programmer to remove error-handling code from the "main line" of the program's execution. This improves program clarity and enhances modifiability. Programmers can decide to handle whatever exceptions they choose—all types of exceptions, all exceptions of a certain type or all exceptions of a group of related types. Such flexibility reduces the likelihood that errors will be overlooked and thereby increases a program's robustness.

Testing and Debugging Tip 10.1

Exception handling helps improve a program's fault tolerance. When it is easy to write error-processing code, programmers are more likely to use it.

Software Engineering Observation 10.1

Although it is possible to do so, do not use exceptions for conventional flow of control. It is difficult to keep track of a larger number of exception cases and programs with a large number of exception cases are hard to read and maintain.

Exception handling is designed to process *synchronous errors*—errors that occur during the normal program flow of control. Common examples of these errors are out-of-range array subscripts, arithmetic overflow (i.e., a value outside the representable range of values), division by zero, invalid method parameters and running out of available memory. Exception handling is not designed to process *asynchronous* events, such as disk I/O completions, network message arrivals, mouse clicks, keystrokes and the like.

Good Programming Practice 10.1

Avoid using exception handling for purposes other than error handling, because this can reduce program clarity.

With programming languages that do not support exception handling, programmers often delay the writing of error-processing code and sometimes simply forget to include it. This results in less robust software products. C# enables the programmer to deal with exception handling easily from the inception of a project. Still, the programmer must put considerable effort into incorporating an exception-handling strategy into software projects.

Software Engineering Observation 10.2

Try to incorporate the exception-handling strategy into a system from the inception of the design process. Adding effective exception handling after a system has been implemented can be difficult.

Software Engineering Observation 10.3

In the past, programmers used many techniques to implement error-processing code. Exception handling provides a single, uniform technique for processing errors. This helps programmers working on large projects to understand each other's error-processing code.

The exception-handling mechanism also is useful for processing problems that occur when a program interacts with software elements, such as methods, constructors, assemblies and classes. Rather than internally handling problems that occur, such software elements often use exceptions to notify programs when problems occur. This enables programmers to implement customized error handling for each application.

Common Programming Error 10.1

Aborting a program component could leave a resource—such as file stream or I/O device—in a state in which other programs are unable to acquire the resource. This is known as a "resource leak."

Performance Tip 10.1

When no exceptions occur, exception-handling code incurs little or no performance penalties. Thus, programs that implement exception handling operate more efficiently than programs that perform error handling throughout the program logic.

Performance Tip 10.2

Exception handling should be used only for problems that occur infrequently. As a "rule of thumb," if a problem occurs at least 30% of the time when a particular statement executes, the program should test for the error inline; otherwise, the overhead of exception handling will cause the program to execute more slowly.[2]

Software Engineering Observation 10.4

*Methods with common error conditions should return **null** (or another appropriate value) rather than throwing exceptions. A program calling such a method simply can check the return value to determine success or failure of the method call.[3]*

Complex applications normally consist of predefined software components (such as those defined in the .NET Framework) and components specific to the application that use the predefined components. When a predefined component encounters a problem, that component needs a mechanism to communicate the problem to the application-specific

2. "Best Practices for Handling Exceptions [C#]," *.NET Framework Developer's Guide*, Visual Studio .NET Online Help.
3. "Best Practices for Handling Exceptions [C#]."

component—the predefined component cannot know in advance how each application will process a problem that occurs. Exception handling simplifies combining software components and having them work together effectively by enabling predefined components to communicate problems that occur to application-specific components, which can then process the problems in an application-specific manner.

Exception handling is geared to situations in which the method that detects an error is unable to handle it. Such a method *throws an exception*. There is no guarantee that there will be an *exception handler*—code that executes when the program detects an exception— to process that kind of exception. If there is, the exception will be *caught* and *handled*. The result of an *uncaught exception* depends on whether the program executes in debug mode or standard execution mode. In debug mode, when the program detects an uncaught exception, a dialog box appears that enables the programmer to view the problem in the debugger or continue program execution by ignoring the problem that occurred. In standard execution mode, a Windows application presents a dialog that enables the user to continue or terminate program execution, and a console application presents a dialog that enables the user to open the program in the debugger or terminate program execution.

C# uses **try** *blocks* to enable exception handling. A **try** block consists of keyword **try** followed by braces (**{}**) that define a block of code in which exceptions may occur. The **try** block encloses statements that could cause exceptions. Immediately following the **try** block are zero or more **catch** *blocks* (also called **catch** *handlers*). Each **catch** handler specifies in parentheses an exception parameter that represents the type of exception the **catch** handler can handle. If an exception parameter includes an optional parameter name, the **catch** handler can use that parameter name to interact with a caught exception object. Optionally, programmers can include a *parameterless* **catch** *handler* that catches all exception types. After the last **catch** handler, an optional **finally** *block* contains code that always executes, regardless of whether an exception occurs.

Common Programming Error 10.2

The parameterless **catch** *handler must be the last* **catch** *handler following a particular* **try** *block; otherwise a syntax error occurs.*

When a method called in a program detects an exception or when the Common Language Runtime detects a problem, the method or CLR *throws an exception*. The point in the program at which an exception occurs is called the *throw point*—an important location for debugging purposes (as we demonstrate in Section 10.6). Exceptions are objects of classes that extend class **Exception** of namespace **System**. If an exception occurs in a **try** block, the **try** block *expires* (i.e., terminates immediately) and program control transfers to the first **catch** handler (if there is one) following the **try** block. C# is said to use the *termination model of exception handling*, because the **try** block enclosing a thrown exception expires immediately when that exception occurs.[4] As with any other block of code, when a **try** block terminates, local variables defined in the block go out of scope. Next, the CLR searches for the first **catch** handler that can process the type of exception that occurred. The CLR locates the matching **catch** by comparing the thrown exception's type to each **catch**'s exception-parameter type until the CLR finds a match. A match

---

4. Some languages use the *resumption model of exception handling*, in which, after the handling of the exception, control returns to the point at which the exception was thrown and execution resumes from that point.

occurs if the types are identical or if the thrown exception's type is a derived class of the exception-parameter type. When a **catch** handler finishes processing, local variables defined within the **catch** handler (including the **catch** parameter) go out of scope. If a match occurs, code contained within the matching **catch** handler is executed. All remaining **catch** handlers for that **try** block are ignored and execution resumes in the **finally** block (if included). The program then continues with the first statement after the **try**/**catch**/**finally** sequence.

If no exceptions occur in a **try** block, the CLR ignores the exception handlers for that block. Program execution resumes with the next statement after the **try**/**catch** sequence. If an exception that occurs in a **try** block has no matching **catch** handler, or if an exception occurs in a statement that is not in a **try** block, the method containing that statement terminates immediately and the CLR attempts to locate an enclosing **try** block in a calling method. This process is called *stack unwinding* (discussed in Section 10.6).

10.3 Example: `DivideByZeroException`

Let us consider a simple example of exception handling. The application in Fig. 10.1 uses **try** and **catch** to specify a block of code that may throw exceptions and to handle those exceptions if they occur. The application displays two **TextBox**es in which the user can type integers. When the user presses the **Click To Divide** button, the program invokes method **divideButton_Click** (lines 44–82), which obtains the user's input, converts the input values to type **int** and divides the first number (**numerator**) by the second number (**denominator**). Assuming that the user provides integers as input and does not specify 0 as the denominator for the division, **divideButton_Click** displays the division result in **outputLabel**. However, if the user inputs a non-integer value or supplies 0 as the denominator, an exception occurs. This program demonstrates how to catch these exceptions.

```
1   // Fig. 10.1: DivideByZeroTest.cs
2   // Basics of C# exception handling.
3
4   using System;
5   using System.Drawing;
6   using System.Collections;
7   using System.ComponentModel;
8   using System.Windows.Forms;
9   using System.Data;
10
11  // class demonstrates how to handle exceptions from
12  // division by zero and from improper numeric formatting
13  public class DivideByZeroTest : System.Windows.Forms.Form
14  {
15      private System.Windows.Forms.Label numeratorLabel;
16      private System.Windows.Forms.TextBox numeratorTextBox;
17      private System.Windows.Forms.Label denominatorLabel;
18      private System.Windows.Forms.TextBox denominatorTextBox;
19
20      private System.Windows.Forms.Button divideButton;
```

Fig. 10.1 Exception handlers for **FormatException** and **DivideByZeroException**. (Part 1 of 3.)

```
21      private System.Windows.Forms.Label outputLabel;
22
23      // required designer variable
24      private System.ComponentModel.Container components = null;
25
26      // default constructor
27      public DivideByZeroTest()
28      {
29         // required for Windows Form Designer support
30         InitializeComponent();
31      }
32
33      // main entry point for the application
34      [STAThread]
35      static void Main()
36      {
37         Application.Run( new DivideByZeroTest() );
38      }
39
40      // Visual Studio .NET generated code
41
42      // obtain integers input by user and divide numerator
43      // by denominator
44      private void divideButton_Click(
45         object sender, System.EventArgs e )
46      {
47         outputLabel.Text = "";
48
49         // retrieve user input and call Quotient
50         try
51         {
52            // Convert.ToInt32 generates FormatException if
53            // argument is not an integer
54            int numerator = Convert.ToInt32( numeratorTextBox.Text );
55            int denominator =
56               Convert.ToInt32( denominatorTextBox.Text );
57
58            // division generates DivideByZeroException if
59            // denominator is 0
60            int result = numerator / denominator;
61
62            outputLabel.Text = result.ToString();
63
64         } // end try
65
66         // process invalid number format
67         catch ( FormatException )
68         {
69            MessageBox.Show( "You must enter two integers",
70               "Invalid Number Format",
71               MessageBoxButtons.OK, MessageBoxIcon.Error );
72         }
```

Fig. 10.1 Exception handlers for **FormatException** and
DivideByZeroException. (Part 2 of 3.)

```
73
74        // user attempted to divide by zero
75        catch ( DivideByZeroException divideByZeroException )
76        {
77           MessageBox.Show( divideByZeroException.Message,
78              "Attempted to Divide by Zero",
79              MessageBoxButtons.OK, MessageBoxIcon.Error );
80        }
81
82     } // end method divideButton_Click
83
84  } // end class DivideByZeroTest
```

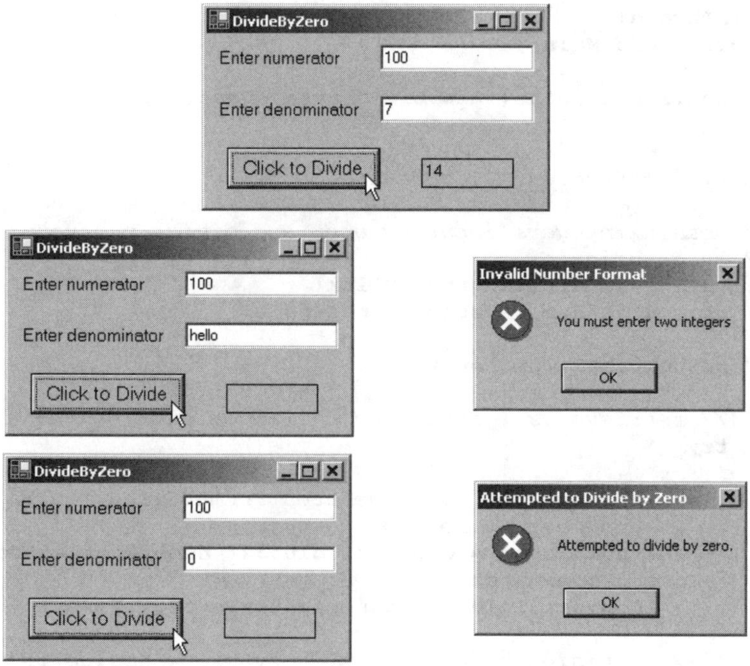

Fig. 10.1   Exception handlers for **FormatException** and **DivideByZeroException**. (Part 3 of 3.)

Before we discuss the program details, consider the sample output windows in Fig. 10.1. The first window shows a successful calculation in which the user inputs the numerator **100** and the denominator **7**. Note that the result (**14**) is an integer, because integer division always yields integer results. The next two windows show the result of inputting a non-integer value—in this case, the user input **"hello"** in the second **TextBox**. When the user presses **Click To Divide**, the program attempts to convert the **string**s the user input into **int** values with method **Convert.ToInt32**. If the argument to **Convert.ToInt32** is not a valid representation of an integer (in this case a valid string representation of an integer), the method generates a **FormatException** (namespace **System**). The program detects the exception and displays an error message dialog, indicating that the user must enter two integers. The last two output windows demonstrate the result after an attempt to divide by zero. In integer arithmetic, the CLR automatically tests for division by zero and generates a *DivideByZeroException* (namespace **System**) if the denominator is zero. The program detects the exception and displays an error-message dialog, indicating an attempt to divide by zero.[5]

Let us consider the user interactions and flow of control that yield the results shown in the sample output windows. The user inputs values into the **TextBox**es that represent the numerator and denominator, then presses **ClicktoDivide**. At this point, the program invokes method **divideButton_Click** (lines 44–82). Line 47 assigns the empty **string** to **outputLabel** to clear any prior result, because the program is about to attempt a new calculation. Lines 50–64 define a **try** block that encloses the code that can throw exceptions, as well as the code that should not execute if an exception occurs. For example, the program should not display a new result in **outputLabel** (line 62) unless the calculation (line 60) completes successfully. Remember that the **try** block terminates immediately if an exception occurs, so the remaining code in the **try** block will not execute.

The two statements that read the integers from the **TextBox**es (lines 54–56) each call method **Convert.ToInt32** to convert **string**s to **int** values. This method throws a **FormatException** if it cannot convert its **string** argument to an integer. If lines 54–56 properly convert the values (i.e., no exceptions occur), then line 60 divides the **numerator** by the **denominator** and assigns the result to variable **result**. If the denominator is zero, line 60 causes the CLR to throw a **DivideByZeroException**. If line 60 does not cause an exception, then line 62 displays the result of the division. If no exceptions occur in the **try** block, the program successfully completes the **try** block by reaching line 64 by ignoring the **catch** handlers at lines 67–72 and 75–80—the program execution continues with the first statement following the **try/catch** sequence. In this example, the program reaches the end of event handler **divideButton_Click**, so the method terminates, and the program awaits the next user interaction.

Immediately following the **try** block are two **catch** handlers (also called *catch blocks*)—lines 67–72 define the exception handler for a **FormatException** and lines 75–80 define the exception handler for the **DivideByZeroException**. Each **catch** handler begins with keyword **catch** followed by an exception parameter in parentheses that specifies the type of exception handled by the **catch** handler. The exception-handling code appears in the **catch** handler. In general, when an exception occurs in a **try** block, a **catch** handler catches the exception and handles it. In Fig. 10.1, the first **catch** handler specifies that it catches the type **FormatException**s (thrown by method **Convert.ToInt32**) and the second **catch** handler specifies that it catches type **DivideByZeroException**s (thrown by the CLR). Only the matching **catch** handler executes if an exception occurs. Both the exception handlers in this example display an error-message dialog to the user. When program control reaches the end of a **catch** handler, the program considers the exception as having been handled, and pro-

---

5. The Common Language Runtime allows floating-point division by zero, which produces a positive or negative infinity result, depending on whether the numerator is positive or negative. Dividing zero by zero is a special case that results in a value called "not a number." Programs can test for these results using constants for positive infinity (*PositiveInfinity*), negative infinity (*NegativeInfinity*) and not a number (*NaN*) that are defined in structures **Double** (for **double** calculations) and **Single** (for **float** calculations).

gram control continues with the first statement after the **try/catch** sequence (the end of the method in this example).

In the second sample output, the user input **hello** as the denominator. When lines 55–56 execute, **Convert.ToInt32** cannot convert this **string** to an **int**, so **Convert.ToInt32** creates a **FormatException** object and throws it to indicate that the method was unable to convert the **string** to an **int**. When an exception occurs, the **try** block expires (terminates). Any local variables defined in the **try** block go out of scope; therefore, those variables are not available to the exception handlers. Next, the CLR attempts to locate a matching **catch** handler, starting with the **catch** at line 67. The program compares the type of the thrown exception (**FormatException**) with the type in parentheses following keyword **catch** (also **FormatException**). A match occurs, so that exception handler executes and the program ignores all other exception handlers following the corresponding **try** block. Once the **catch** handler finishes processing, local variables defined within the **catch** handler go out of scope. If a match did not occur, the program compares the type of the thrown exception with the next **catch** handler in sequence and repeats the process until a match is found.

Software Engineering Observation 10.5

*Enclose in a **try** block a significant logical section of the program in which several statements can throw exceptions, rather than using a separate **try** block for every statement that throws an exception. However, for proper exception-handling granularity, each **try** block should enclose a section of code small enough, that when an exception occurs, the specific context is known and the **catch** handlers can process the exception properly.*

Common Programming Error 10.3

*Attempting to access a **try** block's local variables in one of that **try** block's associated **catch** handlers is a syntax error. Before a corresponding **catch** handler can execute, the **try** block expires, and its local variables go out of scope.*

Common Programming Error 10.4

*Specifying a comma-separated list of exception parameters in a **catch** handler is a syntax error. Each **catch** can have only one exception parameter.*

In the third sample output, the user input **0** as the denominator. When line 60 executes, the CLR throws a **DivideByZeroException** object to indicate an attempt to divide by zero. Once again, the **try** block terminates immediately upon encountering the exception, and the program attempts to locate a matching **catch** handler, starting from the **catch** handler at line 67. The program compares the type of the thrown exception (**DivideByZeroException**) with the type in parentheses following keyword **catch** (**FormatException**). In this case, there is no match, because they are not the same exception types and because **FormatException** is not a base class of **DivideByZeroException**. So, the program proceeds to line 75 and compares the type of the thrown exception (**DivideByZeroException**) with the type in parentheses following keyword **catch** (**DivideByZeroException**). A match occurs, so that exception handler executes. Line 77 in this handler uses property *Message* of class **Exception** to display the error message to the user. If there were additional **catch** handlers, the program would ignore them.

10.4 .NET **Exception** Hierarchy

The exception-handling mechanism allows only objects of class **Exception** and its derived classes to be thrown and caught.[6] This section overviews several of the .NET Framework's exception classes. In addition, we discuss how to determine whether a particular method throws exceptions.

Class **Exception** of namespace **System** is the base class of the .NET Framework exception hierarchy. Two of the most important derived classes of **Exception** are **ApplicationException** and **SystemException**. **ApplicationException** is a base class programmers can extend to create exception data types that are specific to their applications. We discuss creating programmer-defined exception classes in Section 10.7. Programs can recover from most **ApplicationException**s and continue execution.

The CLR can generate **SystemException**s at any point during the execution of the program. Many of these exceptions can be avoided by coding properly. These are called *runtime exceptions* and they derive from class **SystemException**. For example, if a program attempts to access an out-of-range array subscript, the CLR throws an exception of type **IndexOutOfRangeException** (a class derived from **SystemException**). Similarly, a runtime exception occurs when a program uses an object reference to manipulate an object that does not yet exist (i.e., the reference has a **null** value). Attempting to use such a **null** reference causes a **NullReferenceException** (another type of **SystemException**). According to Microsoft's "Best Practices for Handling Exceptions [C#],"[7] programs typically cannot recover from most exceptions the CLR throws. Therefore, programs generally should not throw or catch **SystemException**s. [*Note:* For a complete list of derived classes of **Exception**, look up "**Exception** class" in the **Index** of the Visual Studio .NET online documentation.]

A benefit of using the exception-class hierarchy is that a **catch** handler can catch exceptions of a particular type or can use a base-class type to catch exceptions in a hierarchy of related exception types. For example, a **catch** handler that specifies an exception parameter of type **Exception** also can catch exceptions of all classes that extend **Exception**, because **Exception** is the base class of all exception classes. This allows for processing of related exceptions. The benefit of the latter approach is that the exception handler can use the exception parameter to manipulate the caught exception. If the exception handler does not need access to the caught exception, the exception parameter may be omitted. If no exception type is specified, the catch handler will catch all exceptions.

Using inheritance with exceptions enables an exception handler to catch related exceptions with a concise notation. An exception handler certainly could catch each derived-class exception type individually, but catching the base-class exception type is more concise. However, this makes sense only if the handling behavior is the same for a base class and derived classes. Otherwise, catch each derived-class exception individually.

---

6. Actually, it is possible to **catch** exceptions of types that are not derived from class **Exception** using the parameterless **catch** handler. This is useful for handling exceptions from code written in other languages that do not require all exception types to derive from class **Exception** in the .NET framework.
7. "Best Practices for Handling Exceptions [C#]," *.NET Framework Developer's Guide*, Visual Studio .NET Online Help.

At this point, we know that there are many different exception types. We also know that methods and the CLR can both throw exceptions. But, how do we determine that an exception could occur in a program? For methods in the .NET Framework classes, we can look at the detailed description of the methods in the online documentation. If a method throws an exception, its description contains a section called "Exceptions" that specifies the types of exceptions thrown by the method and briefly describes potential causes for the exceptions. For example, look up "**Convert.ToInt32** method" in the index of the Visual Studio .NET online documentation. In the document that describes the method, click the link "**public static int ToInt32(string);**." In the document that appears, the "Exceptions" section indicates that method **Convert.ToInt32** throws three exception types—**ArgumentException**, **FormatException** and **OverflowException**—and describes the reason that each exception type occurs.

Software Engineering Observation 10.6

*If a method is capable of throwing exceptions, statements that invoke that method should be placed in **try** blocks and those exceptions should be caught and handled.*

Determining when the CLR throws exceptions is more difficult. Typically, such information appears in the *C# Language Specification*, which is located in the online documentation. To access the language specification, select **Contents...** from the **Help** menu in Visual Studio. In the **Contents** window, expand **Visual Studio .NET**, **Visual Basic and Visual C#**, **Reference**, **Visual C# Language** and **C# Language Specification**.

The language specification defines the syntax of the language and specifies cases in which exceptions are thrown. For example, in Fig. 10.1, we demonstrated that the CLR throws a **DivideByZeroException** when a program attempts to divide by zero in integer arithmetic. The language specification, Section 7.7.2 discusses the division operator and its **Exception**s. In this section, you will find the details of when a **DivideByZeroException** occurs.

10.5 **finally** Block

Programs frequently request and release resources dynamically (i.e., at execution time). For example, a program that reads a file from disk first requests the opening of that file. If that request succeeds, the program reads the contents of the file. Operating systems typically prevent more than one program from manipulating a file at once. Therefore, when a program finishes processing a file, the program normally closes the file (i.e., releases the resource). This enables other programs to use the file. Closing the file helps prevent the *resource leak*, in which the file resource is unavailable to other programs because a program using the file never closed it. Programs that obtain certain types of resources (such as files) must return those resources explicitly to the system to avoid resource leaks.

In programming languages, like C and C++, in which the programmer is responsible for dynamic memory management, the most common type of resource leak is a *memory leak*. This happens when a program allocates memory (as we do with operator **new** in C#), but does not deallocate the memory when the memory is no longer needed in the program. In C#, this normally is not an issue, because the CLR performs "garbage collection" of memory no longer needed by an executing program. However, other kinds of resource leaks (such as the unclosed file mentioned previously) can occur in C#.

Testing and Debugging Tip 10.2

The CLR does not completely eliminate memory leaks. The CLR will not garbage-collect an object until the program has no more references to that object. Thus, memory leaks can occur if programmers erroneously keep references to unwanted objects.

Most resources that require explicit release have potential exceptions associated with the processing of the resource. For example, a program that processes a file might receive **IOException**s during the processing. For this reason, file-processing code normally appears in a **try** block. Regardless of whether a program successfully processes a file, the program should close the file when the file is no longer needed. Suppose a program places all resource-request and resource-release code in a **try** block. If no exceptions occur, the **try** block executes normally and releases the resources after using them. However, if an exception occurs, the **try** block may expire before the resource-release code can execute. We could duplicate all resource-release code in the **catch** handlers, but this makes the code more difficult to modify and maintain.

C#'s exception handling mechanism provides the *finally* block, which is guaranteed to execute if program control enters the corresponding **try** block. The **finally** block executes regardless of whether that **try** block executes successfully or an exception occurs. This guarantee makes the **finally** block an ideal location to place resource deallocation code for resources acquired and manipulated in the corresponding **try** block. If the **try** block executes successfully, the **finally** block executes immediately after the **try** block terminates. If an exception occurs in the **try** block, the **finally** block executes immediately after a **catch** handler completes exception handling. If the exception is not caught by a **catch** handler associated with that **try** block or if a **catch** handler associated with that **try** block throws an exception, the **finally** block executes, then the exception is processed by the next enclosing **try** block (if there is one).

Testing and Debugging Tip 10.3

A finally block typically contains code to release resources acquired in the corresponding try block; this makes the finally block an effective way to eliminate resource leaks.

Testing and Debugging Tip 10.4

The only reason a finally block will not execute if program control entered the corresponding try block is that the application terminates before finally can execute.

Performance Tip 10.3

As a rule, resources should be released as soon as it is apparent that they are no longer needed in a program, to make those resources immediately available for reuse, thus enhancing resource utilization in the program.

If one or more **catch** handlers follow a **try** block, the **finally** block is optional. If no **catch** handlers follow a **try** block, a **finally** block must appear immediately after the **try** block. If any **catch** handlers follow a **try** block, the **finally** block appears after the last **catch**. Only whitespace and comments can separate the blocks in a **try**/**catch**/**finally** sequence.

Common Programming Error 10.5

Placing the finally block before a catch handler is a syntax error.

The C# application in Fig. 10.2 demonstrates that the **finally** block always executes, even if no exception occurs in the corresponding **try** block. The program consists of method **Main** (lines 10–59) and four other **static** methods that **Main** invokes to demonstrate **finally**—**DoesNotThrowException** (lines 62–85), **ThrowExceptionWithCatch** (lines 88–114), **ThrowExceptionWithoutCatch** (lines 117–138) and **ThrowExceptionCatchRethrow** (lines 141–173). [*Note:* We use **static** methods in this example so that **Main** can invoke these methods directly without creating any objects of class **UsingExceptions**. This enables us to concentrate on the mechanics of **try/catch/finally**.]

Line 14 of **Main** invokes method **DoesNotThrowException** (lines 62–85). The **try** block (lines 65–68) begins by outputting a message (line 67). The **try** block does not throw any exceptions, so program control reaches the closing brace of the **try** block and the **catch** handler (lines 71–74) and executes the **finally** block (lines 77–81) which outputs a message. At this point, program control continues with the first statement after the **finally** block (line 83), which outputs a message indicating that the end of the method has been reached. Then, program control returns to **Main**.

Line 20 of **Main** invokes method **ThrowExceptionWithCatch** (lines 88–114), which begins in its **try** block (lines 91–97) by outputting a message. Next, the **try** block creates a new **Exception** object and uses a *throw statement* to throw the exception object (lines 95–96). The **string** passed to the constructor becomes the exception object's error message. When a **throw** statement in a **try** block executes, the **try** block expires immediately, and program control continues at the first **catch** (lines 100–103) following this **try** block. In this example, the type thrown (**Exception**) matches the type specified in the **catch**, so line 102 outputs a message indicating the exception that occurred. Then, the **finally** block (lines 106–110) executes and outputs a message. At this point, program control continues with the first statement after the **finally** block (line 112), which outputs a message indicating that the end of the method has been reached, then program control returns to **Main**. Note, that in line 102, we use the exception object's **Message** property to access the error message associated with the exception—(the message passed to the **Exception** constructor). Section 10.6 discusses several properties of class **Exception**.

Common Programming Error 10.6

*The expression of a **throw**—an exception object—must be of either class **Exception** or one of its derived classes.*

Lines 27–30 of **Main** define a **try** block in which **Main** invokes method **ThrowExceptionWithoutCatch** (lines 117–138). The **try** block enables **Main** to catch any exceptions thrown by **ThrowExceptionWithoutCatch**. The **try** block in lines 120–126 of **ThrowExceptionWithoutCatch** begins by outputting a message. Next, the **try** block throws an **Exception** (lines 124–125) and the **try** block expires immediately. Normally, program control would continue at the first **catch** following the **try** block. However, this **try** block does not have any corresponding **catch** handlers. Therefore, the exception is not caught in method **ThrowExceptionWithoutCatch**. Normal program control cannot continue until that exception is caught and processed. Thus, the CLR will terminate **ThrowExceptionWithoutCatch** and program control will return to **Main**. Before control returns to **Main**, the **finally** block (lines 129–133) executes and outputs a message. At this point, program control returns to **Main**—any statements appearing after the **finally** block would not execute. In this example, because the exception thrown at lines 127–128 is not caught, method **ThrowExceptionWithoutCatch** always terminates after the **finally** block executes. In **Main**, the **catch** handler at lines 34–38 catches the exception and displays a message indicating that the exception was caught in **Main**.

```
1   // Fig. 10.2: UsingExceptions.cs
2   // Using finally blocks.
3
4   using System;
5
6   // demonstrating that finally always executes
7   class UsingExceptions
8   {
9      // entry point for application
10     static void Main( string[] args )
11     {
12        // Case 1: No exceptions occur in called method.
13        Console.WriteLine( "Calling DoesNotThrowException" );
14        DoesNotThrowException();
15
16        // Case 2: Exception occurs and is caught
17        // in called method.
18        Console.WriteLine( "\nCalling ThrowExceptionWithCatch" );
19        ThrowExceptionWithCatch();
20
21        // Case 3: Exception occurs, but not caught
22        // in called method, because no catch handlers.
23        Console.WriteLine(
24           "\nCalling ThrowExceptionWithoutCatch" );
25
26        // call ThrowExceptionWithoutCatch
27        try
28        {
29           ThrowExceptionWithoutCatch();
30        }
31
32        // process exception returned from
33        // ThrowExceptionWithoutCatch
34        catch
35        {
36           Console.WriteLine( "Caught exception from " +
37              "ThrowExceptionWithoutCatch in Main" );
38        }
39
40        // Case 4: Exception occurs and is caught
41        // in called method, then rethrown to caller.
42        Console.WriteLine(
43           "\nCalling ThrowExceptionCatchRethrow" );
44
```

Fig. 10.2   Demonstrating that **finally** blocks always execute regardless of whether an exception occurs. (Part 1 of 4.)

```
45              // call ThrowExceptionCatchRethrow
46              try
47              {
48                  ThrowExceptionCatchRethrow();
49              }
50
51              // process exception returned from
52              // ThrowExceptionCatchRethrow
53              catch
54              {
55                  Console.WriteLine( "Caught exception from " +
56                      "ThrowExceptionCatchRethrow in Main" );
57              }
58
59          } // end method Main
60
61          // no exceptions thrown
62          public static void DoesNotThrowException()
63          {
64              // try block does not throw any exceptions
65              try
66              {
67                  Console.WriteLine( "In DoesNotThrowException" );
68              }
69
70              // this catch never executes
71              catch
72              {
73                  Console.WriteLine( "This catch never executes" );
74              }
75
76              // finally executes because corresponding try executed
77              finally
78              {
79                  Console.WriteLine(
80                      "Finally executed in DoesNotThrowException" );
81              }
82
83              Console.WriteLine( "End of DoesNotThrowException" );
84
85          } // end method DoesNotThrowException
86
87          // throws exception and catches it locally
88          public static void ThrowExceptionWithCatch()
89          {
90              // try block throws exception
91              try
92              {
93                  Console.WriteLine( "In ThrowExceptionWithCatch" );
94
```

Fig. 10.2   Demonstrating that **finally** blocks always execute regardless of whether an exception occurs. (Part 2 of 4.)

```
 95              throw new Exception(
 96                  "Exception in ThrowExceptionWithCatch" );
 97          }
 98
 99          // catch exception thrown in try block
100          catch ( Exception error )
101          {
102              Console.WriteLine( "Message: " + error.Message );
103          }
104
105          // finally executes because corresponding try executed
106          finally
107          {
108              Console.WriteLine(
109                  "Finally executed in ThrowExceptionWithCatch" );
110          }
111
112          Console.WriteLine( "End of ThrowExceptionWithCatch" );
113
114      } // end method ThrowExceptionWithCatch
115
116      // throws exception and does not catch it locally
117      public static void ThrowExceptionWithoutCatch()
118      {
119          // throw exception, but do not catch it
120          try
121          {
122              Console.WriteLine( "In ThrowExceptionWithoutCatch" );
123
124              throw new Exception(
125                  "Exception in ThrowExceptionWithoutCatch" );
126          }
127
128          // finally executes because corresponding try executed
129          finally
130          {
131              Console.WriteLine( "Finally executed in " +
132                  "ThrowExceptionWithoutCatch" );
133          }
134
135          // unreachable code; would generate logic error
136          Console.WriteLine( "This will never be printed" );
137
138      } // end method ThrowExceptionWithoutCatch
139
140      // throws exception, catches it and rethrows it
141      public static void ThrowExceptionCatchRethrow()
142      {
143          // try block throws exception
144          try
145          {
146              Console.WriteLine( "In ThrowExceptionCatchRethrow" );
```

Fig. 10.2 Demonstrating that **finally** blocks always execute regardless of whether an exception occurs. (Part 3 of 4.)

```
147
148              throw new Exception(
149                 "Exception in ThrowExceptionCatchRethrow" );
150          }
151
152          // catch any exception, place in object error
153          catch ( Exception error )
154          {
155              Console.WriteLine( "Message: " + error.Message );
156
157              // rethrow exception for further processing
158              throw error;
159
160              // unreachable code; would generate logic error
161          }
162
163          // finally executes because corresponding try executed
164          finally
165          {
166              Console.WriteLine( "Finally executed in " +
167                 "ThrowExceptionCatchRethrow" );
168          }
169
170          // unreachable code; would generate logic error
171          Console.WriteLine( "This will never be printed" );
172
173      } // end method ThrowExceptionCatchRethrow
174
175  } // end class UsingExceptions
```

```
Calling DoesNotThrowException
In DoesNotThrowException
Finally executed in DoesNotThrowException
End of DoesNotThrowException

Calling ThrowExceptionWithCatch
In ThrowExceptionWithCatch
Message: Exception in ThrowExceptionWithCatch
Finally executed in ThrowExceptionWithCatch
End of ThrowExceptionWithCatch

Calling ThrowExceptionWithoutCatch
In ThrowExceptionWithoutCatch
Finally executed in ThrowExceptionWithoutCatch
Caught exception from ThrowExceptionWithoutCatch in Main

Calling ThrowExceptionCatchRethrow
In ThrowExceptionCatchRethrow
Message: Exception in ThrowExceptionCatchRethrow
Finally executed in ThrowExceptionCatchRethrow
Caught exception from ThrowExceptionCatchRethrow in Main
```

Fig. 10.2   Demonstrating that **finally** blocks always execute regardless of whether an exception occurs. (Part 4 of 4.)

Lines 46–49 of **Main** define a **try** block in which **Main** invokes method **Throw-ExceptionCatchRethrow** (lines 141–173). The **try** block enables **Main** to catch any exceptions thrown by **ThrowExceptionCatchRethrow**. The **try** block in lines 144–150 of **ThrowExceptionCatchRethrow** begins by outputting a message. Next, the **try** block throws an **Exception** (lines 148–149). The **try** block expires immediately, and program control continues at the first **catch** (lines 153–161) following the **try** block. In this example, the type thrown (**Exception**) matches the type specified in the **catch**, so line 155 outputs a message indicating the exception that occurred. Line 158 uses the **throw** statement to *rethrow* the exception. This indicates that the **catch** handler performed partial processing (or no processing) of the exception and is now passing the exception back to the calling method (in this case **Main**) for further processing. Note that the expression to the **throw** statement is the reference to the exception that was caught. When rethrowing the original exception, you can also use the statement

> *throw;*

with no expression. Section 10.6 discusses the **throw** statement with an expression. Such a **throw** statement enables programmers to catch an exception, create an exception object, then throw a different type of exception from the **catch** handler. Class library designers often do this to customize the exception types thrown from methods in their class libraries or to provide additional debugging information.

Software Engineering Observation 10.7

Before throwing an exception to a calling method, the method that throws the exception should release any resources acquired within the method before the exception occurred.[8]

Software Engineering Observation 10.8

Whenever possible, a method should handle exceptions that are thrown in that method, rather than passing the exceptions to another region of the program.

The exception handling in method **ThrowExceptionCatchRethrow** did not complete, because the program cannot run code in the **catch** handler placed after the invocation of the **throw** statement (line 158). Therefore, method **ThrowExceptionCatchRethrow** will terminate and return control to **Main**. Once again, the **finally** block (lines 164–168) will execute and output a message before control returns to **Main**. When control returns to **Main**, the **catch** handler at lines 53–57 catches the exception and displays a message indicating that the exception was caught. Then the program terminates.

Note that the point at which program control continues after the **finally** block executes depends on the exception-handling state. If the **try** block successfully completes or if a **catch** handler catches and handles an exception, control continues with the next statement after the **finally** block. If an exception is not caught or if a **catch** handler rethrows an exception, program control continues in the next enclosing **try** block. The enclosing **try** may be in the calling method or one of its callers. Nesting a **try/catch** sequence in a **try** block is also possible, in which case the outer **try** block's catch handlers would process any exceptions that were not caught in the inner **try/catch** sequence. If a **try** block has a cor-

---

8. "Best Practices for Handling Exceptions [C#]," *.NET Framework Developer's Guide*, Visual Studio .NET Online Help.

responding **finally** block, the **finally** block executes even if the **try** block terminates due to a **return** statement; then the **return** occurs.

Common Programming Error 10.7

*Throwing an exception from a **finally** can be dangerous. If an uncaught exception is awaiting processing when the **finally** block executes and the **finally** block throws a new exception that is not caught in the **finally** block, the first exception is lost, and the new exception is the one passed to the next enclosing **try** block.*

Testing and Debugging Tip 10.5

*When placing code that can throw an exception in a **finally** block, always enclose that code in a **try**/**catch** sequence that catches the appropriate exception types. This prevents losing uncaught and rethrown exceptions that occur before the **finally** block executes.*

Software Engineering Observation 10.9

*C#'s exception-handling mechanism removes error-processing code from the main line of a program to improve program clarity. Do not place **try**-**catch**-**finally** around every statement that could throw an exception. Doing so makes programs difficult to read. Rather, place one **try** block around a significant portion of your code. Follow this **try** block with **catch** handlers that handle each of the possible exceptions and follow the **catch** handlers with a single **finally** block.*

10.6 **Exception** Properties

As we discussed in Section 10.4, exception data types derive from class **Exception**, which has several properties. These properties frequently are used to formulate error messages for a caught exception. Two important properties are *Message* and *StackTrace*. Property **Message** stores the error message associated with an **Exception** object. This message may be a default message associated with the exception type or a customized message passed to an exception object's constructor when the exception object is constructed. Property **StackTrace** contains a **string** that represents the *method call stack*. The runtime environment keeps a list of method calls that have been made up to a given moment. The **StackTrace string** represents this sequential list of methods that had not finished processing at the time the exception occurred. The exact location at which the exception occurs in the program is called the exception's *throw point*.

Testing and Debugging Tip 10.6

A stack trace shows the complete method call stack at the time an exception occurred. This lets the programmer view the series of method calls that led to the exception. Information in the stack trace includes names of the methods on the call stack at the time of the exception, names of the classes in which those methods are defined, names of the namespaces in which those classes are defined and line numbers. The first line number in the stack trace indicates the throw point. Subsequent line numbers indicate the locations from which each method in the stack trace was called.

Another property used frequently by class library programmers is *InnerException*. Typically, programmers use this property to "wrap" exception objects caught in their code, then throw new exception types that are specific to their libraries. For example, a programmer implementing an accounting system might have some account-number processing code in which account numbers are input as **string**s but represented with integers in the code. A program can convert **string**s to **int** values with **Convert.ToInt32**, which throws a **FormatException** when it encounters an invalid number format. When an invalid account-number format occurs, the accounting-system programmer might wish either to indicate an error message different from the default one supplied by **FormatException** or to indicate a new exception type, such as **InvalidAccountNumberFormatException**. In these cases, the programmer would provide code to catch the **FormatException**, then create an exception object in the **catch** handler, passing the original exception as one of the constructor arguments. The original exception object becomes the **InnerException** of the new exception object. When an **InvalidAccountNumberFormatException** occurs in code that uses the accounting-system library, the **catch** handler that catches the exception can view the original exception via the property **InnerException**. Thus, the exception indicates that an invalid account number was specified and that the particular problem was an invalid number format.

Our next example (Fig. 10.3) demonstrates properties **Message**, **StackTrace** and **InnerException** and method **ToString**. In addition, this example demonstrates *stack unwinding*—the process that attempts to locate an appropriate **catch** handler for an uncaught exception. As we discuss this example, we keep track of the methods on the call stack, so we can discuss property **StackTrace** and the stack-unwinding mechanism.

Program execution begins with the invocation of **Main**, which becomes the first method on the method call stack. Line 16 of the **try** block in **Main** invokes **Method1** (lines 43–46), which becomes the second method on the stack. If **Method1** throws an exception, the **catch** handler at lines 22–38 handle the exception and output information about the exception that occurred. Line 45 of **Method1** invokes **Method2** (lines 49–52), which becomes the third method on the stack. Then, line 51 of **Method2** invokes **Method3** (defined at lines 55–70) which becomes the fourth method on the stack.

Testing and Debugging Tip 10.7

When reading a stack trace, start from the top of the stack trace and read the error message first. Then, read the remainder of the stack trace, looking for the first line that indicates code that you wrote in your program. Normally, this is the location that caused the exception.

```
1   // Fig. 10.3: Properties.cs
2   // Stack unwinding and Exception class properties.
3
4   using System;
5
6   // demonstrates using the Message, StackTrace and
7   // InnerException properties
8   class Properties
9   {
10     static void Main( string[] args )
11     {
12        // call Method1, any Exception it generates will be
13        // caught in the catch handler that follows
14        try
15        {
16           Method1();
17        }
```

Fig. 10.3 **Exception** properties and stack unwinding. (Part 1 of 3.)

```
18
19          // Output string representation of Exception, then
20          // output values of InnerException, Message,
21          // and StackTrace properties
22          catch ( Exception exception )
23          {
24             Console.WriteLine(
25                "exception.ToString(): \n{0}\n",
26                exception.ToString() );
27
28             Console.WriteLine( "exception.Message: \n{0}\n",
29                exception.Message );
30
31             Console.WriteLine( "exception.StackTrace: \n{0}\n",
32                exception.StackTrace );
33
34             Console.WriteLine(
35                "exception.InnerException: \n{0}",
36                exception.InnerException );
37
38          } // end catch
39
40       } // end Main
41
42       // calls Method2
43       public static void Method1()
44       {
45          Method2();
46       }
47
48       // calls Method3
49       public static void Method2()
50       {
51          Method3();
52       }
53
54       // throws an Exception containing an InnerException
55       public static void Method3()
56       {
57          // attempt to convert non-integer string to int
58          try
59          {
60             Convert.ToInt32( "Not an integer" );
61          }
62
63          // catch FormatException and wrap it in new Exception
64          catch ( FormatException error )
65          {
66             throw new Exception(
67                "Exception occurred in Method3", error );
68          }
69
70       } // end method Method3
```

Fig. 10.3 Exception properties and stack unwinding. (Part 2 of 3.)

```
71
72   } // end class UsingExceptions
```

```
exception.ToString():
System.Exception: Exception occurred in Method3 --->
   System.FormatException: Input string was not in a correct format.
   at System.Number.ParseInt32(String s, NumberStyles style,
      NumberFormatInfo info)
   at System.Convert.ToInt32(String s)
   at Properties.Method3() in
      C:\books\2002\cspapi1\cspapi1_examples\ch10\Fig10_03\
         Properties\Properties.cs:line 60
   --- End of inner exception stack trace ---
   at Properties.Method3() in
      C:\books\2002\cspapi1\cspapi1_examples\ch10\Fig10_03\
         Properties\Properties.cs:line 66
   at Properties.Method2() in
      C:\books\2002\cspapi1\cspapi1_examples\ch10\Fig10_03\
         Properties\Properties.cs:line 51
   at Properties.Method1() in
      C:\books\2002\cspapi1\cspapi1_examples\ch10\Fig10_03\
         Properties\Properties.cs:line 45
   at Properties.Main(String[] args) in
      C:\books\2002\cspapi1\cspapi1_examples\ch10\Fig10_03\
         Properties\Properties.cs:line 16

exception.Message:
Exception occurred in Method3

exception.StackTrace:
   at Properties.Method3() in
      C:\books\2002\cspapi1\cspapi1_examples\ch10\Fig10_03\
         Properties\Properties.cs:line 66
   at Properties.Method2() in
      C:\books\2002\cspapi1\cspapi1_examples\ch10\Fig10_03\
         Properties\Properties.cs:line 51
   at Properties.Method1() in
      C:\books\2002\cspapi1\cspapi1_examples\ch10\Fig10_03\
         Properties\Properties.cs:line 45
   at Properties.Main(String[] args) in
      C:\books\2002\cspapi1\cspapi1_examples\ch10\Fig10_03\
         Properties\Properties.cs:line 16

exception.InnerException:
System.FormatException: Input string was not in a correct format.
   at System.Number.ParseInt32(String s, NumberStyles style,
      NumberFormatInfo info)
   at System.Convert.ToInt32(String s)
   at Properties.Method3() in
      C:\books\2002\cspapi1\cspapi1_examples\ch10\Fig10_03\
         Properties\Properties.cs:line 60
```

Fig. 10.3 **Exception** properties and stack unwinding. (Part 3 of 3.)

At this point, the method call stack for the program is

```
Method3
Method2
Method1
Main
```

with the last method called (**Method3**) at the top and the first method called (**Main**) at the bottom. The **try** block (lines 58–61) in **Method3** invokes method **Convert.ToInt32** (line 60) and attempts to convert a **string** to an **int**. At this point, **Convert.ToInt32** becomes the fifth and final method on the call stack.

The argument to **Convert.ToInt32** is not in integer format, so line 60 throws a **FormatException** that is caught at line 64 in **Method3**. The exception terminates the call to **Convert.ToInt32**, so the method is removed from the method call stack. The **catch** handler creates an **Exception** object, then throws it. The first argument to the **Exception** constructor is the custom error message for our example, "**Exception occurred in Method3.**" The second argument is the **InnerException** object—the **FormatException** that was caught. Note that the **StackTrace** for this new exception object will reflect the point at which the exception was thrown (line 66). Now, **Method3** terminates, because the exception thrown in the **catch** handler is not caught in the method body. Thus, control will be returned to the statement that invoked **Method3** in the prior method in the call stack (**Method2**). This removes or *unwinds* **Method3** from the method-call stack.

Good Programming Practice 10.2

*When catching and rethrowing an exception, provide additional debugging information in the rethrown exception. To do so, create an **Exception** object with more specific debugging information and pass the original caught exception to the new exception object's constructor to initialize the **InnerException** property.*[9]

When control returns to line 51 in **Method2**, the CLR determines that line 51 is not in a **try** block. Therefore, the exception cannot be caught in **Method2**, and **Method2** terminates. This unwinds **Method2** from the method-call stack and returns control to line 45 in **Method1**. Here again, line 45 is not in a **try** block, so the exception cannot be caught in **Method1**. The method terminates and unwinds from the call stack, returning control to line 16 in **Main**, which is in a **try** block. The **try** block in **Main** expires, and the **catch** handler at lines (22–38) catches the exception. The **catch** handler uses method **ToString** and properties **Message**, **StackTrace** and **InnerException** to produce the output. Note that stack unwinding continues until either a **catch** handler catches the exception or the program terminates.

The first block of output (reformatted for readability) in Fig. 10.3 shows the exception's **string** representation returned from method **ToString**. This begins with the name of the exception class followed by the **Message** property value. The next eight lines show the **string** representation of the **InnerException** object. The remainder of that block of output shows the **StackTrace** for the exception thrown in **Method3**. Note that the **StackTrace** represents the state of the method-call stack at the throw

9. "Best Practices for Handling Exceptions [C#]," *.NET Framework Developer's Guide*, Visual Studio .NET Online Help.

point of the exception, not at the point where the exception eventually is caught. Each of the **StackTrace** lines that begins with "**at**" represents a method on the call stack. These lines indicate the method in which the exception occurred, the file in which that method resides and the line number in the file. Also, note that the stack trace includes the inner-exception stack trace.

Testing and Debugging Tip 10.8

When catching and rethrowing an exception, provide additional debugging information in the rethrown exception. To do so, create an **Exception** *object containing more specific debugging information and then pass the original caught exception to the new exception object's constructor to initialize the* **InnerException** *property.*

Method **ToString** of an exception returns a **string** containing the name of the exception, the optional character **string** supplied when the exception was constructed, the inner exception (if there is one) and a stack trace.

The next block of output (two lines) simply displays the **Message** property (**Exception occurred in Method3**) of the exception thrown in **Method3**.

The third block of output displays the **StackTrace** property of the exception thrown in **Method3**. Note that the **StackTrace** property includes the stack trace starting from line 66 in **Method3**, because that is the point at which the **Exception** object was created and thrown. The stack trace always begins from the exception's throw point.

Finally, the last block of output displays the **ToString** representation of the **InnerException** property, which includes the namespace and class names of that exception object, its **Message** property and its **StackTrace** property.

10.7 Programmer-Defined Exception Classes

In many cases, programmers can use existing exception classes from the .NET Framework to indicate exceptions that occur in their programs. However, in some cases, programmers may wish to create exception types that are more specific to the problems that occur in their programs. *Programmer-defined exception classes* should derive directly or indirectly from class **ApplicationException** of namespace **System**.

Good Programming Practice 10.3

Associating each type of malfunction with an appropriately named exception class improves program clarity.

Software Engineering Observation 10.10

Before creating programmer-defined exception classes, investigate the existing exception classes in the .NET Framework to determine whether an appropriate exception type already exists.

Software Engineering Observation 10.11

Programmers should create exception classes only if they need to catch and handle the new exceptions differently from other existing exception types.

Figure 10.4 and Fig. 10.5 demonstrate defining and using a programmer-defined exception class. Class **NegativeNumberException** (Fig. 10.4) is a programmer-defined exception class representing exceptions that occur when a program performs an illegal operation on a negative number, such as the square root of a negative number.

```
1   // Fig. 10.4: NegativeNumberException.cs
2   // NegativeNumberException represents exceptions caused by illegal
3   // operations performed on negative numbers
4
5   using System;
6
7   // NegativeNumberException represents exceptions caused by
8   // illegal operations performed on negative numbers
9   class NegativeNumberException : ApplicationException
10  {
11     // default constructor
12     public NegativeNumberException()
13        : base( "Illegal operation for a negative number" )
14     {
15     }
16
17     // constructor for customizing error message
18     public NegativeNumberException( string message )
19        : base( message )
20     {
21     }
22
23     // constructor for customizing error message and
24     // specifying inner exception object
25     public NegativeNumberException(
26        string message, Exception inner )
27           : base( message, inner )
28     {
29     }
30
31  } // end class NegativeNumberException
```

Fig. 10.4 ApplicationException subclass thrown when a program performs illegal operations on negative numbers.

According to Microsoft,[10] programmer-defined exceptions should extend class **ApplicationException**, should have a class name that ends with "Exception" and should define three constructors—a default constructor, a constructor that receives a **string** argument (the error message) and a constructor that receives a **string** argument and an **Exception** argument (the error message and the inner-exception object).

NegativeNumberExceptions most likely occur during arithmetic operations, so it seems logical to derive class **NegativeNumberException** from class **ArithmeticException**. However, class **ArithmeticException** derives from class **SystemException**—the category of exceptions thrown by the CLR. **ApplicationException** specifically is the base class for exceptions thrown by a user program, not by the CLR.

Class **SquareRootTest** (Fig. 10.5) demonstrates our programmer-defined exception class. The application enables the user to input a numeric value, then invokes method **SquareRoot** (lines 42–52) to calculate the square root of that value. For this

10. "Best Practices for Handling Exceptions [C#]," *.NET Framework Developer's Guide*, Visual Studio .NET Online Help.

purpose, **SquareRoot** invokes class **Math**'s *Sqrt* method, which receives a non-negative **double** value as its argument. If the argument is negative, method **Sqrt** normally returns constant **NaN** from class **Double**. In this program, we would like to prevent the user from calculating the square root of a negative number. If the numeric value received from the user is negative, **SquareRoot** throws a **NegativeNumberException** (lines 46–47). Otherwise, **SquareRoot** invokes class **Math**'s *Sqrt* method to compute the square root.

When the user inputs a value and clicks the **Square Root** button, the program invokes method **squareRootButton_Click** (lines 56–85). The **try** block (lines 62–68) attempts to invoke **SquareRoot** with the value input by the user. If the user input is not a valid number, a **FormatException** occurs, and the **catch** handler at lines 71–76 processes the exception. If the user inputs a negative number, method **SquareRoot** throws a **NegativeNumberException** (lines 46–47). The **catch** handler at lines 79–83 catches and handles that exception.

```
1    // Fig. 10.5: SquareRootTest.cs
2    // Demonstrating a programmer-defined exception class.
3
4    using System;
5    using System.Drawing;
6    using System.Collections;
7    using System.ComponentModel;
8    using System.Windows.Forms;
9    using System.Data;
10
11   // accepts input and computes the square root of that input
12   public class SquareRootTest : System.Windows.Forms.Form
13   {
14      private System.Windows.Forms.Label inputLabel;
15      private System.Windows.Forms.TextBox inputTextBox;
16
17      private System.Windows.Forms.Button squareRootButton;
18
19      private System.Windows.Forms.Label outputLabel;
20
21      // Required designer variable.
22      private System.ComponentModel.Container components = null;
23
24      // default constructor
25      public SquareRootTest()
26      {
27         // Required for Windows Form Designer support
28         InitializeComponent();
29      }
30
31      // Visual Studio .NET generated code
32
```

Fig. 10.5 **SquareRootTest** class throws an exception if error occurs when calculating the square root. (Part 1 of 3.)

```
33        // main entry point for application
34        [STAThread]
35        static void Main()
36        {
37           Application.Run( new SquareRootTest() );
38        }
39
40        // computes square root of its parameter; throws
41        // NegativeNumberException if parameter is negative
42        public double SquareRoot( double operand )
43        {
44           // if negative operand, throw NegativeNumberException
45           if ( operand < 0 )
46              throw new NegativeNumberException(
47                 "Square root of negative number not permitted" );
48
49           // compute the square root
50           return Math.Sqrt( operand );
51
52        } // end class SquareRoot
53
54        // obtain user input, convert to double and calculate
55        // square root
56        private void squareRootButton_Click(
57           object sender, System.EventArgs e )
58        {
59           outputLabel.Text = "";
60
61           // catch any NegativeNumberExceptions thrown
62           try
63           {
64              double result =
65                 SquareRoot( Double.Parse( inputTextBox.Text ) );
66
67              outputLabel.Text = result.ToString();
68           }
69
70           // process invalid number format
71           catch ( FormatException notInteger )
72           {
73              MessageBox.Show( notInteger.Message,
74                 "Invalid Operation", MessageBoxButtons.OK,
75                 MessageBoxIcon.Error );
76           }
77
78           // display MessageBox if negative number input
79           catch ( NegativeNumberException error )
80           {
81              MessageBox.Show( error.Message, "Invalid Operation",
82                 MessageBoxButtons.OK, MessageBoxIcon.Error );
83           }
84
```

Fig. 10.5   SquareRootTest class throws an exception if error occurs when calculating the square root. (Part 2 of 3.)

```
85        } // end method squareRootButton_Click
86
87    } // end class SquareRootTest
```

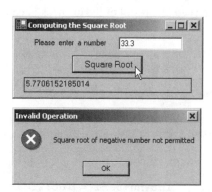

Fig. 10.5 **SquareRootTest** class throws an exception if error occurs when calculating the square root. (Part 3 of 3.)

10.8 Handling Overflows with Operators checked and unchecked

In .NET, the primitive data types are stored in fixed-size structures. For instance, the maximum value of an **int** is 2,147,483,647. In integer arithmetic, a value larger than 2,147,483,647 causes *overflow*—type **int** cannot represent such a number. Overflow also can occur with other C# primitive types. Overflows often cause programs to produce incorrect results.

C# provides operators **checked** and **unchecked** to specify whether integer arithmetic occurs in a *checked context* or *unchecked context*. In a checked context, the CLR throws an **OverflowException** (namespace **System**) if overflow occurs during evaluation of an arithmetic expression. In an unchecked context, the result is truncated if overflow occurs.

The operators **++**, **--**, *****, **/**, **+** and **-** (both unary and binary) may cause overflow when used with integral data types (such as **int** and **long**). Also, explicit conversions between integral data types can cause overflow. For example, converting the integer 1,000,000 from **int** to **short** results in overflow, because a **short** can store a maximum value of 32,767. Figure 10.6 demonstrates overflows occurring in both checked and unchecked contexts.

The program begins by defining **int** variables **number1** and **number2** (lines 11–12) and assigning each variable the maximum value for an **int**—2,147,483,647 (defined by **Int32.MaxValue**). Next, line 13 defines variable **sum** (initialized to 0) to store the **sum** of **number1** and **number2**. Then, lines 15–16 output the values of **number1** and **number2**.

Lines 19–25 define a **try** block in which line 24 adds **number1** and **number2** in a checked context. The expression to evaluate in a checked context appears in parentheses following keyword **checked**. Variables **number1** and **number2** already contain the maximum value for an **int**, so adding these values causes an **OverflowException**. The **catch** handler at lines 28–31 catches the exception and outputs its **string** representation.

Line 39 performs the same calculation in an unchecked context. The result of the calculation should be 4,294,967,294. However, this value requires more memory than an **int** can store, so operator **unchecked** truncates part of the value, resulting in **-2** in the output. As you can see, the result of the unchecked calculation is not the actual sum of the variables.

```
1    // Fig. 10.6: Overflow.cs
2    // Demonstrating operators checked and unchecked.
3
4    using System;
5
6    // demonstrates using the checked and unchecked operators
7    class Overflow
8    {
9       static void Main( string[] args )
10      {
11         int number1 = Int32.MaxValue;   // 2,147,483,647
12         int number2 = Int32.MaxValue;   // 2,147,483,647
13         int sum = 0;
14
15         Console.WriteLine(
16            "number1: {0}\nnumber2: {1}", number1, number2 );
17
18         // calculate sum of number1 and number2
19         try
20         {
21            Console.WriteLine(
22               "\nSum integers in checked context:" );
23
24            sum = checked( number1 + number2 );
25         }
26
27         // catch overflow exception
28         catch ( OverflowException overflowException )
29         {
30            Console.WriteLine( overflowException.ToString() );
31         }
32
33         Console.WriteLine(
34            "\nsum after checked operation: {0}", sum );
35
36         Console.WriteLine(
37            "\nSum integers in unchecked context:" );
38
39         sum = unchecked( number1 + number2 );
40
41         Console.WriteLine(
42            "sum after unchecked operation: {0}", sum );
43
44      } // end method Main
45
46   } // end class Overflow
```

Fig. 10.6 Operators **checked** and **unchecked** and the handling of arithmetic overflow. (Part 1 of 2.)

```
number1: 2147483647
number2: 2147483647

Sum integers in checked context:
System.OverflowException: Arithmetic operation resulted in an over-
flow.
   at Overflow.Overflow.Main(String[] args) in
      C:\books\2001\cspapi1\cspapi1_examples\ch10\Fig10_06\
         Overflow\Overflow.cs:line 24

sum after checked operation: 0

Sum integers in unchecked context:
sum after unchecked operation: -2
```

Fig. 10.6   Operators **checked** and **unchecked** and the handling of arithmetic
overflow. (Part 2 of 2.)

By default, calculations occur in an unchecked context—a dangerous practice, unless
the calculations are performed on constant expressions (such as literal integer values). Constant expressions are evaluated in a checked context at compile time. Overflows in such
expressions results in compile-time errors. It is possible to specify in a project's properties
that the default context for evaluating nonconstant expressions should be to check for arithmetic overflow. In the properties for your project, you can set the checked context as the
default. To do so, first select your project in the **Solution Explorer**. Next, in the **View**
menu, select **Property Pages**. In the **Property Pages** dialog, click the **Configuration
Properties** folder. Under **Code Generation**, change the value of **Check for Arithmetic Overflow/Underflow** to `true`.

Good Programming Practice 10.4

Use a checked context when performing calculations that can result in overflows. The programmer should define exception handlers that can process any overflows that occur.

Software Engineering Observation 10.12

Keywords, **checked** *and* **unchecked** *can be used to evaluate blocks of statements in
checked or unchecked contexts, respectively, by following the appropriate keyword with a
block of code in braces (* **{ }** *).*

In this chapter, we have demonstrated how the exception-handling mechanism works
and discussed how to make applications more robust by writing exception handlers to process potential problems. As programmers develop new applications, it is important to
investigate potential exceptions thrown by the methods your program invokes or by the
CLR and subsequently implement appropriate exception-handling code in order to make
those applications more robust.

10.9 Summary

An exception is an indication of a problem that occurs during a program's execution. Exception handling gives programmers a way to create applications that can resolve exceptions, often allowing a program to continue execution as if no problems were encountered.
Exception handling enables programmers to write clear, robust and more fault-tolerant pro-

grams and enables the programmers to remove error-handling code from the "main line" of a program's execution.

When a method detects an error and is unable to handle it, the method throws an exception. There is no guarantee that there will be an exception handler to process that kind of exception. If there is, the exception will be caught and handled. Exception-handling code uses **try/catch/finally** sequences.

A **try** block encloses the code that could throw exceptions and the code that should not execute if an exception occurs. A **try** block consists of keyword **try** followed by braces (**{}**) that delimit the block of code in which exceptions could occur. If an exception occurs in a **try** block, the block expires, and program control transfers to the first **catch** handler following the **try** block. Each **catch** handler begins with keyword **catch** followed by an optional exception parameter that specifies the type of exception handled by the **catch** handler. The exception-handling code appears in the body of the **catch** handler. The CLR searches for the first **catch** handler that can process the type of exception that occurred. The appropriate handler is the first handler in which the thrown exception's type matches, or is derived from, the exception type specified by the **catch** handler's exception parameter.

After the last **catch** handler, an optional **finally** block contains code that always executes, regardless of whether an exception occurs. The **finally** block is an ideal location to place resource-deallocation code for resources acquired and manipulated in the corresponding **try** block. If no exceptions occur or if an exception is caught and handled, the program resumes execution with the next statement after the **try/catch/finally** sequence.

Class **Exception** (namespace **System**) is the base class of the .NET Framework's exception hierarchy. **ApplicationException** is a base class that programmers can extend to create new exception data types that are specific to their applications. Programs can recover from most **ApplicationException**s and continue execution. The CLR generates **SystemException**s. Programs typically cannot recover from most exceptions thrown by the CLR. Therefore, programs generally should not throw **SystemException**s nor attempt to **catch** such exceptions.

A **throw** statement throws an exception object and can be used in a **catch** handler to rethrow an exception. Such an event indicates that the **catch** handler performed partial processing of the exception and is now passing the exception back to a calling method for further processing.

Exception property **Message** stores the error message associated with an **Exception** object. This message may be a default message associated with the exception type or a customized message passed to an exception object's constructor at the time a program creates the exception. **Exception** property **StackTrace** contains a string that represents the method-call stack at the throw point of the exception. **Exception** property **InnerException** typically is used to "wrap" a caught exception object in a new exception object, and subsequently throw the object of the new exception type.

C# provides operators **checked** and **unchecked** to specify whether arithmetic occurs in a checked context or an unchecked context, respectively. In a checked context, operator **checked** throws an **OverflowException** if an overflow occurs when evaluating an arithmetic expression. In an unchecked context, operator **unchecked** truncates the result if an overflow occurs.

11

Graphical User Interface Concepts

Objectives

- To understand the design principles of graphical user interfaces.
- To understand, use and create events.
- To understand the namespaces containing graphical user interface components and event-handling classes and interfaces.
- To be able to create graphical user interfaces.
- To be able to create and manipulate buttons, labels, lists, textboxes and panels.
- To be able to use mouse and keyboard events.

...the wisest prophets make sure of the event first.
Horace Walpole

...The user should feel in control of the computer; not the other way around. This is achieved in applications that embody three qualities: responsiveness, permissiveness, and consistency.
Inside Macintosh, Volume 1
Apple Computer, Inc. 1985

All the better to see you with my dear.
The Big Bad Wolf to Little Red Riding Hood

11.1 Introduction

A *graphical user interface* (*GUI*) allows users to interact with a program visually. A GUI (pronounced "GOO-EE") gives a program a distinctive "look" and "feel." By providing different applications with a consistent set of intuitive user-interface components, GUIs allow users to spend less time trying to remember which keystroke sequences perform what functions and spend more time using the program in a productive manner.

Look-and-Feel Observation 11.1

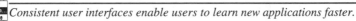

Consistent user interfaces enable users to learn new applications faster.

As an example of a GUI, Fig. 11.1 contains an Internet Explorer window with some of its *GUI components* labeled. In the window, there is a *menu bar* containing *menus*, including **File**, **Edit**, **View**, **Favorites**, **Tools** and **Help**. Below the menu bar is a set of *buttons*; each has a defined task in Internet Explorer. Below the buttons is a *textbox,* in which the user can type the location of a World Wide Web site to visit. To the left of the textbox is a *label* that indicates the textbox's purpose. On the far right and bottom there are *scrollbars*. Scrollbars are used when there is more information in a window than can be displayed at once. By moving the scrollbars back and forth, the user can view different portions of the Web page. The menus, buttons, textboxes, labels and scrollbars are part of Internet Explorer's GUI. They form a user-friendly interface through which the user interacts with the Internet Explorer Web browser.

GUIs are built from GUI components (sometimes called *controls* or *widgets*—short for *window gadgets*). A GUI component is an object with which the user interacts via the mouse or keyboard. Several common GUI components are listed in Fig. 11.2. In the sections that follow, we discuss many of these GUI components in detail.

Fig. 11.1   Sample Internet Explorer window with GUI components.

Control	Description
Label	An area in which icons or uneditable text can be displayed.
TextBox	An area in which the user inputs data from the keyboard. The area also can display information.
Button	An area that triggers an event when clicked.
CheckBox	A GUI control that is either selected or not selected.
ComboBox	A drop-down list of items from which the user can make a selection, by clicking an item in the list or by typing into the box, if permitted.
ListBox	An area in which a list of items is displayed from which the user can make a selection by clicking once on any element. Multiple elements can be selected.
Panel	A container in which components can be placed.
ScrollBar	Allows the user to access a range of values that cannot normally fit in its container.

Fig. 11.2   Some basic GUI components .

11.2 Windows Forms

Windows Forms (also called *WinForms*) create GUIs for programs. A form is a graphical element that appears on the desktop. A form can be a dialog, a window or an *MDI window* (*multiple document interface window*—a window that can contain other windows). A *component* is a class that implements the **IComponent** *interface*, which defines the behaviors that components must implement. A *control*, such as a button or label, is a component with a graphical part. Controls are visible, whereas components, which lack graphical parts, are not.

Figure 11.3 displays the Windows Forms controls and components contained in the Visual Studio .NET **Toolbox**—the first two screens show the controls and the last screen shows the components. When the user selects a component or control, the user then can add that component or control to the form. Note that the **Pointer** (the icon at the top of the list) is not a component; rather it represents the default mouse action. Highlighting it allows the programmer to use the mouse cursor instead of adding an item. In this chapter, we discuss many of these controls.

When interacting with windows, we say that the *active window* has the *focus*. The active window is the frontmost window and has a highlighted title bar. A window becomes the active window when the user clicks somewhere inside it. When a window has focus, the operating system directs user input from the keyboard and mouse to that application.

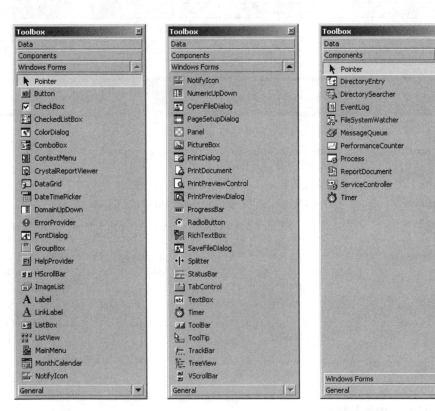

Fig. 11.3　Components and controls for Windows Forms.

The form acts as a *container* for components and controls. Controls must be added to the form using code. When we drag a control from the **Toolbox** onto the form, Visual Studio .NET generates this code for us, which instantiates the control and sets the control's basic properties. We could write the code ourselves, but it is much easier to create and modify controls using the **Toolbox** and **Properties** window, letting Visual Studio .NET handle the details. We introduced such *visual programming* earlier in the book. In later chapters, we build much richer GUIs through visual programming.

When the user interacts with a control by using the mouse or keyboard, events (discussed in Section 11.3) are generated, and event handlers process those events. Events typically cause something to happen in response. For example, clicking the **OK** button in a **MessageBox** generates an event. An event handler in class **MessageBox** closes the **MessageBox** in response to this event.

Each .NET Framework class (i.e., form, component and control) we present in this chapter is in the ***System.Windows.Forms** namespace*. Class **Form**, the basic window used by Windows applications, is fully qualified as **System.Windows.Forms.Form**. Likewise, class **Button** is actually **System.Windows.Forms.Button**.

The general design process for creating Windows applications requires creating a Windows Form, setting its properties, adding controls, setting their properties and implementing the event handlers. Figure 11.4 lists common **Form** properties and events.

Form Properties and Events	Description
Common Properties	
AcceptButton	Which button will be clicked when *Enter* is pressed.
AutoScroll	Whether scrollbars appear when needed (if data fill more than one screen).
CancelButton	Button that is clicked when the *Escape* key is pressed.
FormBorderStyle	Border of the form (e.g., **none**, **single**, **3D**, **sizable**).
Font	Font of text displayed on the form, as well as the default font of controls added to the form.
Text	Text in the form's title bar.
Common Methods	
Close	Closes form and releases all resources. A closed form cannot be reopened.
Hide	Hides form (does not release resources).
Show	Displays a hidden form.
Common Events	
Load	Occurs before a form is shown. Visual Studio .NET generates a default event handler when the programmer double clicks on the form in the designer.

Fig. 11.4   Common **Form** properties and events.

Visual Studio .NET generates most GUI-related code when we create controls and event handlers. Programmers can use Visual Studio .NET to perform most of these tasks graphically, by dragging and dropping components onto the form and setting properties in the **Properties** window. In visual programming, the IDE generally maintains GUI-related code, and the programmer writes the event handlers.

11.3 Event-Handling Model

GUIs are *event driven* (i.e., they generate *events* when the program's user interacts with the GUI). Typical interactions include moving the mouse, clicking the mouse, clicking a button, typing in a textbox, selecting an item from a menu and closing a window. Event handlers are methods that process events and perform tasks. For example, consider a form that changes color when a button is clicked. When clicked, the button generates an event and passes it to the event handler, and the event-handler code changes the form's color.

11.3.1 Delegates

In the event-handling model, objects (called *delegates*) act as intermediaries between objects that generate events and methods that handle those events (Fig. 11.5). Delegates define the signatures for that control's event handlers. Event delegates are *multicast* (class **MulticastDelegate** in namespace **System**)—they contain lists of method references. Each method must have the same *signature* (i.e., the same list of parameters).

Software Engineering Observation 11.1

Delegates enable classes to specify methods that will not be named or implemented until the class is instantiated. This is extremely helpful in creating event handlers. For instance, the creator of the **Form** *class does not need to name or define the method that will handle the* **Click** *event. Using delegates, the class can specify when such an event handler would be called. The programmers that create their own forms then can name and define this event handler. As long as it has been registered with the proper delegate, the method will be called at the proper time.*

Once an event is raised, every method that the delegate references is called. Every method in the delegate must have the same signature, because they are all passed the same information.

Fig. 11.5   Event-handling model using delegates.

11.3.2 Basic Event Handling

In most cases, we do not have to create our own events. Instead, we can handle the events generated by .NET controls such as buttons and text boxes. These controls already have delegates for every event they can raise. The programmer creates the event handler and registers it with the delegate—Visual Studio .NET helps with this task. In the following example, we create a form that displays a message box when clicked. Afterwards, we will analyze the event code that Visual Studio .NET generates.

First, create a new Windows application. To register and define an event handler, click the **Events** icon (the yellow lightning bolt) in the form's **Properties** window (Fig. 11.6). This window allows the programmer to access, modify and create event handlers for a control. The left panel lists the events that the object can generate. The right panel lists the registered event handlers for the corresponding event; this list is initially empty. The drop-down button indicates that multiple handlers can be registered for one event. A brief description of the event appears on the bottom of the window.

In this example, the form will take some action when clicked. Double-click the **Click** event in the **Properties** window to create an empty event handler in the program code.

```
private void FormName_Click( object sender, System.EventArgs e )
{

}
```

This is the method that will be called when the form is clicked. As a response, we will have the form display a message box. To do this, insert the statement

```
MessageBox.Show( "Form was pressed." );
```

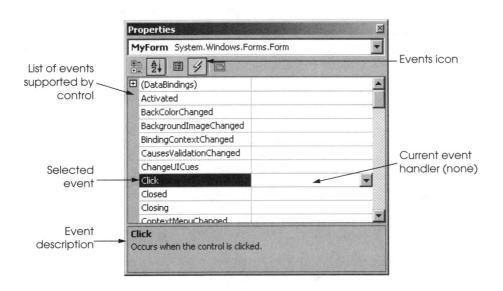

Fig. 11.6 Events section of the **Properties** window.

into the event handler to get

```
private void FormName_Click( object sender, System.EventArgs e )
{
    MessageBox.Show( "Form was pressed" );
}
```

We can now compile and execute the program, which appears in Fig. 11.7. Whenever the form is clicked, a message box appears.

We now discuss the details of the program. First, we create an event handler (lines 26–29). Every event handler must have the signature that the corresponding event delegate specifies. Event handlers are passed two object references. The first is a reference to the object that raised the event (**sender**), and the second is a reference to an event arguments object (**e**). Argument **e** is of type **EventArgs**. Class **EventArgs** is the base class for objects that contain event information.

To create the event handler, we must find the delegate's signature. When we double-click an event name in the **Properties** window, Visual Studio .NET creates a method with the proper signature. The naming convention is *ControlName_EventName*; in our case the event handler is **MyForm_Click**. If we do not use the **Properties** window, we must look up the event arguments class. Consult the documentation index under *ControlName* **class** (i.e., **Form class**) and click the **events** section (Fig. 11.8). This displays a list of all the events the class can generate. Click the name of an event to bring up its delegate, event argument type and a description (Fig. 11.9).

```
1   // Fig. 11.7: SimpleEventExample.cs
2   // Using Visual Studio .NET to create event handlers.
3
4   using System;
5   using System.Drawing;
6   using System.Collections;
7   using System.ComponentModel;
8   using System.Windows.Forms;
9   using System.Data;
10
11  // program that shows a simple event handler
12  public class MyForm : System.Windows.Forms.Form
13  {
14      private System.ComponentModel.Container components = null;
15
16      // Visual Studio .NET generated code
17
18      [STAThread]
19      static void Main()
20      {
21          Application.Run( new MyForm() );
22      }
23
```

Fig. 11.7 Simple event-handling example using visual programming. (Part 1 of 2.)

```
24      // Visual Studio .NET creates an empty handler,
25      // we write definition: show message box when form clicked
26      private void MyForm_Click( object sender, System.EventArgs e )
27      {
28          MessageBox.Show( "Form was pressed" );
29      }
30
31  } // end class MyForm
```

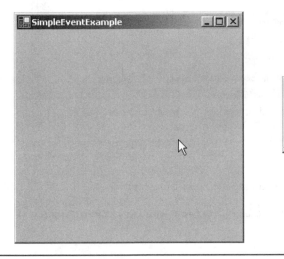

Fig. 11.7 Simple event-handling example using visual programming. (Part 2 of 2.)

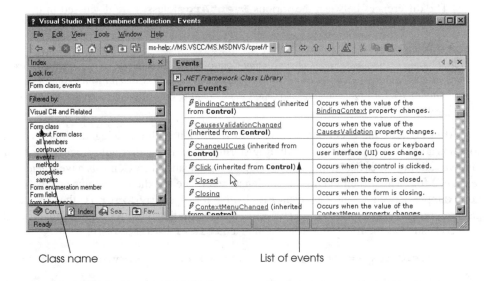

Class name   List of events

Fig. 11.8 List of **Form** events.

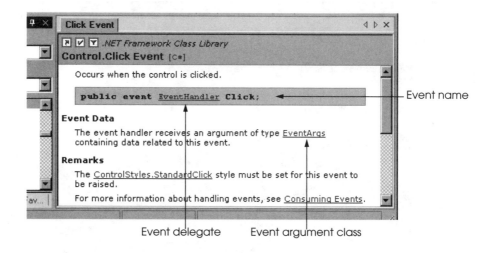

Fig. 11.9 Details of **Click** event.

The format of the event-handling method is, in general,

```
void ControlName_EventName( object sender, EventArgs e )
{
    event-handling code
}
```

where the name of the event handler is by default the name of the control, followed by an underscore (_) and the name of the event. Event handlers have return type **void** and take two arguments—an **object** (usually **sender**) and an instance of an event argument class. The differences between the various **EventArgs** classes are discussed in the following sections.

 Good Programming Practice 11.1

Use the event-handler naming convention ControlName_EventName *to keep methods organized. This informs a programmer which event a method handles, and for which control. Visual Studio .NET uses this naming convention when creating event handlers from the* **Properties** *window.*

After creating the event handler, we must *register* it with the delegate object, which contains a list of event handlers to call. Registering an event handler with a delegate object involves adding the event handler to the delegate's invocation list. Controls have a *delegate reference* for each of their events—the delegate reference has the same name as the event. For example, if we are handling event *EventName* for object **myControl**, then the delegate reference is **myControl.***EventName*. Visual Studio .NET registers events for us with code such as the following from method **InitializeComponent**:

```
this.Click += new System.EventHandler( this.MyForm_Click );
```

The left-hand side is the delegate reference **MyForm.Click**. (**this** refers to an object of class **MyForm**.) The delegate reference is initially empty—we must assign to it an object reference (the right-hand side). We must create a new delegate object for each event handler. We create a new delegate object by writing

> **new System.EventHandler(** *methodName* **)**

which returns a delegate object initialized with method *methodName*. The *methodName* is the name of the event handler, in our case it is **MyForm.MyForm_Click**. The **+=** operator adds an **EventHandler** delegate to the current delegate's invocation list. Because the delegate reference is initially empty, registering the first event handler creates a delegate object. In general, to register an event handler, write

> *objectName.EventName* **+= new System.EventHandler(**
> *MyEventHandler* **);**

We can add more event handlers using similar statements. *Event multicasting* is the ability to have multiple handlers for one event. Each event handler is called when the event occurs, but the order in which the event handlers are called is indeterminate. Use the **-=** operator to remove the method from the delegate object.

Common Programming Error 11.1

Assuming that multiple event handlers registered for the same event are called in a particular order can lead to logic errors. If the order is important, register the first event handler and have it call the others in order, passing the sender and event arguments.

Software Engineering Observation 11.2

*Events for prepackaged .NET components usually have consistent naming schemes. If the event is named **EventName**, then its delegate is **EventNameEventHandler**, and the event arguments class is **EventNameEventArgs**. However, events that use class **EventArgs** use delegate **EventHandler**.*

To review: The information needed to register an event is the **EventArgs** class (a parameter for the event handler) and the **EventHandler** delegate (to register the event handler). Visual Studio .NET can create this code for us, or we can type it in ourselves. If Visual Studio .NET creates the code, the programmer does not have to deal with going through all the steps, but the programmer also does not have complete control of everything that is going on. For simple events and event handlers it is often easier to allow Visual Studio .NET to generate this code. For more complicated solutions, registering your own event handlers might be necessary. In the upcoming sections, we will indicate the **EventArgs** class and the **EventHandler** delegate for each event we cover. To find more information about a particular type of event, search the help documentation for *ClassName* **class** and refer to the **events** subcategory.

11.4 Control Properties and Layout

This section overviews properties that are common to many controls. Controls derive from class *Control* (namespace **System.Windows.Forms**). Figure 11.10 contains a list of common properties and events for class **Control**. The **Text** property specifies the text that appears on a control, which may vary depending on the context. For example, the text of a Windows Form is its title bar, and the text of a button appears on its face. The *Focus* method transfers the focus to a control. When the focus is on a control, it becomes the active control. When the *Tab* key is pressed, the **TabIndex** property determines the order in which controls are given focus. The **TabIndex** property is set by Visual Studio .NET, but can be changed by the programmer. This is helpful for the user who enters information in many different locations—the user can enter information and quickly select the next control by pressing the *Tab* key. The **Enabled** property indicates whether the control can be used. Programs can set property **Enabled** to **false** when an option is unavailable to the user. In most cases, the control's text will appear gray (rather than black), when a control is disabled. Without having to disable a control, the control can be hidden from the user by setting the **Visible** property to **false** or by calling method **Hide**. When a control's **Visible** property is set to **false**, the control still exists, but it is not shown on the form.

Class **Control** Properties and Methods	Description
Common Properties	
BackColor	Background color of the control.
BackgroundImage	Background image of the control.
Enabled	Whether the control is enabled (i.e., if the user can interact with it). A disabled control will still be displayed, but "grayed-out"—portions of the control will become gray.
Focused	Whether a control has focus. (The control that is currently being used in some way.)
Font	**Font** used to display control's **Text**.
ForeColor	Foreground color of the control. This is usually the color used to display the control's **Text** property.
TabIndex	Tab order of the control. When the *Tab* key is pressed, the focus is moved to controls in increasing tab order. This order can be set by the programmer.
TabStop	If **true**, user can use the *Tab* key to select the control.
Text	Text associated with the control. The location and appearance varies with the type of control.
TextAlign	The alignment of the text on the control. One of three horizontal positions (left, center or right) and one of three vertical positions (top, middle or bottom).
Visible	Whether the control is visible.
Common Methods	
Focus	Transfers the focus to the control.
Hide	Hides the control (sets **Visible** to **false**).
Show	Shows the control (sets **Visible** to **true**).

Fig. 11.10 Class **Control** properties and methods.

Visual Studio .NET allows the programmer to *anchor* and *dock* controls, which help to specify the layout of controls inside a container (such as a form). Anchoring allows controls to stay a fixed distance from the sides of the container, even when the control is resized. Docking allows controls to extend themselves along the sides of their containers.

A user may want a control to appear in a certain position (top, bottom, left or right) in a form even when that form is resized. The user can specify this by *anchoring* the control to a side (top, bottom, left or right). The control then maintains a fixed distance from the side to its parent container. In most cases, the parent container is a form; however, other controls can act as a parent container.

When parent containers are resized, all controls move. Unanchored controls move relative to their original position on the form, while anchored controls move so that they will be the same distance from each side that they are anchored to. For example, in Fig. 11.11, the topmost button is anchored to the top and left sides of the parent form. When the form is resized, the anchored button moves so that it remains a constant distance from the top and left sides of the form (its parent). The unanchored button changes position as the form is resized.

Create a simple Windows application that contains two controls. Anchor one control to the right side by setting the **Anchor** property as shown in Fig. 11.12. Leave the other control unanchored. Now, resize the form by dragging the right side farther to the right. Notice that both controls move. The anchored control moves so that it is always the same distance to the right wall. The unanchored control moves so that it is in the same place on the form, relative to each side. This control will continue to be somewhat closer to whatever sides it was originally close to, but will still reposition itself when the user resizes the application window.

Sometimes a programmer wants a control to span the entire side of the form, even when the form is resized. This is useful when we want one control to remain prevalent on the form, such as the status bar that might appear at the bottom of a program. *Docking* allows a control to spread itself along an entire side (left, right, top or bottom) of its parent container. When the parent is resized, the docked control resizes as well. In Fig. 11.13, a button is docked to the top of the form. (It lays across the top portion.) When the form is resized, the button is resized as well—the button always fills the entire top portion of the form. The **Fill** dock option effectively docks the control to all sides of its parent, which causes it to fill its entire parent. Windows Forms contain property **DockPadding**, which sets the distance from docked controls to the edge of the form. The default value is zero, causing the controls to attach to the edge of the form. The control layout properties are summarized in Fig. 11.14.

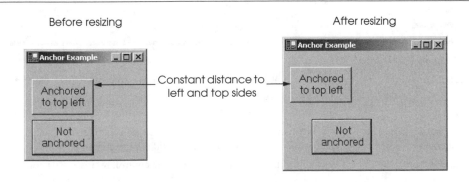

Fig. 11.11 Anchoring demonstration.

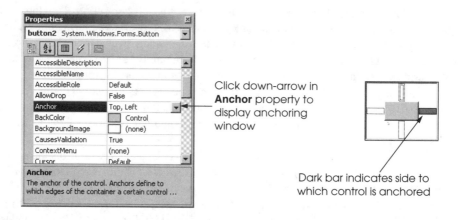

Click down-arrow in **Anchor** property to display anchoring window

Dark bar indicates side to which control is anchored

Fig. 11.12 Manipulating the **Anchor** property of a control.

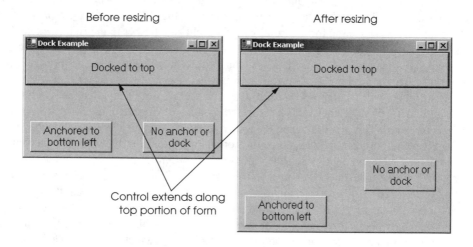

Fig. 11.13 Docking demonstration.

Common Layout Properties	Description
Common Properties	
Anchor	Side of parent container at which to anchor control—values can be combined, such as **Top, Left**.
Dock	Side of parent container to dock control—values cannot be combined.
DockPadding (for containers)	Sets the dock spacing for controls inside the container. Default is zero, so controls appear flush against the side of the container.
Location	Location of the upper left corner of the control, relative to its container.

Fig. 11.14 Class **Control** layout properties. (Part 1 of 2.)

Common Layout Properties	Description
Size	Size of the control. Takes a **Size** structure, which has properties **Height** and **Width**.
MinimumSize, **MaximumSize** (for Windows Forms)	The minimum and maximum size of the form.

Fig. 11.14 Class **Control** layout properties. (Part 2 of 2.)

The docking and anchoring options refer to the parent container, which may be the form. (We learn about other parent containers later this chapter.) The minimum and maximum form sizes can be set using properties **MinimumSize** and **MaximumSize**, respectively. Both properties use the **Size** structure, which has properties **Height** and **Width**, specifying the size of the form. These properties allow the programmer to design the GUI layout for a given size range. To set a form to a fixed size, set its minimum and maximum size to the same value.

Look-and-Feel Observation 11.2

Allow Windows forms to be resized—this enables users with limited screen space or multiple applications running at once to use the application more easily. Check that the GUI layout appears consistent for all permissible form sizes.

11.5 Labels, TextBoxes and Buttons

Labels provide text instructions or information about the program. Labels are defined with class **Label**, which derives from class **Control**. A **Label** displays *read-only text*, or text that the user cannot modify. Once labels are created, programs rarely change their contents. Figure 11.15 lists common **Label** properties.

A *textbox* (class **TextBox**) is an area in which text can be either input by the user from the keyboard or displayed. A *password textbox* is a **TextBox** that hides what the user entered. As the user types in characters, the password textbox displays only a certain character (usually *****). Altering the **PasswordChar** property of a textbox makes it a password textbox and sets the appropriate character to be displayed. Deleting the value of **PasswordChar** in the **Properties** window sets the textbox back to a regular textbox. Figure 11.16 lists the common properties and events of **TextBox**es.

A *button* is a control that the user clicks to trigger a specific action. A program can use several other types of buttons, such as *checkboxes* and *radio buttons*. All the button types are derived from **ButtonBase** (namespace **System.Windows.Forms**), which defines common button features. In this section, we concentrate on the class **Button**, which is often used to initiate a command. The other button types are covered in subsequent sections. The text on the face of a **Button** is called a *button label*. Figure 11.17 lists the common properties and events of **Button**s.

Label Properties	Description / Delegate and Event Arguments
Common Properties	
Font	The font used by the text on the **Label**.
Text	The text to appear on the **Label**.
TextAlign	The alignment of the **Label**'s text on the control. One of three horizontal positions (**left**, **center** or **right**) and one of three vertical positions (**top**, **middle** or **bottom**).

Fig. 11.15 Label properties.

TextBox Properties and Events	Description / Delegate and Event Arguments
Common Properties	
AcceptsReturn	If **true**, pressing *Enter* creates a new line if textbox spans multiple lines. If **false**, pressing *Enter* clicks the default button of the form.
Multiline	If **true**, textbox can span multiple lines. Default is **false**.
PasswordChar	Single character to display instead of typed text, making the **TextBox** a password box. If no character is specified, **Textbox** displays the typed text.
ReadOnly	If **true**, **TextBox** has a gray background and its text cannot be edited. Default is **false**.
ScrollBars	For multiline textboxes, indicates which scrollbars appear (**none**, **horizontal**, **vertical** or **both**).
Text	The text to be displayed in the text box.
Common Events	*(Delegate **EventHandler**, event arguments **EventArgs**)*
TextChanged	Raised when text changes in **TextBox** (the user added or deleted characters). Default event when this control is double clicked in the designer.

Fig. 11.16 TextBox properties and events.

Look-and-Feel Observation 11.3

*Although **Label**s, **TextBox**es and other controls can respond to mouse-button clicks, **Button**s naturally convey this meaning. Use **Button**s (e.g., **OK**), rather than other types of controls, to initiate user actions.*

The program in Fig. 11.18 uses a **TextBox**, a **Button** and a **Label**. The user enters text into a password box and clicks the **Button**. The text then appears in the **Label**. Normally, we would not display this text—the purpose of password textboxes is to hide the text being entered by the user from anyone who may be looking over a person's shoulder.

Button properties and events	Description / Delegate and Event Arguments
Common Properties	
Text	Text displayed on the **Button** face.
Common Events	*(Delegate **EventHandler**, event arguments **EventArgs**)*
Click	Raised when user clicks the control. Default event when this control is double clicked in the designer.

Fig. 11.17 Button properties and events.

```
1   // Fig. 11.18: LabelTextBoxButtonTest.cs
2   // Using a Textbox, Label and Button to display
3   // the hidden text in a password box.
4
5   using System;
6   using System.Drawing;
7   using System.Collections;
8   using System.ComponentModel;
9   using System.Windows.Forms;
10  using System.Data;
11
12  // namespace contains our form to display hidden text
13  namespace LabelTextBoxButtonTest
14  {
15     /// <summary>
16     /// form that creates a password textbox and
17     /// a label to display textbox contents
18     /// </summary>
19     public class LabelTextBoxButtonTest :
20        System.Windows.Forms.Form
21     {
22        private System.Windows.Forms.Button displayPasswordButton;
23        private System.Windows.Forms.Label displayPasswordLabel;
24        private System.Windows.Forms.TextBox inputPasswordTextBox;
25
26        /// <summary>
27        /// Required designer variable.
28        /// </summary>
29        private System.ComponentModel.Container components = null;
30
31        // default contructor
32        public LabelTextBoxButtonTest()
33        {
34           InitializeComponent();
35        }
36
```

Fig. 11.18 Program to display hidden text in a password box. (Part 1 of 4.)

```
37          /// <summary>
38          /// Clean up any resources being used.
39          /// </summary>
40          protected override void Dispose( bool disposing )
41          {
42             if ( disposing )
43             {
44                if ( components != null )
45                {
46                   components.Dispose();
47                }
48             }
49
50             base.Dispose( disposing );
51          }
52
53          #region Windows Form Designer generated code
54          /// <summary>
55          /// Required method for Designer support - do not modify
56          /// the contents of this method with the code editor.
57          /// </summary>
58          private void InitializeComponent()
59          {
60             this.displayPasswordButton =
61                new System.Windows.Forms.Button();
62             this.inputPasswordTextBox =
63                new System.Windows.Forms.TextBox();
64             this.displayPasswordLabel =
65                new System.Windows.Forms.Label();
66             this.SuspendLayout();
67
68             //
69             // displayPasswordButton
70             //
71             this.displayPasswordButton.Location =
72                new System.Drawing.Point( 96, 96 );
73             this.displayPasswordButton.Name =
74                "displayPasswordButton";
75             this.displayPasswordButton.TabIndex = 1;
76             this.displayPasswordButton.Text = "Show Me";
77             this.displayPasswordButton.Click +=
78                new System.EventHandler(
79                this.displayPasswordButton_Click );
80
81             //
82             // inputPasswordTextBox
83             //
84             this.inputPasswordTextBox.Location =
85                new System.Drawing.Point( 16, 16 );
86             this.inputPasswordTextBox.Name =
87                "inputPasswordTextBox";
88             this.inputPasswordTextBox.PasswordChar = '*';
```

Fig. 11.18 Program to display hidden text in a password box. (Part 2 of 4.)

```
89          this.inputPasswordTextBox.Size =
90             new System.Drawing.Size( 264, 20 );
91          this.inputPasswordTextBox.TabIndex = 0;
92          this.inputPasswordTextBox.Text = "";
93
94          //
95          // displayPasswordLabel
96          //
97          this.displayPasswordLabel.BorderStyle =
98             System.Windows.Forms.BorderStyle.Fixed3D;
99          this.displayPasswordLabel.Location =
100            new System.Drawing.Point( 16, 48 );
101         this.displayPasswordLabel.Name =
102            "displayPasswordLabel";
103         this.displayPasswordLabel.Size =
104            new System.Drawing.Size( 264, 23 );
105         this.displayPasswordLabel.TabIndex = 2;
106
107         //
108         // LabelTextBoxButtonTest
109         //
110         this.AutoScaleBaseSize =
111            new System.Drawing.Size( 5, 13 );
112         this.ClientSize =
113            new System.Drawing.Size( 292, 133 );
114         this.Controls.AddRange(
115            new System.Windows.Forms.Control[] {
116               this.displayPasswordLabel,
117               this.inputPasswordTextBox,
118               this.displayPasswordButton});
119         this.Name = "LabelTextBoxButtonTest";
120         this.Text = "LabelTextBoxButtonTest";
121         this.ResumeLayout( false );
122
123      } // end method InitializeComponent
124
125      // end collapsible region started on line 53
126      #endregion
127
128      /// <summary>
129      /// The main entry point for the application.
130      /// </summary>
131      [STAThread]
132      static void Main()
133      {
134         Application.Run( new LabelTextBoxButtonTest() );
135      }
136
137      // display user input on label
138      protected void displayPasswordButton_Click(
139         object sender, System.EventArgs e )
140      {
```

Fig. 11.18 Program to display hidden text in a password box. (Part 3 of 4.)

```
141                // text has not changed
142                displayPasswordLabel.Text =
143                   inputPasswordTextBox.Text;
144            }
145
146       } // end class LabelTextBoxButtonTest
147
148  } // end namespace LabelTextBoxButtonTest
```

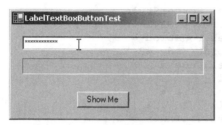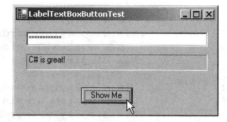

Fig. 11.18 Program to display hidden text in a password box. (Part 4 of 4.)

First, we create the GUI by dragging the components (a **Button**, a **Label** and a **TextBox**) onto the form. Once the components are positioned, we change their names in the **Properties** window (by setting the **(Name)** property) from the default values—**textBox1**, **label1**, **button1**—to the more descriptive **displayPasswordLabel**, **inputPasswordTextBox** and **displayPasswordButton**. Visual Studio .NET creates the code and places it inside method **InitializeComponent**. Now that the reader has an understanding of object-oriented programming, we can mention that the **(Name)** property is not really a property, but a means of changing the variable name of the object reference. For convenience, this value can be changed in the **Properties** window of Visual Studio .NET. This value, however, is not actually manipulated by a property.

We then set **displayPasswordLabel**'s **Text** property to "**Show Me**" and clear the **Text** of **displayPasswordLabel** and **inputPasswordTextBox** so that they are initially blank when the program runs. The **BorderStyle** property of **display-PasswordLabel** is set to **Fixed3D**, to give our **Label** a three-dimensional appearance. Notice that **TextBox**es have their **BorderStyle** property set to **Fixed3D** by default. The password character is set by assigning the asterisk character (*****) to the **PasswordChar** property. This property can take only one character.

Let us examine the code that Visual Studio .NET generates by right-clicking the design and selecting **View Code**. This is important because not every change can be made in the **Properties** window.

We have learned in previous chapters that Visual Studio .NET adds comments to our code. These comments appear throughout the code, such as on lines 15–18. In future examples we remove some of these generated comments to make programs more concise and readable (unless they illustrate a capability we have not yet covered).

Visual Studio .NET inserts declarations for the controls we add to the form (lines 22–24), namely, the **Label**, **TextBox** and **Button**. The IDE manages these declarations for us, making it easy to add and remove controls. Line 29 declares reference **components**—an array to hold the components that we add. We are not using any components in this program (only controls), and thus the reference is **null**.

The constructor for our form is created for us—it calls method **InitializeComponent**. Method **InitializeComponent** creates the components and controls in the form and sets their properties. The usual "to do" comments generated by Visual Studio .NET have been removed, because there is no more code that needs to be added to the constructor. When they existed, they would have appeared as a reminder in the **Task List** window. Method **Dispose** cleans up allocated resources, but is not called explicitly in our programs.

Lines 53–126 contain a collapsible region that encloses our **InitializeComponent** method. Recall that the **#region** and **#endregion** preprocessor directives allow the programmer to collapse code to a single line in Visual Studio .NET. This enables the programmer to focus on certain portions of a program.

Method **InitializeComponent** (lines 58–123) sets the properties of the controls added to the form (the **TextBox**, **Label** and **Button**). Lines 60–66 create new objects for the controls we add (a **Button**, a **TextBox** and a **Label**). Lines 86–88 and 92 set the **Name**, **PasswordChar** and **Text** properties for **inputPasswordTextBox**. The **TabIndex** property is initially set by Visual Studio .NET, but can be changed by the developer.

The comment on lines 54–57 advises us not to modify the contents of method **InitializeComponent**. We have altered it slightly for formatting purposes in this book, but this is not recommended. We have done this only so that the reader is able to see the important portions of the code. Visual Studio .NET examines this method to create the design view of the code. If we change this method, Visual Studio .NET may not recognize our modifications and show the design improperly. It is important to note that the design view is based on the code, and not vice versa.

Testing and Debugging Tip 11.1

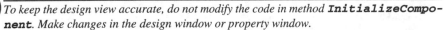

*To keep the design view accurate, do not modify the code in method **InitializeComponent**. Make changes in the design window or property window.*

The **Click** event is triggered when a control is clicked. We create the handler using the procedure described in Section 11.3.2. We want to respond to the **Click** event **displayPasswordButton**, so we double click it in the **Events** window. (Alternately, we could simply have clicked on **displayPasswordButton**.) This creates an empty event handler named **displayPasswordButton_Click** (line 138). Visual Studio .NET also registers the event handler for us (line 77–79). It adds the event handler to the **Click** event, using the **EventHandler** delegate. We must then implement the event handler. Whenever **displayPasswordButton** is clicked, this method is called and displays **inputPasswordTextBox**'s text on **displayPasswordLabel**. Even though **inputPasswordTextBox** displays all asterisks, it still retains its input text in its **Text** property. To show the text, we set **displayPasswordLabel**'s **Text** to **inputPasswordTextBox**'s **Text** (line 142–143). The user must program this line manually. When **displayPasswordButton** is clicked, the **Click** event is triggered, and the event handler **displayPasswordButton_Click** runs (updating **displayPasswordLabel**).

Visual Studio .NET generated most of the code in this program. It simplifies tasks such as creating controls, setting their properties and registering event handlers. However, we should be aware of how this is done—in several programs we may set properties ourselves, using code.

11.6 GroupBoxes and Panels

GroupBoxes and *Panels* arrange components on a GUI. For example, buttons related to a particular task can be placed inside a **GroupBox** or **Panel** inside the Visual Studio .NET form designer. All these buttons move together when the **GroupBox** or **Panel** is moved.

The main difference between the two classes is that **GroupBox**es can display a caption, and **Panel**s can have scrollbars. The scrollbars allow the user to view additional controls inside the **Panel** by scrolling the visible area. **GroupBox**es have thin borders by default, but **Panel**s can be set to have borders by changing their **BorderStyle** property.

Look-and-Feel Observation 11.4

Panels and GroupBoxes can contain other Panels and GroupBoxes.

Look-and-Feel Observation 11.5

*Organize the GUI by anchoring and docking controls (of similar function) inside a **GroupBox** or **Panel**. The **GroupBox** or **Panel** then can be anchored or docked inside a form. This divides controls into functional "groups" that can be arranged easily.*

To create a **GroupBox**, drag it from the toolbar and place it on a form. Create new controls and place them inside the **GroupBox**, causing them to become part of this class. These controls are added to the **GroupBox**'s **Controls** property. The **GroupBox**'s **Text** property determines its caption. The following tables list the common properties of **GroupBox**es (Fig. 11.19) and **Panel**s (Fig. 11.20).

GroupBox Properties	Description
Common Properties	
Controls	The controls that the **GroupBox** contains.
Text	Text displayed on the top portion of the **GroupBox** (its caption).

Fig. 11.19 GroupBox properties.

Panel Properties	Description
Common Properties	
AutoScroll	Whether scrollbars appear when the **Panel** is too small to hold its controls. Default is **false**.
BorderStyle	Border of the **Panel** (default **None**; other options are **Fixed3D** and **FixedSingle**).
Controls	The controls that the **Panel** contains.

Fig. 11.20 Panel properties.

To create a **Panel**, drag it onto the form and add components to it. To enable the scrollbars, set the **Panel**'s **AutoScroll** property to **true**. If the **Panel** is resized and cannot hold its controls, scrollbars appear (Fig. 11.21). These scrollbars then can be used to view all the components in the **Panel** (both when running and designing the form). This allows the programmer to see the GUI exactly as it appears to the client.

Look-and-Feel Observation 11.6

*Use **Panel**s with scrollbars to avoid cluttering a GUI and to reduce the GUI's size.*

The program in Fig. 11.22 uses a **GroupBox** and a **Panel** to arrange buttons. These buttons change the text on a **Label**.

The **GroupBox** (named **mainGroupBox**) has two buttons, **hiButton** (labeled **Hi**) and **byeButton** (labeled **Bye**). The **Panel** (named **mainPanel**) has two buttons as well, **leftButton** (labeled **Far Left**) and **rightButton** (labeled **Far Right**). The **mainPanel** control also has its **AutoScroll** property set to **True**, allowing scrollbars to appear if needed (i.e., if the contents of the **Panel** take up more space than the **Panel** itself). The **Label** (named **messageLabel**) is initially blank.

The event handlers for the four buttons are located in lines 36–61. To create an empty **Click** event handler, double click the button in design mode (instead of using the **Events** window). We add a line in each handler to change the text of **messageLabel**.

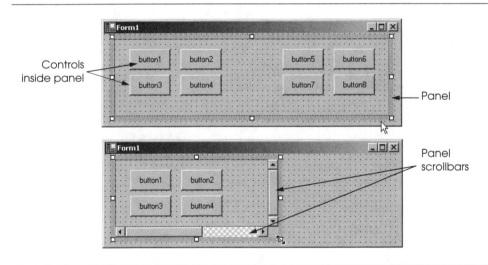

Fig. 11.21 Creating a **Panel** with scrollbars.

```
1   // Fig. 11.22: GroupBoxPanelExample.cs
2   // Using GroupBoxes and Panels to hold buttons.
3
4   using System;
5   using System.Drawing;
6   using System.Collections;
```

Fig. 11.22 Using **GroupBox**es and **Panel**s to arrange **Button**s. (Part 1 of 3.)

```
 7   using System.ComponentModel;
 8   using System.Windows.Forms;
 9   using System.Data;
10
11   // form to display a groupbox versus a panel
12   public class GroupBoxPanelExample : System.Windows.Forms.Form
13   {
14       private System.Windows.Forms.Button hiButton;
15       private System.Windows.Forms.Button byeButton;
16       private System.Windows.Forms.Button leftButton;
17       private System.Windows.Forms.Button rightButton;
18
19       private System.Windows.Forms.GroupBox mainGroupBox;
20       private System.Windows.Forms.Label messageLabel;
21       private System.Windows.Forms.Panel mainPanel;
22
23       private System.ComponentModel.Container components = null;
24
25       // Visual Studio .NET-generated Dispose method
26
27       [STAThread]
28       static void Main()
29       {
30           Application.Run( new GroupBoxPanelExample() );
31       }
32
33       // event handlers to change messageLabel
34
35       // event handler for hi button
36       private void hiButton_Click(
37           object sender, System.EventArgs e )
38       {
39           messageLabel.Text= "Hi pressed";
40       }
41
42       // event handler for bye button
43       private void byeButton_Click(
44           object sender, System.EventArgs e )
45       {
46           messageLabel.Text = "Bye pressed";
47       }
48
49       // event handler for far left button
50       private void leftButton_Click(
51           object sender, System.EventArgs e )
52       {
53           messageLabel.Text = "Far left pressed";
54       }
55
56       // event handler for far right button
57       private void rightButton_Click(
58           object sender, System.EventArgs e )
59       {
```

Fig. 11.22 Using **GroupBox**es and **Panel**s to arrange **Button**s. (Part 2 of 3.)

```
60            messageLabel.Text = "Far right pressed";
61        }
62
63  } // end class GroupBoxPanelExample
```

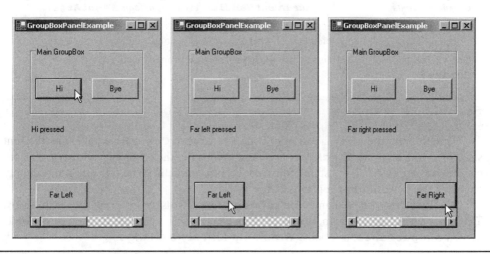

Fig. 11.22 Using **GroupBox**es and **Panel**s to arrange **Button**s. (Part 3 of 3.)

11.7 CheckBoxes and RadioButtons

C# has two types of *state buttons*—*CheckBox* and *RadioButton*—that can be in the on/off or true/false state. Classes **CheckBox** and **RadioButton** are derived from class **ButtonBase**. A **RadioButton** is different from a **CheckBox** in that there are normally several **RadioButton**s grouped together, and only one of the **RadioButton**s in the group can be selected (true) at any time.

A checkbox is a small white square that can be blank or contain a checkmark. When a checkbox is selected, a black checkmark appears in the box. There are no restrictions on how checkboxes are used: Any number may be selected at a time. The text that appears alongside a checkbox is referred to as the *checkbox label*. A list of common properties and events of class **Checkbox** appears in Fig. 11.23.

CheckBox events and properties	Description / Delegate and Event Arguments
Common Properties	
Checked	Whether the **CheckBox** has been checked.
CheckState	Whether the **CheckBox** is checked (contains a black checkmark) or unchecked (blank). An enumeration with values **Checked**, **Unchecked** or **Indeterminate**.
Text	Text displayed to the right of the **CheckBox** (called the label).

Fig. 11.23 CheckBox properties and events. (Part 1 of 2.)

CheckBox events and properties	Description / Delegate and Event Arguments
Common Events	*(Delegate* **EventHandler***, event arguments* **EventArgs***)*
CheckedChanged	Raised every time the **CheckBox** is either checked or unchecked. Default event when this control is double clicked in the designer.
CheckState-Changed	Raised when the **CheckState** property changes.

Fig. 11.23 CheckBox properties and events. (Part 2 of 2.)

The program in Fig. 11.24 allows the user to select a **CheckBox** to change the font style of a **Label**. One **CheckBox** applies a bold style, the other an italic style. If both checkboxes are selected, the style of the font is bold and italic. When the program initially executes, neither **CheckBox** is checked.

The first **CheckBox**, named **boldCheckBox**, has its **Text** property set to **Bold**. The other **CheckBox** is named **italicCheckBox** and is labeled **Italic**. The **Label**, named **outputLabel**, is labeled **Watch the font style change**.

```
1   // Fig. 11.24: CheckBoxTest.cs
2   // Using CheckBoxes to toggle italic and bold styles.
3
4   using System;
5   using System.Drawing;
6   using System.Collections;
7   using System.ComponentModel;
8   using System.Windows.Forms;
9   using System.Data;
10
11  /// form contains checkboxes to allow
12  /// the user to modify sample text
13  public class CheckBoxTest : System.Windows.Forms.Form
14  {
15     private System.Windows.Forms.CheckBox boldCheckBox;
16     private System.Windows.Forms.CheckBox italicCheckBox;
17
18     private System.Windows.Forms.Label outputLabel;
19
20     private System.ComponentModel.Container components = null;
21
22     // Visual Studio .NET-generated Dispose method
23
24     /// The main entry point for the application.
25     [STAThread]
26     static void Main()
27     {
28        Application.Run( new CheckBoxTest() );
29     }
```

Fig. 11.24 Using **CheckBox**es to change font styles. (Part 1 of 2.)

```
30
31       // make text bold if not bold,
32       // if already bold make not bold
33       private void boldCheckBox_CheckedChanged(
34          object sender, System.EventArgs e )
35       {
36          outputLabel.Font =
37             new Font( outputLabel.Font.Name,
38             outputLabel.Font.Size,
39             outputLabel.Font.Style ^ FontStyle.Bold );
40       }
41
42       // make text italic if not italic,
43       // if already italic make not italic
44       private void italicCheckBox_CheckedChanged(
45          object sender, System.EventArgs e )
46       {
47          outputLabel.Font =
48             new Font( outputLabel.Font.Name,
49             outputLabel.Font.Size,
50             outputLabel.Font.Style ^ FontStyle.Italic );
51       }
52
53   } // end class CheckBoxTest
```

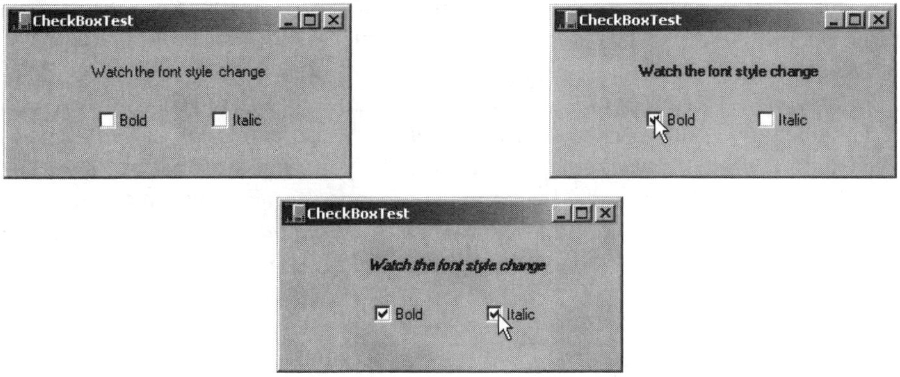

Fig. 11.24 Using **CheckBox**es to change font styles. (Part 2 of 2.)

After creating the components, we define their event handlers. Double clicking **bold-CheckBox** creates and registers an empty **CheckedChanged** event handler. To understand the code added to the event handler, we first discuss **outputLabel**'s **Font** property.

To change the font, the **Font** property must be set to a **Font** object. The **Font** constructor we use takes the font name, size and style. The first two arguments make use of **outputLabel**'s **Font** object, namely, **outputLabel.Font.Name** and **output-Label.Font.Size** (lines 37–38). The style is a member of the **FontStyle** enumeration, which contains the font styles **Regular**, **Bold**, **Italic**, **Strikeout** and **Underline**. (The **Strikeout** style displays text with a line through it, the **Underline** style displays text with a line below it.) A **Font** object's **Style** property is set when the **Font** object is created—the **Style** property itself is read-only.

Styles can be combined using *bitwise operators*, or operators that perform manipulation on bits. In this program, we need to set the font style so that the text will appear bold if it was not bold originally, and vice versa. Notice that on line 39 we use the bitwise XOR operator (**^**) to do this. Applying this operator to two bits does the following: If exactly 1 one of the corresponding bits is 1, set the result to 1. By using the **^** operator as we did on line 39, we are setting the bit values for bold in the same way. The operand on the right (**FontStyle.Bold**) always has bit values set to bold. The operand on the left, then (**outputLabel.Font.Style**) must not be bold for the resulting style to be bold. (Remember for XOR, if one value is set to 1, the other must be 0, or the result will not be 1.) If **outputLable.Font.Style** is bold, then the resulting style will not be bold. This operator also allows us to combine the styles. For instance, if the text were originally italicized, it would now be italicized and bold, rather than just bold.

We could have explicitly tested for the current style and changed it according to what we needed. For example, in the method **boldCheckBox_CheckChanged** we could have tested for the regular style, made it bold, tested for the bold style, made it regular, tested for the italic style, made it bold italic, or the italic bold style and made it italic. However, this method has a drawback—for every new style we add, we double the number of combinations. To add a checkbox for underline, we would have to test for eight possible styles. To add a checkbox for strikeout as well, we would have 16 tests in each event handler. By using the bitwise XOR operator, we save ourselves from this trouble. Each new style needs only a single statement in its event handler. In addition, styles can be removed easily, removing their handler. If we tested for every condition, we would have to remove the handler, and all the unnecessary test conditions in the other handlers.

Radio buttons (defined with class ***RadioButton***) are similar to checkboxes, because they also have two states—*selected* and *not selected* (also called *deselected*). However, radio buttons normally appear as a *group* in which only one radio button can be selected at a time. Selecting a different radio button in the group forces all other radio buttons in the group to be deselected. Radio buttons represent a set of *mutually exclusive* options (i.e., a set in which multiple options cannot be selected at the same time).

Look-and-Feel Observation 11.7

*Use **RadioButton**s when the user should choose only one option in a group.*

Look-and-Feel Observation 11.8

*Use **CheckBox**es when the user should be able to choose many options in a group.*

All radio buttons added to a form become part of the same group. To create new groups, radio buttons must be added to **GroupBox**es or **Panel**s. The common properties and events of class **RadioButton** are listed in Fig. 11.25.

Software Engineering Observation 11.3

*Forms, **GroupBox**es, and **Panel**s can act as logical groups for radio buttons. The radio buttons within each group will be mutually exclusive to each other, but not to radio buttons in different groups.*

RadioButton properties and events	Description / Delegate and Event Arguments
Common Properties	
Checked	Whether the **RadioButton** is checked.
Text	Text displayed to the right of the **RadioButton** (called the label).
Common Events	*(Delegate **EventHandler**, event arguments **EventArgs**)*
Click	Raised when user clicks the control.
CheckedChanged	Raised every time the **RadioButton** is checked or unchecked. Default event when this control is double clicked in the designer.

Fig. 11.25 RadioButton properties and events.

The program in Fig. 11.26 uses radio buttons to select the options for a **MessageBox**. Users select the attributes they want then press the display button, which causes the **MessageBox** to appear. A **Label** in the lower-left corner shows the result of the **MessageBox** (**Yes**, **No**, **Cancel**, etc.). The different **MessageBox** icon and button types have been displayed in tables in Chapter 5, Control Structures: Part 2.

```
1    // Fig. 11.26: RadioButtonsTest.cs
2    // Using RadioButtons to set message window options.
3
4    using System;
5    using System.Drawing;
6    using System.Collections;
7    using System.ComponentModel;
8    using System.Windows.Forms;
9    using System.Data;
10
11   // form contains several radio buttons--user chooses one
12   // from each group to create a custom MessageBox
13   public class RadioButtonsTest : System.Windows.Forms.Form
14   {
15       private System.Windows.Forms.Label promptLabel;
16       private System.Windows.Forms.Label displayLabel;
17       private System.Windows.Forms.Button displayButton;
18
19       private System.Windows.Forms.RadioButton questionButton;
20       private System.Windows.Forms.RadioButton informationButton;
21       private System.Windows.Forms.RadioButton exclamationButton;
22       private System.Windows.Forms.RadioButton errorButton;
23       private System.Windows.Forms.RadioButton retryCancelButton;
24       private System.Windows.Forms.RadioButton yesNoButton;
25       private System.Windows.Forms.RadioButton yesNoCancelButton;
26       private System.Windows.Forms.RadioButton okCancelButton;
27       private System.Windows.Forms.RadioButton okButton;
```

Fig. 11.26 Using **RadioButton**s to set message-window options. (Part 1 of 5.)

```
28         private System.Windows.Forms.RadioButton
29            abortRetryIgnoreButton;
30
31         private System.Windows.Forms.GroupBox groupBox2;
32         private System.Windows.Forms.GroupBox groupBox1;
33
34         private MessageBoxIcon iconType = MessageBoxIcon.Error;
35         private MessageBoxButtons buttonType =
36            MessageBoxButtons.OK;
37
38         // The main entry point for the application.
39         [STAThread]
40         static void Main()
41         {
42            Application.Run( new RadioButtonsTest() );
43         }
44
45         // change button based on option chosen by sender
46         private void buttonType_CheckedChanged(
47            object sender, System.EventArgs e )
48         {
49            if ( sender == okButton ) // display OK button
50               buttonType = MessageBoxButtons.OK;
51
52            // display OK and Cancel buttons
53            else if ( sender == okCancelButton )
54               buttonType = MessageBoxButtons.OKCancel;
55
56            // display Abort, Retry and Ignore buttons
57            else if ( sender == abortRetryIgnoreButton )
58               buttonType = MessageBoxButtons.AbortRetryIgnore;
59
60            // display Yes, No and Cancel buttons
61            else if ( sender == yesNoCancelButton )
62               buttonType = MessageBoxButtons.YesNoCancel;
63
64            // display Yes and No buttons
65            else if ( sender == yesNoButton )
66               buttonType = MessageBoxButtons.YesNo;
67
68            // only one option left--display
69            // Retry and Cancel buttons
70            else
71               buttonType = MessageBoxButtons.RetryCancel;
72
73         } // end method buttonType_CheckedChanged
74
75         // change icon based on option chosen by sender
76         private void iconType_CheckedChanged(
77            object sender, System.EventArgs e )
78         {
79            if ( sender == errorButton ) // display error icon
80               iconType = MessageBoxIcon.Error;
```

Fig. 11.26 Using **RadioButton**s to set message-window options. (Part 2 of 5.)

```
81
82              // display exclamation point
83              else if ( sender == exclamationButton )
84                 iconType = MessageBoxIcon.Exclamation;
85
86              // display information icon
87              else if ( sender == informationButton )
88                 iconType = MessageBoxIcon.Information;
89
90              else // only one option left--display question mark
91                 iconType = MessageBoxIcon.Question;
92
93        } // end method iconType_CheckedChanged
94
95        // display MessageBox and button user pressed
96        protected void displayButton_Click(
97           object sender, System.EventArgs e )
98        {
99           DialogResult result =
100             MessageBox.Show( "This is Your Custom MessageBox.",
101             "Custom MessageBox", buttonType, iconType, 0, 0 );
102
103          // check for dialog result and display it in label
104          switch ( result )
105          {
106             case DialogResult.OK:
107                displayLabel.Text = "OK was pressed.";
108                break;
109
110             case DialogResult.Cancel:
111                displayLabel.Text = "Cancel was pressed.";
112                break;
113
114             case DialogResult.Abort:
115                displayLabel.Text = "Abort was pressed.";
116                break;
117
118             case DialogResult.Retry:
119                displayLabel.Text = "Retry was pressed.";
120                break;
121
122             case DialogResult.Ignore:
123                displayLabel.Text = "Ignore was pressed.";
124                break;
125
126             case DialogResult.Yes:
127                displayLabel.Text = "Yes was pressed.";
128                break;
129
130             case DialogResult.No:
131                displayLabel.Text = "No was pressed.";
132                break;
133
```

Fig. 11.26 Using **RadioButton**s to set message-window options. (Part 3 of 5.)

```
134          } // end switch
135
136      } // end method displayButton_Click
137
138  } // end class RadioButtonsTest
```

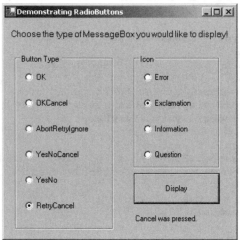

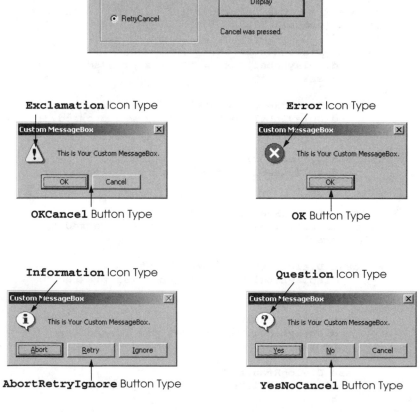

Fig. 11.26 Using **RadioButton**s to set message-window options. (Part 4 of 5.)

YesNo Button Type

RetryCancel Button Type

Fig. 11.26 Using **RadioButton**s to set message-window options. (Part 5 of 5.)

To store the user's choice of options, the objects **iconType** and **buttonType** are created and initialized (lines 34–36). Object **iconType** is a **MessageBoxIcon** enumeration that can have values **Asterisk**, **Error**, **Exclamation**, **Hand**, **Information**, **Question**, **Stop** and **Warning**. In this example we use only **Error**, **Exclamation**, **Information** and **Question**.

Object **buttonType** is a **MessageBoxButton** enumeration with values **Abort-RetryIgnore**, **OK**, **OKCancel**, **RetryCancel**, **YesNo** and **YesNoCancel**. The name indicates which buttons will appear in the **MessageBox**. In this example we use all **MessageBoxButton** enumeration values.

Two **GroupBox**es are created, one for each enumeration. Their captions are **Button Type** and **Icon**. One label is used to prompt the user (**promptLabel**), while the other is used to display which button was pressed, once the custom **MessageBox** has been displayed (**displayLabel**). There is also a button (**displayButton**) that displays the text **Display**. **RadioButton**s are created for the enumeration options, with their labels set appropriately. The radio buttons are grouped, thus only one option can be selected from each **GroupBox**.

For event handling, one event handler exists for all the radio buttons in **groupBox1**, and another for all the radio buttons in **groupBox2**. Each radio button generates a **CheckedChanged** event when clicked.

Remember, to set the event handler for an event, use the events section of the **Properties** window. Create a new **CheckedChanged** event handler for one of the radio buttons in **buttonTypeGroupBox** and rename it **buttonType_CheckedChanged**. Then set the **CheckedChanged** event handlers for all the radio buttons in **buttonType-GroupBox** to method **buttonType_CheckedChanged**. Create a second **Checked-Changed** event handler for a radio button in **iconTypeGroupBox** and rename it **iconType_CheckedChanged**. Finally, set the **CheckedChanged** event handlers for the radio buttons in **iconTypeGroupBox** to method **iconType_CheckedChanged**.

Both handlers compare the **sender** object with every radio button to determine which button was selected. Depending on the radio button selected, either **iconType** or **buttonType** changes (lines 46–93).

The **Click** handler for **displayButton** (lines 96–136) creates a **MessageBox** (lines 99–101). Some of the **MessageBox** options are set by **iconType** and **buttonType**. The result of the message box is a **DialogResult** enumeration, with values **Abort**, **Cancel**, **Ignore**, **No**, **None**, **OK**, **Retry** or **Yes**. The **switch** statement on lines 104–134 tests for the result and sets **displayLabel.Text** appropriately.

11.8 PictureBoxes

A picture box (class **PictureBox**) displays an image. The image, set by an object of class **Image**, can be in a bitmap (**.bmp**), **.gif**, **.jpg**, icon or metafile format. (Images are discussed in Chapter 14, Graphics.) *GIF (Graphics Interchange Format)* and *JPEG (Joint Photographic Expert Group)* files are widely used file formats.

The **Image** property sets the **Image** object to use, and the **SizeMode** property sets how the image is displayed (**Normal**, **StretchImage**, **AutoSize** or **CenterImage**). Figure 11.27 describes the important properties and events of class **PictureBox**.

The program in Fig. 11.28 uses **PictureBox imagePictureBox** to display one of three bitmap images—**image0**, **image1** or **image2**. They are located in the directory **images** (as usual, located in the **bin/debug** directory of our project), where the executable file is located. Whenever the **imagePictureBox** is clicked, the image changes. The **Label** (named **promptLabel**) on the top of the form includes the instructions **Click On Picture Box to View Images**.

PictureBox properties and events	Description / Delegate and Event Arguments
Common Properties	
Image	Image to display in the **PictureBox**.
SizeMode	Enumeration that controls image sizing and positioning. Values **Normal** (default), **StretchImage**, **AutoSize** and **CenterImage**. **Normal** puts image in top-left corner of **PictureBox** and **CenterImage** puts image in middle. (Both cut off image if too large.) **StretchImage** resizes image to fit in **PictureBox**. **AutoSize** resizes **PictureBox** to hold image.
Common Events	*(Delegate **EventHandler**, event arguments **EventArgs**)*
Click	Raised when user clicks the control. Default event when this control is double clicked in the designer.

Fig. 11.27 **PictureBox** properties and events.

```
1   // Fig. 11.28: PictureBoxTest.cs
2   // Using a PictureBox to display images.
3
4   using System;
5   using System.Drawing;
6   using System.Collections;
7   using System.ComponentModel;
8   using System.Windows.Forms;
9   using System.Data;
10  using System.IO;
11
```

Fig. 11.28 Using a **PictureBox** to display images. (Part 1 of 2.)

```
12     /// form to display different images when clicked
13     public class PictureBoxTest : System.Windows.Forms.Form
14     {
15        private System.Windows.Forms.PictureBox imagePictureBox;
16        private System.Windows.Forms.Label promptLabel;
17
18        private int imageNum = -1;
19
20        /// The main entry point for the application.
21        [STAThread]
22        static void Main()
23        {
24           Application.Run( new PictureBoxTest() );
25        }
26
27        // change image whenever PictureBox clicked
28        private void imagePictureBox_Click(
29           object sender, System.EventArgs e )
30        {
31           imageNum = ( imageNum + 1 ) % 3; // imageNum from 0 to 2
32
33           // create Image object from file, display on PictureBox
34           imagePictureBox.Image = Image.FromFile(
35              Directory.GetCurrentDirectory() + "\\images\\image" +
36              imageNum + ".bmp" );
37        }
38
39     } // end class PictureBoxTest
```

Fig. 11.28 Using a **PictureBox** to display images. (Part 2 of 2.)

To respond to the user's clicks, we must handle the **Click** event (lines 28–37). Inside the event handler, we use an integer (**imageNum**) to store the image we want to display. We then set the **Image** property of **imagePictureBox** to an **Image**. Class **Image** is discussed in Chapter 14, Graphics, but here we overview method **FromFile**, which takes a **string** (the path to the image file) and creates an **Image** object.

To find the images, we use class *Directory* (namespace **System.IO**, specified on line 10) method *GetCurrentDirectory* (line 35). This returns the current directory of the executable file (usually **bin\Debug**) as a **string**. To access the **images** subdirectory, we take the current directory and append "**\\images**" followed by "****" and the file name. We use a double slash because an escape sequence is needed to print a single slash.

Alternatively, we could have used **@** to avoid the escape character (i.e., **@"\"** will print a single slash—the slash does not need to be escaped by another slash). We use **imageNum** to append the proper number, so we can load either **image0**, **image1** or **image2**. Integer **imageNum** stays between **0** and **2**, due to the modulus calculation (line 31). Finally, we append **".bmp"** to the filename. Thus, if we want to load **image0**, the string becomes "*CurrentDir***images****image0.bmp**", where **CurrentDir** is the directory of the executable.

11.9 Mouse Event Handling

This section explains how to handle *mouse events,* such as *clicks*, *presses* and *moves*. Mouse events are generated when the mouse interacts with a control. They can be handled for any GUI control that derives from class **System.Windows.Forms.Control**. Mouse event information is passed using class *MouseEventArgs*, and the delegate to create the mouse event handlers is *MouseEventHandler*. Each mouse event-handling method must take an **object** and a **MouseEventArgs** object as arguments. The **Click** event, which we covered earlier, uses delegate **EventHandler** and event arguments **EventArgs**.

Class **MouseEventArgs** contains information about the mouse event, such as the x- and y-coordinates of the mouse pointer, the mouse button pressed, the number of clicks and the number of notches through which the mouse wheel turned. Note that the x- and y-coordinates of the **MouseEventArgs** object are relative to the control that raised the event. Point *(0,0)* is at the upper-left corner of the control. The various mouse events are described in Fig. 11.29.

Mouse Events, Delegates and Event Arguments	
*Mouse Events (Delegate **EventHandler**, event arguments **EventArgs**)*	
MouseEnter	Raised if the mouse cursor enters the area of the control.
MouseLeave	Raised if the mouse cursor leaves the area of the control.
*Mouse Events (Delegate **MouseEventHandler**, event arguments **MouseEventArgs**)*	
MouseDown	Raised if the mouse button is pressed while its cursor is over the area of the control.
MouseHover	Raised if the mouse cursor hovers over the area of the control.
MouseMove	Raised if the mouse cursor is moved while in the area of the control.
MouseUp	Raised if the mouse button is released when the cursor is over the area of the control.
*Class **MouseEventArgs** Properties*	
Button	Mouse button that was pressed (**left**, **right**, **middle** or **none**).
Clicks	The number of times the mouse button was clicked.
X	The x-coordinate of the event, relative to the control.
Y	The y-coordinate of the event, relative to the control.

Fig. 11.29 Mouse events, delegates and event arguments.

Figure 11.30 uses mouse events to draw on the form. Whenever the user drags the mouse (i.e., moves the mouse while holding down a button), a line is drawn on the form.

```
1   // Fig. 11.30: Painter.cs
2   // Using the mouse to draw on a form.
3
4   using System;
5   using System.Drawing;
6   using System.Collections;
7   using System.ComponentModel;
8   using System.Windows.Forms;
9   using System.Data;
10
11  // creates a form as a drawing surface
12  public class Painter : System.Windows.Forms.Form
13  {
14     bool shouldPaint = false; // whether to paint
15
16     // The main entry point for application.
17     [STAThread]
18     static void Main()
19     {
20        Application.Run( new Painter() );
21     }
22
23     // should paint after mouse button has been pressed
24     private void Painter_MouseDown(
25        object sender, System.Windows.Forms.MouseEventArgs e )
26     {
27        shouldPaint = true;
28     }
29
30     // stop painting when mouse button released
31     private void Painter_MouseUp(
32        object sender, System.Windows.Forms.MouseEventArgs e )
33     {
34        shouldPaint = false;
35     }
36
37     // draw circle whenever mouse button
38     // moves (and mouse is down)
39     protected void Painter_MouseMove(
40        object sender, System.Windows.Forms.MouseEventArgs e )
41     {
42        if ( shouldPaint )
43        {
44           Graphics graphics = CreateGraphics();
45           graphics.FillEllipse(
46              new SolidBrush( Color.BlueViolet ),
47              e.X, e.Y, 4, 4 );
48        }
49
50     } // end Painter_MouseMove
```

Fig. 11.30 Using the mouse to draw on a form. (Part 1 of 2.)

```
51
52    } // end class Painter
```

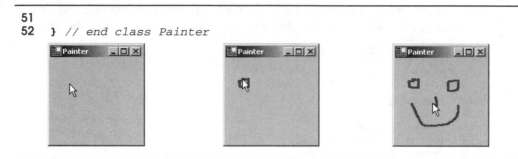

Fig. 11.30 Using the mouse to draw on a form. (Part 2 of 2.)

On line 14 the program creates variable **shouldPaint**, which determines whether we should draw on the form. We want to draw only while the mouse button is pressed down. In the event handler for event **MouseDown**, **shouldPaint** is set to true (line 27). As soon as the mouse button is released the program stops drawing: **shouldPaint** is set to **false** in the **MouseUp** event handler (line 34).

Whenever the mouse moves while the button is pressed down, the **MouseMove** event is generated. The event will be generated repeatedly, at a rate set by the operating system. Inside the **Painter_MouseMove** event handler (lines 39–48), the program draws only if **shouldPaint** is **true** (indicating that the mouse button is down). Line 44 creates the **Graphics** object for the form, which provides methods for drawing various shapes. Method **FillEllipse** (lines 45–47) draws a circle at every point the mouse cursor moves over (while the mouse button is pressed). The first parameter to method **FillEllipse** is a **SolidBrush** object, which determines the color of the shape drawn. We create a new **SolidBrush** object by passing the constructor a **Color** value. Structure **Color** contains numerous predefined color constants—we selected **Color.BlueViolet** (line 46). The **SolidBrush** fills an elliptical region, which lies inside a bounding rectangle. The bounding rectangle is specified by the *x*- and *y*-coordinates of its upper-left corner, its height and its width. These four parameters are the final four arguments to method **FillEllipse**. The *x*- and *y*-coordinates are the location of the mouse event: They can be taken from the mouse event arguments (**e.X** and **e.Y**). To draw a circle, we set the height and width of the bounding rectangle equal—in this case, they are each 4 pixels.

11.10 Keyboard Event Handling

This section explains how to handle *key events*. Key events are generated when keys on the keyboard are pressed and released. These events can be handled by any control that inherits from **System.Windows.Forms.Control**. There are two types of key events. The first is event ***KeyPress***, which fires when a key representing an ASCII character is pressed (determined by ***KeyPressEventArgs*** property ***KeyChar***). ASCII is a 128-character set of alphanumeric symbols. (The full listing can be found in Appendix E, ASCII Character Set.)

Using the **KeyPress** event, we cannot determine if *modifier keys* (such as *Shift*, *Alt* and *Control*) were pressed. To determine such actions, handle the ***KeyUp*** or ***KeyDown*** events, which form the second type of key event. Class ***KeyEventArgs*** contains information about special modifier keys. The key's ***Key*** *enumeration* value can be returned, giving information about a wide range of non-ASCII keys. Modifier keys are often used in conjunction with the mouse to select or highlight information. The delegates for the two classes are **KeyPressEventHandler** (event argument class **KeyPressEventArgs**) and **KeyEventHandler** (event argument class **KeyEventArgs**). Figure 11.31 lists important information about key events.

Figure 11.32 demonstrates using the key event handlers to display the key that was pressed. The program's form contains two **Label**s. It displays the key pressed on one **Label** and modifier information on the other.

The two **Label**s (named **charLabel** and **keyInfoLabel**) are initially empty. The **KeyDown** and **KeyPress** events convey different information; thus, the form (**Key-Demo**) handles them both.

Keyboard Events, Delegates and Event Arguments

*Key Events (Delegate **KeyEventHandler**, event arguments **KeyEventArgs**)*

KeyDown	Raised when key initially is pushed down.
KeyUp	Raised when key is released.

*Key Events (Delegate **KeyPressEventHandler**, event arguments **KeyPressEventArgs**)*

KeyPress	Raised when key is pressed. Occurs repeatedly while key is held down, at a rate specified by the operating system.

*Class **KeyPressEventArgs** Properties*

KeyChar	Returns the ASCII character for the key pressed.
Handled	Whether the **KeyPress** event was handled.

*Class **KeyEventArgs** Properties*

Alt	Indicates whether the *Alt* key was pressed.
Control	Indicates whether the *Control* key was pressed.
Shift	Indicates whether the *Shift* key was pressed.
Handled	Whether the event was handled.
KeyCode	Returns the key code for the key, as a **Keys** enumeration. This does not include modifier key information. Used to test for a specific key.
KeyData	Returns the key code as a **Keys** enumeration, combined with modifier information. Used to determine all information about the key pressed.
KeyValue	Returns the key code as an **int**, rather than as a **Keys** enumeration. Used to obtain a numeric representation of the key pressed.
Modifiers	Returns a **Keys** enumeration for any modifier keys pressed (*Alt*, *Control* and *Shift*). Used to determine modifier key information only.

Fig. 11.31 Keyboard events, delegates and event arguments.

```
1    // Fig. 11.32: KeyDemo.cs
2    // Displaying information about the key the user pressed.
3
4    using System;
5    using System.Drawing;
6    using System.Collections;
7    using System.ComponentModel;
8    using System.Windows.Forms;
9    using System.Data;
10
11   // form to display key press
12   // information--contains two labels
13   public class KeyDemo : System.Windows.Forms.Form
14   {
15      private System.Windows.Forms.Label charLabel;
16      private System.Windows.Forms.Label keyInfoLabel;
17
18      private System.ComponentModel.Container components = null;
19
20      // The main entry point for application.
21      [STAThread]
22      static void Main()
23      {
24         Application.Run( new KeyDemo() );
25      }
26
27      // display the character pressed using key char
28      protected void KeyDemo_KeyPress(
29         object sender, System.Windows.Forms.KeyPressEventArgs e )
30      {
31         charLabel.Text = "Key pressed: " + e.KeyChar;
32      }
33
34      // display modifier keys, key code, key data and key value
35      private void KeyDemo_KeyDown(
36         object sender, System.Windows.Forms.KeyEventArgs e )
37      {
38         keyInfoLabel.Text =
39            "Alt: " + ( e.Alt ? "Yes" : "No") + '\n' +
40            "Shift: " + ( e.Shift ? "Yes" : "No" ) + '\n' +
41            "Ctrl: " + ( e.Control ? "Yes" : "No" ) + '\n' +
42            "KeyCode: " + e.KeyCode + '\n' +
43            "KeyData: " + e.KeyData + '\n' +
44            "KeyValue: " + e.KeyValue;
45      }
46
47      // clear labels when key released
48      private void KeyDemo_KeyUp(
49         object sender, System.Windows.Forms.KeyEventArgs e )
50      {
51         keyInfoLabel.Text = "";
52         charLabel.Text = "";
53      }
```

Fig. 11.32 Demonstrating keyboard events (Part 1 of 2.).

```
54
55   }   // end class KeyDemo
```

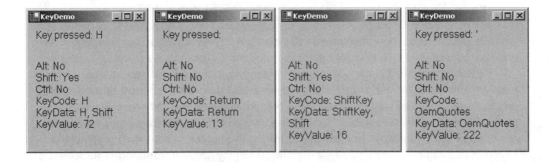

Fig. 11.32 Demonstrating keyboard events (Part 2 of 2.).

The **KeyPress** event handler (lines 28–32) accesses the **KeyChar** property of the **KeyPressEventArgs** object. This returns the key pressed as a **char** and displays in **charLabel** (line 31). If the key pressed was not an ASCII character, then the **KeyPress** event will not fire and **charLabel** remains empty. ASCII is a common encoding format for letters, numbers, punctuation marks and other characters. It does not support keys such as the *function keys* (like *F1*) or the modifier keys (*Alt*, *Control* and *Shift*).

The **KeyDown** event handler (lines 35–45) displays more information, all from its **KeyEventArgs** object. It tests for the *Alt*, *Shift* and *Control* keys (lines 39–41), using the **Alt**, **Shift** and **Control** properties, each of which returns **bool**. It then displays the **KeyCode**, **KeyData** and **KeyValue** properties.

The **KeyCode** property returns a **Keys** enumeration, which is converted to a **string** using method **ToString**. The **KeyCode** property returns the key that was pressed, but does not provide any information about modifier keys. Thus, both a capital and a lowercase "a" are represented as the *A* key.

The **KeyData** property returns a **Keys** enumeration as well, but includes data about modifier keys. Thus, if "A" is input, the **KeyData** shows that the *A* key and the *Shift* key were pressed. Lastly, **KeyValue** returns the key code for the key that was pressed as an integer. This integer is the *Windows virtual key code*, which provides an integer value for a wide range of keys and for mouse buttons. The Windows virtual key code is useful when testing for non-ASCII keys (such as *F12*).

The **KeyUp** event handler clears both labels when the key is released (lines 48–53). As we can see from the output, non-ASCII keys are not displayed in the upper **charLabel** because the **KeyPress** event was not generated. The **KeyDown** event is still raised, and **keyInfoLabel** displays information about the key. The **Keys** enumeration can be used to test for specific keys by comparing the key pressed to a specific **KeyCode**. The Visual Studio. NET documentation has a complete list of the **Keys** enumerations.

Software Engineering Observation 11.4

To cause a control to react when a certain key is pressed (such as Enter*), handle a key event and test for the key pressed. To cause a button to be clicked when the* Enter *key is pressed on a form, set the form's* **AcceptButton** *property.*

11.11 Visual Inheritance

In Chapter 9, Object-Oriented Programming: Inheritance, we discuss how to create classes by inheriting from other classes. In C#, we also can use inheritance to derive classes from class **Form**. This is called *visual inheritance*. The derived **Form** class contains the functionality of its **Form** base class, including any base-class properties, methods, variables and controls. The derived class also inherits all visual aspects—such as sizing, component layout, spacing between GUI components, colors and fonts—from its base class.

Visual inheritance enables developers to achieve visual consistency across applications by reusing code. For example, a company could define a base form that contains a product's logo, a static background color, a predefined menu bar and other elements. Programmers then could use the base form throughout an application for purposes of uniformity and product branding. In Chapter 15, Files and Streams, we create a graphical user interface that can be used by various programs to display account information for a bank's customers.

Class **VisualInheritance** (Fig. 11.33) is a form that we use as a base class for demonstrating visual inheritance. We created this class within a class library project (we demonstrated creating a class library in Section 8.16). By default, a class library in C# contains a file named **Class1.cs**. For this example, we deleted this file and added a Windows Form by right-clicking the project in the **Solution Explorer** and selecting option **Add > Add Windows Form...**. We named the new file **VisualInheritance.cs**. Notice that this file does not contain a **Main** method. Recall that a class library normally does not include a **Main** method because a class library is not an executable application.

The GUI contains two labels (one with text **Bugs, Bugs, Bugs** and one with **Copyright 2002, by Bug2Bug.com**) and one button (displaying the text **Learn More**). When a user presses the **Learn More** button, method **learnMoreButton_Click** (lines 19–26) is invoked. This method displays a message box that provides some informative text.

```
1    // Fig. 11.33: VisualInheritance.cs
2    // Base Form for use with visual inheritance.
3
4    using System;
5    using System.Drawing;
6    using System.Collections;
7    using System.ComponentModel;
8    using System.Windows.Forms;
9    using System.Data;
10
11   public class VisualInheritance : System.Windows.Forms.Form
12   {
13       private System.Windows.Forms.Label bugsLabel;
14       private System.Windows.Forms.Button learnMoreButton;
15       private System.Windows.Forms.Label label1;
16
17       // Visual Studio .NET generated code
18
```

Fig. 11.33 Class **VisualInheritance**, which inherits from class **Form**, contains a button (**Learn More**). (Part 1 of 2.)

```
19      private void learnMoreButton_Click(
20          object sender, System.EventArgs e )
21      {
22          MessageBox.Show(
23              "Bugs, Bugs, Bugs is a product of Bug2Bug.com",
24              "Learn More", MessageBoxButtons.OK,
25              MessageBoxIcon.Information );
26      }
27  }
```

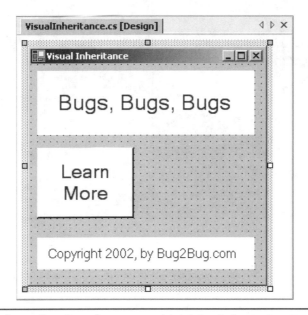

Fig. 11.33 Class **VisualInheritance**, which inherits from class **Form**, contains a button (**Learn More**). (Part 2 of 2.)

We then build the project, packaging class **VisualInheritance** as a **.dll**. The class contained in this **.dll** can now be used to create forms that inherit from the form in Fig. 11.33.

To create the derived form through visual inheritance, create an empty project. From the **Project** menu, select **Add Inherited Form....** This brings up the **Add New Item** window. Select **Inherited Form** from the templates window. Clicking **Open** displays the **Inheritance Picker**. The **Inheritance Picker** tool enables programmers to quickly create a form that inherits from a specified form. Click **Browse**, and select the **.dll** file for class **VisualInheritance**. The **.dll** file normally is located within the **bin\Debug** directory of the **VisualInheritance** project directory. Click **OK**. The Form Designer should now display the inherited form (Fig. 11.34).

Class **VisualInheritanceTest** (Fig. 11.35) derives from class **VisualInheritance**. The GUI contains those components derived from class **VisualInheritance**, plus a button with text **Learn The Program** that we added in class **VisualInheritanceTest**. When a user presses this button, method **learnProgramButton_Click** (lines 18–25) is invoked. This method displays a simple message box. Notice on lines 27–30 that we have added method **Main**, because we want **VisualInheritanceTest** to be used as an executing application.

Figure 11.35 demonstrates that the components, their layouts and the functionality of the base class **VisualInheritance** (Fig. 11.33) are inherited by **VisualInheritanceTest**. If a user clicks button **Learn More**, the base-class event handler **learnMoreButton_Click** displays a **MessageBox**.[1]

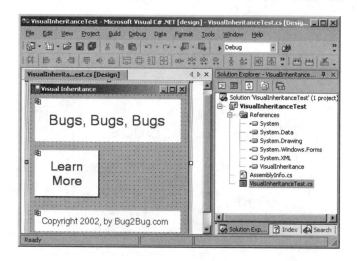

Fig. 11.34 Visual Inheritance through the Form Designer.

```
1   // Fig. 11.35: VisualInheritanceTest.cs
2   // Derived Form using visual inheritance.
3
4   using System;
5   using System.Collections;
6   using System.ComponentModel;
7   using System.Drawing;
8   using System.Windows.Forms;
9
10  public class VisualInheritanceTest :
11     VisualInheritance.VisualInheritance
12  {
13     private System.Windows.Forms.Button learnProgramButton;
14
15     // Visual Studio .NET generated code
16
```

Fig. 11.35 Class **VisualInheritanceTest**, which inherits from class **VisualInheritance.VisualInheritance**, contains an additional button. (Part 1 of 2.)

1. The reader may notice when they run this application that the console window appears in the background. To change this setting, right-click the name of the project in the **Solution Explorer** and select **Properties**. In the dialog that appears, change the **Output Type** property from **Console Application** to **Windows Application**.

```
17          // invoke when user clicks Learn the Program button
18          private void learnProgramButton_Click(
19              object sender, System.EventArgs e )
20          {
21              MessageBox.Show(
22                  "This program was created by Deitel & Associates",
23                  "Learn the Program", MessageBoxButtons.OK,
24                  MessageBoxIcon.Information );
25          }
26
27          public static void Main( string[] args )
28          {
29              Application.Run( new VisualInheritanceTest() );
30          }
31      }
```

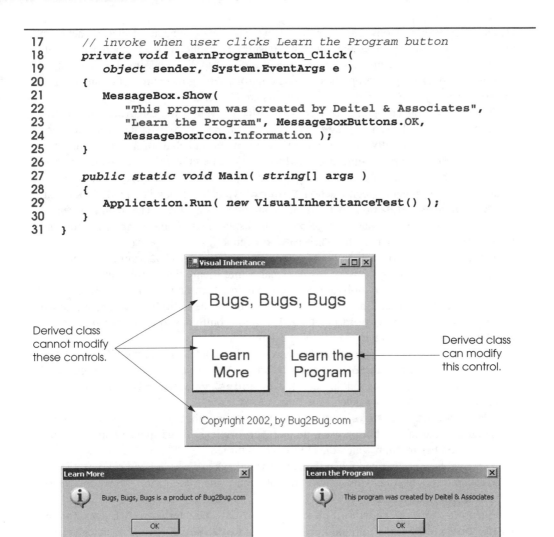

Derived class cannot modify these controls.

Derived class can modify this control.

Fig. 11.35 Class **VisualInheritanceTest**, which inherits from class **VisualInheritance.VisualInheritance**, contains an additional button. (Part 2 of 2.)

11.12 Summary

A graphical user interface (GUI) presents a pictorial interface to a program. A GUI (pronounced "GOO-EE") gives a program a distinctive "look and feel." By providing different applications with a consistent set of intuitive user-interface components, GUIs allow the user to concentrate on using programs productively.

GUIs are built from GUI components (sometimes called controls or widgets). A GUI control is a visual object with which the user interacts via the mouse or keyboard. When the user interacts with a component, an event is generated. This event can trigger methods that respond to the user's actions. Events are based on the notion of delegates. Delegates act as an intermediate step between the object creating (raising) the event and the method handling it.

The general design process for creating Windows applications involves creating a Windows Form, setting its properties, adding controls, setting their properties and configuring event handlers. All forms and components are classes.

The information a programmer needs to register an event is the **EventArgs** class (to define the event handler) and the **EventHandler** delegate (to register the event handler). Visual Studio .NET usually can register the event handler on behalf of the programmer.

A **TextBox** is a single-line area in which text can be entered. A password text box masks each character input with a special character (e.g., *****). A **Button** is a control that the user clicks to trigger a specific action. **Button**s typically respond to the **Click** event.

GroupBoxes and **Panel**s help arrange components on a GUI. The main differences between these classes are that **GroupBox**es can display text, while **Panel**s cannot, and **Panel**s can have scrollbars, while **GroupBox**es cannot.

C# has two types of state buttons—**CheckBox**es and **RadioButton**s—that have on/off or true/false values. A check box is a small white square that is either empty or contains a check mark. Radio buttons appear as a group in which only one radio button can be selected at a time. To create new groups of radio buttons, the radio buttons must be added to a container (e.g., **GroupBox**es or **Panel**s). Radio buttons and check boxes raise the **CheckChanged** event when their value is altered.

Mouse events (clicks, presses and moves) can be handled for any GUI control that derives from **System.Windows.Forms.Control**. Mouse events use class **MouseEventArgs** (whose corresponding delegate is **MouseEventHandler**) and **EventArgs** (whose corresponding delegate is **EventHandler**).

Class **MouseEventArgs** contains information about the x- and y-coordinates of the mouse cursor, the mouse button used, the number of clicks of the mouse button and the number of notches through which the mouse wheel turned.

Key events are generated when the keyboard's keys are pressed and released. These events can be handled by any control that inherits from **System.Windows.Forms.Control**.

Event **KeyPress** can return a **char** for any ASCII character pressed. Events **KeyUp** and **KeyDown** test for special modifier keys (using **KeyEventArgs**). The delegates are **KeyPressEventHandler** (class **KeyPressEventArgs**) and **KeyEventHandler** (class **KeyEventArgs**).

12

Multithreading

Objectives

- To understand the notion of multithreading.
- To appreciate how multithreading can improve program performance.
- To understand how to create, manage and destroy threads.
- To understand the life cycle of a thread.
- To understand thread priorities and scheduling.

The spider's touch, how exquisitely fine!
Feels at each thread, and lives along the line.
Alexander Pope

A person with one watch knows what time it is; a person with two watches is never sure.
Proverb

Learn to labor and to wait.
Henry Wadsworth Longfellow

The most general definition of beauty...Multeity in Unity.
Samuel Taylor Coleridge

Outline

12.1 Introduction

It would be nice if we could perform one action at a time and perform it well, but that is usually difficult to do. The human body performs a great variety of operations *in parallel*— or, as we will say throughout this chapter, *concurrently*. Respiration, blood circulation and digestion, for example, can occur concurrently. All the senses—sight, touch, smell, taste and hearing—can occur at once. Computers, too, perform operations concurrently. It is common for desktop personal computers to be compiling a program, sending a file to a printer and receiving electronic mail messages over a network concurrently.

Ironically, most programming languages do not enable programmers to specify concurrent activities. Rather, programming languages generally provide only a simple set of control structures that enable programmers to perform one action at a time, proceeding to the next action after the previous one has finished. Historically, the type of concurrency that computers perform today generally has been implemented as operating system "primitives" available only to highly experienced "systems programmers."

The Ada programming language, developed by the United States Department of Defense, made concurrency primitives widely available to defense contractors building military command-and-control systems. However, Ada has not been widely used in universities and commercial industry.

The .NET Framework Class Library makes concurrency primitives available to the applications programmer. The programmer specifies that applications contain "threads of execution," each thread designating a portion of a program that may execute concurrently with other threads—this capability is called *multithreading*. Multithreading is available to all .NET programming languages, including C#, Visual Basic and Visual C++.

Software Engineering Observation 12.1

The .NET Framework Class Library includes multithreading capabilities in namespace `System.Threading`*. This encourages the use of multithreading among a larger part of the applications-programming community.*

We discuss many applications of concurrent programming. When programs download large files, such as audio clips or video clips from the World Wide Web, users do not want to wait until an entire clip downloads before starting the playback. To solve this problem, we can put multiple threads to work—one thread downloads a clip, and another plays the clip. These activities, or *tasks*, then may proceed concurrently. To avoid choppy playback, we *synchronize* the threads so that the player thread does not begin until there is a sufficient amount of the clip in memory to keep the player thread busy.

Another example of multithreading is C#'s automatic *garbage collection*. C and C++ place with the programmer the responsibility of reclaiming dynamically allocated memory.

C# provides a *garbage-collector thread* that reclaims dynamically allocated memory that is no longer needed.

Performance Tip 12.1

One of the reasons for the popularity of C and C++ over the years was that their memory-management techniques were more efficient than those of languages that used g*arbage collectors. In fact, memory management in C# often is faster than in C or C++.[1]

Good Programming Practice 12.1

Set an object reference to **null** *when the program no longer needs that object. This enables the garbage collector to determine at the earliest possible moment that the object can be garbage collected. If such an object has other references to it, that object cannot be collected.*

Writing multithreaded programs can be tricky. Although the human mind can perform functions concurrently, people find it difficult to jump between parallel "trains of thought." To see why multithreading can be difficult to program and understand, try the following experiment: Open three books to page 1 and try reading the books concurrently. Read a few words from the first book, then read a few words from the second book, then read a few words from the third book, then loop back and read the next few words from the first book, etc. After this experiment, you will appreciate the challenges of multithreading—switching between books, reading briefly, remembering your place in each book, moving the book you are reading closer so you can see it, pushing books you are not reading aside—and amidst all this chaos, trying to comprehend the content of the books!

Performance Tip 12.2

A problem with single-threaded applications is that lengthy activities must complete before other activities can begin. In a multithreaded application, threads can share a processor (or set of processors), so that multiple tasks are performed in parallel.

12.2 Thread States: Life Cycle of a Thread

At any time, a thread is said to be in one of several *thread states* (illustrated in Fig. 12.1)[2]. This section discusses these states and the transitions between states. Two classes critical for multithreaded applications are **Thread** and **Monitor** (**System.Threading** namespace). This section also discusses several methods of classes **Thread** and **Monitor** that cause state transitions.

A new thread begins its lifecycle in the *Unstarted* state. The thread remains in the *Unstarted* state until the program calls **Thread** method **Start**, which places the thread in the *Started* state (sometimes called the *Ready* or *Runnable* state) and immediately returns control to the calling thread. Then the thread that invoked **Start**, the newly *Started* thread and any other threads in the program execute concurrently.

---

1. E. Schanzer, "Performance Considerations for Run-Time Technologies in the .NET Framework," August 2001 **<http://msdn.microsoft.com/library/default.asp?url= /library/en-us/dndotnet/html/dotnetperftechs.asp>**.
2. As this book went to publication, Microsoft changed the names of the *Started* and *Blocked* thread states to *Running* and *WaitSleepJoin*, respectively.

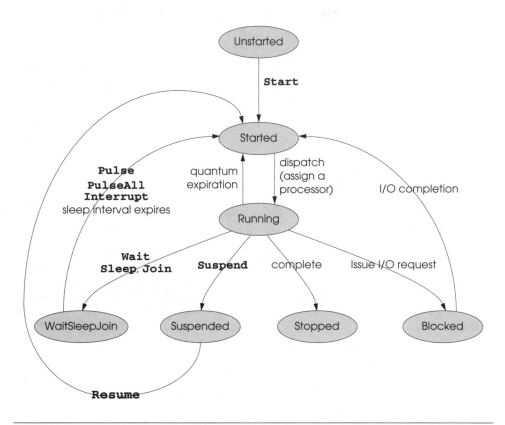

Fig. 12.1 Thread life cycle.

The highest priority *Started* thread enters the *Running* state (i.e., begins executing) when the operating system assigns a processor to the thread (Section 12.3 discusses thread priorities). When a *Started* thread receives a processor for the first time and becomes a *Running* thread, the thread executes its **ThreadStart** delegate, which specifies the actions the thread will perform during its lifecycle. When a program creates a new **Thread**, the program specifies the **Thread**'s **ThreadStart** delegate as the argument to the **Thread** constructor. The **ThreadStart** delegate must be a method that returns **void** and takes no arguments.

A *Running* thread enters the *Stopped* (or *Dead*) state when its **ThreadStart** delegate terminates. Note that a program can force a thread into the *Stopped* state by calling **Thread** method **Abort** on the appropriate **Thread** object. Method **Abort** throws a **ThreadAbortException** in the thread, normally causing the thread to terminate. When a thread is in the *Stopped* state and there are no references to the thread object, the garbage collector can remove the thread object from memory.

A thread enters the *Blocked* state when the thread issues an input/output request. The operating system blocks the thread from executing until the operating system can complete the I/O for which the thread is waiting. At that point, the thread returns to the *Started* state, so it can resume execution. A *Blocked* thread cannot use a processor even if one is available.

There are three ways in which a *Running* thread enters the *WaitSleepJoin* state. If a thread encounters code that it cannot execute yet (normally because a condition is not satisfied), the thread can call **Monitor** method **Wait** to enter the *WaitSleepJoin* state. Once in this state, a thread returns to the *Started* state when another thread invokes **Monitor** method **Pulse** or **PulseAll**. Method **Pulse** moves the next waiting thread back to the *Started* state. Method **PulseAll** moves all waiting threads back to the *Started* state.

A *Running* thread can call **Thread** method **Sleep** to enter the *WaitSleepJoin* state for a period of milliseconds specified as the argument to **Sleep**. A sleeping thread returns to the *Started* state when its designated sleep time expires. Sleeping threads cannot use a processor, even if one is available.

Any thread that enters the *WaitSleepJoin* state by calling **Monitor** method **Wait** or by calling **Thread** method **Sleep** also leaves the *WaitSleepJoin* state and returns to the *Started* state if the sleeping or waiting **Thread**'s **Interrupt** method is called by another thread in the program.

If a thread cannot continue executing (we will call this the dependent thread) unless another thread terminates, the dependent thread calls the other thread's **Join** method to "join" the two threads. When two threads are "joined," the dependent thread leaves the *WaitSleepJoin* state when the other thread finishes execution (enters the *Stopped* state).

If a *Running* **Thread**'s **Suspend** method is called, the *Running* thread enters the *Suspended* state. A *Suspended* thread returns to the *Started* state when another thread in the program invokes the Suspended thread's **Resume** method.

12.3 Thread Priorities and Thread Scheduling

Every thread has a priority in the range between **ThreadPriority.Lowest** to **ThreadPriority.Highest**. These two values come from the **ThreadPriority** enumeration (namespace **System.Threading**). The enumeration consists of the values **Lowest**, **BelowNormal**, **Normal**, **AboveNormal** and **Highest**. By default, each thread has priority **Normal**.

The Windows operating system supports a concept, called *timeslicing,* that enables threads of equal priority to share a processor. Without timeslicing, each thread in a set of equal-priority threads runs to completion (unless the thread leaves the *Running* state and enters the *WaitSleepJoin*, *Suspended* or *Blocked* state) before the thread's peers get a chance to execute. With timeslicing, each thread receives a brief burst of processor time, called a *quantum*, during which the thread can execute. At the completion of the quantum, even if the thread has not finished executing, the processor is taken away from that thread and given to the next thread of equal priority, if one is available.

The job of the thread scheduler is to keep the highest-priority thread running at all times and, if there is more than one highest-priority thread, to ensure that all such threads execute for a quantum in *round-robin* fashion (i.e., these threads can be timesliced). Figure 12.2 illustrates the multilevel priority queue for threads. In Fig. 12.2, assuming a single-processor computer, threads A and B each execute for a quantum in round-robin fashion until both threads complete execution. This means that A gets a quantum of time to run. Then B gets a quantum. Then A gets another quantum. Then B gets another quantum. This continues until one thread completes. The processor then devotes all its power to the thread that remains (unless another thread of that priority is *Started*). Next, thread C runs to completion. Threads D, E and F each execute for a quantum in round-robin fashion until they all complete execution. This process continues until all threads run to completion. Note that, depending on the operating system, new higher-priority threads could postpone—possibly indefinitely—the execution of lower-priority threads. Such *indefinite postponement* often is referred to more colorfully as *starvation*.

A thread's priority can be adjusted with the **Priority** property, which accepts values from the **ThreadPriority** enumeration. If the argument is not one of the valid thread-priority constants, an **ArgumentException** occurs.

A thread executes until it dies, becomes *Blocked* for input/output (or some other reason), calls **Sleep**, calls **Monitor** method **Wait** or **Join**, is preempted by a thread of higher priority or has its quantum expire. A thread with a higher priority than the *Running* thread can become *Started* (and hence preempt the *Running* thread) if a sleeping thread wakes up, if I/O completes for a thread that *Blocked* for that I/O, if either **Pulse** or **PulseAll** is called on an object on which **Wait** was called, or if a thread to which the high-priority thread was **Join**ed completes.

Figure 12.3 demonstrates basic threading techniques, including the construction of a **Thread** object and using the **Thread** class's **static** method **Sleep**. The program creates three threads of execution, each with the default priority **Normal**. Each thread displays a message indicating that it is going to sleep for a random interval of from 0 to 5000 milliseconds, then goes to sleep. When each thread awakens, the thread displays its name, indicates that it is done sleeping, terminates and enters the *Stopped* state. You will see that method **Main** (i.e., the *Main thread of execution*) terminates before the application terminates. The program consists of two classes—**ThreadTester** (lines 8–41), which creates the three threads, and **MessagePrinter** (lines 44–73), which defines a **Print** method containing the actions each thread will perform.

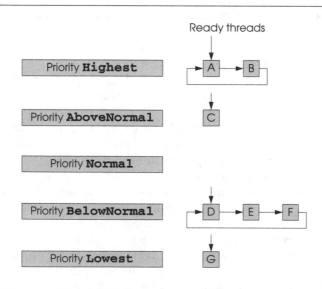

Fig. 12.2   Thread-priority scheduling.

```
1    // Fig. 12.3: ThreadTester.cs
2    // Multiple threads printing at different intervals.
3
4    using System;
5    using System.Threading;
6
7    // class ThreadTester demonstrates basic threading concepts
8    class ThreadTester
9    {
10      static void Main( string[] args )
11      {
12         // Create and name each thread. Use MessagePrinter's
13         // Print method as argument to ThreadStart delegate.
14         MessagePrinter printer1 = new MessagePrinter();
15         Thread thread1 =
16            new Thread ( new ThreadStart( printer1.Print ) );
17         thread1.Name = "thread1";
18
19         MessagePrinter printer2 = new MessagePrinter();
20         Thread thread2 =
21            new Thread ( new ThreadStart( printer2.Print ) );
22         thread2.Name = "thread2";
23
24         MessagePrinter printer3 = new MessagePrinter();
25         Thread thread3 =
26            new Thread ( new ThreadStart( printer3.Print  ) );
27         thread3.Name = "thread3";
28
29         Console.WriteLine( "Starting threads" );
30
31         // call each thread's Start method to place each
32         // thread in Started state
33         thread1.Start();
34         thread2.Start();
35         thread3.Start();
36
37         Console.WriteLine( "Threads started\n" );
38
39      } // end method Main
40   } // end class ThreadTester
41
42   // Print method of this class used to control threads
43   class MessagePrinter
44   {
45      private int sleepTime;
46      private static Random random = new Random();
47
48      // constructor to initialize a MessagePrinter object
49      public MessagePrinter()
50      {
51         // pick random sleep time between 0 and 5 seconds
52         sleepTime = random.Next( 5001 );
53      }
```

Fig. 12.3   Threads sleeping and printing. (Part 1 of 2)

```
54
55      // method Print controls thread that prints messages
56      public void Print()
57      {
58         // obtain reference to currently executing thread
59         Thread current = Thread.CurrentThread;
60
61         // put thread to sleep for sleepTime amount of time
62         Console.WriteLine(
63            current.Name + " going to sleep for " + sleepTime );
64
65         Thread.Sleep ( sleepTime );
66
67         // print thread name
68         Console.WriteLine( current.Name + " done sleeping" );
69
70      } // end method Print
71
72   } // end class MessagePrinter
```

```
Starting threads
Threads started

thread1 going to sleep for 1977
thread2 going to sleep for 4513
thread3 going to sleep for 1261
thread3 done sleeping
thread1 done sleeping
thread2 done sleeping
```

```
Starting threads
Threads started

thread1 going to sleep for 1466
thread2 going to sleep for 4245
thread3 going to sleep for 1929
thread1 done sleeping
thread3 done sleeping
thread2 done sleeping
```

Fig. 12.3   Threads sleeping and printing. (Part 2 of 2)

Objects of class **MessagePrinter** (lines 44–73) control the lifecycle of each of the three threads class **ThreadTester**'s **Main** method creates. Class **MessagePrinter** consists of instance variable **sleepTime** (line 46), **static** variable **random** (line 47), a constructor (lines 50–54) and a **Print** method (lines 57–71). Variable **sleepTime** stores a random integer value chosen when a new **MessagePrinter** object's constructor is called. Each thread controlled by a **MessagePrinter** object sleeps for the amount of time specified by the corresponding **MessagePrinter** object's **sleepTime**

The **MessagePrinter** constructor (lines 50–54) initializes **sleepTime** to a random integer from 0 up to, but not including, 5001 (i.e., from 0 to 5000).

Method **Print** begins by obtaining a reference to the currently executing thread (line 60) via class **Thread**'s **static** property *CurrentThread*. The currently executing thread is the one that invokes method **Print**. Next, lines 63–64 display a message indicating the name of the currently executing thread and stating that the thread is going to sleep for a certain number of milliseconds. Note that line 64 uses the currently executing thread's **Name** property to obtain the thread's name (set in method **Main** when each thread is created). Line 66 invokes **static Thread** method **Sleep** to place the thread into the *Wait-SleepJoin* state. At this point, the thread loses the processor and the system allows another thread to execute. When the thread awakens, it reenters the *Started* state again until the system assigns a processor to the thread. When the **MessagePrinter** object enters the *Running* state again, line 69 outputs the thread's name in a message that indicates the thread is done sleeping, and method **Print** terminates.

Class **ThreadTester**'s **Main** method (lines 10–39) creates three objects of class **MessagePrinter**, at lines 14, 19 and 24, respectively. Lines 15–16, 20–21 and 25–26 create and initialize three **Thread** objects. Lines 17, 22 and 27 set each **Thread**'s **Name** property, which we use for output purposes. Note that each **Thread**'s constructor receives a **ThreadStart** delegate as an argument. Remember that a **ThreadStart** delegate specifies the actions a thread performs during its lifecyle. Line 16 specifies that the delegate for **thread1** will be method **Print** of the object to which **printer1** refers. When **thread1** enters the *Running* state for the first time, **thread1** will invoke **printer1**'s **Print** method to perform the tasks specified in method **Print**'s body. Thus, **thread1** will print its name, display the amount of time for which it will go to sleep, sleep for that amount of time, wake up and display a message indicating that the thread is done sleeping. At that point method **Print** will terminate. A thread completes its task when the method specified by a **Thread**'s **ThreadStart** delegate terminates, placing the thread in the *Stopped* state. When **thread2** and **thread3** enter the *Running* state for the first time, they invoke the **Print** methods of **printer2** and **printer3**, respectively. Threads **thread2** and **thread3** perform the same tasks as **thread1** by executing the **Print** methods of the objects to which **printer2** and **printer3** refer (each of which has its own randomly chosen sleep time).

Testing and Debugging Tip 12.1

*Naming threads helps in the debugging of a multithreaded program. Visual Studio .NET's debugger provides a **Threads** window that displays the name of each thread and enables you to view the execution of any thread in the program.*

Lines 33–35 invoke each **Thread**'s **Start** method to place the threads in the *Started* state (sometimes called *launching a thread*). Method **Start** returns immediately from each invocation, then line 37 outputs a message indicating that the threads were started, and the **Main** thread of execution terminates. The program itself does not terminate, however, because there are still threads that are alive (i.e., the threads were *Started* and have not reached the *Stopped* state yet). The program will not terminate until its last thread dies. When the system assigns a processor to a thread, the thread enters the *Running* state and calls the method specified by the thread's **ThreadStart** delegate. In this program, each thread invokes method **Print** of the appropriate **MessagePrinter** object to perform the tasks discussed previously.

Note that the sample outputs for this program show each thread and the thread's sleep time as the thread goes to sleep. The thread with the shortest sleep time normally awakens first, indicates that it is done sleeping and terminates.

12.4 Summary

Computers perform multiple operations concurrently. Programming languages generally provide only a simple set of control structures that enable programmers to perform just one action at a time and proceed to the next action only after the previous one finishes. The FCL, however, provides the C# programmer with the ability to specify that applications contain threads of execution, where each thread designates a portion of a program that may execute concurrently with other threads. This capability is called multithreading.

A thread is initialized using the **Thread** class's constructor, which receives a **ThreadStart** delegate. This delegate specifies the method that contains the tasks a thread will perform. A thread remains in the *Unstarted* state until the thread's **Start** method is called, which the thread enters the *Started* state. A thread in the *Started* state enters the *Running* state when the system assigns a processor to the thread. The system assigns the processor to the highest-priority *Started* thread. A thread enters the *Stopped* state when its **ThreadStart** delegate completes or terminates. A thread is forced into the *Stopped* state when its **Abort** method is called (by itself or by another thread). A *Running* thread enters the *Blocked* state when the thread issues an input/output request. A *Blocked* thread becomes *Started* when the I/O it is waiting for completes. A *Blocked* thread cannot use a processor, even if one is available.

If a thread needs to sleep, it calls method **Sleep**. A thread wakes up when the designated sleep interval expires. If a thread cannot continue executing unless another thread terminates, the first thread, referred to as the dependent thread, calls the other thread's **Join** method to "join" the two threads. When two threads are joined, the dependent thread leaves the *WaitSleepJoin* state when the other thread finishes execution.

When a thread encounters code that it cannot yet run, the thread can call **Monitor** method **Wait** until certain actions occur that enable the thread to continue executing. This method call puts the thread into the *WaitSleepJoin* state. Any thread in the *WaitSleepJoin* state can leave that state if another thread invokes **Thread** method **Interrupt** on the thread in the *WaitSleepJoin* state. If a thread has called **Monitor** method **Wait**, a corresponding call to **Monitor** method **Pulse** or **PulseAll** by another thread in the program will transition the original thread from the *WaitSleepJoin* state to the *Started* state.

If **Thread** method **Suspend** is called on a thread, the thread enters the *Suspended* state. A thread leaves the *Suspended* state when a separate thread invokes **Thread** method **Resume** on the suspended thread.

Every C# thread has a priority. The job of the thread scheduler is to keep the highest-priority thread running at all times and, if there is more than one highest-priority thread, to ensure that all equally high-priority threads execute for a quantum at a time in round-robin fashion. A thread's priority can be adjusted with the **Priority** property, which is assigned an argument from the **ThreadPriority** enumeration.

Strings and Characters

Objectives

- To be able to create and manipulate immutable character string objects of class **String**.
- To be able to create and manipulate mutable character string objects of class **StringBuilder**.
- To be able to use **Char** methods to process characters.

The chief defect of Henry King
Was chewing little bits of string.
Hilaire Belloc

Vigorous writing is concise. A sentence should contain no unnecessary words, a paragraph no unnecessary sentences.
William Strunk, Jr.

I have made this letter longer than usual, because I lack the time to make it short.
Blaise Pascal

The difference between the almost-right word & the right word is really a large matter—it's the difference between the lightning bug and the lightning.
Mark Twain

Mum's the word.
Miguel de Cervantes

Outline

13.1 Introduction

In this chapter, we introduce the Framework Class Library's string and character processing capabilities. The techniques presented in this chapter can be employed to develop text editors, word processors, page-layout software, computerized typesetting systems and other kinds of text-processing software. Previous chapters have already presented several string-processing capabilities. In this chapter, we expand on this information by detailing the capabilities of class *String* and type *char* from the **System** namespace and class *StringBuilder* from the *System.Text* namespace.

13.2 Fundamentals of Characters and Strings

Characters are the fundamental building blocks of C# source code. Every program is composed of characters that, when grouped together meaningfully, create a sequence that the compiler interprets as a series of instructions that describe how to accomplish a task. In addition to normal characters, a program also can contain *character constants*. A character constant is a character that is represented as an integer value, called a *character code*. For example, the integer value **122** corresponds to the character constant **'z'**. The integer value **10** corresponds to the new line character **'\n'**. Character constants are established according to the *Unicode character set*, an international character set that contains many more symbols and letters than does the ASCII character set (see Appendix E, ASCII Character Set). To learn more about Unicode®, see Appendix F.

A string is a series of characters treated as a single unit. These characters can be uppercase letters, lowercase letters, digits and various *special characters,* such as **+, -, *, /, $** and others. A string is an object of class **String** in the **System** namespace.[1] We write *string literals*, or *string constants* (often called *literal **string**s*), as sequences of characters in double quotation marks, as follows:

```
"John Q. Doe"
"9999 Main Street"
"Waltham, Massachusetts"
"(201) 555-1212"
```

A declaration can assign a **string** literal to a **string** reference. The declaration

```
string color = "blue";
```

initializes **string** reference **color** to refer to the **string** literal object **"blue"**.

Performance Tip 13.1

*If there are multiple occurrences of the same **string** literal object in an application, a single copy of the **string** literal object will be referenced from each location in the program that uses that **string** literal. It is possible to share the object in this manner, because **string** literal objects are implicitly constant. Such sharing conserves memory.*

On occasion, a **string** will contain multiple backslash characters (this often occurs in the name of a file). It is possible to exclude escape sequences and interpret all the characters in a **string** literally, using the **@** character. Backslashes within the double quotation marks are not considered escape sequences, but rather regular backslash charac*ters. Often this simplifies programming and makes the code easier to read. For example, consider the string "**C:\MyFolder\MySubFolder\MyFile.txt**" with the following assignment:

```
string file = "C:\\MyFolder\\MySubFolder\\MyFile.txt";
```

Using the verbatim string syntax, the assignment can be altered to

```
string file = @"C:\MyFolder\MySubFolder\MyFile.txt";
```

This approach also has the advantage of allowing strings to span multiple lines by preserving all newlines, spaces and tabs.

---

1. C# provides the **string** keyword as an alias for class **String**. In this book, we use **String** to refer to the class **String** and **string** to refer to an object of class **String**.

13.3 `String` Constructors

Class **String** provides eight constructors for initializing **string**s in various ways. Figure 13.1 demonstrates the use of three of the constructors.

Lines 14–16 declare **string**s **output**, **originalString**, **string1**, **string2**, **string3** and **string4**. Lines 18–19 allocate the **char** array **characterArray**, which contains nine characters. Line 22 assigns literal **string "Welcome to C# programming!"** to **string** reference **originalString**. Line 23 sets **string1** to reference the same **string** literal.

Line 24 assigns to **string2** a new **string**, using the **String** constructor that takes a character array as an argument. The new **string** contains a copy of the characters in array **characterArray**.

```
1   // Fig. 13.1: StringConstructor.cs
2   // Demonstrating String class constructors.
3
4   using System;
5   using System.Windows.Forms;
6
7   // test several String class constructors
8   class StringConstructor
9   {
10     // the main entry point for application.
11     [STAThread]
12     static void Main( string[] args )
13     {
14        string output;
15        string originalString, string1, string2,
16           string3, string4;
17
18        char[] characterArray =
19           { 'b', 'i', 'r', 't', 'h', ' ', 'd', 'a', 'y' };
20
21        // string initialization
22        originalString = "Welcome to C# programming!";
23        string1 = originalString;
24        string2 = new string( characterArray );
25        string3 = new string( characterArray, 6, 3 );
26        string4 = new string( 'C', 5 );
27
28        output = "string1 = " + "\"" + string1 + "\"\n" +
29           "string2 = " + "\"" + string2 + "\"\n" +
30           "string3 = " + "\"" + string3 + "\"\n" +
31           "string4 = " + "\"" + string4 + "\"\n";
32
33        MessageBox.Show( output, "String Class Constructors",
34           MessageBoxButtons.OK, MessageBoxIcon.Information );
35
36     } // end method Main
37
38  } // end class StringConstructor
```

Fig. 13.1 String constructors. (Part 1 of 2.)

Fig. 13.1 **String** constructors. (Part 2 of 2.)

Software Engineering Observation 13.1

*In most cases, it is not necessary to make a copy of an existing **string**. All **string**s are immutable—their character contents cannot be changed after they are created. Also, if there are one or more references to a **string** (or any object for that matter), the object cannot be reclaimed by the garbage collector.*

Line 25 assigns to **string3** a new **string**, using the **String** constructor that takes a **char** array and two **int** arguments. The second argument specifies the starting index position (the *offset*) from which characters in the array are copied. The third argument specifies the number of characters (the *count*) to be copied from the specified starting position in the array. The new **string** contains a copy of the specified characters in the array. If the specified offset or count indicates that the program should access an element outside the bounds of the character array, an ***ArgumentOutOfRangeException*** is thrown.

Line 26 assigns to **string4** a new **string**, using the **String** constructor that takes as arguments a character and an **int** specifying the number of times to repeat that character in the **string**.

13.4 **String** Indexer, **Length** Property and **CopyTo** Method

The application in Fig. 13.2 presents the **String** indexer, which facilitates the retrieval of any character in the **string**, and the **String** property **Length**, which returns the length of the **string**. The **String** method **CopyTo** copies a specified number of characters from a **string** into a **char** array.

In this example, we create an application that determines the length of a **string**, reverses the order of the characters in the **string** and copies a series of characters from the **string** into a character array.

```
1   // Fig. 13.2: StringMethods.cs
2   // Using the indexer, property Length and method CopyTo
3   // of class String.
4
5   using System;
6   using System.Windows.Forms;
7
```

Fig. 13.2 **String** indexer, **Length** property and **CopyTo** method. (Part 1 of 2.)

```
 8      // creates string objects and displays results of using
 9      // indexer and methods Length and CopyTo
10      class StringMethods
11      {
12          // the main entry point for application.
13          [STAThread]
14          static void Main( string[] args )
15          {
16              string string1, output;
17              char[] characterArray;
18
19              string1 = "hello there";
20              characterArray = new char[ 5 ];
21
22              // output string
23              output =
24                  "string1: \"" + string1 + "\"";
25
26              // test Length property
27              output += "\nLength of string1: " + string1.Length;
28
29              // loop through character in string1 and display
30              // reversed
31              output += "\nThe string reversed is: ";
32
33              for ( int i = string1.Length - 1; i >= 0; i-- )
34                  output += string1[ i ];
35
36              // copy characters from string1 into characterArray
37              string1.CopyTo( 0, characterArray, 0, 5 );
38              output += "\nThe character array is: ";
39
40              for ( int i = 0 ; i < characterArray.Length; i++ )
41                  output += characterArray[ i ];
42
43              MessageBox.Show( output, "Demonstrating the string " +
44                  "Indexer, Length Property and CopyTo method",
45                  MessageBoxButtons.OK, MessageBoxIcon.Information );
46
47          } // end method Main
48
49      } // end class StringMethods
```

Fig. 13.2 **String** indexer, **Length** property and **CopyTo** method. (Part 2 of 2.)

Line 27 uses **String** property **Length** to determine the number of characters in **string string1**. Like arrays, **string**s always know their own size.

Lines 33–34 append to **output** the characters of the **string string1** in reverse order. The **string** indexer returns the character at a specific position in the **string**. The **string** indexer treats a **string** as an array of **char**s. The indexer receives an integer argument as the *position number* and returns the character at that position. As with arrays, the first element of a **string** is considered to be at position 0.

Common Programming Error 13.1

*Attempting to access a character that is outside the bounds of a **string** (i.e., an index less than 0 or an index greater than or equal to the **string**'s length) results in an **Index-OutOfRangeException**.*

Line 37 uses **String** method **CopyTo** to copy the characters of a **string** (**string1**) into a character array (**characterArray**). The first argument given to method **CopyTo** is the index from which the method begins copying characters in the **string**. The second argument is the character array into which the characters are copied. The third argument is the index specifying the location at which the method places the copied characters in the character array. The last argument is the number of characters that the method will copy from the **string**. Lines 40–41 append the **char** array contents to **string output** one character at a time.

13.5 Comparing Strings

The next two examples demonstrate the various methods that C# provides for comparing **string**s. To understand how one **string** can be "greater than" or "less than" another **string**, consider the process of alphabetizing a series of last names. The reader would, no doubt, place **"Jones"** before **"Smith"**, because the first letter of **"Jones"** comes before the first letter of **"Smith"** in the alphabet. The alphabet is more than just a set of 26 letters—it is an ordered list of characters in which each letter occurs in a specific position. For example, **z** is more than just a letter of the alphabet; **z** is specifically the twenty-sixth letter of the alphabet.

Computers can order characters alphabetically because the characters are represented internally as Unicode numeric codes. When comparing two **string**s, C# simply compares the numeric codes of the characters in the **string**s.

Class **String** provides several ways to compare **string**s. The application in Fig. 13.3 demonstrates the use of method **Equals**, method **CompareTo** and the equality operator (**==**).

The condition in the **if** structure (line 27) uses instance method **Equals** to compare **string1** and literal **string "hello"** to determine whether they are equal. Method **Equals** (inherited by **String** from class **Object**) tests any two objects for equality (i.e., checks whether the objects contain identical contents). The method returns **true** if the objects are equal and **false** otherwise. In this instance, the preceding condition returns **true**, because **string1** references **string** literal object **"hello"**. Method **Equals** uses a *lexicographical comparison*—the integer Unicode values that represent each character in each **string** are compared. Method **Equals** compares the numeric Unicode values that represent the characters in each **string**. A comparison of the **string "hello"** with the **string "HELLO"** would return **false**, because the numeric representations of lowercase letters are different from the numeric representations of corresponding uppercase letters.

The condition in the second **if** structure (line 33) uses the equality operator (**==**) to compare **string string1** with the literal **string "hello"** for equality. In C#, the equality operator also uses a lexicographical comparison to compare two **string**s. Thus, the condition in the **if** structure evaluates to **true**, because the values of **string1** and **"hello"** are equal. To compare the references of two **string**s, we must explicitly cast the **string**s to type **object** and use the equality operator (**==**).

```
1   // Fig. 13.3: StringCompare.cs
2   // Comparing strings.
3
4   using System;
5   using System.Windows.Forms;
6
7   // compare a number of strings
8   class StringCompare
9   {
10      // the main entry point for application
11      [STAThread]
12      static void Main( string[] args )
13      {
14          string string1 = "hello";
15          string string2 = "good bye";
16          string string3 = "Happy Birthday";
17          string string4 = "happy birthday";
18          string output;
19
20          // output values of four strings
21          output = "string1 = \"" + string1 + "\"" +
22              "\nstring2 = \"" + string2 + "\"" +
23              "\nstring3 = \"" + string3 + "\"" +
24              "\nstring4 = \"" + string4 + "\"\n\n";
25
26          // test for equality using Equals method
27          if ( string1.Equals( "hello" ) )
28              output += "string1 equals \"hello\"\n";
29          else
30              output += "string1 does not equal \"hello\"\n";
31
32          // test for equality with ==
33          if ( string1 == "hello" )
34              output += "string1 equals \"hello\"\n";
35          else
36              output += "string1 does not equal \"hello\"\n";
37
38          // test for equality comparing case
39          if ( String.Equals( string3, string4 ) )
40              output += "string3 equals string4\n";
41          else
42              output += "string3 does not equal string4\n";
43
```

Fig. 13.3 **String** test to determine equality. (Part 1 of 2.)

```
44          // test CompareTo
45          output += "\nstring1.CompareTo( string2 ) is " +
46              string1.CompareTo( string2 ) + "\n" +
47              "string2.CompareTo( string1 ) is " +
48              string2.CompareTo( string1 ) + "\n" +
49              "string1.CompareTo( string1 ) is " +
50              string1.CompareTo( string1 ) + "\n" +
51              "string3.CompareTo( string4 ) is " +
52              string3.CompareTo( string4 ) + "\n" +
53              "string4.CompareTo( string3 ) is " +
54              string4.CompareTo( string3 ) + "\n\n";
55
56          MessageBox.Show( output, "Demonstrating string " +
57              "comparisons", MessageBoxButtons.OK,
58              MessageBoxIcon.Information );
59
60      } // end method Main
61
62  } // end class StringCompare
```

Fig. 13.3   String test to determine equality. (Part 2 of 2.)

We present the test for **string** equality between **string3** and **string4** (line 39) to illustrate that comparisons are indeed case sensitive. Here, **static** method **Equals** (as opposed to the instance method in line 27) is used to compare the values of two **string**s. **"Happy Birthday"** does not equal **"happy birthday"**, so the condition of the **if** structure fails, and the message **"string3 does not equal string4"** is added to the output message (line 42).

Lines 46–54 use the **String** method **CompareTo** to compare **string**s. Method **CompareTo** returns **0** if the **string**s are equal, a **-1** if the **string** that invokes **CompareTo** is less than the **string** that is passed as an argument and a **1** if the **string** that invokes **CompareTo** is greater than the **string** that is passed as an argument. Method **CompareTo** uses a lexicographical comparison.

Notice that **CompareTo** considers **string3** to be larger than **string4**. The only difference between these two **string**s is that **string3** contains two uppercase letters. This example illustrates that an uppercase letter has a lower value in the Unicode character set than its corresponding lowercase letter.

The application in Fig. 13.4 shows how to test whether a **string** instance begins or ends with a given **string**. Method *StartsWith* determines whether a **string** instance starts with the **string** text passed to it as an argument. Method *EndsWith* determines whether a **string** instance ends with the **string** text passed to it as an argument. Application **StringStartEnd**'s **Main** method defines an array of **string**s (called **strings**), which contains **"started"**, **"starting"**, **"ended"** and **"ending"**. The remainder of method **Main** tests the elements of the array to determine whether they start or end with a particular set of characters.

Line 21 uses method **StartsWith**, which takes a **string** argument. The condition in the **if** structure determines whether the **string** at index **i** of the array starts with the characters **"st"**. If so, the method returns **true** and appends **strings[i]** to **string output** for display purposes.

Line 30 uses method **EndsWith**, which also takes a **string** argument. The condition in the **if** structure determines whether the **string** at index **i** of the array ends with the characters **"ed"**. If so, the method returns **true**, and **strings[i]** is appended to **string output** for display purposes.

```
1   // Fig. 13.4: StringStartEnd.cs
2   // Demonstrating StartsWith and EndsWith methods.
3
4   using System;
5   using System.Windows.Forms;
6
7   // testing StartsWith and EndsWith
8   class StringStartEnd
9   {
10     // the main entry point for application
11     [STAThread]
12     static void Main( string[] args )
13     {
14        string[] strings =
15              { "started", "starting", "ended", "ending" };
16        string output = "";
17
18        // test every string to see if it starts with "st"
19        for ( int i = 0; i < strings.Length; i++ )
20
21           if ( strings[ i ].StartsWith( "st" ) )
22              output += "\"" + strings[ i ] + "\"" +
23                 " starts with \"st\"\n";
24
25        output += "\n";
26
27        // test every string to see if it ends with "ed"
28        for ( int i = 0; i < strings.Length; i ++ )
29
30           if ( strings[ i ].EndsWith( "ed" ) )
31              output += "\"" + strings[ i ] + "\"" +
32                 " ends with \"ed\"\n";
33
```

Fig. 13.4 **StartsWith** and **EndsWith** methods. (Part 1 of 2.)

```
34            MessageBox.Show( output, "Demonstrating StartsWith and " +
35                "EndsWith methods", MessageBoxButtons.OK,
36                MessageBoxIcon.Information );
37
38        } // end method Main
39
40    } // end class StringStartEnd
```

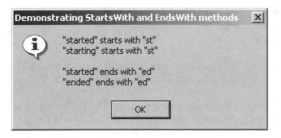

Fig. 13.4 **StartsWith** and **EndsWith** methods. (Part 2 of 2.)

13.6 String Method GetHashCode

Often, it is necessary to store **string**s and other data types in a manner that enables the information to be found quickly. One of the best ways to make information easily accessible is to store it in a hash table. A *hash table* stores an object by performing a special calculation on that object, which produces a *hash code*. The object then is stored at a location in the hash table determined by the calculated hash code. When a program needs to retrieve the information, the same calculation is performed, generating the same hash code. Any object can be stored in a hash table. Class **Object** defines method **GetHashCode** to perform the hash-code calculation. Although all classes inherit this method from class **Object**, it is recommended that they override **Object**'s default implementation. Class **String overrides** method **GetHashCode** to provide a good hash-code distribution based on the contents of the **string**. We will discuss hashing in detail in Chapter 21, FCL Collections.

The example in Fig. 13.5 demonstrates the application of the **GetHashCode** method to two **string**s (**"hello"** and **"Hello"**). Here, the hash-code value for each **string** is different. However, **string**s that are not identical can have the same hash-code value.

```
1   // Fig. 13.5: StringHashCode.cs
2   // Demonstrating method GetHashCode of class String.
3
4   using System;
5   using System.Windows.Forms;
6
```

Fig. 13.5 **GetHashCode** method demonstration. (Part 1 of 2.)

```
7     // testing the GetHashCode method
8     class StringHashCode
9     {
10        // the main entry point for application
11        [STAThread]
12        static void Main( string[] args )
13        {
14
15            string string1 = "hello";
16            string string2 = "Hello";
17            string output;
18
19            output = "The hash code for \"" + string1 +
20               "\" is " + string1.GetHashCode() + "\n";
21
22            output += "The hash code for \"" + string2 +
23               "\" is " + string2.GetHashCode() + "\n";
24
25            MessageBox.Show( output, "Demonstrating String " +
26               "method GetHashCode", MessageBoxButtons.OK,
27               MessageBoxIcon.Information );
28
29        } // end method Main
30
31    } // end class StringHashCode
```

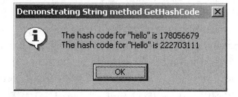

Fig. 13.5   GetHashCode method demonstration. (Part 2 of 2.)

13.7 Locating Characters and Substrings in **Strings**

In many applications, it is necessary to search for a character or set of characters in a **string**. For example, a programmer creating a word processor would want to provide capabilities for searching through documents. The application in Fig. 13.6 demonstrates some of the many versions of **String** methods *IndexOf*, *IndexOfAny*, *LastIndexOf* and *LastIndexOfAny*, which search for a specified character or substring in a **string**. We perform all searches in this example on the **string letters** (initialized with **"abcdefghijklmabcdefghijklm"**) located in method **Main** of class **StringIndexMethods**.

```
1     // Fig. 13.6: StringIndexMethods.cs
2     // Using String searching methods.
3
```

Fig. 13.6   Searching for characters and substrings in **string**s. (Part 1 of 3.)

```
 4    using System;
 5    using System.Windows.Forms;
 6
 7    // testing indexing capabilities of strings
 8    class StringIndexMethods
 9    {
10        // the main entry point for application
11        [STAThread]
12        static void Main( string[] args )
13        {
14            string letters = "abcdefghijklmabcdefghijklm";
15            string output = "";
16            char[] searchLetters = { 'c', 'a', '$' };
17
18            // test IndexOf to locate a character in a string
19            output += "'c' is located at index " +
20                letters.IndexOf( 'c' );
21
22            output += "\n'a' is located at index " +
23                letters.IndexOf( 'a', 1 );
24
25            output += "\n'$' is located at index " +
26                letters.IndexOf( '$', 3, 5 );
27
28            // test LastIndexOf to find a character in a string
29            output += "\n\nLast 'c' is located at " +
30                "index " + letters.LastIndexOf( 'c' );
31
32            output += "\nLast 'a' is located at index " +
33                letters.LastIndexOf( 'a', 25 );
34
35            output += "\nLast '$' is located at index " +
36                letters.LastIndexOf( '$', 15, 5 );
37
38            // test IndexOf to locate a substring in a string
39            output += "\n\n\"def\" is located at" +
40                " index " + letters.IndexOf( "def" );
41
42            output += "\n\"def\" is located at index " +
43                letters.IndexOf( "def", 7 );
44
45            output += "\n\"hello\" is located at index " +
46                letters.IndexOf( "hello", 5, 15 );
47
48            // test LastIndexOf to find a substring in a string
49            output += "\n\nLast \"def\" is located at index " +
50                letters.LastIndexOf( "def" );
51
52            output += "\nLast \"def\" is located at " +
53                letters.LastIndexOf( "def", 25 );
54
55            output += "\nLast \"hello\" is located at index " +
56                letters.LastIndexOf( "hello", 20, 15 );
```

Fig. 13.6   Searching for characters and substrings in **string**s. (Part 2 of 3.)

```
57
58        // test IndexOfAny to find first occurrence of character
59        // in array
60        output += "\n\nFirst occurrence of 'c', 'a', '$' is " +
61           "located at " + letters.IndexOfAny( searchLetters );
62
63        output += "\nFirst occurrence of 'c, 'a' or '$' is " +
64           "located at " + letters.IndexOfAny( searchLetters, 7 );
65
66        output += "\nFirst occurrence of 'c', 'a' or '$' is " +
67           "located at " + letters.IndexOfAny( searchLetters, 20, 5 );
68
69        // test LastIndexOfAny to find last occurrence of character
70        // in array
71        output += "\n\nLast occurrence of 'c', 'a' or '$' is " +
72           "located at " + letters.LastIndexOfAny( searchLetters );
73
74        output += "\nLast occurrence of 'c', 'a' or '$' is " +
75           "located at " + letters.LastIndexOfAny( searchLetters, 1 );
76
77        output += "\nLast occurrence of 'c', 'a' or '$' is " +
78           "located at " + letters.LastIndexOfAny(
79           searchLetters, 25, 5 );
80
81        MessageBox.Show( output,
82           "Demonstrating class index methods",
83           MessageBoxButtons.OK, MessageBoxIcon.Information );
84
85     } // end method Main
86
87  } // end class StringIndexMethods
```

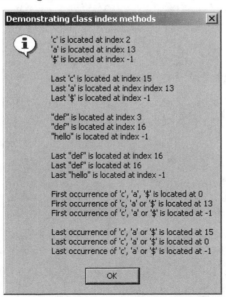

Fig. 13.6   Searching for characters and substrings in **string**s. (Part 3 of 3.)

Lines 20, 23 and 26 use method **IndexOf** to locate the first occurrence of a character or substring in a **string**. If **IndexOf** finds a character, **IndexOf** returns the index of the specified character in the **string**; otherwise, **IndexOf** returns **−1**. The expression on line 23 uses a version of method **IndexOf** that takes two arguments—the character to search for and the starting index at which the search of the **string** should begin. The method does not examine any characters that occur prior to the starting index (in this case **1**). The expression in line 26 uses another version of method **IndexOf** that takes three arguments—the character to search for, the index at which to start searching and the number of characters to search.

Lines 30, 33 and 36 use method **LastIndexOf** to locate the last occurrence of a character in a **string**. Method **LastIndexOf** performs the search from the end of the **string** toward the beginning of the **string**. If method **LastIndexOf** finds the character, **LastIndexOf** returns the index of the specified character in the **string**; otherwise, **LastIndexOf** returns **−1**. There are three versions of **LastIndexOf** that search for characters in a **string**. The expression in line 30 uses the version of method **LastIndexOf** that takes as an argument the character for which to search. The expression in line 33 uses the version of method **LastIndexOf** that takes two arguments—the character for which to search and the highest index from which to begin searching backward for the character. The expression in line 36 uses a third version of method **LastIndexOf** that takes three arguments—the character for which to search, the starting index from which to start searching backward and the number of characters (the portion of the **string**) to search.

Lines 40–56 use versions of **IndexOf** and **LastIndexOf** that take a **string** instead of a character as the first argument. These versions of the methods perform identically to those described above except that they search for sequences of characters (or substrings) that are specified by their **string** arguments.

Lines 61–79 use methods **IndexOfAny** and **LastIndexOfAny**, which take an array of characters as the first argument. These versions of the methods also perform identically to those described above except that they return the index of the first occurrence of any of the characters in the character array argument.

Common Programming Error 13.2

*In the overloaded methods **LastIndexOf** and **LastIndexOfAny** that take three parameters, the second argument must always be greater than or equal to the third argument. This might seem counterintuitive, but remember that the search moves from the end of the string toward the start of the string.*

13.8 Extracting Substrings from Strings

Class **String** provides two *Substring* methods, which are used to create a new **string** by copying part of an existing **string**. Each method returns a new **string**. The application in Fig. 13.7 demonstrates the use of both methods.

```
1   // Fig. 13.7: SubString.cs
2   // Demonstrating the String Substring method.
3
```

Fig. 13.7   Substrings generated from **string**s. (Part 1 of 2.)

```
4  using System;
5  using System.Windows.Forms;
6
7  // creating substrings
8  class SubString
9  {
10     // The main entry point for the application.
11     [STAThread]
12     static void Main( string[] args )
13     {
14        string letters = "abcdefghijklmabcdefghijklm";
15        string output = "";
16
17        // invoke Substring method and pass it one parameter
18        output += "Substring from index 20 to end is \"" +
19           letters.Substring( 20 ) + "\"\n";
20
21        // invoke Substring method and pass it two parameters
22        output += "Substring from index 0 to 6 is \"" +
23           letters.Substring( 0, 6 ) + "\"";
24
25        MessageBox.Show( output,
26           "Demonstrating String method Substring",
27           MessageBoxButtons.OK, MessageBoxIcon.Information );
28
29     } // end method Main
30
31  } // end class SubString
```

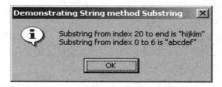

Fig. 13.7 Substrings generated from **string**s. (Part 2 of 2.)

The statement in line 19 uses the **Substring** method that takes one **int** argument. The argument specifies the starting index from which the method copies characters in the original **string**. The substring returned contains a copy of the characters from the starting index to the end of the **string**. If the index specified in the argument is outside the bounds of the **string**, the program throws an **ArgumentOutOfRangeException**.

The second version of method **Substring** (line 23) takes two **int** arguments. The first argument specifies the starting index from which the method copies characters from the original **string**. The second argument specifies the length of the substring to be copied. The substring returned contains a copy of the specified characters from the original **string**.

13.9 Concatenating Strings

The **+** operator (discussed in Chapter 3, Introduction to C# Programming) is not the only way to perform **string** concatenation. The **static** method *Concat* of class **String** (Fig. 13.8) concatenates two **string**s and returns a new **string** containing the combined characters from both original **string**s. Line 23 appends the characters from **string2** to the end of **string1**, using method **Concat**. The statement on line 23 does not modify the original **string**s.

13.10 Miscellaneous **String** Methods

Class **String** provides several methods that return modified copies of **string**s. The application in Fig. 13.9 demonstrates the use of these methods, which include **String** methods *Replace*, *ToLower*, *ToUpper*, *Trim* and *ToString*.

```
1   // Fig. 13.8: SubConcatenation.cs
2   // Demonstrating String class Concat method.
3
4   using System;
5   using System.Windows.Forms;
6
7   // concatenates strings using String method Concat
8   class StringConcatenation
9   {
10      // the main entry point for application
11      [STAThread]
12      static void Main( string[] args )
13      {
14         string string1 = "Happy ";
15         string string2 = "Birthday";
16         string output;
17
18         output = "string1 = \"" + string1 + "\"\n" +
19            "string2 = \"" + string2 + "\"";
20
21         output +=
22            "\n\nResult of String.Concat( string1, string2 ) = " +
23            String.Concat( string1, string2 );
24
25         output += "\nstring1 after concatenation = " + string1;
26
27         MessageBox.Show( output,
28            "Demonstrating String method Concat",
29            MessageBoxButtons.OK, MessageBoxIcon.Information );
30
31      } // end method Main
32
33   } // end class StringConcatenation
```

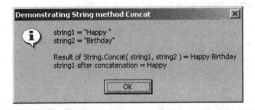

Fig. 13.8   **Concat static** method.

Line 27 uses **String** method **Replace** to return a new **string**, replacing every occurrence in **string1** of character **'e'** with character **'E'**. Method **Replace** takes two arguments—a **string** for which to search and another **string** with which to replace all matching occurrences of the first argument. The original **string** remains unchanged. If there are no occurrences of the first argument in the **string**, the method returns the original **string**.

String method **ToUpper** generates a new **string** (line 31) that replaces any lowercase letters in **string1** with their uppercase equivalent. The method returns a new **string** containing the converted **string**; the original **string** remains unchanged. If there are no characters to convert to uppercase, the method returns the original **string**. Line 32 uses **String** method **ToLower** to return a new **string** in which any uppercase letters in **string2** are replaced by their lowercase equivalents. The original **string** is unchanged. As with **ToUpper**, if there are no characters to convert to lowercase, method **ToLower** returns the original **string**.

```
1   // Fig. 13.9: StringMiscellaneous2.cs
2   // Demonstrating String methods Replace, ToLower, ToUpper, Trim
3   // and ToString.
4
5   using System;
6   using System.Windows.Forms;
7
8   // creates strings using methods Replace, ToLower, ToUpper, Trim
9   class StringMethods2
10  {
11     // the main entry point for application
12     [STAThread]
13     static void Main( string[] args )
14     {
15        string string1 = "cheers!";
16        string string2 = "GOOD BYE ";
17        string string3 = "   spaces   ";
18        string output;
19
20        output = "string1 = \"" + string1 + "\"\n" +
21           "string2 = \"" + string2 + "\"\n" +
22           "string3 = \"" + string3 + "\"";
23
24        // call method Replace
25        output +=
26           "\n\nReplacing \"e\" with \"E\" in string1: \"" +
27           string1.Replace( 'e', 'E' ) + "\"";
28
29        // call ToLower and ToUpper
30        output += "\n\nstring1.ToUpper() = \"" +
31           string1.ToUpper() + "\"\nstring2.ToLower() = \"" +
32           string2.ToLower() + "\"";
33
```

Fig. 13.9 **String** methods **Replace**, **ToLower**, **ToUpper**, **Trim** and **ToString**. (Part 1 of 2.)

```
34          // call Trim method
35          output += "\n\nstring3 after trim = \"" +
36              string3.Trim() + "\"";
37
38          // call ToString method
39          output += "\n\nstring1 = \"" + string1.ToString() + "\"";
40
41          MessageBox.Show( output,
42              "Demonstrating various string methods",
43              MessageBoxButtons.OK, MessageBoxIcon.Information );
44
45      } // end method Main
46
47   } // end class StringMethods2
```

Fig. 13.9 **String** methods **Replace**, **ToLower**, **ToUpper**, **Trim** and **ToString**. (Part 2 of 2.)

Line 36 uses **String** method **Trim** to remove all whitespace characters that appear at the beginning and end of a **string**. Without otherwise altering the original **string**, the method returns a new **string** that contains the **string**, but omits leading or trailing whitespace characters. Another version of method **Trim** takes a character array and returns a **string** that does not contain the characters in the array argument.

Line 39 uses class **String**'s method **ToString** to show that the various other methods employed in this application have not modified **string1**. Why is the **ToString** method provided for class **String**? In C#, all objects are derived from class **Object**, which defines **virtual** method **ToString**. Thus, method **ToString** can be called to obtain a **string** representation of any object. If a class that inherits from **Object** (such as **String**) does not override method **ToString**, the class uses the default version from class **Object**, which returns a **string** consisting of the object's class name. Classes usually override method **ToString** to express the contents of an object as text. Class **String** overrides method **ToString** so that, instead of returning the class name, it simply returns the **string**.

13.11 Class **StringBuilder**

The **String** class provides many capabilities for processing **string**s. However a **string**'s contents can never change. Operations that seem to concatenate **string**s are in fact assigning **string** references to newly created **string**s (e.g., the **+=** operator creates a new **string** and assigns the initial **string** reference to the newly created **string**).

The next several sections discuss the features of class **StringBuilder** (namespace **System.Text**), used to create and manipulate dynamic string information—i.e., mutable strings. Every **StringBuilder** can store a certain number of characters that is specified by its capacity. Exceeding the capacity of a **StringBuilder** causes the capacity to expand to accommodate the additional characters. As we will see, members of class **StringBuilder**, such as methods **Append** and **AppendFormat**, can be used for concatenation like the operators **+** and **+=** for class **String**.

Software Engineering Observation 13.2

*Objects of class **String** are constant strings, whereas object of class **StringBuilder** are mutable strings. C# can perform certain optimizations involving **string**s (such as the sharing of one **string** among multiple references), because it knows these objects will not change.*

Performance Tip 13.2

*When given the choice between using a **string** to represent a string and using a **StringBuilder** object to represent that string, always use a **string** if the contents of the object will not change. When appropriate, using **string**s instead of **StringBuilder** objects improves performance.*

Class **StringBuilder** provides six overloaded constructors. Class **StringBuilderConstructor** (Fig. 13.10) demonstrates the use of three of these overloaded constructors.

```
1    // Fig. 13.10: StringBuilderConstructor.cs
2    // Demonstrating StringBuilder class constructors.
3
4    using System;
5    using System.Windows.Forms;
6    using System.Text;
7
8    // creates three StringBuilder with three constructors
9    class StringBuilderConstructor
10   {
11       // the main entry point for application
12       [STAThread]
13       static void Main( string[] args )
14       {
15           StringBuilder buffer1, buffer2, buffer3;
16           string output;
17
18           buffer1 = new StringBuilder();
19           buffer2 = new StringBuilder( 10 );
20           buffer3 = new StringBuilder( "hello" );
21
22           output = "buffer1 = \"" + buffer1.ToString() + "\"\n";
23
24           output += "buffer2 = \"" + buffer2.ToString() + "\"\n";
25
```

Fig. 13.10 StringBuilder class constructors. (Part 1 of 2.)

```
26              output += "buffer3 = \"" + buffer3.ToString() + "\"\n";
27
28          MessageBox.Show( output,
29              "Demonstrating StringBuilder class constructors",
30                  MessageBoxButtons.OK, MessageBoxIcon.Information );
31
32      } // end method Main
33
34  } // end class StringBuilderConstructor
```

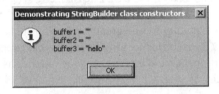

Fig. 13.10 `StringBuilder` class constructors. (Part 2 of 2.)

Line 18 employs the no-argument **StringBuilder** constructor to create a **StringBuilder** that contains no characters and has a default initial capacity of 16 characters. Line 19 uses the **StringBuilder** constructor that takes an **int** argument to create a **StringBuilder** that contains no characters and has the initial capacity specified in the **int** argument (i.e., **10**). Line 20 uses the **StringBuilder** constructor that takes a **string** argument to create a **StringBuilder** containing the characters of the **string** argument. The initial capacity is the smallest power of two greater than the number of characters in the **string** passed as an argument.

Lines 22–26 use **StringBuilder** method **ToString** to obtain a **string** representation of the **StringBuilder**s' contents. This method returns the **StringBuilder**s' underlying string.

13.12 StringBuilder Indexer, Length and Capacity Properties, and EnsureCapacity Method

Class **StringBuilder** provides the *Length* and *Capacity* properties to return the number of characters currently in a **StringBuilder** and the number of characters that a **StringBuilder** can store without allocating more memory, respectively. These properties also can increase or decrease the length or the capacity of the **StringBuilder**.

Method *EnsureCapacity* allows programmers to guarantee that a **StringBuilder** has a capacity that reduces the number of times the capacity must be increased. Method **EnsureCapacity** doubles the **StringBuilder** instance's current capacity. If this doubled value is greater than the value that the programmer wishes to ensure, it becomes the new capacity. Otherwise, **EnsureCapacity** alters the capacity to make it one more than the requested number. For example, if the current capacity is 17 and we wish to make it 40, 17 multiplied by 2 is not greater than 40, so the call will result in a new capacity of 41. If the current capacity is 23 and we wish to make it 40, 23 will be multiplied by 2 to result in a new capacity of 46. Both 41 and 46 are greater than 40, and so a capacity of 40 is indeed ensured by method **EnsureCapacity**. The program in Fig. 13.11 demonstrates the use of these methods and properties.

The program contains one **StringBuilder**, called **buffer**. Lines 15–16 of the program use the **StringBuilder** constructor that takes a **string** argument to instantiate the **StringBuilder** and initialize its value to **"Hello, how are you?"**. Lines 19–21 append to **output** the content, length and capacity of the **StringBuilder**. In the output window, notice that the capacity of the **StringBuilder** is initially 32. Remember, the **StringBuilder** constructor that takes a **string** argument creates a **StringBuilder** object with an initial capacity that is the smallest power of two greater than the number of characters in the **string** passed as an argument.

Line 24 expands the capacity of the **StringBuilder** to a minimum of 75 characters. The current capacity (**32**) multiplied by two is less than 75, so method **EnsureCapacity** increases the capacity to one greater than 75 (i.e., 76). If new characters are added to a **StringBuilder** so that its length exceeds its capacity, the capacity grows to accommodate the additional characters in the same manner as if method **EnsureCapacity** had been called.

```
1   // Fig. 13.11: StringBuilderFeatures.cs
2   // Demonstrating some features of class StringBuilder.
3
4   using System;
5   using System.Windows.Forms;
6   using System.Text;
7
8   // uses some of class StringBuilder's methods
9   class StringBuilderFeatures
10  {
11     // the main entry point for application
12     [STAThread]
13     static void Main( string[] args )
14     {
15        StringBuilder buffer =
16           new StringBuilder( "Hello, how are you?" );
17
18        // use Length and Capacity properties
19        string output = "buffer = " + buffer.ToString() +
20           "\nLength = " + buffer.Length +
21           "\nCapacity = " + buffer.Capacity;
22
23        // use EnsureCapacity method
24        buffer.EnsureCapacity( 75 );
25
26        output += "\n\nNew capacity = " +
27           buffer.Capacity;
28
29        // truncate StringBuilder by setting Length property
30        buffer.Length = 10;
31
32        output += "\n\nNew length = " +
33           buffer.Length + "\nbuffer = ";
34
```

Fig. 13.11 **StringBuilder** size manipulation. (Part 1 of 2.)

```
35          // use StringBuilder indexer
36          for ( int i = 0; i < buffer.Length; i++ )
37             output += buffer[ i ];
38
39          MessageBox.Show( output, "StringBuilder features",
40             MessageBoxButtons.OK, MessageBoxIcon.Information );
41
42       } // end method Main
43
44    } // end class StringBuilderFeatures
```

Fig. 13.11 StringBuilder size manipulation. (Part 2 of 2.)

Line 30 uses **Length**'s **Set** accessor to set the length of the **StringBuilder** to **10**. If the specified length is less than the current number of characters in the **StringBuilder**, the contents of **StringBuilder** are truncated to the specified length (i.e., the program discards all characters in the **StringBuilder** that occur after the specified length). If the specified length is greater than the number of characters currently in the **StringBuilder**, null characters (characters with the numeric representation **0** that signal the end of a **string**) are appended to the **StringBuilder** until the total number of characters in the **StringBuilder** is equal to the specified length.

Common Programming Error 13.3

*Assigning **null** to a **string** reference can lead to logic errors. The keyword **null** is a null reference, not a **string**. Do not confuse **null** with the empty string, **""** (the **string** that is of length 0 and contains no characters).*

13.13 StringBuilder Append and AppendFormat Methods

Class **StringBuilder** provides 19 overloaded *Append* methods that allow various data-type values to be added to the end of a **StringBuilder**. C# provides versions for each of the primitive data types and for character arrays, **String**s and **Object**s. (Remember that method **ToString** produces a **string** representation of any **Object**.) Each of the methods takes an argument, converts it to a **string** and appends it to the **StringBuilder**. Figure 13.12 demonstrates the use of several **Append** methods.

Lines 29–47 use 10 different overloaded **Append** methods to attach the objects created in lines 15–26 to the end of the **StringBuilder**. **Append** behaves similarly to the **+** operator which is used with **string**s. Just as **+** seems to append objects to a **string**, method **Append** can append data types to a **StringBuilder**'s underlying string.

Class **StringBuilder** also provides method ***AppendFormat***, which converts a **string** to a specified format and then appends it to the **StringBuilder**. The example in Fig. 13.13 demonstrates the use of this method.

```
1   // Fig. 13.12: StringBuilderAppend.cs
2   // Demonstrating StringBuilder Append methods.
3
4   using System;
5   using System.Windows.Forms;
6   using System.Text;
7
8   // testing the Append method
9   class StringBuilderAppend
10  {
11     // the main entry point for application
12     [STAThread]
13     static void Main( string[] args )
14     {
15        object objectValue = "hello";
16        string stringValue = "good bye";
17        char[] characterArray = { 'a', 'b', 'c', 'd',
18                                  'e', 'f' };
19
20        bool booleanValue = true;
21        char characterValue = 'Z';
22        int integerValue = 7;
23        long longValue = 1000000;
24        float floatValue = 2.5F;
25        double doubleValue = 33.333;
26        StringBuilder buffer = new StringBuilder();
27
28        // use method Append to append values to buffer
29        buffer.Append( objectValue );
30        buffer.Append( "  " );
31        buffer.Append( stringValue );
32        buffer.Append( "  " );
33        buffer.Append( characterArray );
34        buffer.Append( "  " );
35        buffer.Append( characterArray, 0, 3 );
36        buffer.Append( "  " );
37        buffer.Append( booleanValue );
38        buffer.Append( "  " );
39        buffer.Append( characterValue );
40        buffer.Append( "  " );
41        buffer.Append( integerValue );
42        buffer.Append( "  " );
43        buffer.Append( longValue );
44        buffer.Append( "  " );
45        buffer.Append( floatValue );
46        buffer.Append( "  " );
47        buffer.Append( doubleValue );
48
```

Fig. 13.12 Append methods of **StringBuilder**. (Part 1 of 2.)

```
49            MessageBox.Show( "buffer = " + buffer.ToString(),
50               "Demonstrating StringBuilder append method",
51               MessageBoxButtons.OK, MessageBoxIcon.Information );
52
53        } // end method Main
54
55    } // end class StringBuilderAppend
```

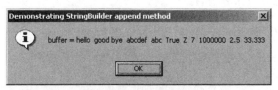

Fig. 13.12 Append methods of **StringBuilder**. (Part 2 of 2.)

```
1    // Fig. 13.13: StringBuilderAppendFormat.cs
2    // Demonstrating method AppendFormat.
3
4    using System;
5    using System.Windows.Forms;
6    using System.Text;
7
8    // use the AppendFormat method
9    class StringBuilderAppendFormat
10   {
11       // the main entry point for application
12       [STAThread]
13       static void Main( string[] args )
14       {
15          StringBuilder buffer = new StringBuilder();
16          string string1, string2;
17
18          // formatted string
19          string1 = "This {0} costs: {1:C}.\n";
20
21          // string1 argument array
22          object[] objectArray = new object[ 2 ];
23
24          objectArray[ 0 ] = "car";
25          objectArray[ 1 ] = 1234.56;
26
27          // append to buffer formatted string with argument
28          buffer.AppendFormat( string1, objectArray );
29
30          // formatted string
31          string2 = "Number:{0:d3}.\n" +
32             "Number right aligned with spaces:{0, 4}.\n" +
33             "Number left aligned with spaces:{0, -4}.";
34
```

Fig. 13.13 StringBuilder's **AppendFormat** method. (Part 1 of 2.)

```
35          // append to buffer formatted string with argument
36          buffer.AppendFormat( string2, 5 );
37
38          // display formatted strings
39          MessageBox.Show( buffer.ToString(), "Using AppendFormat",
40             MessageBoxButtons.OK, MessageBoxIcon.Information );
41
42      } // end method Main
43
44   } // end class StringBuilderAppendFormat
```

Fig. 13.13 **StringBuilder**'s **AppendFormat** method. (Part 2 of 2.)

Line 19 creates a **string** that contains formatting information. The information enclosed within the braces determines how to format a specific piece of information. Formats have the form **{X[,Y][:FormatString]}**, where **X** is the number of the argument to be formatted, counting from zero. **Y** is an optional argument, which can be positive or negative, indicating how many characters should be in the result of formatting. If the resulting **string** is less than the number **Y**, the **string** will be padded with spaces to make up for the difference. A positive integer aligns the **string** to the right; a negative integer aligns it to the left. The optional **FormatString** applies a particular format to the argument: Currency, decimal or scientific, among others. In this case, "**{0}**" means the first argument will be printed out. "**{1:C}**" specifies that the second argument will be formatted as a currency value.

Line 28 shows a version of **AppendFormat**, which takes two parameters—a **string** specifying the format and an array of objects to serve as the arguments to the format **string**. The argument referred to by "**{0}**" is in the object array at index **0**, and so on.

Lines 31–33 define another **string** used for formatting. The first format "**{0:D3}**" specifies that the first argument will be formatted as a three-digit decimal, meaning any number that has fewer than three digits will have leading zeros placed in front to make up the difference. The next format, "**{0, 4}**" specifies that the formatted **string** should have four characters and should be right aligned. The third format, "**{0, -4}**" specifies that the **string**s should be aligned to the left. For more formatting options, please refer to the documentation.

Line 36 uses a version of **AppendFormat** that takes two parameters: A **string** containing a format and an object to which the format is applied. In this case, the object is the number **5**. The output of Fig. 13.13 displays the result of applying these two versions of **AppendFormat** with their respective arguments.

13.14 `StringBuilder` Insert, Remove and `Replace` Methods

Class **StringBuilder** provides 18 overloaded *Insert* methods to allow various data-type values to be inserted at any position in a **StringBuilder**. The class provides versions for each of the primitive data types and for character arrays, **String**s and **Object**s. (Remember that method **ToString** produces a **string** representation of any **Object**.) Each method takes its second argument, converts it to a **string** and inserts the **string** into the **StringBuilder** in front of the index specified by the first argument. The index specified by the first argument must be greater than or equal to **0** and less than the length of the **StringBuilder**; otherwise, the program throws an **ArgumentOutOfRange-Exception**.

Class **StringBuilder** also provides method *Remove* for deleting any portion of a **StringBuilder**. Method **Remove** takes two arguments—the index at which to begin deletion and the number of characters to delete. The sum of the starting subscript and the number of characters to be deleted must always be less than the length of the **String-Builder**; otherwise, the program throws an **ArgumentOutOfRangeException**. The **Insert** and **Remove** methods are demonstrated in Fig. 13.14.

```
1   // Fig. 13.14: StringBuilderInsertRemove.cs
2   // Demonstrating methods Insert and Remove of the
3   // StringBuilder class.
4
5   using System;
6   using System.Windows.Forms;
7   using System.Text;
8
9   // test the Insert and Remove methods
10  class StringBuilderInsertRemove
11  {
12     // the main entry point for application
13     [STAThread]
14     static void Main( string[] args )
15     {
16        object objectValue = "hello";
17        string stringValue = "good bye";
18        char[] characterArray = { 'a', 'b', 'c',
19                                  'd', 'e', 'f' };
20
21        bool booleanValue = true;
22        char characterValue = 'K';
23        int integerValue = 7;
24        long longValue = 10000000;
25        float floatValue = 2.5F;
26        double doubleValue = 12.345;
27        StringBuilder buffer = new StringBuilder();
28        string output;
29
30        // insert values into buffer
31        buffer.Insert(0, objectValue);
```

Fig. 13.14 **StringBuilder** text insertion and removal. (Part 1 of 2.)

```
32              buffer.Insert(0, "  ");
33              buffer.Insert(0, stringValue);
34              buffer.Insert(0, "  ");
35              buffer.Insert(0, characterArray);
36              buffer.Insert(0, "  ");
37              buffer.Insert(0, booleanValue);
38              buffer.Insert(0, "  ");
39              buffer.Insert(0, characterValue);
40              buffer.Insert(0, "  ");
41              buffer.Insert(0, integerValue);
42              buffer.Insert(0, "  ");
43              buffer.Insert(0, longValue);
44              buffer.Insert(0, "  ");
45              buffer.Insert(0, floatValue);
46              buffer.Insert(0, "  ");
47              buffer.Insert(0, doubleValue);
48              buffer.Insert(0, "  ");
49
50          output = "buffer after inserts: \n" +
51              buffer.ToString() + "\n\n";
52
53          buffer.Remove( 10, 1 ); // delete 2 in 2.5
54          buffer.Remove( 2, 4 );  // delete 12.3 in 12.345
55
56          output += "buffer after Removes:\n" +
57              buffer.ToString();
58
59          MessageBox.Show( output, "Demonstrating StringBuilder " +
60              "Insert and Remove methods", MessageBoxButtons.OK,
61              MessageBoxIcon.Information );
62
63      } // end method Main
64
65  } // end class StringBuilderInsertRemove
```

Fig. 13.14 StringBuilder text insertion and removal. (Part 2 of 2.)

Another useful method included with **StringBuilder** is **Replace**. **Replace** searches for a specified **string** or character and substitutes another **string** or character in its place. Figure 13.15 demonstrates this method.

```
1   // Fig. 13.15: StringBuilderReplace.cs
2   // Demonstrating method Replace.
3
```

Fig. 13.15 StringBuilder text replacement. (Part 1 of 2.)

```
4   using System;
5   using System.Windows.Forms;
6   using System.Text;
7
8   // testing the Replace method
9   class StringBuilderReplace
10  {
11      // the main entry point for application
12      [STAThread]
13      static void Main( string[] args )
14      {
15          StringBuilder builder1 =
16              new StringBuilder( "Happy Birthday Jane" );
17
18          StringBuilder builder2 =
19              new StringBuilder( "good bye greg" );
20
21          string output = "Before replacements:\n" +
22              builder1.ToString() + "\n" + builder2.ToString();
23
24          builder1.Replace( "Jane", "Greg" );
25          builder2.Replace( 'g', 'G', 0, 5 );
26
27          output += "\n\nAfter replacements:\n" +
28              builder1.ToString() + "\n" + builder2.ToString();
29
30          MessageBox.Show( output,
31              "Using StringBuilder method Replace",
32              MessageBoxButtons.OK, MessageBoxIcon.Information );
33
34      } // end method Main
35
36  } // end class StringBuilderReplace
```

Fig. 13.15 StringBuilder text replacement. (Part 2 of 2.)

Line 24 uses method **Replace** to replace all instances of the **string "Jane"** with the **string "Greg"** in **builder1**. Another overload of this method takes two characters as parameters and replaces each occurrence of the first with one of the second. Line 25 uses an overload of **Replace** that takes four parameters, the first two of which are characters and the second two of which are **int**s. The method replaces all instances of the first character with the second, beginning at the index specified by the first **int** and continuing for a count specified by the second. Thus, in this case, **Replace** looks through only five characters starting with the character at index **0**. As the outputs illustrates, this version of

Replace replaces **g** with **G** in the word **"good"**, but not in **"greg"**. This is because the **g**s in **"greg"** do not fall in the range indicated by the **int** arguments (i.e., between indexes **0** and **4**).

13.15 Char Methods

C# provides a data type, called a *structure*, that is similar to a class. Although structures and classes are comparable in many ways, structures are a value type. Like classes, structures include methods and properties. Both use the same modifiers (such as **public**, **private** and **protected**) and access members via the member access operator (**.**). However, classes are created by using the keyword **class**, but structures are created using the keyword *struct*.

Many of the primitive data types that we have used in this book are actually aliases for different structures. For instance, an **int** is defined by structure **System.Int32**, a **Long** by **System.Int64**, and so on. These structures are derived from class *ValueType*, which in turn is derived from class **Object**. In this section, we present structure *Char*, which is the structure for characters.

Most **Char** methods are **static**, take at least one character argument and perform either a test or a manipulation on the character. We present several of these methods in the next example. Figure 13.16 demonstrates **static** methods that test characters to determine whether they are of a specific character type and **static** methods that perform case conversions on characters.

This Windows application contains a prompt, a **TextBox** into which the user can input a character, a button that the user can press after entering a character and a second **TextBox** that displays the output of our analysis. When the user clicks the **Analyze Character** button, event handler **analyzeButton_Click** (lines 32–37) is invoked. This method converts the entered data from a **string** to a **Char**, using method **Convert.ToChar** (line 35). On line 36, we call method **BuildOutput**, which is defined in lines 40–72.

Line 45 uses **Char** method *IsDigit* to determine whether character **input-Character** is defined as a digit. If so, the method returns **true**; otherwise, it returns **false**.

Line 48 uses **Char** method *IsLetter* to determine whether character **inputCharacter** is a letter. If so, the method returns **true**; otherwise, it returns **false**. Line 51 uses **Char** method *IsLetterOrDigit* to determine whether character **inputCharacter** is a letter or a digit. If so, the method returns **true**; otherwise, it returns **false**.

```
1   // Fig. 13.16: CharMethods.cs
2   // Demonstrates static character testing methods
3   // from Char structure
4
5   using System;
6   using System.Drawing;
7   using System.Collections;
8   using System.ComponentModel;
9   using System.Windows.Forms;
10  using System.Data;
```

Fig. 13.16 **Char**'s **static** character-testing methods and case-conversion methods. (Part 1 of 3.)

```
11
12    // Form displays information about specific characters.
13    public class StaticCharMethods : System.Windows.Forms.Form
14    {
15       private System.Windows.Forms.Label enterLabel;
16       private System.Windows.Forms.TextBox inputTextBox;
17       private System.Windows.Forms.Button analyzeButton;
18       private System.Windows.Forms.TextBox outputTextBox;
19
20       private System.ComponentModel.Container components = null;
21
22       // the main entry point for application
23       [STAThread]
24       static void Main()
25       {
26          Application.Run( new StaticCharMethods() );
27       }
28
29       // Visual Studio .NET generated code
30
31       // handle analyzeButton_Click
32       private void analyzeButton_Click(
33          object sender, System.EventArgs e )
34       {
35          char character = Convert.ToChar( inputTextBox.Text );
36          BuildOutput( character );
37       }
38
39       // display character information in outputTextBox
40       private void BuildOutput( char inputCharacter )
41       {
42          string output;
43
44          output = "is digit: " +
45             Char.IsDigit( inputCharacter ) + "\r\n";
46
47          output += "is letter: " +
48             Char.IsLetter( inputCharacter ) + "\r\n";
49
50          output += "is letter or digit: " +
51             Char.IsLetterOrDigit( inputCharacter ) + "\r\n";
52
53          output += "is lower case: " +
54             Char.IsLower( inputCharacter ) + "\r\n";
55
56          output += "is upper case: " +
57             Char.IsUpper( inputCharacter ) + "\r\n";
58
59          output += "to upper case: " +
60             Char.ToUpper( inputCharacter ) + "\r\n";
61
```

Fig. 13.16 Char's static character-testing methods and case-conversion methods. (Part 2 of 3.)

```
62              output += "to lower case: " +
63                  Char.ToLower( inputCharacter ) + "\r\n";
64
65              output += "is punctuation: " +
66                  Char.IsPunctuation( inputCharacter ) + "\r\n";
67
68              output += "is symbol: " + Char.IsSymbol( inputCharacter );
69
70              outputTextBox.Text = output;
71
72          } // end method BuildOutput
73
74    } // end class StaticCharMethods
```

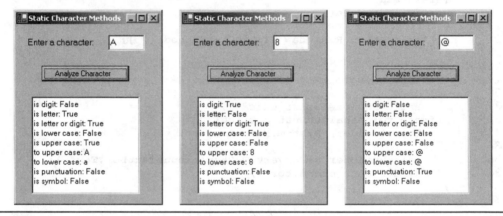

Fig. 13.16 Char's static character-testing methods and case-conversion methods. (Part 3 of 3.)

Line 54 uses **Char** method *IsLower* to determine whether character **inputCharacter** is a lowercase letter. If so, the method returns **true**; otherwise, it returns **false**. Line 57 uses **Char** method *IsUpper* to determine whether character **inputCharacter** is an uppercase letter. If so, the method returns **true**; otherwise, it returns **false**. Line 60 uses **Char** method *ToUpper* to convert the character **inputCharacter** to its uppercase equivalent. The method returns the converted character if the character has an uppercase equivalent; otherwise, the method returns its original argument. Line 63 uses **Char** method *ToLower* to convert the character **inputCharacter** to its lowercase equivalent. The method returns the converted character if the character has a lowercase equivalent; otherwise, the method returns its original argument.

Line 66 uses **Char** method *IsPunctuation* to determine whether character **inputCharacter** is a punctuation mark. If so, the method returns **true**; otherwise, it returns **false**. Line 68 uses **Char** method *IsSymbol* to determine whether character **inputCharacter** is a symbol. If so, the method returns **true**; otherwise it returns **false**.

Structure type **Char** also contains other methods not shown in this example. Many of the **static** methods are similar; for instance, *IsWhiteSpace* is used to determine whether a certain character is a whitespace character (e.g., newline, tab or space). The structure also contains several **public** instance methods; many of these, such as methods

ToString and **Equals**, are methods that we have seen before in other classes. This group includes method **CompareTo**, which is used to compare two character values with one another.

13.16 Card Shuffling and Dealing Simulation

In this section, we use random-number generation to develop a program that simulates the shuffling and dealing of cards. Once created, this program can be implemented in programs that imitate specific card games.

Class **Card** (Fig. 13.17) contains two **string** instance variables—**face** and **suit**—that store references to the face name and suit name of a specific card. The constructor for the class receives two **string**s that it uses to initialize **face** and **suit**. Method **ToString** (lines 20–24) creates a **string** consisting of the **face** of the card and the **suit** of the card.

We develop application **DeckForm** (Fig. 13.18), which creates a deck of 52 playing cards, using **Card** objects. Users can deal each card by clicking the **Deal Card** button. Each dealt card is displayed in a **Label**. Users can also shuffle the deck at any time by clicking the **Shuffle Cards** button.

Method **DeckForm_Load** (lines 35–53 of Fig. 13.18) uses the **for** structure (lines 50–51) to fill the **deck** array with **Card**s. Note that each **Card** is instantiated and initialized with two **string**s—one from the **faces** array (**string**s **"Ace"** through **"King"**) and one from the **suits** array (**"Hearts"**, **"Diamonds"**, **"Clubs"** or **"Spades"**). The calculation **i % 13** always results in a value from **0** to **12** (the thirteen subscripts of the **faces** array), and the calculation **i % 4** always results in a value from **0** to **3** (the four subscripts in the **suits** array). The initialized **deck** array contains the cards with faces ace through king for each suit.

```
1   // Fig. 13.17: Card.cs
2   // Stores suit and face information on each card.
3
4   using System;
5
6   // the representation of a card
7   public class Card
8   {
9      private string face;
10     private string suit;
11
12     public Card( string faceValue,
13        string suitValue )
14     {
15        face = faceValue;
16        suit = suitValue;
17
18     } // end constructor
19
```

Fig. 13.17 Card class. (Part 1 of 2.)

```
20      public override string ToString()
21      {
22         return face + " of " + suit;
23
24      } // end method ToString
25
26   } // end class Card
```

Fig. 13.17 Card class. (Part 2 of 2.)

```
1    // Fig. 13.18: DeckOfCards.cs
2    // Simulating card drawing and shuffling.
3
4    using System;
5    using System.Drawing;
6    using System.Collections;
7    using System.ComponentModel;
8    using System.Windows.Forms;
9    using System.Data;
10
11   // provides the functionality for the form
12   public class DeckForm : System.Windows.Forms.Form
13   {
14      private System.Windows.Forms.Button dealButton;
15      private System.Windows.Forms.Button shuffleButton;
16
17      private System.Windows.Forms.Label displayLabel;
18      private System.Windows.Forms.Label statusLabel;
19
20      private System.ComponentModel.Container components = null;
21
22      private Card[] deck = new Card[ 52 ];
23      private int currentCard;
24
25      // main entry point for application
26      [STAThread]
27      static void Main()
28      {
29         Application.Run( new deckForm() );
30      }
31
32      // Visual Studio .NET generated code
33
34      // handles form at load time
35      private void DeckForm_Load(
36         object sender, System.EventArgs e )
37      {
38         string[] faces = { "Ace", "Deuce", "Three", "Four",
39                            "Five", "Six", "Seven", "Eight",
40                            "Nine", "Ten", "Jack", "Queen",
41                            "King" };
```

Fig. 13.18 Card-dealing and -shuffling simulation. (Part 1 of 4.)

```
42
43          string[] suits = { "Hearts", "Diamonds", "Clubs",
44                             "Spades" };
45
46          // no cards have been drawn
47          currentCard = -1;
48
49          // initialize deck
50          for ( int i = 0; i < deck.Length; i++ )
51             deck[ i ] = new Card( faces[ i % 13 ], suits[ i % 4 ] );
52
53       } // end method deckForm_Load
54
55       // handles dealButton Click
56       private void dealButton_Click(
57          object sender, System.EventArgs e )
58       {
59          Card dealt = DealCard();
60
61          // if dealt card is null, then no cards left
62          // player must shuffle cards
63          if ( dealt != null )
64          {
65             displayLabel.Text = dealt.ToString();
66             statusLabel.Text = "Card #: " + currentCard;
67          }
68          else
69          {
70             displayLabel.Text = "NO MORE CARDS TO DEAL";
71             statusLabel.Text = "Shuffle cards to continue";
72          }
73       }
74
75       // shuffle cards
76       private void Shuffle()
77       {
78          Random randomNumber = new Random();
79          Card temporaryValue;
80
81          currentCard = -1;
82
83          // swap each card with random card
84          for ( int i = 0; i < deck.Length; i++ )
85          {
86             int j = randomNumber.Next( 52 );
87
88             // swap cards
89             temporaryValue = deck[ i ];
90             deck[ i ] = deck[ j ];
91             deck[ j ] = temporaryValue;
92          }
93
```

Fig. 13.18 Card-dealing and -shuffling simulation. (Part 2 of 4.)

```
94              dealButton.Enabled = true;
95
96          } // end method Shuffle
97
98          private Card DealCard()
99          {
100             // if there is a card to deal then deal it
101             // otherwise signal that cards need to be shuffled by
102             // disabling dealButton and returning null
103             if ( currentCard + 1 < deck.Length )
104             {
105                 currentCard++;
106                 return deck[ currentCard ];
107             }
108             else
109             {
110                 dealButton.Enabled = false;
111                 return null;
112             }
113
114         } // end method DealCard
115
116         // handles shuffleButton Click
117         private void shuffleButton_Click(
118             object sender, System.EventArgs e )
119         {
120             displayLabel.Text = "SHUFFLING...";
121             Shuffle();
122             displayLabel.Text = "DECK IS SHUFFLED";
123             statusLabel.Text = "";
124         } // end method shuffleButton_Click
125
126     } // end class deckForm
```

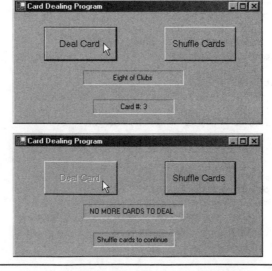

Fig. 13.18 Card-dealing and -shuffling simulation. (Part 3 of 4.)

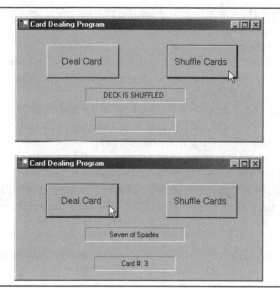

Fig. 13.18 Card-dealing and -shuffling simulation. (Part 4 of 4.)

When users click the **Deal Card** button, event handler **dealButton_Click** (lines 56–73) invokes method **DealCard** (defined in lines 98–114) to get the next card in the **deck** array. If the **deck** is not empty, the method returns a **Card** object reference; otherwise, it returns **null**. If the reference is not **null**, lines 65–66 display the **Card** in **displayLabel** and display the card number in the **statusLabel**.

If **DealCard** returns a **null** reference, the **string "NO MORE CARDS TO DEAL"** is displayed in **displayLabel**, and the **string "Shuffle cards to continue"** is displayed in **statusLabel**.

When users click the **Shuffle Cards** button, the button's event-handling method, **shuffleButton_Click** (lines 117–124), invokes method **Shuffle** (defined on lines 76–96) to shuffle the cards. The method loops through all 52 cards (array subscripts **0–51**). For each card, the method randomly picks a number between **0** and **51**. Then the current **Card** object and the randomly selected **Card** object are swapped in the array. To shuffle the cards, method **Shuffle** makes a total of only 52 swaps during a single pass of the entire array. When the shuffling is complete, **displayLabel** displays the **string "DECK IS SHUFFLED"** and **statusLabel** is cleared.

13.17 Summary

Characters are the fundamental building blocks of C# program code. Every program is composed of a sequence of characters that is interpreted by the compiler as a series of instructions used to accomplish a task.

A **string** is a series of characters treated as a single unit. A **string** may include letters, digits, and various special characters, such as **+, -, *, /, $** and others. All characters correspond to numeric codes. When the computer compares two **string**s, it actually compares the numeric codes of the characters in the **string**s. Once a **string** is created, its contents can never change. Class **StringBuilder** provides a modifiable **string**-like entity that can grow and shrink in size.

A hash table stores information, using a special calculation on the object to be stored that produces a hash code. The hash code is used to choose the location in the table at which to store the object. Class **Object** defines method **GetHashCode** to perform the hash-code calculation.

The braces in a format **string** specify how to format a particular piece of information. Formats have the form **{X[,Y] [:FormatString]}**, where **X** is the number of the argument to be formatted, counting from zero. **Y** is an optional argument that can be positive or negative. **Y** indicates how many characters should be in the formatted result; if the resulting **string** has fewer characters than this number, the string will be padded with spaces to make up for the difference. If **Y** is positive, the **string** will be right aligned; if it is negative, the string will be left aligned. The optional **FormatString** indicates what kind of formatting should be applied to the argument—currency, decimal or scientific, among others.

Structures are, in many ways, similar to classes, the primary difference between them being that structures encapsulate value types, whereas classes encapsulate reference types. Many of the primitive data types that we have been using are actually aliases for different structures. These structures are derived from class **ValueType**, which, in turn, is derived from class **Object**. **Char** is a structure that represents characters.

14

Graphics

Objectives

- To understand graphics contexts and graphics objects.
- To be able to manipulate colors and fonts.
- To understand and be able to use GDI+ **Graphics** methods to draw lines, rectangles, **string**s and images.
- To be able to use class **Image** to manipulate and display images.

One picture is worth ten thousand words.
Chinese proverb

Treat nature in terms of the cylinder, the sphere, the cone, all in perspective.
Paul Cezanne

Nothing ever becomes real till it is experienced—even a proverb is no proverb to you till your life has illustrated it.
John Keats

A picture shows me at a glance what it takes dozens of pages of a book to expound.
Ivan Sergeyevich

Outline

14.1 Introduction

In this chapter, we overview C#'s tools for drawing two-dimensional shapes and for controlling colors and fonts. C# supports graphics that enable programmers to enhance their Windows applications visually. The FCL contains many sophisticated drawing capabilities as part of namespace *System.Drawing* and the other namespaces that make up the .NET resource *GDI+*. GDI+, an extension of the Graphical Device Interface, is an application programming interface (API) that provides classes for creating two-dimensional vector graphics (a way of describing graphics so that they may be easily manipulated with high-performance techniques), manipulating fonts and inserting images. GDI+ expands GDI by simplifying the programming model and introducing several new features, such as extended image file format support and alpha blending. Using the GDI+ API, programmers can create images without worrying about the platform-specific details of their graphics hardware.

We begin with an introduction to the .NET framework's drawing capabilities. In the remainder of this chapter, we discuss class *Image*, which can store and manipulate images from various file formats.

Figure 14.1 depicts a portion of the **System.Drawing** class hierarchy, which includes several of the basic graphics classes and structures covered in this chapter. The most commonly used components of GDI+ reside in the **System.Drawing** and *System.Drawing.Drawing2D* namespaces.

Class *Graphics* contains methods used for drawing **string**s, lines, rectangles and other shapes on a **Control**. The drawing methods of class **Graphics** usually require a *Pen* or *Brush* object to render a specified shape. The **Pen** draws shape outlines; the **Brush** draws solid objects.

Structure **Color** contains numerous **static** properties, which set the colors of various graphical components, plus methods that allow users to create new colors. Class *Font* contains properties that define unique fonts. Class *FontFamily* contains methods for obtaining font information.

To begin drawing in C#, we first must understand GDI+'s *coordinate system* (Fig. 14.2), a scheme for identifying every point on the screen. By default, the upper-left corner of a GUI component (such as a **Panel** or a **Form**) has the coordinates *(0, 0)*. A coordinate pair has both an *x-coordinate* (the *horizontal coordinate*) and a *y-coordinate* (the *vertical coordinate*). The *x*-coordinate is the horizontal distance (to the right) from the upper-left corner. The *y*-coordinate is the vertical distance (downward) from the upper-left corner. The *x-axis* defines every horizontal coordinate, and the *y-axis* defines every vertical coordinate. Programmers position text and shapes on the screen by specifying their (*x*, *y*) coordinates. Coordinate units are measured in *pixels* ("picture elements"), which are the smallest units of resolution on a display monitor.

The **System.Drawing** namespace provides structures **Rectangle** and **Point**. The ***Rectangle*** *structure* defines rectangular shapes and dimensions. The ***Point*** *structure* represents the *x-y* coordinates of a point on a two-dimensional plane.

Portability Tip 14.1

Different display monitors have different resolutions, so the density of pixels on such monitors will vary. This might cause the sizes of graphics to appear different on other monitors.

Good Programming Practice 14.1

Familiarize yourself with the rich set of capabilities provided by the **System.Drawing** *namespace.*

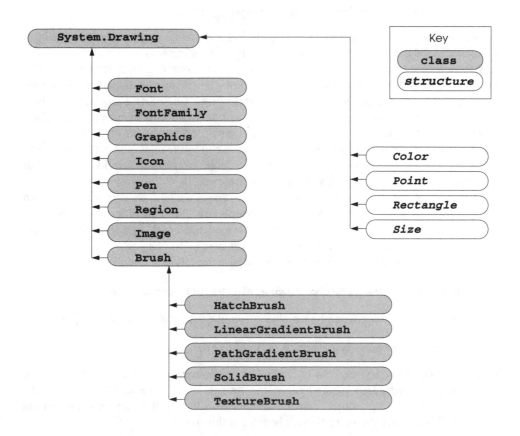

Fig. 14.1 System.Drawing namespace's classes and structures.

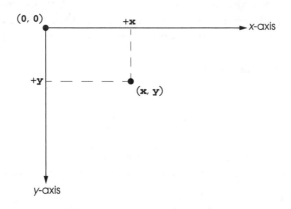

Fig. 14.2 GDI+ coordinate system. Units are measured in pixels.

14.2 Graphics Contexts and Graphics Objects

A C# *graphics context* represents a drawing surface that enables drawing on the screen. A **Graphics** object manages a graphics context by controlling how information is drawn. **Graphics** objects contain methods for drawing, font manipulation, color manipulation and other graphics-related actions. Every Windows application that derives from class **System.Windows.Forms.Form** inherits a **virtual *OnPaint*** event handler where most graphics operations are performed. The arguments to the **OnPaint** method include a **PaintEventArgs** object from which we can obtain a **Graphics** object for the control. We must obtain the **Graphics** object on each call to the method, because the properties of the graphics context that the graphics object represents could change. The **OnPaint** method triggers the **Control**'s **Paint** event.

When displaying graphical information on a **Form**'s client area, programmers can override the **OnPaint** method to retrieve a **Graphics** object from argument **PaintEventArgs** or to create a new **Graphics** object associated with the appropriate surface. We demonstrate these techniques of drawing in C# later in the chapter.

To override the inherited **OnPaint** method, use the following method definition:

```
protected override void OnPaint( PaintEventArgs e )
```

Next, extract the incoming **Graphics** object from the **PaintEventArgs** argument:

```
Graphics graphicsObject = e.Graphics;
```

Variable **graphicsObject** now is available to draw shapes and **string**s on the form.

Calling the **OnPaint** method raises the **Paint** event. Instead of overriding the **OnPaint** method, programmers can add an event handler for the **Paint** event. Visual Studio .NET generates the **Paint** event handler in this form:

```
protected void MyEventHandler_Paint(
    object sender, PaintEventArgs e )
```

Programmers seldom call the **OnPaint** method directly, because the drawing of graphics is an *event-driven process*. An event—such as the covering, uncovering or resizing of a window—calls the **OnPaint** method of that form. Similarly, when any control (such as a **TextBox** or **Label**) is displayed, the program calls that control's **Paint** method.

If programmers need to cause method **OnPaint** to run explicitly, they should not call method **OnPaint**. Rather, they can call the *Invalidate* method (inherited from **Control**). This method refreshes a control's client area and implicitly repaints all graphical components. C# contains several overloaded **Invalidate** methods that allow programmers to update portions of the client area.

Performance Tip 14.1

*Calling the **Invalidate** method to refresh the **Control** often is inefficient. Instead, call **Invalidate** with a **Rectangle** parameter to refresh only the area designated by the rectangle. This improves program performance.*

Controls, such as **Label**s and **Button**s, do not have their own graphics contexts, but one can be created. To draw on a control, first create its graphics object by invoking the **CreateGraphics** method:

```
Graphics graphicsObject = controlName.CreateGraphics();
```

where *graphicsObject* represents an instance of class **Graphics** and *controlName* is any control. Now, a programmer can use the methods provided in class **Graphics** to draw on the control.

14.3 Color Control

Colors can enhance a program's appearance and help convey meaning. For example, a red traffic light indicates stop, yellow indicates caution and green indicates go.

Structure **Color** defines methods and constants used to manipulate colors. Because it is a lightweight object that performs only a handful of operations and stores **static** fields, **Color** is implemented as a structure, rather than as a class.

Every color can be created from a combination of alpha, red, green and blue components. Together, these components are called *ARGB values*. All four ARGB components are **byte**s that represent integer values in the range from 0 to 255. The alpha value determines the opacity of the color. For example, the alpha value 0 results in a transparent color, the value 255 in an opaque color. Alpha values between 0 and 255 result in a weighted blending effect of the color's RGB value with that of any background color, causing a semi-transparent effect. The first number in the RGB value defines the amount of red in the color, the second defines the amount of green and the third defines the amount of blue. The larger the value, the greater the amount of that particular color. C# enables programmers to choose from almost 17 million colors. If a particular computer cannot display all these colors, it will display the color closest to the one specified. Figure 14.3 summarizes some predefined **Color** constants, and Fig. 14.4 describes several **Color** methods and properties.

The table in Fig. 14.4 describes two *FromArgb* method calls. One takes three **int** arguments, and one takes four **int** arguments (all argument values must be between 0 and 255). Both take **int** arguments specifying the amount of red, green and blue. The overloaded version takes four arguments and allows the user to specify alpha; the three-argument version defaults the alpha to 255. Both methods return a **Color** object representing the specified values. **Color** properties **A**, **R**, **G** and **B** return **byte**s that represent **int** values from 0 to 255, corresponding to the amounts of alpha, red, green and blue, respectively.

Programmers draw shapes and **string**s with **Brush**es and **Pen**s. A **Pen**, which functions similarly to an ordinary pen, is used to draw lines. Most drawing methods require a **Pen** object. The overloaded **Pen** constructors allow programmers to specify the colors and widths of the lines that they wish to draw. The **System.Drawing** namespace also provides a **Pens** collection containing predefined **Pen**s.

All classes derived from class **Brush** define objects that color the interiors of graphical shapes (for example, the **SolidBrush** constructor takes a **Color** object—the color to draw). In most **Fill** methods, **Brush**es fill a space with a color, pattern or image. Figure 14.5 summarizes various **Brush**es and their functions.

Constants in structure Color (all are public static)	RGB value	Constants in structure Color (all are public static)	RGB value
Orange	255, 200, 0	**White**	255, 255, 255
Pink	255, 175, 175	**Gray**	128, 128, 128
Cyan	0, 255, 255	**DarkGray**	64, 64, 64
Magenta	255, 0, 255	**Red**	255, 0, 0
Yellow	255, 255, 0	**Green**	0, 255, 0
Black	0, 0, 0	**Blue**	0, 0, 255

Fig. 14.3   **Color** structure **static** constants and their RGB values.

Structure Color methods and properties	Description
Common Methods	
static FromArgb	Creates a color based on red, green and blue values expressed as **int**s from 0 to 255. Overloaded version allows specification of alpha, red, green and blue values.
static FromName	Creates a color from a name, passed as a **string**.
Common Properties	
A	**byte** between 0 and 255, representing the alpha component.
R	**byte** between 0 and 255, representing the red component.
G	**byte** between 0 and 255, representing the green component.
B	**byte** between 0 and 255, representing the blue component.

Fig. 14.4   **Color** structure members.

The application in Fig. 14.6 demonstrates several of the methods and properties described in Fig. 14.4. It displays two overlapping rectangles, allowing the user to experiment with color values and color names.

When the application begins its execution, it calls class **ShowColors**'s **OnPaint** method to paint the window. Line 44 gets a reference to **PaintEventArgs e**'s **Graphics** object and assigns it to **Graphics** object **graphicsObject**. Lines 47–50 create a black and a white **SolidBrush** for drawing on the form. Class **SolidBrush** derives from base class **Brush**; programmers can draw solid shapes with the **Solid-Brush**.

Class	Description
HatchBrush	Uses a rectangular brush to fill a region with a pattern. The pattern is defined by a member of the **HatchStyle** enumeration, a foreground color (with which the pattern is drawn) and a background color.
LinearGradient-Brush	Fills a region with a gradual blend of one color into another. Linear gradients are defined along a line. They can be specified by the two colors, the angle of the gradient and either the width of a rectangle or two points.
SolidBrush	Fills a region with one color. Defined by a **Color** object.
TextureBrush	Fills a region by repeating a specified **Image** across the surface.

Fig. 14.5 Classes that derive from class **Brush**.

```
1   // Fig. 14.6: ShowColors.cs
2   // Using different colors in C#.
3
4   using System;
5   using System.Drawing;
6   using System.Collections;
7   using System.ComponentModel;
8   using System.Windows.Forms;
9   using System.Data;
10
11  // allows users to change colors using the name of
12  // the color or argb values
13  class ShowColors : System.Windows.Forms.Form
14  {
15     private System.ComponentModel.Container components = null;
16
17     // color for back rectangle
18     private Color behindColor = Color.Wheat;
19     private System.Windows.Forms.GroupBox nameGroup;
20     private System.Windows.Forms.GroupBox colorValueGroup;
21     private System.Windows.Forms.TextBox colorNameTextBox;
22     private System.Windows.Forms.TextBox alphaTextBox;
```

Fig. 14.6 Color value and alpha demonstration. (Part 1 of 3.)

```
23        private System.Windows.Forms.TextBox redTextBox;
24        private System.Windows.Forms.TextBox greenTextBox;
25        private System.Windows.Forms.TextBox blueTextBox;
26        private System.Windows.Forms.Button colorValueButton;
27        private System.Windows.Forms.Button colorNameButton;
28
29        // color for front rectangle
30        private Color frontColor =
31           Color.FromArgb( 100, 0 , 0, 255 );
32
33        [STAThread]
34        static void Main()
35        {
36           Application.Run( new ShowColors() );
37        }
38
39        // Visual Studio .NET generated code
40
41        // override Form OnPaint method
42        protected override void OnPaint( PaintEventArgs e )
43        {
44           Graphics graphicsObject = e.Graphics; // get graphics
45
46           // create text brush
47           SolidBrush textBrush = new SolidBrush( Color.Black );
48
49           // create solid brush
50           SolidBrush brush = new SolidBrush( Color.White );
51
52           // draw white background
53           graphicsObject.FillRectangle( brush, 4, 4, 275, 180 );
54
55           // display name of behindColor
56           graphicsObject.DrawString( behindColor.Name, this.Font,
57              textBrush, 40, 5 );
58
59           // set brush color and display back rectangle
60           brush.Color = behindColor;
61
62           graphicsObject.FillRectangle( brush, 45, 20, 150, 120 );
63
64           // display Argb values of front color
65           graphicsObject.DrawString( "Alpha: " + frontColor.A +
66              " Red: " + frontColor.R + " Green: " + frontColor.G
67              + " Blue: " + frontColor.B, this.Font, textBrush,
68              55, 165 );
69
70           // set brush color and display front rectangle
71           brush.Color = frontColor;
72
73           graphicsObject.FillRectangle( brush, 65, 35, 170, 130 );
74
75        } // end method OnPaint
```

Fig. 14.6 Color value and alpha demonstration. (Part 2 of 3.)

```
76
77      // handle colorValueButton click event
78      private void colorValueButton_Click(
79         object sender, System.EventArgs e )
80      {
81         // obtain new front color from text boxes
82         frontColor = Color.FromArgb( Convert.ToInt32(
83            alphaTextBox.Text ),
84            Convert.ToInt32( redTextBox.Text ),
85            Convert.ToInt32( greenTextBox.Text ),
86            Convert.ToInt32( blueTextBox.Text ) );
87
88         Invalidate(); // refresh Form
89      }
90
91      // handle colorNameButton click event
92      private void colorNameButton_Click(
93         object sender, System.EventArgs e )
94      {
95         // set behindColor to color specified in text box
96         behindColor = Color.FromName( colorNameTextBox.Text );
97
98         Invalidate(); // refresh Form
99      }
100
101 } // end class ShowColors
```

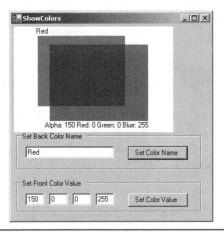

Fig. 14.6 Color value and alpha demonstration. (Part 3 of 3.)

Graphics method *FillRectangle* draws a solid white rectangle with the **Brush** supplied as a parameter (line 53). It takes as parameters a brush, the *x*- and *y*-coordinates of a point and the width and height of the rectangle to draw. The point represents the upper-left corner of the rectangle. Lines 56–57 display the **string Name** property of the **Brush**'s **Color** property with the **Graphics DrawString** method. The programmer has access to several overloaded **DrawString** methods; the version demonstrated in lines 56–57 takes a **string** to display, the display **Font**, a **Brush** and the x- and y-coordinates of the location for the **string**'s first character.

Lines 60–62 assign the **Color behindColor** value to the **Brush**'s **Color** property and display a rectangle. Lines 65–68 extract and display the ARGB values of **Color frontColor** and then display a filled rectangle that overlaps the first.

Button event handler **colorValueButton_Click** (lines 78–89) uses **Color** method **FromArgb** to construct a new **Color** object from the ARGB values that a user specifies via text boxes. It then assigns the newly created **Color** to **frontColor**. **Button** event handler **colorNameButton_Click** (lines 92–99) uses the **Color** method **FromName** to create a new **Color** object from the **colorName** that a user enters in a text box. This **Color** is assigned to **behindColor**.

If the user assigns an alpha value between 0 and 255 for the **frontColor**, the effects of alpha blending are apparent. In the screenshot output, the red back rectangle blends with the blue front rectangle to create purple where the two overlap.

Software Engineering Observation 14.1

*No methods in class **Color** enable programmers to change the characteristics of the current color. To use a different color, create a new **Color** object.*

The predefined GUI component ***ColorDialog*** is a dialog that allows users to select from a palette of available colors. It also offers the option of creating custom colors. The program in Fig. 14.7 demonstrates the use of such a dialog. When a user selects a color and presses **OK**, the application retrieves the user's selection via the **ColorDialog**'s ***Color*** property.

The GUI for this application contains two **Button**s. The top one, **backgroundColorButton**, allows the user to change the form and button background colors. The bottom one, **textColorButton**, allows the user to change the button text colors.

Lines 28–45 define the event handler that is called when the user clicks **Button textColorButton**. The event handler creates a new **ColorDialog** named **colorChooser** and invokes its **ShowDialog** method, which displays the window. Property **Color** of **colorChooser** stores users' selections. Lines 42–43 set the text color of both buttons to the selected color.

Lines 48–65 define the event handler for button **backgroundColorButton**. The method modifies the background color of the form by setting **BackColor** equal to the dialog's **Color** property. The method creates a new **ColorDialog** and sets the dialog's ***FullOpen*** property to **true**. The dialog now displays all available colors, as shown in the screen capture in Fig. 14.7. The regular color display does not show the right-hand portion of the screen.

Users are not restricted to the **ColorDialog**'s 48 colors. To create a custom color, users can click anywhere in the **ColorDialog**'s large rectangle—this displays the various color shades. Adjust the slider, hue and other features to refine the color. When finished, click the **Add to Custom Colors** button, which adds the custom color to a square in the custom colors section of the dialog. Clicking **OK** sets the **Color** property of the **ColorDialog** to that color. Selecting a color and pressing the dialog's **OK** button causes the application's background color to change.

```
1   // Fig. 14.7: ShowColorsComplex.cs
2   // Change the background and text colors of a form.
```

Fig. 14.7 ColorDialog used to change background and text color. (Part 1 of 3.)

```
3
4   using System;
5   using System.Drawing;
6   using System.Collections;
7   using System.ComponentModel;
8   using System.Windows.Forms;
9   using System.Data;
10
11  // allows users to change colors using a ColorDialog
12  public class ShowColorsComplex : System.Windows.Forms.Form
13  {
14     private System.Windows.Forms.Button backgroundColorButton;
15     private System.Windows.Forms.Button textColorButton;
16
17     private System.ComponentModel.Container components = null;
18
19     [STAThread]
20     static void Main()
21     {
22        Application.Run( new ShowColorsComplex() );
23     }
24
25     // Visual Studio .NET generated code
26
27     // change text color
28     private void textColorButton_Click(
29        object sender, System.EventArgs e )
30     {
31        // create ColorDialog object
32        ColorDialog colorChooser = new ColorDialog();
33        DialogResult result;
34
35        // get chosen color
36        result = colorChooser.ShowDialog();
37
38        if ( result == DialogResult.Cancel )
39           return;
40
41        // assign forecolor to result of dialog
42        backgroundColorButton.ForeColor = colorChooser.Color;
43        textColorButton.ForeColor = colorChooser.Color;
44
45     } // end method textColorButton_Click
46
47     // change background color
48     private void backgroundColorButton_Click(
49        object sender, System.EventArgs e )
50     {
51        // create ColorDialog object
52        ColorDialog colorChooser = new ColorDialog();
53        DialogResult result;
54
```

Fig. 14.7 `ColorDialog` used to change background and text color. (Part 2 of 3.)

```
55          // show ColorDialog and get result
56          colorChooser.FullOpen = true;
57          result = colorChooser.ShowDialog();
58
59          if ( result == DialogResult.Cancel )
60              return;
61
62          // set background color
63          this.BackColor = colorChooser.Color;
64
65      }   // end method backgroundColorButton_Click
66
67  }   // end class ShowColorsComplex
```

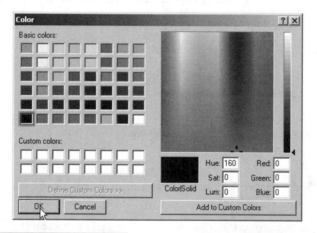

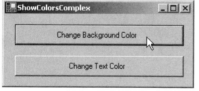 

Fig. 14.7 **ColorDialog** used to change background and text color. (Part 3 of 3.)

14.4 Font Control

This section introduces methods and constants that are related to font control. Once a **Font** has been created, its properties cannot be modified. If programmers require a different **Font**, they must create a new **Font** object—there are many overloaded versions of the **Font** constructor for creating custom **Font**s. Some properties of class **Font** are summarized in Fig. 14.8.

Note that the **Size** property returns the font size as measured in design units, whereas **SizeInPoints** returns the font size as measured in points (the more common measurement). When we say that the **Size** property measures the size of the font in *design units*, we mean that the font size can be specified in a variety of ways, such as inches or millimeters. Some versions of the **Font** constructor accept a **GraphicsUnit** argument—an enumeration that allows users to specify the unit of measurement employed to describe the font size. Members of the **GraphicsUnit** enumeration include **Point** (1/72 inch), **Display** (1/75 inch), **Document** (1/300 inch), **Millimeter**, **Inch** and **Pixel**. If this argument is provided, the **Size** property contains the size of the font as measured in the specified design unit, and the **SizeInPoints** property converts the size of the font into points. For example, if we create a **Font** having size **1** and specify that **GraphicsUnit.Inch** be used to measure the font, the **Size** property will be **1**, and the **SizeInPoints** property will be **72**. If we employ a constructor that does not accept a member of the **GraphicsUnit**, the default measurement for the font size is **GraphicsUnit.Point** (thus, the **Size** and **SizeInPoints** properties will be equal).

Class **Font** has a number of constructors. Most require a *font name*, which is a **string** representing a font currently supported by the system. Common fonts include Microsoft *SansSerif* and *Serif*. Constructors also usually require the *font size* as an argument. Lastly, **Font** constructors usually require a *font style*, specified by the **FontStyle** enumeration: **Bold**, **Italic**, **Regular**, **Strikeout**, **Underline**. Font styles can be combined via the '**|**' operator (for example, **FontStyle.Italic** | **FontStyle.Bold**, makes a font both italic and bold).

Graphics method **DrawString** sets the current drawing font—the font in which the text displays—to its **Font** argument.

Common Programming Error 14.1

Specifying a font that is not available on a system is a logic error. If this occurs, C# will substitute that system's default font.

The program in Fig. 14.9 displays text in four different fonts, each of a different size. The program uses the **Font** constructor to initialize **Font** objects (lines 32–47). Each call to the **Font** constructor passes a font name (e.g., Arial, Times New Roman, Courier New or Tahoma) as a **string**, a font size (a **float**) and a **FontStyle** object (**style**). **Graphics** method **DrawString** sets the font and draws the text at the specified location. Note that line 29 creates a **DarkBlue SolidBrush** object (**brush**), causing all **string**s drawn with that brush to appear in **DarkBlue**.

Property	Description
Bold	Tests a font for a bold font style. Returns *true* if the font is bold.
FontFamily	Represents the **FontFamily** of the **Font** (a grouping structure to organize fonts and define their similar properties).
Height	Represents the height of the font.
Italic	Tests a font for an italic font style. Returns *true* if the font is italic.
Name	Represents the font's name as a *string*.
Size	Returns a *float* value indicating the current font size measured in design units (design units are any specified units of measurement for the font).

Fig. 14.8   **Font** class read-only properties. (Part 1 of 2.)

Property	Description
SizeInPoints	Returns a *float* value indicating the current font size measured in points.
Strikeout	Tests a font for a strikeout font style. Returns *true* if the font is in strikeout format.
Underline	Tests a font for a underline font style. Returns *true* if the font is underlined.

Fig. 14.8 **Font** class read-only properties. (Part 2 of 2.)

 Software Engineering Observation 14.2

There is no way to change the properties of a **Font** *object—to use a different font, programmers must create a new* **Font** *object.*

```
1   // Fig. 14.9: UsingFonts.cs
2   // Demonstrating various font settings.
3
4   using System;
5   using System.Drawing;
6   using System.Collections;
7   using System.ComponentModel;
8   using System.Windows.Forms;
9   using System.Data;
10
11  // demonstrate font constructors and properties
12  public class UsingFonts : System.Windows.Forms.Form
13  {
14     private System.ComponentModel.Container components = null;
15
16     [STAThread]
17     static void Main()
18     {
19        Application.Run( new UsingFonts() );
20     }
21
22     // Visual Studio .NET generated code
23
24     // demonstrate various font and style settings
25     protected override void OnPaint(
26        PaintEventArgs paintEvent )
27     {
28        Graphics graphicsObject = paintEvent.Graphics;
29        SolidBrush brush = new SolidBrush( Color.DarkBlue );
30
31        // arial, 12 pt bold
32        FontStyle style = FontStyle.Bold;
33        Font arial =
34           new Font( new FontFamily( "Arial" ), 12, style );
```

Fig. 14.9 **Font**s and **FontStyle**s. (Part 1 of 2.)

```
35
36        // times new roman, 12 pt regular
37        style = FontStyle.Regular;
38        Font timesNewRoman =
39           new Font( "Times New Roman", 12, style );
40
41        // courier new, 16 pt bold and italic
42        style = FontStyle.Bold | FontStyle.Italic;
43        Font courierNew = new Font( "Courier New", 16, style );
44
45        // tahoma, 18 pt strikeout
46        style = FontStyle.Strikeout;
47        Font tahoma = new Font( "Tahoma", 18, style );
48
49        graphicsObject.DrawString( arial.Name +
50           " 12 point bold.", arial, brush, 10, 10 );
51
52        graphicsObject.DrawString( timesNewRoman.Name +
53           " 12 point plain.", timesNewRoman, brush, 10, 30 );
54
55        graphicsObject.DrawString( courierNew.Name +
56           " 16 point bold and italic.", courierNew,
57           brush, 10, 54 );
58
59        graphicsObject.DrawString( tahoma.Name +
60           " 18 point strikeout.", tahoma, brush, 10, 75 );
61
62     } // end method OnPaint
63
64  } // end class UsingFonts
```

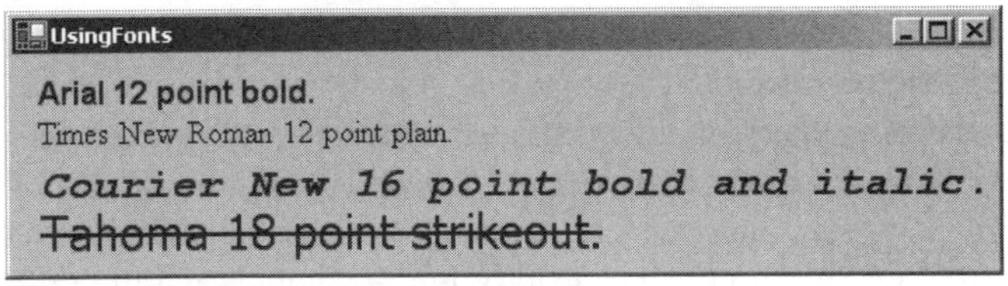

Fig. 14.9 Fonts and FontStyles. (Part 2 of 2.)

14.5 Drawing Lines, Rectangles and Ovals

This section presents a variety of **Graphics** methods for drawing lines, rectangles and ovals. Each of the drawing methods has several overloaded versions. When employing methods that draw shape outlines, we use versions that take a **Pen** and four **int**s; when employing methods that draw solid shapes, we use versions that take a **Brush** and four **int**s. In both instances, the first two **int** arguments represent the coordinates of the upper-left corner of the shape or its enclosing area, and the last two **int**s indicate the shape's width and height. Figure 14.10 summarizes the **Graphics** methods and their parameters.

The application in Fig. 14.11 draws lines, rectangles and ellipses. In this application, we also demonstrate methods that draw filled and unfilled shapes.

Graphics Drawing Methods and Descriptions.

Note: Many of these methods are overloaded—consult the documentation for a full listing.

DrawLine(Pen p, *int* x1, *int* y1, *int* x2, *int* y2)
Draws a line from (**x1, y1**) to (**x2, y2**). The **Pen** determines the color, style and width of the line.

DrawRectangle(Pen p, *int* x, *int* y, *int* width, *int* height)
Draws a rectangle of the specified width and height. The top-left corner of the rectangle is at point (**x, y**). The **Pen** determines the color, style, and border width of the rectangle.

FillRectangle(Brush b, *int* x, *int* y, *int* width, *int* height)
Draws a solid rectangle of the specified width and height. The top-left corner of the rectangle is at point (**x, y**). The **Brush** determines the fill pattern inside the rectangle.

DrawEllipse(Pen p, *int* x, *int* y, *int* width, *int* height)
Draws an ellipse inside a rectangle. The width and height of the rectangle are as specified, and its top-left corner is at point (**x, y**). The **Pen** determines the color, style and border width of the ellipse.

FillEllipse(Brush b, *int* x, *int* y, *int* width, *int* height)
Draws a filled ellipse inside a rectangle. The width and height of the rectangle are as specified, and its top-left corner is at point (**x, y**). The **Brush** determines the pattern inside the ellipse.

Fig. 14.10 Graphics methods that draw lines, rectangles and ovals.

Methods **DrawRectangle** and **FillRectangle** (lines 33 and 42) draw rectangles on the screen. For each method, the first argument specifies the drawing object to use. The **DrawRectangle** method uses a **Pen** object, whereas the **FillRectangle** method uses a **Brush** object (in this case, an instance of **SolidBrush**—a class that derives from **Brush**). The next two arguments specify the coordinates of the upper-left corner of the *bounding rectangle*, which represents the area in which the rectangle will be drawn. The fourth and fifth arguments specify the rectangle's width and height. Method **DrawLine** (lines 36–39) takes a **Pen** and two pairs of **int**s, specifying the start and endpoint of the line. The method then draws a line, using the **Pen** object passed to it.

Methods **DrawEllipse** and **FillEllipse** each provide overloaded versions that take five arguments. In both methods, the first argument specifies the drawing object to use. The next two arguments specify the upper-left coordinates of the bounding rectangle representing the area in which the ellipse will be drawn. The last two arguments specify the bounding rectangle's width and height, respectively. Figure 14.12 depicts an ellipse bounded by a rectangle. The ellipse touches the midpoint of each of the four sides of the bounding rectangle. The bounding rectangle is not displayed on the screen.

```
1    // Fig. 14.11: LinesRectanglesOvals.cs
2    // Demonstrating lines, rectangles and ovals.
```

Fig. 14.11 Demonstration that draw lines, rectangles and ellipses. (Part 1 of 3.)

```
3
4   using System;
5   using System.Drawing;
6   using System.Collections;
7   using System.ComponentModel;
8   using System.Windows.Forms;
9   using System.Data;
10
11  // draws shapes on Form
12  public class LinesRectanglesOvals : System.Windows.Forms.Form
13  {
14     private System.ComponentModel.Container components = null;
15
16     [STAThread]
17     static void Main()
18     {
19        Application.Run( new LinesRectanglesOvals() );
20     }
21
22     // Visual Studio .NET generated code
23
24     protected override void OnPaint(
25        PaintEventArgs paintEvent )
26     {
27        // get graphics object
28        Graphics g = paintEvent.Graphics;
29        SolidBrush brush = new SolidBrush( Color.Blue );
30        Pen pen = new Pen( Color.AliceBlue );
31
32        // create filled rectangle
33        g.FillRectangle( brush, 90, 30, 150, 90 );
34
35        // draw lines to connect rectangles
36        g.DrawLine( pen, 90, 30, 110, 40 );
37        g.DrawLine( pen, 90, 120, 110, 130 );
38        g.DrawLine( pen, 240, 30, 260, 40 );
39        g.DrawLine( pen, 240, 120, 260, 130 );
40
41        // draw top rectangle
42        g.DrawRectangle( pen, 110, 40, 150, 90 );
43
44        // set brush to red
45        brush.Color = Color.Red;
46
47        // draw base Ellipse
48        g.FillEllipse( brush, 280, 75, 100, 50 );
49
50        // draw connecting lines
51        g.DrawLine( pen, 380, 55, 380, 100 );
52        g.DrawLine( pen, 280, 55, 280, 100 );
53
54        // draw Ellipse outline
55        g.DrawEllipse( pen, 280, 30, 100, 50 );
```

Fig. 14.11 Demonstration that draw lines, rectangles and ellipses. (Part 2 of 3.)

```
56
57      } // end method OnPaint
58
59   } // end class LinesRectanglesOvals
```

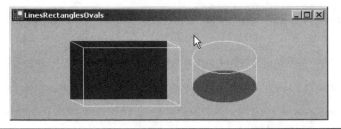

Fig. 14.11 Demonstration that draw lines, rectangles and ellipses. (Part 3 of 3.)

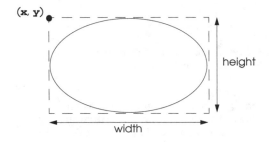

Fig. 14.12 Ellipse bounded by a rectangle.

14.6 Loading, Displaying and Scaling Images

C#'s multimedia capabilities include graphics, images, animations and video. Previous sections demonstrated C#'s vector-graphics capabilities; this section concentrates on image manipulation. The Windows form that we create in Fig. 14.13 demonstrates the loading of an **Image** (**System.Drawing** namespace). The application allows users to enter a desired height and width for the **Image**, which then is displayed in the specified size.

Lines 23–24 declare **Image** reference **image**. The **static Image** method *From-File* then retrieves an image stored on disk and assigns it to **image** (line 24). Line 31 uses **Form** method *CreateGraphics* to create a **Graphics** object associated with the **Form**; we use this object to draw on the **Form**. Method **CreateGraphics** is inherited from class **Control**; all Windows controls, such as **Button**s and **Panel**s, also provide this method. When users click **Set**, the width and height parameters are validated to ensure that they are not too large. If the parameters are valid, line 59 calls **Graphics** method *Clear* to paint the entire **Form** in the current background color. Lines 62–63 call **Graphics** method *DrawImage* with the following parameters: the image to draw, the x-coordinate of the upper-left corner, the y-coordinate of the upper-left corner, the width of the image and the height of the image. If the width and height do not correspond to the image's original dimensions, the image is scaled to fit the new specifications.

In this chapter, we have explored various graphics capabilities of GDI+, including pens, brushes and images. In the next chapter, we cover the reading, writing and accessing of sequential-access files.

```
1   // Fig. 14.13: DisplayLogoForm.cs
2   // Displaying and resizing an image.
3
4   using System;
5   using System.Drawing;
6   using System.Collections;
7   using System.ComponentModel;
8   using System.Windows.Forms;
9   using System.Data;
10
11  // displays an image and allows the user to resize it
12  public class DisplayLogoForm : System.Windows.Forms.Form
13  {
14     private System.Windows.Forms.Button setButton;
15     private System.Windows.Forms.TextBox heightTextBox;
16     private System.Windows.Forms.Label heightLabel;
17     private System.Windows.Forms.TextBox widthTextBox;
18     private System.Windows.Forms.Label widthLabel;
19
20     private
21        System.ComponentModel.Container components = null;
22
23     private
24        Image image = Image.FromFile( "images/Logo.gif" );
25     private Graphics graphicsObject;
26
27     public DisplayLogoForm()
28     {
29        InitializeComponent();
30
31        graphicsObject = this.CreateGraphics();
32     }
33
34     [STAThread]
35     static void Main()
36     {
37        Application.Run( new DisplayLogoForm() );
38     }
39
40     // Visual Studio .NET generated code
41
42     private void setButton_Click(
43        object sender, System.EventArgs e )
44     {
45        // get user input
46        int width = Convert.ToInt32( widthTextBox.Text );
47        int height = Convert.ToInt32( heightTextBox.Text );
48
```

Fig. 14.13 Image resizing. (Part 1 of 2.)

```
49              // if dimensions specified are too large
50              // display problem
51              if ( width > 375 || height > 225 )
52              {
53                  MessageBox.Show( "Height or Width too large" );
54
55                  return;
56              }
57
58              // clear Windows Form
59              graphicsObject.Clear( this.BackColor );
60
61              // draw image
62              graphicsObject.DrawImage(
63                  image, 5, 5, width, height );
64
65        } // end method setButton_Click
66
67  } // end class DisplayLogoForm
```

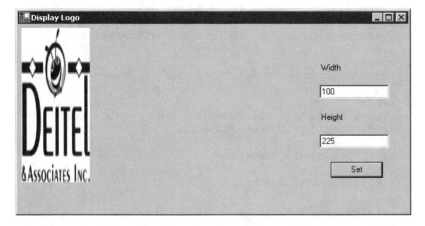

Fig. 14.13 Image resizing. (Part 2 of 2.)

14.7 Summary

A coordinate system identifies every possible point on the screen. The upper left corner of a GUI component has coordinates *(0, 0)*. A coordinate pair is composed of an *x*-coordinate (the horizontal coordinate) and a *y*-coordinate (the vertical coordinate). Coordinate units are measured in pixels. A pixel is the smallest unit of resolution on a display monitor.

A graphics context represents a drawing surface on the screen. A **Graphics** object provides access to the graphics context of a control. **Graphics** objects contain methods for drawing, font manipulation, color manipulation and other graphics-related actions.

Class **Graphics** provides methods **DrawLine**, **DrawRectangle**, **DrawEllipse**, **DrawArc**, **DrawLines**, **DrawPolygon** and **DrawPie**, which draw lines and outlines of shapes. Methods **FillRectangle**, **FillEllipse**, **FillPolygon** and **FillPie** draw solid shapes. Classes **HatchBrush**, **LinearGradientBrush**, **PathGradientBrush** and **TextureBrush** all derive from class **Brush** and represent shape-filling styles.

Method **OnPaint** normally is called in response to an event, such as the uncovering of a window. This method, in turn, triggers a **Paint** event.

Structure **Color** defines constants for manipulating colors in a C# program. **Color** properties **R**, **G** and **B** return **int** values from **0** to **255**, representing the amounts of red, green and blue, respectively, that exist in a **Color**. The larger the value, the greater is the amount of that particular color.

Class **Font**'s constructors all take at least three arguments—the font name, the font size and the font style. The font name is the name of any font currently supported by the system. The font style is a member of the **FontStyle** enumeration.

15

Files and Streams

Objectives

- To be able to create, read, write and update files.
- To understand the C# streams class hierarchy.
- To be able to use the **FileStream** and **BinaryFormatter** classes to read objects from, and write objects to, files.
- To become familiar with sequential-access file processing.

I can only assume that a "Do Not File" document is filed in a "Do Not File" file.
Senator Frank Church
Senate Intelligence Subcommittee Hearing, 1975

Consciousness ... does not appear to itself chopped up in bits. ... A "river" or a "stream" are the metaphors by which it is most naturally described.
William James

I read part of it all the way through.
Samuel Goldwyn

Outline

15.1 Introduction

Variables and arrays offer only temporary storage of data—the data are lost when an object is garbage collected or when the program terminates. By contrast, *files* are used for long-term storage of large amounts of data and can retain data even after the program that created the data terminates. Data maintained in files often are called *persistent data*. Computers can store files on *secondary storage devices*, such as magnetic disks, optical disks and magnetic tapes. In this chapter, we explain how to create, update and process data files in C# programs. We have two goals in this chapter: To introduce the sequential-access file-processing paradigm and to provide the reader with sufficient stream-processing capabilities to support the networking features that we introduce in Chapter 20, Networking: Streams-Based Sockets.

File processing is one of a programming language's most important capabilities, because it enables a language to support commercial applications that typically process massive amounts of persistent data. This chapter discusses C#'s powerful and abundant file-processing and stream-input/output features.

15.2 Data Hierarchy

Ultimately, all data items processed by a computer are reduced to combinations of zeros and ones. This is because it is simple and economical to build electronic devices that can assume two stable states—**0** represents one state, and **1** represents the other. It is remarkable that the impressive functions performed by computers involve only the most fundamental manipulations of **0**s and **1**s.

The smallest data items that computers support are called *bits* (short for "*binary digit*"—a digit that can assume one of two values). Each data item, or bit, can assume either the value **0** or the value **1**. Computer circuitry performs various simple bit manipulations, such as examining the value of a bit, setting the value of a bit and reversing a bit (from **1** to **0** or from **0** to **1**).

Programming with data in the low-level form of bits is cumbersome. It is preferable to program with data in forms such as *decimal digits* (i.e., 0, 1, 2, 3, 4, 5, 6, 7, 8 and 9), *letters* (i.e., A through Z and a through z) and *special symbols* (i.e., $, @, %, &, *, (,), -, +, ", :, ?, / and many others). Digits, letters and special symbols are referred to as *characters*. The set of all characters used to write programs and represent data items on a particular computer is called that computer's *character set*. Because computers can process only **1**s and **0**s, every character in a computer's character set is represented as a pattern of **1**s and **0**s. *Bytes* are composed of eight bits (characters in C# are *Unicode* characters, which are composed of 2 bytes). Programmers create programs and data items with characters; computers manipulate and process these characters as patterns of bits.

In the same way that characters are composed of bits, *fields* are composed of characters. A field is a group of characters that conveys some meaning. For example, a field consisting of uppercase and lowercase letters can represent a person's name.

The various kinds of data items processed by computers form a *data hierarchy* (Fig. 15.1) in which data items become larger and more complex in structure as we progress from bits, to characters, to fields and up to larger data structures.

Typically, a *record* is composed of several fields. In a payroll system, for example, a record for a particular employee might include the following fields:

1. Employee identification number

2. Name

3. Address

4. Hourly pay rate

5. Number of exemptions claimed

6. Year-to-date earnings

7. Amount of taxes withheld

Thus, a record is a group of related fields. In the preceding example, each field is associated with the same employee. A *file* is a group of related records.[1] A company's payroll file normally contains one record for each employee. Thus, a payroll file for a small company might contain only 22 records, whereas a payroll file for a large company might contain 100,000 records. It is not unusual for a company to have many files, some containing millions, billions or even trillions of bits of information.

To facilitate the retrieval of specific records from a file, at least one field in each record is chosen as a unique *record key*. A record key identifies a record as belonging to a particular person or entity and distinguishes that record from all other records. In the payroll record described previously, the employee identification number normally would be chosen as the record key.

There are many ways of organizing records in a file. The most common type of organization is called a *sequential file*, in which records typically are stored in order by the record-key field. In a payroll file, records usually are ordered by employee-identification numbers. The first employee record in the file contains the lowest employee-identification number, and subsequent records contain increasingly higher employee-identification numbers.

Most businesses use many different files to store data. For example, a company might have payroll files, accounts receivable files (listing money due from clients), accounts payable files (listing money due to suppliers), inventory files (listing facts about all the items handled by the business) and many other types of files. Sometimes, a group of related files is called a *database*. A collection of programs designed to create and manage databases is called a *database management system* (DBMS). We discuss databases in detail in Chapter 16, Database, SQL and ADO .NET.

---

1. More generally, a file can contain arbitrary data in arbitrary formats. In some operating systems, a file is viewed as nothing more than a collection of bytes. In such an operating system, any organization of the bytes in a file (such as organizing the data into records) is a view created by the applications programmer.

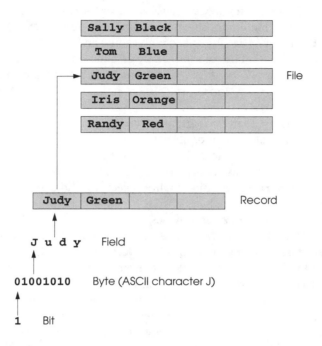

Fig. 15.1   Data hierarchy.

15.3 Files and Streams

C# views each file as a sequential *stream* of bytes (Fig. 15.2). Each file ends either with an *end-of-file marker* or at a specific byte number that is recorded in a system-maintained administrative data structure. When a file is *opened*, C# creates an object, then associates a stream with that object. The runtime environment creates three stream objects upon program execution, which are accessible via properties **Console.Out**, **Console.In** and **Console.Error**, respectively. These objects facilitate communication between a program and a particular file or device. Property **Console.In** returns the *standard input stream object*, which enables a program to input data from the keyboard. Property **Console.Out** returns the *standard output stream object*, which enables a program to output data to the screen. Property **Console.Error** returns the *standard error stream object*, which enables a program to output error messages to the screen. We have been using **Console.Out** and **Console.In** in our console applications—**Console** methods **Write** and **WriteLine** use **Console.Out** to perform output, and methods **Read** and **ReadLine** use **Console.In** to perform input.

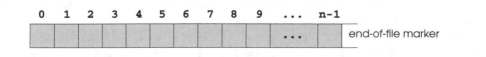

Fig. 15.2   C#'s view of an *n-byte* file.

To perform file processing in C#, namespace **System.IO** must be referenced. This namespace includes definitions for stream classes such as *StreamReader* (for text input from a file), *StreamWriter* (for text output to a file) and **FileStream** (for both input from and output to a file). Files are opened by creating objects of these stream classes, which inherit from classes *TextReader*, *TextWriter* and *Stream*, respectively. Actually, **Console.In** and **Console.Out** are properties of class **TextReader** and **TextWriter**, respectively.

C# provides class *BinaryFormatter*, which is used in conjunction with a **Stream** object to perform input and output of objects. *Serialization* involves converting an object into a format that can be written to a file without losing any of that object's data. *Deserialization* consists of reading this format from a file and reconstructing the original object from it. A **BinaryFormatter** can serialize objects to, and deserialize objects from, a specified **Stream**.

Class *System.IO.Stream* provides functionality for representing streams as bytes. Classes *FileStream*, *MemoryStream* and *BufferedStream* (all from namespace **System.IO**) inherit from class **Stream**. Later in the chapter, we use **FileStream** to read data to, and write data from, sequential-access files. Class **MemoryStream** enables the transferal of data directly to and from memory—this type of transfer is much faster than are other types of data transfer (e.g., to and from disk). Class **BufferedStream** uses *buffering* to transfer data to or from a stream. Buffering is an I/O-performance-enhancement technique in which each output operation is directed to a region in memory called a *buffer* that is large enough to hold the data from many output operations. Then, actual transfer to the output device is performed in one large *physical output operation* each time the buffer fills. The output operations directed to the output buffer in memory often are called *logical output operations*.

C# offers many classes for performing input and output. In this chapter, we use several key stream classes to implement a variety of file-processing programs that create, manipulate and destroy sequential-access files. In Chapter 20, Networking: Streams-Based Sockets, we use stream classes extensively to implement networking applications.

15.4 Creating a Sequential-Access File

C# imposes no structure on files. Thus, concepts like that of a "record" do not exist in C# files. This means that the programmer must structure files to meet the requirements of applications. In this example, we use text and special characters to organize our own concept of a "record."

The following examples demonstrate file processing in a bank-account maintenance application. These programs have similar user interfaces, so we created class **BankUIForm** (Fig. 15.3) to encapsulate a base-class GUI (see the screen capture in Fig. 15.3). Class **BankUIForm** contains four **Label**s (lines 15, 18, 21 and 24) and four **TextBox**es (lines 16, 19, 22 and 25). Methods **ClearTextBoxes** (lines 49–64), **SetTextBoxValues** (lines 67–91) and **GetTextBoxValues** (lines 94–110) clear, set the values of, and get the values of the text in the **TextBox**es, respectively.

To reuse class **BankUIForm**, we compile the GUI into a DLL library by creating a project of type **Windows Control Library** (the DLL we create is called **BankLibrary**). This library, as well as all the code in this book, can be found at our Web site, **www.deitel.com**, under the **Downloads/Resources** link. However, readers might need to change the reference to this library, as it most likely resides in a different location on their systems.

Figure 15.4 contains class **Record** that Fig. 15.5, Fig. 15.7 and Fig. 15.8 use for reading records from, and writing records to, a file sequentially. This class also belongs to the **BankLibrary** DLL, so it is located in the same project as is class **BankUIForm**.

The *Serializable* attribute (line 6) indicates to the compiler that objects of class **Record** can be *serialized*, or represented as sets of bytes—we can read and write these bytes to our streams. Objects that we wish to write to or read from a stream must include this attribute in their class definitions.

Class **Record** contains **private** data members **account**, **firstName**, **lastName** and **balance** (lines 9–12), which collectively represent all information necessary to store record data. The default constructor (lines 15–17) sets these members to their default (i.e., empty) values, and the overloaded constructor (lines 20–28) sets these members to specified parameter values. Class **Record** also provides properties **Account** (lines 31–43), **FirstName** (lines 46–58), **LastName** (lines 61–73) and **Balance** (lines 76–88) for accessing the account number, first name, last name and balance of each customer, respectively.

Class **CreateFileForm** (Fig. 15.5) uses instances of class **Record** to create a sequential-access file that might be used in an accounts receivable system—i.e., a program that organizes data regarding money owed by a company's credit clients. For each client, the program obtains an account number and the client's first name, last name and balance (i.e., the amount of money that the client owes to the company for previously received goods or services). The data obtained for each client constitutes a record for that client. In this application, the account number represents the record key—files are created and maintained in account-number order. This program assumes that the user enters records in account-number order. However, a comprehensive accounts receivable system would provide a sorting capability. The user could enter the records in any order, and the records then could be sorted and written to the file in order. (Note that all outputs in this chapter should be read row by row, from left to right in each row.)

Figure 15.5 contains the code for class **CreateFileForm**, which either creates or opens a file (depending on whether one exists), then allows the user to write bank information to that file. Line 16 imports the **BankLibrary** namespace; this namespace contains class **BankUIForm**, from which class **CreateFileForm** inherits (line 18). Because of this inheritance relationship, the **CreateFileForm** GUI is similar to that of class **BankUIForm** (shown in the Fig. 15.5 output), except that the inherited class contains buttons **Save As**, **Enter** and **Exit**.

When the user clicks the **Save As** button, the program invokes method **saveButton_Click** (lines 41–85). Line 45 instantiates an object of class **SaveFileDialog**, which belongs to the **System.Windows.Forms** namespace. Objects of this class are used for selecting files (see the second screen in Fig. 15.5). Line 46 calls method **ShowDialog** of the **SaveFileDialog** object to display the **SaveFileDialog**. When displayed, a **SaveFileDialog** prevents the user from interacting with any other window in the program until the user closes the **SaveFileDialog** by clicking either **Save** or **Cancel**. Dialogs that behave in this fashion are called *modal dialogs*. The user selects the appropriate drive, directory and file name, then clicks **Save**. Method **ShowDialog** returns an integer specifying which button (**Save** or **Cancel**) the user clicked to close the dialog. In this example, the **Form** property **DialogResult** receives this integer. Line 53 tests whether the user clicked **Cancel** by comparing the value returned by property **DialogResult** to constant *DialogResult.Cancel*. If the values are equal, method **saveButton_Click** returns (line 54). If the values are unequal (i.e., the user clicked **Save**, instead of clicking **Cancel**), line 57 uses property *FileName* of class **SaveFileDialog** to obtain the user-selected file.

```
1    // Fig. 15.3: BankUI.cs
2    // A reusable windows form for the examples in this chapter.
3
4    using System;
5    using System.Drawing;
6    using System.Collections;
7    using System.ComponentModel;
8    using System.Windows.Forms;
9    using System.Data;
10
11   public class BankUIForm : System.Windows.Forms.Form
12   {
13       private System.ComponentModel.Container components = null;
14
15       public System.Windows.Forms.Label accountLabel;
16       public System.Windows.Forms.TextBox accountTextBox;
17
18       public System.Windows.Forms.Label firstNameLabel;
19       public System.Windows.Forms.TextBox firstNameTextBox;
20
21       public System.Windows.Forms.Label lastNameLabel;
22       public System.Windows.Forms.TextBox lastNameTextBox;
23
24       public System.Windows.Forms.Label balanceLabel;
25       public System.Windows.Forms.TextBox balanceTextBox;
26
27       // number of TextBoxes on Form'
28       protected int TextBoxCount = 4;
29
30       // enumeration constants specify TextBox indices
31       public enum TextBoxIndices
32       {
33          ACCOUNT,
34          FIRST,
35          LAST,
36          BALANCE
37
38       } // end enum
39
40       [STAThread]
41       static void Main()
42       {
43          Application.Run( new BankUIForm() );
44       }
45
```

Fig. 15.3   Base class for GUIs in our file-processing applications. (Part 1 of 3.)

```
46       // Visual Studio .NET generated code
47
48       // clear all TextBoxes
49       public void ClearTextBoxes()
50       {
51          // iterate through every Control on form
52          for ( int i = 0; i < Controls.Count; i++ )
53          {
54             Control myControl = Controls[ i ]; // get control
55
56             // determine whether Control is TextBox
57             if ( myControl is TextBox )
58             {
59                // clear Text property (set to empty strng)
60                myControl.Text = "";
61             }
62          }
63
64       } // end method ClearTextBoxes
65
66       // set text box values to string array values
67       public void SetTextBoxValues( string[] values )
68       {
69          // determine whether string array has correct length
70          if ( values.Length != TextBoxCount )
71          {
72             // throw exception if not correct length
73             throw( new ArgumentException( "There must be " +
74                (TextBoxCount + 1) + " strings in the array" ) );
75          }
76
77          // set array values if array has correct length
78          else
79          {
80             // set array values to text box values
81             accountTextBox.Text =
82                values[ ( int )TextBoxIndices.ACCOUNT ];
83             firstNameTextBox.Text =
84                values[ ( int )TextBoxIndices.FIRST ];
85             lastNameTextBox.Text =
86                values[ ( int )TextBoxIndices.LAST ];
87             balanceTextBox.Text =
88                values[ ( int )TextBoxIndices.BALANCE ];
89          }
90
91       } // end method SetTextBoxValues
92
93       // return text box values as string array
94       public string[] GetTextBoxValues()
95       {
96          string[] values = new string[ TextBoxCount ];
97
```

Fig. 15.3   Base class for GUIs in our file-processing applications. (Part 2 of 3.)

```
98          // copy text box fields to string array
99          values[ ( int )TextBoxIndices.ACCOUNT ] =
100            accountTextBox.Text;
101         values[ ( int )TextBoxIndices.FIRST ] =
102            firstNameTextBox.Text;
103         values[ ( int )TextBoxIndices.LAST ] =
104            lastNameTextBox.Text;
105         values[ ( int )TextBoxIndices.BALANCE ] =
106            balanceTextBox.Text;
107
108         return values;
109      } // end method GetTextBoxValues
110
111   } // end class BankUIForm
```

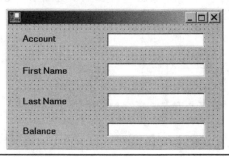

Fig. 15.3   Base class for GUIs in our file-processing applications. (Part 3 of 3.)

```
1    // Fig. 15.4: Record.cs
2    // Serializable class that represents a data record.
3
4    using System;
5
6    [Serializable]
7    public class Record
8    {
9       private int account;
10      private string firstName;
11      private string lastName;
12      private double balance;
13
14      // default constructor sets members to default values
15      public Record() : this( 0, "", "", 0.0 )
16      {
17      }
18
19      // overloaded constructor sets members to parameter values
20      public Record( int accountValue, string firstNameValue,
21         string lastNameValue, double balanceValue )
22      {
23         Account = accountValue;
24         FirstName = firstNameValue;
```

Fig. 15.4   Record for sequential-access file-processing applications. (Part 1 of 3.)

```
25            LastName = lastNameValue;
26            Balance = balanceValue;
27
28        } // end constructor
29
30        // property Account
31        public int Account
32        {
33           get
34           {
35              return account;
36           }
37
38           set
39           {
40              account = value;
41           }
42
43        } // end property Account
44
45        // property FirstName
46        public string FirstName
47        {
48           get
49           {
50              return firstName;
51           }
52
53           set
54           {
55              firstName = value;
56           }
57
58        } // end property FirstName
59
60        // property LastName
61        public string LastName
62        {
63           get
64           {
65              return lastName;
66           }
67
68           set
69           {
70              lastName = value;
71           }
72
73        } // end property LastName
74
75        // property Balance
76        public double Balance
77        {
```

Fig. 15.4   Record for sequential-access file-processing applications. (Part 2 of 3.)

```
78          get
79          {
80              return balance;
81          }
82
83          set
84          {
85              balance = value;
86          }
87
88      } // end property Balance
89
90  } // end class Record
```

Fig. 15.4   Record for sequential-access file-processing applications. (Part 3 of 3.)

```
 1   // Fig. 15.5: CreateSequentialAccessFile.cs
 2   // Creating a sequential-access file.
 3
 4   // C# namespaces
 5   using System;
 6   using System.Drawing;
 7   using System.Collections;
 8   using System.ComponentModel;
 9   using System.Windows.Forms;
10   using System.Data;
11   using System.IO;
12   using System.Runtime.Serialization.Formatters.Binary;
13   using System.Runtime.Serialization;
14
15   // Deitel namespace
16   using BankLibrary;
17
18   public class CreateFileForm : BankUIForm
19   {
20       private System.Windows.Forms.Button saveButton;
21       private System.Windows.Forms.Button enterButton;
22       private System.Windows.Forms.Button exitButton;
23
24       private System.ComponentModel.Container components = null;
25
26       // serializes Record in binary format
27       private BinaryFormatter formatter = new BinaryFormatter();
28
29       // stream through which serializable data is written to file
30       private FileStream output;
31
```

Fig. 15.5   Create and write to a sequential-access file. (Part 1 of 6.)

```
32        [STAThread]
33        static void Main()
34        {
35           Application.Run( new CreateFileForm() );
36        }
37
38        // Visual Studio .NET generated code
39
40        // invoked when user clicks Save button
41        private void saveButton_Click(
42           object sender, System.EventArgs e )
43        {
44           // create dialog box enabling user to save file
45           SaveFileDialog fileChooser = new SaveFileDialog();
46           DialogResult result = fileChooser.ShowDialog();
47           string fileName; // name of file to save data
48
49           // allow user to create file
50           fileChooser.CheckFileExists = false;
51
52           // exit event handler if user clicked "Cancel"
53           if ( result == DialogResult.Cancel )
54              return;
55
56           // get specified file name
57           fileName = fileChooser.FileName;
58
59           // show error if user specified invalid file
60           if ( fileName == "" || fileName == null )
61              MessageBox.Show( "Invalid File Name", "Error",
62                 MessageBoxButtons.OK, MessageBoxIcon.Error );
63           else
64           {
65              // save file via FileStream if user specified valid file
66              try
67              {
68                 // open file with write access
69                 output = new FileStream( fileName,
70                    FileMode.OpenOrCreate, FileAccess.Write );
71
72                 // disable Save button and enable Enter button
73                 saveButton.Enabled = false;
74                 enterButton.Enabled = true;
75              }
76
77              // handle exception if file does not exist
78              catch ( FileNotFoundException )
79              {
80                 // notify user if file does not exist
81                 MessageBox.Show( "File Does Not Exist", "Error",
82                    MessageBoxButtons.OK, MessageBoxIcon.Error );
83              }
84           }
```

Fig. 15.5   Create and write to a sequential-access file. (Part 2 of 6.)

```
85      } // end method saveButton_Click
86
87      // invoke when user clicks Enter button
88      private void enterButton_Click(
89         object sender, System.EventArgs e )
90      {
91         // store TextBox values string array
92         string[] values = GetTextBoxValues();
93
94         // Record containing TextBox values to serialize
95         Record record = new Record();
96
97         // determine whether TextBox account field is empty
98         if ( values[ ( int )TextBoxIndices.ACCOUNT ] != "" )
99         {
100           // store TextBox values in Record and serialize Record
101           try
102           {
103              // get account number value from TextBox
104              int accountNumber = Int32.Parse(
105                 values[ ( int )TextBoxIndices.ACCOUNT ] );
106
107              // determine whether accountNumber is valid
108              if ( accountNumber > 0 )
109              {
110                 // store TextBox fields in Record
111                 record.Account = accountNumber;
112                 record.FirstName =
113                    values[ ( int )TextBoxIndices.FIRST ];
114                 record.LastName =
115                    values[ ( int )TextBoxIndices.LAST ];
116                 record.Balance = Double.Parse( values[
117                    ( int )TextBoxIndices.BALANCE ] );
118
119                 // write Record to FileStream (serialize object)
120                 formatter.Serialize( output, record );
121              }
122              else
123              {
124                 // notify user if invalid account number
125                 MessageBox.Show( "Invalid Account Number", "Error",
126                    MessageBoxButtons.OK, MessageBoxIcon.Error );
127              }
128           }
129
130           // notify user if error occurs in serialization
131           catch( SerializationException )
132           {
133              MessageBox.Show( "Error Writing to File", "Error",
134                 MessageBoxButtons.OK, MessageBoxIcon.Error );
135           }
136
```

Fig. 15.5   Create and write to a sequential-access file. (Part 3 of 6.)

```
137              // notify user if error occurs regarding parameter format
138              catch( FormatException )
139              {
140                  MessageBox.Show( "Invalid Format", "Error",
141                      MessageBoxButtons.OK, MessageBoxIcon.Error );
142              }
143          }
144
145          ClearTextBoxes(); // clear TextBox values
146
147      } // end method enterButton_Click
148
149      // invoked when user clicks Exit button
150      private void exitButton_Click(
151          object sender, System.EventArgs e )
152      {
153          // determine whether file exists
154          if ( output != null )
155          {
156              // close file
157              try
158              {
159                  output.Close();
160              }
161
162              // notify user of error closing file
163              catch( IOException )
164              {
165                  MessageBox.Show( "Cannot close file", "Error",
166                      MessageBoxButtons.OK, MessageBoxIcon.Error );
167              }
168          }
169
170          Application.Exit();
171
172      } // end method exitButton_Click
173
174  } // end class CreateFileForm
```

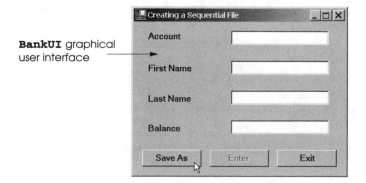

BankUI graphical user interface

Fig. 15.5   Create and write to a sequential-access file. (Part 4 of 6.)

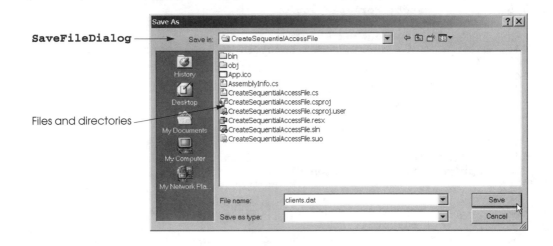

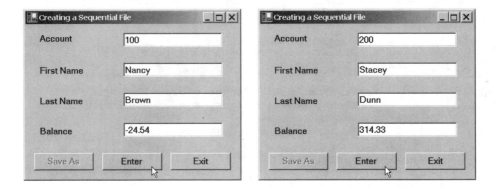

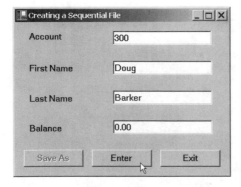

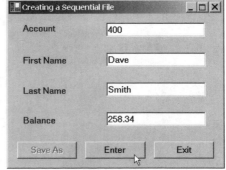

Fig. 15.5   Create and write to a sequential-access file. (Part 5 of 6.)

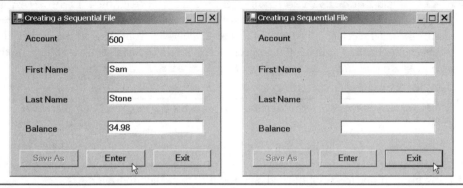

Fig. 15.5   Create and write to a sequential-access file. (Part 6 of 6.)

As we stated previously in this chapter, we can open files to perform text manipulation by creating objects of classes **FileStream**. In this example, we want the file to be opened for output, so lines 69–70 instantiate a **FileStream** object. The **FileStream** constructor that we use receives three arguments—a **string** containing the name of the file to be opened, a constant describing how to open the file and a constant describing the file permissions. Line 70 passes constant **FileMode.OpenOrCreate** to the **FileStream** constructor as the constructor's second argument. This constant indicates that the **FileStream** object should open the file if the file exists or create the file if the file does not exist. C# offers other **FileMode** constants describing how to open files; we introduce these constants as we use them in examples. Line 70 passes constant **FileAccess.Write** to the **FileStream** constructor as the constructor's third argument. This constant ensures that the program can perform write-only operations on the **FileStream** object. C# provides two other constants for this parameter—**FileAccess.Read** for read-only access and **FileAccess.ReadWrite** for both read and write access.

 Good Programming Practice 15.1

*When opening files, use the **FileAccess** enumeration to control user access to these files.*

After the user types information in each **TextBox**, the user clicks the **Enter** button, which calls method **enterButton_Click** (lines 88–147) to save data from the **TextBox** in the user-specified file. If the user entered a valid account number (i.e., an integer greater than zero), lines 112–118 store the **TextBox** values in an object of type **Record**. If the user entered invalid data in one of the **TextBox**es (such as entering non-numeric characters in the **Balance** field), the program throws a **FormatException**. The **catch** block in lines 138–142 handles such an exception by notifying the user (via a **MessageBox**) of the improper format. If the user entered valid data, line 120 writes the record to the file by invoking method **Serialize** of the **BinaryFormatter** object (instantiated in line 27). Class **BinaryFormatter** uses methods *Serialize* and *Deserialize* to write and read objects into streams, respectively. Method **Serialize** writes the object's representation to a file. Method **Deserialize** reads this representation from a file and reconstructs the original object. Both methods throw a **SerializationException** if an error occurs during serialization or deserialization (errors result when the methods attempt to access streams or records that do not exist). Both methods

Serialize and **Deserialize** require a **Stream** object (e.g., the **FileStream**) as a parameter so that the **BinaryFormatter** can access the correct file; the **Binary-Formatter** must receive an instance of a class that derives from class **Stream**, because **Stream** cannot be used to instantiate objects. Class **BinaryFormatter** belongs to the *System.Runtime.Serialization.Formatters.Binary* namespace.

Common Programming Error 15.1

Failure to open a file before attempting to reference it in a program is a logic error.

When the user clicks the **Exit** button, the program invokes method **exitButton_Click** (lines 150–172) to exit the application. Line 159 closes the **FileStream** if one has been opened, and line 170 exits the program.

Performance Tip 15.1

Close each file explicitly when the program no longer needs to reference the file. This can reduce resource usage in programs that continue executing long after they finish using a specific file. The practice of explicitly closing files also improves program clarity.

Performance Tip 15.2

Releasing resources explicitly when they are no longer needed makes them immediately available for reuse by the program, thus improving resource utilization.

In the sample execution for the program in Fig. 15.5, we entered information for five accounts (Fig. 15.6). The program does not depict how the data records are rendered in the file. To verify that the file has been created successfully, in the next section, we create a program to read and display the file.

15.5 Reading Data from a Sequential-Access File

Data are stored in files so that they can be retrieved for processing when they are needed. The previous section demonstrated how to create a file for use in sequential-access applications. In this section, we discuss how to read (or retrieve) data sequentially from a file.

Class **ReadSequentialAccessFileForm** (Fig. 15.7) reads records from the file created by the program in Fig. 15.5, then displays the contents of each record. Much of the code in this example is similar to that of Fig. 15.5, so we discuss only the unique aspects of the application.

Account Number	First Name	Last Name	Balance
100	Nancy	Brown	-25.54
200	Stacey	Dunn	314.33
300	Doug	Barker	0.00
400	Dave	Smith	258.34
500	Sam	Stone	34.98

Fig. 15.6 Sample data for the program of Fig. 15.5.

When the user clicks the **Open File** button, the program calls method **open-Button_Click** (lines 40–70). Line 44 instantiates an object of class *OpenFile-Dialog*, and line 45 calls the object's *ShowDialog* method to display the **Open** dialog (see the second screenshot in Fig. 15.7). The behavior and GUI for the two dialog types are the same (except that **Save** is replaced by **Open**). If the user inputs a valid file name, lines 63–64 create a **FileStream** object and assign it to reference **input**. We pass constant **FileMode.Open** as the second argument to the **FileStream** constructor. This constant indicates that the **FileStream** should open the file if the file exists or should throw a **FileNotFoundException** if the file does not exist. (In this example, the **FileStream** constructor will not throw a **FileNotFoundException**, because the **OpenFileDialog** requires the user to enter a name of a file that exists.) In the last example (Fig. 15.5), we wrote text to the file using a **FileStream** object with write-only access. In this example, (Fig. 15.7), we specify read-only access to the file by passing constant **FileAccess.Read** as the third argument to the **FileStream** constructor.

Testing and Debugging Tip 15.1

Open a file with the **FileAccess.Read** *file-open mode if the contents of the file should not be modified. This prevents unintentional modification of the file's contents.*

When the user clicks the **Next Record** button, the program calls method **nextButton_Click** (lines 73–113), which reads the next record from the user-specified file. (The user must click **Next Record** after opening the file to view the first record.) Lines 80–81 call method **Deserialize** of the **BinaryFormatter** object to read the next record. Method **Deserialize** reads the data and casts the result to a **Record**—this cast is necessary, because **Deserialize** returns a reference of type **Object**. Lines 84–91 then display the **Record** values in the **TextBox**es. When method **Deserialize** attempts to deserialize a record that does not exist in the file (i.e., the program has displayed all file records), the method throws a **SerializationException**. The **catch** block (lines 95–111) that handles this exception closes the **FileStream** object (line 98) and notifies the user that there are no more records (lines 109–110).

To retrieve data sequentially from a file, programs normally start from the beginning of the file, reading data consecutively until the desired data are found. It sometimes is necessary to process a file sequentially several times (from the beginning of the file) during the execution of a program. A **FileStream** object can reposition its *file-position pointer* (which contains the byte number of the next byte to be read from or written to the file) to any position in the file—we show this feature when we introduce random-access file-processing applications. When a **FileStream** object is opened, its file-position pointer is set to zero (i.e., the beginning of the file).

```
1   // Fig. 15.7: ReadSequentialAccessFile.cs
2   // Reading a sequential-access file.
3
4   // C# namespaces
5   using System;
6   using System.Drawing;
7   using System.Collections;
```

Fig. 15.7   Reading sequential-access files. (Part 1 of 5.)

```
 8   using System.ComponentModel;
 9   using System.Windows.Forms;
10   using System.Data;
11   using System.IO;
12   using System.Runtime.Serialization.Formatters.Binary;
13   using System.Runtime.Serialization;
14
15   // Deitel namespace
16   using BankLibrary;
17
18   public class ReadSequentialAccessFileForm : BankUIForm
19   {
20      System.Windows.Forms.Button openButton;
21      System.Windows.Forms.Button nextButton;
22
23      private System.ComponentModel.Container components = null;
24
25      // stream through which serializable data are read from file
26      private FileStream input;
27
28      // object for deserializing Record in binary format
29      private BinaryFormatter reader = new BinaryFormatter();
30
31      [STAThread]
32      static void Main()
33      {
34         Application.Run( new ReadSequentialAccessFileForm() );
35      }
36
37      // Visual Studio .NET generated code
38
39      // invoked when user clicks Open button
40      private void openButton_Click(
41         object sender, System.EventArgs e )
42      {
43         // create dialog box enabling user to open file
44         OpenFileDialog fileChooser = new OpenFileDialog();
45         DialogResult result = fileChooser.ShowDialog();
46         string fileName; // name of file containing data
47
48         // exit event handler if user clicked Cancel
49         if ( result == DialogResult.Cancel )
50            return;
51
52         // get specified file name
53         fileName = fileChooser.FileName;
54         ClearTextBoxes();
55
56         // show error if user specified invalid file
57         if ( fileName == "" || fileName == null )
58            MessageBox.Show( "Invalid File Name", "Error",
59               MessageBoxButtons.OK, MessageBoxIcon.Error );
```

Fig. 15.7   Reading sequential-access files. (Part 2 of 5.)

```
60          else
61          {
62              // create FileStream to obtain read access to file
63              input = new FileStream( fileName, FileMode.Open,
64                  FileAccess.Read );
65
66              // enable next record button
67              nextButton.Enabled = true;
68          }
69
70      } // end method openButton_Click
71
72      // invoked when user clicks Next button
73      private void nextButton_Click(
74          object sender, System.EventArgs e )
75      {
76          // deserialize Record and store data in TextBoxes
77          try
78          {
79              // get next Record available in file
80              Record record =
81                  ( Record )reader.Deserialize( input );
82
83              // store Record values in temporary string array
84              string[] values = new string[] {
85                  record.Account.ToString(),
86                  record.FirstName.ToString(),
87                  record.LastName.ToString(),
88                  record.Balance.ToString() };
89
90              // copy string array values to TextBox values
91              SetTextBoxValues( values );
92          }
93
94          // handle exception when no Records in file
95          catch( SerializationException )
96          {
97              // close FileStream if no Records in file
98              input.Close();
99
100             // enable Open Record button
101             openButton.Enabled = true;
102
103             // disable Next Record button
104             nextButton.Enabled = false;
105
106             ClearTextBoxes();
107
108             // notify user if no Records in file
109             MessageBox.Show( "No more records in file", "",
110                 MessageBoxButtons.OK, MessageBoxIcon.Information );
111         }
112
```

Fig. 15.7   Reading sequential-access files. (Part 3 of 5.)

```
113        } // end method nextButton_Click
114
115  } // end class ReadSequentialAccessFileForm
```

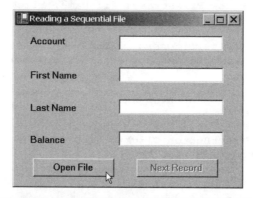

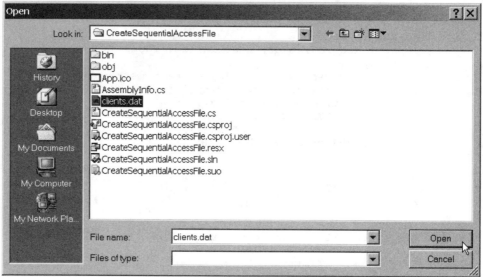

Fig. 15.7   Reading sequential-access files. (Part 4 of 5.)

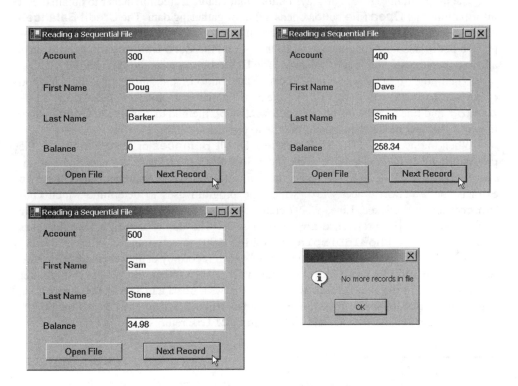

Fig. 15.7   Reading sequential-access files. (Part 5 of 5.)

Performance Tip 15.3

It is time-consuming to close and reopen a file for the purpose of moving the file-position pointer to the file's beginning. Doing so frequently could slow program performance.

We now present a more substantial program that builds on the concepts employed in Fig. 15.7. Class **creditInquiryForm** (Fig. 15.8) is a credit-inquiry program that enables a credit manager to display account information for those customers with credit balances (i.e., customers to whom the company owes money), zero balances (i.e., customers who do not owe the company money) and debit balances (i.e., customers who owe the company money for previously received goods and services). Note that line 21 declares a ***RichTextBox*** that will display the account information. **RichTextBox**es provide more functionality than do regular **TextBox**es—for example, **RichTextBox**es offer method ***Find*** for searching individual strings and method ***LoadFile*** for displaying file contents. Class **RichTextBox** does not inherit from class **TextBox**; rather, both classes inherit directly from class ***System.Windows.Forms.TextBoxBase***. We use a **RichTextBox** in this example, because a **RichTextBox** displays multiple lines of text by default, whereas a regular **TextBox** displays only one. Alternatively, we could have specified that a **TextBox** object display multiple lines of text by setting its **Multiline** property to **true**

The program in Fig. 15.8 displays buttons that enable a credit manager to obtain credit information. The **Open File** button opens a file for gathering data. The **Credit Balances** button displays a list of accounts that have credit balances, the **Debit Balances** button displays a list of accounts that have debit balances, and the **Zero Balances** button displays a list of accounts that have zero balances. The **Done** button exits the application.

When the user clicks the **Open File** button, the program calls method **openButton_Click** (lines 49–76). Line 53 instantiates an object of class *OpenFile-Dialog*, and line 54 calls the object's *ShowDialog* method to display the **Open** dialog, in which the user inputs the name of the file to open.

When the user clicks **Credit Balances**, **Debit Balances** or **Zero Balances**, the program invokes method **get_Click** (lines 80–142). Line 83 casts the **sender** parameter, which is a reference to the object that sent the event, to a **Button** object. Line 86 extracts the **Button** object's text, which the program uses to determine which GUI **Button** the user clicked. Lines 96–97 create a **FileStream** object with read-only file access and assign it to reference **input**. Lines 102–125 define a **while** loop that uses **private** method **ShouldDisplay** (lines 145–170) to determine whether to display each record in the file. The **while** loop obtains each record by calling method **Deserialize** of the **FileStream** object repeatedly (line 105). When the file-position pointer reaches the end of file, method **Deserialize** throws a **SerializationException**, which the **catch** block in lines 136–140 handles: Line 139 calls the **Close** method of **FileStream** to close the file, and method **get_Click** returns.

```
1   // Fig. 15.8: CreditInquiry.cs
2   // Read a file sequentially and display contents based on
3   // account type specified by user(credit, debit or zero balances).
4
5   // C# namespaces
6   using System;
7   using System.Drawing;
8   using System.Collections;
9   using System.ComponentModel;
10  using System.Windows.Forms;
11  using System.Data;
12  using System.IO;
13  using System.Runtime.Serialization.Formatters.Binary;
14  using System.Runtime.Serialization;
15
16  // Deitel namespace
17  using BankLibrary;
18
19  public class CreditInquiryForm : System.Windows.Forms.Form
20  {
21      private System.Windows.Forms.RichTextBox displayTextBox;
22
23      private System.Windows.Forms.Button doneButton;
24      private System.Windows.Forms.Button zeroButton;
25      private System.Windows.Forms.Button debitButton;
26      private System.Windows.Forms.Button creditButton;
```

Fig. 15.8   Credit-inquiry program. (Part 1 of 6.)

```
27        private System.Windows.Forms.Button openButton;
28
29        private System.ComponentModel.Container components = null;
30
31        // stream through which serializable data are read from file
32        private FileStream input;
33
34        // object for deserializing Record in binary format
35        BinaryFormatter reader = new BinaryFormatter();
36
37        // name of file that stores credit, debit and zero balances
38        private string fileName;
39
40        [STAThread]
41        static void Main()
42        {
43           Application.Run( new CreditInquiryForm() );
44        }
45
46        // Visual Studio .NET generated code
47
48        // invoked when user clicks Open File button
49        private void openButton_Click(
50           object sender, System.EventArgs e )
51        {
52           // create dialog box enabling user to open file
53           OpenFileDialog fileChooser = new OpenFileDialog();
54           DialogResult result = fileChooser.ShowDialog();
55
56           // exit event handler if user clicked Cancel
57           if ( result == DialogResult.Cancel )
58              return;
59
60           // get name from user
61           fileName = fileChooser.FileName;
62
63           // show error if user specified invalid file
64           if ( fileName == "" || fileName == null )
65              MessageBox.Show( "Invalid File Name", "Error",
66                 MessageBoxButtons.OK, MessageBoxIcon.Error );
67           else
68           {
69              // enable all GUI buttons, except for Open file button
70              openButton.Enabled = false;
71              creditButton.Enabled = true;
72              debitButton.Enabled = true;
73              zeroButton.Enabled = true;
74           }
75
76        } // end method openButton_Click
77
78        // invoked when user clicks credit balances,
79        // debit balances or zero balances button
```

Fig. 15.8   Credit-inquiry program. (Part 2 of 6.)

```
80      private void get_Click( object sender, System.EventArgs e )
81      {
82         // convert sender explicitly to object of type button
83         Button senderButton = ( Button )sender;
84
85         // get text from clicked Button, which stores account type
86         string accountType = senderButton.Text;
87
88         // read and display file information
89         try
90         {
91            // close file from previous operation
92            if ( input != null )
93               input.Close();
94
95            // create FileStream to obtain read access to file
96            input = new FileStream( fileName, FileMode.Open,
97               FileAccess.Read );
98
99            displayTextBox.Text = "The accounts are:\r\n";
100
101           // traverse file until end of file
102           while ( true )
103           {
104              // get next Record available in file
105              Record record = ( Record )reader.Deserialize( input );
106
107              // store record's last field in balance
108              Double balance = record.Balance;
109
110              // determine whether to display balance
111              if ( ShouldDisplay( balance, accountType ) )
112              {
113                 // display record
114                 string output = record.Account + "\t" +
115                    record.FirstName + "\t" + record.LastName +
116                    new string( ' ', 6 ) + "\t";
117
118                 // display balance with correct monetary format
119                 output += String.Format(
120                    "{0:C}", balance ) + "\r\n";
121
122                 // copy output to screen
123                 displayTextBox.Text += output;
124              }
125           }
126        }
127
128        // handle exception when file cannot be closed
129        catch( IOException )
130        {
131           MessageBox.Show( "Cannot Close File", "Error",
132              MessageBoxButtons.OK, MessageBoxIcon.Error );
```

Fig. 15.8   Credit-inquiry program. (Part 3 of 6.)

```
133            }
134
135            // handle exception when no more records
136            catch( SerializationException )
137            {
138                // close FileStream if no Records in file
139                input.Close();
140            }
141
142         } // end method get_Click
143
144         // determine whether to display given record
145         private bool ShouldDisplay( double balance, string accountType )
146         {
147            if ( balance > 0 )
148            {
149                // display credit balances
150                if ( accountType == "Credit Balances" )
151                    return true;
152            }
153
154            else if ( balance < 0 )
155            {
156                // display debit balances
157                if ( accountType == "Debit Balances" )
158                    return true;
159            }
160
161            else // balance == 0
162            {
163                // display zero balances
164                if ( accountType == "Zero Balances" )
165                    return true;
166            }
167
168            return false;
169
170         } // end method ShouldDisplay
171
172         // invoked when user clicks Done button
173         private void doneButton_Click(
174            object sender, System.EventArgs e )
175         {
176            // determine whether file exists
177            if ( input != null )
178            {
179                // close file
180                try
181                {
182                    input.Close();
183                }
184
```

Fig. 15.8   Credit-inquiry program. (Part 4 of 6.)

```
185              // handle exception if FileStream does not exist
186              catch( IOException )
187              {
188                  // notify user of error closing file
189                  MessageBox.Show( "Cannot close file", "Error",
190                      MessageBoxButtons.OK, MessageBoxIcon.Error);
191              }
192          }
193
194          Application.Exit();
195
196      } // end method doneButton_Click
197
198  } // end class CreditInquiryForm
```

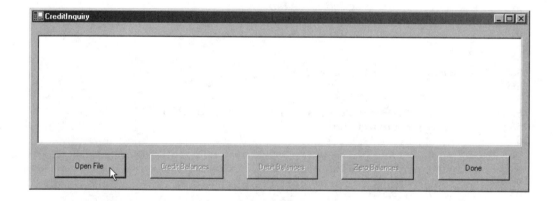

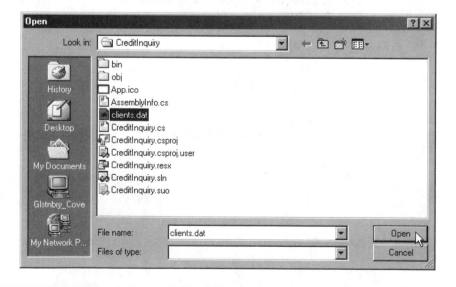

Fig. 15.8   Credit-inquiry program. (Part 5 of 6.)

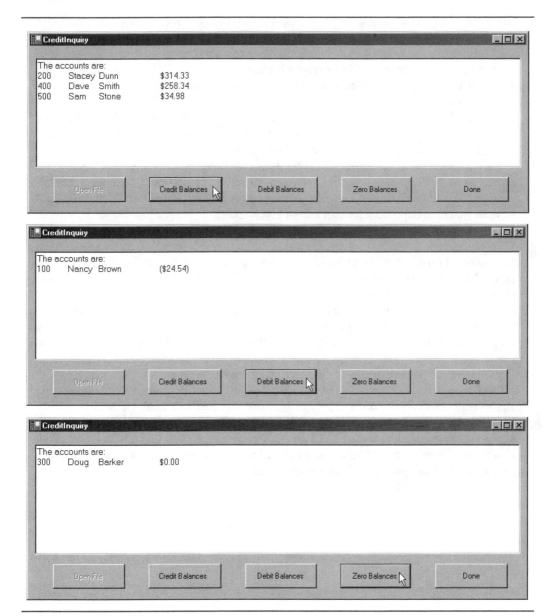

Fig. 15.8   Credit-inquiry program. (Part 6 of 6.)

15.6 Summary

All data items processed by a computer ultimately are reduced to combinations of zeros and ones. The smallest data items that computers support are called bits and can assume either the value **0** or the value **1**. Digits, letters and special symbols are referred to as characters. The set of all characters used to write programs and represent data items on a particular computer is called that computer's character set. Every character in a computer's character set is represented as a pattern of **1**s and **0**s.

A field is a group of characters that conveys some meaning. A record is a group of related fields. At least one field in a record is chosen as a record key, which identifies that record as belonging to a particular person or entity and distinguishes that record from all other records in the file.

A file is a group of related records. Files are used for long-term retention of large amounts of data and can store the data even after the program that created the data terminates. Data maintained in files often are called persistent data.

C# imposes no structure on files. This means that concepts like that of a "record" do not exist in C#. The programmer must structure each file appropriately to meet the requirements of an application. C# views each file as a sequential stream of bytes. Each file ends in some machine-dependent form of end-of-file marker.

To perform file processing in C#, the namespace **System.IO** must be referenced. This namespace includes definitions for stream classes such as **StreamReader**, **StreamWriter** and **FileStream**. Files are opened by instantiating objects of these classes. When a file is opened, an object is created, and a stream is associated with the object. Streams provide communication channels between files and programs.

The most common type of file organization is the sequential file, in which records typically are stored in order by the record-key field. To retrieve data sequentially from a file, programs normally start from the beginning of the file, reading all data consecutively until the desired data are found. With a sequential-access file, each successive input/output request reads or writes the next consecutive set of data in the file.

BinaryFormatter provides methods **Serialize** and **Deserialize** to write and to read objects, respectively. Only classes with the **Serializable** attribute can be serialized to and deserialized from files. Method **Serialize** writes the object's representation to a stream. Method **Deserialize** reads this representation from a stream and reconstructs the original object. Methods **Serialize** and **Deserialize** each require a **Stream** object as a parameter, enabling the **BinaryFormatter** to access the correct file.

16

Database, SQL and ADO .NET

Objectives

- To understand the relational database model.
- To understand basic database queries using Structured Query Language (SQL).
- To use the classes of namespace **System.Data** to manipulate databases.
- To understand and use ADO .NET's disconnected model.
- To use the classes of namespace **System.Data.OleDb**.

It is a capital mistake to theorize before one has data.
Arthur Conan Doyle

Now go, write it before them in a table, and note it in a book, that it may be for the time to come for ever and ever.
The Holy Bible: The Old Testament

Let's look at the record.
Alfred Emanuel Smith

Get your facts first, and then you can distort them as much as you please.
Mark Twain

I like two kinds of men: domestic and foreign.
Mae West

16.1 Introduction

A *database* is an integrated collection of data. Many different strategies exist for organizing data in databases to facilitate easy access to and manipulation of the data. A *database management system* (*DBMS*) provides mechanisms for storing and organizing data in a manner that is consistent with the database's format. Database management systems enable programmers to access and store data without worrying about the internal representation of databases.

Today's most popular database systems are *relational databases*. Almost universally, relational databases use a language called *Structured Query Language* (*SQL*—pronounced as its individual letters or as "sequel") to perform *queries* (i.e., to request information that satisfies given criteria) and to manipulate data. [*Note*: The writing in this chapter assumes that SQL is pronounced as its individual letters. For this reason, we often precede SQL with the article "an," as in "an SQL database" or "an SQL statement."]

Some popular, enterprise-level relational database systems include Microsoft SQL Server, Oracle™, Sybase™, DB2™, Informix™ and MySQL™. This chapter presents examples using Microsoft Access—a relational database system that is packaged with Microsoft Office.

A programming language connects to, and interacts with, a relational database via an *interface*—software that facilitates communication between a database management system and a program. C# programmers communicate with databases and manipulate their data through *Microsoft ActiveX Data Objects*™ (ADO), *ADO .NET*.

16.2 Relational Database Model

The *relational database model* is a logical representation of data that allows relationships among data to be considered without concern for the physical structure of the data. A relational database is composed of *tables*. Figure 16.1 illustrates an example table that might be used in a personnel system. The table name is **Employee**, and its primary purpose is to illustrate the specific attributes of various employees. A particular row of the table is called a *record* (or *row*). This table consists of six records. The **number** *field* (or *column*) of each record in the table is the *primary key* for referencing data in the table. A primary key is a field (or fields) in a table that contain(s) unique data—i.e, data that is not duplicated in other records of that table. This guarantees that each record can be identified by at least one distinct value. Examples of primary-key fields are columns that contain social security numbers, employee IDs and part numbers in an inventory system. The records of Fig. 16.1 are *ordered* by primary key. In this case, the records are listed in increasing order (they also could be listed in decreasing order).

Each column of the table represents a different field. Records normally are unique (by primary key) within a table, but particular field values might be duplicated in multiple records. For example, three different records in the **Employee** table's **Department** field contain the number 413.

Often, different users of a database are interested in different data and different relationships among those data. Some users require only subsets of the table columns. To obtain table subsets, we use SQL statements to specify certain data we wish to *select* from a table. SQL provides a complete set of commands (including ***SELECT***) that enable programmers to define complex *queries* to select data from a table. The results of a query commonly are called *result sets* (or *record sets*). For example, we might select data from the table in Fig. 16.1 to create a new result set containing only the location of each department. This result set appears in Fig. 16.2. SQL queries are discussed in detail in Section 16.4.

number	name	department	salary	location
23603	Jones	413	1100	New Jersey
24568	Kerwin	413	2000	New Jersey
34589	Larson	642	1800	Los Angeles
35761	Myers	611	1400	Orlando
47132	Neumann	413	9000	New Jersey
78321	Stephens	611	8500	Orlando

Record/Row {

Primary key   Field/Column

Fig. 16.1   Relational-database structure of an **Employee** table.

16.3 Relational Database Overview: Books Database

The next section provides an overview of SQL in the context of a sample **Books** database that we created for this chapter. However, before we discuss SQL, we must explain the various tables of the **Books** database. We use this database to introduce various database concepts, including the use of SQL to manipulate and obtain useful information from the database.

The database consists of four tables: **Authors**, **Publishers**, **AuthorISBN** and **Titles**. The **Authors** table (described in Fig. 16.3) consists of three fields (or columns) that maintain each author's unique ID number, first name and last name. Figure 16.4 contains the data from the **Authors** table of the **Books** database.

The **Publishers** table (described in Fig. 16.5) consists of two fields, representing each publisher's unique ID and name. Figure 16.6 contains the data from the **Publishers** table of the **Books** database.

The **AuthorISBN** table (described in Fig. 16.7) consists of two fields that maintain the authors' ID numbers and the corresponding ISBN numbers of their books. This table helps associate the names of the authors with the titles of their books. Figure 16.8 contains the data from the **AuthorISBN** table of the **Books** database. ISBN is an abbreviation for "International Standard Book Number"—a numbering scheme by which publishers worldwide assign every book a unique identification number. [*Note*: To save space, we have split the contents of this figure into two columns, each containing the **authorID** and **isbn** fields.

department	location
413	New Jersey
611	Orlando
642	Los Angeles

Fig. 16.2 Result set formed by selecting **Department** and **Location** data from the **Employee** table.

Field	Description
authorID	Author's ID number in the database. In the **Books** database, this **int** field is defined as an *auto-incremented field*. For each new record inserted in this table, the database increments the **authorID** value, ensuring that each record has a unique **authorID**. This field represents the table's primary key.

Fig. 16.3 **Authors** table from **Books**. (Part 1 of 2.)

Field	Description
firstName	Author's first name (a **string**).
lastName	Author's last name (a **string**).

Fig. 16.3 Authors table from **Books**. (Part 2 of 2.)

authorID	firstName	lastName
1	Harvey	Deitel
2	Paul	Deitel
3	Tem	Nieto
4	Kate	Steinbuhler
5	Sean	Santry
6	Ted	Lin
7	Praveen	Sadhu
8	David	McPhie
9	Cheryl	Yaeger
10	Marina	Zlatkina
11	Ben	Wiedermann
12	Jonathan	Liperi
13	Jeffrey	Listfield

Fig. 16.4 Data from the **Authors** table of **Books**.

Field	Description
publisherID	The publisher's ID number in the database. This auto-incremented **int** field is the table's primary-key field.
publisherName	The name of the publisher (a **string**).

Fig. 16.5 Publishers table from **Books**.

publisherID	publisherName
1	Prentice Hall
2	Prentice Hall PTG

Fig. 16.6 Data from the **Publishers** table of **Books**.

Field	Description
authorID	The author's ID number, which allows the database to associate each book with a specific author. The integer ID number in this field must also appear in the **Authors** table.
isbn	The ISBN number for a book (a **string**).

Fig. 16.7   **AuthorISBN** table from **Books**.

authorID	isbn	authorID	isbn
1	0130895725	2	0139163050
1	0132261197	2	013028419x
1	0130895717	2	0130161438
1	0135289106	2	0130856118
1	0139163050	2	0130125075
1	013028419x	2	0138993947
1	0130161438	2	0130852473
1	0130856118	2	0130829277
1	0130125075	2	0134569555
1	0138993947	2	0130829293
1	0130852473	2	0130284173
1	0130829277	2	0130284181
1	0134569555	2	0130895601
1	0130829293	3	013028419x
1	0130284173	3	0130161438
1	0130284181	3	0130856118
1	0130895601	3	0134569555
2	0130895725	3	0130829293
2	0132261197	3	0130284173
2	0130895717	3	0130284181
2	0135289106	4	0130895601

Fig. 16.8   Data from **AuthorISBN** table in **Books**.

The **Titles** table (described in Fig. 16.9) consists of seven fields that maintain general information about the books in the database. This information includes each book's ISBN number, title, edition number, copyright year and publisher's ID number, as well as the name of a file containing an image of the book cover and, finally, each book's price. Figure 16.10 contains the data from the **Titles** table.

Field	Description
isbn	ISBN number of the book (a **string**).
title	Title of the book (a **string**).
editionNumber	Edition number of the book (a **string**).
copyright	Copyright year of the book (an **int**).
publisherID	Publisher's ID number (an **int**). This value must correspond to an ID number in the **Publishers** table.
imageFile	Name of the file containing the book's cover image (a **string**).
price	Suggested retail price of the book (a real number). [*Note*: The prices shown in this database are for example purposes only.]

Fig. 16.9 **Titles** table from **Books**.

isbn	title	edition-Number	publish-erID	copy-right	imageFile	price
0130923613	Python How to Program	1	1	2002	**python.jpg**	$69.95
0130622214	C# How to Program	1	1	2002	**cshtp.jpg**	$69.95
0130341517	Java How to Program	4	1	2002	**jhtp4.jpg**	$69.95
0130649341	The Complete Java Training Course	4	2	2002	**javactc4.jpg**	$109.95
0130895601	Advanced Java 2 Platform How to Program	1	1	2002	**advjhtp1.jpg**	$69.95
0130308978	Internet and World Wide Web How to Program	2	1	2002	**iw3htp2.jpg**	$69.95
0130293636	Visual Basic .NET How to Program	2	1	2002	**vbnet.jpg**	$69.95
0130895636	The Complete C++ Training Course	3	2	2001	**cppctc3.jpg**	$109.95
0130895512	The Complete e-Business & e-Commerce Programming Training Course	1	2	2001	**ebecctc.jpg**	$109.95

Fig. 16.10 Data from the **Titles** table of **Books**. (Part 1 of 3.)

isbn	title	edition-Number	publish-erID	copy-right	imageFile	price
013089561X	The Complete Internet & World Wide Web Programming Training Course	2	2	2001	`iw3ctc2.jpg`	$109.95
0130895547	The Complete Perl Training Course	1	2	2001	`perl.jpg`	$109.95
0130895563	The Complete XML Programming Training Course	1	2	2001	`xmlctc.jpg`	$109.95
0130895725	C How to Program	3	1	2001	`chtp3.jpg`	$69.95
0130895717	C++ How to Program	3	1	2001	`cpphtp3.jpg`	$69.95
013028419X	e-Business and e-Commerce How to Program	1	1	2001	`ebechtp1.jpg`	$69.95
0130622265	Wireless Internet and Mobile Business How to Program	1	1	2001	`wireless.jpg`	$69.95
0130284181	Perl How to Program	1	1	2001	`perlhtp1.jpg`	$69.95
0130284173	XML How to Program	1	1	2001	`xmlhtp1.jpg`	$69.95
0130856118	The Complete Internet and World Wide Web Programming Training Course	1	2	2000	`iw3ctc1.jpg`	$109.95
0130125075	Java How to Program (Java 2)	3	1	2000	`jhtp3.jpg`	$69.95
0130852481	The Complete Java 2 Training Course	3	2	2000	`javactc3.jpg`	$109.95
0130323640	e-Business and e-Commerce for Managers	1	1	2000	`ebecm.jpg`	$69.95
0130161438	Internet and World Wide Web How to Program	1	1	2000	`iw3htp1.jpg`	$69.95
0130132497	Getting Started with Visual C++ 6 with an Introduction to MFC	1	1	1999	`gsvc.jpg`	$49.95

Fig. 16.10 Data from the **Titles** table of **Books**. (Part 2 of 3.)

isbn	title	edition-Number	publish-erID	copy-right	imageFile	price
0130829293	The Complete Visual Basic 6 Training Course	1	2	1999	vbctc1.jpg	$109.95
0134569555	Visual Basic 6 How to Program	1	1	1999	vbhtp1.jpg	$69.95
0132719746	Java Multimedia Cyber Classroom	1	2	1998	javactc.jpg	$109.95
0136325890	Java How to Program	1	1	1998	jhtp1.jpg	$69.95
0139163050	The Complete C++ Training Course	2	2	1998	cppctc2.jpg	$109.95
0135289106	C++ How to Program	2	1	1998	cpphtp2.jpg	$49.95
0137905696	The Complete Java Training Course	2	2	1998	javactc2.jpg	$109.95
0130829277	The Complete Java Training Course (Java 1.1)	2	2	1998	javactc2.jpg	$99.95
0138993947	Java How to Program (Java 1.1)	2	1	1998	jhtp2.jpg	$49.95
0131173340	C++ How to Program	1	1	1994	cpphtp1.jpg	$69.95
0132261197	C How to Program	2	1	1994	chtp2.jpg	$49.95
0131180436	C How to Program	1	1	1992	chtp.jpg	$69.95

Fig. 16.10 Data from the **Titles** table of **Books**. (Part 3 of 3.)

Figure 16.11 illustrates the relationships among the tables in the **Books** database. The first line in each table is the table's name. The field whose name appears in italics contains that table's primary key. A table's primary key uniquely identifies each record in the table. Every record must have a value in the primary-key field, and the value must be unique. This is known as the *Rule of Entity Integrity*. Note that the **AuthorISBN** table contains two fields whose names are italicized. This indicates that these two fields form a *compound primary key*—each record in the table must have a unique **authorID–isbn** combination. For example, several records might have an **authorID** of **2**, and several records might have an **isbn** of **0130895601**, but only one record can have both an **authorID** of **2** and an **isbn** of **0130895601**.

Common Programming Error 16.1

Failure to provide a value for a primary-key field in every record breaks the Rule of Entity Integrity and causes the DBMS to report an error.

Common Programming Error 16.2

Providing duplicate values for the primary-key field of multiple records causes the DBMS to report an error.

The lines connecting the tables in Fig. 16.11 represent the *relationships* among the tables. Consider the line between the **Publishers** and **Titles** tables. On the **Publishers** end of the line, there is a **1**, and, on the **Titles** end, there is an infinity (∞) symbol. This line indicates a *one-to-many relationship*, in which every publisher in the **Publishers** table can have an arbitrarily large number of books in the **Titles** table. Note that the relationship line links the **publisherID** field in the **Publishers** table to the **publisherID** field in **Titles** table. In the **Titles** table, the **publisherID** field is a *foreign key*—a field for which every entry has a unique value in another table and where the field in the other table is the primary key for that table (e.g., **publisherID** in the **Publishers** table). Programmers specify foreign keys when creating a table. The foreign key helps maintain the *Rule of Referential Integrity*: Every foreign-key field value must appear in another table's primary-key field. Foreign keys enable information from multiple tables to be *joined* together for analysis purposes. There is a one-to-many relationship between a primary key and its corresponding foreign key. This means that a foreign-key field value can appear many times in its own table, but must appear exactly once as the primary key of another table. The line between the tables represents the link between the foreign key in one table and the primary key in another table.

Common Programming Error 16.3

Providing a foreign-key value that does not appear as a primary-key value in another table breaks the Rule of Referential Integrity and causes the DBMS to report an error.

The line between the **AuthorISBN** and **Authors** tables indicates that, for each author in the **Authors** table, the **AuthorISBN** table can contain an arbitrary number of ISBNs for books written by that author. The **authorID** field in the **AuthorISBN** table is a foreign key of the **authorID** field (the primary key) of the **Authors** table. Note, again, that the line between the tables links the foreign key in table **AuthorISBN** to the corresponding primary key in table **Authors**. The **AuthorISBN** table links information in the **Titles** and **Authors** tables.

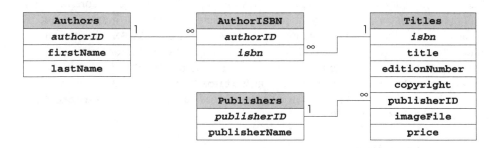

Fig. 16.11 Table relationships in **Books**.

The line between the **Titles** and **AuthorISBN** tables illustrates another one-to-many relationship; a title can be written by any number of authors. In fact, the sole purpose of the **AuthorISBN** table is to represent a many-to-many relationship between the **Authors** and **Titles** tables; an author can write any number of books, and a book can have any number of authors.

16.4 Structured Query Language (SQL)

In this section, we provide an overview of Structured Query Language (SQL) in the context of our **Books** sample database. The SQL queries discussed here form the foundation for the SQL used in the chapter examples.

Figure 16.12 lists SQL keywords and provides a description of each. In the next several subsections, we discuss these SQL keywords in the context of complete SQL queries. Other SQL keywords exist, but are beyond the scope of this text.

16.4.1 Basic SELECT Query

Let us consider several SQL queries that extract information from database **Books**. A typical SQL query "selects" information from one or more tables in a database. Such selections are performed by *SELECT queries*. The basic format for a **SELECT** query is:

>   *SELECT * FROM* tableName

In this query, the asterisk (*) indicates that all columns from the *tableName* table of the database should be selected. For example, to select the entire contents of the **Authors** table (i.e., all data depicted in Fig. 16.4), use the query:

>   *SELECT * FROM* Authors

To select specific fields from a table, replace the asterisk (*) with a comma-separated list of the field names to select. For example, to select only the fields **authorID** and **lastName** for all rows in the **Authors** table, use the query:

SQL keyword	Description
SELECT	Selects (retrieves) fields from one or more tables.
FROM	Specifies tables from which to get fields or delete records. Required in every *SELECT* and *DELETE* statement.
WHERE	Specifies criteria that determine the rows to be retrieved.
INNER JOIN	Joins records from multiple tables to produce a single set of records.
GROUP BY	Specifies criteria for grouping records.
ORDER BY	Specifies criteria for ordering records.
INSERT	Inserts data into a specified table.

Fig. 16.12 SQL query keywords. (Part 1 of 2.)

SQL keyword	Description
UPDATE	Updates data in a specified table.
DELETE	Deletes data from a specified table.

Fig. 16.12 SQL query keywords. (Part 2 of 2.)

> **SELECT** authorID, lastName *FROM* Authors

This query returns only the data presented in Fig. 16.13. [*Note*: If a field name contains spaces, the entire field name must be enclosed in square brackets (**[ ]**) in the query. For example, if the field name is **first name**, it must appear in the query as **[first name]**.]

Common Programming Error 16.4

If a program assumes that an SQL statement using the asterisk ( ) to select fields always returns those fields in the same order, the program could process the result set incorrectly. If the field order in the database table(s) changes, the order of the fields in the result set would change accordingly.*

Performance Tip 16.1

If a program does not know the order of fields in a result set, the program must process the fields by name. This could require a linear search of the field names in the result set. If users specify the field names that they wish to select from a table (or several tables), the application receiving the result set knows the order of the fields in advance. When this occurs, the program can process the data more efficiently, because fields can be accessed directly by column number.

16.4.2 WHERE Clause

In most cases, users search a database for records that satisfy certain *selection criteria*. Only records that match the selection criteria are selected. SQL uses the optional *WHERE* clause in a **SELECT** query to specify the selection criteria for the query. The simplest format for a **SELECT** query that includes selection criteria is:

> *SELECT* fieldName1, fieldName2, ... *FROM* tableName *WHERE* criteria

For example, to select the **title**, **editionNumber** and **copyright** fields from those rows of table **Titles** in which the **copyright** date is greater than **1999**, use the query:

authorID	lastName	authorID	lastName
1	Deitel	8	McPhie
2	Deitel	9	Yaeger
3	Nieto	10	Zlatkina

Fig. 16.13 **authorID** and **lastName** from the **Authors** table. (Part 1 of 2.)

authorID	lastName	authorID	lastName
4	Steinbuhler	12	Wiedermann
5	Santry	12	Liperi
6	Lin	13	Listfield
7	Sadhu		

Fig. 16.13 `authorID` and `lastName` from the **Authors** table. (Part 2 of 2.)

```
SELECT title, editionNumber, copyright
FROM Titles
WHERE copyright > 1999
```

Figure 16.14 shows the result set of the preceding query. [*Note*: When we construct a query for use in C#, we simply create a **string** containing the entire query. However, when we display queries in the text, we often use multiple lines and indentation to enhance readability.]

Performance Tip 16.2

Using selection criteria improves performance, because queries that involve such criteria normally select a portion of the database that is smaller than the entire database. Working with a smaller portion of the data is more efficient than working with the entire set of data stored in the database.

title	editionNumber	copyright
Internet and World Wide Web How to Program	2	2002
Java How to Program	4	2002
The Complete Java Training Course	4	2002
The Complete e-Business & e-Commerce Programming Training Course	1	2001
The Complete Internet & World Wide Web Programming Training Course	2	2001
The Complete Perl Training Course	1	2001
The Complete XML Programming Training Course	1	2001
C How to Program	3	2001
C++ How to Program	3	2001
The Complete C++ Training Course	3	2001
e-Business and e-Commerce How to Program	1	2001
Internet and World Wide Web How to Program	1	2000
The Complete Internet and World Wide Web Programming Training Course	1	2000
Java How to Program (Java 2)	3	2000

Fig. 16.14 Titles with copyrights after 1999 from table **Titles**. (Part 1 of 2.)

title	editionNumber	copyright
The Complete Java 2 Training Course	3	2000
XML How to Program	1	2001
Perl How to Program	1	2001
Advanced Java 2 Platform How to Program	1	2002
e-Business and e-Commerce for Managers	1	2000
Wireless Internet and Mobile Business How to Program	1	2001
C# How To Program	1	2002
Python How to Program	1	2002
Visual Basic .NET How to Program	2	2002

Fig. 16.14 Titles with copyrights after 1999 from table **Titles**. (Part 2 of 2.)

The **WHERE** clause condition can contain operators **<, >, <=, >=, =, <>** and **LIKE**. Operator **LIKE** is used for *pattern matching* with wildcard characters *asterisk* (*****) and *question mark* (**?**). Pattern matching allows SQL to search for strings that "match a pattern."

A pattern that contains an asterisk (*****) searches for strings in which zero or more characters take the asterisk character's place in the pattern. For example, the following query locates the records of all authors whose last names start with the letter **D**:

```
SELECT authorID, firstName, lastName
FROM Authors
WHERE lastName LIKE 'D*'
```

The preceding query selects the two records shown in Fig. 16.15, because two of the authors in our database have last names that begin with the letter **D** (followed by zero or more characters). The ***** in the **WHERE** clause's **LIKE** pattern indicates that any number of characters can appear after the letter **D** in the **lastName** field. Notice that the pattern string is surrounded by single-quote characters.

Portability Tip 16.1

*Not all database systems support the **LIKE** operator, so be sure to read the database system's documentation carefully before employing this operator.*

Portability Tip 16.2

*Most databases use the **%** character in place of the ***** character in **LIKE** expressions.*

Portability Tip 16.3

In some databases, string data is case sensitive.

Portability Tip 16.4

In some databases, table names and field names are case sensitive.

Good Programming Practice 16.1

By convention, SQL keywords should be written entirely in uppercase letters on systems that are not case sensitive. This emphasizes the SQL keywords in an SQL statement.

A pattern string including a question mark (**?**) character searches for strings in which exactly one character takes the question mark's place in the pattern. For example, the following query locates the records of all authors whose last names start with any character (specified with **?**), followed by the letter **i**, followed by any number of additional characters (specified with *****):

```
SELECT authorID, firstName, lastName
FROM Authors
WHERE lastName LIKE '?i*'
```

The preceding query produces the records listed in Fig. 16.16; five authors in our database have last names in which the letter **i** is the second letter.

Portability Tip 16.5

Most databases use the _ character in place of the ? character in LIKE expressions.

16.4.3 ORDER BY Clause

The results of a query can be arranged in ascending or descending order using the optional ***ORDER BY*** *clause*. The simplest forms for an **ORDER BY** clause are:

> **SELECT** *fieldName1,* *fieldName2,* ... **FROM** *tableName* **ORDER BY** *field* **ASC**
> **SELECT** *fieldName1,* *fieldName2,* ... **FROM** *tableName* **ORDER BY** *field* **DESC**

where **ASC** specifies ascending order (lowest to highest), **DESC** specifies descending order (highest to lowest) and *field* specifies the field whose values determine the sorting order.

For example, to obtain a list of authors arranged in ascending order by last name (Fig. 16.17), use the query:

```
SELECT authorID, firstName, lastName
FROM Authors
ORDER BY lastName ASC
```

Note that the default sorting order is ascending; therefore, **ASC** is optional.

To obtain the same list of authors arranged in descending order by last name (Fig. 16.18), use the query:

```
SELECT authorID, firstName, lastName
FROM Authors
ORDER BY lastName DESC
```

authorID	firstName	lastName
1	Harvey	Deitel
2	Paul	Deitel

Fig. 16.15 Authors from the **Authors** table whose last names start with **D**.

authorID	firstName	lastName
3	Tem	Nieto
6	Ted	Lin
11	Ben	Wiedermann
12	Jonathan	Liperi
13	Jeffrey	Listfield

Fig. 16.16 Authors from table **Authors** whose last names contain **i** as the second letter.

authorID	firstName	lastName
2	Paul	Deitel
1	Harvey	Deitel
6	Ted	Lin
12	Jonathan	Liperi
13	Jeffrey	Listfield
8	David	McPhie
3	Tem	Nieto
7	Praveen	Sadhu
5	Sean	Santry
4	Kate	Steinbuhler
11	Ben	Wiedermann
9	Cheryl	Yaeger
10	Marina	Zlatkina

Fig. 16.17 Authors from table **Authors** in ascending order by **lastName**.

authorID	firstName	lastName
10	Marina	Zlatkina
9	Cheryl	Yaeger
11	Ben	Wiedermann
4	Kate	Steinbuhler

Fig. 16.18 Authors from table **Authors** in descending order by **lastName**. (Part 1 of 2.)

authorID	firstName	lastName
5	Sean	Santry
7	Praveen	Sadhu
3	Tem	Nieto
8	David	McPhie
13	Jeffrey	Listfield
12	Jonathan	Liperi
6	Ted	Lin
2	Paul	Deitel
1	Harvey	Deitel

Fig. 16.18 Authors from table **Authors** in descending order by **lastName**. (Part 2 of 2.)

The **ORDER BY** clause also can be used to order records by multiple fields. Such queries are written in the form:

> **ORDER BY** *field1 sortingOrder, field2 sortingOrder, ...*

where *sortingOrder* is either **ASC** or **DESC**. Note that the *sortingOrder* does not have to be identical for each field.

For example, the query:

```
SELECT authorID, firstName, lastName
FROM Authors
ORDER BY lastName, firstName
```

sorts all authors in ascending order by last name, then by first name. This means that, if any authors have the same last name, their records are returned sorted by first name (Fig. 16.19).

WHERE and **ORDER BY** clauses can be combined in one query. For example, the query:

```
SELECT isbn, title, editionNumber, copyright, price
FROM Titles
WHERE title
LIKE '*How to Program' ORDER BY title ASC
```

returns the ISBN, title, edition number, copyright and price of each book in the **Titles** table that has a **title** ending with "**How to Program**"; it lists these records in ascending order by **title**. The results of the query are depicted in Fig. 16.20.

authorID	firstName	lastName
1	Harvey	Deitel
2	Paul	Deitel

Fig. 16.19 Authors from table **Authors** in ascending order by **lastName** and by **firstName**. (Part 1 of 2.)

authorID	firstName	lastName
6	Ted	Lin
12	Jonathan	Liperi
13	Jeffrey	Listfield
8	David	McPhie
3	Tem	Nieto
7	Praveen	Sadhu
5	Sean	Santry
4	Kate	Steinbuhler
11	Ben	Wiedermann
9	Cheryl	Yaeger
10	Marina	Zlatkina

Fig. 16.19 Authors from table **Authors** in ascending order by **lastName** and by **firstName**. (Part 2 of 2.)

isbn	title	edition-Number	copy-right	price
0130895601	Advanced Java 2 Platform How to Program	1	2002	$69.95
0131180436	C How to Program	1	1992	$69.95
0130895725	C How to Program	3	2001	$69.95
0132261197	C How to Program	2	1994	$49.95
0130622214	C# How To Program	1	2002	$69.95
0135289106	C++ How to Program	2	1998	$49.95
0131173340	C++ How to Program	1	1994	$69.95
0130895717	C++ How to Program	3	2001	$69.95
013028419X	e-Business and e-Commerce How to Program	1	2001	$69.95
0130308978	Internet and World Wide Web How to Program	2	2002	$69.95
0130161438	Internet and World Wide Web How to Program	1	2000	$69.95
0130341517	Java How to Program	4	2002	$69.95
0136325890	Java How to Program	1	1998	$49.95
0130284181	Perl How to Program	1	2001	$69.95

Fig. 16.20 Books from table **Titles** whose titles end with **How to Program** in ascending order by **title**. (Part 1 of 2.)

isbn	title	edition-Number	copy-right	price
0130923613	Python How to Program	1	2002	$69.95
0130293636	Visual Basic .NET How to Program	2	2002	$69.95
0134569555	Visual Basic 6 How to Program	1	1999	$69.95
0130622265	Wireless Internet and Mobile Business How to Program	1	2001	$69.95
0130284173	XML How to Program	1	2001	$69.95

Fig. 16.20 Books from table **Titles** whose titles end with **How to Program** in ascending order by **title**. (Part 2 of 2.)

16.4.4 INSERT Statement

The **INSERT** statement inserts a new record in a table. The simplest form for this statement is:

> **INSERT INTO** *tableName* **(** *fieldName1***,** *fieldName2***,** *...***,** *fieldNameN* **)**
>   **VALUES (** *value1***,** *value2***,** *...***,** *valueN* **)**

where *tableName* is the table in which to insert the record. The *tableName* is followed by a comma-separated list of field names in parentheses. The list of field names is followed by the SQL keyword **VALUES** and a comma-separated list of values in parentheses. The specified values in this list must match the field names listed after the table name in both order and type (for example, if *fieldName1* is specified as the **firstName** field, then *value1* should be a string in single quotes representing the first name). The **INSERT** statement:

> **INSERT INTO** Authors **(** firstName**,** lastName **)**
>   **VALUES (** 'Sue'**,** 'Smith' **)**

inserts a record into the **Authors** table. The first comma-separated list indicates that the statement provides data for the **firstName** and **lastName** fields. The corresponding values to insert, which are contained in the second comma-separated list, are **'Sue'** and **'Smith'**. We do not specify an **authorID** in this example, because **authorID** is an auto-increment field in the database. Every new record that we add to this table is assigned a unique **authorID** value that is the next value in the auto-increment sequence (i.e., 1, 2, 3, etc.). In this case, **Sue Smith** would be assigned **authorID** number 14. Figure 16.21 shows the **Authors** table after we perform the **INSERT** operation.

authorID	firstName	lastName
1	Harvey	Deitel
2	Paul	Deitel

Fig. 16.21 Authors after an **INSERT** operation to add a record. (Part 1 of 2.)

authorID	firstName	lastName
3	Tem	Nieto
4	Kate	Steinbuhler
5	Sean	Santry
6	Ted	Lin
7	Praveen	Sadhu
8	David	McPhie
9	Cheryl	Yaeger
10	Marina	Zlatkina
11	Ben	Wiedermann
12	Jonathan	Liperi
13	Jeffrey	Listfield
14	Sue	Smith

Fig. 16.21 `Authors` after an `INSERT` operation to add a record. (Part 2 of 2.)

Common Programming Error 16.5

SQL statements use the single-quote (') character as a delimiter for strings. To specify a string containing a single quote (such as O'Malley) in an SQL statement, the string must include two single quotes in the position where the single-quote character should appear in the string (e.g., `'O''Malley'` *). The first of the two single-quote characters acts as an escape character for the second. Failure to escape single-quote characters in a string that is part of an SQL statement is an SQL syntax error.*

16.4.5 UPDATE Statement

An *UPDATE* statement modifies data in a table. The simplest form for an **UPDATE** statement is:

> *UPDATE* *tableName*
>   *SET* *fieldName1* = *value1,* *fieldName2* = *value2,* ..., *fieldNameN* = *valueN*
>   *WHERE* *criteria*

where *tableName* is the table in which to update a record (or records). The *tableName* is followed by keyword *SET* and a comma-separated list of field name/value pairs written in the format, *fieldName* = *value*. The **WHERE** clause specifies the criteria used to determine which record(s) to update. For example, the **UPDATE** statement:

> *UPDATE* Authors
>   *SET* lastName = 'Jones'
>   *WHERE* lastName = 'Smith' *AND* firstName = 'Sue'

updates a record in the **Authors** table. The statement indicates that **lastName** will be assigned the new value **Jones** for the record in which **lastName** currently is equal to **Smith** and **firstName** is equal to **Sue**. If we know the **authorID** in advance of the

UPDATE operation (possibly because we searched for the record previously), the **WHERE** clause could be simplified as follows:

```
WHERE AuthorID = 14
```

Figure 16.22 depicts the **Authors** table after we perform the **UPDATE** operation.

Common Programming Error 16.6

*Failure to use a **WHERE** clause with an **UPDATE** statement could lead to logic errors.*

16.4.6 DELETE Statement

An SQL **DELETE** statement removes data from a table. The simplest form for a **DELETE** statement is:

```
DELETE FROM tableName WHERE criteria
```

where *tableName* is the table from which to delete a record (or records). The **WHERE** clause specifies the criteria used to determine which record(s) to delete. For example, the **DELETE** statement:

```
DELETE FROM Authors
    WHERE lastName = 'Jones' AND firstName = 'Sue'
```

deletes the record for **Sue Jones** from the **Authors** table.

authorID	firstName	lastName
1	Harvey	Deitel
2	Paul	Deitel
3	Tem	Nieto
4	Kate	Steinbuhler
5	Sean	Santry
6	Ted	Lin
7	Praveen	Sadhu
8	David	McPhie
9	Cheryl	Yaeger
10	Marina	Zlatkina
11	Ben	Wiedermann
12	Jonathan	Liperi
13	Jeffrey	Listfield
14	Sue	Jones

Fig. 16.22 Table **Authors** after an **UPDATE** operation to change a record.

Common Programming Error 16.7

WHERE clauses can match multiple records. When deleting records from a database, be sure to define a WHERE clause that matches only the records to be deleted.

Figure 16.23 depicts the **Authors** table after we perform the **DELETE** operation.

16.5 ADO .NET Object Model

The ADO .NET object model provides an API for accessing database systems programmatically. ADO .NET was created for the .NET Framework and is the next generation of *ActiveX Data Objects*™ (ADO).

Namespace **System.Data** is the root namespace for the ADO .NET API. The primary namespaces for ADO .NET, **System.Data.OleDb** and **System.Data.SqlClient**, contain classes that enable programs to connect with and modify datasources. Namespace **System.Data.OleDb** contains classes that are designed to work with any datasource, whereas the **System.Data.SqlClient** namespace contains classes that are optimized to work with Microsoft SQL Server 2000 databases.

Instances of class **System.Data.DataSet**, which consist of a set of **DataTable**s and relationships among those **DataTable**s, represent *caches* of data—data that a program stores temporarily in local memory. The structure of a **DataSet** mimics the structure of a relational database. An advantage of using class **DataSet** is that it is *disconnected*—the program does not need a persistent connection to the datasource to work with data in a **DataSet**. The program connects to the datasource only during the initial population of the **DataSet** and then to store any changes made in the **DataSet**. Hence, the program does not require any active, permanent connection to the datasource.

authorID	firstName	lastName
1	Harvey	Deitel
2	Paul	Deitel
3	Tem	Nieto
4	Kate	Steinbuhler
5	Sean	Santry
6	Ted	Lin
7	Praveen	Sadhu
8	David	McPhie
9	Cheryl	Yaeger
10	Marina	Zlatkina
11	Ben	Wiedermann
12	Jonathan	Liperi
13	Jeffrey	Listfield

Fig. 16.23 Table **Authors** after a **DELETE** operation to remove a record.

Instances of class *OleDbConnection* (namespace **System.Data.OleDb**) represent connections to a datasource. An instance of class *OleDbDataAdapter* connects to a datasource through an instance of class **OleDbConnection** and can populate a **DataSet** with data from that datasource. We discuss the details of creating and populating **DataSet**s momentarily. An instance of class *OleDbCommand* (namespace **System.Data.OleDb**) represents an arbitrary SQL command to be executed on a datasource. A program can use instances of class **OleDbCommand** to manipulate a datasource through an **OleDbConnection**. The programmer must close the active connection to the datasource explicitly once no further changes are to be made. Unlike **DataSet**s, **OleDbCommand** objects do not cache data in local memory.

Instances of classes **SqlDataReader** (namespace **System.Data.SqlClient**) and **OleDbDataReader** (namespace **System.Data.OleDb**) represent read-only connections to a datasource. Data readers provide a performance-optimized way to retrieve large amounts of data. Chapter 17, ASP .NET, Web Forms and Web Controls, contains an application using an **OleDbDataReader**.

16.6 Programming with ADO .NET: Extracting Information from a Database

In this section, we present examples that introduce how to connect to a database, query the database and display the results of the query. The database used in these examples is the Microsoft Access **Books** database that we have discussed throughout this chapter. It can be found in the project directory for the application of Fig. 16.24. This program must specify the location of the database on the computer's hard drive. When executing these examples, readers must update this location. For example, before readers can run the application in Fig. 16.24 on their computers, they must change lines 234–247 so that the code specifies the correct location of the database file.

16.6.1 Connecting to and Querying an Access Data Source

Figure 16.24 performs a simple query on the **Books** database that retrieves the entire **Authors** table and displays the data in a *DataGrid* (a **System.Windows.Forms** component class that can display a datasource in a GUI). The program illustrates the process of connecting to the database, querying the database and displaying the results in a **DataGrid**. The discussion following the example presents the key aspects of the program. [*Note*: We present all of Visual Studio's auto-generated code in Fig. 16.24 so that readers are aware of the code that Visual Studio generates for the example.]

This example uses an Access database. To register the **Books** database as a datasource, select **View > Server Explorer**. Right click the **Data Connections** node in the **Server Explorer** and then select **Add Connection....** In the **Provider** tab of the window that appears, select "**Microsoft Jet 4.0 OLE DB Provider**," which is the driver for Access databases. In the **Connection** tab, click the ellipses button (**...**) to the right of the textbox for the database name, which opens the **Select Access Database** dialog. Go to the appropriate folder, select the **Books** database and click **OK**. Now, this database is listed as a connection in the **Server Explorer**. Drag the database node onto the Windows Form. This creates an **OleDbConnection** to the source, which the Windows Form designer displays as **oleDbConnection1**.

```
1    // Fig. 16.24: TableDisplay.cs
2    // Displays data from a database table.
3
4    using System;
5    using System.Drawing;
6    using System.Collections;
7    using System.ComponentModel;
8    using System.Windows.Forms;
9    using System.Data;
10
11   // Summary description for TableDisplay.cs.
12   public class TableDisplay : System.Windows.Forms.Form
13   {
14      private System.Data.DataSet dataSet1;
15      private System.Data.OleDb.OleDbDataAdapter oleDbDataAdapter1;
16      private System.Windows.Forms.DataGrid dataGrid1;
17      private System.Data.OleDb.OleDbCommand oleDbSelectCommand1;
18      private System.Data.OleDb.OleDbCommand oleDbInsertCommand1;
19      private System.Data.OleDb.OleDbCommand oleDbUpdateCommand1;
20      private System.Data.OleDb.OleDbCommand oleDbDeleteCommand1;
21      private System.Data.OleDb.OleDbConnection oleDbConnection1;
22
23      private System.ComponentModel.Container components = null;
24
25      public TableDisplay()
26      {
27         InitializeComponent();
28
29         // Fill dataSet1 with data
30         oleDbDataAdapter1.Fill( dataSet1, "Authors" );
31
32         // bind data in Authors table in dataSet1 to dataGrid1
33         dataGrid1.SetDataBinding( dataSet1, "Authors" );
34      }
35
36      private void InitializeComponent()
37      {
38         this.dataSet1 = new System.Data.DataSet();
39         this.oleDbDataAdapter1 =
40            new System.Data.OleDb.OleDbDataAdapter();
41         this.dataGrid1 = new System.Windows.Forms.DataGrid();
42         this.oleDbSelectCommand1 =
43            new System.Data.OleDb.OleDbCommand();
44         this.oleDbInsertCommand1 =
45            new System.Data.OleDb.OleDbCommand();
46         this.oleDbUpdateCommand1 =
47            new System.Data.OleDb.OleDbCommand();
48         this.oleDbDeleteCommand1 =
49            new System.Data.OleDb.OleDbCommand();
50         this.oleDbConnection1 =
51            new System.Data.OleDb.OleDbConnection();
52         ((System.ComponentModel.ISupportInitialize)
53            (this.dataSet1)).BeginInit();
```

Fig. 16.24 Accessing and displaying a database's data. (Part 1 of 6.)

```
54              ((System.ComponentModel.ISupportInitialize)
55                  (this.dataGrid1)).BeginInit();
56          this.SuspendLayout();
57          //
58          // dataSet1
59          //
60          this.dataSet1.DataSetName = "NewDataSet";
61          this.dataSet1.Locale =
62              new System.Globalization.CultureInfo("en-US");
63          //
64          // oleDbDataAdapter1
65          //
66          this.oleDbDataAdapter1.DeleteCommand =
67              this.oleDbDeleteCommand1;
68          this.oleDbDataAdapter1.InsertCommand =
69              this.oleDbInsertCommand1;
70          this.oleDbDataAdapter1.SelectCommand =
71              this.oleDbSelectCommand1;
72          this.oleDbDataAdapter1.TableMappings.AddRange(
73              new System.Data.Common.DataTableMapping[] {
74                  new System.Data.Common.DataTableMapping(
75                      "Table", "Authors",
76                      new System.Data.Common.DataColumnMapping[] {
77                          new System.Data.Common.DataColumnMapping(
78                              "authorID", "authorID"),
79                          new System.Data.Common.DataColumnMapping(
80                              "firstName", "firstName"),
81                          new System.Data.Common.DataColumnMapping(
82                              "lastName", "lastName")})});
83          this.oleDbDataAdapter1.UpdateCommand =
84              this.oleDbUpdateCommand1;
85          //
86          // dataGrid1
87          //
88          this.dataGrid1.DataMember = "";
89          this.dataGrid1.HeaderForeColor =
90              System.Drawing.SystemColors.ControlText;
91          this.dataGrid1.Location =
92              new System.Drawing.Point(16, 16);
93          this.dataGrid1.Name = "dataGrid1";
94          this.dataGrid1.Size = new System.Drawing.Size(264, 248);
95          this.dataGrid1.TabIndex = 0;
96          //
97          // oleDbSelectCommand1
98          //
99          this.oleDbSelectCommand1.CommandText =
100             "SELECT authorID, firstName, lastName FROM Authors";
101         this.oleDbSelectCommand1.Connection =
102             this.oleDbConnection1;
103         //
104         // oleDbInsertCommand1
105         //
106         this.oleDbInsertCommand1.CommandText =
```

Fig. 16.24 Accessing and displaying a database's data. (Part 2 of 6.)

```
107              "INSERT INTO Authors(firstName, lastName) VALUES " +
108              "(?, ?)";
109         this.oleDbInsertCommand1.Connection =
110              this.oleDbConnection1;
111         this.oleDbInsertCommand1.Parameters.Add(
112              new System.Data.OleDb.OleDbParameter("firstName",
113                  System.Data.OleDb.OleDbType.VarWChar, 50,
114                  "firstName"));
115         this.oleDbInsertCommand1.Parameters.Add(
116              new System.Data.OleDb.OleDbParameter("lastName",
117                  System.Data.OleDb.OleDbType.VarWChar, 50,
118                  "lastName"));
119         //
120         // oleDbUpdateCommand1
121         //
122         this.oleDbUpdateCommand1.CommandText =
123              "UPDATE Authors SET firstName = ?, lastName = ? WHERE" +
124              " (authorID = ?) AND (firstNam" +
125              "e = ? OR ? IS NULL AND firstName IS NULL) AND " +
126              "(lastName = ? OR ? IS NULL AND las" +
127              "tName IS NULL)";
128         this.oleDbUpdateCommand1.Connection =
129              this.oleDbConnection1;
130         this.oleDbUpdateCommand1.Parameters.Add(
131              new System.Data.OleDb.OleDbParameter(
132                  "firstName",
133                  System.Data.OleDb.OleDbType.VarWChar,
134                  50, "firstName"));
135         this.oleDbUpdateCommand1.Parameters.Add(
136              new System.Data.OleDb.OleDbParameter(
137              "lastName",
138              System.Data.OleDb.OleDbType.VarWChar, 50,
139              "lastName"));
140         this.oleDbUpdateCommand1.Parameters.Add(
141              new System.Data.OleDb.OleDbParameter(
142                  "Original_authorID",
143                  System.Data.OleDb.OleDbType.Integer, 0,
144                  System.Data.ParameterDirection.Input, false,
145                  ((System.Byte)(10)), ((System.Byte)(0)),
146                  "authorID", System.Data.DataRowVersion.Original,
147                  null));
148         this.oleDbUpdateCommand1.Parameters.Add(
149              new System.Data.OleDb.OleDbParameter(
150                  "Original_firstName",
151                  System.Data.OleDb.OleDbType.VarWChar, 50,
152                  System.Data.ParameterDirection.Input, false,
153                  ((System.Byte)(0)), ((System.Byte)(0)),
154                  "firstName", System.Data.DataRowVersion.Original,
155                  null));
156         this.oleDbUpdateCommand1.Parameters.Add(
157              new System.Data.OleDb.OleDbParameter(
158                  "Original_firstName1",
159                  System.Data.OleDb.OleDbType.VarWChar, 50,
```

Fig. 16.24 Accessing and displaying a database's data. (Part 3 of 6.)

```
160              System.Data.ParameterDirection.Input, false,
161              ((System.Byte)(0)), ((System.Byte)(0)),
162              "firstName", System.Data.DataRowVersion.Original,
163              null));
164          this.oleDbUpdateCommand1.Parameters.Add(
165              new System.Data.OleDb.OleDbParameter(
166                  "Original_lastName",
167                  System.Data.OleDb.OleDbType.VarWChar, 50,
168                  System.Data.ParameterDirection.Input, false,
169                  ((System.Byte)(0)), ((System.Byte)(0)),
170                  "lastName", System.Data.DataRowVersion.Original,
171                  null));
172          this.oleDbUpdateCommand1.Parameters.Add(
173              new System.Data.OleDb.OleDbParameter(
174                  "Original_lastName1",
175                  System.Data.OleDb.OleDbType.VarWChar, 50,
176                  System.Data.ParameterDirection.Input, false,
177                  ((System.Byte)(0)), ((System.Byte)(0)),
178                  "lastName", System.Data.DataRowVersion.Original,
179                  null));
180          //
181          // oleDbDeleteCommand1
182          //
183          this.oleDbDeleteCommand1.CommandText =
184              "DELETE FROM Authors WHERE (authorID = ?) AND " +
185              "(firstName = ? OR ? IS NULL AND firs" +
186              "tName IS NULL) AND (lastName = ? OR ? IS NULL AND " +
187              "lastName IS NULL)";
188          this.oleDbDeleteCommand1.Connection =
189              this.oleDbConnection1;
190          this.oleDbDeleteCommand1.Parameters.Add(
191              new System.Data.OleDb.OleDbParameter(
192                  "Original_authorID",
193                  System.Data.OleDb.OleDbType.Integer, 0,
194                  System.Data.ParameterDirection.Input, false,
195                  ((System.Byte)(10)), ((System.Byte)(0)),
196                  "authorID", System.Data.DataRowVersion.Original,
197                  null));
198          this.oleDbDeleteCommand1.Parameters.Add(
199              new System.Data.OleDb.OleDbParameter(
200                  "Original_firstName",
201                  System.Data.OleDb.OleDbType.VarWChar, 50,
202                  System.Data.ParameterDirection.Input, false,
203                  ((System.Byte)(0)), ((System.Byte)(0)),
204                  "firstName", System.Data.DataRowVersion.Original,
205                  null));
206          this.oleDbDeleteCommand1.Parameters.Add(
207              new System.Data.OleDb.OleDbParameter(
208                  "Original_firstName1",
209                  System.Data.OleDb.OleDbType.VarWChar, 50,
210                  System.Data.ParameterDirection.Input, false,
211                  ((System.Byte)(0)), ((System.Byte)(0)),
212                  "firstName", System.Data.DataRowVersion.Original,
```

Fig. 16.24 Accessing and displaying a database's data. (Part 4 of 6.)

```
213                  null));
214           this.oleDbDeleteCommand1.Parameters.Add(
215              new System.Data.OleDb.OleDbParameter(
216                 "Original_lastName",
217                 System.Data.OleDb.OleDbType.VarWChar, 50,
218                 System.Data.ParameterDirection.Input, false,
219                 ((System.Byte)(0)), ((System.Byte)(0)),
220                 "lastName", System.Data.DataRowVersion.Original,
221                 null));
222           this.oleDbDeleteCommand1.Parameters.Add(
223              new System.Data.OleDb.OleDbParameter(
224                 "Original_lastName1",
225                 System.Data.OleDb.OleDbType.VarWChar, 50,
226                 System.Data.ParameterDirection.Input, false,
227                 ((System.Byte)(0)), ((System.Byte)(0)),
228                 "lastName", System.Data.DataRowVersion.Original,
229                 null));
230           //
231           // oleDbConnection1
232           //
233           this.oleDbConnection1.ConnectionString =
234              @"Provider=Microsoft.Jet.OLEDB.4.0;Password="""";" +
235              @"User ID=Admin;Data Source=C:\Books\2001\csphtp1\" +
236              @"csphtp1_examples\ch19\Books.mdb;Mode=Share " +
237              @"Deny None;Extended Properties="""";Jet OLEDB:" +
238              @"System database="""";Jet OLEDB:Registry " +
239              @"Path="""";Jet OLEDB:Database Password="""";" +
240              @"Jet OLEDB:Engine Type=5;Jet OLEDB:Database " +
241              @"Locking Mode=1;Jet OLEDB:Global Partial Bulk " +
242              @"Ops=2;Jet OLEDB:Global Bulk Transactions=1;Jet " +
243              @"OLEDB:New Database Password="""";Jet OLEDB:" +
244              @"Create System Database=False;Jet OLEDB:Encrypt " +
245              @"Database=False;Jet OLEDB:Don't Copy Locale on " +
246              @"Compact=False;Jet OLEDB:Compact Without Replica " +
247              @"Repair=False;Jet OLEDB:SFP=False";
248           //
249           // TableDisplay
250           //
251           this.AutoScaleBaseSize = new System.Drawing.Size(5, 13);
252           this.ClientSize = new System.Drawing.Size(292, 273);
253           this.Controls.AddRange(
254              new System.Windows.Forms.Control[] {
255                 this.dataGrid1});
256           this.Name = "TableDisplay";
257           this.Text = "TableDisplay";
258           ((System.ComponentModel.ISupportInitialize)
259              (this.dataSet1)).EndInit();
260           ((System.ComponentModel.ISupportInitialize)
261              (this.dataGrid1)).EndInit();
262           this.ResumeLayout(false);
263
264        }    // end of InitializeComponent
265
```

Fig. 16.24 Accessing and displaying a database's data. (Part 5 of 6.)

```
266     [STAThread]
267     static void Main()
268     {
269         Application.Run( new TableDisplay() );
270     }
271 }
```

Fig. 16.24 Accessing and displaying a database's data. (Part 6 of 6.)

Next, drag an *OleDbDataAdapter* from the **Toolbox**'s *Data* group onto the Windows Form designer. This displays the **Data Adapter Configuration Wizard** for configuring the **OleDbDataAdapter** instance with a custom query for populating a **DataSet**. Click **Next** to select a connection to use. Select the connection created in the previous step from the drop-down list and click **Next**. The resulting screen allows us to choose how the **OleDbDataAdapter** should access the database. Keep the default **Use SQL Statement** option and then click **Next**. Click the **Query Builder** button, select the **Authors** table from the **Add** menu and **Close** that menu. Place a check mark in the ***All Columns** box from the **Authors** window. Notice how that particular window lists all columns of the **Authors** table.

Next, we must create a **DataSet** to store the query results. To do so, drag **DataSet** from the **Data** group in the **Toolbox**. This displays the **Add DataSet** window. Choose the **Untyped DataSet (no schema)**, because the query with which we populate the **DataSet** dictates the **DataSet**'s *schema*, or structure.

Figure 16.24 shows all of the code generated by Visual Studio. Normally, we omit this code, because it usually only contains GUI related code. In this case, however, the code contains database functionality that we must discuss. Furthermore, we have left the default naming conventions of Visual Studio in this example to demonstrate the exact format of the auto-generated code that Visual Studio creates. Normally, we would change these names to conform to our programming conventions and style. The code generated by Visual Studio has also been formatted for presentation purposes.

 Good Programming Practice 16.2

Use clear, descriptive variable names in code. This makes programs easier to understand.

Lines 233–247 initialize the **oleDbConnection** for this program. The **ConnectionString** property specifies the path to the database file on the computer's hard drive.

An instance of class **OleDbDataAdapter** populates the **DataSet** in this example with data from the **Books** database. The instance properties *DeleteCommand* (lines 66–67), *InsertCommand* (lines 68–69), *SelectCommand* (lines 70–71) and *Update-Command* (lines 83–84) are **OleDbCommand** objects that specify how the **OleDbData-Adapter** deletes, inserts, selects and updates data in the database, respectively.

Each **OleDbCommand** object must have an **OleDbConnection** through which the **OleDbCommand** can communicate with the database. Property **Connection** is set to the **OleDbConnection** to the **Books** database. For **oleDbUpdateCommand1**, lines 128–129 set the **Connection** property, and lines 122–127 set the **CommandText**.

Although Visual Studio generates most of this program's code, we enter code in the **TableDisplay** constructor (lines 25–34) for populating **dataSet1** using an **OleDb-DataAdapter**. Line 30 calls **OleDbDataAdapter** method *Fill* to retrieve information from the database associated with the **OleDbConnection**, placing the information in the **DataSet** provided as an argument. The second argument to this method is a **string** that specifies the name of the table in the database from which to **Fill** the **DataSet**.

Line 33 invokes **DataGrid** method *SetDataBinding* to bind the **DataGrid** to a data source. The first argument is the **DataSet**—in this case, **dataSet1**—whose data the **DataGrid** should display. The second argument is a **string** representing the name of the table within the data source we want to bind to the **DataGrid**. Once this line executes, the **DataGrid** is filled with the information in the **DataSet**—the number of rows and number of columns are set from the information in **dataSet1**.

16.6.2 Querying the Books Database

The example in Fig. 16.25 demonstrates how to execute SQL **SELECT** statements on database **Books.mdb** and display the results. Although Fig. 16.25 uses only **SELECT** statements to query the data, the same program could be used to execute many different SQL statements if we made a few minor modifications.

Method **submitButton_Click** is the key part of this program. When the program invokes this event handler, lines 47–48 assign the **SELECT** query **string** to **OleDb-DataAdapter**'s **SelectCommand** property. This **string** is parsed into an SQL query and executed on the database via the **OleDbDataAdapter**'s **Fill** method (line 55). As we discussed in the previous section, method **Fill** places data from the database into **dataSet1**.

```
1   // Fig. 16.25: DisplayQueryResults.cs
2   // Displays the contents of the authors database.
3
4   using System;
5   using System.Drawing;
6   using System.Collections;
7   using System.ComponentModel;
```

Fig. 16.25 Execute SQL statements on a database. (Part 1 of 3.)

```
 8   using System.Windows.Forms;
 9   using System.Data;
10
11   public class DisplayQueryResults : System.Windows.Forms.Form
12   {
13      private System.Data.OleDb.OleDbConnection oleDbConnection1;
14      private System.Data.DataSet dataSet1;
15      private System.Data.OleDb.OleDbDataAdapter oleDbDataAdapter1;
16      private System.Data.OleDb.OleDbCommand oleDbSelectCommand1;
17      private System.Data.OleDb.OleDbCommand oleDbInsertCommand1;
18      private System.Data.OleDb.OleDbCommand oleDbUpdateCommand1;
19      private System.Data.OleDb.OleDbCommand oleDbDeleteCommand1;
20      private System.Windows.Forms.TextBox queryTextBox;
21      private System.Windows.Forms.Button submitButton;
22      private System.Windows.Forms.DataGrid dataGrid1;
23      private System.ComponentModel.Container components = null;
24
25      public DisplayQueryResults()
26      {
27
28         InitializeComponent();
29      }
30
31      // Visual Studio.NET generated code
32
33      [STAThread]
34      static void Main()
35      {
36         Application.Run( new DisplayQueryResults() );
37      }
38
39      // perform SQL query on data
40      private void submitButton_Click( object sender,
41         System.EventArgs e )
42      {
43         try
44         {
45            // set SQL query to what user
46            // input into queryTextBox
47            oleDbDataAdapter1.SelectCommand.CommandText =
48               queryTextBox.Text;
49
50            // clear DataSet from previous operation
51            dataSet1.Clear();
52
53            // Fill data set with information that results
54            // from SQL query
55            oleDbDataAdapter1.Fill( dataSet1, "Authors" );
56
57            // bind DataGrid to contents of DataSet
58            dataGrid1.SetDataBinding( dataSet1, "Authors" );
59         }
60
```

Fig. 16.25 Execute SQL statements on a database. (Part 2 of 3.)

```
61              catch ( System.Data.OleDb.OleDbException oleException )
62              {
63                  MessageBox.Show( "Invalid query" );
64              }
65
66          }  // end of submitButton_Click
67      }
```

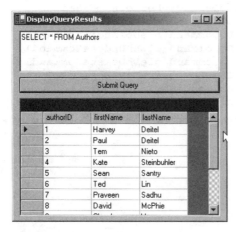

Fig. 16.25 Execute SQL statements on a database. (Part 3 of 3.)

Common Programming Error 16.8

*If a **DataSet** has been **Fill**ed at least once, forgetting to call a **DataSet**'s **Clear** method before calling the **Fill** method again will lead to logic errors.*

To display or redisplay contents in the **DataGrid**, use method **SetDataBinding**. The first argument is the data source to be displayed in the table—a **DataSet** in this case. The second argument is the **string** name of the data-source member to be displayed (line 58). Readers can try entering their own query in the text box and pressing the **Submit Query** button to execute the query.

16.7 Summary

A database is an integrated collection of data. A database management system (DBMS) provides mechanisms for storing and organizing data. Today's most popular database systems are relational databases.

A relational database is composed of tables. A row of a table is called a record. A primary key is a field that contains unique data, or data that are not duplicated in other records of that table. Each column in a table represents a different field. A primary key can be composed of more than one column (or field) in the database. A one-to-many relationship between tables indicates that a record in one table can have many corresponding records in a separate table. A foreign key is a field for which every entry in one table has a unique value in another table, where the field in the second table is the primary key for that table.

A language called Structured Query Language (SQL) is used almost universally with relational-database systems to perform queries and manipulate data. SQL provides a complete set of commands, enabling programmers to define complex queries to select data from a table. The results of a query commonly are called result sets (or record sets).

The **SELECT** query is used to extract data from a database. The optional **WHERE** clause specifies the selection criteria for the query. The condition of the **WHERE** clause can contain operators **<**, **>**, **<=**, **>=**, **=**, **<>** and **LIKE**. Operator **LIKE** is used for pattern matching with wildcard characters asterisk (*****) and question mark (**?**). The results of a query can be arranged in ascending or descending order via the optional **ORDER BY** clause. A join merges records from two or more tables by testing for matching values in a field that is common to both tables. An **INSERT** statement inserts a new record in a table. An **UPDATE** statement modifies data in a table. A **DELETE** statement removes data from a table.

A programming language connects to, and interacts with, relational databases via an interface. C# programmers communicate with databases and manipulate their data via ADO .NET. **System.Data**, **System.Data.OleDb** and **System.Data.Sql-Client** are the three main namespaces in ADO .NET. Class **DataSet** is from the **System.Data** namespace. Instances of this class represent in-memory caches of data. The advantage of using class **DataSet** is that it allows the contents of a datasource to be modified without having to maintain an active connection to the database. Class **OleDb-Command** of the **System.Data.OleDb** namespace enables the programmer to execute SQL statements directly on the datasource.

The **Add Connection** option is used to create a database connection. The **Data Adapter Configuration Wizard** is used to set up an **OleDbDataAdapter** and generate queries. **OleDbCommand** commands are what the **OleDbDataAdapter** executes on the database in the form of SQL queries. **OleDbCommand** instance property **Connection** is set to the **OleDbConnection** on which the command will be executed, and the instance property **CommandText** is set to the SQL query that will be executed on the database.

ASP .NET, Web Forms and Web Controls

Objectives

- To become familiar with Web Forms in ASP .NET.
- To be able to create Web Forms.
- To become familiar with Web controls.
- To become familiar with the Simple Object Access Protocol (SOAP).

If any man will draw up his case, and put his name at the foot of the first page, I will give him an immediate reply. Where he compels me to turn over the sheet, he must wait my leisure.
Lord Sandwich

Rule One: Our client is always right
Rule Two: If you think our client is wrong, see Rule One.
Anonymous

A fair question should be followed by a deed in silence.
Dante Alighieri

You will come here and get books that will open your eyes, and your ears, and your curiosity, and turn you inside out or outside in.
Ralph Waldo Emerson

Outline

17.1 Introduction

In previous chapters, we used Windows Forms and Windows controls to develop Windows applications. In this chapter, we introduce *Web-based application development* with Microsoft's ASP .NET technology. Web-based applications create content for Web browser clients. This Web content can include HyperText Markup Language (HTML),[1] client-side scripting, images and binary data.

We present an example that demonstrates Web-based applications development using *Web Forms* (also known as *Web Form pages*), *Web controls* (also known as *ASP .NET server controls*) and C# programming. Web Form files have the file extension **.aspx** and contain the Web page's GUI. Programmers customize Web Forms by adding Web controls, which include labels, text boxes, images, buttons and other GUI components. [*Note:* From this point onward, we refer to Web Form files as *ASPX files*.]

Every ASPX file created in Visual Studio has a corresponding class written in a .NET-compliant language, such as C#. This class includes event handlers, initialization code, utility methods and other supporting code for the user interface in the ASPX file. The C# file that contains this class is called the *code-behind file* and provides the ASPX file's programmatic implementation.

17.2 Simple HTTP Transaction

Before exploring Web-based applications development further, a basic understanding of networking and the World Wide Web is necessary. In this section, we examine the inner workings of the *HyperText Transfer Protocol (HTTP)* and discuss what occurs behind the scenes when a browser displays a Web page. HTTP is a protocol that specifies a set of *methods* and *headers* that allow clients and servers to interact and exchange information in a uniform and predictable way.

In their simplest form, Web pages are HTML documents, these are plain-text files that contains markings (*markup* or *tags*) describing the structures of the documents. For example, the HTML markup:

```
<title>My Web Page</title>
```

indicates that the text contained between the **<title>** *start tag* and the **</title>** *end tag* is the Web page's title. HTML documents also can contain *hyperlinks*, which enable

---

1. Readers not familiar with HTML should read Appendices G–H before studying this chapter.

users to navigate their Web browsers to other Web pages. When the user activates a hyperlink (usually by clicking it with the mouse), the requested Web page (or different part of the same Web page) is loaded into the user's browser window.

Any HTML document available on the Web has a *Uniform Resource Locator (URL)*, which indicates the location of a resource. The URL contains information that directs Web browsers to the document. Computers that run *Web server* software provide such resources. Microsoft *Internet Information Services (IIS)* is the Web server that programmers use when developing ASP .NET Web applications in Visual Studio.

Let us examine the components of the URL:

```
http://www.deitel.com/books/downloads.htm
```

The **http://** indicates that the resource is to be obtained using HTTP. The middle portion—**www.deitel.com**—is the fully qualified *hostname* of the server. The hostname is the name of the computer on which the resource resides. This computer usually is referred to as the *host*, because it houses and maintains resources. The hostname **www.deitel.com** is translated into an *IP address* (**207.60.134.230**) that identifies the server in a manner similar to that by which a telephone number uniquely defines a particular phone line. The translation of the hostname into an IP address normally is performed by a *domain name server (DNS)*—a computer that maintains a database of hostnames and their corresponding IP addresses. This translation operation is called a *DNS lookup*.

The remainder of the URL provides the name and location of the requested resource, **/books/downloads.htm** (an HTML document). This portion of the URL specifies both the name of the resource (**downloads.htm**) and its path, or location (**/books**), on the Web server. The path could specify the location of an actual directory on the Web server's file system. However, for security reasons, paths often specify the locations of a *virtual directory*. In such systems, the server translates the virtual directory into a real location on the server (or on another computer on the server's network), thus hiding the true location of the resource. Furthermore, some resources are created dynamically and do not reside anywhere on the server computer. The hostname in the URL for such a resource specifies the correct server, and the path and resource information identifies the location of the resource with which to respond to the client's request.

When given a URL, a browser performs a simple HTTP transaction to retrieve and display a Web page. Figure 17.1 illustrates this transaction in detail. The transaction consists of interaction between the Web browser (the client side) and the Web-server application (the server side).

In Fig. 17.1, the Web browser sends an HTTP request to the server. The request (in its simplest form) is

```
GET /books/downloads.htm HTTP/1.1
```

The word **GET** is an HTTP method indicating that the client wishes to obtain a resource from the server. The remainder of the request provides the path name of the resource and the protocol's name and version number (**HTTP/1.1**).

Any server that understands HTTP (version 1.1) can translate this request and respond appropriately. Figure 17.2 depicts a Web server's response when it a successful request. The server first responds by sending a line of text that indicates the HTTP version, followed by a numeric code and phrase, both of which describe the status of the transaction. For example,

```
HTTP/1.1 200 OK
```

indicates success, whereas

```
HTTP/1.1 404 Not found
```

informs the client that the Web server could not locate the requested resource.

The server then sends one or more *HTTP headers,* which provide information about the data that will be sent. In this case, the server is sending an HTML text document, so the HTTP header for this example reads:

```
Content-type: text/html
```

This header specifies the *Multipurpose Internet Mail Extensions* (*MIME*) type of the content that the server is transmitting to the browser. MIME is an Internet standard used to identify various types of data so that programs can interpret those data correctly. For example, the MIME type **text/plain** indicates that the information is plain-text, which a Web browser can display directly without any special formatting. Similarly, the MIME type **image/gif** indicates that the transmitted content is a GIF image, enabling the Web browser to display the image appropriately.

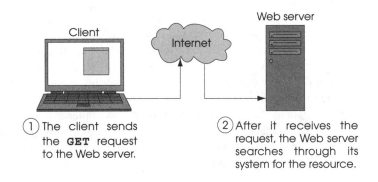

① The client sends the **GET** request to the Web server.

② After it receives the request, the Web server searches through its system for the resource.

Fig. 17.1 Web server/client interaction. Step 1: The **GET** request, **GET /books/downloads.htm HTTP/1.1**.

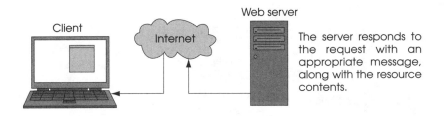

The server responds to the request with an appropriate message, along with the resource contents.

Fig. 17.2 Client interacting with Web server. Step 2: The HTTP response, **HTTP/1.1 200 OK**.

The set of headers is followed by a blank line, which indicates to the client that the server is finished sending HTTP headers. The server then sends the contents of the requested HTML document (**downloads.htm**). The server terminates the connection when the transfer of the resource is complete. At this point, the client-side browser parses the HTML it has received and *renders* (or displays) the results.

17.3 System Architecture

Most Web-based applications are *multi-tier applications* (sometimes referred to as *n*-tier applications). Multi-tier applications divide functionality into separate *tiers* (i.e., logical groupings of functionality). Although tiers can be located on the same computer, the tiers of Web-based applications typically reside on separate computers. Figure 17.3 presents the basic structure of a three-tier Web-based application.

The *information tier* (also called the *data tier* or the *bottom tier*) maintains data that pertains to the application. This tier typically stores data in a *relational database management system (RDBMS)*. We discussed RDBMSs in Chapter 16, Database, SQL and ADO .NET. For example, a retail store might maintain a database for storing product information, such as descriptions, prices and quantities in stock. The same database also might contain customer information, such as user names, billing addresses and credit-card numbers. This tier can be comprised of multiple databases, which together contain the data needed for our application.

The *middle tier* implements *business logic*, *controller logic* and *presentation logic* to control interactions between application clients and application data. The middle tier acts as an intermediary between data in the information tier and the application's clients. The middle-tier controller logic processes client requests (such as requests to view a product catalog) and retrieves data from the database. The middle-tier presentation logic then processes data from the information tier and presents the content to the client. Web applications typically present data to clients in the form of HTML documents.

Business logic in the middle tier enforces *business rule*s and ensures that data are reliable before the server application updates the database or presents data to users. Business rules dictate how clients can and cannot access application data and how applications process data.

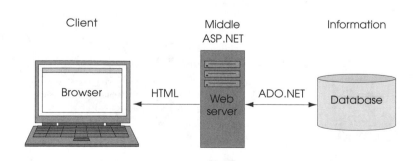

Fig. 17.3 Three-tier architecture.

The *client tier*, or *top tier*, is the application's user interface, which typically is a Web browser. Users interact directly with the application through the user interface. The client tier interacts with the middle tier to make requests and to retrieve data from the information tier. The client tier then displays to the user the data retrieved by the middle tier.

17.4 Creating and Running a Simple Web Form Example

In this section, we present an ASP .NET application. When run, this program displays the text **A Simple Web Form Example**, followed by the Web server's time. As mentioned previously, the program consists of two related files—an ASPX file (Fig. 17.4) and a C# code-behind file (Fig. 17.5). We present the markup in the ASPX file, the code in the code-behind file and the output of the application first; then, we carefully guide the reader through the step-by-step process of creating this program. [*Note*: The markup in Fig. 17.4 has been reformatted for presentation purposes.]

```
1   <%-- Fig. 17.4: WebTime.aspx          --%>
2   <%-- A page that contains two labels. --%>
3
4   <%@ Page language="c#" Codebehind="WebTime.aspx.cs"
5       AutoEventWireup="false" Inherits="WebTime.WebTimeTest"%>
6
7   <!DOCTYPE HTML PUBLIC "-//W3C//DTD HTML 4.0 Transitional//EN" >
8
9   <HTML>
10     <HEAD>
11        <title>WebTime</title>
12           <meta name="GENERATOR"
13              Content="Microsoft Visual Studio 7.0">
14           <meta name="CODE_LANGUAGE" Content="C#">
15           <meta name="vs_defaultClientScript"
16              content="JavaScript">
17           <meta name="vs_targetSchema"
18              content="http://schemas.microsoft.com/intellisense/ie5">
19     </HEAD>
20
21     <body MS_POSITIONING="GridLayout">
22        <form id="WebForm1" method="post" runat="server">
23           <asp:Label id="promptLabel" style="Z-INDEX: 101;
24              LEFT: 25px; POSITION: absolute; TOP: 23px"
25              runat="server" Font-Size="Medium">
26              A Simple Web Form Example
27           </asp:Label>
28
29           <asp:Label id="timeLabel" style="Z-INDEX: 102;
30              LEFT: 25px; POSITION: absolute; TOP: 55px"
31              runat="server" Font-Size="XX-Large"
32              BackColor="Black" ForeColor="LimeGreen">
33           </asp:Label>
34        </form>
35     </body>
36  </HTML>
```

Fig. 17.4 ASPX page that displays the Web server's time.

Visual Studio generates the markup shown in Fig. 17.4 when the programmer drags two **Label**s onto a Web Form and sets their properties. Notice that the ASPX file contains other information, in addition to HTML.

Lines 1–2 of Fig. 17.4 are *ASP .NET comments* that indicate the figure number, the file name and the purpose of the file. ASP.NET comments begin with **<%--** and terminate with **--%>**. Lines 4–5 use a **<%@ Page...%>** *directive* to specify information needed to process this file. The **language** of the code-behind file is specified as **C#**, and the code-behind file is named **WebTime.aspx.cs**.

The **AutoEventWireup** attribute determines how event handlers are linked to a control's events. When **AutoEventWireup** is set to **true**, ASP .NET determines which methods in the class to call in response to an event generated by a user's interaction with the Web page. ASP .NET will call the proper event handlers for a Web control (based on a specific naming convention for event handlers) without using a delegate, thus eliminating the need for the programmer to add a delegate for the event handler. This elimination is particularly convenient when developers are not using Visual Studio and therefore must add all code themselves. When Visual Studio .NET generates an ASPX file, it sets **AutoEventWireup** to **false**, because Visual Studio generates the necessary event delegates for us. If we were to set **AutoEventWireup** to **true** in Visual Studio (where all the delegates are added automatically) an event handler could be called twice—once through the delegate, and once as a result of **AutoEventWireup**.

The **Inherits** attribute specifies the class in the code-behind file from which this ASP .NET document inherits—in this case, **WebTimeTest**. We say more about **Inherits** momentarily.

Line 7 is called the *document type declaration*, which specifies the document element name (**HTML**) and the uniform resource identifier (URI) for the DTD. Lines 9–10 contain the **<HTML>** and **<HEAD>** start tags, respectively. **HTML** documents have root element **HTML** and mark up information about the document in the **HEAD** element. Line 11 sets the title for this Web page. Lines 12–18 display a series of **meta** *elements* that contain information about the document. Two important **meta**-element attributes are **name**, which identifies the **meta** element, and **content**, which stores the **meta** element's data. Visual Studio generates these **meta** elements when an ASPX file is created.

Line 21 contains the **<body>** start tag, which marks the beginning of the Web page's viewable content; the body contains the content that the browser displays. The **Form** that contains our controls is defined in lines 22–34. Notice the **runat** attribute in line 22, which is set to **"server"**. This attribute indicates that the server processes the **form** and generates HTML to send to the client.

Lines 23–27 and 29–33 display the markup for two **Label** Web controls. The properties that we set in the **Properties** window, such as **Font-Size** and **Text**, are attributes here. The **asp:** *tag prefix* in the declaration of the **Label** tag indicates that the label is an ASP .NET Web control. Each Web control maps to a corresponding HTML element.

Portability Tip 17.1

A single type of Web control can map to different HTML elements, depending on the client browser and the Web control's property settings.

In this example, the **asp:Label** control maps to the HTML *span* element. A **span** element simply contains text. This particular element is used because **span** elements facilitate the application of styles to text. Several of the property values that were applied to our labels are represented as part of the **style** attribute of the **span** element. We will see the **span** elements that are created by this control shortly.

Each Web control in our example contains the **runat="server"** attribute-value pair, because these controls must be processed on the server. If this attribute pair is not present, the **asp:Label** element is written to the client. (i.e., the control will not be converted into a **span** element, and the Web browser will not render the element properly.)

Figure 17.5 presents the code-behind file for our example. Recall that the ASPX file in Fig. 17.4 references this file in line 4.

Notice the **using** statements on lines 10–16. These statements specify namespaces that contain classes for developing Web-based applications. The key namespace on which we initially focus is *System.Web*, which contains classes that manage client requests and server responses. Some of the other namespaces define the available controls and various manipulations of these controls; we discuss the other namespaces throughout the chapter as they become more relevant.

Line 23 begins the class definition for **WebTimeTest**, which inherits from class *Page*. This class defines the requested Web page and is located in the *System.Web.UI* namespace (line 14), which contains classes for the creation of Web-based applications and controls. Class **Page** also provides event handlers and objects necessary for creating Web-based applications. In addition to the **Page** class (from which all Web Forms directly or indirectly inherit), **System.Web.UI** also includes the *Control* class. This class is the base class that provides common functionality for all Web controls.

```
1   // Fig. 17.5: WebTime.aspx.cs
2   // The code-behind file for a page
3   // that displays the Web server's time.
4
5   using System;
6   using System.Collections;
7   using System.ComponentModel;
8   using System.Data;
9   using System.Drawing;
10  using System.Web;
11  using System.Web.SessionState;
12
13  // definitions for graphical controls used in Web Forms
14  using System.Web.UI;
15  using System.Web.UI.WebControls;
16  using System.Web.UI.HtmlControls;
17
18  namespace WebTime
19  {
20     /// <summary>
21     /// display current time
22     /// </summary>
23     public class WebTimeTest : System.Web.UI.Page
24     {
25        protected System.Web.UI.WebControls.Label promptLabel;
26        protected System.Web.UI.WebControls.Label timeLabel;
27
```

Fig. 17.5   Code-behind file for a page that displays the Web server's time. (Part 1 of 2.)

```
28          // event handler for Load event
29          private void Page_Load(
30              object sender, System.EventArgs e )
31          {
32              // display current time
33              timeLabel.Text =
34                  String.Format( "{0:D2}:{1:D2}:{2:D2}",
35                  DateTime.Now.Hour, DateTime.Now.Minute,
36                  DateTime.Now.Second );
37          }
38
39          // event handler for Init event; sets
40          // timeLabel to Web server's time
41          #region Web Form Designer generated code
42          override protected void OnInit( EventArgs e )
43          {
44              //
45              // CODEGEN: This call is required by the
46              // ASP.NET Web Form Designer.
47              //
48              InitializeComponent();
49              base.OnInit( e );
50          }
51
52          /// <summary>
53          /// Required method for Designer support - do not modify
54          /// the contents of this method with the code editor.
55          /// </summary>
56          private void InitializeComponent()
57          {
58              this.Load += new System.EventHandler(
59                  this.Page_Load );
60          }
61          #endregion
62
63      } // end class WebTimeTest
64
65  } // end namespace WebTime
```

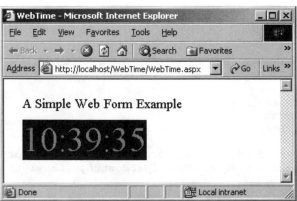

Fig. 17.5   Code-behind file for a page that displays the Web server's time. (Part 2 of 2.)

Lines 25–26 declare references to two **Label**s. These **Label**s are Web controls, defined in namespace *System.Web.UI.WebControls* (line 15). This namespace contains Web controls employed in the design of the page's user interface. Web controls in this namespace derive from class *WebControl*.

Lines 42–50 define method *OnInit*, which is called when the *Init* event is raised. This event, which is the first event raised when a client requests the Web form, indicates that the page is ready to be initialized. Method **OnInit** calls method **InitializeComponent** (defined in lines 56–60). As in Windows Forms, this method is used to set some initial properties of the application's components. The method also can be used to register events. Method **InitializeComponent** creates and attaches an event handler for the *Load* event, which is raised when the page loads (this event occurs after all the Web controls on the page have been initialized and loaded). After **InitializeComponent** executes, method **OnInit** calls the base class's (**Page**'s) **OnInit** method to perform any additional initialization that might be required (line 49).

How are the ASPX file and the code-behind file used to create the Web page that is sent to the client? First, recall that class **WebTimeTest** is the base class specified in line 5 of the ASPX file (Fig. 17.4). Class **WebTimeTest** inherits from **Page**, which defines the general functionality of a Web page. In addition to inheriting this functionality, **WebTimeTest** defines some of its own (i.e., displaying the current time). The code-behind file is the file that defines this functionality, whereas the ASPX file defines the GUI. When a client requests an ASPX file, a class is created behind the scenes that contains both the visual aspect of our page (defined in the ASPX file) and the logic of our page (defined in the code-behind file). The new class inherits from **Page**. The first time that our Web page is requested, this class is compiled, and an instance is created. This instance represents our page—it creates the HTML that is sent to the client. The assembly created from our compiled class is placed in the project's **bin** directory.

Performance Tip 17.1

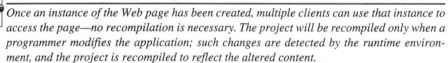

Once an instance of the Web page has been created, multiple clients can use that instance to access the page—no recompilation is necessary. The project will be recompiled only when a programmer modifies the application; such changes are detected by the runtime environment, and the project is recompiled to reflect the altered content.

Let us look briefly at how the code in our Web page executes. When the Web server creates an instance of our page to serve a client request, the **Init** event occurs first, invoking method **OnInit**. This method calls **InitializeComponent**. In addition, method **OnInit** might contain code for initializing objects. After this occurs, the **Load** event is generated, which calls method **Page_Load**. This event handler executes any processing that is necessary to restore data that was used in previous requests to the page. Lines 33–36 of the **Load** event handler set **timeLabel**'s **Text** property to the Web server's time. We include this code in the **Load** event handler so that the time will be updated with every page request. After this event handler finishes executing, the page processes any events raised by the page's controls. This includes the handling of any events generated by the user, such as button clicks. When the Web Form object is ready for garbage collection, an *Unload* event is generated. Although not present in our example, event handler *Page_Unload* is inherited from class **Page**. This event handler contains code that releases resources, especially any *unmanaged resources* (i.e., resources not managed by the CLR).

Figure 17.6 depicts the HTML generated by the ASP .NET application. To view this HTML, select **View > Source** in Internet Explorer.

The contents of this page are similar to those of the ASPX file. Lines 7–15 define a document header similar to the one in Fig. 17.4. Lines 17–37 define the body of the document. Line 18 begins the form, which is a mechanism for collecting user information and sending it to the Web server. In this particular program, the user does not submit data to the Web server for processing.

HTML forms can contain visual and nonvisual components. Visual components include buttons and other GUI components with which users interact. Nonvisual components, called *hidden inputs*, store any data that the document author specifies, such as e-mail addresses entered by users of the Web page. One of these hidden inputs is defined in lines 20–23. Attribute *method* of element **form** (line 18) specifies the method by which the Web browser submits the form to the server (in this example **post**). The *action* attribute in the **form** element identifies the name and location of the resource that will be requested when this form is submitted; in this case, **WebTime.aspx**. Recall that the ASPX file's **form** element contained the **runat="server"** attribute-value pair. When the **form** is processed on the server, the **name="WebForm1"** and **action="WebTime.aspx"** attribute-value pairs are added to the HTML **form** sent to the client browser.

```
1   <!-- Fig. 17.6: WebTime.html                        -->
2   <!-- The HTML generated when WebTime is loaded. -->
3
4   <!DOCTYPE HTML PUBLIC "-//W3C//DTD HTML 4.0 Transitional//EN" >
5
6   <HTML>
7      <HEAD>
8         <title>WebTime</title>
9         <meta name="GENERATOR"
10           Content="Microsoft Visual Studio 7.0">
11        <meta name="CODE_LANGUAGE" Content="C#">
12        <meta name="vs_defaultClientScript" content="JavaScript">
13        <meta name="vs_targetSchema"
14           content="http://schemas.microsoft.com/intellisense/ie5">
15     </HEAD>
16
17     <body MS_POSITIONING="GridLayout">
18        <form name="WebForm1" method="post"
19           action="WebTime.aspx" id="WebForm1">
20           <input type="hidden" name="__VIEWSTATE"
21                  value="dDwtNjA2MTkwMTQ5O3Q8O2w8aTwxPjs+O2w8dDw7bDxp
22                  PDM+Oz47bDx0PHA8cDxsPFR1eHQ7PjtsPDIzOjA1OjIwOz4+Oz4
23                  7Oz47Pj47Pj47PjRRGUKr1WZTYjdISduCHSyBXEzO" />
24
25           <span id="promptLabel"
26              style="font-size:Medium;Z-INDEX: 101; LEFT: 25px;
27              POSITION: absolute; TOP: 23px">
28              A Simple Web Form Example
29           </span>
```

Fig. 17.6 HTML response when the browser requests **WebTime.aspx**. (Part 1 of 2.)

```
30
31            <span id="timeLabel" style="color:LimeGreen;
32               background-color:Black;font-size:XX-Large;
33               Z-INDEX: 102; LEFT: 25px; POSITION: absolute;
34               TOP: 55px">10:39:35
35            </span>
36         </form>
37      </body>
38   </HTML>
```

Fig. 17.6   HTML response when the browser requests `WebTime.aspx`. (Part 2 of 2.)

In the ASPX file, the form's labels were Web controls. Here, we are viewing the HTML created by our application, so the **form** contains **span** elements to represent the text in our labels. In this particular case, ASP .NET maps the **Label** Web controls to HTML **span** elements. Each **span** element contains formatting information, such as size and placement of the text being displayed. Most of the information specified as properties of **timeLabel** and **promptLabel** are specified in the **style** attribute of each **span**.

Now that we have presented the ASPX file and the code-behind file, we outline the process by which we created this application:[2]

1. *Create the project.* Select **File > New > Project...** to display the **New Project** dialog (Fig. 17.7). In this dialog, select **Visual C# Projects** in the left pane and then **ASP.NET Web Application** in the right pane. Notice that the field for the project is grayed out. Rather than using this field, we specify the name and location of the project in the **Location** field. We want the project to be located at the Web address **http://localhost**, which is the URL for IIS's root directory (typically **C:\InetPub\wwwroot**). The name *localhost* indicates that the client and server reside on the same machine. If the Web server were located on a different machine, **localhost** would be replaced with the appropriate IP address or hostname. By default, Visual Studio assigns the project name **WebApplication1**, which we changed to **WebTime**. IIS must be running to create the project successfully. IIS can be started by executing **inetmgr.exe**, right clicking **Default Web Site** in the dialog that appears and selecting **Start**. [*Note*: Readers might need to expand the node representing their computer to display the **Default Web Site**.] Below the **Location** text box, the text "**Project will be created at http://localhost/WebTime**" appears. This indicates that the project's folder is located in the Web server's root directory. When the developer clicks **OK**, the project is created; this action also produces a virtual directory, which is linked to the project folder. The **Create New Web** dialog is displayed next, while Visual Studio creates the Web site on the server (Fig. 17.8).

2. The steps provided in this chapter enable readers to create Web applications of their own. If the readers would like to run the example for this chapter (located on our Web site), they must first create a virtual directory in Microsoft Internet Information Services. For instructions, visit the **Downloads/Resources** link at **www.deitel.com**. Once the virtual directory has been created and the application has been opened, readers will need to set the start page for the Web application. To do this, right-click the ASPX file and select **Set as Start Page**.

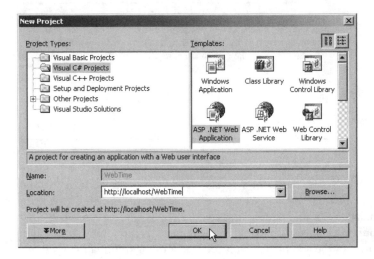

Fig. 17.7   Creating an **ASP.NET Web Application** in Visual Studio.

Fig. 17.8   Visual Studio creating and linking a virtual directory for the **WebTime** project folder.

2. *Examine the newly created project.* The next several figures describe the new project's content; we begin with the **Solution Explorer**, shown in Fig. 17.9. As with Windows applications, Visual Studio creates several files when a new **ASP .NET Web Application** is created. **WebForm1.aspx** is the Web Form. (**WebForm1** is the default name for this file.) A code-behind file also is included as part of the project. To view the ASPX file's code-behind file, right click the ASPX file and select **View Code**. Alternatively, the programmer can click an icon to display all files, then expand the node for our ASPX page (see Fig. 17.9.). [*Note*: To see the code-behind file listed in the **Solution Explorer**, the reader might need to select the icon that displays all files.]

The next figure, Fig. 17.10, shows the **Web Forms** listed in the **Toolbox**. The left figure displays the beginning of the Web controls list, and the right figure displays the remaining Web controls. Notice that some controls are similar to the Windows controls presented earlier in the book.

Figure 17.11 shows the Web Form designer for **WebForm1.aspx**. It consists of a grid on which users drag and drop components, such as buttons and labels, from the **Toolbox**.

The Web Form designer's *HTML* mode (Fig. 17.12) allows the programmer to view the markup that represents the user interface. Clicking the **HTML** button in the lower-left corner of the Web Form designer switches the Web Form designer to HTML mode. Similarly, clicking the *Design* button (to the left of the **HTML** button) returns the Web Form designer to design mode.

The next figure (Fig. 17.13) displays **WebForm1.aspx.cs**—the code-behind file for **WebForm1.aspx**. Recall that Visual Studio .NET generates this code-behind file when the project is created. This file can be viewed by right-clicking the ASPX file in the **Solution Explorer** and selecting **View Code**.

3. *Rename the ASPX file.* We have displayed the contents of the default ASPX and code-behind files. We now rename these files. Right click the ASPX file in the **Solution Explorer** and select **Rename**. Enter the new file name and hit *Enter*. This updates the name of both the ASPX file and the code-behind file. In this example, we use the name **WebTime.aspx**.

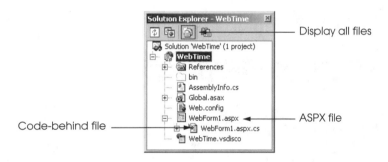

Fig. 17.9   **Solution Explorer** window for project **WebTime**.

Fig. 17.10 **Web Forms** menu in the **Toolbox**.

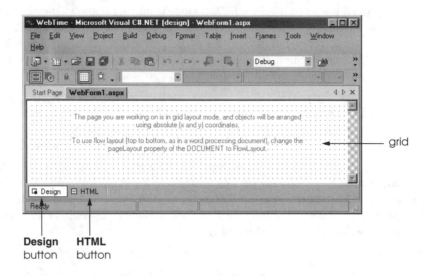

Fig. 17.11 Design mode of Web Form designer.

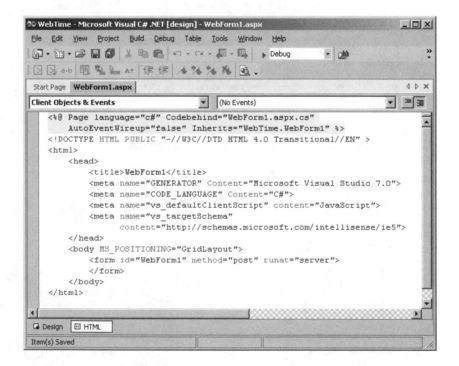

Fig. 17.12 HTML mode of Web Form designer.

4. *Design the page*. Designing a Web Form is as simple as designing a Windows
    Form. To add controls to the page, drag and drop them from the **Toolbox** onto
    the Web Form. Like the Web Form itself, each control is an object that has prop-

erties, methods and events. Developers can set these properties and events using the **Properties** window.

The *PageLayout* property determines how controls are arranged on the form (Fig. 17.14). By default, property **PageLayout** is set to *GridLayout*, which specifies that all controls are located exactly where they are dropped on the Web Form. This is called *absolute positioning*. Alternatively, the developer can set the Web Form's **PageLayout** property to *FlowLayout*, which causes controls to be placed sequentially on the Web Form. This is called *relative positioning*, because the controls' positions are relative to the Web Form's upper left corner. We use **GridLayout** in this example. To view the Web Form's properties, select *Document* from the drop-down list in the **Properties** window; **Document** is the name used to represent the Web Form in the **Properties** window.

In this example, we use two **Label**s, which developers can place on the Web Form either by drag-and-drop or by double-clicking the **Toolbox**'s **Label** control. Name the first **Label promptLabel** and the second **timeLabel**. We delete **timeLabel**'s text, because this text is set in the code-behind file. When a **Label** does not contain text, the **Label** displays its name in square brackets in the Web Form designer (Fig. 17.15), but this name is not displayed at runtime. We set the text for **promptLabel** to **A Simple Web Form Example**.

We set **timeLabel**'s **BackColor**, **ForeColor** and **Font-Size** properties to **Black**, **LimeGreen** and **XX-Large**, respectively. To change font properties, the programmer must expand the **Font** node in the **Properties** window, then change each relevant property individually. We also set the labels' locations and sizes by dragging the controls. Once the **Label**s' properties are set in the **Properties** window, Visual Studio updates the ASPX file's contents. Figure 17.15 shows the IDE after these properties are set.

5. *Add page logic.* Once the user interface has been designed, C# code must be added to the code-behind file. In this example, lines 33–36 of Fig. 17.5 are added to the code-behind file. The statement retrieves the current time and formats it so that the time is in the format *HH:MM:SS*. For example, 9 a.m. is formatted as **09:00:00**.

6. *Run the program.* Select **Debug > Start**. An Internet Explorer window opens and loads the Web page (the ASPX file). Notice that the URL is **http://localhost/WebTime/WebTime.aspx** (Fig. 17.4), indicating that our ASPX file is located within the directory **WebTime**, which is located in the Web server's root directory.

After the Web Form is created, the programmer can view it three different ways. First, the programmer can select **Debug > Start** (as described previously), which runs the application by opening a browser window. The IDE exits **Run** or **Debug** mode when the browser is closed.

The programmer also can right-click either the Web Form designer or the ASPX file name (in the **Solution Explorer**) and select *View In Browser*. This opens a browser window within Visual Studio and displays a preview of the page. This technique allows developers to view what the page will look like when it is requested by a client, but does not compile the code-behind file. The third way to run an ASP .NET application is to open a browser window and type in the Web page's URL. When testing an ASP .NET application on the local computer, type **http://localhost/***ProjectFolder***/***PageName***.aspx**, where *ProjectFolder* is the folder in which the page resides (usually the name of the project), and *PageName* is the name of the ASP .NET page. Note that, if this technique is used, the page must already be compiled.

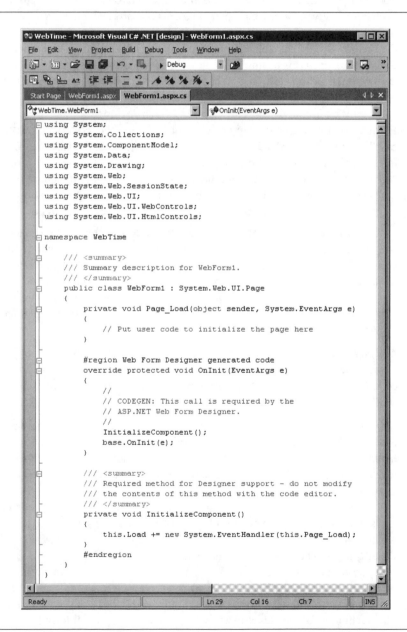

```csharp
using System;
using System.Collections;
using System.ComponentModel;
using System.Data;
using System.Drawing;
using System.Web;
using System.Web.SessionState;
using System.Web.UI;
using System.Web.UI.WebControls;
using System.Web.UI.HtmlControls;

namespace WebTime
{
    /// <summary>
    /// Summary description for WebForm1.
    /// </summary>
    public class WebForm1 : System.Web.UI.Page
    {
        private void Page_Load(object sender, System.EventArgs e)
        {
            // Put user code to initialize the page here
        }

        #region Web Form Designer generated code
        override protected void OnInit(EventArgs e)
        {
            //
            // CODEGEN: This call is required by the
            // ASP.NET Web Form Designer.
            //
            InitializeComponent();
            base.OnInit(e);
        }

        /// <summary>
        /// Required method for Designer support - do not modify
        /// the contents of this method with the code editor.
        /// </summary>
        private void InitializeComponent()
        {
            this.Load += new System.EventHandler(this.Page_Load);
        }
        #endregion
    }
}
```

Fig. 17.13 Code-behind file for **WebForm1.aspx** generated by Visual Studio .NET.

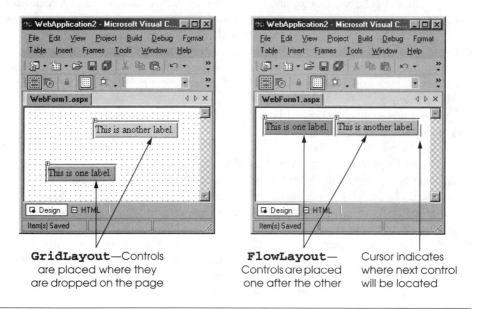

GridLayout—Controls are placed where they are dropped on the page

FlowLayout— Controls are placed one after the other

Cursor indicates where next control will be located

Fig. 17.14 **GridLayout** and **FlowLayout** illustration.

Labels   Web Form

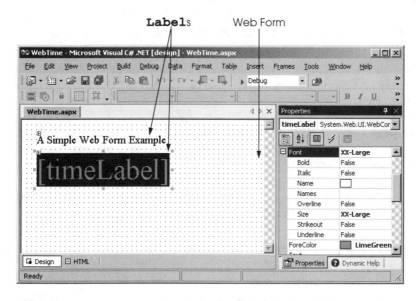

Fig. 17.15 **WebForm.aspx** after adding two **Label**s and setting their properties.

17.5 Summary

Microsoft's ASP .NET is a technology for developing Web-based applications that create Web content for Web-browser clients. The Web-Form file represents the Web page that is sent to the client browser. Programmers customize Web Forms by adding Web controls, which include text boxes, images and buttons. Every ASPX file created in Visual Studio .NET has a code-behind file that provides the ASPX file's programmatic implementation.

Visual Studio .NET generates markup in the ASPX page when controls are dragged onto the Web Form. When a control's **runat** attribute is set to **"server"**, the control is executed on a server, which results in HTML markup being sent to the client. The **asp:** tag prefix indicates that a control is an ASP .NET Web control. Each Web control maps to an HTML element.

Class **Page** defines a standard Web page, providing event handlers and objects necessary for creating Web-based applications. All code-behind classes for ASPX forms inherit from class **Page**. When a client requests an ASPX file, a class is created behind the scenes that contains the page's user interface (defined in the ASPX file) and the page's logic (defined in the code-behind file). This new class inherits from **Page**. The first time that a Web page is requested, the class is compiled, and an instance that represents the page is created.

Method **OnInit** is called when the **Init** event is raised. This event indicates that the page is ready to be initialized. The **Load** event is raised each time a page is requested or reloaded. The **Page_Load** event handler executes any processing that is necessary to restore data from previous requests. After **Page_Load** has finished executing, the page processes any events raised by the page's controls.

The **PageLayout** property determines how controls are arranged on the form. By default, property **PageLayout** is set to **GridLayout**, meaning that all controls remain exactly where they are dropped on the Web Form.

17.6 Internet and World Wide Web Resources

www.asp.net
The Microsoft site overviews ASP .NET and provides a link for downloading ASP .NET. This site includes the IBuy Spy e-commerce storefront example that uses ASP .NET. Links to the Amazon and Barnes & Noble Web sites, at which the user can purchase books, also are included.

www.asp101.com/aspdotnet/aspplus/index.asp
This site overviews ASP .NET and includes articles, code examples and links to ASP .NET resources. The code samples demonstrate the use of cookies in an ASP .NET application and show how to establish a connection to a database—two key capabilities of multi-tier applications.

www.411asp.net
This resource site provides programmers with ASP .NET tutorials and code samples. The community pages allows programmers to ask questions, answer questions and post messages.

www.aspfree.com
This site provides free ASP .NET demos and source code. The site also provides a list of articles for various topics and a frequently asked questions (FAQs) page.

www.aspng.com/aspng/index.asp
This site offers tutorials, links and recommendations for books on ASP. NET. Links to different mailing lists also are provided. These links are organized by topic. This site also contains articles related to many ASP. NET topics, such as "Performance Tips and Tricks."

www.aspnetfaq.com
This site provides answers to frequently asked questions (FAQs) about ASP. NET.

www.123aspx.com
This site offers a directory of links to ASP .NET resources. The site also includes daily and weekly newsletters.

Extensible Markup Language (XML)

Objectives

- To be able to mark up data, using XML.
- To be able to create elements.
- To be able to create attributes.
- To understand what an XML parser is and the role it has in XML processing.
- To understand the concept of an XML namespace.
- To understand what the Document Object Model (DOM) is.
- To use C# to process XML documents.

Knowing trees, I understand the meaning of patience.
Knowing grass, I can appreciate persistence.
Hal Borland

Like everything metaphysical, the harmony between thought
and reality is to be found in the grammar of the language.
Ludwig Wittgenstein

I played with an idea and grew willful, tossed it into the air;
transformed it; let it escape and recaptured it; made it
iridescent with fancy, and winged it with paradox.
Oscar Wilde

Outline

18.1 Introduction

The *Extensible Markup Language* (XML) was developed in 1996 by the *World Wide Web Consortium's (W3C's) XML Working Group*. XML is a portable, widely supported, *open technology* (i.e., non-proprietary technology) for describing data. XML is becoming the standard for storing data that is exchanged between applications. Using XML, document authors can describe any type of data, including mathematical formulas, software-configuration instructions, music, recipes and financial reports. XML documents are readable by both humans and machines.

The .NET Framework uses XML extensively. The Framework Class Library (FCL) provides an extensive set of XML-related classes. Much of Visual Studio's internal implementation also employs XML. In this chapter, we introduce XML, XML-related technologies and key classes for creating and manipulating XML documents.

18.2 XML Documents

In this section, we present our first XML document, which describes an article (Fig. 18.1). [*Note:* The line numbers shown are not part of the XML document.

This document begins with an optional *XML declaration* (line 1), which identifies the document as an XML document. The **version** *information parameter* specifies the version of XML that is used in the document. XML comments (lines 3–4), which begin with **<!--** and end with **-->**, can be placed almost anywhere in an XML document. As in a C# program, comments are used in XML for documentation purposes.

 Common Programming Error 18.1

The placement of any characters, including whitespace, before the XML declaration is an error.

```
1    <?xml version = "1.0"?>
2
3    <!-- Fig. 18.1: article.xml        -->
4    <!-- Article structured with XML -->
5
6    <article>
7
8        <title>Simple XML</title>
9
```

Fig. 18.1   XML used to mark up an article. (Part 1 of 2.)

```
10     <date>December 6, 2001</date>
11
12     <author>
13        <firstName>John</firstName>
14        <lastName>Doe</lastName>
15     </author>
16
17     <summary>XML is pretty easy.</summary>
18
19     <content>In this chapter, we present a wide variety of examples
20        that use XML.
21     </content>
22
23  </article>
```

Fig. 18.1   XML used to mark up an article. (Part 2 of 2.)

Portability Tip 18.1

Although the XML declaration is optional, documents should include the declaration to iden-tify the version of XML used. Otherwise, in the future, a document that lacks an XML decla-ration might be assumed to conform to the latest version of XML, and errors could result.

In XML, data are marked up using *tags*, which are names enclosed in *angle brackets* (**<>**). Tags are used in pairs to delimit character data (e.g., **Simple XML** in line 8). A tag that begins *markup* (i.e., XML data) is called a *start tag*, whereas a tag that terminates markup is called an *end tag*. Examples of start tags are **<article>** and **<title>** (lines 6 and 8, respectively). End tags differ from start tags in that they contain a *forward slash* (**/**) character immediately after the **<** character. Examples of end tags are **</title>** and **</article>** (lines 8 and 23, respectively). XML documents can contain any number of tags.

Common Programming Error 18.2

Failure to provide a corresponding end tag for a start tag is an error.

Individual units of markup (i.e., everything included between a start tag and its corre-sponding end tag) are called *elements*. An XML document includes one element (called a *root element*) that contains every other element. The root element must be the first element after the XML declaration. In Fig. 18.1, **article** (line 6) is the root element. Elements are *nested* within each other to form hierarchies—with the root element at the top of the hierarchy. This allows document authors to create explicit relationships between data. For example, elements **title**, **date**, **author**, **summary** and **content** are nested within **article**. Elements **firstName** and **lastName** are nested within **author**.

Common Programming Error 18.3

Attempting to create more than one root element in an XML document is a syntax error.

Element **title** (line 8) contains the title of the article, **Simple XML**, as character data. Similarly, **date** (line 10), **summary** (line 17) and **content** (lines 19–21) contain as character data the date, summary and content, respectively. XML element names can be of any length and may contain letters, digits, underscores, hyphens and periods—they must begin with a letter or an underscore.

Common Programming Error 18.4

XML is case sensitive. The use of the wrong case for an XML element name is a syntax error.

By itself, this document is simply a text file named **article.xml**. Although it is not required, most XML documents end in the file extension **.xml**. The processing of XML documents requires a program called an *XML parser* also called *XML processors*. Parsers are responsible for checking an XML document's syntax and making the XML document's data available to applications. Often, XML parsers are built into applications such as Visual Studio or available for download over the Internet. Popular parsers include Microsoft's *msxml*, the Apache Software Foundation's *Xerces* and IBM's *XML4J*. In this chapter, we use msxml.

When the user loads **article.xml** into Internet Explorer (IE),[1] msxml parses the document and passes the parsed data to IE. IE then uses a built-in *style sheet* to format the data. Notice that the resulting format of the data (Fig. 18.2) is similar to the format of the XML document shown in Fig. 18.1. As we soon demonstrate, style sheets play an important and powerful role in the transformation of XML data into formats suitable for display.

Notice the minus (–) and plus (+) signs in Fig. 18.2. Although these are not part of the XML document, IE places them next to all *container elements* (i.e., elements that contain other elements). Container elements also are called *parent elements*. A minus sign indicates that the parent element's *child elements* (i.e., nested elements) are being displayed. When clicked, a minus sign becomes a plus sign (which collapses the container element and hides all children). Conversely, clicking a plus sign expands the container element and changes the plus sign to a minus sign. This behavior is similar to the viewing of the directory structure on a Windows system using Windows Explorer. In fact, a directory structure often is modeled as a series of tree structures, in which each drive letter (e.g., **C:**, etc.) represents the *root* of a tree. Each folder is a *node* in the tree. Parsers often place XML data into trees to facilitate efficient manipulation, as discussed in Section 18.4.

Common Programming Error 18.5

*Nesting XML tags improperly is a syntax error. For example, **<x><y>hello</x></y>** is a error, because the **</y>** tag must precede the **</x>** tag.*

We now present a second XML document (Fig. 18.3), which marks up a business letter. This document contains significantly more data than did the previous XML document.

Root element **letter** (lines 6–45) contains the child elements **contact** (lines 7–16 and 18–27), **salutation**, **paragraph** (lines 31–36 and 38–40), **closing** and **signature**. In addition to being placed between tags, data also can be placed in *attributes*, which are name-value pairs in start tags. Elements can have any number of attributes in their start tags. The first **contact** element (lines 7–16) has attribute **type** with attribute *value* **"from"**, which indicates that this **contact** element marks up information about the letter's sender. The second **contact** element (lines 18–27) has attribute **type** with value **"to"**, which indicates that this **contact** element marks up information about the letter's recipient. Like element names, attribute names are case sensitive, can be any length; may contain letters, digits, underscores, hyphens and periods; and must begin with either a letter or underscore character. A **contact** element stores a contact's name, address and

---

1. IE 5 and higher.

phone number. Element **salutation** (line 29) marks up the letter's salutation. Lines 31–40 mark up the letter's body with **paragraph** elements. Elements **closing** (line 42) and **signature** (line 44) mark up the closing sentence and the signature of the letter's author, respectively.

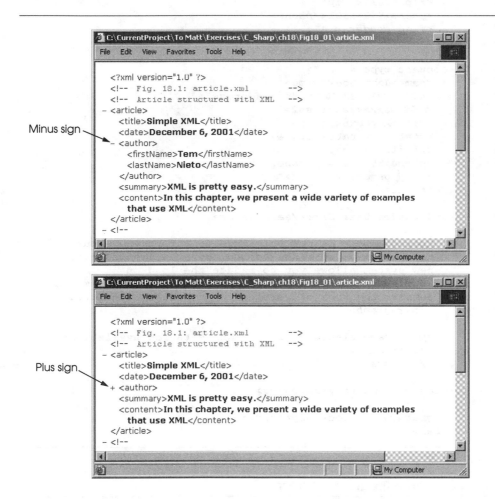

Fig. 18.2 **article.xml** displayed by Internet Explorer.

```
1   <?xml version = "1.0"?>
2
3   <!-- Fig. 18.3: letter.xml              -->
4   <!-- Business letter formatted with XML -->
5
6   <letter>
7      <contact type = "from">
8         <name>Jane Doe</name>
```

Fig. 18.3 XML to mark up a business letter. (Part 1 of 2.)

```
 9          <address1>Box 12345</address1>
10          <address2>15 Any Ave.</address2>
11          <city>Othertown</city>
12          <state>Otherstate</state>
13          <zip>67890</zip>
14          <phone>555-4321</phone>
15          <flag gender = "F" />
16      </contact>
17
18      <contact type = "to">
19          <name>John Doe</name>
20          <address1>123 Main St.</address1>
21          <address2></address2>
22          <city>Anytown</city>
23          <state>Anystate</state>
24          <zip>12345</zip>
25          <phone>555-1234</phone>
26          <flag gender = "M" />
27      </contact>
28
29      <salutation>Dear Sir:</salutation>
30
31          <paragraph>It is our privilege to inform you about our new
32          database managed with <technology>XML</technology>. This
33          new system allows you to reduce the load on
34          your inventory list server by having the client machine
35          perform the work of sorting and filtering the data.
36          </paragraph>
37
38          <paragraph>Please visit our Web site for availability
39          and pricing.
40          </paragraph>
41
42      <closing>Sincerely</closing>
43
44      <signature>Ms. Doe</signature>
45  </letter>
```

Fig. 18.3 XML to mark up a business letter. (Part 2 of 2.)

Common Programming Error 18.6

Failure to enclose attribute values in either double (" ") or single (' ') quotes is a syntax error.

Common Programming Error 18.7

Attempting to provide two attributes with the same name for an element is a syntax error.

In line 15, we introduce *empty element* **flag**, which indicates the gender of the contact. Empty elements do not contain character data (i.e., they do not contain text between the start and end tags). Such elements are closed either by placing a slash at the end of the element (as shown in line 15) or by explicitly writing a closing tag, as in

```
<flag gender = "F"></flag>
```

18.3 XML Namespaces

Object-oriented programming languages, such as C# and Visual Basic .NET, provide massive class libraries that group their features into namespaces. These namespaces prevent *naming collisions* between programmer-defined identifiers and identifiers in class libraries. For example, we might use class **Book** to represent information on one of our publications; however, a stamp collector might use class **Book** to represent a book of stamps. A naming collision would occur if we use these two classes in the same assembly, without using namespaces to differentiate them.

Like C#, XML also provides *namespaces*, which provide a means of uniquely identifying XML elements. In addition, XML-based languages—called *vocabularies*, such as XML Schema (for describing an XML document's contents) and the Extensible Stylesheet Language (for transforming an XML document's contents into another format)—often use namespaces to identify their elements.

Elements are differentiated via *namespace prefixes*, which identify the namespace to which an element belongs. For example,

> `<deitel:book>C# A Programmer's Introduction</deitel:book>`

qualifies element **book** with namespace prefix **deitel**. This indicates that element **book** is part of namespace **deitel**. Document authors can use any name for a namespace prefix except the reserved namespace prefix **xml**.

Common Programming Error 18.8

*Attempting to create a namespace prefix named **xml** in any mixture of case is an error.*

The mark up in Fig. 18.4 demonstrates the use of namespaces. This XML document contains two **file** elements that are differentiated using namespaces.

```
1   <?xml version = "1.0"?>
2
3   <!-- Fig. 18.4: namespace.xml -->
4   <!-- Demonstrating namespaces -->
5
6   <text:directory xmlns:text = "urn:deitel:textInfo"
7      xmlns:image = "urn:deitel:imageInfo">
8
9      <text:file filename = "book.xml">
10        <text:description>A book list</text:description>
11     </text:file>
12
13     <image:file filename = "funny.jpg">
14        <image:description>A funny picture</image:description>
15        <image:size width = "200" height = "100" />
16     </image:file>
17
18  </text:directory>
```

Fig. 18.4 XML namespaces demonstration. (Part 1 of 2.)

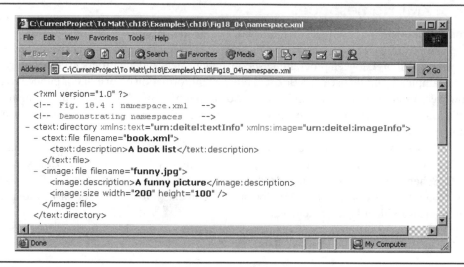

```
C:\CurrentProject\To Matt\ch18\Examples\ch18\Fig18_04\namespace.xml

File   Edit   View   Favorites   Tools   Help

Back             Search      Favorites     Media

Address   C:\CurrentProject\To Matt\ch18\Examples\ch18\Fig18_04\namespace.xml           Go

  <?xml version="1.0" ?>
  <!-- Fig. 18.4 : namespace.xml    -->
  <!-- Demonstrating namespaces      -->
- <text:directory xmlns:text="urn:deitel:textInfo" xmlns:image="urn:deitel:imageInfo">
  - <text:file filename="book.xml">
      <text:description>A book list</text:description>
    </text:file>
  - <image:file filename="funny.jpg">
      <image:description>A funny picture</image:description>
      <image:size width="200" height="100" />
    </image:file>
  </text:directory>

Done                                                          My Computer
```

Fig. 18.4   XML namespaces demonstration. (Part 2 of 2.)

Software Engineering Observation 18.1

A programmer has the option of qualifying an attribute with a namespace prefix. However, it is not required, because attributes always are associated with elements.

Lines 6–7 use attribute **xmlns** to create two namespace prefixes: **text** and **image**. Each namespace prefix is bound to a series of characters called a *uniform resource identifier (URI)* that uniquely identifies the namespace. Document authors create their own namespace prefixes and URIs.

To ensure that namespaces are unique, document authors must provide unique URIs. Here, we use the text **urn:deitel:textInfo** and **urn:deitel:imageInfo** as URIs. A common practice is to use *Universal Resource Locators (URLs)* for URIs, because the domain names (such as, **www.deitel.com**) used in URLs are guaranteed to be unique. For example, lines 6–7 could have been written as

```
<text:directory xmlns:text =
    "http://www.deitel.com/xmlns-text"
    xmlns:image = "http://www.deitel.com/xmlns-image">
```

In this example, we use URLs related to the Deitel & Associates, Inc, domain name to identify namespaces. The parser never visits these URLs—they simply represent a series of characters used to differentiate names. The URLs need not refer to actual Web pages or be formed properly.

Lines 9–11 use the namespace prefix **text** to qualify elements **file** and **description** as belonging to the namespace **"urn:deitel:textInfo"**. Notice that the namespace prefix **text** is applied to the end tags as well. Lines 13–16 apply namespace prefix **image** to elements **file**, **description** and **size**.

To eliminate the need to precede each element with a namespace prefix, document authors can specify a *default namespace*. Figure 18.5 demonstrates the creation and use of default namespaces.

```
1   <?xml version = "1.0"?>
2
3   <!-- Fig. 18.5: defaultnamespace.xml -->
4   <!-- Using default namespaces         -->
5
6   <directory xmlns = "urn:deitel:textInfo"
7       xmlns:image = "urn:deitel:imageInfo">
8
9       <file filename = "book.xml">
10          <description>A book list</description>
11      </file>
12
13      <image:file filename = "funny.jpg">
14          <image:description>A funny picture</image:description>
15          <image:size width = "200" height = "100" />
16      </image:file>
17
18  </directory>
```

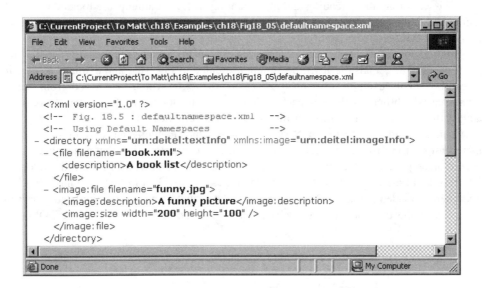

Fig. 18.5   Default namespaces demonstration.

Line 6 declares a default namespace using attribute **xmlns** with a URI as its value. Once we define this default namespace, child elements belonging to the namespace need not be qualified by a namespace prefix. Element **file** (line 9–11) is in the namespace **urn:deitel:textInfo**. Compare this to Fig. 18.4, where we prefixed **file** and **description** with **text** (lines 9–11).

The default namespace applies to the **directory** element and all elements that are not qualified with a namespace prefix. However, we can use a namespace prefix to specify a different namespace for particular elements. For example, the **file** element in line 13 is prefixed with **image** to indicate that it is in the namespace **urn:deitel:imageInfo**, rather than the default namespace.

18.4 Document Object Model (DOM)

Although XML documents are text files, retrieving data from them via sequential-file access techniques is neither practical nor efficient, especially in situations where data must be added or deleted dynamically.

Upon successful parsing of documents, some XML parsers store document data as tree structures in memory. Figure 18.6 illustrates the tree structure for the document **article.xml** discussed in Fig. 18.1. This hierarchical tree structure is called a *Document Object Model (DOM)* tree, and an XML parser that creates this type of structure is known as a *DOM parser*. The DOM tree represents each component of the XML document (e.g., **article**, **date**, **firstName**, etc.) as a node in the tree. Nodes (such as, **author**) that contain other nodes (called *child nodes*) are called *parent nodes*. Nodes that have the same parent (such as, **firstName** and **lastName**) are called *sibling nodes*. A node's *descendant nodes* include that node's children, its children's children and so on. Similarly, a node's *ancestor nodes* include that node's parent, its parent's parent and so on. Every DOM tree has a single *root node* that contains all other nodes in the document, such as comments, elements, etc.

Classes for creating, reading and manipulating XML documents are located in the C# namespace **System.Xml**. This namespace also contains additional namespaces that contain other XML-related operations.

In this section, we present an example that uses DOM trees. Our first example, the program in Fig. 18.7, loads the XML document presented in Fig. 18.1 and displays its data in a text box. This example uses class **XmlNodeReader** which is derived from **XmlReader**, which iterates through each node in the XML document. Class **XmlReader** is a class that defines the interface for reading XML documents.

Line 6 includes the **System.Xml** namespace, which contains the XML classes used in this example. Line 18 creates a reference to an **XmlDocument** object that conceptually represents an empty XML document. The XML document **article.xml** is parsed and loaded into this **XmlDocument** object when method **Load** is invoked in line 19. Once an XML document is loaded into an **XmlDocument**, its data can be read and manipulated programmatically. In this example, we read each node in the **XmlDocument**, which is the DOM tree.

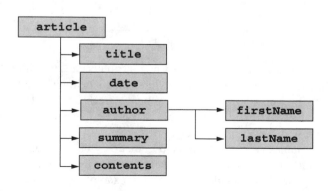

Fig. 18.6   Tree structure for Fig. 18.1.

In line 22, we create an **XmlNodeReader** and assign it to reference **reader**, which enables us to read one node at a time from the **XmlDocument**. Method *Read* of **XmlReader** reads one node from the DOM tree. Placing this statement in the **while** loop (lines 31–78) makes **reader Read** all the document nodes. The **switch** statement (lines 33–77) processes each node. Either the *Name* property (line 41), which contains the node's name, or the *Value* property (line 53), which contains the node's data, is formatted and concatenated to the **string** assigned to the text box **Text** property. The **NodeType** property contains the node type (specifying whether the node is an element, comment, text, etc.). Notice that each **case** specifies a node type, using *XmlNodeType* enumeration constants.

Notice that the displayed output emphasizes the structure of the XML document. Variable **depth** (line 28) sets the number of tab characters used to indent each element. The depth is incremented each time an **Element** type is encountered and is decremented each time an **EndElement** or empty element is encountered. We use a similar technique in the next example to emphasize the tree structure of the XML document in the display.

```
1   // Fig. 18.7: XmlReaderTest.cs
2   // Reading an XML document.
3
4   using System;
5   using System.Windows.Forms;
6   using System.Xml;
7
8   public class XmlReaderTest : System.Windows.Forms.Form
9   {
10      private System.Windows.Forms.TextBox outputTextBox;
11      private System.ComponentModel.Container components = null;
12
13      public XmlReaderTest()
14      {
15         InitializeComponent();
16
17         // reference to "XML document"
18         XmlDocument document = new XmlDocument();
19         document.Load( "..\\..\\article.xml" );
20
21         // create XmlNodeReader for document
22         XmlNodeReader reader = new XmlNodeReader( document );
23
24         // show form before outputTextBox is populated
25         this.Show();
26
27         // tree depth is -1, no indentation
28         int depth = -1;
29
30         // display each node's content
31         while ( reader.Read() )
32         {
33            switch ( reader.NodeType )
34            {
```

Fig. 18.7   **XmlNodeReader** used to iterate through an XML document. (Part 1 of 3.)

```
35                   // if Element, display its name
36                   case XmlNodeType.Element:
37
38                      // increase tab depth
39                      depth++;
40                      TabOutput( depth );
41                      outputTextBox.Text += "<" + reader.Name + ">" +
42                         "\r\n";
43
44                      // if empty element, decrease depth
45                      if ( reader.IsEmptyElement )
46                         depth--;
47
48                      break;
49
50                   // if Comment, display it
51                   case XmlNodeType.Comment:
52                      TabOutput( depth );
53                      outputTextBox.Text +=
54                         "<!--" + reader.Value + "-->\r\n";
55                      break;
56
57                   // if Text, display it
58                   case XmlNodeType.Text:
59                      TabOutput( depth );
60                      outputTextBox.Text += "\t" + reader.Value +
61                         "\r\n";
62                      break;
63
64                   // if XML declaration, display it
65                   case XmlNodeType.XmlDeclaration:
66                      TabOutput( depth );
67                      outputTextBox.Text += "<?" + reader.Name + " "
68                         + reader.Value + " ?>\r\n";
69                      break;
70
71                   // if EndElement, display it and decrement depth
72                   case XmlNodeType.EndElement:
73                      TabOutput( depth );
74                      outputTextBox.Text += "</" + reader.Name
75                         + ">\r\n";
76                      depth--;
77                      break;
78               } // end switch statement
79            } // end while loop
80         } // end XmlReaderTest constructor
81
82         // insert tabs
83         private void TabOutput( int number )
84         {
85            for ( int i = 0; i < number; i++ )
86               outputTextBox.Text += "\t";
87         } // end TabOutput
```

Fig. 18.7 XmlNodeReader used to iterate through an XML document. (Part 2 of 3.)

```
88
89      // Windows Form Designer generated code
90
91      [STAThread]
92      static void Main()
93      {
94          Application.Run( new XmlReaderTest() );
95      } // end Main
96  } // end XmlReaderTest
```

Fig. 18.7 **XmlNodeReader** used to iterate through an XML document. (Part 3 of 3.)

Notice that our line breaks use the character sequence **"\r\n"**, which denotes a carriage return followed by a line feed. This is the standard line break for Windows-based applications and controls.

18.5 Summary

XML is a widely supported, open (i.e., nonproprietary) technology for data exchange. It is becoming the standard by which applications maintain data. XML is highly portable. Any text editor that supports ASCII or Unicode characters can render or display XML documents. Because XML elements describe the data they contain, they are both human and machine readable.

XML permits document authors to create custom markup for virtually any type of information. This extensibility enables document authors to create entirely new markup languages that describe specific types of data, including mathematical formulas, chemical molecular structures, music and recipes.

The processing of XML documents—which programs typically store in files whose names end with the **.xml** extension—requires a program called an XML parser. An XML parser is responsible for identifying components of XML documents and for storing those components in a data structure for manipulation.

Data are marked up with tags whose names are enclosed in angle brackets (**<>**). Tags are used in pairs to delimit markup. A tag that begins markup is called a start tag, and a tag that terminates markup is called an end tag. End tags differ from start tags in that they contain a forward-slash (**/**) character.

Individual units of markup are called elements, which are the most fundamental XML building blocks. XML documents contain one element, called a root element, that contains every other element in the document. Elements are embedded or nested within each other to form hierarchies, with the root element at the top of the hierarchy.

In addition to being placed between tags, data also can be placed in attributes, which are name-value pairs in start tags. Elements can have any number of attributes.

Because XML allows document authors to create their own tags, naming collisions (i.e., when two different elements have the same name) can occur. As in C#, XML namespaces provide a means for document authors to prevent collisions: Elements are qualified with namespace prefixes to specify the namespace to which they belong.

Each namespace prefix is bound to a uniform resource identifier (URI) that uniquely identifies the namespace. A URI is a series of characters that differentiates names. Document authors create their own namespace prefixes. Virtually any name can be used as a namespace prefix, except the reserved namespace prefix **xml**. To eliminate the need to place a namespace prefix in each element, document authors can specify a default namespace for an element and its children.

When an XML parser successfully parses a document, the parser stores a tree structure containing the document's data in memory. This hierarchical tree structure is called a Document Object Model (DOM) tree. The DOM tree represents each component of the XML document as a node in the tree. Nodes that contain other nodes are called parent nodes. Nodes that have the same parent are called sibling nodes. A node's descendant nodes include that node's children, its children's children and so on. A node's ancestor nodes include that node's parent, its parent's parent and so on. The DOM tree has a single root node that contains all other nodes in the document.

18.6 Internet and World Wide Web Resources

www.w3.org/xml
The W3C (World Wide Web Consortium) facilitates the development of common protocols to ensure interoperability on the Web. Their XML page includes information about upcoming events, publications, software and discussion groups. Visit this site to read about the latest developments in XML.

www.xml.org
xml.org is a reference for XML.

www.w3.org/TR
This is the W3C technical reports and publications page. It contains links to working drafts, proposed recommendations and other resources.

www.devx.com/xml/
The Development Exchange XML Zone is a complete resource for XML information. This site includes a FAQ, news, articles and links to other XML sites and newsgroups.

wdvl.internet.com/Authoring/Languages/XML
Web Developer's Virtual Library XML site includes tutorials, a FAQ, the latest news and extensive links to XML sites and software downloads.

www.xml.com

XML.com provides the latest news and information about XML, conference listings, links to XML Web resources organized by topic, tools and other resources.

msdn.microsoft.com/xml

The MSDN Online XML Development Center features articles on XML, Ask the Experts chat sessions, samples and demos, newsgroups and other helpful information.

www.oasis-open.org/cover/xml.html

The SGML/XML Web Page is an extensive resource that includes links to several FAQs, online resources, industry initiatives, demos, conferences and tutorials.

www-106.ibm.com/developerworks/xml

The IBM XML Zone site is a great resource for developers. It provides news, tools, a library, case studies, and information about events and standards.

developer.netscape.com/tech/xml/index.html

The XML and Metadata Developer Central site has demos, technical notes and news articles related to XML.

www.devx.com/projectcool/developer/xmlz/

The Project Cool Developer Zone site includes several tutorials covering introductory through advanced XML topics.

www.ucc.ie/xml

This site provides a detailed set of XML FAQs. Developers can check out responses to some popular questions or submit their own questions through the site.

ASP .NET and Web Services

Objectives

- To understand what a Web service is.
- To be able to create Web services.
- To understand the elements that comprise a Web service, such as service descriptions and discovery files.
- To be able to create a client that uses a Web service.
- To be able to use Web services with Windows applications.

A client is to me a mere unit, a factor in a problem.
Sir Arthur Conan Doyle

...if the simplest things of nature have a message that you understand, rejoice, for your soul is alive.
Eleonora Duse

Protocol is everything.
Francoise Giuliani

They also serve who only stand and wait.
John Milton

Outline

19.1 Introduction[1]

Throughout this book, we have created dynamic link libraries (DLLs) to facilitate software reusability and modularity—the cornerstones of good object-oriented programming. However, the use of DLLs is limited by the fact that DLLs must reside on the same machine as the programs that use them. This chapter introduces the use of Web services (sometimes called *XML Web services*) to promote software reusability in distributed systems. Distributed-systems technologies allow applications to execute across multiple computers on a network. A Web service is an application that enables distributed computing by allowing one machine to call methods on other machines via common data formats and protocols, such as XML and HTTP. In .NET, these method calls are implemented using the Simple Object Access Protocol (SOAP), an XML-based protocol describing how to mark up requests and responses so that they can be transferred via protocols such as HTTP. Using SOAP, applications represent and transmit data in a standardized format—XML. The underlying implementation of the Web service is irrelevant to clients using the Web service.

Microsoft is encouraging software vendors and e-businesses to deploy Web services. As more and more people worldwide connect to the Internet via networks, applications that call methods across a network become more practical. Earlier in this text, we discussed the merits of object-oriented programming. Web services represents the next step in object-oriented programming: Instead of developing software from a small number of class libraries provided at one location, programmers can access countless libraries in multiple locations.

This technology also makes it easier for businesses to collaborate and grow together. By purchasing Web services that are relevant to their businesses, companies that create applications can spend less time coding and more time developing new products from existing components. In addition, e-businesses can employ Web services to provide their customers with an enhanced shopping experience. As a simple example, consider an online music store that enables users to purchase music CDs or to obtain information about artists. Now, suppose another company that sells concert tickets provides a Web service that determines the dates of upcoming concerts by various artists and allows users to buy concert tickets. By licensing the concert-ticket Web service for use on its site, the online music store can sell concert tickets to its customers, which likely will result in increased traffic to its site. The company that sells concert tickets also benefits from the business relationship. In addition to selling more tickets, the company receives revenue from the online music store in exchange for the use of its Web service.

---

1. Internet Information Services (IIS) must be running to create a Web service in Visual Studio.

Visual Studio and the .NET Framework provide a simple way to create Web services like the one discussed in this example. In this chapter, we explore the steps involved in both the creation and accessing of Web services.

19.2 Web Services

A Web service is an application stored on one machine that can be accessed on another machine over a network. Due to the nature of this relationship, the machine on which the Web service resides commonly is referred to as a *remote machine*. The application that accesses the Web service sends a method call to the remote machine, which processes the call and sends a response to the application. This kind of distributed computing benefits various systems, including those without access to certain data and those lacking the processing power necessary to perform specific computations.

A Web service is, in its simplest form, a class. In previous chapters, when we wanted to include a class in a project, we would either define the class in our project or add a reference to the compiled DLL. This compiled DLL is placed in the **bin** directory of an application by default. As a result, all pieces of our application reside on one machine. When using Web services, the class (and its compiled DLL) we wish to include in our project are stored on a remote machine—a compiled version of this class is not placed in the current application.

Methods in a Web service are remotely invoked using a *Remote Procedure Call* (*RPC*). These methods, which are marked with the **WebMethod** attribute, often are referred to as *Web-service methods*. Declaring a method with this attribute makes the method accessible to other classes via an RPC. The declaration of a Web-service method with attribute **WebMethod** is known as *exposing* the method, or enabling it to be called remotely.

Common Programming Error 19.1

Attempting to call a remote method from a Web service if the method is not declared with the **WebMethod** *attribute is a compilation error.*

Most requests to and responses from Web services are transmitted via SOAP. This means that any client capable of generating and processing SOAP messages can use a Web service, regardless of the language in which the Web service is written.

Web services have important implications for *business-to-business* (*B2B*) *transactions*, (i.e., transactions that occur between two or more businesses). Now, instead of using proprietary applications, businesses can conduct transactions via Web services—a much simpler and more efficient means of conducting business. Because Web services and SOAP are platform-independent, companies can collaborate and use Web services without worrying about the compatibility of various technologies or programming languages. In this way, Web services are an inexpensive, readily-available solution to facilitate B2B transactions.

A Web service created in Visual Studio .NET has two parts: An *ASMX* file and a code-behind file. The ASMX file by default can be viewed in any Web browser and contains valuable information about the Web service, such as descriptions of Web-service methods and ways to test these methods. The code-behind file provides the implementation for the methods that the Web service encompasses. Figure 19.1 depicts Internet Explorer rendering an ASMX file.

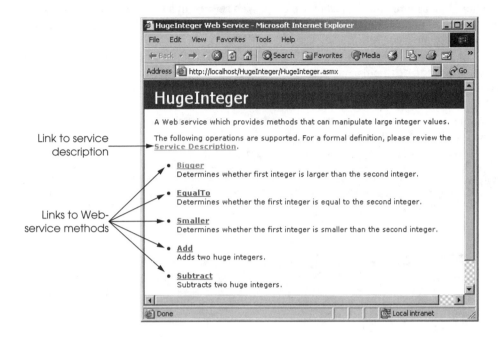

Link to service description

Links to Web-service methods

Fig. 19.1　ASMX file rendered in Internet Explorer.

The top of the page provides a link to the Web service's ***Service Description***. A service description is an XML document that conforms to the *Web Service Description Language* (*WSDL*), an XML vocabulary that defines the methods that the Web service makes available and the ways in which clients can interact with those methods. The WSDL document also specifies lower-level information that clients might need, such as the required formats for requests and responses. Visual Studio .NET generates the WSDL service description. Client programs can use the service description to confirm the correctness of method calls when the client programs are compiled.

The programmer should not alter the service description, as it defines how a Web service works. When a user clicks the **Service Description** link at the top of the ASMX page, WSDL is displayed that defines the service description for this Web service (Fig. 19.2).

Below the **Service Description** link, the Web page shown in Fig. 19.1 lists the methods that the Web service provides (i.e., all methods in the application that are declared with **WebMethod** attributes). Clicking any method name requests a test page that describes the method (Fig. 19.3). After explaining the method's arguments, the test page allows users to test the method by entering the proper parameters and clicking **Invoke**. (We discuss the process of testing a Web-service method shortly.) Below the **Invoke** button, the page displays sample request and response messages using SOAP, HTTP GET and HTTP POST. These protocols are the three options for sending and receiving messages in Web services. The protocol used to transmit request and response messages is sometimes known as the Web service's *wire protocol* or *wire format*, because the protocol specifies how information is sent "along the wire." Notice that Fig. 19.3 uses the HTTP GET protocol to test a method. Later in this chapter, when we use a Web service in a C# program, we use SOAP as the wire protocol. The advantages of using SOAP over HTTP GET and HTTP POST are discussed in the next section.

On the page depicted in Fig. 19.3, users can test a method by entering **Value**s in the **first:** and **second:** fields and then clicking **Invoke** (in this example, we tested method **Bigger**). The method executes, and a new Web browser window opens to display an XML document containing the result (Fig. 19.4). Now that we have introduced a simple example using a Web service, the next several sections explore the role of XML in Web services, as well as other aspects of Web service functionality.

Testing and Debugging Tip 19.1

Using the ASMX page of a Web service to test and debug methods makes that Web service more reliable and robust; it also reduces the likelihood that clients using the Web service will encounter errors.

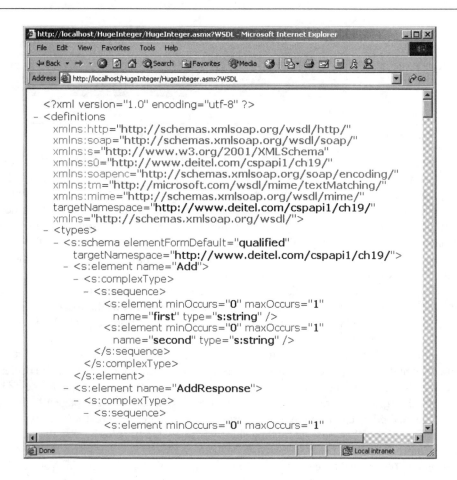

Fig. 19.2   Service description for a Web service.

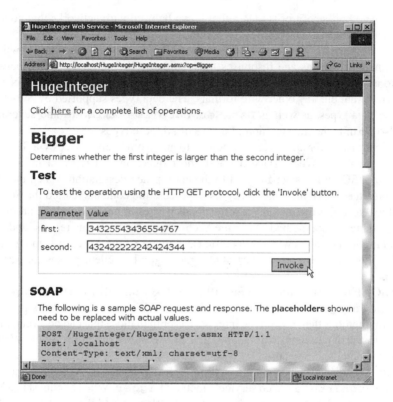

Fig. 19.3 Invoking a method of a Web service from a Web browser.

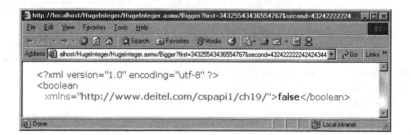

Fig. 19.4 Results of invoking a Web-service method from a Web browser.

19.3 Simple Object Access Protocol (SOAP) and Web Services

The Simple Object Access Protocol (SOAP) is a platform-independent protocol that uses XML to make remote-procedure calls over HTTP. Each request and response is packaged in a *SOAP message*—an XML message that contains all the information necessary to process its contents. SOAP messages are quite popular, because they are written in the easy-to-understand and platform-independent XML. Similarly, HTTP was chosen to transmit SOAP messages, because HTTP is a standard protocol for sending information across the Internet. The use of XML and HTTP enables different operating systems to send and receive SOAP messages. Another benefit of HTTP is that it can be used with networks that contain *fire-walls*—security barriers that restrict communication among networks.

SOAP supports an extensive set of data types. Readers should note that the wire format used to transmit requests and responses must support all data types passed between the applications. Web services that use SOAP support a wider variety of data types than do Web services that employ other wire formats. The data types supported by SOAP include most basic data types, as well as **DataSet**, **DateTime**, **XmlNode** and several others. SOAP also permits the transmission of arrays of all these types.

Applications send requests and responses to and from Web services via SOAP. When a program invokes a Web-service method, the request and all relevant information are packaged in a SOAP message and sent to the appropriate destination. When the Web service receives the SOAP message, it begins to process the contents (called the *SOAP envelope*), which specifies the method that the client wishes to execute and the arguments the client is passing to that method. After the Web service receives this request and parses it, the proper method is called with the specified arguments (if there are any), and the response is sent back to the client in another SOAP message. The client parses the response to retrieve the result of the method call.

The SOAP request portrayed in Fig. 19.5 was taken directly from the **Bigger** method of the **HugeInteger** Web service (Fig. 19.3). This Web service provides programmers with several methods that manipulate integers larger than those that can be stored in a **long** variable. Most programmers do not manipulate SOAP messages, allowing the Web service to handle the details of transmission.

Figure 19.5 displays a standard SOAP request that is created when a client wishes to execute the **HugeInteger** Web service's method **Bigger**. When a request to a Web service causes such a SOAP request to be created, the elements **first** and **second**'s character data (**string**s) would contain the actual values that the user entered (lines 16–17). If this envelope contained the request from Fig. 19.3, element **first** and element **second** would contain the values entered in Fig. 19.3. Placeholder **length** would contain the length of this SOAP message.

```
1    POST /HugeIntegerWebService/HugeInteger.asmx HTTP/1.1
2    Host: localhost
3    Content-Type: text/xml; charset=utf-8
4    Content-Length: length
5    SOAPAction: "http://www.deitel.com/cspapi1/ch19/Bigger"
6
7    <?xml version="1.0" encoding="utf-8"?>
8
9    <soap:Envelope
10       xmlns:xsi="http://www.w3.org/2001/XMLSchema-instance"
11       xmlns:xsd="http://www.w3.org/2001/XMLSchema"
12       xmlns:soap="http://schemas.xmlsoap.org/soap/envelope/">
13
14       <soap:Body>
15          <Bigger xmlns="http://www.deitel.com/cspapi1/ch19/">
16             <first>string</first>
17             <second>string</second>
```

Fig. 19.5   SOAP request for the **HugeInteger** Web service. (Part 1 of 2.)

```
18          </Bigger>
19      </soap:Body>
20
21  </soap:Envelope>
```

Fig. 19.5 SOAP request for the **HugeInteger** Web service. (Part 2 of 2.)

19.4 Publishing and Consuming Web Services

This section presents an example of creating (also known as *publishing*) and using (also known as *consuming*) a Web service. An application that consumes a Web service actually consists of two parts: A *proxy* class that represents the Web service and a client application that accesses the Web service via an instance of the proxy class. The proxy class handles the transferal of the arguments for the Web-service method from the client application to the Web service, as well as the transferal of the result from the Web-service method back to the client application. Visual Studio .NET can generate proxy classes—we demonstrate how to do this momentarily.

Figure 19.6 presents the code-behind file for the **HugeInteger** Web service (Fig. 19.1). The name of the Web service is based on the name of the class that defines it (in this case, **HugeInteger**). This Web service is designed to perform calculations with integers that contain a maximum of 100 digits. As we mentioned earlier, **long** variables cannot handle integers of this size (i.e., an overflow would occur). The Web service provides a client with methods that take two "huge integers" and determine which one is larger or smaller, whether the two numbers are equal, their sum or their difference. The reader can think of these methods as services that one application provides for the programmers of other applications (hence the term, "Web services"). Any programmer can access this Web service, use its methods and thus avoid the writing, testing and debugging of over 200 lines of code.

Line 13 places class **HugeInteger** in namespace **HugeIntegerWebService**. Line 19 assigns the Web service namespace to **www.deitel.com/cspapi1/ch19/** to uniquely identify this Web service. The namespace is specified using the **Namespace** property of the **WebService** attribute. In lines 20–21, we use property **Description** to provide information about our Web service that appears in the ASMX file. Line 22 specifies that our class derives from **System.Web.Services.WebService**. By default, Visual Studio defines our Web service so that it inherits from the **WebService** class. Although a Web service class is not required to subclass **WebService**, class **WebService** provides members that are useful in determining information about the client and the Web service itself. Several methods in class **HugeInteger** are tagged with the **WebMethod** attribute, which *exposes* the method such that it can be called remotely. When this attribute is absent, the method is not accessible through the Web service. Notice that the **WebMethod** attribute, like the **WebService** attribute, contains a **Description** property, which provides information about the method to the ASMX page. Readers can see these descriptions in the output of Fig. 19.6.

```
1   // Fig. 19.6: HugeInteger.asmx.cs
2   // HugeInteger Web Service.
```

Fig. 19.6 **HugeInteger** Web service. (Part 1 of 6.)

```
3
4    using System;
5    using System.Text;
6    using System.Collections;
7    using System.ComponentModel;
8    using System.Data;
9    using System.Diagnostics;
10   using System.Web;
11   using System.Web.Services; // contains Web service related classes
12
13   namespace HugeIntegerWebService
14   {
15      /// <summary>
16      /// performs operations on large integers
17      /// </summary>
18      [ WebService(
19         Namespace = "http://www.deitel.com/cspapi1/ch19/",
20         Description = "A Web service which provides methods that" +
21         " can manipulate large integer values." ) ]
22      public class HugeInteger : System.Web.Services.WebService
23      {
24         // default constructor
25         public HugeInteger()
26         {
27            // CODEGEN: This call is required by the ASP .NET Web
28            // Services Designer
29            InitializeComponent();
30
31            number = new int[ MAXIMUM ];
32         }
33
34         #region Component Designer generated code
35         /// <summary>
36         /// Required method for Designer support - do not modify
37         /// the contents of this method with the code editor.
38         /// </summary>
39         private void InitializeComponent()
40         {
41         }
42         #endregion
43
44         /// <summary>
45         /// Clean up any resources being used.
46         /// </summary>
47         protected override void Dispose( bool disposing )
48         {
49         }
50
51         // WEB SERVICE EXAMPLE
52         // The HelloWorld() example service returns
53         // the string Hello World
54         // To build, uncomment the following lines
55         // then save and build the project
```

Fig. 19.6 HugeInteger Web service. (Part 2 of 6.)

```
56          // To test this web service, press F5
57
58          //    [WebMethod]
59          //    public string HelloWorld()
60          //    {
61          //        return "Hello World";
62          //    }
63
64          private const int MAXIMUM = 100;
65
66          public int[] number;
67
68          // indexer that accepts an integer parameter
69          public int this[ int index ]
70          {
71             get
72             {
73                return number[ index ];
74             }
75
76             set
77             {
78                number[ index ] = ( value >= 0 ? value : 0 );
79             }
80
81          } // end indexer
82
83          // returns string representation of HugeInteger
84          public override string ToString()
85          {
86             StringBuilder returnString = new StringBuilder();
87
88             foreach ( int digit in number )
89                returnString.Insert( 0, digit );
90
91             return returnString.ToString();
92          }
93
94          // creates HugeInteger based on argument
95          public static HugeInteger FromString( string integer )
96          {
97             HugeInteger parsedInteger = new HugeInteger();
98
99             for ( int i = 0; i < integer.Length; i++ )
100               parsedInteger[ i ] = Int32.Parse(
101                  integer[ integer.Length - i - 1 ].ToString() );
102
103            return parsedInteger;
104         }
105
106         // WebMethod that performs integer addition
107         // represented by string arguments
```

Fig. 19.6 HugeInteger Web service. (Part 3 of 6.)

```
108        [ WebMethod ( Description = "Adds two huge integers." ) ]
109        public string Add( string first, string second )
110        {
111           int carry = 0;
112
113           HugeInteger operand1 = HugeInteger.FromString( first );
114           HugeInteger operand2 =
115              HugeInteger.FromString( second );
116
117           // store result of addition
118           HugeInteger result = new HugeInteger();
119
120           // perform addition algorithm for each digit
121           for ( int i = 0; i < MAXIMUM; i++ )
122           {
123              // add two digits in same column
124              // result is their sum, plus carry from
125              // previous operation modulus 10
126              result[ i ] =
127                 ( operand1[ i ] + operand2[ i ] ) % 10 + carry;
128
129              // store remainder of dividing
130              // sums of two digits by 10
131              carry = ( operand1[ i ] + operand2[ i ] ) / 10;
132           }
133
134           return result.ToString();
135
136        } // end method Add
137
138        // WebMethod that performs the subtraction of integers
139        // represented by string arguments
140        [ WebMethod (
141           Description = "Subtracts two huge integers." ) ]
142        public string Subtract( string first, string second )
143        {
144           HugeInteger operand1 = HugeInteger.FromString( first );
145           HugeInteger operand2 =
146              HugeInteger.FromString( second );
147           HugeInteger result = new HugeInteger();
148
149           // subtract top digit from bottom digit
150           for ( int i = 0; i < MAXIMUM; i++ )
151           {
152              // if top digit is smaller than bottom
153              // digit we need to borrow
154              if ( operand1[ i ] < operand2[ i ] )
155                 Borrow( operand1, i );
156
157              // subtract bottom from top
158              result[ i ] = operand1[ i ] - operand2[ i ];
159           }
160
```

Fig. 19.6 HugeInteger Web service. (Part 4 of 6.)

```
161            return result.ToString();
162
163        } // end method Subtract
164
165        // borrows 1 from next digit
166        private void Borrow( HugeInteger integer, int place )
167        {
168            // if no place to borrow from, signal problem
169            if ( place >= MAXIMUM - 1 )
170                throw new ArgumentException();
171
172            // otherwise if next digit is zero,
173            // borrow from digit to left
174            else if ( integer[ place + 1 ] == 0 )
175                Borrow( integer, place + 1 );
176
177            // add ten to current place because we borrowed
178            // and subtract one from previous digit -
179            // this is digit borrowed from
180            integer[ place ] += 10;
181            integer[ place + 1 ] -= 1;
182
183        } // end method Borrow
184
185        // WebMethod that returns true if first integer is
186        // bigger than second
187        [ WebMethod ( Description = "Determines whether first " +
188            "integer is larger than the second integer." ) ]
189        public bool Bigger( string first, string second )
190        {
191            char[] zeroes = { '0' };
192
193            try
194            {
195                // if elimination of all zeroes from result
196                // of subtraction is an empty string,
197                // numbers are equal, so return false,
198                // otherwise return true
199                if ( Subtract( first, second ).Trim( zeroes ) == "" )
200                    return false;
201                else
202                    return true;
203            }
204
205            // if ArgumentException occurs, first number
206            // was smaller, so return false
207            catch ( ArgumentException )
208            {
209                return false;
210            }
211
212        } // end method Bigger
213
```

Fig. 19.6 HugeInteger Web service. (Part 5 of 6.)

```
214          // WebMethod returns true if first integer is
215          // smaller than second
216          [ WebMethod ( Description = "Determines whether the " +
217             "first integer is smaller than the second integer." ) ]
218          public bool Smaller( string first, string second )
219          {
220             // if second is bigger than first, then first is
221             // smaller than second
222             return Bigger( second, first );
223          }
224
225          // WebMethod that returns true if two integers are equal
226          [ WebMethod ( Description = "Determines whether the " +
227             "first integer is equal to the second integer." ) ]
228          public bool EqualTo( string first, string second )
229          {
230             // if either first is bigger than second, or first is
231             // smaller than second, they are not equal
232             if ( Bigger( first, second ) ||
233                Smaller( first, second ) )
234                return false;
235             else
236                return true;
237          }
238
239       } // end class HugeInteger
240
241    } // end namespace HugeIntegerWebService
```

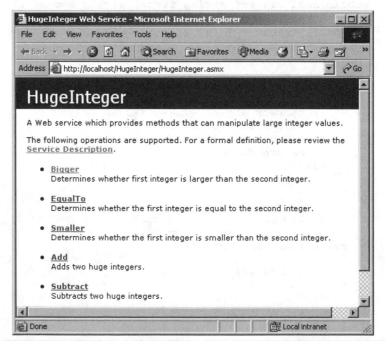

Fig. 19.6   HugeInteger Web service. (Part 6 of 6.)

Good Programming Practice 19.1

Specify a namespace for each Web service so that it can be uniquely identified.

Good Programming Practice 19.2

Specify descriptions for all Web services and Web-service methods so that clients can obtain additional information about the Web service and its contents.

Common Programming Error 19.2

Web-service methods cannot be declared **static**, *or a runtime error will occur when attempting to view the ASMX page. For a client to access a Web-service method, an instance of that Web service must exist.*

Lines 69–81 define an indexer for our class. This enables us to access any digit in **HugeInteger** as if we were accessing it through array **number**. Lines 108–136 and 142–163 define **WebMethod**s **Add** and **Subtract**, which perform addition and subtraction, respectively. Method **Borrow** (lines 166–183) handles the case in which the digit in the left operand is smaller than the corresponding digit in the right operand. For instance, when we subtract 19 from 32, we usually go digit by digit, starting from the right. The number 2 is smaller than 9, so we add 10 to 2 (resulting in 12), which subtracts 9, resulting in 3 for the rightmost digit in the solution. We then subtract 1 from the next digit over (3), making it 2. The corresponding digit in the right operand is now the "1" in 19. The subtraction of 1 from 2 is 1, making the corresponding digit in the result 1. The final result, when both resulting digits are combined, is 13. Method **Borrow** adds 10 to the appropriate digits and subtracts 1 from the digit to the left. Because this is a utility method that is not intended to be called remotely, it is not qualified with attribute **WebMethod**.

The screen capture in Fig. 19.6 is identical to the one in Fig. 19.1. A client application can invoke only the five methods listed in the screen shot (i.e., the methods qualified with the **WebMethod** attribute).

Now, let us demonstrate how to create this Web service. To begin, we must create a project of type **ASP.NET Web Service**. Like Web Forms, Web services are by default placed in the Web server's **wwwroot** directory on the server (**localhost**). By default, Visual Studio places the solution file (**.sln**) in the **Visual Studio Projects** folder, in a directory for the solution. (The **Visual Studio Projects** folder is usually located in the **My Documents** folder.)

Notice that, when the project is created, the code-behind file is displayed in design view by default (Fig. 19.7). If this file is not open, it can be opened by clicking **Service1.asmx**. The file that will be opened, however, is **Service1.asmx.cs** (the code-behind file for our Web service). This is because, when creating Web services in Visual Studio, programmers work almost exclusively in the code-behind file. In fact, if a programmer were to open the ASMX file, it would contain only the lines:

```
<%@ WebService Language="c#" Codebehind="Service1.asmx.cs"
    Class="WebService1.Service1" %>
```

indicating the name of the code-behind file, the programming language in which the code-behind file is written and the class that defines our Web service. This is the extent of the information that this file must contain. [*Note*: By default, the code-behind file is not listed in the **Solution Explorer**. The code-behind file is displayed when the ASMX file is double clicked in the **Solution Explorer**. This file can be listed in the **Solution Explorer** by clicking the icon to show all files.]

It might seem strange that there is a design view for Web services, given that Web services do not have graphical user interfaces. A design view is provided because more sophisticated Web services contain methods that manipulate more than just strings or numbers. For example, a Web-service method could manipulate a database. Instead of typing all the code necessary to create a database connection, developers can simply drop the proper ADO .NET components into the design view and manipulate them as we would in a Windows or Web application.

Now that we have defined our Web service, we demonstrate how to use it. First, a client application must be created. In this first example, we create a Windows application as our client. Once this application has been created, the client must add a proxy class for accessing the Web service. A proxy class (or proxy) is a class created from the Web service's WSDL file that enables the client to call Web-service methods over the Internet. The proxy class handles all the "plumbing" required for Web-service method calls. Whenever a call is made in the client application to a Web-service method, the application actually calls a corresponding method in the proxy class. This method takes the name of the method and its arguments, then formats them so that they can be sent as a request in a SOAP message. The Web service receives this request and executes the method call, sending back the result as another SOAP message. When the client application receives the SOAP message containing the response, the proxy class decodes it and formats the results so that they are understandable to the client. This information then is returned to the client. It is important to note that the proxy class essentially is hidden from the programmer. We cannot, in fact, view it in the **Solution Explorer** unless we choose to show all the files. The purpose of the proxy class is to make it seem to clients as though they are calling the Web-service methods directly. It is rarely necessary for the client to view or manipulate the proxy class.

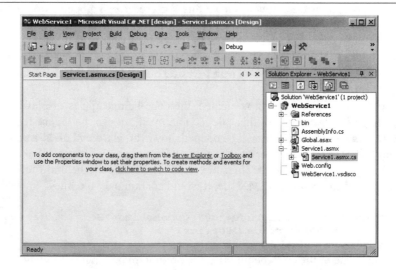

Fig. 19.7   Design view of a Web service.

The next example demonstrates how to create a Web service client and its corresponding proxy class. We must begin by creating a project and adding a *Web reference* to that project. When we add a Web reference to a client application, the proxy class is created. The client then creates an instance of the proxy class, which is used to call methods included in the Web service.

To create a proxy in Visual Studio, right click the **References** folder in **Solution Explorer** and select *Add Web Reference* (Fig. 19.8). In the **Add Web Reference** dialog that appears (Fig. 19.9), enter the Web address of the Web service and press *Enter*. Once a Web service is chosen the description of that Web service appears, and the developer can click **Add Reference**. This adds to the **Solution Explorer** (Fig. 19.10) a **Web References** folder with a node named for the domain where the Web service is located. In this case, the name is **localhost**, because we are using the local Web server. This means that, when we reference class **HugeInteger**, we will be doing so through class **HugeInteger** in namespace **localhost**, instead of class **HugeInteger** in namespace **HugeIntegerWebService** [*Note*: The Web service class and the proxy class have the same name. Visual Studio generates a proxy for the Web service and adds it as a reference (Fig. 19.10).]

The steps that we described previously work well if the programmer knows the appropriate Web services reference. However, what if we are trying to locate a new Web service? There are two technologies that facilitate this process: *Universal Description, Discovery and Integration* (*UDDI*) and *Discovery files* (*DISCO*). UDDI is a project for developing a set of specifications that define how Web services should be published so that programmers searching for Web services can find them. Microsoft began this ongoing project to facilitate the locating of Web services that conform to certain specifications, allowing programmers to find different Web services using search engines. UDDI organizes and describes Web services and then places this information in a central location. Although UDDI is beyond the scope of what we are teaching, the reader can learn more about this project and view a demonstration by visiting **www.uddi.org** and **uddi.microsoft.com**. These sites contain search tools that make finding Web services fast and easy.

Good Programming Practice 19.3

When creating a program that will use Web services, add the Web reference first. This will enable Visual Studio to recognize an instance of the Web service class, allowing Intellisense to help the developer use the Web service.

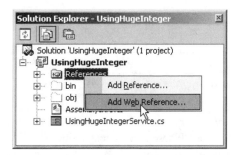

Fig. 19.8   Adding a Web service reference to a project.

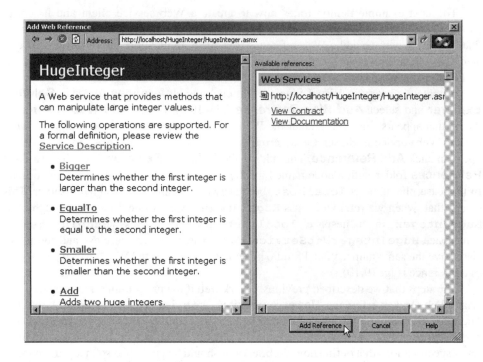

Fig. 19.9   Web reference selection and description.

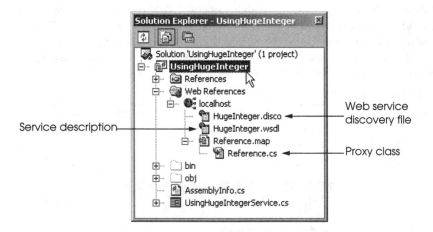

Fig. 19.10 Solution Explorer after adding a Web reference to a project.

A DISCO file catalogs Web services in a particular directory. There are two types of discovery files: *Dynamic discovery* files (with a `.vsdisco` extension) and *static discovery* files (with a `.disco` extension). These files indicate both the location of the ASMX file and the service description (a WSDL file) for each Web service in the current directory, as well as any Web services in the current directory's subdirectories. When a programmer creates a Web service, Visual Studio generates a dynamic discovery file for that Web service. When a Web reference is added, the client can use the dynamic discovery file to select the desired Web service. Once the Web reference is created, a static discovery file is placed in the client's project. The static discovery file hard codes the location for the ASMX and WSDL files. (By "hard code," we mean that the location is entered directly into the file.) Dynamic discovery files, on the other hand, are created such that list of Web services is created dynamically on the server when a client is searching for a Web service. The use of dynamic discovery enables certain extra options, such as hiding of certain Web services in subdirectories. Discovery files are a Microsoft-specific technology, whereas UDDI is not. However, the two can work together to enable a client to find a Web service. Using both technologies, the client can use a search engine to find a location with various Web services on a topic, and then use discovery files to view all the Web services in that location.

Once the Web reference is added, the client can access the Web service through our proxy. Because our proxy class is named **HugeInteger** and is located in namespace **localhost**, we must use **localhost.HugeInteger** to reference this class. The Windows Form in Fig. 19.11 uses the **HugeInteger** Web service to perform computations with positive integers up to **100** digits long. [*Note*: If using the examples for this book located on our Web site, the reader might need to regenerate the proxy.]

```
1   // Fig. 19.11: UsingHugeIntegerService.cs
2   // Using the HugeInteger Web Service.
3
4   using System;
5   using System.Drawing;
6   using System.Collections;
7   using System.ComponentModel;
8   using System.Windows.Forms;
9   using System.Web.Services.Protocols;
10
11  // allows user to perform operations on large integers
12  public class UsingHugeIntService : System.Windows.Forms.Form
13  {
14     private System.Windows.Forms.Label promptLabel;
15     private System.Windows.Forms.Label resultLabel;
16
17     private System.Windows.Forms.TextBox firstTextBox;
18     private System.Windows.Forms.TextBox secondTextBox;
19
20     private System.Windows.Forms.Button addButton;
21     private System.Windows.Forms.Button subtractButton;
22     private System.Windows.Forms.Button biggerButton;
23     private System.Windows.Forms.Button smallerButton;
24     private System.Windows.Forms.Button equalButton;
25
26     private System.ComponentModel.Container components = null;
27
28     // declare a reference Web service
29     private localhost.HugeInteger remoteInteger;
30
31     private char[] zeroes = { '0' };
32
```

Fig. 19.11 Using the **HugeInteger** Web service. (Part 1 of 5.)

```
33      // default constructor
34      public UsingHugeIntService()
35      {
36          InitializeComponent();
37
38          // instantiate remoteInteger
39          remoteInteger = new localhost.HugeInteger();
40      }
41
42      // Visual Studio .NET generated code
43
44      [STAThread]
45      static void Main()
46      {
47          Application.Run( new UsingHugeIntService() );
48
49      } // end Main
50
51      // checks whether two numbers user input are equal
52      protected void equalButton_Click(
53          object sender, System.EventArgs e )
54      {
55          // make sure HugeIntegers do not exceed 100 digits
56          if ( CheckSize( firstTextBox, secondTextBox ) )
57              return;
58
59          // call Web-service method to determine
60          // whether integers are equal
61          if ( remoteInteger.EqualTo(
62              firstTextBox.Text, secondTextBox.Text ) )
63
64              resultLabel.Text =
65                  firstTextBox.Text.TrimStart( zeroes ) +
66                  " is equal to " +
67                  secondTextBox.Text.TrimStart( zeroes );
68          else
69              resultLabel.Text =
70                  firstTextBox.Text.TrimStart( zeroes ) +
71                  " is NOT equal to " +
72                  secondTextBox.Text.TrimStart( zeroes );
73
74      } // end method equalButton_Click
75
76      // checks whether first integer input
77      // by user is smaller than second
78      protected void smallerButton_Click(
79          object sender, System.EventArgs e )
80      {
81          // make sure HugeIntegers do not exceed 100 digits
82          if ( CheckSize( firstTextBox, secondTextBox ) )
83              return;
84
```

Fig. 19.11 Using the **HugeInteger** Web service. (Part 2 of 5.)

```
85          // call Web-service method to determine whether first
86          // integer is smaller than second
87          if ( remoteInteger.Smaller(
88             firstTextBox.Text, secondTextBox.Text ) )
89
90             resultLabel.Text =
91                firstTextBox.Text.TrimStart( zeroes ) +
92                " is smaller than " +
93                secondTextBox.Text.TrimStart( zeroes );
94          else
95             resultLabel.Text =
96                firstTextBox.Text.TrimStart( zeroes ) +
97                " is NOT smaller than " +
98                secondTextBox.Text.TrimStart( zeroes );
99
100      } // end method smallerButton_Click
101
102      // checks whether first integer input
103      // by user is bigger than second
104      protected void biggerButton_Click(
105         object sender, System.EventArgs e )
106      {
107         // make sure HugeIntegers do not exceed 100 digits
108         if ( CheckSize( firstTextBox, secondTextBox ) )
109            return;
110
111         // call Web-service method to determine whether first
112         // integer is larger than the second
113         if ( remoteInteger.Bigger( firstTextBox.Text,
114            secondTextBox.Text ) )
115
116            resultLabel.Text =
117               firstTextBox.Text.TrimStart( zeroes ) +
118               " is larger than " +
119               secondTextBox.Text.TrimStart( zeroes );
120         else
121            resultLabel.Text =
122               firstTextBox.Text.TrimStart( zeroes ) +
123               " is NOT larger than " +
124               secondTextBox.Text.TrimStart( zeroes );
125
126      } // end method biggerButton_Click
127
128      // subtract second integer from first
129      protected void subtractButton_Click(
130         object sender, System.EventArgs e )
131      {
132         // make sure HugeIntegers do not exceed 100 digits
133         if ( CheckSize( firstTextBox, secondTextBox ) )
134            return;
135
```

Fig. 19.11 Using the **HugeInteger** Web service. (Part 3 of 5.)

```
136          // perform subtraction
137          try
138          {
139              string result = remoteInteger.Subtract(
140                  firstTextBox.Text,
141                  secondTextBox.Text ).TrimStart( zeroes );
142
143              resultLabel.Text = ( ( result == "" ) ? "0" : result );
144          }
145
146          // if WebMethod throws an exception, then first
147          // argument was smaller than second
148          catch ( SoapException )
149          {
150              MessageBox.Show(
151                  "First argument was smaller than the second" );
152          }
153
154      } // end method subtractButton_Click
155
156      // adds two integers input by user
157      protected void addButton_Click(
158          object sender, System.EventArgs e )
159      {
160          // make sure HugeInteger does not exceed 100 digits
161          // and is not situation where both integers are 100
162          // digits long--result in overflow
163          if ( firstTextBox.Text.Length > 100 ||
164              secondTextBox.Text.Length > 100   ||
165              ( firstTextBox.Text.Length == 100 &&
166              secondTextBox.Text.Length == 100 ) )
167          {
168              MessageBox.Show( "HugeIntegers must not be more "
169                  + "than 100 digits\nBoth integers cannot be of"
170                  + " length 100: this causes an overflow",
171                  "Error", MessageBoxButtons.OK,
172                  MessageBoxIcon.Information );
173
174              return;
175          }
176
177          // perform addition
178          resultLabel.Text = remoteInteger.Add( firstTextBox.Text,
179              secondTextBox.Text ).TrimStart( zeroes ).ToString();
180
181      } // end method addButton_Click
182
183      // determines whether size of integers is too big
184      private bool CheckSize( TextBox first, TextBox second )
185      {
186          if ( first.Text.Length > 100 || second.Text.Length > 100 )
187          {
```

Fig. 19.11 Using the **HugeInteger** Web service. (Part 4 of 5.)

```
188              MessageBox.Show( "HugeIntegers must be less than 100"
189                 + " digits", "Error", MessageBoxButtons.OK,
190                 MessageBoxIcon.Information );
191
192          return true;
193       }
194
195       return false;
196
197    } // end method CheckSize
198
199 } // end class UsingHugeIntegerService
```

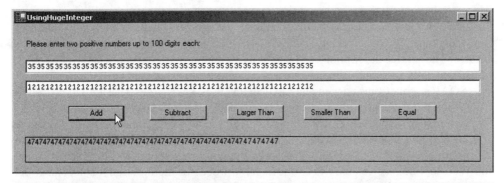

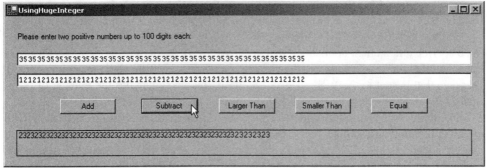

Fig. 19.11 Using the **HugeInteger** Web service. (Part 5 of 5.)

The user inputs two integers, each up to 100 digits long. The clicking of any button invokes a remote method to perform the appropriate calculation and return the result. The return value of each operation is displayed, and all leading zeroes are eliminated, using **string** method **TrimStart**. Note that **UsingHugeInteger** does not have the capability to perform operations with 100-digit numbers. Instead, it creates **string** representations of these numbers and passes them as arguments to Web-service methods that handle such tasks for us.

19.5 Summary

A Web service in .NET has two parts—an ASMX file and a code-behind file. The ASMX file can be viewed in any Web browser and displays information about the Web service. The code-behind file contains the definition of the methods in the Web service.

A service description is an XML document that conforms to the Web Service Description Language (WSDL). WSDL is an XML vocabulary that describes how Web services behave. The service description can be used by a client program to confirm the correctness of method calls at compile time.

SOAP is a platform-independent protocol that uses XML to describe remote-procedure calls over HTTP. Requests to and responses from a Web-service method are packaged in a SOAP message—an XML message containing all the information necessary to process its contents. When a program invokes a Web-service method, the request and all relevant information are packaged in a SOAP message and sent to the appropriate destination. When the Web service receives the SOAP message, it processes the message's contents, which specify the method to invoke and the arguments the client is passing to that method. The method is executed, and the response is sent back to the client as another SOAP message.

An application that uses a Web service consists of two parts—a proxy class for the Web service and a client application that accesses the Web service via the proxy. A proxy class handles the task of transferring the arguments passed from the client into a SOAP message that is sent to the Web service. Likewise, the proxy handles the transfer of information in the SOAP response to the client. A proxy class is created from the Web service's WSDL file, which enables the client to call Web-service methods over the Internet. Whenever a call is made in a client application to a Web-service method, a method in the proxy class is called. This method takes the method name and arguments passed by the client and formats them so that they can be sent as a request in a SOAP message.

Class **WebService** provides members that determine information about the user, the application and other topics relevant to the Web service. A Web service is not required to inherit from class **WebService**. A programmer specifies a class as a Web service by tagging it with the **WebService** attribute.

UDDI (Universal Description, Discovery and Integration) is a project for developing a set of specifications that define how Web services should be discovered, so that clients searching for Web services can find them. A DISCO (discovery) file specifies any Web services that are available in the current directory. There are two types of discovery files—dynamic discovery files (**.vsdisco** extension) and static discovery files (**.disco** extension). Once a Web reference is created, a static discovery file is placed in the client's project. The static discovery file specifies the locations of the ASMX and WSDL files. Dynamic discovery files are created so that a list of Web services is constructed when a client is searching for Web services.

20

Networking: Streams-Based Sockets

Objectives

- To understand the fundamentals of socket-based networking.
- To be able to implement C# networking applications that use sockets.
- To understand how to implement C# clients and servers that communicate with one another.

If the presence of electricity can be made visible in any part of a circuit, I see no reason why intelligence may not be transmitted instantaneously by electricity.
Samuel F. B. Morse

Mr. Watson, come here, I want you.
Alexander Graham Bell

What networks of railroads, highways and canals were in another age, the networks of telecommunications, information and computerization ... are today.
Bruno Kreisky

Science may never come up with a better office-communication system than the coffee break.
Earl Wilson

20.1 Introduction

The Internet and the World Wide Web have generated a great deal of excitement in the business and computing communities. The Internet ties the "information world" together; the Web makes the Internet easy to use while providing the flair of multimedia. Organizations see both the Internet and the Web as crucial to their information-systems strategies. C# and the .NET Framework offer a number of built-in networking capabilities that facilitate Internet-based and Web-based applications development. C# not only can specify parallelism through multithreading, but also can enable programs to search the Web for information and collaborate with programs running on other computers internationally.

In Chapters 17 and 19, we began our presentation of C#'s networking and distributed-computing capabilities. We discussed Web Forms and Web Services, two high-level networking technologies that enable programmers to develop distributed applications in C#. In this chapter, we focus on the networking technologies that support C#'s ASP.NET capabilities and can be used to build distributed applications.

Our discussion of networking focuses on both sides of a *client-server relationship*. The *client* requests that some action be performed; the *server* performs the action and responds to the client. A common implementation of this request-response model is between Web browsers and Web servers. When users select Web sites that they wish to view through a browser (the client application), the browser makes a request to the appropriate Web server (the server application). The server normally responds to the client by sending the appropriate HTML Web pages.

C#'s networking capabilities are grouped into several namespaces. The fundamental networking capabilities are defined by classes of namespace **System.Net.Sockets**. Through this namespace, C# offers *socket-based communications*, which enable developers to view networking as if it were file I/O. This means that a program can read from a *socket* (network connection) or write to a socket as easily as it can read from or write to a file. Sockets are the fundamental way to perform network communications in the .NET Framework. The term "socket" refers to the Berkeley Sockets Interface, which was developed in 1978 for network programming with UNIX and was popularized by C and C++ programmers.

Socket-based communications in C# employ *stream sockets*. With stream sockets, a *process* (running program) establishes a *connection* to another process. While the connection is in place, data flows between the processes in continuous *streams*. For this reason, stream sockets are said to provide a *connection-oriented service*. The popular *TCP (Transmission Control Protocol)* facilitates stream-socket transmission.

Portability Tip 20.1

The TCP protocol and its related set of protocols enable intercommunication among a wide variety of heterogeneous computer systems (i.e., computer systems with different processors and different operating systems).

20.2 Establishing a Simple Server (Using Stream Sockets)

Typically, with TCP and stream sockets, a server "waits" for a connection request from a client. Often, the server program contains a control structure or block of code that executes continuously until the server receives a request. On receiving a request, the server establishes a connection with the client. The server then uses this connection to handle future requests from that client and to send data to the client.

The establishment of a simple server with TCP and stream sockets in C# requires five steps. The first step is to create an object of class **TcpListener**, which belongs to namespace **System.Net.Sockets**. This class represents a TCP stream socket through which a server can listen for requests. A call to the **TcpListener** constructor, such as

```
TcpListener server = new TcpListener( port );
```

binds (assigns) the server to the specified *port number*. A port number is a numeric identifier that a process uses to identify itself at a given *network address*, also known as an *Internet Protocol Address* (*IP Address*). IP addresses identify computers on the Internet. In fact, Web-site names, such as **www.deitel.com**, are aliases for IP addresses. Any process that performs networking identifies itself via an *IP address/port number pair*. Hence, no two processes can have the same port number at a given IP address. The explicit binding of a socket to a port (using method **Bind** of class **Socket**) is usually unnecessary, because class **TcpListener** and other classes discussed in this chapter hide this binding (i.e., bind sockets to ports implicitly), plus they perform other socket-initialization operations.

Software Engineering Observation 20.1

Port numbers can have values between 0 and 65535. Many operating systems reserve port numbers below 1024 for system services (such as e-mail and Web servers). Applications must be granted special privileges to use these reserved port numbers. Usually, a server-side application should not specify port numbers below 1024 as connection ports, because some operating systems might reserve these numbers.

Common Programming Error 20.1

Attempting to bind an already assigned port at a given IP address is a logic error.

To receive requests, the **TcpListener** first must listen for them. The second step in our connection process is to call **TcpListener**'s *Start* method, which causes the **TcpListener** object to begin listening for connection requests. The third step establishes the connection between the server and client. The server listens indefinitely for a request—i.e., the execution of the server-side application waits until some client attempts to connect with it. The server creates a connection to the client upon receipt of a connection request. An object of class *System.Net.Sockets.Socket* manages each connection to the client. Method *AcceptSocket* of class **TcpListener** waits for a connection request, then creates a connection when a request is received. This method returns a **Socket** object upon connection, as in the statement

```
Socket connection = server.AcceptSocket();
```

When the server receives a request, method **AcceptSocket** calls method **Accept** of the **TcpListener**'s underlying **Socket** to make the connection. This is an example of C#'s hiding of networking complexity from the programmer. The programmer can write the preceding statement into a server-side program, then allow the classes of namespace **System.Net.Sockets** to handle the details of accepting requests and establishing connections.

Step four is the processing phase, in which the server and the client communicate via methods **Receive** and **Send** of class **Socket**. Note that these methods, as well as TCP and stream sockets, can be used only when the server and client are connected.

The fifth step is the connection-termination phase. When the client and server have finished communicating, the server uses method **Close** of the **Socket** object to close the connection. Most servers then return to step two (i.e., wait for another client's connection request).

One problem associated with the server scheme described in this section is that step four *blocks* other requests while processing a client's request, so that no other client can connect with the server while the code that defines the processing phase is executing. The most common technique for addressing this problem is to use multithreaded servers, which place the processing-phase code in a separate thread. When the server receives a connection request, the server *spawns*, or creates, a **Thread** to process the connection, leaving its **TcpListener** (or **Socket**) free to receive other connections.

Software Engineering Observation 20.2

Using C#'s multithreading capabilities, we can create servers that can manage simultaneous connections with multiple clients. This multithreaded-server architecture is precisely what popular UNIX and Windows network servers use.

Software Engineering Observation 20.3

*A multithreaded server can be implemented to create a thread that manages network I/O across a reference to a **Socket** object returned by method **AcceptSocket**. A multithreaded server also can be implemented to maintain a pool of threads that manage network I/O across newly created **Socket**s.*

Performance Tip 20.1

*In high-performance systems with abundant memory, a multithreaded server can be implemented to create a pool of threads. These threads can be assigned quickly to handle network I/O across each multiple **Socket**. Thus, when a connection is received, the server does not incur the overhead of thread creation.*

20.3 Establishing a Simple Client (Using Stream Sockets)

We create TCP-stream-socket clients via a process that requires four steps. In the first step, we create an object of class **TcpClient** (which belongs to namespace **System.Net.Sockets**) to connect to the server. This connection is established through method **Connect** of class **TcpClient**. One overloaded version of this method receives two arguments—the server's IP address and the port number—as in the following:

```
TcpClient client = new TcpClient();
client.Connect( serverAddress, serverPort );
```

Here, **serverPort** is an **int** that represents the server's port number; **serverAddress** can be either an *IPAddress* instance (that encapsulates the server's IP address) or a **string** that specifies the server's hostname. Alternatively, the programmer could pass an object reference of class *IPEndPoint*, which represents an IP address/port number pair, to a different overload of method **Connect**. Method **Connect** of class **TcpClient** calls method *Connect* of class **Socket** to establish the connection. If the connection is successful, method **TcpClient.Connect** returns a positive integer; otherwise, it returns **0**.

In step two, the **TcpClient** uses its method *GetStream* to get a *NetworkStream* so that it can write to and read from the server. **NetworkStream** methods *WriteByte* and *Write* can be used to output individual bytes or sets of bytes to the server, respectively; similarly, **NetworkStream** methods *ReadByte* and *Read* can be used to input individual bytes or sets of bytes from the server, respectively.

The third step is the processing phase, in which the client and the server communicate. In this phase, the client uses methods **Read**, **ReadByte**, **Write** and **WriteByte** of class **NetworkStream** to perform the appropriate communications. Using a process similar to that used by servers, a client can employ threads to prevent blocking of communications with other servers while processing data from one connection.

After the transmission is complete, step four requires the client to close the connection by calling method *Close* of the **NetworkStream** object. This closes the underlying **Socket** (if the **NetworkStream** has a reference to that **Socket**). Then, the client calls method *Close* of class **TcpClient** to terminate the TCP connection. At this point, a new connection can be established through method **Connect**, as we have described.

20.4 Client/Server Interaction with Stream-Socket Connections

The applications in Fig. 20.1 and Fig. 20.2 use the classes and techniques discussed in the previous two sections to construct a simple *client/server chat application*. The server waits for a client's request to make a connection. When a client application connects to the server, the server application sends an array of bytes to the client, indicating that the connection was successful. The client then displays a message notifying the user that a connection has been established.

Both the client and the server applications contain **TextBox**es that enable users to type messages and send them to the other application. When either the client or the server sends message "**TERMINATE**," the connection between the client and the server terminates. The server then waits for another client to request a connection. Figure 20.1 and Fig. 20.2 provide the code for classes **Server** and **Client**, respectively. Figure 20.2 also contains screen captures displaying the execution between the client and the server.

```
1   // Fig. 20.1: Server.cs
2   // Set up a Server that will receive a connection from a client,
3   // send a string to the client, and close the connection.
4
5   using System;
6   using System.Drawing;
```

Fig. 20.1   Server portion of a client/server stream-socket connection. (Part 1 of 4.)

```
 7   using System.Collections;
 8   using System.ComponentModel;
 9   using System.Windows.Forms;
10   using System.Threading;
11   using System.Net.Sockets;
12   using System.IO;
13
14   // server that awaits client connections (one at a time) and
15   // allows a conversation between client and server
16   public class Server : System.Windows.Forms.Form
17   {
18      private System.Windows.Forms.TextBox inputTextBox;
19      private System.Windows.Forms.TextBox displayTextBox;
20      private Socket connection;
21      private Thread readThread;
22
23      private System.ComponentModel.Container components = null;
24      private NetworkStream socketStream;
25      private BinaryWriter writer;
26      private BinaryReader reader;
27
28      // default constructor
29      public Server()
30      {
31         InitializeComponent();
32
33         // create a new thread from the server
34         readThread = new Thread( new ThreadStart( RunServer ) );
35         readThread.Start();
36      }
37
38      // Visual Studio .NET generated code
39
40      [STAThread]
41      static void Main()
42      {
43         Application.Run( new Server() );
44      }
45
46      protected void Server_Closing(
47         object sender, CancelEventArgs e )
48      {
49         System.Environment.Exit( System.Environment.ExitCode );
50      }
51
52      // sends the text typed at the server to the client
53      protected void inputTextBox_KeyDown(
54         object sender, KeyEventArgs e )
55      {
56         // sends the text to the client
57         try
58         {
```

Fig. 20.1   Server portion of a client/server stream-socket connection. (Part 2 of 4.)

```
59              if ( e.KeyCode == Keys.Enter && connection != null )
60              {
61                  writer.Write( "SERVER>>> " + inputTextBox.Text );
62
63                  displayTextBox.Text +=
64                      "\r\nSERVER>>> " + inputTextBox.Text;
65
66                  // if the user at the server signaled termination
67                  // sever the connection to the client
68                  if ( inputTextBox.Text == "TERMINATE" )
69                      connection.Close();
70
71                  inputTextBox.Clear();
72              }
73          }
74          catch ( SocketException )
75          {
76              displayTextBox.Text += "\nError writing object";
77          }
78      } // inputTextBox_KeyDown
79
80      // allows a client to connect and displays the text it sends
81      public void RunServer()
82      {
83          TcpListener listener;
84          int counter = 1;
85
86          // wait for a client connection and display the text
87          // that the client sends
88          try
89          {
90              // Step 1: create TcpListener
91              listener = new TcpListener( 5000 );
92
93              // Step 2: TcpListener waits for connection request
94              listener.Start();
95
96              // Step 3: establish connection upon client request
97              while ( true )
98              {
99                  displayTextBox.Text = "Waiting for connection\r\n";
100
101                  // accept an incoming connection
102                  connection = listener.AcceptSocket();
103
104                  // create NetworkStream object associated with socket
105                  socketStream = new NetworkStream( connection );
106
107                  // create objects for transferring data across stream
108                  writer = new BinaryWriter( socketStream );
109                  reader = new BinaryReader( socketStream );
110
```

Fig. 20.1 Server portion of a client/server stream-socket connection. (Part 3 of 4.)

```
111            displayTextBox.Text += "Connection " + counter +
112               " received.\r\n";
113
114            // inform client that connection was successfull
115            writer.Write( "SERVER>>> Connection successful" );
116
117            inputTextBox.ReadOnly = false;
118            string theReply = "";
119
120            // Step 4: read String data sent from client
121            do
122            {
123               try
124               {
125                  // read the string sent to the server
126                  theReply = reader.ReadString();
127
128                  // display the message
129                  displayTextBox.Text += "\r\n" + theReply;
130               }
131
132               // handle exception if error reading data
133               catch ( Exception )
134               {
135                  break;
136               }
137
138            } while ( theReply != "CLIENT>>> TERMINATE"  &&
139               connection.Connected );
140
141            displayTextBox.Text +=
142               "\r\nUser terminated connection";
143
144            // Step 5: close connection
145            inputTextBox.ReadOnly = true;
146            writer.Close();
147            reader.Close();
148            socketStream.Close();
149            connection.Close();
150
151            ++counter;
152         }
153      } // end try
154
155      catch ( Exception error )
156      {
157         MessageBox.Show( error.ToString() );
158      }
159
160   } // end method RunServer
161
162 } // end class Server
```

Fig. 20.1 Server portion of a client/server stream-socket connection. (Part 4 of 4.)

```
1   // Fig. 20.2: Client.cs
2   // Set up a Client that will read information sent from a Server
3   // and display the information.
4
5   using System;
6   using System.Drawing;
7   using System.Collections;
8   using System.ComponentModel;
9   using System.Windows.Forms;
10  using System.Threading;
11  using System.Net.Sockets;
12  using System.IO;
13
14  // connects to a chat server
15  public class Client : System.Windows.Forms.Form
16  {
17     private System.Windows.Forms.TextBox inputTextBox;
18     private System.Windows.Forms.TextBox displayTextBox;
19
20     private NetworkStream output;
21     private BinaryWriter writer;
22     private BinaryReader reader;
23
24     private string message = "";
25
26     private Thread readThread;
27
28     private System.ComponentModel.Container components = null;
29
30     // default constructor
31     public Client()
32     {
33        InitializeComponent();
34
35        readThread = new Thread( new ThreadStart( RunClient ) );
36        readThread.Start();
37     }
38
39     // Visual Studio .NET-generated code
40
41     [STAThread]
42     static void Main()
43     {
44        Application.Run( new Client() );
45     }
46
47     protected void Client_Closing(
48        object sender, CancelEventArgs e )
49     {
50        System.Environment.Exit( System.Environment.ExitCode );
51     }
52
```

Fig. 20.2   Client portion of a client/server stream-socket connection. (Part 1 of 4.)

```
53        // sends text the user typed to server
54        protected void inputTextBox_KeyDown (
55           object sender, KeyEventArgs e )
56        {
57           try
58           {
59              if ( e.KeyCode == Keys.Enter )
60              {
61                 writer.Write( "CLIENT>>> " + inputTextBox.Text );
62
63                 displayTextBox.Text +=
64                    "\r\nCLIENT>>> " + inputTextBox.Text;
65
66                 inputTextBox.Clear();
67              }
68           }
69           catch ( SocketException ioe )
70           {
71              displayTextBox.Text += "\nError writing object";
72           }
73
74        } // end method inputTextBox_KeyDown
75
76        // connect to server and display server-generated text
77        public void RunClient()
78        {
79           TcpClient client;
80
81           // instantiate TcpClient for sending data to server
82           try
83           {
84              displayTextBox.Text += "Attempting connection\r\n";
85
86              // Step 1: create TcpClient and connect to server
87              client = new TcpClient();
88              client.Connect( "localhost", 5000 );
89
90              // Step 2: get NetworkStream associated with TcpClient
91              output = client.GetStream();
92
93              // create objects for writing and reading across stream
94              writer = new BinaryWriter( output );
95              reader = new BinaryReader( output );
96
97              displayTextBox.Text += "\r\nGot I/O streams\r\n";
98
99              inputTextBox.ReadOnly = false;
100
101             // loop until server signals termination
102             do
103             {
104
```

Fig. 20.2   Client portion of a client/server stream-socket connection. (Part 2 of 4.)

```
105                    // Step 3: processing phase
106                    try
107                    {
108                        // read message from server
109                        message = reader.ReadString();
110                        displayTextBox.Text += "\r\n" + message;
111                    }
112
113                    // handle exception if error in reading server data
114                    catch ( Exception )
115                    {
116                        System.Environment.Exit(
117                            System.Environment.ExitCode );
118                    }
119            } while( message != "SERVER>>> TERMINATE" );
120
121            displayTextBox.Text += "\r\nClosing connection.\r\n";
122
123            // Step 4: close connection
124            writer.Close();
125            reader.Close();
126            output.Close();
127            client.Close();
128            Application.Exit();
129        }
130
131        // handle exception if error in establishing connection
132        catch ( Exception error )
133        {
134            MessageBox.Show( error.ToString() );
135        }
136
137    } // end method RunClient
138
139 } // end class Client
```

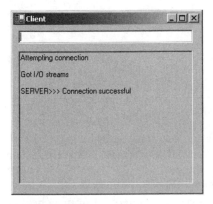

Fig. 20.2   Client portion of a client/server stream-socket connection. (Part 3 of 4.)

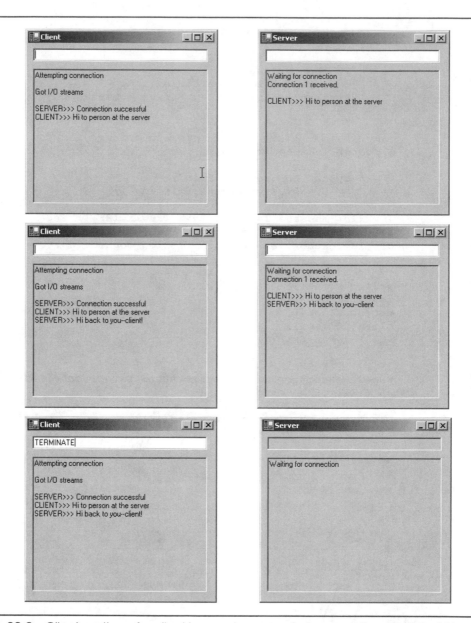

Fig. 20.2   Client portion of a client/server stream-socket connection. (Part 4 of 4.)

As we analyze this example, we begin by discussing class **Server** (Fig. 20.1). In the constructor, line 34 creates a **Thread** that will accept connections from clients. Line 35 starts the **Thread**, which invokes method **RunServer** (lines 81–160). Method **Run-Server** initializes the server to receive connection requests and process connections. Line 91 instantiates the **TcpListener** to listen for a connection request from a client at port **5000** (Step 1). Line 94 then calls method **Start** of the **TcpListener** object, which causes the **TcpListener** to begin waiting for requests (Step 2).

Lines 97–152 declare an infinite **while** loop that establishes connections requested by clients (Step 3). Line 102 calls method **AcceptSocket** of the **TcpListener** object, which returns a **Socket** upon successful connection. The thread in which method **AcceptSocket** is called stops executing until a connection is established. The **Socket** object will manage the connection. Line 105 passes this **Socket** object as an argument to the constructor of a **NetworkStream** object. Class **NetworkStream** provides access to streams across a network—in this example, the **NetworkStream** object provides access to the **Socket** connection. Lines 108–109 create instances of the *BinaryWriter* and *BinaryReader* classes for writing and reading data. We pass the **Network-Stream** object as an argument to each constructor; **BinaryWriter** can write bytes to the **NetworkStream**, and **BinaryReader** can read bytes from **NetworkStream**. Lines 111–112 append text to the **TextBox**, indicating that a connection was received.

BinaryWriter method *Write* has many overloaded versions, which enable the method to write various types to a stream. Line 115 uses method **Write** to send to the client a **string** notifying the user of a successful connection. Lines 121–139 declare a **do/while** structure that executes until the server receives a message indicating connection termination (i.e., **CLIENT>>> TERMINATE**). Line 126 uses **BinaryReader** method *ReadString* to read a **string** from the stream (Step 4). Method **Read-String** blocks until a **string** is read. To prevent the whole server from blocking, we use a separate **Thread** to handle the transfer of information. The **while** statement loops until there is more information to read—this results in I/O blocking, which causes the program always to appear frozen. However, if we run this portion of the program in a separate **Thread**, the user can interact with the Windows **Form** and send messages while the program waits in the background for incoming messages.

When the chat is complete, lines 146–149 close the **BinaryWriter**, **BinaryReader**, **NetworkStream** and **Socket** (Step 5) by invoking their respective **Close** methods. The server then waits for another client connection request by returning to the beginning of the **while** loop (line 97).

When the user of the server application enters a **string** in the **TextBox** and presses the *Enter* key, event handler **inputTextBox_KeyDown** (lines 53–78) reads the **string** and sends it via method **Write** of class **BinaryWriter**. If a user terminates the server application, line 69 calls method **Close** of the **Socket** object to close the connection.

Lines 46–50 define the **Server_Closing** event handler for the **Closing** event. The event closes the application and uses **System.Environment.Exit** method with parameter **System.Environment.ExitCode** to terminate all threads. Method **Exit** of class **Environment** closes all threads associated with the application.

Figure 20.2 lists the code for the **Client** object. Like the **Server** object, the **Client** object creates a **Thread** (lines 35–36) in its constructor to handle all incoming messages. **Client** method **RunClient** (lines 77–137) connects to the **Server**, receives data from the **Server** and sends data to the **Server** (when the user presses the *Enter Key*). Lines 87–88 instantiate a **TcpClient** object and call its method **Connect** to establish a connection (Step 1). The first argument to method **Connect** is the name of the server; in our example, the server's name is *"localhost"*, meaning that the server is located on the same machine as the client. The **localhost** is also known as the *loopback IP address* and is equivalent to the IP address *127.0.0.1*. This value sends the data transmission back to the sender's IP address. [*Note*: We chose to demonstrate the client/ server relationship by connecting between programs that are executing on the same computer (**localhost**). Normally, this argument would contain the Internet address of another computer.] The second argument to method **Connect** is the server's port number. This number must match the port number at which the server waits for connections.

The **Client** uses a **NetworkStream** to send data to and receive data from the server. The client obtains the **NetworkStream** on line 91 through a call to **TcpClient** method **GetStream** (Step 2). The **do/while** structure in lines 102–119 loops until the client receives the connection-termination message (**SERVER>>> TERMINATE**). Line 109 uses **BinaryReader** method **ReadString** to obtain the next message from the server (Step 3). Line 110 displays the message, and lines 124–127 close the **BinaryWriter**, **BinaryReader**, **NetworkStream** and **TcpClient** objects (Step 4).

When the user of the client application enters a **string** in the **TextBox** and presses the *Enter* key, the event handler **inputTextBox_KeyDown** (lines 54–74) reads the **string** from the **TextBox** and sends it via **BinaryWriter** method **Write**. Notice that, here, the **Server** receives a connection, processes it, closes it and waits for the next one. In a real-world application, a server would likely receive a connection, set up the connection to be processed as a separate thread of execution and wait for new connections. The separate threads that process existing connections can continue to execute while the **Server** concentrates on new connection requests.

20.5 Summary

Stream sockets provide a connection-oriented service, meaning that one process establishes a connection to another process, and data can flow between the processes in continuous streams. Transmission Control Protocol (TCP) is the preferred protocol for stream sockets. It is a reliable and relatively fast way to send data through a network.

The establishment of a simple server with TCP and stream sockets in C# requires five steps. Step 1 is to create a **TcpListener** object. This class represents a TCP stream socket that a server can use to receive connections. To receive connections, the **TcpListener** must be listening for them. For the **TcpListener** to listen for client connections, its **Start** method must be called (Step 2). **TcpListener** method **AcceptSocket** blocks indefinitely until a connection is established, at which point it returns a **Socket** (Step 3). Step 4 is the processing phase, in which the server and the client communicate using methods **Read** and **Write** via a **NetworkStream** object. When the client and server have finished communicating, the server closes the connection by calling the **Close** method on the **Socket** (Step 5). Most servers will then, by means of a control loop, return to the **AcceptSocket** call step to wait for another client's connection.

A port number is a numeric ID number that a process uses to identify itself at a given network address; it is also known as an Internet Protocol Address (IP Address). An individual process running on a computer is identified by an IP-address/port-number pair. Hence, no two processes can have the same port number at a given IP address. Class **IPAddress** represents an Internet Protocol address. Class **IPEndPoint** represents an end point on a network, including an IP-address/port-number pair.

The establishment of a simple client requires four steps. Step 1 is to create a **Tcp-Client** to connect to the server. This connection is established through a call to the **Tcp-**

Client method **Connect**, containing two arguments—the server's IP address and the port number. In Step 2, the **TcpClient** calls method **GetStream** to get a **Stream** to write to and read from the server. Step 3 is the processing phase, in which the client and the server communicate. Step 4 has the client close the connection by calling the **Close** method on the **NetworkStream. NetworkStream** methods **WriteByte** and **Write** can be used to output individual bytes or sets of bytes to a stream, respectively. **Network-Stream** methods **ReadByte** and **Read** can be used to read individual bytes or sets of bytes from a stream, respectively.

21

FCL Collections

Objectives

- To become familiar with the collections provided by the FCL.
- To be able to use class **Array**.
- To be able to use class **ArrayList**.
- To be able to use class **Stack**.
- To be able to use class **Hashtable**.

Much that I bound, I could not free;
Much that I freed returned to me.
Lee Wilson Dodd

Will you walk a little faster? said a whiting to a snail,
There's a porpoise close behind us, and he's treading
on my tail.
Lewis Carroll

There is always room at the top.
Daniel Webster

Push on—keep moving.
Thomas Morton

I think that I shall never see
A poem lovely as a tree.
Joyce Kilmer

Outline

21.1 Introduction

In this chapter, we consider the prepackaged data-structure classes provided by the .NET Framework. These classes are known as *collection classes*; they store collections of data. Each instance of one of these classes is known as a *collection*, which is a set of items.

21.2 Collection Classes

With collection classes, instead of creating data structures, the programmer simply uses existing data structures, without concern for how the data structures are implemented. This methodology is a marvelous example of code reuse. By using collection classes, programmers can code faster and can expect excellent performance, maximizing execution speed and minimizing memory consumption.

Some examples of collections are the cards you hold in a card game, your favorite songs stored in your computer and the real-estate records in your local registry of deeds (which map book numbers and page numbers to property owners). The .NET Framework provides several collections. In this chapter, we demonstrate four collection classes— *Array*, *ArrayList*, *Stack* and *Hashtable*—most from namespace **System.Collections**, as well as the capabilities of built-in arrays. In addition, namespace **System.Collections** provides several other data structures, including *BitArray* (a collection of true/false values), *Queue* and *SortedList* (a collection of key/value pairs that are sorted by key and can be accessed either by key or by index).

The .NET Framework provides ready-to-go, reusable components; you do not need to write your own collection classes. The collections are standardized so that applications can share them easily, without having to take account of the details of their implementation. These collections are written for broad reuse. They are tuned for rapid execution and for efficient use of memory. As new data structures and algorithms are developed that fit this framework, a large base of programmers already will be familiar with the interfaces and algorithms implemented by those data structures.

21.2.1 Class **Array**

Chapter 7 presented basic array-processing capabilities, and many subsequent chapters used the techniques shown there. We discussed briefly that all arrays inherit from class **Array** (of namespace **System**), which defines a **Length** property that specifies the number of elements in an array. In addition, class **Array** supplies **static** methods that provide algorithms for processing arrays. Typically, class **Array** overloads these methods to provide multiple options for performing algorithms. For example, **Array** method **Reverse** can reverse the order of the elements in an entire array or can reverse the elements in a specified range of elements in an array. For a complete list of class **Array**'s **static** methods and their overloaded versions, see the online documentation for the class. Figure 21.1 demonstrates several **static** methods of class **Array**.

Line 28 uses **static Array** method *Sort* to sort an array of **double** values. When this method returns, the array contains its original elements, sorted in ascending order.

Lines 31–32 uses **static Array** method *Copy* to copy elements from array **intArray** into array **intArrayCopy**. The first argument is the array to copy (**intValues**), the second argument is the destination array (**intValuesCopy**) and the third argument is an integer representing the number of elements to copy (in this case, **intValues.Length** specifies all elements).

Lines 39 and 45 invoke **static Array** method *BinarySearch* to perform binary searches on array **intValues**. Method **BinarySearch** receives the *sorted* array in which to search and the key for which to search. The method returns the index in the array at which it finds the key (for a negative number if the key was not found).

Other **static Array** methods include *Clear* (to set a range of elements to **0** or **null**), *CreateInstance* (to create a new array of a specified data type), *IndexOf* (to locate the first occurrence of an object in an array or portion of an array), *LastIndexOf* (to locate the last occurrence of an object in an array or portion of an array) and *Reverse* (to reverse the contents of an array or portion of an array).

```
1    // Fig. 21.1: UsingArray.cs
2    // Using Array class to perform common array manipulations.
3
4    using System;
5    using System.Windows.Forms;
6    using System.Collections;
7
8    namespace UsingArray
9    {
10      // demonstrate algorithms of class Array
11      class UsingArray
12      {
13         private int[] intValues = { 1, 2, 3, 4, 5, 6 };
14         private double[] doubleValues =
15            { 8.4, 9.3, 0.2, 7.9, 3.4 };
16         private int[] intValuesCopy;
17         private string output;
18
19         // method to build and display program output
20         public void Start()
21         {
22            intValuesCopy = new int[ intValues.Length ];
23
24            output = "Initial array values:\n";
```

Fig. 21.1 Program that demonstrates class **Array**. (Part 1 of 3.)

```
25                PrintArray();   // output initial array contents
26
27                // sort doubleValues
28                Array.Sort( doubleValues );
29
30                // copy intValues into intValuesCopy
31                Array.Copy( intValues, intValuesCopy,
32                   intValues.Length );
33
34                output += "\nArray values after Sort and Copy:\n";
35                PrintArray();   // output array contents
36                output += "\n";
37
38                // search for 5 in intValues
39                int result = Array.BinarySearch( intValues, 5 );
40                output +=
41                   ( result >= 0 ? "5 found at element " + result :
42                       "5 not found" ) + " in intValues\n";
43
44                // search for 8763 in intValues
45                result = Array.BinarySearch( intValues, 8763 );
46                output +=
47                   ( result >= 0 ? "8763 found at element " + result :
48                       "8763 not found" ) + " in intValues";
49
50                MessageBox.Show( output, "Using Class Array",
51                   MessageBoxButtons.OK, MessageBoxIcon.Information );
52             }
53
54             // append array content to output string
55             private void PrintArray()
56             {
57                output += "doubleValues: ";
58
59                foreach ( double element in doubleValues )
60                   output += element + " ";
61
62                output += "\nintValues: ";
63
64                foreach ( int element in intValues )
65                   output += element + " ";
66
67                output += "\nintValuesCopy: ";
68
69                foreach ( int element in intValuesCopy )
70                   output += element + " ";
71
72                output += "\n";
73             }
74
75             // main entry point for application
76             static void Main( string[] args )
77             {
```

Fig. 21.1   Program that demonstrates class **Array**. (Part 2 of 3.)

```
78              UsingArray application = new UsingArray();
79
80              application.Start();
81          }
82
83      } // end class UsingArray
84  }
```

Fig. 21.1   Program that demonstrates class **Array**. (Part 3 of 3.)

21.2.2 Class **ArrayList**

In most programming languages, conventional arrays have a fixed size—they cannot be changed dynamically to conform to an application's execution-time memory requirements. In some applications, this fixed-size limitation presents a problem for programmers. They must choose between using fixed-size arrays that are large enough to store the maximum number of elements the program may require and using dynamic data structures that can grow and shrink the amount of memory required to store data in response to the changing requirements of a program at execution time.

The .NET Framework's class **ArrayList** collection mimics the functionality of conventional arrays and provides dynamic resizing of the collection through the class's methods. At any time, an **ArrayList** contains a certain number of elements that is less than or equal to the **ArrayList**'s *capacity*—the number of elements currently reserved for an **Array-List**. A program can manipulate the capacity with **ArrayList** property **Capacity**. If an **ArrayList** needs to grow, it doubles its current **Capacity**, by default.

Performance Tip 21.1

*As with linked lists it is a fast operation to insert additional elements into an **ArrayList** whose current size is less than its capacity.*

Performance Tip 21.2

*It is a slow operation to insert an element into an **ArrayList** that needs to grow larger to accommodate the new element.*

Performance Tip 21.3

*The default capacity increment—doubling the size of the **ArrayList**—may seem to waste storage, but doubling is an efficient way for an **ArrayList** to grow quickly to "about the right size." This operation is a much more efficient use of time than growing the **ArrayList** by one element at a time in response to insert operations.*

Performance Tip 21.4

*If storage is at a premium, use method **TrimToSize** of class **ArrayList** to trim an **ArrayList** to its exact size. This operation will optimize an **ArrayList**'s memory use. Be careful, however: If the program needs to insert additional elements, the process will be slower, because the **ArrayList** must grow dynamically (because trimming leaves no room for growth).*

ArrayLists store references to **object**s. All classes derive from class **Object**, so an **ArrayList** can contain objects of any type. Figure 21.2 lists some useful methods of class **ArrayList**.

Figure 21.3 demonstrates class **ArrayList** and several of its methods. Users can type a **string** into the user interface's **TextBox** and press a button representing an **ArrayList** method to see a demonstration of that method's functionality. A **TextBox** displays messages indicating each operation's results.

The **ArrayList** in this example stores **string**s that users input in the **TextBox**. Line 35 creates an **ArrayList** with an initial capacity of one element. This **ArrayList** will double in size each time the user fills the array and attempts to add another element.

ArrayList method *Add* appends a new element at the end of an **ArrayList**. When the user clicks the **Add** button, event handler **addButton_Click** (lines 53–60) invokes method **Add** (line 56) to append the **string** in the **inputTextBox** to the **ArrayList**.

Method	Description
Add	Adds an **object** to the **ArrayList**. Returns an **int** specifying the index at which the **object** was added.
Clear	Removes all the elements from the **ArrayList**.
Contains	Returns **true** if the specified **object** is in the **ArrayList**; otherwise, returns **false**.
IndexOf	Returns the index of the first occurrence of the specified **object** in the **ArrayList**.
Insert	Inserts an **object** at the specified index.
Remove	Removes the first occurrence of the specified **object**.
RemoveAt	Removes an object at the specified index.
RemoveRange	Removes a specified number of elements, starting at a specified index in the **ArrayList**.
Sort	Sorts the **ArrayList**.
TrimToSize	Sets the **Capacity** of the **ArrayList** to be the number of elements the **ArrayList** currently contains.

Fig. 21.2 Some methods of class **ArrayList**.

```
1   // Fig. 21.3: ArrayListTest.cs
2   // Using class ArrayList.
```

Fig. 21.3 Demonstrating the **ArrayList** class. (Part 1 of 5.)

```
 3
 4   using System;
 5   using System.Drawing;
 6   using System.Collections;
 7   using System.ComponentModel;
 8   using System.Windows.Forms;
 9   using System.Data;
10   using System.Text;
11
12   namespace ArrayListTest
13   {
14      // demonstrating ArrayList functionality
15      public class ArrayListTest : System.Windows.Forms.Form
16      {
17         private System.Windows.Forms.Button addButton;
18         private System.Windows.Forms.TextBox inputTextBox;
19         private System.Windows.Forms.Label inputLabel;
20         private System.Windows.Forms.Button removeButton;
21         private System.Windows.Forms.Button firstButton;
22         private System.Windows.Forms.Button lastButton;
23         private System.Windows.Forms.Button isEmptyButton;
24         private System.Windows.Forms.Button containsButton;
25         private System.Windows.Forms.Button locationButton;
26         private System.Windows.Forms.Button trimButton;
27         private System.Windows.Forms.Button statisticsButton;
28         private System.Windows.Forms.Button displayButton;
29
30         // Required designer variable.
31         private System.ComponentModel.Container components = null;
32         private System.Windows.Forms.TextBox consoleTextBox;
33
34         // ArrayList for manipulating strings
35         private ArrayList arrayList = new ArrayList( 1 );
36
37         public ArrayListTest()
38         {
39            // Required for Windows Form Designer support
40            InitializeComponent();
41         }
42
43         // Visual Studio.NET generated code
44
45         // main entry point for the application
46         [STAThread]
47         static void Main()
48         {
49            Application.Run( new ArrayListTest() );
50         }
51
52         // add item to end of arrayList
53         private void addButton_Click(
54            object sender, System.EventArgs e )
55         {
```

Fig. 21.3   Demonstrating the **ArrayList** class. (Part 2 of 5.)

```
56              arrayList.Add( inputTextBox.Text );
57              consoleTextBox.Text =
58                 "Added to end: " + inputTextBox.Text;
59              inputTextBox.Clear();
60           }
61
62           // remove specified item from arrayList
63           private void removeButton_Click(
64              object sender, System.EventArgs e )
65           {
66              arrayList.Remove( inputTextBox.Text );
67              consoleTextBox.Text = "Removed: " + inputTextBox.Text;
68              inputTextBox.Clear();
69           }
70
71           // display first element
72           private void firstButton_Click(
73              object sender, System.EventArgs e )
74           {
75              // get first element
76              try
77              {
78                 consoleTextBox.Text =
79                    "First element: " + arrayList[ 0 ];
80              }
81
82              // show exception if no elements in arrayList
83              catch ( ArgumentOutOfRangeException outOfRange )
84              {
85                 consoleTextBox.Text = outOfRange.ToString();
86              }
87           }
88
89           // display last element
90           private void lastButton_Click(
91              object sender, System.EventArgs e )
92           {
93              // get last element
94              try
95              {
96                 consoleTextBox.Text = "Last element: " +
97                    arrayList[ arrayList.Count - 1 ];
98              }
99
100             // show exception if no elements in arrayList
101             catch ( ArgumentOutOfRangeException outOfRange )
102             {
103                consoleTextBox.Text = outOfRange.ToString();
104             }
105          }
106
```

Fig. 21.3 Demonstrating the **ArrayList** class. (Part 3 of 5.)

```
107         // determine whether arrayList is empty
108         private void isEmptyButton_Click(
109            object sender, System.EventArgs e )
110         {
111            consoleTextBox.Text = ( arrayList.Count == 0 ?
112               "arrayList is empty" : "arrayList is not empty" );
113         }
114
115         // determine whether arrayList contains specified object
116         private void containsButton_Click(
117            object sender, System.EventArgs e )
118         {
119            if ( arrayList.Contains( inputTextBox.Text ) )
120               consoleTextBox.Text = "arrayList contains " +
121                  inputTextBox.Text;
122            else
123               consoleTextBox.Text = inputTextBox.Text +
124                  " not found";
125         }
126
127         // determine location of specified object
128         private void locationButton_Click(
129            object sender, System.EventArgs e )
130         {
131            consoleTextBox.Text = "Element is at location " +
132               arrayList.IndexOf( inputTextBox.Text );
133         }
134
135         // trim arrayList to current size
136         private void trimButton_Click(
137            object sender, System.EventArgs e )
138         {
139            arrayList.TrimToSize();
140            consoleTextBox.Text = "Vector trimmed to size";
141         }
142
143         // show arrayList current size and capacity
144         private void statisticsButton_Click(
145            object sender, System.EventArgs e )
146         {
147            consoleTextBox.Text = "Size = " + arrayList.Count +
148               "; capacity = " + arrayList.Capacity;
149         }
150
151         // display contents of arrayList
152         private void displayButton_Click(
153            object sender, System.EventArgs e )
154         {
155            IEnumerator enumerator = arrayList.GetEnumerator();
156            StringBuilder buffer = new StringBuilder();
157
158            while ( enumerator.MoveNext() )
159               buffer.Append( enumerator.Current + "   " );
```

Fig. 21.3   Demonstrating the **ArrayList** class. (Part 4 of 5.)

```
160
161              consoleTextBox.Text = buffer.ToString();
162        }
163    }
164 }
```

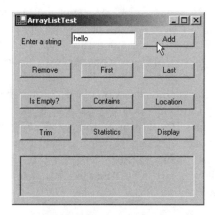

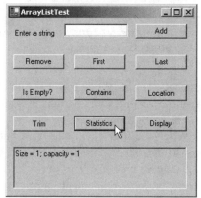

Fig. 21.3   Demonstrating the **ArrayList** class. (Part 5 of 5.)

ArrayList method *Remove* deletes a specified item from an **ArrayList**. When the user clicks the **Remove** button, event handler **removeButton_Click** (line 63–69) invokes **Remove** (line 66) to remove the **string** specified in the **inputTextBox** from the **ArrayList**. If the object passed to **Remove** is in the **ArrayList**, the first occurrence of that object is removed, and all subsequent elements shift toward the beginning of the **ArrayList** to fill the empty position.

A program can access **ArrayList** elements as it would access conventional-array elements—that is, by following the **ArrayList** reference name with the array subscript operator (**[]**) and the desired index of the element. Event handlers **firstButton_Click** (lines 72–87) and **lastButton_Click** (lines 90–105) use the **ArrayList** subscript operator to retrieve the first element (line 79) and last element (line 97), respectively. An **ArgumentOutOfRangeException** occurs if the specified index is not both greater than zero and less than the number of elements currently stored in the **ArrayList**.

Event handler **isEmptyButton_Click** (lines 108–113) uses **ArrayList** property *Count* (line 111) to determine whether the **ArrayList** is empty. Event handler **containsButton_Click** (lines 116–125) uses **ArrayList** method **Contains** (line 119) to determine whether the given object is currently in the **ArrayList**. If so, the method returns **true**; otherwise, it returns **false**.

Performance Tip 21.5

*ArrayList method **Contains** performs a linear search, which is a costly operation for large **ArrayLists**. If the **ArrayList** is sorted, use **ArrayList** method **Binary-Search** to perform a more efficient search.*

When the user clicks the **Location** button, event handler **locationButton_Click** (lines 128–133) invokes **ArrayList** method *IndexOf* (line 132) to determine the index of a particular object in the **ArrayList**. **IndexOf** returns **-1** if the element is not found.

When the user clicks the **Trim** button, event handler **trimButton_Click** (lines 136–141) invokes method *TrimToSize* (line 139) to set the *Capacity* property equal to the **Count** property. This operation reduces the storage capacity of the **ArrayList** to the exact number of elements currently in the **ArrayList**.

When the user clicks the **Statistics** button, **statisticsButton_Click** (lines 144–149) uses the **Count** and **Capacity** properties to display the current number of elements in the **ArrayList** and the maximum number of elements that can be stored without allocating more memory to the **ArrayList**.

When the user clicks the **Display** button, **displayButton_Click** (lines 152–162) outputs the contents of the **ArrayList**. This event handler uses an *IEnumerator* (sometimes called an *enumerator* or an *iterator*) to traverse the elements of an **ArrayList** one element at a time. **IEnumerator** is an *interface*. An interface is similar to a class, except that objects cannot be instantiated from it. Classes that implement (i.e., inherit) an interface must override all the interface's methods and properties. When an interface is implemented, the "is-a" relationship applies: The interface is a base class to the class that implements it. Therefore, objects of the implementing class can be assigned to **IEnumerator** references. This capability allows programmers to process a large number of similar collections in a generic manner. Many of the collection classes in .NET implement interface **IEnumerator**.

Interface **IEnumerator** defines methods **MoveNext** and **Reset** and property **Current**. **MoveNext** moves the enumerator to the next element in the **ArrayList**. The first call to **MoveNext** positions the enumerator at the first element of the **ArrayList**. **MoveNext** returns **true** if there is at least one more element in the **ArrayList**; otherwise, it returns **false**. Method **Reset** positions the enumerator before the first element of the **ArrayList**. Methods **MoveNext** and **Reset** throw an **InvalidOperation-Exception** if the contents of the collection are modified in any way after the enumerator's creation. Property **Current** returns the object at the current location in the **ArrayList**.

Line 155 creates an **IEnumerator** called **enumerator** and assigns to it the result of a call to **ArrayList** method *GetEnumerator*. Lines 158–159 iterate while **MoveNext** returns **true**, retrieve the current item via property **Count** and append it to **buffer**. When the loop terminates, line 161 displays the contents of **buffer**.

21.2.3 Class Stack

The **Stack** class, as its name implies, implements a *stack* (i.e., a data structure for which insertions and deletions are made at only one end—its *top*.). The application in Fig. 21.4 provides a GUI that enables the user to test many **Stack** methods. Line 38 of the **StackTest** constructor creates a **Stack** with the default initial capacity (10 elements).

Class **Stack** has methods **Push** and **Pop** to perform the basic stack operations. Method **Push** takes an **object** as an argument and adds it to the top of the **Stack**. If the number of items on the **Stack** (represented by the **Count** property) is equal to the capacity at the time of the **Push** operation, the **Stack** grows to accommodate more **object**s. Event handler **pushButton_Click** (lines 51–56) uses method **Push** to add a user-specified string to the stack (line 54).

Method **Pop** takes no arguments. This method removes and returns the object currently on top of the **Stack**. Event handler **popButton_Click** (lines 59–73) calls method **Pop** (line 57) to remove an object from the **Stack**. An **InvalidOperation-Exception** occurs if the **Stack** is empty when the program calls **Pop**.

Method **Peek** returns the value of the element on top of the stack, but does not remove the element from the **Stack**. We demonstrate **Peek** on line 82, in event handler **peekButton_Click** (lines 76–90). As with **Pop**, an **InvalidOperationException** occurs if the **Stack** is empty when the program calls **Peek**.

```
1   // Fig. 21.4: StackTest.cs
2   // Demonstrates class Stack of namespace System.Collections.
3
4   using System;
5   using System.Drawing;
6   using System.Collections;
7   using System.ComponentModel;
8   using System.Windows.Forms;
9   using System.Data;
10  using System.Text;
11
```

Fig. 21.4 Using the **Stack** class. (Part 1 of 4.)

```
12    namespace StackTest
13    {
14       // demonstrate Stack collection
15       public class StackTest : System.Windows.Forms.Form
16       {
17          private System.Windows.Forms.Label inputLabel;
18          private System.Windows.Forms.TextBox inputTextBox;
19          private System.Windows.Forms.Button pushButton;
20          private System.Windows.Forms.Button popButton;
21          private System.Windows.Forms.Button peekButton;
22          private System.Windows.Forms.Button isEmptyButton;
23          private System.Windows.Forms.Button searchButton;
24          private System.Windows.Forms.Button displayButton;
25          private System.Windows.Forms.Label statusLabel;
26
27          // Required designer variable.
28          private System.ComponentModel.Container components = null;
29
30          private Stack stack;
31
32          public StackTest()
33          {
34             // Required for Windows Form Designer support
35             InitializeComponent();
36
37             // create Stack
38             stack = new Stack();
39          }
40
41          // Visual Studio.NET generated code
42
43          // main entry point for the application
44          [STAThread]
45          static void Main()
46          {
47             Application.Run( new StackTest() );
48          }
49
50          // push element onto stack
51          private void pushButton_Click(
52             object sender, System.EventArgs e )
53          {
54             stack.Push( inputTextBox.Text );
55             statusLabel.Text = "Pushed: " + inputTextBox.Text;
56          }
57
58          // pop element from stack
59          private void popButton_Click(
60             object sender, System.EventArgs e )
61          {
62             // pop element
63             try
64             {
```

Fig. 21.4   Using the **Stack** class. (Part 2 of 4.)

```
65                  statusLabel.Text = "Popped: " + stack.Pop();
66              }
67
68          // print message if stack is empty
69          catch ( InvalidOperationException invalidOperation )
70          {
71              statusLabel.Text = invalidOperation.ToString();
72          }
73      }
74
75      // peek at top element of stack
76      private void peekButton_Click(
77          object sender, System.EventArgs e )
78      {
79          // view top element
80          try
81          {
82              statusLabel.Text = "Top: " + stack.Peek();
83          }
84
85          // print message if stack is empty
86          catch ( InvalidOperationException invalidOperation )
87          {
88              statusLabel.Text = invalidOperation.ToString();
89          }
90      }
91
92      // determine whether stack is empty
93      private void isEmptyButton_Click(
94          object sender, System.EventArgs e )
95      {
96          statusLabel.Text = ( stack.Count == 0 ?
97              "Stack is empty" : "Stack is not empty" );
98      }
99
100     // determine whether specified element is on stack
101     private void searchButton_Click(
102         object sender, System.EventArgs e )
103     {
104         string result = stack.Contains( inputTextBox.Text ) ?
105             " found" : " not found";
106
107         statusLabel.Text = inputTextBox.Text + result;
108     }
109
110     // display stack contents
111     private void displayButton_Click(
112         object sender, System.EventArgs e )
113     {
114         IEnumerator enumerator = stack.GetEnumerator();
115         StringBuilder buffer = new StringBuilder();
116
```

Fig. 21.4 Using the **Stack** class. (Part 3 of 4.)

```
117              // while the enumerator can move on to the next element
118              // print that element out.
119              while ( enumerator.MoveNext() )
120                 buffer.Append( enumerator.Current + " " );
121
122              statusLabel.Text = buffer.ToString();
123           }
124        }
125  }
```

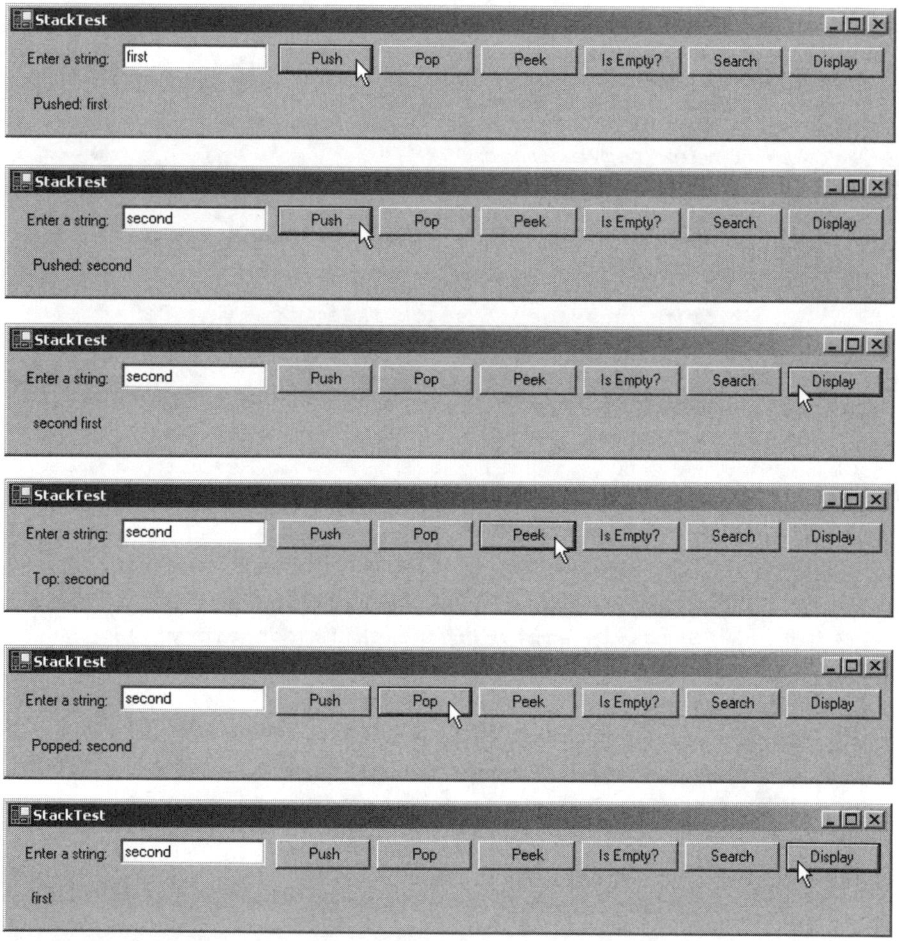

Fig. 21.4   Using the **Stack** class. (Part 4 of 4.)

Common Programming Error 21.1

*Attempting to **Peek** or **Pop** an empty **Stack** (i.e., a **Stack** whose **Count** property equals 0) causes an **InvalidOperationException**.*

Event handler **isEmptyButton_Click** (lines 93–98) determines whether the **Stack** is empty by comparing the **Stack**'s **Count** property with **0**. If it equals **0**, the **Stack** is empty; otherwise, it is not. Event handler **searchButton_Click** (lines 101–

108) uses **Stack** method **Contains** (lines 104–105) to determine whether the **Stack** contains the object specified as its argument. **Contains** returns **true** if the **Stack** contains the specified object and **false** otherwise.

Event handler **isEmptyButton_Click** (lines 111–123) uses an **IEnumerator** to traverse the **Stack** and display its contents.

21.2.4 Class **Hashtable**

Object-oriented programming languages facilitate the creation of new types. When a program creates objects of new or existing types, it needs to manage those objects efficiently. This responsibility includes sorting and retrieving objects. Sorting and retrieving information with arrays is efficient if some aspect of your data directly matches the value of the keys and if those keys are unique and tightly packed. For example, if you have 100 employees, each of whom has a unique nine-digit Social Security numbers, and you want to store and retrieve employee data by using the Social Security number as a key, the task would nominally require an array with 999,999,999 elements, because there are 999,999,999 unique nine-digit numbers. An array of this size is impractical for virtually all applications that key on Social Security numbers. If you could have an array that large, however, you could achieve very high performance in storing and retrieving employee records simply by using the Social Security number as the array index.

A large variety of applications have this problem—namely, that either the keys are of the wrong type (i.e., not nonnegative integers), or they are of the right type, but they are sparsely spread over a large range.

What is needed is a high-speed scheme for converting keys such as Social Security numbers and inventory part numbers into unique array subscripts. Then, when an application needs to store something, the scheme could convert the application key rapidly into a subscript, and the record of information could be stored at that location in the array. Retrieval occurs in the same way: Once the application has a key for which it wants to retrieve the data record, the application simply applies the conversion to the key, which produces the array subscript where the data reside, retrieves the data.

The scheme we have described here is the basis of a technique called *hashing*. It has this name because, when we convert a key into an array subscript, we literally scramble the bits, forming a kind of "mishmash" number. The number actually has no real significance beyond its usefulness in storing and retrieving the particular data record.

A glitch in the scheme occurs when *collisions* happen [i.e., when two different keys "hash into" the same cell (or element) in the array, called a *hash table*]. Because we cannot sort two different data records into the same space, we need to find an alternative space for all records beyond the first that hash into the same array subscript. Many schemes exist for finding alternative subscripts. One is to "hash again" (i.e., to reapply the hashing transformation to the key in order to provide the next candidate cell in the array). The hashing process is designed to be quite random, so the assumption is that, with just a few hashes, an available cell will be found.

Another scheme uses one hash to locate the first candidate cell. If the cell is occupied, successive cells are searched linearly until an available cell is found. Retrieval works in the same way: The key is hashed once, and the resulting cell is checked to determine whether it contains the desired data. If it does, the search is complete. If it does not, successive cells are searched linearly until the desired data are found.

The most popular solution to hash-table collisions is to have each cell of the table be a hash "bucket," typically a linked list of all the key/value pairs that hash to that cell. This is the solution that the .NET Framework's *Hashtable* class implements.

The *load factor* affects the performance of hashing schemes. The load factor is the ratio of the number of occupied cells in the hash table to the size of the hash table. The closer the ratio gets to 1.0, the greater is the chance of collisions.

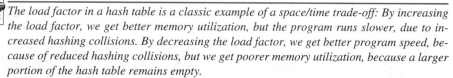

Performance Tip 21.6

The load factor in a hash table is a classic example of a space/time trade-off: By increasing the load factor, we get better memory utilization, but the program runs slower, due to increased hashing collisions. By decreasing the load factor, we get better program speed, because of reduced hashing collisions, but we get poorer memory utilization, because a larger portion of the hash table remains empty.

Programming hash tables properly is too complex for most casual programmers. Computer science students study hashing schemes thoroughly in courses on Data Structures and Algorithms. Recognizing the value of hashing, C#'s creators provided class **Hashtable** and some related features to enable programmers to take advantage of hashing without having to deal with the complex details.

The preceding sentence expresses a concept that is profoundly important in our study of object-oriented programming. Classes encapsulate and hide complexity (i.e., details of implementation) and offer user-friendly interfaces. Crafting classes properly is one of the most valued skills in the field of object-oriented programming.

A *hash function* performs a calculation that determines where to place data in a hashtable. The hash function is applied to the key in a key/value pair of objects. Class **Hashtable** can accept any object as a key. For this reason, class **Object** defines method **GetHashCode**, which all objects in C# inherit. Most classes that are candidates to be used as keys in a hash table override this method to provide one that performs efficient hashcode calculations for a specific data type. For example, a **string** should have a hash-code calculation that is based on the contents of the **string**. Figure 21.5 demonstrates several methods of class **Hashtable**.

Event handler **addButton_Click** (lines 57–75) reads the first name and last name of an employee from the user interface, creates an object of class Employee (defined on lines 153–170) and uses method *Add* (line 66) to add that **Employee** to the **Hashtable**. This method receives two arguments——a key object and a value object. In this example, the key is the last name of the **Employee** (a **string**), and the value is the corresponding **Employee** object. An **ArgumentException** occurs if the **Hashtable** already contains the key or if the key is **null**.

```
1    // Fig. 21.5: HashtableTest.cs
2    // Demonstrate class Hashtable of namespace System.Collections.
3
4    using System;
5    using System.Drawing;
6    using System.Collections;
7    using System.ComponentModel;
8    using System.Windows.Forms;
```

Fig. 21.5 Using the **Hashtable** class. (Part 1 of 5.)

```
 9    using System.Data;
10    using System.Text;
11
12    namespace HashTableTest
13    {
14        // demonstrate Hashtable functionality
15        public class HashTableTest : System.Windows.Forms.Form
16        {
17            private System.Windows.Forms.Label firstNameLabel;
18            private System.Windows.Forms.Label lastNameLabel;
19            private System.Windows.Forms.Button addButton;
20            private System.Windows.Forms.TextBox lastNameTextBox;
21            private System.Windows.Forms.TextBox consoleTextBox;
22            private System.Windows.Forms.TextBox firstNameTextBox;
23            private System.Windows.Forms.Button getButton;
24            private System.Windows.Forms.Button removeButton;
25            private System.Windows.Forms.Button emptyButton;
26            private System.Windows.Forms.Button containsKeyButton;
27            private System.Windows.Forms.Button clearTableButton;
28            private System.Windows.Forms.Button listObjectsButton;
29            private System.Windows.Forms.Button listKeysButton;
30            private System.Windows.Forms.Label statusLabel;
31
32            // Required designer variable.
33            private System.ComponentModel.Container components = null;
34
35            // Hashtable to demonstrate functionality
36            private Hashtable table;
37
38            public HashTableTest()
39            {
40                // Required for Windows Form Designer support
41                InitializeComponent();
42
43                // create Hashtable object
44                table = new Hashtable();
45            }
46
47            // Visual Studio.NET generated code
48
49            // main entry point for application
50            [STAThread]
51            static void Main()
52            {
53                Application.Run( new HashTableTest() );
54            }
55
56            // add last name and Employee object to table
57            private void addButton_Click(
58                object sender, System.EventArgs e )
59            {
60                Employee employee = new Employee( firstNameTextBox.Text,
61                    lastNameTextBox.Text );
```

Fig. 21.5 Using the **Hashtable** class. (Part 2 of 5.)

```
62
63          // add new key/value pair
64          try
65          {
66             table.Add( lastNameTextBox.Text, employee );
67             statusLabel.Text = "Put: " + employee.ToString();
68          }
69
70          // if key is null or already in table, output message
71          catch ( ArgumentException argumentException )
72          {
73             statusLabel.Text = argumentException.ToString();
74          }
75       }
76
77       // get object for given key
78       private void getButton_Click(
79          object sender, System.EventArgs e )
80       {
81          object result = table[ lastNameTextBox.Text ];
82
83          if ( result != null )
84             statusLabel.Text = "Get: " + result.ToString();
85          else
86             statusLabel.Text = "Get: " + lastNameTextBox.Text +
87                " not in table";
88       }
89
90       // remove key/value pair from table
91       private void removeButton_Click(
92          object sender, System.EventArgs e )
93       {
94          table.Remove( lastNameTextBox.Text );
95          statusLabel.Text = "Object Removed";
96       }
97
98       // determine whether table is empty
99       private void emptyButton_Click(
100         object sender, System.EventArgs e )
101      {
102         statusLabel.Text = "Table is " + (
103            table.Count == 0 ? "empty" : "not empty" );
104      }
105
106      // determine whether table contains specified key
107      private void containsKeyButton_Click(
108         object sender, System.EventArgs e )
109      {
110         statusLabel.Text = "Contains key: " +
111            table.ContainsKey( lastNameTextBox.Text );
112      }
113
```

Fig. 21.5   Using the **Hashtable** class. (Part 3 of 5.)

```
114            // discard all table contents
115            private void clearTableButton_Click(
116               object sender, System.EventArgs e )
117            {
118               table.Clear();
119               statusLabel.Text = "Clear: Table is now empty";
120            }
121
122            // display list of objects in table
123            private void listObjectsButton_Click(
124               object sender, System.EventArgs e )
125            {
126               IDictionaryEnumerator enumerator =
127                  table.GetEnumerator();
128               StringBuilder buffer = new StringBuilder();
129
130               while ( enumerator.MoveNext() )
131                  buffer.Append( enumerator.Value + "\r\n" );
132
133               consoleTextBox.Text = buffer.ToString();
134            }
135
136            // display list of keys in table
137            private void listKeysButton_Click(
138               object sender, System.EventArgs e )
139            {
140               IDictionaryEnumerator enumerator =
141                  table.GetEnumerator();
142               StringBuilder buffer = new StringBuilder();
143
144               while ( enumerator.MoveNext() )
145                  buffer.Append( enumerator.Key + "\r\n" );
146
147               consoleTextBox.Text = buffer.ToString();
148            }
149
150         } // end class HashtableTest
151
152         // class Employee for use with HashtableTest
153         class Employee
154         {
155            private string first, last;
156
157            // constructor
158            public Employee( string fName, string lName )
159            {
160               first = fName;
161               last = lName;
162            }
163
164            // return Employee first and last names as string
165            public override string ToString()
166            {
```

Fig. 21.5 Using the **Hashtable** class. (Part 4 of 5.)

```
167            return first + " " + last;
168        }
169
170    } // end class Employee
171
172 } // end namespace HashTableTest
```

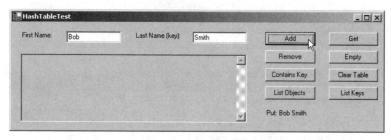

Fig. 21.5   Using the **Hashtable** class. (Part 5 of 5.)

Event handler **getButton_Click** (lines 78–88) retrieves the object associated with a specific key, using the **Hashtable**'s subscript operator, as shown on line 81. The expression in square brackets is the key for which the **Hashtable** should return the corresponding object. If the key is not found, the result is **null**.

Event handler **removeButton_Click** (lines 91–96) invokes **Hashtable** method *Remove* to delete a key and its associated object from the **Hashtable**. If the key does not exist in the table, nothing happens.

Event handler **emptyButton_Click** (lines 99–104) uses **Hashtable** property *Count* to determine whether the **Hashtable** is empty (i.e., whether **Count** is **0**).

Event handler **containsKeyButton_Click** (lines 107–112) invokes **Hashtable** method *ContainsKey* to determine whether the **Hashtable** contains the specified key. If so, the method returns **true**; otherwise, it returns **false**.

Event handler **clearTableButton_Click** (lines 115–120) invokes **Hashtable** method *Clear* to delete all **Hashtable** entries.

Class **Hashtable** provides method **GetEnumerator** that returns an enumerator of type *IDictionaryEnumerator*, which derives from **IEnumerator**. Such enumerators provide properties *Key* and *Value* to access the information for a key/value pair. The event handler on lines 123–134 (**listObjectsButton_click**) uses the **Value** property of the enumerator to output the objects in the **Hashtable**. The event handler on lines 123–134 (**listKeysButton_click**) uses the **Key** property of the enumerator to output the keys in the **Hashtable**.

21.3 Summary

Collection classes store collections of data. Each instance of one of these classes is known as a collection, which is a set of items. With collection classes, instead of creating data structures, the programmer simply uses existing data structures, without concern for how the data structures are implemented.

The .NET Framework provides several collection classes, including **Array**, **ArrayList**, **Stack** and **Hashtable**—most of which are from namespace **System.Collections**—as well as built-in array capabilities.

All arrays inherit from class **Array**, which defines a **Length** property that specifies the number of elements in an array. In addition, class **Array** provides **static** methods that provide algorithms for processing arrays.

The .NET Framework's class **ArrayList** collection mimics the functionality of conventional arrays and, through its methods, provides dynamic resizing of the collection. At any time, an **ArrayList** contains a certain number of elements that is less than or equal to the **ArrayList**'s capacity—the number of elements currently reserved for an **ArrayList**. **ArrayList**s store references to **object**s. All classes derive from class **Object**, so an **ArrayList** can contain objects of any type. A program can access **ArrayList** elements as it would access conventional-array elements—that is, by following the **ArrayList** reference name with the array subscript operator (**[]**) and the desired index of the element.

The **Stack** class implements a stack (i.e., a data structure for which insertions and deletions are made at only one end—its top.). Class **Stack** has methods **Push** and **Pop** to perform the basic stack operations. Method **Push** takes an **object** as an argument and adds it to the top of the **Stack**. If the number of items on the **Stack** (represented by the **Count** property) is equal to the capacity at the time of the **Push** operation, the **Stack** grows to accommodate more **object**s. Method **Peek** returns the value of the element on top of the stack, but does not remove the element from the **Stack**.

A hash function performs a calculation that determines where to place data in a hashtable. The hash function is applied to the key in a key/value pair of objects. Class **Hashtable** can accept any object as a key. For this reason, class **Object** defines method **GetHashCode**, which all objects in C# inherit. Most classes that are candidates to be used as keys in a hash table override this method to provide one that performs efficient hashcode calculations for a specific data type.

Class **Hashtable** provides method **GetEnumerator** that returns an enumerator of type **IDictionaryEnumerator**, which derives from **IEnumerator**. Such enumerators provide properties **Key** and **Value** to access the information for a key/value pair.

22

Accessibility

Objectives

- To introduce the World Wide Web Consortium's Web Content Accessibility Guidelines 1.0 (WCAG 1.0).
- To understand how to use the **alt** attribute of the XHTML **<img>** tag to describe images to people with visual impairments, mobile-Web-device users and others unable to view images.
- To understand how to make tables more accessible to page readers.
- To understand how to verify that XHTML tags are used properly and to ensure that Web pages can be viewed on any type of display or reader.
- To understand how VoiceXML™ and CallXML™ are changing the way in which people with disabilities access information on the Web.
- To introduce the various accessibility aids offered in Windows 2000.

'Tis the good reader that makes the good book...
Ralph Waldo Emerson

I once was lost, but now am found,
Was blind, but now I see.
John Newton

Outline

22.1 Introduction

Throughout this book, we discuss the creation of C# applications. Later chapters also introduced the development of Web-based content using Web Forms, ASP .NET, HTML and XML. In this chapter, we explore the topic of *accessibility*, which refers to the level of usability that an application or Web site provides to people with various disabilities. Disabilities that might affect an individual's computer or Internet usage are common; they include visual impairments, hearing impairments, other physical injuries (such as the inability to use a keyboard or a mouse) and learning disabilities. In today's computing environment, such impediments prevent many users from taking full advantage of applications and Web content.

The design of applications and sites to meet the needs of individuals with disabilities should be a priority for all software companies and e-businesses. People affected by disabilities represent a significant portion of the population, and legal ramifications could exist for companies that discriminate by failing to provide adequate and universal access to their resources. In this chapter, we explore the World Wide Web Consortium's *Web Accessibility Initiative* and its guidelines and review various laws regarding the availability of computing and Internet resources to people with disabilities. We also highlight companies that have developed systems, products and services that meet the needs of this demographic. As readers use C# and its related technologies to design applications and Web sites, they should keep in mind the accessibility requirements and recommendations that we discuss in this chapter.

22.2 Regulations and Resources

Over the past several years, the United States has taken legislative steps to ensure that people with disabilities are given the tools they need to use computers and access the Web. A wide variety of legislation, including the *Americans With Disabilities Act* (ADA) of 1990, governs the provision of computer and Web accessibility (Fig. 22.1). These laws have inspired significant legal action. For example, according to the ADA, companies are required to offer equal access to individuals with visual problems. The National Federation for the Blind (NFB) cited this law in a 1999 suit against AOL, responding to the company's failure to make its services available to individuals with disabilities.

There are 54 million Americans with disabilities, and these individuals represent an estimated $1 trillion in annual purchasing power. In addition to legislation, many organizations and resources focus on assisting individuals with disabilities to access computers and the Internet. **WeMedia.com**™ (Fig. 22.2) is a Web site that provides news, information, products and services to the millions of people with disabilities and to their families, friends and caregivers.

Act	Purpose
Americans with Disabilities Act	The ADA prohibits discrimination on the basis of disability in employment, state and local government, public accommodations, commercial facilities, transportation and telecommunications.
Telecommunications Act of 1996	The Telecommunications Act of 1996 contains two amendments to Section 255 and Section 251(a)(2) of the Communications Act of 1934. These amendments require that communication devices, such as cell phones, telephones and pagers, be accessible to individuals with disabilities.

Fig. 22.1 Acts designed to improve Internet and computer accessibility for people with disabilities. (Part 1 of 2.)

Act	Purpose
Individuals with Disabilities Education Act of 1997	The Individuals with Disabilities Education Act stipulates that education materials in schools must be made accessible to children with disabilities.
Rehabilitation Act	Section 504 of the Rehabilitation Act states that college sponsored activities receiving federal funding cannot discriminate against individuals with disabilities. Section 508 mandates that all government institutions receiving federal funding must design their Web sites so that they are accessible to individuals with disabilities. Businesses that sell services to the government also must abide by this act.

Fig. 22.1 Acts designed to improve Internet and computer accessibility for people with disabilities. (Part 2 of 2.)

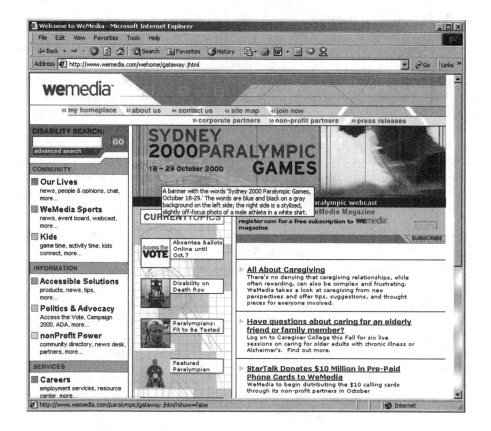

Fig. 22.2 We Media's home page. (**Wemedia.com** home page courtesy of WeMedia, Inc.)

As these laws and resources exemplify, computer and Internet accessibility for individuals with disabilities is quickly becoming a reality. Such accessibility enables individuals with disabilities to work in a vast array of new fields. This is partly because the Internet provides a medium through which disabled people can telecommute to jobs and interact easily with others without traveling. Such technologies as voice activation, visual enhancers and auditory aids create additional employment opportunities. For example, people with visual impairments can use computer monitors with enlarged text, and people with physical impairments can use head pointers with on-screen keyboards. In the remaining sections of this chapter, we explore various organizations, techniques, products and services that help provide computer and Internet access to people with disabilities.

22.3 Web Accessibility Initiative

Currently, most Web sites are considered to be either partially or totally inaccessible to people with visual, learning or mobility impairments. Total accessibility is difficult to achieve, because of the variety of disabilities that must be accommodated and because of problems resulting from language barriers and hardware and software inconsistencies. However, a high level of accessibility is attainable. As more people with disabilities begin to use the Internet, it is imperative that Web-site designers increase the accessibility of their sites. Although computer and Web accessibility is the focus of some recent legislation, standards organizations also see the need for industry recommendations. In an attempt to address issues of accessibility, the World Wide Web Consortium (W3C) launched the *Web Accessibility Initiative* (WAI™) in April 1997. To learn more about the WAI or to read its mission statement, visit **www.w3.org/WAI**.

This chapter explains various techniques used to develop accessible Web sites. In 1999, the WAI published the *Web Content Accessibility Guidelines* (*WCAG*) *1.0* to help businesses determine whether their Web sites are universally accessible. The WCAG 1.0 (available at **www.w3.org/TR/WCAG10**) uses checkpoints to list specific accessibility requirements. Each checkpoint is accompanied by a corresponding priority rating that indicates the requirement's level of importance. *Priority-one checkpoints* are goals that must be met to ensure accessibility; we focus on these points in this chapter. *Priority-two checkpoints*, though not essential, are highly recommended. If these checkpoints are not satisfied, people with certain disabilities will experience difficulty accessing Web sites. *Priority-three checkpoints* slightly improve accessibility.

At the time of publication, the WAI was working on *WCAG 2.0*; a working draft of this publication can be found at **www.w3.org/TR/WCAG20**. A single checkpoint in the WCAG 2.0 Working Draft might encompass several checkpoints from WCAG 1.0. Once WCAG 2.0 has been reviewed and published by the W3C, its checkpoints will supersede those of WCAG 1.0. Furthermore, the new version can be applied to a wider range of markup languages (i.e., XML, WML, etc.) and content types than can its predecessor.

The WAI also presents a supplemental checklist of *quick tips*, which reinforce ten important points relating to accessible Web–site design. More information on the WAI Quick Tips can be found at **www.w3.org/WAI/References/Quicktips**.

22.4 Providing Alternatives for Images

One important WAI requirement specifies that every image on a Web page should be accompanied by a textual description that clearly defines the purpose of the image. To accomplish this task, Web developers can use the **alt** attribute of the **img** and **input** tags to include a textual equivalent for every image or graphic included on a site.

Web developers who do not use the **alt** attribute to provide text equivalents increase the difficulties that people with visual impairments experience in navigating the Web. Specialized *user agent*s (or *accessibility aids*), such as *screen readers* (programs that allow users to hear all text that is displayed on their screens) and *braille displays* (devices that receive data from screen-reading software and then output the data as braille), enable people with visual impairments to access text-based information that normally is displayed on the screen. A user agent visually interprets Web-page source code and translates it into a format that is accessible to people with various disabilities. Web browsers and the screen readers mentioned throughout this chapter are examples of user agents.

Similarly, Web pages that do not provide text equivalents for video and audio clips are difficult for people with visual and hearing impairments to access. Screen readers cannot interpret images, movies and most other non-XHTML[1] content from these Web pages. However, by providing multimedia-based information in a variety of ways (e.g., using the **alt** attribute or providing in-line descriptions of images), Web designers can help maximize the accessibility of their sites' content.

Web designers should provide useful and appropriate text equivalents in the **alt** attribute for use by nonvisual user agents. For example, if the **alt** attribute describes a sales-growth chart, it should provide a brief summary of the data, but should not describe the data in the chart. Instead, a complete description of the chart's data should be included in the ***longdesc*** (long description) *attribute*, which is intended to augment the **alt** attribute's description. The **longdesc** attribute contains a link to a Web page describing the image or multimedia content. Currently, most Web browsers do not support the **longdesc** attribute. An alternative to the **longdesc** attribute is *D-link*, which provides descriptive text about graphs and charts. More information on D-links can be obtained at the *CORDA Technologies* Web site (**www.corda.com**).

The use of a screen reader to facilitate Web-site navigation can be time-consuming and frustrating, because screen readers cannot interpret pictures and other graphical content. The inclusion of a link at the top of each Web page providing direct access to the page's content could allow disabled users to bypass long lists of navigation links and other irrelevant or inaccessible content. This jump can save time and eliminate frustration for individuals with visual impairments.

Emacspeak (**www.cs.cornell.edu/home/raman/emacspeak/emacspeak.html**) is a screen interface that improves the quality of Internet access for individuals with visual disabilities by translating text to voice data. The open-source product also implements auditory icons that play various sounds. Emacspeak can be customized with Linux operating systems and provides support for the IBM *ViaVoice* speech engine.

In March 2001, We Media introduced another user agent, the *WeMedia Browser*, which allows people with vision impairments and cognitive disabilities (such as dyslexia) to use the Internet more conveniently. The WeMedia Browser enhances traditional browser capabilities by providing oversized buttons and keystroke commands that assist in naviga-

---

1. XHTML has replaced the HyperText Markup Language (HMTL) as the primary means of describing Web content. XHTML provides more robust, richer and extensible features than HTML. For more on XHTML/HTML visit **www.w3.org/markup**.

tion. The browser "reads" text that the user selects, allowing the user to control the speed and volume at which the browser reads the contents of the Web page. The WeMedia Browser free download is available at **www.wemedia.com**.

IBM Home Page Reader (HPR) is another browser that "reads" text selected by the user. The HPR uses IBM ViaVoice technology to synthesize an audible voice. A trial version of HPR is available at **www-3.ibm.com/able/hpr.html**.

22.5 Maximizing Readability by Focusing on Structure

Many Web sites use XHTML tags for aesthetic purposes, ignoring the tags' intended functions. For example, the **<h1>** heading tag often is used erroneously to make text large and bold, rather than to indicate a major section head for content. This practice might create a desired visual effect, but it causes problems for screen readers. When the screen-reader software encounters the **<h1>** tag, it might verbally inform the user that a new section has been reached. If this is not in fact the case, the **<h1>** tag might confuse users. Therefore, developers should use the **h1** only in accordance with its XHTML specifications (e.g., to mark up a heading that introduces an important section of a document). Instead of using **h1** to make text large and bold, developers can use CSS (Cascading Style Sheets) or XSL (Extensible Stylesheet Language) to format and style the text. For further examples of this nature, refer to the WCAG 1.0 Web site at **www.w3.org/TR/WCAG10**. [*Note:* The **<strong>** tag also can be used to make text bold; however, screen readers emphasize bold text, which affects the inflection of what is spoken.]

Another accessibility issue is *readability*. When creating a Web page intended for the general public, it is important to consider the reading level (i.e., level of difficulty to read and understand) at which content is written. Web-site designers can make their sites easier to read by using shorter words. Furthermore, slang terms and other nontraditional language could be problematic for users from other countries, so developers should limit the use of such words.

WCAG 1.0 suggests using a paragraph's first sentence to convey its subject. When a Web site states the point of a paragraph in this paragraph's first sentence, it is easier for individuals with disabilities both to find crucial information and to bypass unwanted material.

The *Gunning Fog Index*, a formula that produces a readability grade when applied to a text sample, can evaluate a Web site's readability. To obtain more information about the Gunning Fog Index, visit **www.trainingpost.org/3-2-inst.htm**.

22.6 Accessibility in Visual Studio .NET

In the previous sections, we have outlined various accessibility guidelines presented in the W3C's Web Accessibility initiative. However, Visual Studio .NET provides its own guidelines for designing accessible software within its programming environment. For instance, one guideline recommends reserving the use of color for the enhancement or emphasis of information, instead of for aesthetic purposes. A second guideline recommends providing information about objects (e.g., desktop icons and open windows) to the accessibility aids (specialized software that renders applications to individuals with disabilities). Such information might include the name, location and size of a window. A third guideline recommends designing user interfaces so that they can accommodate user preferences. For example, people with visual disabilities should be able to modify the font size of a user interface. A fourth guideline recommends allowing users to adjust the time setting for applications that have time constraints. For example, users with mobility or speech disabilities might experience difficulty when using applications that require users to enter input within a predetermined period of time (such as 10 seconds). However, if such applications provide adjustable time settings, users can modify the settings to suit their needs.

In addition to suggesting guidelines the help developers create accessible applications, Visual Studio .NET also offers features that enable disabled individuals to use the development environment itself. For example, users can enlarge icons and text, customize the toolbox and keyboard and rearrange windows. The next subsections illustrate these capabilities.

22.6.1 Enlarging Toolbar Icons

To enlarge icons in Visual Studio, select **Customize** from the **Tools** menu. In the **Customize** window's **Options** tab, select the **Large Icons** check box (Fig. 22.3), and select **Close**. Figure 22.4 depicts the enlarged icons on the Visual Studio development window.

Fig. 22.3   Enlarging icons using the **Customize** feature.

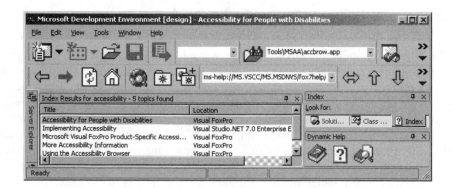

Fig. 22.4   Enlarged icons in the development window.

22.6.2 Enlarging the Text

Visual Studio uses the default operating-system font settings when displaying text. However, some individuals cannot read these default font settings, causing the applications to be inaccessible to them. To remedy this, Visual Studio allows users to modify the font size. Select **Options** from the **Tools** menu. In the **Options** window, open the **Environment** directory and choose **Fonts and Colors**. In the **Show settings for** drop-down box, select **Text Editor**. In the **Font** drop-down box, select a different style of font and, in the **Size** drop-down box, select a different font size. Figure 22.5 depicts the **Text Editor** before we modified the font size, Fig. 22.6 shows the **Options** window with new font settings and Fig. 22.7 displays the **Text Editor** after the changes have been applied.

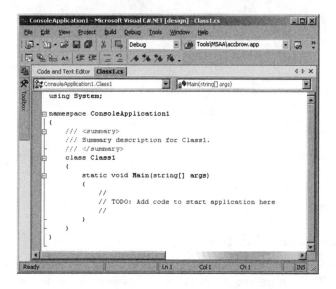

Fig. 22.5   Text Editor before modifying the font size.

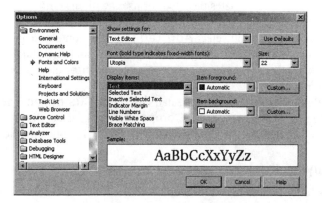

Fig. 22.6   Enlarging text in the **Options** window.

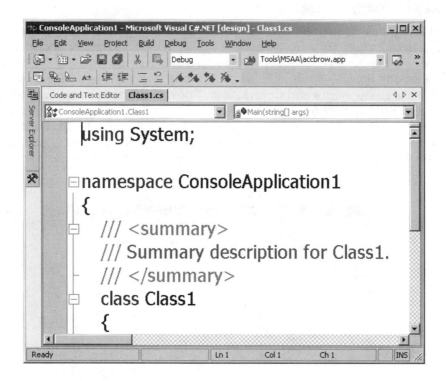

Fig. 22.7   Text Editor after the font size is modified.

22.6.3 Modifying the Toolbox

The **Toolbox** feature of Visual Studio contains numerous design elements that facilitate the creation of Web applications; however, some developers might use only a few of these design elements. To accommodate the needs of individual developers, Visual Studio allows programmers to customize the toolbox by creating new tabs and then inserting design elements into the tabs. This eliminates the need for users with disabilities to navigate among multiple tabs or scroll through long lists in search of design elements. To create a new tab, right-click any existing tab and select **Add Tab** from the context menu. In the text box, type an identifier for the tab (such as "Frequently Used") and click *Enter*. By default, the **Pointer** element is placed in all tabs (Fig. 22.8). The **Pointer** element simply allows the cursor to function normally.

To insert elements into the newly created tab, select **Customize Toolbox** from the **Tools** menu. In the **.NET Framework Components** tab, select the elements to include in the new tab and click **OK**. The selected elements now will appear in the tab.

22.6.4 Modifying the Keyboard

Another accessibility feature in Visual Studio .NET allows individuals with disabilities to customize their keyboards by creating *shortcut keys* (i.e., combinations of keyboard keys that, when pressed together, perform frequent tasks; for example, *Ctrl* + *V* causes text to be pasted from the clipboard). To create a shortcut key, begin by selecting **Options** from the **Tools** menu. In the **Options** window, select the **Keyboard** item from the **Environment** directory. From the **Keyboard mapping scheme** drop-down list, select a scheme and click the **Save As** button. Then, assign a name to the scheme in the **Save Scheme** dialog box and click **OK**. Enter the task of the shortcut key in the **Show commands containing** text box. For example, if we were creating a shortcut key for the paste function, we would enter **Paste** in the text box, or we would select the proper task from the selection list directly below the text box. Then, in the **Use new shortcut** drop-down list, select the applications that will use the shortcut key. If the shortcut key will be used in all applications, select **Global**. Finally, in the **Press shortcut key(s)** text box, assign a shortcut key to the task in the form *non-text key + text key*. Valid non-text keys include *Ctrl*, *Shift* and *Alt*; valid text keys include A–Z, inclusive. [*Note*: To enter a non-text key, select the key itself—do not type the word *Ctrl*, *Shift* or *Alt*. It is possible to include more than one non-text key as part of a shortcut key. Do not enter the + symbol.] Thus, a valid shortcut key might be *Ctrl+Alt+D*. After assigning a shortcut key, select **Assign** and then **OK**. Figure 22.9 illustrates the process of creating a shortcut key for the **NewBreakpoint** function. The shortcut key (*Ctrl+Alt+D*) is valid only in the **Text Editor**.

22.6.5 Rearranging Windows

Some screen readers have difficulty interpreting user interfaces that include multiple tabs; this is because most screen readers can read information on only one screen. To accommodate such screen readers, Visual Studio allows developers to customize their user interfaces so that only the console window appears. To remove tabs, select **Options** from the **Tools** menu. Then, in the **Options** window, select the **General** item from the **Environment** directory. In the **Settings** section, select the **MDI environment** radio button and click **OK**. Figure 22.10 depicts the **Options** window, and Fig. 22.11 illustrates a console window with and without tabs.

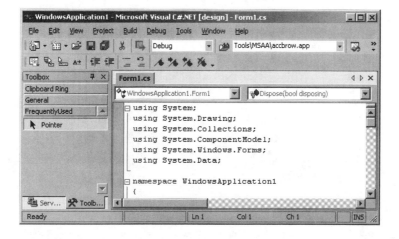

Fig. 22.8   Adding tabs to the **Toolbox**.

operation selection   application to
apply shortcuts   mapping scheme   key designation

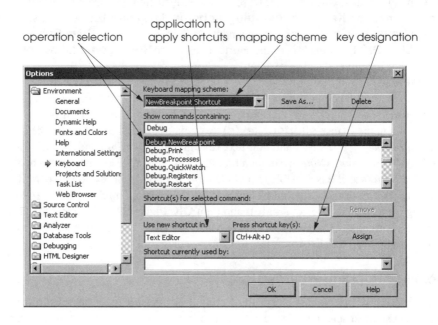

Fig. 22.9 Shortcut key creation.

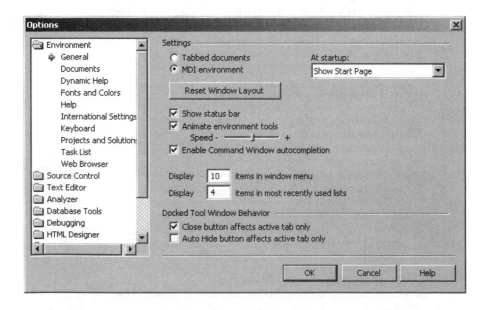

Fig. 22.10 Removing tabs from Visual Studio environment.

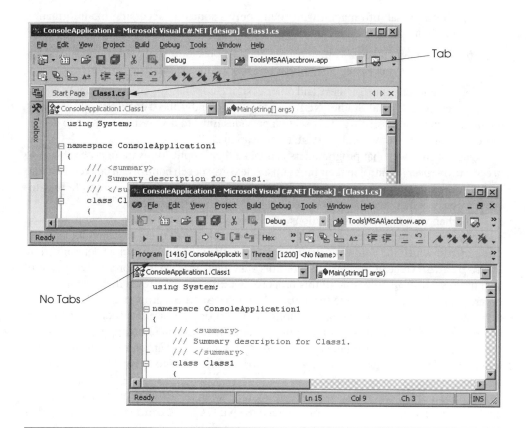

Fig. 22.11 Console windows with tabs and without tabs.

22.7 Accessibility in C#

Visual Studio .NET provides extensive accessibility features and also presents guidelines for creating accessible applications in its development environment. Similar recommendations guide the development of C# applications that are accessible to people with disabilities. It is important that C# programmers gear applications toward as many potential users as possible, rather then toward only the average user. With some modifications, most applications can be made accessible to a wide variety of individuals. General guidelines for designing accessible applications are:

1. Use larger-sized fonts—this helps people with visual impairments see the text.

2. Create flexible applications that provide keyboard shortcuts for all features within the application—this allows people to use the application without employing a mouse.

3. Allow information to be conveyed to the user both in a visual and in an audio context.

4. Use graphics and images whenever helpful—visual cues can increase accessibility for people who have trouble reading text on the screen.

5. Never signal information with sound only—someone accessing the information might not have speakers or might have hearing impairments.[2]

6. Test the application without using either a mouse or a keyboard. Access to an application's functionality should not be limited to one input device.

For more information on these and other design guidelines for accessible applications, please refer to the Visual Studio .NET documentation under the **overview** subsection of the index topic **accessibility**. This section provides links to discussions of how to design more accessible Windows and ASP.NET applications.

One specific way that programmers can make their applications more accessible is to use a *text-to-speech* control in their programs. A text-to-speech control can convert text into speech—a computerized voice speaks the words provided as text to the control. Text-to-speech controls facilitate access for people who cannot see the screen.

Another way to make applications more accessible is to use *tab stops*. A tab stop occurs when the user presses the *Tab* key, causing the focus to transfer to another control. The order in which the controls gain focus is called the *tab order*, which is determined by the **TabIndex** value of the controls (controls gain focus in ascending order). Each control also has a **TabStop** property—if this property is **true**, the control is included in the tab order; otherwise, it is not. Using the **TabIndex** and **TabStop** properties makes it simple to create more easily navigable applications. If these properties are set incorrectly, the logical ordering of the application might not be maintained. Consider an application that has **TextBox**es in which a user inputs a first name, a last name and an address. The logical tab order would take the user from the **TextBox** for the first name to the one for the last name and then to the one for the address.

A third and important way in which programmers can increase the accessibility of their applications is to use specific classes provided by .NET. Class **Control**, for example, has many properties designed for conveying information to users. These applications can then, in turn, find the required information stored as properties. Figure 22.12 lists some properties of class **Control** that are designed to provide information to users.

Property	Purpose
AccessibleDescription	Describes the control to an accessibility client application. For example, a **CheckBox** that says **"New User"** would not require more description, but a **CheckBox** with an image of a cat would have its **AccessibleDescription** property set to something like, **"A CheckBox with an image of a cat on it"**.
AccessibleName	Contains a short name or identifier for the control.

Fig. 22.12 Properties of class **Control** related to accessibility. (Part 1 of 2.)

---

2. "Basic Principles of Accessible Design," *.NET Framework Developer's Guide*, Visual Studio .NET Online Help

Property	Purpose
AccessibleRole	Member of the **AccessibleRole** enumeration. Represents the role of this control in the application—this information might help the accessibility client application determine what actions it should take.
IsAccessible	Contains a **bool** value specifying whether the control is visible to accessibility client applications.

Fig. 22.12 Properties of class **Control** related to accessibility. (Part 2 of 2.)

The application in Fig. 22.13 uses a text-to-speech control, tab stops and class **Control**'s accessibility-related properties. It consists of a form with three **Label**s, three **TextBox**es and a **Button**, enabling a user to submit the information. Submitting the information simply terminates the application—the application is intended only to demonstrate the use of the text-to-speech control.

The accessibility features in this program work as follows: When the mouse is over a **Label**, the text-to-speech control prompts the user to enter the appropriate information in the **TextBox** located to the right of the **Label**. If the mouse is over a **TextBox**, the contents of the **TextBox** are spoken. Lastly, if the mouse is over **Button Submit**, the user is told that the button should be clicked to submit the information. The tab order is the following: The **TextBox**es where the user inputs the name, phone number and password, then the **Button**. The **Label**s and text-to-speech control are not included in the tab order, because the user cannot interact with them, and their inclusion would serve no purpose. The accessibility properties are set so that accessibility client applications will obtain appropriate information about the controls. Please note that only the relevant code generated by Visual Studio .NET is included in Fig. 22.13. To use the text-to-speech control, first add it to the **Toolbox**. This is accomplished by selecting **Customize Toolbox** from the **Tools** menu. The **Customize Toolbox** dialog pops up—check the box next to the **TextToSpeech Class** option. Click **OK** to dismiss the dialog box. The **VText** control now is in the **ToolBox** and can be dragged onto a form int he same way that any other control.

The application has three **Label**s that prompts for the user's name, phone number and password. Three corresponding **TextBox**es accept the user's input and, a **Button** allows the user to submit the form. Line 25 declares a text-to-speech control named **speaker**. We want the user to hear audio descriptions of controls when the mouse is located over those controls. Lines 112–139 define the **controls_MouseHover** event handler—we attach this method to the three **TextBox**es and the **Button** as the event handler for the **MouseHover** event.

```
1   // Fig. 22.13: TextToSpeech.cs
2   // Providing audio for people with visual impairments.
3
4   using System;
5   using System.Drawing;
```

Fig. 22.13 Application with accessibility features. (Part 1 of 4.)

```
 6   using System.Collections;
 7   using System.ComponentModel;
 8   using System.Windows.Forms;
 9   using System.Data;
10
11   // helps users navigate form with aid of audio cues
12   public class TextToSpeech : System.Windows.Forms.Form
13   {
14       private System.Windows.Forms.Label nameLabel;
15       private System.Windows.Forms.Label phoneLabel;
16
17       private System.Windows.Forms.TextBox nameTextBox;
18       private System.Windows.Forms.TextBox phoneTextBox;
19       private System.Windows.Forms.TextBox passwordTextBox;
20
21       private System.Windows.Forms.Button submitButton;
22
23       private System.Windows.Forms.Label passwordLabel;
24
25       private AxHTTSLib.AxTextToSpeech speaker;
26
27       private System.ComponentModel.Container components = null;
28
29       // default constructor
30       public TextToSpeech()
31       {
32           InitializeComponent();
33
34           // set Form to be visible to accessibility applications
35           this.IsAccessible = true;
36
37           // let all controls be visible to accessibility applications
38           foreach ( Control current in this.Controls )
39               current.IsAccessible = true;
40       }
41
42       private void InitializeComponent()
43       {
44           this.nameLabel.AccessibleDescription = "User Name";
45           this.nameLabel.AccessibleName = "User Name";
46           this.nameLabel.TabIndex = 5;
47           this.nameLabel.MouseHover +=
48               new System.EventHandler( this.controls_MouseHover );
49
50           this.phoneLabel.AccessibleDescription =
51               "Phone Number Label";
52           this.phoneLabel.AccessibleName = "Phone Number Label";
53           this.phoneLabel.TabIndex = 6;
54           this.phoneLabel.MouseHover +=
55               new System.EventHandler( this.controls_MouseHover );
56
57           this.nameTextBox.AccessibleDescription =
58               "Enter User Name";
```

Fig. 22.13 Application with accessibility features. (Part 2 of 4.)

```
59          this.nameTextBox.AccessibleName = "User Name TextBox";
60          this.nameTextBox.TabIndex = 1;
61          this.nameTextBox.MouseHover +=
62             new System.EventHandler( this.controls_MouseHover );
63
64          this.phoneTextBox.AccessibleDescription =
65             "Enter Phone Number";
66          this.phoneTextBox.AccessibleName = "Phone Number TextBox";
67          this.phoneTextBox.TabIndex = 2;
68          this.phoneTextBox.MouseHover +=
69             new System.EventHandler( this.controls_MouseHover );
70
71          this.passwordTextBox.AccessibleDescription =
72             "Enter Password";
73          this.passwordTextBox.AccessibleName = "Password TextBox";
74          this.passwordTextBox.TabIndex = 3;
75          this.passwordTextBox.MouseHover +=
76             new System.EventHandler( this.controls_MouseHover );
77
78          this.submitButton.AccessibleDescription =
79             "Submit the Information";
80          this.submitButton.AccessibleName = "Submit Information";
81          this.submitButton.TabIndex = 4;
82          this.submitButton.Text = "&Submit";
83          this.submitButton.Click +=
84             new System.EventHandler( this.submitButton_Click );
85          this.submitButton.MouseHover +=
86             new System.EventHandler( this.controls_MouseHover );
87
88          this.passwordLabel.AccessibleDescription =
89             "Password Label";
90          this.passwordLabel.AccessibleName = "Password Label";
91          this.passwordLabel.TabIndex = 7;
92          this.passwordLabel.MouseHover +=
93             new System.EventHandler( this.controls_MouseHover );
94
95          this.speaker.AccessibleDescription =
96             "Give Information about Form";
97          this.speaker.AccessibleName = "Speaker";
98          this.speaker.TabIndex = 8;
99          this.speaker.TabStop = false;
100
101         this.AccessibleDescription = "Registration Form";
102         this.AccessibleName = "Registration Form";
103      }
104
105      [STAThread]
106      static void Main()
107      {
108         Application.Run( new TextToSpeech() );
109      }
110
```

Fig. 22.13 Application with accessibility features. (Part 3 of 4.)

```
111   // tell user over which control mouse is
112   private void controls_MouseHover(
113      object sender, System.EventArgs e )
114   {
115      // if mouse is over Label, tell user to enter information
116      if ( sender.GetType() == nameLabel.GetType() )
117      {
118         Label temporary = ( Label) sender;
119         speaker.Speak( "Please enter your " + temporary.Text +
120            " in the textbox to the right" );
121      }
122
123      // if mouse is over TextBox, tell user what
124      // information was entered
125      else if ( sender.GetType() == nameTextBox.GetType() )
126      {
127         TextBox temporary = ( TextBox ) sender;
128         speaker.Speak( "You have entered " +
129            ( temporary.Text == "" ? "nothing" :
130            temporary.Text ) + " in the " + temporary.Name );
131      }
132
133      // otherwise, user is over Button, so tell user to click
134      // it to submit information
135      else
136         speaker.Speak(
137            "Click on this button to submit your information" );
138
139   } // end method controls_MouseHover
140
141   // thank user for information submission
142   private void submitButton_Click(
143      object sender, System.EventArgs e )
144   {
145      speaker.Speak(
146         "Thank you, your information has been submitted." );
147
148      Application.Exit();
149   }
150
151 } // end class TextToSpeech
```

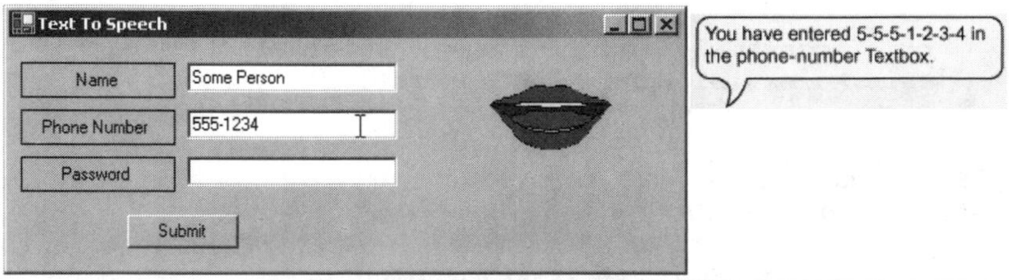

Fig. 22.13 Application with accessibility features. (Part 4 of 4.)

Method **controls_MouseHover** determines which type of control the mouse is hovering over and generates the appropriate audio. Line 116 determines whether the type of the control calling the method is the same as that of **nameLabel**. Here, we use method **GetType** of class **Type**, which returns an instance of class **Type**; this class represents information about a particular class. We call method **GetType** on object **sender**. Event-handler argument **sender** is a reference to the control that triggered the event. When the condition at line 116 evaluates to **true** (i.e., the control that triggered the event is **nameLabel**), lines 118–120 execute. Line 118 casts **sender** to a **Label** (now that we know it is one) and assigns it to **Label temporary**. Lines 119–120 call **speaker**'s method **Speak**, which provides the **string** that should be converted to speech.

A similar process is performed to determine whether the mouse is over a **TextBox** (line 125) and to generate the appropriate audio (lines 127–130). Lastly, if the control over which the mouse is hovering is neither a **Label** nor a **TextBox**, it must be the **Button**; lines 136–137 tell the user to click the button to submit information. Method **submitButton_Click** (lines 142–149) executes when the user clicks the **Button**. This event handler calls **speaker**'s method **Speak**, providing as an argument a thank-you message, and then exits the application.

Line 82 sets the **Text** property of **submitButton** to **"&Submit"**. This is an example of providing keyboard access to the functionality of the application. Placing an ampersand character, **&** in front of a letter creates a shortcut key. Here, we do the same for **submitButton**—pressing **Alt+S** on the keyboard is equivalent to clicking the **submitButton**.

We establish the tab order in this application by setting the **TabIndex** and **TabStop** properties. The **TabIndex** properties of the controls are assigned in lines 46, 60, 67, 74, 81, 91 and 98. The **TextBox**es are assigned the tab indices 1–3, in order of their appearance (vertically) on the form. The **Button** is assigned tab index 4, and the rest of the controls are given tab indices 5–8. We want the tab order to include only the **TextBox**es and the **Button**. The default setting for the **TabStop** property of **Label**s is **false**—thus, we do not need to change it; the labels will not be included in the tab order. The **TabStop** property of **TextBox**es and **Button**s is **true**, which means that we do not need to change the values for those controls either. The **TabStop** property of **speaker**, however, is **true** by default. We set it to **false**, indicating that we do not want **speaker** included in the tab order. In general, those controls with which the user cannot directly interact should have their **TabStop** properties set to **false**.

The last accessibility feature in this application involves setting the accessibility properties of the controls so that client accessibility applications can access and process the controls properly. Lines 44, 50–51, 57–58, 64–65, 71–72, 78–79, 88–89 and 95–96 set the **AccessibleDescription** properties of all the controls (including the Form). Lines 45, 52, 59, 66, 73, 80, 90 and 97 set the **AccessibleName** properties of all the controls (again including the Form). The **IsAccessible** property is not visible in the **Properties** window during design time, so we must write code to set it to **true**. Line 35 sets the **IsAccessible** property of **TextToSpeech** to **true**. Lines 38–39 loop through each control on the form and set each **IsAccessible** property to **true**. The Form and all its controls now will be visible to client accessibility applications.

22.8 Accessibility in XHTML Tables

Complex Web pages often contain tables that format content and present data. However, many screen readers are incapable of translating tables correctly unless developers design

the tables with screen-reader requirements in mind. For example, the *CAST eReader*, a
screen reader developed by the Center for Applied Special Technology
(**www.cast.org**), starts at the top-left-hand cell and reads columns from left to right, top
to bottom. This technique of reading data from a table is referred to as *linearized*.
Figure 22.14 creates a simple table listing the costs of various fruits; later, we provide this
table to the CAST eReader to demonstrate its linear reading of the table. The CAST eReader reads the table in Fig. 22.14 as follows:

> *Price of Fruit Fruit Price Apple $0.25 Orange $0.50 Banana*
> *$1.00 Pineapple $2.00*

This reading does not present the content of the table adequately: The reading neither
specifies caption and header information nor links data contained in cells to the column
headers that describe them. WCAG 1.0 recommends using Cascading Style Sheets (CSS)
instead of tables, unless a table's content linearizes in an understandable manner.

```
1    <?xml version = "1.0"?>
2    <!DOCTYPE html PUBLIC "-//W3C//DTD XHTML 1.0 Strict//EN"
3        "http://www.w3.org/TR/xhtml1/DTD/xhtml1-strict.dtd">
4
5    <!-- Fig. 22.14: withoutheaders.html -->
6    <!-- Table without headers            -->
7
8    <html xmlns = "http://www.w3.org/1999/xhtml">
9       <head>
10         <title>XHTML Table Without Headers</title>
11
12         <style type = "text/css">
13            body { background-color: #ccffaa;
14                   text-align: center }
15         </style>
16      </head>
17
18      <body>
19
20         <p>Price of Fruit</p>
21
22         <table border = "1" width = "50%">
23
24            <tr>
25               <td>Fruit</td>
26               <td>Price</td>
27            </tr>
28
29            <tr>
30               <td>Apple</td>
31               <td>$0.25</td>
32            </tr>
33
```

Fig. 22.14 XHTML table without accessibility modifications. (Part 1 of 2.)

```
34                <tr>
35                    <td>Orange</td>
36                    <td>$0.50</td>
37                </tr>
38
39                <tr>
40                    <td>Banana</td>
41                    <td>$1.00</td>
42                </tr>
43
44                <tr>
45                    <td>Pineapple</td>
46                    <td>$2.00</td>
47                </tr>
48
49            </table>
50
51        </body>
52    </html>
```

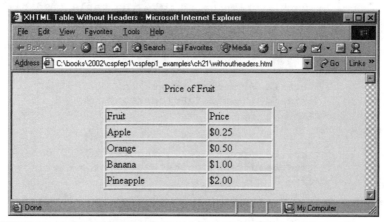

Fig. 22.14 XHTML table without accessibility modifications. (Part 2 of 2.)

If the table in Fig. 22.14 were large, the screen reader's linearized reading would be even more confusing to users. However, modifying the **<td>** tag with the **headers** attribute and modifying *header cells* (cells specified by the **<th>** tag) with the **id** attribute causes the table to be read as intended. Figure 22.15 demonstrates how these modifications change the way in which a screen reader interprets the table.

```
1    <?xml version = "1.0"?>
2    <!DOCTYPE html PUBLIC "-//W3C//DTD XHTML 1.0 Strict//EN"
3        "http://www.w3.org/TR/xhtml1/DTD/xhtml1-strict.dtd">
4
5    <!-- Fig. 22.15: withheaders.html  -->
6    <!-- Table with headers           -->
7
```

Fig. 22.15 Table optimized for screen reading, using attribute **headers**. (Part 1 of 3.)

```
 8    <html xmlns = "http://www.w3.org/1999/xhtml">
 9       <head>
10          <title>XHTML Table With Headers</title>
11
12          <style type = "text/css">
13             body { background-color: #ccffaa;
14                    text-align: center }
15          </style>
16       </head>
17
18       <body>
19
20       <!-- This table uses the id and headers attributes to    -->
21       <!-- ensure readability by text-based browsers. It also   -->
22       <!-- uses a summary attribute, used by screen readers to  -->
23       <!-- describe the table.                                  -->
24
25          <table width = "50%" border = "1"
26             summary = "This table uses th elements and id and
27             headers attributes to make the table readable
28             by screen readers">
29
30             <caption><strong>Price of Fruit</strong></caption>
31
32             <tr>
33                <th id = "fruit">Fruit</th>
34                <th id = "price">Price</th>
35             </tr>
36
37             <tr>
38                <td headers = "fruit">Apple</td>
39                <td headers = "price">$0.25</td>
40             </tr>
41
42             <tr>
43                <td headers = "fruit">Orange</td>
44                <td headers = "price">$0.50</td>
45             </tr>
46
47             <tr>
48                <td headers = "fruit">Banana</td>
49                <td headers = "price">$1.00</td>
50             </tr>
51
52             <tr>
53                <td headers = "fruit">Pineapple</td>
54                <td headers = "price">$2.00</td>
55             </tr>
56
57          </table>
58
59       </body>
60    </html>
```

Fig. 22.15 Table optimized for screen reading, using attribute **headers**. (Part 2 of 3.)

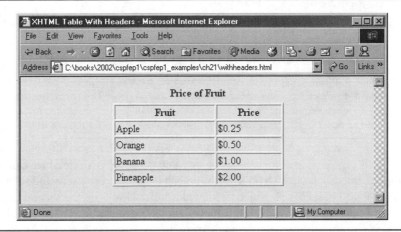

Fig. 22.15 Table optimized for screen reading, using attribute **headers**. (Part 3 of 3.)

This table does not appear to be different from the standard XHTML table shown in Fig. 22.14. However, the formatting of this table allows a screen reader to read the contained data more intelligently. A screen reader vocalizes the data from the table in Fig. 22.15 as follows:

```
Caption: Price of Fruit
Summary: This table uses th elements and id and headers
attributes to make the table readable by screen readers
Fruit: Apple, Price: $0.25
Fruit: Orange, Price: $0.50
Fruit: Banana, Price: $1.00
Fruit: Pineapple, Price: $2.00
```

Every cell in the table is preceded by its corresponding header when read by the screen reader. This format helps the listener understand the table. The **headers** *attribute* is intended specifically for use in tables that hold large amounts of data. Most small tables linearize fairly well, as long as the **<th>** tag is used properly. We also suggest using the **summary** attribute and **caption** element to enhance clarity. To view additional examples that demonstrate how to make tables accessible, visit **www.w3.org/TR/WCAG**.

22.9 Accessibility in XHTML Frames

Web designers often use frames to display more than one XHTML file in a single browser window. Frames are a convenient way to ensure that certain content always displays on the screen. Unfortunately, frames often lack proper descriptions, and this prevents users with text-based browsers and users listening via speech synthesizers from navigating the Web site.

A site that uses frames must provide a meaningful description of each frame in the frame's **<title>** tag. Examples of good titles include "*Navigation Frame*" and "*Main Content Frame.*" Users navigating via text-based browsers, such as Lynx, must choose which frame they want to open; descriptive titles make this choice simpler. However, the assignment of titles to frames does not solve all the navigation problems associated with frames. Web designers also should use the **<noframes>** tag, which provides alternative content for browsers that do not support frames.

Look-and-Feel Observation 22.1

Always provide titles for frames to ensure that user agents that do not support frames have alternatives.

Look-and-Feel Observation 22.2

*Include a title for each frame's contents with the **frame** element; if possible, provide links to the individual pages within the frameset, so that users still can navigate through the Web pages. To provide alternative content to browsers that do not support frames, use the **<nof-rames>** tag. This also improves access for browsers that offer limited support for frames.*

WCAG 1.0 suggests using Cascading Style Sheets (CSS) as an alternative to frames, because CSS can provide similar functionality and is highly customizible. Unfortunately, the ability to display multiple XHTML documents in a single browser window requires the complete support of HTML 4, which is not widespread. However, the second generation of Cascading Style Sheets (CSS2) can display a single document as if it were several documents. CSS2 is not yet fully supported by many user agents.

22.10 Accessibility in XML

XML gives developers the freedom to create new markup languages. Although this feature provides many advantages, the new languages might not incorporate accessibility features. To prevent the proliferation of inaccessible languages, the WAI is developing guidelines—the *XML Guidelines (XML GL)*—to facilitate the creation of accessible XML documents. The XML Guidelines recommend including a text description, similar to XHTML's **<alt>** tag, for each non-text object on a page. To enhance accessibility further, element types should allow grouping and classification and should identify important content. Without an accessible user interface, other efforts to implement accessibility are less effective. Therefore, it is essential to create stylesheets that can produce multiple outputs, including document outlines.

Many XML languages, including Synchronized Multimedia Integration Language (SMIL) and Scalable Vector Graphics (SVG), have implemented several of the WAI guidelines. The WAI XML Accessibility Guidelines can be found at **www.w3.org/WAI/PF/xmlgl.htm**.

22.11 Using Voice Synthesis and Recognition with VoiceXML™

A joint effort by AT&T®, IBM®, Lucent™ and Motorola® has created an XML vocabulary that marks up information for use by *speech synthesizers*, or tools that enable computers to speak to users. This technology, called *VoiceXML*, can provide tremendous benefits to people with visual impairments and to people who are illiterate. VoiceXML-enabled applications read Web pages to the user and then employ *speech recognition* technology to understand words spoken into a microphone. An example of a speech-recognition tool is IBM's *ViaVoice* (**www-4.ibm.com/software/speech**).

The VoiceXML interpreter and the VoiceXML browser process VoiceXML. In the future, Web browsers might incorporate these interpreters. VoiceXML is derived from XML, so VoiceXML is platform–independent. When a VoiceXML document is loaded, a *voice server* sends a message to the VoiceXML browser and begins a verbal conversation between the user and the computer.

The IBM *WebSphere Voice Server SDK 1.5* is a VoiceXML interpreter that can be used to test VoiceXML documents on the desktop. To download the VoiceServer SDK, visit **www.alphaworks.ibm.com/tech/voiceserversdk**. [*Note*: To run the VoiceXML program in Fig. 22.16, download *Java 2 Platform Standard Edition* (Java SDK) 1.4 from **www.java.sun.com/j2se/1.4**. Installation instructions for both the VoiceServerSDK and the Java SDK are located on the Deitel & Associates, Inc., Web site at **www.deitel.com**.]

Figure 22.16 and Fig. 22.17 depict examples of VoiceXML that could be included on a Web site. The computer speaks a document's text to the user, and the text embedded in the VoiceXML tags enables verbal interaction between the user and the browser. The output included in Fig. 22.17 demonstrates a conversation that might take place between a user and a computer after this document is loaded.

```
1    <?xml version = "1.0"?>
2    <vxml version = "1.0">
3
4    <!-- Fig. 22.16: main.vxml -->
5    <!-- Voice page           -->
6
7    <link next = "#home">
8       <grammar>home</grammar>
9    </link>
10
11   <link next = "#end">
12      <grammar>exit</grammar>
13   </link>
14
15   <var name = "currentOption" expr = "'home'"/>
16
17   <form>
18      <block>
19         <emp>Welcome</emp> to the voice page of Deitel and
20         Associates. To exit any time say exit.
21         To go to the home page any time say home.
22      </block>
23
24      <subdialog src = "#home"/>
25   </form>
26
27   <menu id = "home">
28      <prompt count = "1" timeout = "10s">
29         You have just entered the Deitel home page.
30         Please make a selection by speaking one of the
31         following options:
32         <break msecs = "1000" />
33         <enumerate/>
34      </prompt>
35
36      <prompt count = "2">
37         Please say one of the following.
38         <break msecs = "1000" />
```

Fig. 22.16 Home page written in VoiceXML. (Part 1 of 3.)

```
39          <enumerate/>
40      </prompt>
41
42      <choice next = "#about">About us</choice>
43      <choice next = "#directions">Driving directions</choice>
44      <choice next = "publications.vxml">Publications</choice>
45   </menu>
46
47   <form id = "about">
48      <block>
49          About Deitel and Associates, Inc.
50          Deitel and Associates, Inc. is an internationally
51          recognized corporate training and publishing
52          organization, specializing in programming languages,
53          Internet and World Wide Web technology and object
54          technology education. Deitel and Associates, Inc. is a
55          member of the World Wide Web Consortium. The company
56          provides courses on Java, C++, Visual Basic, C, Internet
57          and World Wide Web programming and Object Technology.
58          <assign name = "currentOption" expr = "'about'"/>
59          <goto next = "#repeat"/>
60      </block>
61   </form>
62
63   <form id = "directions">
64      <block>
65          Directions to Deitel and Associates, Inc.
66          We are located on Route 20 in Sudbury,
67          Massachusetts, equidistant from route
68          <sayas class = "digits">128</sayas> and route
69          <sayas class = "digits">495</sayas>.
70          <assign name = "currentOption" expr = "'directions'"/>
71          <goto next = "#repeat"/>
72      </block>
73   </form>
74
75   <form id = "repeat">
76      <field name = "confirm" type = "boolean">
77          <prompt>
78              To repeat say yes. To go back to home, say no.
79          </prompt>
80
81          <filled>
82              <if cond = "confirm == true">
83                  <goto expr = "'#' + currentOption"/>
84              <else/>
85                  <goto next = "#home"/>
86              </if>
87          </filled>
88
89      </field>
90   </form>
91
```

Fig. 22.16 Home page written in VoiceXML. (Part 2 of 3.)

```
92    <form id = "end">
93       <block>
94          Thank you for visiting Deitel and Associates voice page.
95          Have a nice day.
96          <exit/>
97       </block>
98    </form>
99
100   </vxml>
```

Fig. 22.16 Home page written in VoiceXML. (Part 3 of 3.)

```
101   <?xml version = "1.0"?>
102   <vxml version = "1.0">
103
104   <!-- Fig. 22.17: publications.vxml       -->
105   <!-- Voice page for various publications -->
106
107   <link next = "main.vxml#home">
108      <grammar>home</grammar>
109   </link>
110
111   <link next = "main.vxml#end">
112      <grammar>exit</grammar>
113   </link>
114
115   <link next = "#publication">
116      <grammar>menu</grammar>
117   </link>
118
119   <var name = "currentOption" expr = "'home'"/>
120
121   <menu id = "publication">
122
123      <prompt count = "1" timeout = "12s">
124         Following are some of our publications. For more
125         information visit our web page at www.deitel.com.
126         To repeat the following menu, say menu at any time.
127         Please select by saying one of the following books:
128         <break msecs = "1000" />
129         <enumerate/>
130      </prompt>
131
132      <prompt count = "2">
133         Please select from the following books.
134         <break msecs = "1000" />
135         <enumerate/>
136      </prompt>
137
138      <choice next = "#java">Java.</choice>
139      <choice next = "#c">C.</choice>
```

Fig. 22.17 Publication page of Deitel and Associates' VoiceXML page. (Part 1 of 4.)

```
140        <choice next = "#cplus">C plus plus.</choice>
141    </menu>
142
143    <form id = "java">
144        <block>
145           Java How to program, third edition.
146           The complete, authoritative introduction to Java.
147           Java is revolutionizing software development with
148           multimedia-intensive, platform-independent,
149           object-oriented code for conventional, Internet,
150           Intranet and Extranet-based applets and applications.
151           This Third Edition of the world's most widely used
152           university-level Java textbook carefully explains
153           Java's extraordinary capabilities.
154           <assign name = "currentOption" expr = "'java'"/>
155           <goto next = "#repeat"/>
156        </block>
157    </form>
158
159    <form id = "c">
160        <block>
161           C How to Program, third edition.
162           This is the long-awaited, thorough revision to the
163           world's best-selling introductory C book! The book's
164           powerful "teach by example" approach is based on
165           more than 10,000 lines of live code, thoroughly
166           explained and illustrated with screen captures showing
167           detailed output.World-renowned corporate trainers and
168           best-selling authors Harvey and Paul Deitel offer the
169           most comprehensive, practical introduction to C ever
170           published with hundreds of hands-on exercises, more
171           than 250 complete programs written and documented for
172           easy learning, and exceptional insight into good
173           programming practices, maximizing performance, avoiding
174           errors, debugging, and testing. New features include
175           thorough introductions to C++, Java, and object-oriented
176           programming that build directly on the C skills taught
177           in this book; coverage of graphical user interface
178           development and C library functions; and many new,
179           substantial hands-on projects.For anyone who wants to
180           learn C, improve their existing C skills, and understand
181           how C serves as the foundation for C++, Java, and
182           object-oriented development.
183           <assign name = "currentOption" expr = "'c'"/>
184           <goto next = "#repeat"/>
185        </block>
186    </form>
187
188    <form id = "cplus">
189        <block>
190           The C++ how to program, second edition.
191           With nearly 250,000 sold, Harvey and Paul Deitel's C++
192           How to Program is the world's best-selling introduction
```

Fig. 22.17 Publication page of Deitel and Associates' VoiceXML page. (Part 2 of 4.)

```
193          to C++ programming. Now, this classic has been thoroughly
194          updated! The new, full-color Third Edition has been
195          completely revised to reflect the ANSI C++ standard, add
196          powerful new coverage of object analysis and design with
197          UML, and give beginning C++ developers even better live
198          code examples and real-world projects. The Deitels' C++
199          How to Program is the most comprehensive, practical
200          introduction to C++ ever published with hundreds of
201          hands-on exercises, roughly 250 complete programs written
202          and documented for easy learning, and exceptional insight
203          into good programming practices, maximizing performance,
204          avoiding errors, debugging, and testing. This new Third
205          Edition covers every key concept and technique ANSI C++
206          developers need to master: control structures, functions,
207          arrays, pointers and strings, classes and data
208          abstraction, operator overloading, inheritance, virtual
209          functions, polymorphism, I/O, templates, exception
210          handling, file processing, data structures, and more. It
211          also includes a detailed introduction to Standard
212          Template Library containers, container adapters,
213          algorithms, and iterators.
214          <assign name = "currentOption" expr = "'cplus'"/>
215          <goto next = "#repeat"/>
216       </block>
217    </form>
218
219    <form id = "repeat">
220       <field name = "confirm" type = "boolean">
221
222          <prompt>
223             To repeat say yes. Say no, to go back to home.
224          </prompt>
225
226          <filled>
227             <if cond = "confirm == true">
228                <goto expr = "'#' + currentOption"/>
229             <else/>
230                <goto next = "#publication"/>
231             </if>
232          </filled>
233       </field>
234    </form>
235    </vxml>
```

Computer speaks:
**Welcome to the voice page of Deitel and Associates. To exit any time
say exit. To go to the home page any time say home.**

User speaks:
Home

(continued on next page)

Fig. 22.17 Publication page of Deitel and Associates' VoiceXML page. (Part 3 of 4.)

(continued from previous page)

Computer speaks:
You have just entered the Deitel home page. Please make a selection by speaking one of the following options: About us, Driving directions, Publications.

User speaks:
Driving directions

Computer speaks:
Directions to Deitel and Associates, Inc.
We are located on Route 20 in Sudbury,
Massachusetts, equidistant from route 128
and route 495.
To repeat say yes. To go back to home, say no.

Fig. 22.17 Publication page of Deitel and Associates' VoiceXML page. (Part 4 of 4.)

A VoiceXML document contains a series of dialogs and subdialogs, resulting in spoken interaction between the user and the computer. The **<form>** and **<menu>** tags implement the dialogs. A **form** element both presents information to the user and gathers data from the user. A **menu** element provides the user with list options and then transfers control to another dialog in response to the user's selection.

Lines 7–9 (of Fig. 22.16) use element **link** to create an active link to the home page. Attribute **next** specifies the URL to which the browser is directed when a user selects the link. Element **grammar** marks up the text that the user must speak to select the link. In the **link** element, we navigate to the element containing **id home** when a user speaks the word **home**. Lines 11–13 use element **link** to create a link to **id end** when a user speaks the word **exit**.

Lines 17–25 create a form dialog using element **form**, which collects information from the user. Lines 18–22 present introductory text. Element **block**, which can exist only within a **form** element, groups together elements that perform an action or an event. Element **emp** indicates that a section of text should be spoken with emphasis. If the level of emphasis is not specified, then the default level—*moderate*—is used. Our example uses the default level. [*Note*: To specify an emphasis level, use the **level** attribute. This attribute accepts the following values: *strong*, *moderate*, *none* and *reduced*.]

The **menu** element in line 27 enables users to select the page to which they would like to link. The **choice** element, which always is part of either a **menu** or a **form**, presents the options. The **next** attribute indicates the page that is loaded when a user makes a selection. The user selects a **choice** element by speaking the text marked up between the tags into a microphone. In this example, the first and second **choice** elements in lines 42–43 transfer control to a *local dialog* (i.e., a location within the same document) when they are selected. The third **choice** element transfers the user to the document **publications.vxml**. Lines 28–34 use element **prompt** to instruct the user to make a selection. Attribute **count** maintains a record of the number of times that a prompt is spoken (i.e., each time the computer reads a prompt, **count** increments by one). The **count** attribute transfers control to another prompt once a certain limit has been reached. Attribute

timeout specifies how long the program should wait after outputting the prompt for users to respond. In the event that the user does not respond before the timeout period expires, lines 36–40 provide a second, shorter prompt that reminds the user to make a selection.

When the user chooses the **publications** option, **publications.vxml** (Fig. 22.17) loads into the browser. Lines 107–113 define **link** elements that provide links to **main.vxml**. Lines 115–117 provide links to the **menu** element (lines 121–141), which asks users to select one of the following publications: Java, C or C++. The **form** elements in lines 143–217 describe books that correspond to these topics. Once the browser speaks the description, control transfers to the **form** element with an **id** attribute whose value equals **repeat** (lines 219–234).

Figure 22.18 provides a brief description of each VoiceXML tag that we used in the previous example (Fig. 22.17).

VoiceXML Tag	Description
<assign>	Assigns a value to a variable.
<block>	Presents information to users without any interaction between the user and the computer (i.e., the computer does not expect any input from the user).
<break>	Instructs the computer to pause its speech output for a specified period of time.
<choice>	Specifies an option in a *menu* element.
<enumerate>	Lists all the available options to the user.
<exit>	Exits the program.
<filled>	Contains elements that execute when the computer receives input for a *form* element from the user.
<form>	Gathers information from the user for a set of variables.
<goto>	Transfers control from one dialog to another.
<grammar>	Specifies grammar for the expected input from the user.
<if>, *<else>*, *<elseif>*	Indicates a control statement used for making logic decisions.
<link>	Performs a transfer of control similar to the *goto* statement, but a *link* can be executed at any time during the program's execution.
<menu>	Provides user options and then transfers control to other dialogs on the basis of the selected option.
<prompt>	Specifies text to be read to users when they must make a selection.
<subdialog>	Calls another dialog. After executing the subdialog, the calling dialog resumes control.
<var>	Declares a variable.
<vxml>	Top-level tag that specifies that the document should be processed by a VoiceXML interpreter.

Fig. 22.18 VoiceXML tags.

22.12 CallXML™

Another advancement benefiting people with visual impairments is *CallXML*, a voice technology created and supported by *Voxeo* (**www.voxeo.com**). CallXML creates phone-to-Web applications that control incoming and outgoing telephone calls. Examples of CallXML applications include voice mail, interactive voice-response systems and Internet call waiting. VoiceXML allows computers to read Web pages to users with visual impairments; CallXML reads Web content to users via a telephone. CallXML has important implications for individuals who do not have a computer, but do have a telephone.

When users access CallXML applications, a *text-to-speech (TTS)* engine converts text to an automated voice. The TTS engine then reads information contained within CallXML elements to the users. CallXML applications are tailored to respond to input from callers. [*Note*: Users must have a touch-tone phone to access CallXML applications.]

Typically, CallXML applications play prerecorded audio clips or text as output, requesting responses as input. An audio clip might contain a greeting that introduces callers to the application, or it might recite a menu of options, requesting that callers make a touch-tone entry. Certain applications, such as voice mail, might require both verbal and touch-tone input. Once the application receives the necessary input, it responds by invoking CallXML elements (such as **text**) that contain the information a TTS engine reads to users. If the application does not receive input within a designated time frame, it prompts the user to enter valid input.

When a user accesses a CallXML application, the incoming telephone call is referred to as a *session*. A CallXML application can support multiple sessions, which means that the application can process multiple telephone calls at once. Each session is independent of the others and is assigned a unique *sessionID* for identification. A session terminates either when the user hangs up the telephone or when the CallXML application invokes the **hangup** element.

Our first CallXML application demonstrates the classic "Hello World" example (Fig. 22.19). Line 1 contains the optional *XML declaration*. Value **version** indicates the XML version to which the document conforms. The current XML recommendation is version **1.0**. Value **encoding** indicates the type of *Unicode* encoding that the application uses. For this example, we empty UTF-8, which requires eight bits to transfer and receive data. More information on Unicode® can be found in Appendix F, Unicode®.

The **<callxml>** tag in line 6 declares that the content is a CallXML document. Line 7 contains the **Hello World text**. All text that is to be spoken by a text-to-speech (TTS) engine must be placed within **<text>** tags.

```
1    <?xml version = "1.0" encoding = "UTF-8"?>
2
3    <!-- Fig. 22.19: hello.xml            -->
4    <!-- The classic Hello World example -->
5
6    <callxml>
7       <text>Hello World.</text>
8    </callxml>
```

Fig. 22.19 Hello World CallXML example. (Part 1 of 2.) (Courtesy of Voxeo, © Voxeo Corporation 2000–2002.)

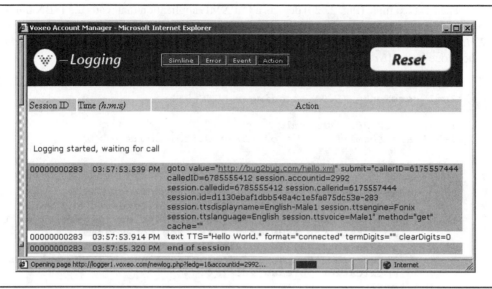

Fig. 22.19 Hello World CallXML example. (Part 2 of 2.) (Courtesy of Voxeo, © Voxeo Corporation 2000–2002.)

To deploy a CallXML application, register with the *Voxeo* Community (`community.voxeo.com`), a Web resource that facilitates the creation, debugging and deployment of phone applications. For the most part, Voxeo resources are free, but the company does charge fees when CallXML applications are deployed commercially. The Voxeo Community assigns a unique telephone number to each CallXML application so that external users can access and interact with the application. [*Note*: Voxeo assigns telephone numbers only to applications that reside on the Internet. If you have access to a Web server (such as IIS, PWS or Apache), use it to post your CallXML application. Otherwise, open an Internet account through one of the many Internet-service companies (such as `www.geocities.com`, `angelfire.lycos.com`, `www.stormpages.com`, `www.freewebsites.com`, or `www.brinkster.com`). These companies allow individuals to post documents on the Internet using their Web servers.]

Figure 22.19 also demonstrates the *logging* feature of the **Voxeo Account Manager**, which is accessible to registered members. The logging feature records and displays the "conversation" between the user and the application. The first row of the logging feature lists the URL of the CallXML application and the *global variables* associated with that session. When a session begins, the application creates and assigns values to global variables that the entire application can access and modify. The subsequent row(s) display the "conversation." This example demonstrates a one-way conversation (i.e., the application does not accept any input from the user) in which the TTS engine says **Hello World**. The last row displays the **end of session** message, which states that the phone call has terminated. The logging feature assists developers in the debugging of their applications. By observing a CallXML "conversation," a developer can determine the point at which the application terminates. If the application terminates abruptly ("crashes"), the logging feature displays information regarding the type and location of the error, pointing the developer toward the section of the application that is causing the problem.

The next example (Fig. 22.20) depicts a CallXML application that reads the ISBN numbers of three Deitel books—*Internet and World Wide Web How to Program: Second Edition*, *XML How to Program* and *Java How to Program: Fourth Edition*—on the basis of a user's touch-tone input. [*Note*: The code has been formatted for presentation purposes.]

```xml
1   <?xml version = "1.0" encoding = "UTF-8"?>
2
3   <!-- Fig. 22.20: isbn.xml                      -->
4   <!-- Reads the ISBN value of three Deitel books -->
5
6   <callxml>
7      <block>
8         <text>
9            Welcome. To obtain the ISBN of the Internet and World
10           Wide Web How to Program: Second Edition, please enter 1.
11           To obtain the ISBN of the XML How to Program,
12           please enter 2. To obtain the ISBN of the Java How
13           to Program: Fourth Edition, please enter 3. To exit the
14           application, please enter 4.
15        </text>
16
17        <!-- Obtains the numeric value entered by the user and -->
18        <!-- stores it in the variable ISBN. The user has 60   -->
19        <!-- seconds to enter one numeric value                -->
20        <getDigits var = "ISBN"
21           maxDigits = "1"
22           termDigits = "1234"
23           maxTime = "60s" />
24
25        <!-- Requests that the user enter a valid numeric -->
26        <!-- value after the elapsed time of 60 seconds   -->
27        <onMaxSilence>
28           <text>
29              Please enter either 1, 2, 3 or 4.
30           </text>
31
32           <getDigits var = "ISBN"
33              termDigits = "1234"
34              maxDigits = "1"
35              maxTime = "60s" />
36
37        </onMaxSilence>
38
39        <onTermDigit value = "1">
40           <text>
41              The ISBN for the Internet book is 0130308978.
42              Thank you for calling our CallXML application.
43              Good-bye.
44           </text>
45        </onTermDigit>
46
```

Fig. 22.20 CallXML example that reads three ISBN values. (Part 1 of 2.) (Courtesy of Voxeo, © Voxeo Corporation 2000–2002.)

```
47          <onTermDigit value = "2">
48             <text>
49                The ISBN for the XML book is 0130284173.
50                Thank you for calling our CallXML application.
51                Good-bye.
52             </text>
53          </onTermDigit>
54
55          <onTermDigit value = "3">
56             <text>
57                The ISBN for the Java book is 0130341517.
58                Thank you for calling our CallXML application.
59                Good-bye.
60             </text>
61          </onTermDigit>
62
63          <onTermDigit value = "4">
64             <text>
65                Thank you for calling our CallXML application.
66                Good-bye.
67             </text>
68          </onTermDigit>
69       </block>
70
71       <!-- Event handler that terminates the call -->
72       <onHangup />
73    </callxml>
```

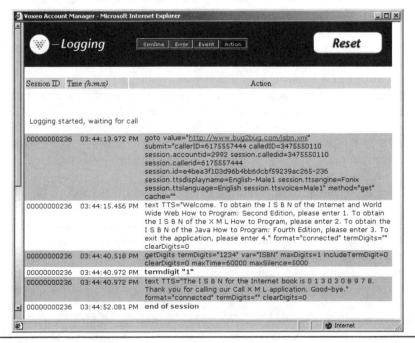

Fig. 22.20 CallXML example that reads three ISBN values. (Part 2 of 2.) (Courtesy of Voxeo, © Voxeo Corporation 2000–2002.)

The **<block>** tag (line 7) encapsulates other CallXML tags. Usually, sets of CallXML tags that perform similar tasks are enclosed within **<block>...</block>**. The **block** element in this example encapsulates the **<text>**, **<getDigits>**, **<onMaxSilence>** and **<onTermDigit>** tags. A **block** element also can be nested in other **block** elements.

Lines 20–23 contain some attributes of the **<getDigits>** tag. The **getDigits** element obtains the user's touch-tone response and stores it in the variable declared by the **var** attribute (i.e., **ISBN**). The **maxDigits** attribute (line 21) indicates the maximum number of digits that the application can accept. This application accepts only one character. If no maximum is stated, then the application uses the default value, *nolimit*.

The **termDigits** attribute (line 22) contains the list of characters that terminate user input. When a user inputs a character from this list, the application is notified that it has received the last acceptable input; any character entered after this point is invalid. These characters do not terminate the call; they simply notify the application to proceed to the next instruction, because the necessary input has been received. In our example, the values for **termDigits** are **1**, **2**, **3** and **4**. The default value for **termDigits** is the null value (**""**).

The **maxTime** attribute (line 23) indicates the maximum amount of time that the application will wait for a user response. If the user fails to enter input within the given time frame, then the CallXML application invokes the event handler **onMaxSilence**. The default value for this attribute is 30 seconds.

The **onMaxSilence** element (lines 27–37) is an event handler that is invoked when attribute **maxTime** (or **maxSilence**) expires. The event handler notifies the application of the appropriate action to perform when a user fails to respond. In this case, the application asks the user to enter a value, because the **maxTime** has expired. After receiving input, **getDigits** (line 32) stores the entered value in the **ISBN** variable.

The **onTermDigit** element (lines 39–68) is an event handler that notifies the application of the appropriate action to perform when a user selects one of the **termDigits** characters. At least one **<onTermDigit>** tag must be associated with (i.e., must appear after) the **getDigits** element, even if the default value (**""**) is used. We provide four actions that the application can perform in response to the specific **termDigits** value entered by the user. For example, if the user enters **1**, the application reads the ISBN value for the *Internet and World Wide Web How to Program: Second Edition* textbook.

Line 72 contains the **<onHangup/>** event handler, which terminates the telephone call when the user hangs up the telephone. Our **<onHangup>** event handler is an empty tag (i.e., no action is performed when this tag is invoked).

The logging feature (Fig. 22.20) displays the "conversation" between the application and the user. As in the previous example, the first row specifies the URL of the application and the global variables of the session. The subsequent rows display the "conversation": The application asks the caller which ISBN value to read; the caller enters **1** (*Internet and World Wide Web How to Program: Second Edition*), and the application reads the corresponding ISBN. The **end of session** message states that the application has terminated.

We provide brief descriptions of various logic and action CallXML elements in Fig. 22.21. *Logic elements* assign values to, and clear values from, the session variables; *action elements* perform specified tasks, such as answering and terminating a telephone call during the current session. A complete list of CallXML elements is available at:

www.oasis-open.org/cover/callxmlv2.html

22.13 JAWS® for Windows

JAWS (Job Access with Sound) is one of the leading screen readers currently on the market. Henter-Joyce, a division of Freedom Scientific™, created this application to help people with visual impairments interact with technology.

To download a demonstration version of JAWS, visit **www.freedomscientific.com**. The JAWS demo is fully functional and includes an extensive, highly customized help system. Users can select the voice that "reads" Web content and the rate at which text is spoken. Users also can create keyboard shortcuts. Although the demo is in English, the full version of JAWS allows the user to choose one of several supported languages.

JAWS also includes special key commands for popular programs, such as Microsoft Internet Explorer and Microsoft Word. For example, when browsing in Internet Explorer, JAWS' capabilities extend beyond the reading of content on the screen. If JAWS is enabled, pressing *Insert + F7* in Internet Explorer opens a **Links List** dialog, which displays all the links available on a Web page. For more information about JAWS and the other products offered by Henter-Joyce, visit **www.freedomscientific.com**.

Elements	Description
assign	Assigns a **value** to a variable, **var**.
clear	Clears the contents of the **var** attribute.
clearDigits	Clears all digits that the user has entered.
goto	Navigates to another section of the current CallXML application or to a different CallXML application. The **value** attribute specifies the URL of the invoked application. The **submit** attribute lists the variables that are passed to the invoked application. The **method** attribute states whether to use the HTTP *get* or *post* request type when sending and retrieving information. A *get* request retrieves data from a Web server without modifying the contents, whereas the *post* request receives modified data.
run	Starts a new CallXML session for each call. The **value** attribute specifies the CallXML application to retrieve. The **submit** attribute lists the variables that are passed to the invoked application. The **method** attribute states whether to use the HTTP *get* or *post* request type. The **var** attribute stores the identification number of the session.
sendEvent	Allows multiple sessions to exchange messages. The **value** attribute stores the message, and the **session** attribute specifies the identification number of the session that receives the message.
answer	Answers an incoming telephone call.
call	Calls the URL specified by the **value** attribute. The **callerID** attribute contains the phone number that is displayed on a CallerID device. The **maxTime** attribute specifies the length of time to wait for the call to be answered before disconnecting.

Fig. 22.21 CallXML elements. (Part 1 of 2.)

Elements	Description
`conference`	Connects multiple sessions so that individuals can participate in a conference call. The **`targetSessions`** attribute specifies the identification numbers of the sessions, and the **`termDigits`** attribute indicates the touch-tone keys that terminate the call.
`wait`	Waits for user input. The **`value`** attribute specifies how long to wait. The **`termDigits`** attribute indicates the touch-tone keys that terminate the **`wait`** element.
`play`	Plays an audio file or pronounces a value that is stored as a number, date or amount of money and is indicated by the **`format`** attribute. The **`value`** attribute contains the information (location of the audio file, number, date or amount of money) that corresponds to the **`format`** attribute. The **`clearDigits`** attribute specifies whether or not to delete the previously entered input. The **`termDigits`** attribute indicates the touch-tone keys that terminate the audio file, etc.
`recordAudio`	Records an audio file and stores it at the URL specified by **`value`**. The **`format`** attribute indicates the file extension of the audio clip. Other attributes include **`termDigits`**, **`clearDigits`**, **`maxTime`** and **`maxSilence`**.

Fig. 22.21 CallXML elements. (Part 2 of 2.)

22.14 Other Accessibility Tools

Many accessibility products are available to assist people with disabilities. One such technology, Microsoft's *Active Accessibility*®, establishes a protocol by which an accessibility aid can retrieve information about an application's user interface in a consistent manner. Accessibility aids require information such as the name, location and layout of particular GUI elements within an application, so that the accessibility aid can render the information properly to the intended audience. Active Accessibility also enables software developers and accessibility-aid developers to design programs and products that are compatible with each other. Moreover, Active Accessibility is packaged in two components, enabling both programmers and individuals who use accessibility aids to employ the software. The *Software Development Kit (SDK)* component is intended for programmers: It includes testing tools, programmatic libraries and header files. The *Redistribution Kit (RDK)* component is intended for those who use accessibility aids: It installs a runtime component into the Microsoft operating system. Accessibility aids use the Active Accessibility runtime component to interact with and obtain information from any application software. For more information on Active Accessibility, visit:

```
www.msdn.microsoft.com/library/default.asp?url=/nhp/
Default.asp?contentid=28000544
```

Another important accessibility tool for individuals with visual impairments is the *braille keyboard*. In addition to providing keys labeled with the letters they represent, a braille keyboard also has the equivalent braille symbol printed on each key. Most often, braille keyboards are combined with a speech synthesizer or a braille display, enabling users to interact with the computer to verify that their typing is correct.

Speech synthesis also provides benefits to people with disabilities. *Speech synthesizers* have been used for many years to aid people who are unable to communicate verbally. However, the growing popularity of the Web has prompted a surge of interest in the fields of speech synthesis and speech recognition. Now, these technologies are allowing individuals with disabilities to use computers more than ever before. The development of speech synthesizers also is enabling the improvement of other technologies, such as VoiceXML and *AuralCSS* (**www.w3.org/TR/REC-CSS2/aural.html**). These tools allow people with visual impairments and illiterate people to access Web sites.

Despite the existence of adaptive software and hardware for people with visual impairments, the accessibility of computers and the Internet is still hampered by the high costs, rapid obsolescence and unnecessary complexity of current technology. Moreover, almost all software currently available requires installation by a person who can see. *Ocularis* is a project launched in the open-source community that aims to address these problems. (Open-source software for people with visual impairments already exists; although it is often superior to its proprietary, closed-source counterparts, it has not yet reached its full potential.) Ocularis ensures that the blind can access and use all aspects of the Linux operating system. Products that integrate with Ocularis include word processors, calculators, basic finance applications, Internet browsers and e-mail clients. In addition, a screen reader is included for use with programs that have a command-line interface. The official Ocularis Web site is located at

ocularis.sourceforge.net.

People with visual impairments are not the only beneficiaries of efforts to improve markup languages. People with hearing impairments also have a number of tools to help them interpret auditory information delivered over the Web. One of these tools, *Synchronized Multimedia Integration Language* (SMIL™), is designed to add extra *tracks* (layers of content found within a single audio or video file) to multimedia content. The additional tracks can contain closed captioning.

Technologies are being designed to help people with severe disabilities, such as quadriplegia, a form of paralysis that affects the body from the neck down. One such technology, *EagleEyes*, developed by researchers at Boston College (**www.bc.edu/eagleeyes**), is a system that translates eye movements into mouse movements. A user moves the mouse cursor by moving his or her eyes or head and is thereby able to control the computer.

GW Micro, Henter-Joyce and Adobe Systems, Inc., also are working on software that assists people with disabilities. Adobe Acrobat 5.0 complies with Microsoft's application programming interface (API) to allow businesses to provide information to a wider audience. JetForm Corp is also accommodating the needs of people with disabilities by developing server-based XML software. The new software allows users to download information in a format that best meets their needs.

There are many services on the Web that assist e-businesses in designing Web sites so that they are accessible to individuals with disabilities. For additional information, the U.S. Department of Justice (**www.usdoj.gov**) provides extensive resources detailing legal and technical issues related to people with disabilities.

22.15 Accessibility in Microsoft® Windows® 2000

Because of the prominence of the Windows operating system, it is crucial that this operating system provide proper accessibility to individuals with disabilities. Beginning with Microsoft *Windows 95*, Microsoft has included accessibility features in its operating systems and many of its applications, including *Office 97*, *Office 2000* and *Netmeeting*. In Microsoft *Windows 2000*, Microsoft significantly enhanced the operating system's accessibility features. All the accessibility options provided by Windows 2000 are available through the **Accessibility Wizard**, which guides users through Windows 2000 accessibility features and then configures users' computers in accordance with the chosen specifications. This section uses the **Accessibility Wizard** to guide users through the configuration of their Windows 2000 accessibility options.

To access the **Accessibility Wizard**, users' computers must be equipped with Microsoft Windows 2000. Click the **Start** button and select **Programs**, followed by **Accessories**, **Accessibility** and **Accessibility Wizard**. When the wizard starts, the **Welcome** screen displays. Click **Next**. The next dialog (Fig. 22.22) asks the user to select a font size. Modify the font size if necessary and then click **Next**.

Figure 22.22 depicts the **Display Settings** dialog. This dialog allows the user to activate the font-size settings chosen in the previous window, change the screen resolution, enable the *Microsoft Magnifier* (a program that displays an enlarged section of the screen in a separate window) and disable personalized menus. Personalized menus hide rarely used programs from the start menu and can be a hindrance to users with disabilities. Make appropriate selections and click **Next**.

The **Set Wizard Options** dialog (Fig. 22.23) asks questions about the user's disabilities; the answers to these questions allow the **Accessibility Wizard** to customize Windows to better suit the user's needs. For demonstration purposes, we selected every type of disability included in the dialogue. Click **Next** to continue.

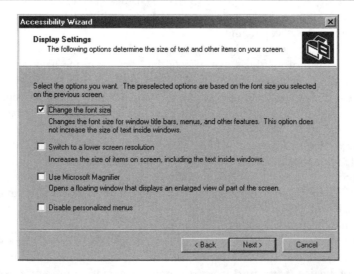

Fig. 22.22 Display Settings dialog.

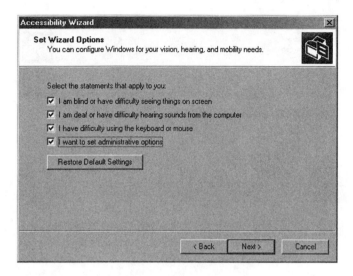

Fig. 22.23 **Accessibility Wizard** initialization options.

22.15.1 Tools for People with Visual Impairments

When we check all the options in Fig. 22.23, the wizard begins to configure Windows so that it is accessible to people with visual impairments. The dialog box shown in Fig. 22.24 allows the user to resize the scroll bars and window borders to increase their visibility. Click **Next** to proceed to the next dialog.

Figure 22.25 contains a dialog that allows the user to resize icons. Users with poor vision and users who are illiterate or have trouble reading benefit from large icons.

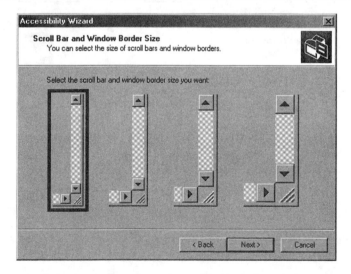

Fig. 22.24 **Scroll Bar and Window Border Size** dialog.

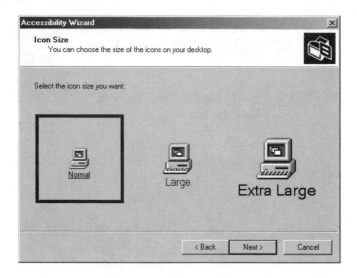

Fig. 22.25 Adjusting window-element sizes.

Clicking **Next** displays the **Display Color Settings** dialog (Fig. 22.26). These settings enable the user to change the Windows color scheme and resize various screen elements.

Click **Next** to view the dialog (Fig. 22.27) that enables customization of the mouse cursor. Anyone who has ever used a laptop computer knows how difficult it can be to see the mouse cursor. This is even more problematic for people with visual impairments. To address this problem, the wizard offers users the options of larger cursors, black cursors and cursors that invert the colors of objects underneath them. Click **Next**.

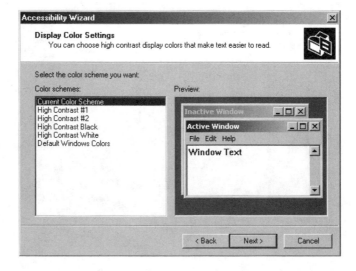

Fig. 22.26 Display Color Settings options.

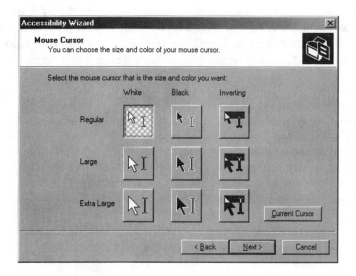

Fig. 22.27 Accessibility Wizard mouse cursor adjustment tool.

22.15.2 Tools for People with Hearing Impairments

This section, which focuses on accessibility for people with hearing impairments, begins with the **SoundSentry** window (Fig. 22.28). **SoundSentry** is a tool that creates visual signals to notify users of system events. For example, people with hearing impairments are unable to hear the beeps that normally indicate warnings, so **SoundSentry** flashes the screen when a beep occurs. To continue on to the next dialog, click **Next**.

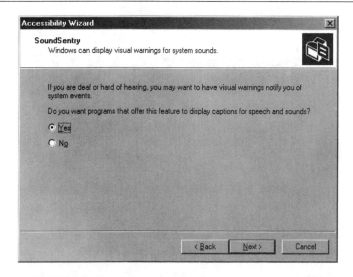

Fig. 22.28 SoundSentry dialog.

The next window is the ***ShowSounds*** window (Fig. 22.29). **ShowSounds** adds captions to spoken text and other sounds produced by today's multimedia-rich software. Note that, for **ShowSounds** to work in a specific application, developers must provide the captions and spoken text specifically within their software. Make selections and click **Next**.

22.15.3 Tools for Users Who Have Difficulty Using the Keyboard

The next dialog describes **StickyKeys** (Fig. 22.30). ***StickyKeys*** is a program that helps users who have difficulty pressing multiple keys at the same time. Many important computer commands can be invoked only by pressing specific key combinations. For example, the reboot command requires the user to press *Ctrl+Alt+Delete* simultaneously. **Sticky-Keys** enables the user to press key combinations in sequence, rather than at the same time. Click **Next** to continue to the **BounceKeys** dialog (Fig. 22.31).

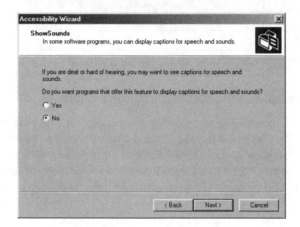

Fig. 22.29 ShowSounds dialog.

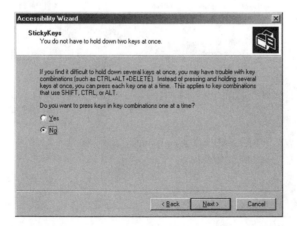

Fig. 22.30 StickyKeys window.

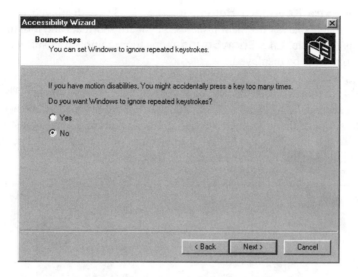

Fig. 22.31 BounceKeys dialog.

Another common problem that affects certain users with disabilities is the accidental pressing of the same key multiple times. This problem typically is caused by holding a key down too long. **BounceKeys** forces the computer to ignore repeated keystrokes. Click **Next**.

ToggleKeys (Fig. 22.32) alerts users that they have pressed one of the lock keys (i.e., *Caps Lock*, *Num Lock* or *Scroll Lock*) by sounding an audible beep. Make selections and click **Next**.

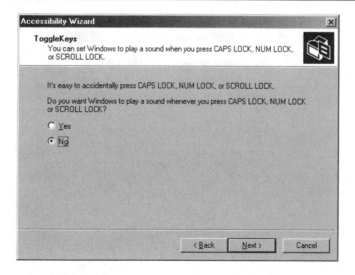

Fig. 22.32 ToggleKeys window.

Next, the **Extra Keyboard Help** dialog (Fig. 22.33) is displayed. This dialog can activate a tool that displays information such as keyboard shortcuts and tool tips when such information is available. Like **ShowSounds**, this tool requires that software developers provide the content to be displayed.

Clicking **Next** will load the **MouseKeys** (Fig. 22.34) customization window. **_MouseKeys_** is a tool that uses the keyboard to imitate mouse movements. The arrow keys direct the mouse, and the 5 key indicates a single click. To double click, the user must press the + key; to simulate the holding down of the mouse button, the user must press the *Ins* (Insert) key. To release the mouse button, the user must press the *Del* (Delete) key. Choose whether to enable **MouseKeys** and then click **Next.**

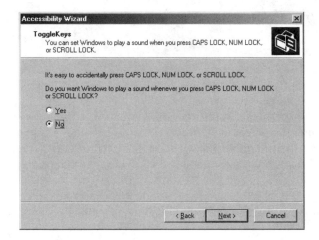

Fig. 22.33 Extra Keyboard Help dialog.

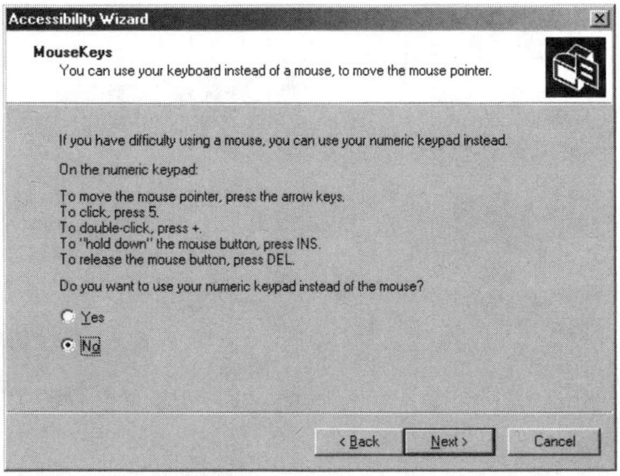

Fig. 22.34 MouseKeys window.

Today's computer tools, including most mice, are designed almost exclusively for right-handed users. Microsoft recognized this problem and added the ***Mouse Button* Settings** window (Fig. 22.35) to the **Accessibility Wizard**. This tool allows the user to create a virtual left-handed mouse by swapping the button functions. Click **Next**.

Users can adjust mouse speed through the **MouseSpeed** (Fig. 22.36) section of the **Accessibility Wizard**. Dragging the scroll bar changes the speed. Clicking the **Next** button sets the speed and displays the wizard's **Set Automatic Timeouts** window (Fig. 22.37). Although accessibility tools are important to users with disabilities, they can be a hindrance to users who do not need them. In situations where varying accessibility needs exist, it is important that the user be able to turn the accessibility tools on and off as necessary. The ***Set Automatic Timeouts*** window specifies a *timeout* period for enabling or disabling accessibility tools. A timeout either enables or disables a certain action after the computer has idled for a specified amount of time. A screen saver is a common example of a program with a timeout period. Here, a timeout is set to toggle the accessibility tools.

After the user clicks **Next**, the **Save Settings to File** dialog appears (Fig. 22.38). This dialog determines whether the accessibility settings should be used as the *default settings*, which are loaded when the computer is rebooted or after a timeout. Set the accessibility settings as the default if the majority of users needs them. Users also can save multiple accessibility settings. The user can create an **.acw** file, which, when chosen, activates the saved accessibility settings on any Windows 2000 computer.

22.15.4 Microsoft Narrator

Microsoft Narrator is a text-to-speech program designed for people with visual impairments. It reads text, describes the current desktop environment and alerts the user when certain Windows events occur. **Narrator** is intended to aid in the configuration of Microsoft Windows. It is a screen reader that works with Internet Explorer, Wordpad, Notepad and most programs in the **Control Panel**. Although its capabilities are limited outside these applications, **Narrator** is excellent at navigating the Windows environment.

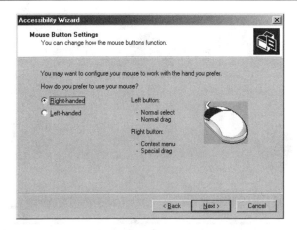

Fig. 22.35 Mouse Button Settings window.

To explore **Narrator**'s functionality, we explain how to use the program in conjunction with several Windows applications. Click the **Start** button and select **Programs**, followed by **Accessories**, **Accessibility** and **Narrator**. Once **Narrator** is open, it describes the current foreground window. It then reads the text inside the window aloud to the user. When the user clicks **OK**, the dialog in Fig. 22.39 displays.

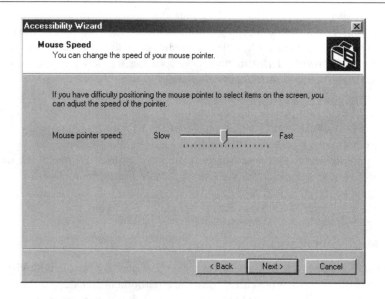

Fig. 22.36 Mouse Speed dialog.

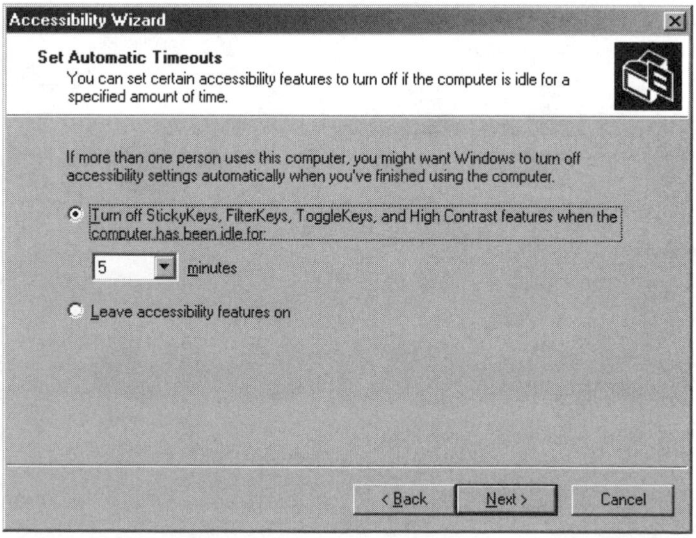

Fig. 22.37 Set Automatic Timeouts dialog.

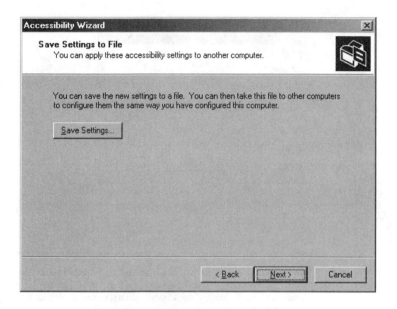

Fig. 22.38 Saving new accessibility settings.

Fig. 22.39 Narrator window.

Checking the first option instructs **Narrator** to describe menus and new windows when they are opened. The second option instructs **Narrator** to speak the characters that users type as they type them. The third option moves the mouse cursor to the region currently being read by **Narrator**. Clicking the **Voice...** button enables the user to change the pitch, volume and speed of the narrator voice (Fig. 22.40).

Now, we demonstrate **Narrator** in various applications. When **Narrator** is running, open **Notepad** and click the **File** menu. **Narrator** announces the opening of the program and begins to describe the items in the **File** menu. As a user scrolls down the list, **Narrator** reads the item to which the mouse currently is pointing. Type some text and press *Ctrl-Shift-Enter* to hear **Narrator** read it (Fig. 22.41). If the **Read typed characters** option is checked, **Narrator** reads each character as it is typed. Users also can employ the keyboard's direction arrows to make **Narrator** read. The up and down arrows cause **Narrator** to speak the lines adjacent to the current mouse position, and the left and right arrows cause **Narrator** to speak the characters adjacent to the current mouse position.

Fig. 22.40 Voice-settings window.

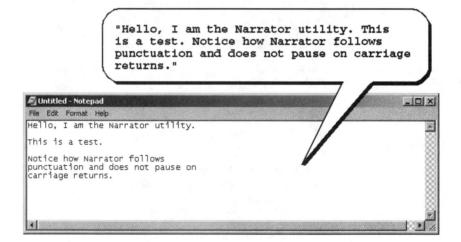

Fig. 22.41 Narrator reading **Notepad** text.

22.15.5 Microsoft On-Screen Keyboard

Some computer users lack the ability to use a keyboard, but are able to use a pointing device, such as a mouse. For these users, the ***On-Screen Keyboard*** is helpful. To access the On-Screen Keyboard, click the **Start** button and select **Programs**, followed by **Accessories**, **Accessibility** and **On-Screen Keyboard**. Figure 22.42 depicts the layout of the Microsoft On-Screen Keyboard.

Users who have difficulty using the On-Screen Keyboard can purchase more sophisticated products, such as *Clicker 4*™ by *Inclusive Technology*. Clicker 4 is an aid designed for people who cannot use a keyboard effectively. Its best feature is that it can be customized. Keys can have letters, numbers, entire words or even pictures on them. For more information regarding Clicker 4, visit **www.inclusive.co.uk/catalog/ clicker.shtml**.

Fig. 22.42 Microsoft **On-Screen Keyboard**.

22.15.6 Accessibility Features in Microsoft Internet Explorer 6

Internet Explorer 6 offers a variety of options that can improve usability. To access IE6's accessibility features, launch the program, click the **Tools** menu and select **Internet Options...**. Then, from the **Internet Options** menu, press the button labeled **Accessibility...** to open the accessibility options (Fig. 22.43).

The accessibility options in IE6 are designed to improve the Web browsing experiences of users with disabilities. Users are able to ignore Web colors, Web fonts and font-size tags. This eliminates accessibility problems arising from poor Web-page design and allows users to customize their Web browsing. Users can even specify a *style sheet,* which formats every Web site that users visit according to their personal preferences.

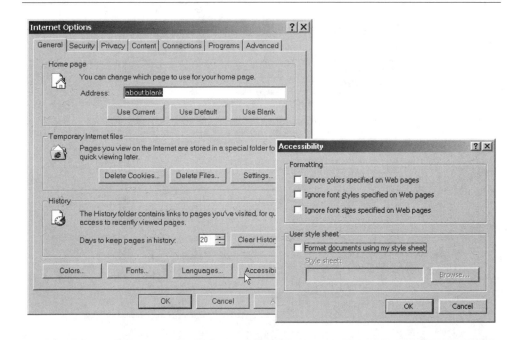

Fig. 22.43 Microsoft Internet Explorer 6's accessibility options.

In the **Internet Options** dialog, click the **Advanced** tab. This opens the dialog depicted in Fig. 22.44. The first available option is labeled **Always expand ALT text for images**. By default, IE6 hides some of the `<alt>` text if the size of the text exceeds that of the image it describes. This option forces IE6 to show all the text. The second option reads: **Move system caret with focus/selection changes**. This option is intended to make screen reading more effective. Some screen readers use the *system caret* (the blinking vertical bar associated with editing text) to determine what to read. If this option is not activated, screen readers might not read Web pages correctly.

Web designers often forget to take accessibility into account when creating Web sites, and, in attempts to provide large amounts of content, they use fonts that are too small. Many user agents have addressed this problem by allowing the user to adjust the text size. Click the **View** menu and select **Text Size** to change the font size in pages rendered by IE6. By default, the text size is set to **Medium**.

This chapter presented a wide variety of technologies that help people with various disabilities use computers and the Internet. We hope that all our readers will join us in emphasizing the importance of these capabilities in their schools and workplaces.

22.16 Summary

In 1997, the World Wide Web Consortium (W3C) launched the Web Accessibility Initiative (WAI). The WAI is an attempt to make the Web more accessible; its mission is described at **www.w3.org/WAI**. One important WAI requirement is to ensure that every image, movie and sound on a Web site is accompanied by a description that clearly defines the item's purpose; the description is called an `<alt>` tag.

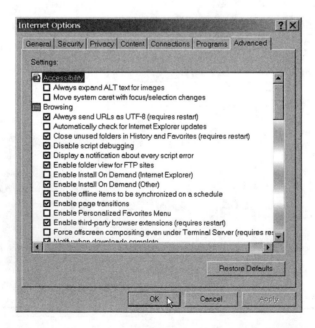

Fig. 22.44 Advanced accessibility settings in Microsoft Internet Explorer 6.

Accessibility refers to the level of usability of an application or Web site for people with disabilities. Total accessibility is difficult to achieve, because there are many different disabilities, language barriers, and hardware and software inconsistencies.

Specialized user agents, such as screen readers (programs that allow users to hear what is being displayed on their screen) and braille displays (devices that receive data from screen-reading software and output the data as braille), allow people with visual impairments to access text-based information that normally is displayed on the screen.

Web pages with large amounts of multimedia content are difficult for user agents to interpret unless they are designed properly. Images, movies and most non-XHTML objects cannot be read by screen readers.

When creating a Web page for the general public, it is important to consider the reading level at which it is written. Web site designers can make their sites more readable through the use of shorter words; some users may have difficulty understanding slang and other nontraditional language.

Web designers often use frames to display more than one XHTML file at a time. Unfortunately, frames often lack proper descriptions, which prevents users with text-based browsers and users with visual impairments from navigating the Web site.

VoiceXML has tremendous implications for people with visual impairments and for illiterate people. VoiceXML, a speech recognition and synthesis technology, reads Web pages to users and understands words spoken into a microphone.

CallXML, a language created and supported by Voxeo, creates phone-to-Web applications. These applications tailor themselves to the user's input.

Braille keyboards are similar to standard keyboards, except that in addition to having each key labeled with the letter it represents, braille keyboards have the equivalent braille symbol printed on the key. Most often, braille keyboards are combined with a speech synthesizer or a braille display, so that users are able to interact with the computer to verify that their typing is correct.

People with visual impairments are not the only beneficiaries of the effort being made to improve markup languages. Individuals with hearing impairments also have a great number of tools to help them interpret auditory information delivered over the Web.

People with hearing impairments will soon benefit from what is called Synchronized Multimedia Integration Language (SMIL). This markup language is designed to add extra tracks—layers of content found within a single audio or video file. The additional tracks can contain such data as closed captioning.

EagleEyes, developed by researchers at Boston College, is a system that translates eye movements into mouse movements. Users move the mouse cursor by moving their eyes or head and are thereby able to control the computer.

All of the accessibility options provided by Windows 2000 are available through the **Accessibility Wizard**. The **Accessibility Wizard** guides users step by step through all of the Windows accessibility features and configures their computer according to the chosen specifications.

22.17 Internet and Web Resources

There are many accessibility resources available on the Internet and World Wide Web; this section lists a variety of these resources.

General Information, Guidelines and Definitions

www.w3.org/WAI

The World Wide Web Consortium's *Web Accessibility Initiative (WAI)* site promotes the design of universally accessible Web sites. This site contains the current guidelines and forthcoming standards for Web accessibility.

www.w3.org/TR/xhtml1

The *XHTML 1.0 Recommendation* contains XHTML 1.0 general information, compatibility issues, document type definition information, definitions, terminology and much more.

www.abledata.com/text2/icg_hear.htm

This page contains a consumer guide that discusses technologies designed for people with hearing impairments.

www.washington.edu/doit

The University of Washington's DO-IT (Disabilities, Opportunities, Internetworking and Technology) site provides information and Web-development resources for the creation of universally accessible Web sites.

www.webable.com

The *WebABLE* site contains links to many disability-related Internet resources; the site is geared towards those developing technologies for people with disabilities.

www.webaim.org

The *WebAIM* site provides a number of tutorials, articles, simulations and other useful resources that demonstrate how to design accessible Web sites. The site provides a screen-reader simulation.

deafness.about.com/health/deafness/msubvib.htm

This site provides information on vibrotactile devices, which allow individuals with hearing impairments to experience audio in the form of vibrations.

Developing Accessible Applications with Existing Technologies

wdvl.com/Authoring/Languages/XML/XHTML

The Web Developers Virtual Library provides an introduction to XHTML. This site also contains articles, examples and links to other technologies.

www.w3.org/TR/1999/xhtml-modularization-19990406/DTD/doc

The XHTML 1.0 DTD documentation site provides links to DTD documentation for the strict, transitional and frameset document type definitions.

www.webreference.com/xml/reference/xhtml.html

This Web page contains a list of the frequently used XHTML tags, such as header tags, table tags, frame tags and form tags. It also provides a description of each tag.

www.w3.org/TR/REC-CSS2/aural.html

This site discusses Aural Style Sheets, outlining the purpose and uses of this new technology.

www.islandnet.com

Lynxit is a development tool that allows users to view any Web site as if they were using a text-only browser. The site's form allows you to enter a URL and returns the Web site in text-only format.

www.trill-home.com/lynx/public_lynx.html

This site allows users to browse the Web with a Lynx browser. Users can view how Web pages appear to users who are not using the most current technologies.

java.sun.com/products/java-media/speech/forDevelopers/JSML
This site outlines the specifications for JSML, Sun Microsystem's Java Speech Markup Language. This language, like VoiceXML, helps improve accessibility for people with visual impairments.

ocfo.ed.gov/coninfo/clibrary/software.htm
This is the U.S. Department of Education's Web site that outlines software accessibility requirements. The site helps developers produce accessible products.

www.speech.cs.cmu.edu/comp.speech/SpeechLinks.html
The *Speech Technology Hyperlinks* page has over 500 links to sites related to computer-based speech and speech-recognition tools.

www.islandnet.com/accessibility.html
This page provides a list of tips for creating accessible Web pages.

www.chantinc.com/technology
This page is the *Chant* Web site, which discusses speech technology and how it works. Chant also provides speech–synthesis and speech-recognition software.

www.searchWebServices.com
This site provides definitions and information about several topics, including CallXML. Its thorough definition of CallXML differentiates CallXML from VoiceXML, another technology developed by Voxeo. The site also contains links to other published articles that discuss CallXML.

www.oasis-open.org/cover/callxmlv2.html
This site provides a comprehensive list of the CallXML tags, complete with a description of each tag. The site also provides short examples on how to apply the tags in various applications.

www.freedomscientific.com
Henter-Joyce is a division of Freedom Scientific that provides software for people with visual impairments. It is the homepage of JAWS (Job Access with Sound).

www-3.ibm.com/able/
This is the homepage of IBM's accessibility site. It provides information on IBM products and their accessibility and discusses hardware, software and Web accessibility.

www.w3.org/TR/voice-tts-reqs
This page explains the speech-synthesis markup requirements for voice markup languages.

www.cast.org
CAST (Center for Applied Special Technology) offers software, including a valuable accessibility checker, that can help individuals with disabilities use computers. The accessibility checker is a Web-based program that validates the accessibility of Web sites.

www.cs.cornell.edu/home/raman/emacspeak/emacspeak.html
The site for Emacspeak, a screen interface that improves the quality of Internet access for individuals with visual disabilities.

Information on Disabilities

deafness.about.com/health/deafness/msubmenu6.htm
This is the home page of **deafness.about.com**. It provides a wealth of information on the history of hearing loss, the current state of medical developments and other resources related to these topics.

www.trainingpost.org/3-2-inst.htm
This site presents a tutorial on the Gunning Fog Index. The Gunning Fog Index is a method of grading text according to its readability.

**laurence.canlearn.ca/English/learn/accessibility2001/neads/
index.shtml**
INDIE stands for "Integrated Network of Disability Information and Education." This site is home to a search engine that helps users find information on disabilities.

www.wgbh.org/wgbh/pages/ncam/accesslinks.html
This page provides links to other accessibility pages across the Web.

23

Mobile Internet Toolkit

Objectives

- To become familiar with the Mobile Internet Toolkit (MIT).
- To be able to use ASP .NET and C# to create mobile Web content.
- To be able to use mobile Web controls.
- To create code-behind files.
- To create scripts for mobile Web forms.

It was ordained at the beginning of the world that certain signs should prefigure certain events.
Marcus Tullius Cicero

Oh, never mind the fashion. When one has a style of one's own, it is always twenty times better.
Margaret Oliphant

Outline

23.1 Introduction

Wireless technologies bring the power of communications and the Internet to users worldwide. Wireless communications affect many aspects of society, including business management and operations, employee productivity, consumer purchasing behavior, marketing strategies and personal communications. In addition to Web applications and Windows applications, programmers must develop for wireless platforms.

In this chapter, we introduce the Microsoft® *Mobile Internet Toolkit (MIT)*,[1] which allows programmers to create mobile Web applications. The MIT extends Visual Studio .NET's functionality and uses the .NET Framework to create Web content for mobile devices using languages such as C# and Visual Basic .NET. In this chapter, we show how to use Visual Studio .NET and the functionality provided by the MIT to create simple applications for mobile devices.

23.2 Mobile Internet Toolkit Client Devices

In 1997, the *Wireless Application Protocol (WAP)* was developed by dominant cell-phone manufacturers Nokia, Ericsson, Motorola and others to facilitate the introduction and standardization of wireless Internet access.[2] WAP is a set of communications protocols that are designed to enable wireless devices to access the Internet.

The *Wireless Markup Language (WML)*, which is an XML vocabulary, is the markup language used to describe content for WAP devices. *Microbrowsers*, browsers designed with limited bandwidth and memory requirements, can access the Web via the wireless Internet. WAP supports WML to deliver the content.

Although WAP and WML have many proponents, they also have many opponents. WAP technology is viewed as a short-term solution for the delivery of wireless Internet access. WAP opponents cite various disadvantages that are associated with the protocol, including possible security breaches, limited bandwidth and unreliability.[3] Another disadvantage cited is that the WAP standard has been implemented only loosely for the various WAP microbrowsers on the market. This means that various microbrowsers may only support a subset of WML tags and thus limited functionality.

---

1. Setup instructions for the Mobile Internet Toolkit 5.0, Microsoft Mobile Explorer (MME) 3.0 and Pocket PC 2002 can be downloaded from the **Downloads/Resources** page at **deitel.com**.
2. T. Hughes, "The Web Unwired," *Global Technology Business* December 1999: 33.
3. Further information about WAP can be found at the WAP Forum Web site, **www.wapforum.org**.

Portability Tip 23.1

Different WAP microbrowsers can have inconsistent WML implementations. This makes it difficult to use WML uniformly across a wide variety of WAP microbrowsers.

The fast pace at which the wireless community is growing has let to the development of other standards, some of which will be discussed shortly. Multiple standards have created a significant challenge for wireless developers. In a world of clients attempting to communicate over the disparate technologies, it is a difficult task to build one application that will run correctly on a variety of wireless devices. This chapter introduces the MIT and it helps developers handle disparate mobile devices uniformly. Before we begin our discussion of the MIT's features, let us briefly overview the types of devices that can be targeted by the Mobile Internet Toolkit.

The MIT supports three main clients—*HTML devices*, *WAP* (*Wireless Application Protocol*) *devices* and *iMode devices*. HTML devices are those that display HTML markup, such as Internet Explorer, Pocket PC and Palm-based browses. WAP devices are those that support *WAP microbrowsers*, which render WML markup. WAP devices can include mobile phones equipped with Nokia or Openwave WAP microbrowsers.

The relationship between WAP browsers and WML is similar to that of Internet Explorer (IE) and HTML. WML's design fits the needs of small devices with low memory capabilities and limited display screens.

Finally, iMode devices are those that support *cHTML* (*compact HyperText Markup Language*) *content*. cHTML conforms to a subset of the HTML 2.0 specification. Unlike HTML, cHTML does not support image maps, tables, frames or JPEG images. cHTML uses a smaller set of tags than that of HTML and supports fewer character fonts and styles. cHTML pages cannot have a background color or image. Style sheets (e.g., CSS) and scripts (e.g., JavaScript) cannot be used with cHTML.

When learning about mobile communications, it is vital to understand that the process by which mobile devices connect to and interact with the Internet is different for each application type. For example, WAP applications communicate with a WAP gateway using WAP, and the WAP gateway communicates with a Web server via HTTP; whereas iMode applications communicate with a Web server directly via HTTP. The MIT eliminates the burden of understanding the various protocols and languages. Rather then creating WML markup for WAP devices, cHTML markup for iMode devices and HTML markup for HTML devices, the developer can now create one application that produces the proper markup needed for disparate devices. For a list of mobile devices supported by the MIT, visit **msdn.microsoft.com/vstudio/device/mitdevices.asp**.

23.3 Mobile Internet Toolkit and Mobile Web Forms

The MIT extends ASP .NET (Chapter 17) functionality to include mobile clients. When an ASPX page is requested by the *incoming device* (i.e., the mobile device), the MIT generates HTML for IE 6.0 and Pocket IE, cHTML for iMode clients, and WML for WAP clients.

Creating a mobile Web application in Visual Studio .NET generates an ASPX page (with the **.aspx** file extension), which contains the markup for the page's user interface. The business logic (e.g., event handlers for buttons) for the application can be embedded in the ASPX file as a script or in a code-behind file. The business logic is executed on the Web server. In this chapter, we use both methods of code containment.

Software Engineering Observation 23.1

Most developers use a code-behind file, especially when an application contains significant amounts of code. Using a code-behind file makes programs easier to maintain, debug and modify because the interface is separated from the implementation.

In this section, we present two mobile Web applications and guide the reader through the steps necessary to create the applications. Figure 23.1 displays the **Welcome.aspx** Web page. The markup in this example is generated by Visual Studio .NET when the user interface is created in design view. Lines 6–7 use the ***Page*** directive to set the language in which the code-behind file is written to C# (***Language*** attribute) and set the code-behind file as **Welcome.aspx.cs** (**CodeBehind** attribute). We discuss this code-behind file momentarily. Attribute ***Inherits*** indicates the class from which this page inherits. In this example, we are inheriting from the class **Welcome.WelcomePage**, defined in the code-behind file.

The ***Register*** directive (lines 9–11) specifies the namespace and assembly to which this mobile Web Form's controls belong and the *tag prefix*, which qualifies the mobile control tag names. The tag prefix is assigned to the ***TagPrefix*** attribute. The default value for this attribute is **mobile**. Setting the ***Namespace*** attribute (line 10) to **System.Web.UI.MobileControls** indicates that any control with the prefix **mobile** is defined in the namespace **System.Web.UI.MobileControls**. The ***Assembly*** attribute's value (***System.Web.Mobile***) specifies the library file where the mobile FCL classes are located.

```
1    <%-- Fig. 23.1: Welcome.aspx --%>
2    <%-- A simple Web Form.        --%>
3
4    <%-- directive specifies file where code is stored and --%>
5    <%-- programming language in which the code is written --%>
6    <%@ Page language="c#" Codebehind="Welcome.aspx.cs"
7        Inherits="Welcome.WelcomePage" AutoEventWireup="false" %>
8
9    <%@ Register TagPrefix="mobile"
10       Namespace="System.Web.UI.MobileControls"
11       Assembly="System.Web.Mobile, Version=1.0.3300.0,
Culture=neutral, PublicKeyToken=b03f5f7f11d50a3a" %>
12
13   <meta name="GENERATOR" content="Microsoft Visual Studio 7.0">
14   <meta name="CODE_LANGUAGE" content="C#">
15   <meta name="vs_targetSchema"
16       content="http://schemas.microsoft.com/Mobile/Page">
17
18   <body Xmlns:mobile="http://schemas.microsoft.com/Mobile/WebForm">
19
20       <mobile:Form id="startForm" runat="server">
21
22           <mobile:Label id="startLabel" runat="server">
23               Click Start!
24           </mobile:Label>
25
```

Fig. 23.1   Multiple forms in a mobile Web Form page. (Part 1 of 2.)

```
26          <%-- Command control --%>
27          <%-- invokes method startCommand_Click when clicked --%>
28          <mobile:Command id="startCommand" runat="server">
29             Start
30          </mobile:Command>
31       </mobile:Form>
32
33       <%-- Form resultForm --%>
34       <%-- when activated, method resultForm_Activate is called --%>
35       <mobile:Form id="resultForm" runat="server">
36          <mobile:Label id="resultLabel" runat="server"></mobile:Label>
37       </mobile:Form>
38
39    </body>
```

Fig. 23.1   Multiple forms in a mobile Web Form page. (Part 2 of 2.)

The **Body** element (lines 18–39) of the ASPX page encapsulates all the forms and their controls used in the application. The **Body** element used in MIT markup is similar to the HTML element introduced in Chapter 17, ASP .NET, Web Forms and Web Controls.

Mobile Web form controls (or *mobile controls*) are the objects used to create mobile applications. Some basic mobile controls include labels and buttons. Every mobile control's start tag has its *runat* attribute set to **"server"** to indicate that the control must be executed on the server. Lines 20–31 define the first mobile control, a **Form**, which is used to create a mobile Web Form. The *id* attribute's value (line 20) provides a programmatic identifier for the control. In this case, we chose the identifier **startForm**, because this is the initial form that is displayed to mobile clients. Programmers can assign almost any value to the **id** attribute, provided that it is a valid C# identifier. Programmers can access and manipulate this control in their code-behind files using the identifier **startForm**.

This form contains a *Label* control and a *Command* control. Like Web Form **Label** controls, mobile **Label** controls display textual information. Setting the **Label**'s **Text** property to **Click Start!** in design view creates a **Label** control in the markup, such as

```
<mobile:Label id="startLabel" runat="server">
   Click Start!
</mobile:Label>
```

In design view, **Command** controls look like buttons. However, some mobile browsers, such as the Openwave™ 5.0 browser, render **Command** controls as hyperlinks. When a **Command** control is clicked, method **startCommand_Click** is called to handle the **Click** event. This method is defined in the code-behind file (discussed in Fig. 23.2). Notice that, in the output of Fig. 23.2, the **Command** control appears below the **Label** control. By default, controls are placed below each other on the form. We discuss how to change this grouping later in this chapter. Screen size is limited on most mobile devices; therefore, content usually is divided into multiple forms, which reduces the user's need to scroll a page. On lines 36–38 of Fig. 23.1, the second form is provided, which is the equivalent of another Web page. When the form becomes *active* (i.e., is being displayed), the form is displayed and the code-behind file's **resultForm_Activate** method is called. [*Note*: The form being displayed is called the *active form*. Only one form can be active at a time.]

Common Programming Error 23.1

Web Form pages must contain a minimum of one form. A page with no forms results in a compilation error.

On line 18 of **Welcome.aspx.cs** (Fig. 23.2), we add a reference to namespace ***System.Web.UI.MobileControls*** that includes base class ***MobilePage***. This class is required for mobile Web forms. Class **WelcomePage** begins on line 27 and is the base class specified on line 7 in Fig. 23.1. On lines 46–52, we define method **startCommand_Click** that handles the **Click** event raised when the user presses the **Start** button. Line 50 sets the active form. Forms must be activated in this manner because ASPX files can contain multiple forms. Only one form can be active at a time. Method **resultForm_Activate** (lines 55–62) sets **resultLabel**'s **Text** property of label to a welcome message (lines 59–60). In this example, the text displayed by **result-Label** is set to **"Welcome to the Microsoft Mobile Internet Toolkit!"**.

The Microsoft Mobile Explorer is a phone emulator that includes two *soft keys* (labeled in Fig. 23.2). These keys allow users to interact with the application. For example, the first output window in Fig. 23.2 shows the **Start** button highlighted with a label above the left soft key, **OK**. Pressing the left soft key selects (i.e., presses) the **Start** button. The *scroll keys* allow users to scroll through Web pages.

```
1   // Fig. 23.2: Welcome.aspx.cs
2   // Code-behind file for Welcome.aspx.
3
4   using System;
5   using System.Collections;
6   using System.ComponentModel;
7   using System.Data;
8   using System.Drawing;
9
10  // contains classes that manage client requests and
11  // server responses
12  using System.Web;
13  using System.Web.Mobile;
14  using System.Web.SessionState;
15
16  // definitions for graphical controls used in Web Forms
17  using System.Web.UI;
18  using System.Web.UI.MobileControls;
19  using System.Web.UI.WebControls;
20  using System.Web.UI.HtmlControls;
21
22  namespace Welcome
23  {
24     public class WelcomePage :
25        System.Web.UI.MobileControls.MobilePage
26     {
27        // forms
28        protected System.Web.UI.MobileControls.Form startForm;
```

Fig. 23.2 Code-behind file for a mobile application that displays a welcome message. (Part 1 of 3.)

```
29           protected System.Web.UI.MobileControls.Form resultForm;
30
31       // labels
32       protected System.Web.UI.MobileControls.Label startLabel;
33       protected System.Web.UI.MobileControls.Label resultLabel;
34
35       // button
36       protected System.Web.UI.MobileControls.Command startCommand;
37
38       private void Page_Load( object sender, System.EventArgs e )
39       {
40          // Put user code to initialize the page here
41       }
42
43       // Visual Studio .NET generated code
44
45       // sets resultForm to be active form when Start is clicked
46       private void startCommand_Click(
47          object sender, System.EventArgs e )
48       {
49          // change current form to resultForm
50          ActiveForm = resultForm;
51
52       } // end startCommand_Click
53
54       // displays text when resultForm becomes active
55       private void resultForm_Activate(
56          object sender, System.EventArgs e )
57       {
58          // set value to be displayed
59          resultLabel.Text =
60             "Welcome to the Microsoft Mobile Internet Toolkit!";
61
62       } // end resultForm_Activate
63
64    } // end class WelcomePage
65
66  } // end namespace Welcome
```

Fig. 23.2   Code-behind file for a mobile application that displays a welcome message. (Part 2 of 3.)

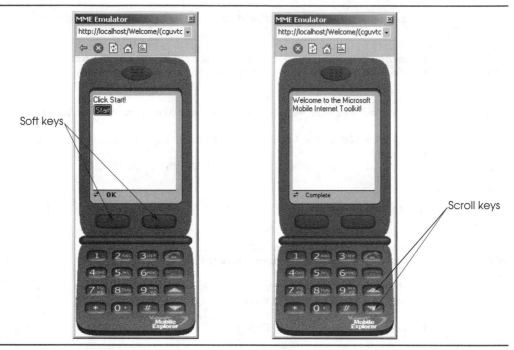

Fig. 23.2   Code-behind file for a mobile application that displays a welcome message. (Part 3 of 3.)

Now that we have presented the ASPX file and the code-behind file,[4] we outline the process by which we created this application. To create the application, perform the following steps:[5]

1. *Create the project.* Open Visual Studio .NET, and select **File > New > Project...** to display the **New Project** dialog (Fig. 23.3). In this dialog, select **Visual C# Projects** in the left pane and then *Mobile Web Application* in the right pane. Notice that the field for the project name is disabled (i.e., grayed out). Rather than using this field, we specify the name and location of the project in the **Location** field. We want our project to be located in **http://localhost**, which is the URL for IIS' root directory (typically **C:\InetPub\wwwroot**). The name *localhost* indicates that the client and server reside on the same machine. If the Web server were located on a different machine, **localhost** would be replaced with the appropriate IP address or hostname. By default, Visual Studio .NET assigns the project name **MobileWebApplication1**, which we change to **Welcome**. Below the **Location** textbox, the text **Project will be created at http://localhost/Welcome** appears. This indicates that the project's folder is located in the

---

4. To run the chapter examples provided at **www.deitel.com**, you must create a virtual directory in IIS. For instructions on how to create a virtual directory, visit the **Downloads/Resources** link at **www.deitel.com**.
5. IIS must be running for this project to be created successfully. IIS can be started by executing **inetmgr.exe**, right-clicking **Default Web Site** and selecting **Start**. You might need to expand the node representing your computer to display the **Default Web Site**.

root directory on the Web server. Clicking **OK** creates the project and creates a virtual directory, which is linked to the project folder. The ***Create New Web*** dialog is displayed next, while Visual Studio .NET is creating the Web site on the server (Fig. 23.4).

2. *Examine the newly created project.* The next several figures describe the new project's content; we begin with the **Solution Explorer** shown in Fig. 23.5. Visual Studio .NET generates several files when a new **Mobile Web Application** project is created. **MobileWebForm1.aspx** is the mobile Web Form, which includes a code-behind file. To view the ASPX file's code-behind file, right click the ASPX file, and select **View Code**. Alternatively, the programmer can click the icon to display all files, then expand the node for the ASPX page as shown in Fig. 23.5.

Figure 23.6 shows the Mobile Web Form Designer for **MobileWebForm1.aspx**. It consists of a form on which programmers drag and drop controls, such as buttons and labels, from the **Toolbox**.

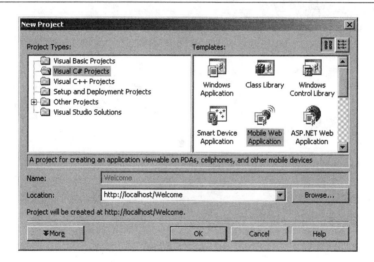

Fig. 23.3   Creating a **Mobile Web Application** in Visual Studio .NET.

Fig. 23.4   Visual Studio .NET creating and linking a virtual directory for the **Welcome** project folder.

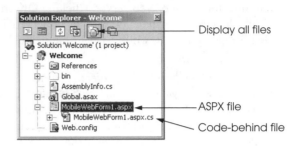

Fig. 23.5   **Solution Explorer** window for project **Welcome**.

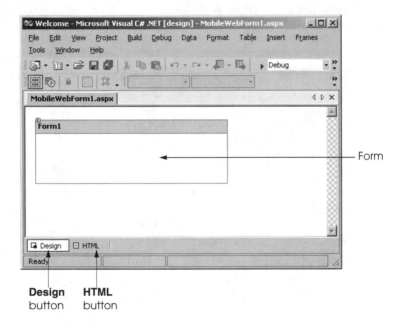

Fig. 23.6   **Design** mode of the Mobile Web Form Designer.

Figure 23.7 shows the Mobile Web Form Designer in *HTML mode*, which allows the programmer to view the markup that represents the user interface shown in *design mode*. A developer can switch to HTML mode by clicking the **HTML** *button* in the lower-left corner of the Mobile Web Form Designer. Similarly, clicking the **Design** button (to the left of the **HTML** button) returns the Mobile Web Form Designer to design mode.

The next figure (Fig. 23.8) displays **MobileWebForm1.aspx.cs**—the code-behind file for **MobileWebForm1.aspx**. Recall that Visual Studio .NET generates this code-behind file when the project is created; we have reformatted the file's contents for presentation purposes.

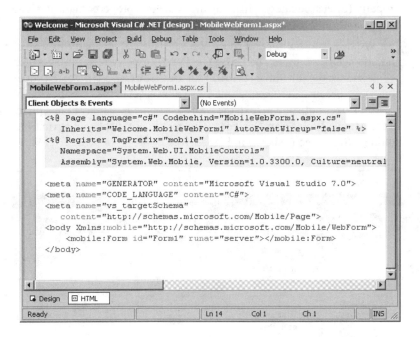

Fig. 23.7 HTML mode of Mobile Web Form Designer.

3. *Rename the ASPX file.* We have displayed the contents of the default ASPX and code-behind files. We now rename these files. Right click the ASPX file in the **Solution Explorer**, and select **Rename**. Enter the new file name, and press *Enter*. This updates the name of both the ASPX file and the code-behind file. In this example, we use the name **Welcome.aspx**.

4. *Design the page.* The process of designing a mobile Web Form is the same as designing a Web Form. To add mobile controls to the page, drag and drop them from the **Toolbox** onto the mobile Web Form. Like the mobile Web Form itself, each control is an object that has properties, methods and events. Programmers can set these properties and events using the **Properties** window. To view the properties of the mobile Web Form, select *Document* from the drop-down list in the **Properties** window.

Figure 23.9 shows the **Mobile Web Forms** controls listed in the **Toolbox**. The left figure displays the beginning of the mobile Web controls list, and the right figure displays the remaining mobile Web controls. Many of these controls are similar to the Windows controls and Web controls presented earlier in the book.

We set the form's **(ID)** property to **startForm**. We then add a **Label** control and a **Command** control to the form. We set the **Label**'s **(ID)** property to **startLabel** and its **Text** property to **Click Start!**. Notice that the **Command** control appears below the **Label** control. In the Mobile Web Form Designer, each control is placed one on top of the other. Changing how the form is rendered by a client can be altered using properties such as the **BreakAfter** property (discussed later). Changing the value of a property in the designer changes that controls corresponding markup in the ASPX document.]

We now add the second form. We set its **(ID)** property to **resultForm** and add a **Label** to it. The **Label**'s **(ID)** property is set to **resultLabel**. We delete the default value (**Label**) for **resultLabel**'s **Text** property in design view, because the **Text** property's value is set in the code-behind file. When a **Label** does not contain text, the **Label**'s name is displayed in square brackets in the Mobile Web Form Designer. This text is not displayed at runtime. The resulting ASPX page is shown in Fig. 23.10.

Fig. 23.8 Code-behind file for **MobileWebForm1.aspx** generated by Visual Studio .NET.

Fig. 23.9 **Mobile Web Forms** group in the **Toolbox**.

Labels   Web Form

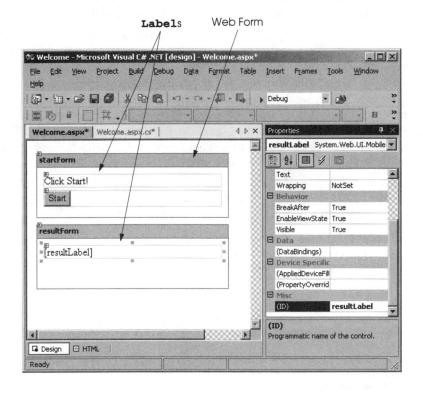

Fig. 23.10 **Welcome.aspx** after adding two **Label**s and setting their properties.

5. *Add page logic.* Once the user interface has been designed, C# code must be added to the code-behind file. In this example, lines 46–62 of Fig. 23.2 are added to the code-behind file. When the command button in **startForm** is clicked, method

startCommand_Click (lines 46–52) is called to handle the **Click** event. The statement within this method sets **resultForm** as the active form. When **resultForm** becomes the active form, the method **resultForm_Activate** (lines 55–62) is called. This method sets and displays the contents of **resultLabel**.

6. *Run the program*[6]. Select **Build > Build Solution** to build the solution. Next, select **File > Browse With...**. From the list of browsers on the left side of the dialog, select *Microsoft Mobile Explorer Emulator*, and click **Browse**. The Mobile Explorer window opens and loads the Web page (the ASPX file). Notice that the URL is **http://localhost/Welcome/Welcome.aspx** (Fig. 23.2), indicating that our ASPX file is located within the directory **Welcome**.

After the mobile Web Form is created, the programmer can view it by opening the Mobile Explorer Emulator outside Visual Studio .NET and typing the Web page's URL in the emulator's combo box. When testing an ASP .NET application on the same computer, type **http://localhost/***ProjectFolder***/***PageName***.aspx**, where *ProjectFolder* is the folder in which the page resides (usually the name of the project) and *PageName* is the name of the ASP .NET page.

In the next example (Fig. 23.11), we create a tip calculator, which calculates a tip amount based on the total amount of a meal and the tip percentage. We also demonstrate how to embed a C# script in an ASPX file. The script begins with a *<script>* tag on line 18, wherein we specify the language (using the *language* attribute) that is used in the script. On lines 21–38, we define method **calculateCommand_Click**, which calculates the tip amount based on the amount and tip percentage information entered by the user. This method is called when the user clicks the **Calculate Tip** button. Users enter information into two **TextBox** controls (lines 61–62 and 75–76). [Note: For simplicity, we do not check the user input for numeric values.]

```
1   <%-- Fig. 23.11: TipCalculator.aspx   --%>
2   <%-- A Web Form that calculates tips. --%>
3
4   <%@ Page language="c#" Codebehind="TipCalculator.aspx.cs"
5       Inherits="TipCalculator.TipCalulator"
6       AutoEventWireup="false" %>
7
8   <%@ Register TagPrefix="mobile"
9       Namespace="System.Web.UI.MobileControls"
10      Assembly="System.Web.Mobile, Version=1.0.3300.0,
Culture=neutral, PublicKeyToken=b03f5f7f11d50a3a" %>
11
12  <meta name="GENERATOR" content="Microsoft Visual Studio 7.0">
13  <meta name="CODE_LANGUAGE" content="C#">
14  <meta name="vs_targetSchema"
15      content="http://schemas.microsoft.com/Mobile/Page">
```

Fig. 23.11 Web Form with embedded C# code. (Part 1 of 4.) (Image courtesy Openwave Systems, Inc.)

6. Before performing this step, the MME must be installed.

```
16
17    <%-- embedded script containing C# code --%>
18    <script runat="server" language="C#">
19
20       // calculate tip
21       protected void calculateCommand_Click(
22          object sender, System.EventArgs e )
23       {
24          if ( Page.IsValid )
25          {
26             decimal tip;
27             string dollarAmount;
28
29             tip = Decimal.Parse( totalTextBox.Text ) *
30                Decimal.Parse( tipTextBox.Text ) /
31                ( decimal ) 100;
32
33             // change tip to dollar value
34             dollarAmount = String.Format( "{0:C}", tip );
35             resultLabel.Text = "Tip Amount: " + dollarAmount;
36          }
37
38       } // end calculateCommand_Click
39
40       // clear form
41       protected void clearCommand_Click(
42          object sender, System.EventArgs e )
43       {
44          tipTextBox.Text = "";
45          totalTextBox.Text = "";
46          resultLabel.Text = "";
47
48       } // end clearCommand_Click
49
50    </script>
51
52    <body Xmlns:mobile="http://schemas.microsoft.com/Mobile/WebForm">
53
54       <mobile:Form id="tipCalculatorForm" runat="server">
55
56          <mobile:Label id="instructionLabel1" runat="server"
57             BreakAfter="False">
58             Enter Tip Percentage:
59          </mobile:Label>
60
61          <mobile:TextBox id="tipTextBox" runat="server">
62          </mobile:TextBox>
63
64          <mobile:RequiredFieldValidator id="tipValidator"
65             runat="server" ControlToValidate="tipTextBox"
66             ErrorMessage="RequiredFieldValidator">
67             Please enter the tip percentage
```

Fig. 23.11 Web Form with embedded C# code. (Part 2 of 4.) (Image courtesy Openwave Systems, Inc.)

```
68           </mobile:RequiredFieldValidator>
69
70           <mobile:Label id="instructionLabel2" runat="server"
71              BreakAfter="False">
72              Enter Total Amount:
73           </mobile:Label>
74
75           <mobile:TextBox id="totalTextBox" runat="server">
76           </mobile:TextBox>
77
78           <mobile:RequiredFieldValidator id="totalValidator"
79              runat="server" ControlToValidate="totalTextBox"
80              ErrorMessage="RequiredFieldValidator">
81              Please enter the total amount
82           </mobile:RequiredFieldValidator>
83
84           <mobile:Label id="resultLabel" runat="server">
85           </mobile:Label>
86
87           <mobile:Command id="calculateCommand"
88              OnClick="calculateCommand_Click" runat="server"
89              BreakAfter="False">
90              Calculate Tip
91           </mobile:Command>
92
93           <mobile:Command id="clearCommand" runat="server"
94              OnClick="clearCommand_Click">
95              Clear
96           </mobile:Command>
97
98       </mobile:Form> <%-- end form tipCalculatorForm --%>
99
100  </body>
```

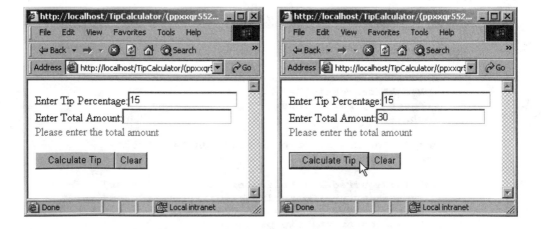

Fig. 23.11 Web Form with embedded C# code. (Part 3 of 4.) (Image courtesy Openwave Systems, Inc.)

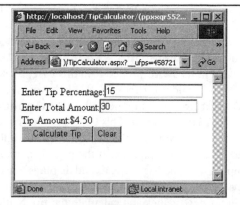

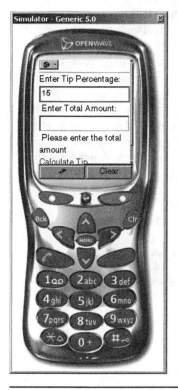

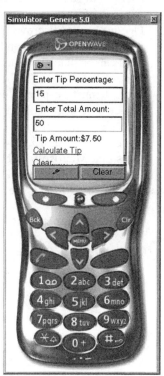

Fig. 23.11 Web Form with embedded C# code. (Part 4 of 4.) (Image courtesy Openwave Systems, Inc.)

Below each **TextBox** control, we included a *validation control*. Validation controls examine user input. If users enter incorrect information, such as an invalid phone number, most Web designers will not want their page to proceed because the user has not provided information in the proper format. In this example, we use the **RequiredFieldValidator** control, which ensures that another control contains data when users attempt to submit the page. In this example, the two **TextBox**es are required to have data because both the tip percentage and the total amount are required to perform the calculation. The first of these validation controls (**tipValidator**) is defined on lines 64–68. The ***ControlToValidate*** attribute (line 65) specifies which control is validated. In this case, our validator is set to validate the **TextBox** named **tipTextBox**. If this **TextBox** is empty when the user clicks **Calculate Tip**, the **RequiredFieldValidator** displays the error message specified in its **Text** property (in this case, **Please enter the tip percentage**). The second validator (lines 78–82) behaves in a similar manner, but is used to validate **totalTextBox**. Calling method **calculateCommand_Click** tests the condition **Page.IsValid** on line 24. This condition determines whether the page is *valid* (i.e., no errors were raised by the validators). If valid, the remainder of **calculateCommand_Click** will execute. If the page is not valid (i.e., one or both of the **TextBox**es are empty), then the page reloads and displays one or more error messages.

Once **calculateCommand_Click** calculates the tip amount and displays it, the user has the ability to enter new values and calculate the tip. Notice, however, that there are some differences between the way this program renders on the IE browser and on the Openwave WAP browser. For example, the **TextBox**es are displayed next to their respective labels in IE and the Openwave browser displays them on separate lines. Controls can be placed on the same line by setting the ***BreakAfter*** *property* for a **Label** control to **False**. The MIT determines if the control can fit on the same line, or if the control must be placed on the next line, by checking the device's screen size. Each device's screen size and other device-specific information, such as support for color graphics or the ability to initiate a phone call, are stored in the **machine.config** file. For example, Fig. 23.12 shows a section of the **machine.config** file that lists the features that Microsoft Mobile Explorer supports. The markup in Fig 23.12 indicates that the MME supports HTML markup (line 6) and GIF images (line 7). The **machine.config** file is located in the

C:\WINDOWS\Microsoft.NET\Framework\v1.0.3705\CONFIG

directory. [*Note*: The version number (i.e., **v1.0.3705**) is subject to change.]

```
1    <!-- HTML-oriented capabilities of the HTML MME browsers -->
2    <filter
3       match=".+"
4       with="${httpRequest}">
5       preferredRenderingType = "html32"
6       preferredRenderingMime = "text/html"
7       preferredImageMime = "image/gif"
8       supportsImageSubmit = "true"
9       supportsBold = "true"
10      supportsItalic = "true"
11      supportsFontSize = "true"
12      supportsFontName = "true"
13      supportsFontColor = "true"
14      supportsBodyColor = "true"
15      supportsDivAlign = "true"
16      supportsDivNoWrap = "false"
17   </filter>
```

Fig. 23.12 Section of **machine.config** file.

23.4 Summary

The Mobile Internet Toolkit (MIT) allows programmers to create mobile Web applications. The MIT extends the functionality of Visual Studio .NET and is a powerful tool that uses the .NET Framework to create Web content for mobile devices using languages such as C# and Visual Basic .NET.

The MIT supports three main clients—HTML devices, WAP (Wireless Application Protocol) devices and iMode devices. HTML devices are those that display HTML markup. WAP devices use WAP microbrowsers to render WML markup. WML is a markup language, designed for small devices with low memory capabilities and limited display screens. iMode devices render cHTML (compact HyperText Markup Language) content. cHTML is a subset of HTML 2.0.

The MIT can be used to create content specific to the incoming device, whether it be HTML for Internet Explorer 6.0 and Pocket IE, cHTML for iMode browsers or WML for WAP microbrowsers.

The business logic for the application (such as event handlers for buttons) can be embedded in the ASPX file as a script or in a code-behind file. Mobile Web applications can contain multiple forms, each representing a separate mobile Web page. The form that is being displayed is known as the active form. Only one form can be displayed at a time. When a form becomes active, the **Activate** event is raised.

The process of designing a mobile Web Form is the same as designing a non-mobile Web Form. To add mobile Web controls to the page, drag and drop them from the **Toolbox** onto the mobile Web Form. Like the mobile Web Form itself, each control is an object that has properties, methods and events. Programmers can set these properties and events using the **Properties** window. Changing the properties of a control will cause the markup in the ASPX page to be modified accordingly. Once the user interface has been designed, C# code must be added either to the code-behind file or to the script.

23.5 Internet and Web Resources

msdn.microsoft.com/vstudio/device/mitdevices.asp
This site lists the devices supported by the Mobile Internet Toolkit and the browser that is on each device.

msdn.microsoft.com/vstudio/nextgen/technology/mobilewebforms.asp
This site presents an online introduction to mobile Web Forms.

www.devx.com
This online information source does not yet contain information about the Mobile Internet Toolkit, but it does offer information on both wireless technology and .NET, including discussions, help and code.

www.csharphelp.com
This site covers several topics of C#, including a message board where programmers can post questions and receive answers.

Newsgroups

microsoft.public.dotnet.framework.aspnet.mobile
Questions and answers on several Mobile Internet Toolkit topics are posted on this Microsoft newsgroup. This newsgroup provides a way for all levels of programmers to communicate and learn from each other.

Operator Precedence Chart

Operators are shown in decreasing order of precedence from top to bottom with each level of precedence separated by a horizontal line.[1]

Operator	Type	Associativity
.	member access	left-to-right
( )	parenthesized expression	
[ ]	element access	
++	post increment	
--	post decrement	
new	object creation	
typeof	typeof	
checked	checked	
unchecked	unchecked	
+	unary plus	left-to-right
-	unary minus	
!	unary	
~	unary	
++	pre-increment	
--	pre-decrement	

Fig. A.1   Operator precedence chart. (Part 1 of 2.)

---

1. This operator-precedence chart is based on Section 7.2.1, *Operator precedence and associativity*, of the C# Language Specification (for more information, visit **msdn.microsoft.com/library/default.asp?url=/library/en-us/csspec/html/CSharpSpec-Start.asp**).

Operator	Type	Associativity
* / %	multiplication division modulus	left-to-right
+ -	addition subtraction	left-to-right
<< >>	shift left shift right	left-to-right
< > <= >= *is*	relational less than relational greater than relational less than or equal to relational greater than or equal to type comparison	left-to-right
== !=	relational is equal to relational is not equal to	left-to-right
&	logical AND	left-to-right
^	logical exclusive OR	left-to-right
|	logical inclusive OR	left-to-right
&&	conditional AND	left-to-right
||	conditional OR	left-to-right
?:	conditional	right-to-left
= *= /= += -= <<= >>= &= ^= |=	assignment multiplication assignment division assignment addition assignment subtraction assignment shift left assignment shift right assignment logical AND assignment logical exclusive OR assignment logical inclusive OR assignment	right-to-left

Fig. A.1   Operator precedence chart. (Part 2 of 2.)

Number Systems

Objectives

- To understand basic number system concepts such as base, positional value and symbol value.
- To understand how to work with numbers represented in the binary, octal and hexadecimal number systems
- To be able to abbreviate binary numbers as octal numbers or hexadecimal numbers.
- To be able to convert octal numbers and hexadecimal numbers to binary numbers.
- To be able to covert back and forth between decimal numbers and their binary, octal and hexadecimal equivalents.
- To understand binary arithmetic and how negative binary numbers are represented using two's complement notation.

Here are only numbers ratified.
William Shakespeare

Nature has some sort of arithmetic-geometrical coordinate system, because nature has all kinds of models. What we experience of nature is in models, and all of nature's models are so beautiful.

It struck me that nature's system must be a real beauty, because in chemistry we find that the associations are always in beautiful whole numbers—there are no fractions.
Richard Buckminster Fuller

Outline

B.1 Introduction

In this appendix, we introduce the key number systems that programmers use, especially when they are working on software projects that require close interaction with "machine-level" hardware. Projects like this include operating systems, computer networking software, compilers, database systems, and applications requiring high performance.

When we write an integer such as 227 or –63 in a program, the number is assumed to be in the *decimal (base 10) number system*. The *digits* in the decimal number system are 0, 1, 2, 3, 4, 5, 6, 7, 8, and 9. The lowest digit is 0 and the highest digit is 9—one less than the *base* of 10. Internally, computers use the *binary (base 2) number system*. The binary number system has only two digits, namely 0 and 1. Its lowest digit is 0 and its highest digit is 1—one less than the base of 2. Fig. B.1 summarizes the digits used in the binary, octal, decimal and hexadecimal number systems.

As we will see, binary numbers tend to be much longer than their decimal equivalents. Programmers who work in assembly languages and in high-level languages that enable programmers to reach down to the "machine level," find it cumbersome to work with binary numbers. So two other number systems the *octal number system (base 8)* and the *hexadecimal number system (base 16)*—are popular primarily because they make it convenient to abbreviate binary numbers.

In the octal number system, the digits range from 0 to 7. Because both the binary number system and the octal number system have fewer digits than the decimal number system, their digits are the same as the corresponding digits in decimal.

The hexadecimal number system poses a problem because it requires sixteen digits—a lowest digit of 0 and a highest digit with a value equivalent to decimal 15 (one less than the base of 16). By convention, we use the letters A through F to represent the hexadecimal digits corresponding to decimal values 10 through 15. Thus in hexadecimal we can have numbers like 876 consisting solely of decimal-like digits, numbers like 8A55F consisting of digits and letters, and numbers like FFE consisting solely of letters. Occasionally, a hexadecimal number spells a common word such as FACE or FEED—this can appear strange to programmers accustomed to working with numbers. Fig. B.2 summarizes each of the number systems.

Each of these number systems uses positional notation—each position in which a digit is written has a different positional value. For example, in the decimal number 937 (the 9, the 3, and the 7 are referred to as symbol values), we say that the 7 is written in the ones position, the 3 is written in the tens position, and the 9 is written in the hundreds position. Notice that each of these positions is a power of the base (base 10), and that these powers begin at 0 and increase by 1 as we move left in the number (Fig. B.3).

For longer decimal numbers, the next positions to the left would be the thousands position (10 to the 3rd power), the ten-thousands position (10 to the 4th power), the hundred-thousands position (10 to the 5th power), the millions position (10 to the 6th power), the ten-millions position (10 to the 7th power) and so on.

In the binary number 101, we say that the rightmost 1 is written in the ones position, the 0 is written in the twos position, and the leftmost 1 is written in the fours position. Notice that each of these positions is a power of the base (base 2), and that these powers begin at 0 and increase by 1 as we move left in the number (Fig. B.4).

For longer binary numbers, the next positions to the left would be the eights position (2 to the 3rd power), the sixteens position (2 to the 4th power), the thirty-twos position (2 to the 5th power), the sixty-fours position (2 to the 6th power), and so on.

In the octal number 425, we say that the 5 is written in the ones position, the 2 is written in the eights position, and the 4 is written in the sixty-fours position. Notice that each of these positions is a power of the base (base 8), and that these powers begin at 0 and increase by 1 as we move left in the number (Fig. B.5).

Binary digit	Octal digit	Decimal digit	Hexadecimal digit
0	0	0	0
1	1	1	1
	2	2	2
	3	3	3
	4	4	4
	5	5	5
	6	6	6
	7	7	7
		8	8
		9	9
			A (decimal value of 10)
			B (decimal value of 11)
			C (decimal value of 12)
			D (decimal value of 13)
			E (decimal value of 14)
			F (decimal value of 15)

Fig. B.1   Digits of the binary, octal, decimal and hexadecimal number systems.

Attribute	Binary	Octal	Decimal	Hexadecimal
Base	2	8	10	16
Lowest digit	0	0	0	0
Highest digit	1	7	9	F

Fig. B.2 Comparison of the binary, octal, decimal and hexadecimal number systems.

Positional values in the decimal number system			
Decimal digit	9	3	7
Position name	Hundreds	Tens	Ones
Positional value	100	10	1
Positional value as a power of the base (10)	10^2	10^1	10^0

Fig. B.3 Positional values in the decimal number system.

For longer octal numbers, the next positions to the left would be the five-hundred-and-twelves position (8 to the 3rd power), the four-thousand-and-ninety-sixes position (8 to the 4th power), the thirty-two-thousand-seven-hundred-and-sixty eights position (8 to the 5th power), and so on.

In the hexadecimal number 3DA, we say that the A is written in the ones position, the D is written in the sixteens position, and the 3 is written in the two-hundred-and-fifty-sixes position. Notice that each of these positions is a power of the base (base 16), and that these powers begin at 0 and increase by 1 as we move left in the number (Fig. B.6).

For longer hexadecimal numbers, the next positions to the left would be the four-thousand-and-ninety-sixes position (16 to the 3rd power), the sixty-five-thousand-five-hundred-and-thirty-six position (16 to the 4th power), and so on.

Positional values in the binary number system			
Binary digit	1	0	1
Position name	Fours	Twos	Ones
Positional value	4	2	1
Positional value as a power of the base (2)	2^2	2^1	2^0

Fig. B.4 Positional values in the binary number system.

Positional values in the octal number system			
Decimal digit	4	2	5
Position name	Sixty-fours	Eights	Ones
Positional value	64	8	1
Positional value as a power of the base (8)	8^2	8^1	8^0

Fig. B.5   Positional values in the octal number system.

Positional values in the hexadecimal number system			
Decimal digit	3	D	A
Position name	Two-hundred-and-fifty-sixes	Sixteens	Ones
Positional value	256	16	1
Positional value as a power of the base (16)	16^2	16^1	16^0

Fig. B.6   Positional values in the hexadecimal number system.

B.2 Abbreviating Binary Numbers as Octal Numbers and Hexadecimal Numbers

The main use for octal and hexadecimal numbers in computing is for abbreviating lengthy binary representations. Figure B.7 highlights the fact that lengthy binary numbers can be expressed concisely in number systems with higher bases than the binary number system.

Decimal number	Binary representation	Octal representation	Hexadecimal representation
0	0	0	0
1	1	1	1
2	10	2	2
3	11	3	3
4	100	4	4
5	101	5	5
6	110	6	6
7	111	7	7

Fig. B.7   Decimal, binary, octal, and hexadecimal equivalents. (Part 1 of 2.)

Decimal number	Binary representation	Octal representation	Hexadecimal representation
8	1000	10	8
9	1001	11	9
10	1010	12	A
11	1011	13	B
12	1100	14	C
13	1101	15	D
14	1110	16	E
15	1111	17	F
16	10000	20	10

Fig. B.7   Decimal, binary, octal, and hexadecimal equivalents. (Part 2 of 2.)

A particularly important relationship that both the octal number system and the hexadecimal number system have to the binary system is that the bases of octal and hexadecimal (8 and 16 respectively) are powers of the base of the binary number system (base 2). Consider the following 12-digit binary number and its octal and hexadecimal equivalents. See if you can determine how this relationship makes it convenient to abbreviate binary numbers in octal or hexadecimal. The answer follows the numbers.

Binary Number	Octal equivalent	Hexadecimal equivalent
100011010001	4321	8D1

To see how the binary number converts easily to octal, simply break the 12-digit binary number into groups of three consecutive bits each, and write those groups over the corresponding digits of the octal number as follows

100	011	010	001
4	3	2	1

Notice that the octal digit you have written under each group of thee bits corresponds precisely to the octal equivalent of that 3-digit binary number as shown in Fig. B.7.

The same kind of relationship may be observed in converting numbers from binary to hexadecimal. In particular, break the 12-digit binary number into groups of four consecutive bits each and write those groups over the corresponding digits of the hexadecimal number as follows

1000	1101	0001
8	D	1

Notice that the hexadecimal digit you wrote under each group of four bits corresponds precisely to the hexadecimal equivalent of that 4-digit binary number as shown in Fig. B.7.

B.3 Converting Octal Numbers and Hexadecimal Numbers to Binary Numbers

In the previous section, we saw how to convert binary numbers to their octal and hexadecimal equivalents by forming groups of binary digits and simply rewriting these groups as their equivalent octal digit values or hexadecimal digit values. This process may be used in reverse to produce the binary equivalent of a given octal or hexadecimal number.

For example, the octal number 653 is converted to binary simply by writing the 6 as its 3-digit binary equivalent 110, the 5 as its 3-digit binary equivalent 101, and the 3 as its 3-digit binary equivalent 011 to form the 9-digit binary number 110101011.

The hexadecimal number FAD5 is converted to binary simply by writing the F as its 4-digit binary equivalent 1111, the A as its 4-digit binary equivalent 1010, the D as its 4-digit binary equivalent 1101, and the 5 as its 4-digit binary equivalent 0101 to form the 16-digit 1111101011010101.

B.4 Converting from Binary, Octal or Hexadecimal to Decimal

Because we are accustomed to working in decimal, it is often convenient to convert a binary, octal, or hexadecimal number to decimal to get a sense of what the number is "really" worth. Our diagrams in Section B.1 express the positional values in decimal. To convert a number to decimal from another base, multiply the decimal equivalent of each digit by its positional value, and sum these products. For example, the binary number 110101 is converted to decimal 53 as shown in Fig. B.8.

To convert octal 7614 to decimal 3980, we use the same technique, this time using appropriate octal positional values as shown in Fig. B.9.

Converting a binary number to decimal					
Positional values:	32	16	8	4	2	1
Symbol values:	1	1	0	1	0	1
Products:	1*32=32	1*16=16	0*8=0	1*4=4	0*2=0	1*1=1
Sum:	= 32 + 16 + 0 + 4 + 0 + 1 = 53					

Fig. B.8   Converting a binary number to decimal.

Converting an octal number to decimal			
Positional values:	512	64	8	1
Symbol values:	7	6	1	4
Products	7*512=3584	6*64=384	1*8=8	4*1=4
Sum:	= 3584 + 384 + 8 + 4 = 3980			

Fig. B.9   Converting an octal number to decimal.

To convert hexadecimal AD3B to decimal 44347, we use the same technique, this time using appropriate hexadecimal positional values as shown in Fig. B.10.

B.5 Converting from Decimal to Binary, Octal or Hexadecimal

The conversions of the previous section follow naturally from the positional notation conventions. Converting from decimal to binary, octal or hexadecimal also follows these conventions.

Suppose we wish to convert decimal 57 to binary. We begin by writing the positional values of the columns right to left until we reach a column whose positional value is greater than the decimal number. We do not need that column, so we discard it. Thus, we first write:

Positional values:**6432168421**

Then we discard the column with positional value 64 leaving:

Positional values:**321684 2 1**

Next we work from the leftmost column to the right. We divide 32 into 57 and observe that there is one 32 in 57 with a remainder of 25, so we write 1 in the 32 column. We divide 16 into 25 and observe that there is one 16 in 25 with a remainder of 9 and write 1 in the 16 column. We divide 8 into 9 and observe that there is one 8 in 9 with a remainder of 1. The next two columns each produce quotients of zero when their positional values are divided into 1 so we write 0s in the 4 and 2 columns. Finally, 1 into 1 is 1 so we write 1 in the 1 column. This yields:

Positional values:**321684 2 1**
Symbol values:**11 1   0 0 1**

and thus decimal 57 is equivalent to binary 111001.

To convert decimal 103 to octal, we begin by writing the positional values of the columns until we reach a column whose positional value is greater than the decimal number. We do not need that column, so we discard it. Thus, we first write:

Positional values:**5126481**

Then we discard the column with positional value 512, yielding:

Positional values:**6481**

Converting a hexadecimal number to decimal			
Positional values:	4096	256	16	1
Symbol values:	A	D	3	B
Products	A*4096=40960	D*256=3328	3*16=48	B*1=11
Sum:	= 40960 + 3328 + 48 + 11 = 44347			

Fig. B.10   Converting a hexadecimal number to decimal.

Next we work from the leftmost column to the right. We divide 64 into 103 and observe that there is one 64 in 103 with a remainder of 39, so we write 1 in the 64 column. We divide 8 into 39 and observe that there are four 8s in 39 with a remainder of 7 and write 4 in the 8 column. Finally, we divide 1 into 7 and observe that there are seven 1s in 7 with no remainder so we write 7 in the 1 column. This yields:

> Positional values:**6481**
> Symbol values:**14 7**

and thus decimal 103 is equivalent to octal 147.

To convert decimal 375 to hexadecimal, we begin by writing the positional values of the columns until we reach a column whose positional value is greater than the decimal number. We do not need that column, so we discard it. Thus, we first write

> Positional values:**4096256161**

Then we discard the column with positional value 4096, yielding:

> Positional values:**256161**

Next we work from the leftmost column to the right. We divide 256 into 375 and observe that there is one 256 in 375 with a remainder of 119, so we write 1 in the 256 column. We divide 16 into 119 and observe that there are seven 16s in 119 with a remainder of 7 and write 7 in the 16 column. Finally, we divide 1 into 7 and observe that there are seven 1s in 7 with no remainder so we write 7 in the 1 column. This yields:

> Positional values:**256161**
> Symbol values:**17 7**

and thus decimal 375 is equivalent to hexadecimal 177.

B.6 Negative Binary Numbers: Two's Complement Notation

The discussion in this appendix has been focussed on positive numbers. In this section, we explain how computers represent negative numbers using *two's complement notation*. First we explain how the two's complement of a binary number is formed, and then we show why it represents the negative value of the given binary number.

Consider a machine with 32-bit integers. Suppose

```
int number = 13;
```

The 32-bit representation of **number** is

```
00000000 00000000 00000000 00001101
```

To form the negative of **number** we first form its *one's complement* by applying C#'s ^ operator:

```
onesComplement = number ^ 0x7FFFFFFF;
```

Internally, **onesComplement** is now **number** with each of its bits reversed—ones become zeros and zeros become ones as follows:

number:
```
00000000 00000000 00000000 00001101
```

onesComplement:
```
11111111 11111111 11111111 11110010
```

To form the two's complement of **number**, we simply add one to the one's complement of **number**.

Thus, the two's complement of **number** is

```
11111111 11111111 11111111 11110011
```

Now, if this is in fact equal to −13, we should be able to add it to binary 13 and obtain a result of 0. Let us try this:

```
 00000000 00000000 00000000 00001101
+11111111 11111111 11111111 11110011
-------------------------------------
 00000000 00000000 00000000 00000000
```

The carry bit coming out of the leftmost column is discarded, and we indeed get zero as a result. If we add the one's complement of a number to the number, the result would be all ones. The key to getting a result of all zeros is that the twos complement is one more than the one's complement. The addition of one causes each column to add to zero with a carry of one. The carry keeps moving leftward until it is discarded from the leftmost bit, and hence the resulting number is all zeros.

Computers actually perform a subtraction such as

```
x = a - number;
```

by adding the two's complement of **number** to **a** as follows:

```
x = a + ( onesComplement + 1 );
```

Suppose **a** is 27 and **number** is 13 as before. If the two's complement of **number** is actually the negative of **number**, then adding the two's complement of **number** to **a** should produce the result 14. Let us try this:

```
a  (i.e., 27)              00000000 00000000 00000000 00011011
+( onesComplement + 1 )   +11111111 11111111 11111111 11110011
                          -------------------------------------
                           00000000 00000000 00000000 00001110
```

which is indeed equal to 14.

B.7 Summary

When programmers write an integer such as 19, 227 or −63 in a C# program, the number is considered to be in the decimal (base-10) number system. The digits in the decimal number system are 0, 1, 2, 3, 4, 5, 6, 7, 8 and 9. The lowest digit is 0 and the highest digit is 9— one less than the base of 10.

Internally, computers use the binary (base-2) number system. The binary number system has only two digits, namely, 0 and 1. Its lowest digit is 0 and its highest digit is 1—

one less than the base of 2. Computers represent negative numbers using two's-complement notation.

The digits of the octal number system (base 8) range from 0 to 7. The hexadecimal number system (base 16) requires 16 digits—a lowest digit of 0 and a highest digit with a value equivalent to decimal 15 (one less than the base of 16). By convention, letters A through F are the hexadecimal digits representing decimal values 10 through 15.

Career Opportunities

Objectives

- To explore the various online career services.
- To examine the advantages and disadvantages of posting and finding jobs online.
- To review the major online career services Web sites available to job seekers.
- To explore the various online services available to employers seeking to build their workforces.

What is the city but the people?
William Shakespeare

A great city is that which has the greatest men and women,
If it be a few ragged huts it is still the greatest city in the
whole world.
Walt Whitman

To understand the true quality of people, you must look into
their minds, and examine their pursuits and aversions.
Marcus Aurelius

The soul is made for action, and cannot rest till it be
employed. Idleness is its rust. Unless it will up and think and
taste and see, all is in vain.
Thomas Traherne

Outline

C.1 Introduction

There are approximately 40,000 career-advancement services on the Internet today.[1] These services include large, comprehensive job sites, such as **Monster.com** (see the upcoming **Monster.com** feature), as well as interest-specific job sites such as **JustJava-Jobs.com**. Companies can reduce the amount of time spent searching for qualified employees by building recruiting features on their Web sites or establishing accounts with career sites. This results in a larger pool of qualified applicants, as online services can automatically select and reject resumes based on user-designated criteria. Online interviews, testing services and other resources also expedite the recruiting process.

Applying for a position online is a relatively new method of exploring career opportunities. Online recruiting services streamline the process and allow job seekers to concentrate their energies in careers that are of interest to them. Job seekers can explore opportunities according to geographic location, position, salary or benefits packages.

Job seekers can learn how to write resumes and cover letters, post them online and search through job listings to find the jobs that best suit their needs. *Entry-level positions*, or positions commonly sought by individuals who are entering a specific field or the job market for the first time; contracting positions; executive-level positions and middle-management-level positions are all available on the Web.

Job seekers will find a number of time-saving features when searching for jobs online. These include storing and distributing resumes digitally, e-mail notification of possible positions, salary and relocation calculators, job coaches, self-assessment tools and information on continuing education.

In this chapter, we explore online career services from the employer and employee's perspective. We suggest sites on which applications can be submitted, jobs can be searched and applicants can be reviewed. We also review services that build recruiting pages directly into e-businesses.

C.2 Resources for the Job Seeker

Finding a job online can greatly reduce the amount of time spent applying for a position. Instead of searching through newspapers and mailing resumes, job seekers can request a specific positions in specific industries through search engines. Some sites allow job seekers to setup intelligent agents to find jobs that meet their requirements. Intelligent agents are programs that search and arrange large amounts of data and report answers based on that data. When the agent finds a potential match, it sends it to the job seeker's inbox. Resumes can be stored digitally, customized quickly to meet job requirements and e-mailed instantaneously. A potential candidate also can learn more about a company by visiting its Web site. Most employment sites are free to job seekers. These sites typically generate their revenues by charging employers for posting job opportunities and by selling advertising space on their Web pages (see the **Monster.com** feature).

Career services, such as **FlipDog.com**, search a list of employer job sites to find positions. By searching links to employer Web sites, **FlipDog.com** is able to identify positions from companies of all sizes. This feature enables job seekers to find jobs that employers may not have posted outside the corporation's Web site.

Monster.com

Super Bowl ads and effective marketing have made **Monster.com** one of the most recognizable online brands (see Fig. C.1). In fact, in the 24 hours following Super Bowl XXXIV, 5 million job searches occurred on **Monster.com**.[2] The site allows people looking for jobs to post their resumes, search job listings, read advice and information about the job-search process and take proactive steps to improve their careers. These services are free to job seekers. Employers can post job listings, search resume databases and become featured employers.

Posting a resume at **Monster.com** is simple and free. **Monster.com** has a resume builder that allows users to post a resume to its site in 15–30 minutes. Each user can store up to 5 resumes and cover letters on the **Monster.com** server. Some companies offer their employment applications directly through the **Monster.com** site. **Monster.com** has job postings in every state and all major categories. Users can limit access to their personal identification information. As one of the leading recruiting sites on the Web, **Monster.com** is a good place to begin a job search or to find out more about the search process.

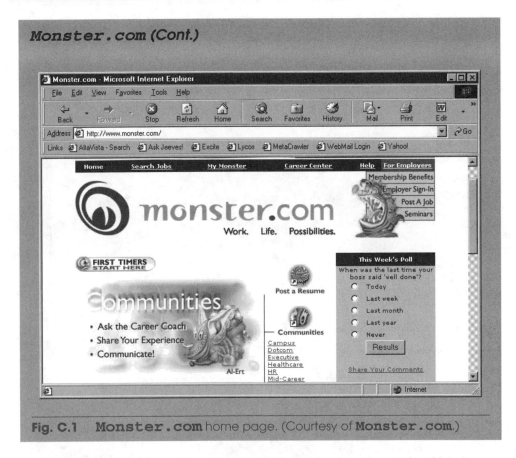

Fig. C.1 **Monster.com** home page. (Courtesy of **Monster.com**.)

Job seekers can visit **FlipDog.com** and choose, by state, the area in which they are looking for positions. Applicants also can conduct worldwide searches. After a user selects a region, **FlipDog.com** requests the user to choose a job category containing several specific positions. The user's choice causes a list of local employers to appear. The user can specify an employer or request that **FlipDog.com** search the employment databases for jobs offered by all employers (see Fig. C.2).

Other services, such as employment networks, also help job seekers in their search. Sites such as **Vault.com** (see the **Vault.com** feature) and **WetFeet.com** allow job seekers to post questions in designated chat rooms or on electronic bulletin boards about employers and positions.

C.3 Online Opportunities for Employers

Recruiting on the Internet provides several benefits over traditional recruiting. For example, Web recruiting reaches a much larger audience than posting an advertisement in a local newspaper. Given the breadth of the services provided by most online career services Web sites, the cost of posting online can be considerably less than posting positions through traditional means. Even newspapers, which depend greatly on career opportunity advertising, are starting online career sites.[3]

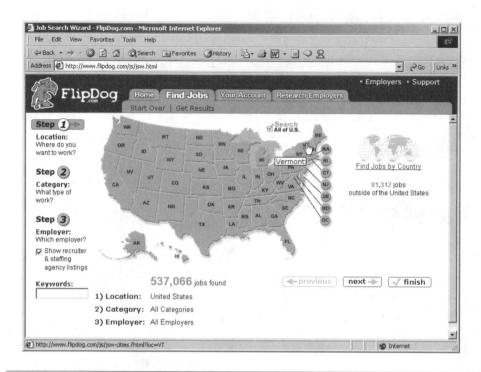

Fig. C.2 **FlipDog.com** job search. (Courtesy of **Flipdog.com**.)

Vault.com: Finding the Right Job on the Web[4]

Vault.com allows potential employees to seek out additional, third-party information for over 3000 companies. By visiting the *Insider Research* page, Web users have access to a profile on the company of their choice, as long as it exists in **Vault.com**'s database. In addition to **Vault.com**'s profile, there is a link to additional commentary by company employees. Most often anonymous, these messages can provide prospective employees with potentially valuable decision-making information. However, users must consider the integrity of the source. For example, a disgruntled employee may leave a posting that is not an accurate representation of the corporate culture of his or her company.

The **Vault.com** *Electronic Watercooler*™ is a message board that allows visitors to post stories, questions and concerns and to advise employees and job seekers. In addition, the site provides e-newsletters and feature stories designed to help job seekers in their search. Individuals seeking information on business, law and graduate schools can also find information on **Vault.com**.

Job-posting and career-advancement services for the job seeker are featured on **Vault.com**. These services include *VaultMatch*, a career service that e-mails job postings as requested, and *Salary Wizard*™, which helps job seekers determine the salary they are worth. Online guides with advice for fulfilling career ambitions are also available.

> ## Vault.com: Finding the Right Job on the Web[4] (Cont.)
>
> Employers can also use the site. *HR Vault*, a feature of **Vault.com**, provides employers with a free job-posting site. It offers career-management advice, employer-to-employee relationship management and recruiting resources.

e-Fact C.1

According to Forrester Research, 33 percent of today's average company's hiring budget goes toward online career services, while the remaining 66 percent is used for traditional recruiting mechanisms. Online use is expected to increase to 42 percent by 2004, while traditional mechanisms may be reduced to 10 percent.[5]

Generally, jobs posted online are viewed by a larger number of job seekers than jobs posted through traditional means. However, it is important not to overlook the benefits of combining online efforts with human-to-human interaction. There are many job seekers who are not yet comfortable with the process of finding a job online. Often, online recruiting is used as a means of freeing up a recruiter's time for the interviewing process and final selection.

e-Fact C.2

Cisco Systems cites a 39 percent reduction in cost-per-hire expenses, and a 60 percent reduction in the time spent hiring.[6]

C.3.1 Posting Jobs Online

When searching for job candidates online, there are many things employers need to consider. The Internet is a valuable tool for recruiting, but one that takes careful planning to acquire the best results. It provides a good supplementary tool, but should not be considered the complete solution for filling positions. Web sites, such as WebHire (**www.webhire.com**), enhance a company's online employment search (see the WebHire feature).

There are a variety of sites that allow employers to post jobs online. Some of these sites require a fee, which generally runs between $100–$200. Postings typically remain on the Web site for 30–60 days. Employers should be careful to post to sites that are most likely to be visited by eligible candidates. As we discovered in the previous section, there are a variety of online career services focused on specific industries, and many of the larger, more comprehensive sites have categorized their databases by job category.

When designing a posting, the recruiter should consider the vast number of postings already on the Web. Defining what makes the job position unique, including information such as benefits and salary, might convince a qualified candidate to further investigate the position (see Fig. C.3).[7]

HotJobs.com career postings are cross-listed on a variety of other sites, thus increasing the number of potential employees who see the job listings. Like **Monster.com** and **jobfind.com**, **HotJobs.com** requires a fee per listing. Employers also have the option of becoming **HotJobs.com** members. Employers can gain access to HotJob's *Private Label Job Board*s (private corporate employment sites), online recruiting technology and online career fairs.

WebHire™[8]

Designed specifically for recruiters and employers, WebHire is a multifaceted service that provides employers with *end-to-end recruiting solutions*. The service offers job-posting services as well as candidate searches. The most comprehensive of the services, *WebHire™ Enterprise*, locates and ranks candidates found through resume-scanning mechanisms. Clients will also receive a report indicating the best resources for their search. Other services available through the *WebHire™ Employment Services Network* include preemployment screening, tools for assessing employees' skill levels and information on compensation packages. An employment law advisor helps organizations design interview questions.

WebHire™ Agent is an intelligent agent that searches for qualified applicants based on job specifications. When WebHire Agent identifies a potential candidate, an e-mail is sent to the candidate to generate interest. WebHire Agent then ranks applicants according to the skills information it gains from the Web search; the information is stored so that new applicants are distinguished from those who have already received an e-mail from the site.

Yahoo!® Resumes, a feature of WebHire, allows recruiters to find potential employees by typing in keywords on the Yahoo! Resumes search engine. Employers can purchase a year's membership to the recruiting solution for a flat fee; there are no per-use charges.

Job Seeker's Criteria

Position (responsibilities)

Salary

Location

Benefits (health, dental, stock options)

Advancement

Time Commitment

Training Opportunities

Tuition Reimbursement

Corporate Culture

Fig. C.3   List of a job seeker's criteria.

Boston Herald *Job Find* (`www.jobfind.com`) also charges employers to post on its site. The initial fee entitles the employer to post up to three listings. Employers have no limitations on the length of their postings.

Other Web sites providing employers with employee recruitment services include **CareerPath.com**, America's Job Bank (`www.ajb.dni.us/employer`), CareerWeb (`www.cweb.com`), **Jobs.com** and **Career.com**.

C.3.2 Problems with Recruiting on the Web

The large number of applicants presents a challenge to both job seekers and employers. On many recruitment sites, matching resumes to positions is conducted by *resume-filtering software*. The software scans a pool of resumes for keywords that match the job description. While this software increases the number of resumes that receive attention, it is not a foolproof system. For example, the resume-filtering software might overlook someone with similar skills to those listed in the job description, or someone whose abilities would enable them to learn the skills required for the position. Digital transmissions can also create problems because certain software platforms are not always acceptable by the recruiting software. This sometimes results in an unformatted transmission, or a failed transmission.

A lack of confidentiality is another disadvantage of online career services. In many cases, a job candidate will want to search for job opportunities anonymously. This reduces the possibility of offending the candidate's current employer. Posting a resume on the Web increases the likelihood that the candidate's employer might come across it when recruiting new employees. The traditional method of mailing resumes and cover letters to potential employers does not impose the same risk.

According to recent studies, the number of individuals researching employment positions through traditional means, such as referrals, newspapers and temporary agencies, far outweighs the number of job seekers researching positions through the Internet.[9] Optimists feel, however, that this disparity is largely due to the early stages of e-business development. Given time, online career services will become more refined in their posting and searching capabilities, decreasing the amount of time it takes for a job seeker to find jobs and employers to fill positions.

C.3.3 Diversity in the Workplace

Every workplace inevitably develops its own culture. Responsibilities, schedules, deadlines and projects all contribute to a working environment. Perhaps the most defining elements of a *corporate culture* are the employees. For example, if all employees were to have the same skills, same backgrounds and the same ideas, the workplace would lack diversity. It also might lack creativity and enthusiasm. One way to increase the dynamics of an organization is to employ people of different backgrounds and cultures.

The Internet hosts demographic-specific sites for employers seeking to increase diversity in the workplace. By recruiting people from different backgrounds, new ideas and perspectives are brought forth, helping businesses meet the needs of a larger, more diverse target audience.[10]

Blackvoices.com and **hirediversity.com** are demographic-specific Web sites. BlackVoices™, which functions primarily as a portal (a site offering news, sports and weather information, as well as Web searches), features job searching capabilities and the ability for prospective employees to post resumes. HireDiversity is divided into several categories, including opportunities for African Americans, Hispanics and women. Other online recruiting services place banner advertisements on ethnic Web sites for companies seeking diverse workforces.

The Diversity Directory (**www.mindexchange.com**) offers international career-searching capabilities. Users selecting the **Diversity** site can find job opportunities, information and additional resources to help them in their career search. The site can be searched according to demographics (African American, Hispanic, alternative lifestyle, etc.) or by subject (employer, position, etc.) via hundreds of links. Featured sites include **BilingualJobs.com**, *Latin World* and *American Society for Female Entrepreneurs*.

Many sites have sections dedicated to job seekers with disabilities. In addition to providing job-searching capabilities, these sites include additional resources, such as equal opportunity documents and message boards. The *National Business and Disability Council* (*NBDC*) provides employers with integration and accessibility information for employing people with disabilities, and the site also lists opportunities for job seekers.

C.4 Recruiting Services

There are many services on the Internet that help employers match individuals to positions. The time saved by conducting preliminary searches on the Internet can be dedicated to interviewing qualified candidates and making the best matches possible.

Advantage Hiring, Inc. (**www.advantagehiring.com**) provides employers with a resume-screening service. When a prospective employee submits a resume for a particular position, Advantage Hiring, Inc. presents *Net-Interview™*, a small questionnaire to supplement the information presented on the resume. The site also offers *SiteBuilder*, a service that helps employers build an employee recruitment site. An online demonstration can be found at **www.advantagehiring.com**. The demonstration walks the user through the Net-Interview software, as well as a number of other services offered by Advantage Hiring (see Fig. C.4).

Recruitsoft.com is an application service provider (ASP) that offers companies recruiting software on a *pay-per-hire* basis (Recruitsoft receives a commission on hires made via its service). *Recruiter WebTop™* is the company's online recruiting software. It includes features such as Web-site hosting, an employee-referral program, skill-based resume screening, applicant-tracking capabilities and job-board posting capabilities. A demonstration of Recruiter WebTop's *Corporate Recruiting Solutions* can be found at **www.recruitsoft.com/process**. Other online recruiting services include **Hire.com**, and **Futurestep.com**™.

The Internet also provides employers with a cost-effective means of testing their prospective employees in such categories as decision making, problem solving and personality. Services such *eTest* help to reduce the cost of in-house testing and to make the interview process more effective. Test results, given in paragraph form, present employers with the interested individual's strengths and weaknesses. Based on these results, the report suggests interview methods, such as asking *open-ended questions*, which are questions that require more than a "yes" or "no" response. Sample reports and a free-trial test can be found at **www.etest.net**.

Employers and job seekers can also find career placement exercises at **www.advisorteam.net/User/ktsintro.asp**. Some of these services require a fee. The tests ask several questions regarding the individual's interests and working style. Results help candidates determine the best career for their skills and interests.

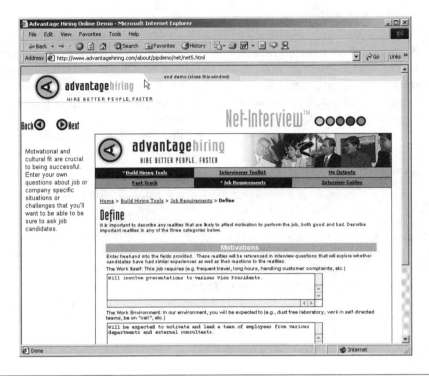

Fig. C.4   Advantage Hiring, Inc.'s Net-Interview™ service. (Courtesy of
Advantage Hiring, Inc.)

C.5 Career Sites

Online career sites can be comprehensive or industry specific. In this section, we explore a
variety of sites on the Web that accommodate the needs of both the job seeker and the employer. We review sites offering technical positions, free-lancing opportunities and contracting positions.

C.5.1 Comprehensive Career Sites

As mentioned previously, there are many sites on the Web that provide job seekers with
career opportunities in multiple fields. **Monster.com** is the largest of these sites, attract-
ing the greatest number of unique visitors per month. Other popular online recruiting sites
include **JobsOnline.com**, **HotJobs.com**, **www.jobtrak.com** (a **Monster.com**
site) and **Headhunter.net**.

Searching for a job online can be a conducted in a few steps. For example, during an
initial visit to **JobsOnline.com**, a user is required to fill out a registration form. The
form requests basic information, such as name, address and area of interest. After registering, members can search through job postings according to such criteria as job category,
location and the number of days the job has been posted. Contact information is provided
for additional communication.

C.5.2 Technical Positions

Technical positions are becoming widely available as the Internet grows more pervasive. Limited job loyalty and high turnover rates in technical positions allow job seekers to find jobs that best suit their needs and skills. Employers are required to rehire continuously to keep positions filled and productivity levels high. The amount of time for an employer to fill a technical position can be greatly reduced by using an industry-specific site. Career sites designed for individuals seeking technical positions are among the most popular online career sites. In this section, we review several sites that offer recruiting and hiring opportunities for technical positions.

e-Fact C.3

It costs a company 25 percent more to hire a new technical employee than it does to pay an already employed individual's salary.[11]

Dice.com (**www.dice.com**) is a recruiting Web site that focuses on technical fields. Company fees are based on the number of jobs the company posts and the frequency with which the postings are updated. Job seekers can post their resumes and search the job database for free. **JustTechJobs.com** directs job seekers toward 39 specific computer technologies for their job search. Language-specific sites include **JustJavaJobs.com**, **JustCJobs.com** and **JustPerlJobs.com**. Hardware, software and communications technology sites are also available. Other technology recruiting sites include **Hire-Ability.com**, and **HotDispatch.com**.

C.5.3 Wireless Positions

The wireless industry is developing rapidly. According to **WirelessResumes.com**, the number of wireless professionals is 328,000. This number is expected to increase 40 percent each year for the next five years. To accommodate this growth, and the parallel demand for professionals, **WirelessResumes.com** has created an online career site specifically for the purpose of filling wireless jobs (see the **WirelessResumes.com** feature).

WirelessResumes.com: *Filling Wireless Positions*

WirelessResumes.com is an online career site focused specifically on matching wireless professionals with careers in the industry. This narrow focus enables businesses to locate new employees quickly—reducing the time and expense attached to traditional recruiting methods. Similarly, candidates can limit their searches to precisely the job category of interest. Wireless carriers, device manufacturers, WAP and Bluetooth developers, e-commerce companies and application service providers (ASPs) are among those represented on the site.

In addition to searching for jobs and posting a resume, **WirelessResumes.com** provides job seekers with resume writing tips, interviewing techniques, relocation tools and assistance in obtaining a Visa or the completion of other necessary paperwork. Employers can use the site to search candidates and post job opportunities.

The Caradyne Group (**www.pcsjobs.com**), an executive search firm, connects job seekers to employers in the wireless technology field. Interested job seekers must first fill out a "Profile Questionnaire." This information is then entered into The Caradyne Group's database and is automatically matched to an open position in the job seeker's field of expertise. If there are no open positions, a qualified consultant from The Caradyne Group will contact the job seeker for further a interview and discussion.

C.5.4 Contracting Online

The Internet also serves as a forum for job seekers to find employment on a project-by-project basis. *Online contracting services* allow businesses to post positions for which they wish to hire outside resources, and individuals can identify projects that best suit their interests, schedules and skills.

e-Fact C.4

Approximately six percent of America's workforce falls into the category of independent contractor.[12]

Guru.com (**www.guru.com**) is a recruiting site for contract employees. Independent contractors, private consultants and trainers use **guru.com** to find short-term and long-term contract assignments. Tips, articles and advice are available for contractors who wish to learn more about their industry. Other sections of the site teach users how to manage their businesses, buy the best equipment and deal with legal issues. **Guru.com** includes an online store where contractors can buy products associated with small-business management, such as printing services and office supplies. Companies wishing to hire contractors must register with **guru.com**, but individuals seeking contract assignments do not.

Monster.com's Talent Market™ offers online auction-style career services to free agents. Interested users design a profile, listing their qualifications. After establishing a profile, free agents "Go Live" to start the bidding on their services. The bidding lasts for five days during which users can view the incoming bids. At the close of five days, the user can choose the job of his or her choice. The service is free for users, and bidding employers pay a commission on completed transactions.

Elance.com is another site where individuals can find contracting work. Interested applicants can search Elance's database by category, including business, finance and marketing (Fig. C.5). These projects, or *requests for proposals* (RFPs), are posted by companies worldwide. When users find projects for which they feel qualified, they submit bids on the projects. Bids must contain a user's required payment, a statement detailing the user's skills and a feedback rating drawn from other projects on which the user has worked. If a user's bid is accepted, the user is given the project, and the work is conducted over Elance's file-sharing system, enabling both the contractor and the employer to contact one another quickly and easily. For an online demonstration, visit **www.Elance.com** and click on the **take a tour...** link.

Other Web sites that provide contractors with projects and information include eWork® Exchange (**www.ework.com**), **MBAFreeAgent.com**, **Aquent.com** and **WorkingSolo.com**.

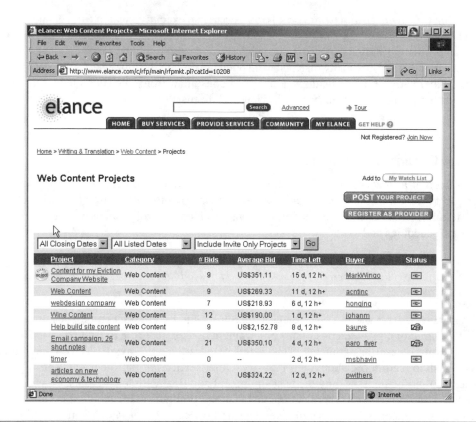

Fig. C.5   **Elance.com** request for proposal (RFP) example. (Copyright 2002 Elance, Inc. All rights reserved.)

C.5.5 Executive Positions

In this section, we discuss the advantages and disadvantages of finding an executive position online. Executive career advancement sites usually include many of the features found on comprehensive job-search sites. Searching for an executive position online differs from finding an entry-level position online. The Internet allows individuals to continually survey the job market. However, candidates for executive-level positions must exercise a higher level of caution when determining who is able to view their resume. Applying for an executive position online is an extensive process. As a result of the high level of scrutiny passed on a candidate during the hiring process, the initial criteria presented by an executive level candidate often are more specific than the criteria presented by the first-time job seeker. Executive positions often are difficult to fill, due to the high demands and large amount of experience required for the jobs.

SixFigureJobs (**www.sixfigurejobs.com**) is a recruitment site designed for experienced executives. Resume posting and job searching is free to job seekers. Other sites, including **www.execunet.com**, **Monster.com**'s ChiefMonster™ (**www.chiefmonster.com**) and **www.nationjob.com** are designed for helping executives find positions.

C.5.6 Students and Young Professionals

The Internet provides students and young professionals with tools to get them started in the job market. Individuals still in school and seeking internships, individuals who are just graduating and individuals who have been in the workforce for a few years make up the target market. Additional tools specifically designed for this *demographic* (a population defined by a specific characteristic) are available. For example, journals kept by previous interns provide prospective interns with information regarding what to look for in an internship, what to expect and what to avoid. Many sites will provide information to lead young professionals in the right direction, such as matching positions to their college or university major.

Experience.com is a career services Web site geared toward the younger population. Members can search for positions according to specific criteria, such as geographic location, job category, keywords, commitment (i.e. full time, part time, internship), amount of vacation and amount of travel time. After applicants register, they can send their resumes directly to the companies posted on the site. In addition to the resume, candidates provide a personal statement, a list of applicable skills and their language proficiency. Registered members also receive access to the site's *Job Agent*. Up to three Job Agents can be used by each member. The agents search for available positions, based on the criteria posted by the member. If a match is made, the site contacts the candidate via e-mail.[13,14]

Internships.wetfeet.com helps students find internships. In addition to posting a resume and searching for an internship, students can use the relocation calculator to compare the cost of living in different regions. Tips on building resumes and writing essays are provided. The *City Intern* program provides travel, housing and entertainment guides to interns interviewing or accepting a position in an unfamiliar city, making them feel more at home in a new location.

In addition to its internship locators, undergraduate, graduate, law school, medical school and business school services, the Princeton Review's Web site (**www.review.com**) offers career services to graduating students. While searching for a job, students and young professionals can also read through the site's news reports or even increase their vocabulary by visiting the "word for the day." Other career sites geared toward the younger population include **campuscareercenter.com**, **brassring-campus.com** and **collegegrad.com**.

C.5.7 Other Online Career Services

In addition to Web sites that help users find and post jobs online, there are a number of Web sites that offer features that will enhance searches, prepare users to search online, help applicants design resumes or help users calculate the cost of relocating.

Salary.com helps job seekers gauge their expected income, based on position, level of responsibility and years of experience. The search requires job category, ZIP code and specific job title. Based on this information, the site will return an estimated salary for an individual living in the specified area and employed in the position described. Estimates are returned based on the average level of income for the position.

In addition to helping applicants find employment, **www.careerpower.com** provides individuals with tests that will help them realize their strengths, weaknesses, values, skills and personality traits. Based on the results, which can be up to 10–12 pages per test, users can best decide what job categories they are qualified for and what career choice will be best suited to their personal ambitions. The service is available for a fee.

InterviewSmart™ is another service offered through CareerPower that prepares job seekers of all levels for the interviewing process. The service can be downloaded for a minimal fee or can be used on the Web for free. Both versions are available at **www.career-power.com/CareerPerfect/interviewing.htm#is.start.anchor**.

Additional services will help applicants find positions that meet their unique needs or help them design their resumes to attract the attention of specific employers. **Dog-friendly.com**, organized by geographic location, helps job seekers find opportunities that allow them to bring their pets to work, and **cooljobs.com** is a searchable database of unique job opportunities.

C.6 Summary

The Internet can improve an employer's ability to recruit employees and can help users find career opportunities worldwide. Job seekers can learn how to write a resume and cover letter, post them online and search through job listings to find the jobs that best suit their needs. Employers are able to post jobs that can be searched by an enormous pool of applicants. Job seekers can store and distribute resumes digitally, receive e-mail notification of possible positions, use salary and relocation calculators, consult job coaches and use self-assessment tools when searching for a job on the Web.

There are approximately 40,000 career-advancement services on the Internet today. Finding a job online can greatly reduce the amount of time spent applying for a position. Potential candidates also can learn more about a company by visiting its Web site. Most sites are free to job seekers. These sites typically generate their revenues by charging employers who post their job opportunities and by selling advertising space on their Web pages. On many recruitment sites, the match of a resume to a position is conducted with resume-filtering software. Career sites designed for individuals seeking technical positions are among the most popular online career sites. Online contracting services but allow businesses to post positions for which they wish to hire outside resources and allow individuals to identify projects that best suit their interests, schedules and skills.

The Internet provides students and young professionals with some of the necessary tools to get them started in the job market. The target market is made up of individuals still in school and seeking internships, individuals who are just graduating and individuals who have been in the workforce for a few years. A number of Web sites offer features that enhance job searches, prepare users to search online, help design applicants' resumes or help users calculate the cost of relocating. Web recruiting reaches a much larger audience than does posting an advertisement in the local newspaper. A variety of sites allow employers to post jobs online. Some of these sites require a fee, which generally runs between $100 and $200. Postings remain on the Web site for approximately 30–60 days.

In designing a job posting, defining what makes a job position unique and including information such as benefits and salary might convince a qualified candidate to investigate the position further. The Internet hosts demographic-specific sites for employers seeking to increase diversity in the workplace. The Internet has provided employers with a cost-effective means of testing their prospective employees in such categories as decision making, problem solving and personality.

C.7 Internet and World Wide Web Resources

Information Technology (IT) Career Sites

www.dice.com
This is a recruiting Web site that focuses on the computer industry.

www.guru.com
This is a recruiting site for contract employees. Independent contractors, private consultants and trainers can use **guru.com** to find short-term and long-term work.

www.hallkinion.com
This is a Web recruiting service for individuals seeking IT positions.

www.techrepublic.com
This site provides employers and job seekers with recruiting capabilities and information regarding developing technology.

www.justcomputerjobs.com
This site serves as a portal with access to language-specific sites, including Java, Perl, C and C++.

www.hotdispatch.com
This forum provides software developers with the opportunity to share projects, discuss code and ask questions.

www.techjobs.bizhosting.com/jobs.htm
This site directs job seekers to links of numerous technological careers listed by location, internet, type of field, etc.

Career Sites

www.careerbuilder.com
A network of career sites, including IT Careers, *USA Today* and MSN, CareerBuilder attracts 3 million unique job seekers per month. The site provides resume-builder and job-searching agents.

www.recruitek.com
This free site caters to jobs seekers, employers and contractors.

www.monster.com
This site, the largest of the online career sites, allows people looking for jobs to post their resumes, search job listings and read advice and information about the job-search process. It also provides a variety of recruitment services for employers.

www.jobsonline.com
Similar to **Monster.com**, this site provides opportunities for job seekers and employers.

www.hotjobs.com
This online recruiting site offers cross-listing possibilities on additional sites.

www.jobfind.com
This job site is an example of locally targeted job-search resources. **JobFind.com** targets the Boston area.

www.flipdog.com
This site allows online job candidates to search for career opportunities. It employs intelligent agents to scour the Web and return jobs matching the candidate's request.

www.cooljobs.com
This site highlights unique job opportunities.

`www.inetsupermall.com`
This site aids job searchers in creating professional resumes and connecting with employers.

`www.wirelessnetworksonline.com`
This site helps connect job searchers to careers for which they are qualified.

`www.careerweb.com`
This site highlights featured employers and jobs and allows job seekers and employers to post and view resumes, respectively.

`www.jobsleuth.com`
On this site job seekers can fill out a form that indicates their desired field of employment. Job Sleuth™ searches the Internet and returns potential matches to the user's inbox. The service is free.

`www.ajb.org`
America's Job Bank is an online recruiting service provided through the Department of Labor and the state employment service. Searching for and posting positions on the site are free.

Executive Positions

`www.sixfigurejobs.com`
This is a recruitment site designed for experienced executives.

`www.leadersonline.com`
This career services Web site offers confidential job searches for mid-level professionals. Potential job matches are e-mailed to job candidates.

`www.ecruitinginc.com`
This site is designed to search for employees for executive positions.

Diversity

`www.latpro.com`
This site is designed for Spanish-speaking and Portuguese-speaking job seekers. In addition to providing resume-posting services, the site enables job seekers to receive matching positions via e-mail. Advice and information services are available.

`www.blackvoices.com`
This portal site hosts a career center designed to match African American job seekers with job opportunities.

`www.hirediversity.com`
In addition to services for searching for and posting positions, resume-building and updating services are also available on this site. The site targets a variety of demographics including African Americans, Asian Americans, people with disabilities, women and Latin Americans.

People with Disabilities

`www.halftheplanet.com`
This site represents people with disabilities. The site is large and includes many different resources and information services. A special section is dedicated to job seekers and employers.

`www.wemedia.com`
This site is designed to meet the needs of people with disabilities. It includes a section for job seekers and employers.

www.disabilities.com
This site provides users with a host of links to information resources on career opportunities.

www.mindexchange.com
The diversity section of this site provides users with several links to additional resources regarding people with disabilities and employment.

www.usdoj.gov/crt/ada/adahom1.htm
This is the Americans with Disabilities Act home page.

www.abanet.org/publicserv/mental.html
This is the Web site for The Commission on Mental and Physical Disability Law.

janweb.icdi.wvu.edu
The Job Accommodation Web site offers consulting services to employers regarding integration of people with disabilities into the workplace.

General Resources

www.vault.com
This site provides potential employees with "insider information" on over 3000 companies. In addition, job seekers can search through available positions and post and answer questions on the message board.

www.wetfeet.com
Similar to **vault.com**, this site allows visitors to ask questions and receive "insider information" on companies that are hiring.

Special Interest

www.eharvest.com/careers
This Web site provides job seekers interested in agricultural positions with online career services.

www.opportunitynocs.org
This career services site is for both employers and job seekers interested in non-profit opportunities.

www.experience.com
This Web site is designed specifically for young professionals and students seeking full-time, part-time and internship positions.

www.internships.wetfeet.com
Students seeking internships can search job listings on this site. It also features City Intern, to help interns become acquainted with a new location.

www.brassringcampus.com
This site provides college grads and young professionals with less than five years of experience with job opportunities. Additional features help users buy cars or find apartments.

Online Contracting

www.ework.com
This online recruiting site matches outside contractors with companies needing project specialists. Other services provided through eWork include links to online training sites, benefits packages and payment services and online meeting and management resources.

www.Elance.com
Similar to **eWork.com**, Elance matches outside contractors with projects.

www.MBAFreeAgent.com
This site is designed to match MBAs with contracting opportunities.

www.aquent.com
This site provides access to technical contracting positions.

www.WorkingSolo.com
This site helps contractors begin their own projects.

Recruiting Services

www.advantagehiring.com
This site helps employers screen resumes.

www.etest.net
This site provides employers with testing services to assess the strengths and weaknesses of prospective employees. This information can be used for better hiring strategies.

www.hire.com
Hire.com's eRecruiter is an application service provider that helps organizations streamline their Web-recruiting process.

www.futurestep.com
Executives can register confidentially at **Futurestep.com** to be considered for senior executive positions. The site connects registered individuals to positions. It also offers career management services.

www.webhire.com
This site provides employers with end-to-end recruiting solutions.

Wireless Career Resources

www.wirelessresumes.com
This site connects employers and job seekers with resumes that focus on jobs revolving around wireless technology.

www.msua.org/job.htm
This site contains links to numerous wireless job-seeking Web sites.

www.wiwc.org
This site's focus is wireless communication job searching for women.

www.firstsearch.com
At this site a job seeker is able to discover part-time, full-time and salary-based opportunities in the wireless industry.

www.pcsjobs.com
This is the site for The Caradyne Group, which is an executive search firm that focuses on finding job seekers wireless job positions.

www.cnijoblink.com
CNI Career Networks offers confidential, no-charge job placement in the wireless and telecommunications industries.

WORKS CITED

The notation **<www.domain-name.com>** indicates that the citation is for information found at the Web site.

1.   J. Gaskin, "Web Job Sites Face Tough Tasks," *Inter@ctive Week*, 14 August 2000: 50.

2.   J. Gaskin, 50.

3.   M. Berger, "Jobs Supermarket," *Upside*, November 2000: 224.

4.   **<www.vault.com>.**

5.   M. Berger, 224.

6.   Cisco Advertisement, *The Wall Street Journal,* 19 October 2000: B13.

7.   M. Feffer, "Posting Jobs on the Internet," 18 August 2000 **<www.webhire.com/hr/spot-light.asp>.**

8.   **<www.webhire.com>.**

9.   J. Gaskin, 51.

10. C. Wilde, "Recruiters Discover Diverse Value in Web Sites," *Information Week* 7, February 2000: 144.

11. A.K. Smith, "Charting Your Own Course," *U.S. News and World Report*, 6 November 2000: 58.

12. D. Lewis, "Hired! By the Highest Bidder," *The Boston Globe*, 9 July 2000: G1.

13. **<www.experience.com>.**

14. M. French, "Experience Inc., E-Recruiting for Jobs for College Students," *Mass High Tech*, 7 February–13 February 2000: 29.

Visual Studio .NET Debugger

Objectives

- To understand syntax and logic errors.
- To become familiar with the Visual Studio .NET debugging tools.
- To understand the use of breakpoints to suspend program execution.
- To be able to examine data using expressions in the debugging windows.
- To be able to debug methods and objects.

And often times excusing of a fault
Doth make the fault the worse by the excuse.
William Shakespeare

To err is human, to forgive divine.
Alexander Pope

Outline

D.1 Introduction

Two types of errors occur during software development: syntax errors and logic errors. Syntax errors (or compilation errors) occur when program statements violate the grammatical rules of a programming language, such as failure to end a statement with a semicolon. When a compiler detects syntax errors, the compiler terminates without building the application. By contrast, logic errors do not prevent programs from compiling or executing, but rather prevent programs from operating as expected.

Syntax errors are easier to fix than are logic errors. Upon detecting a syntax error, the compiler provides the description and line number in the ***Task List*** window (Fig. D.1). This information gives the programmer a "clue" as to how to eliminate the error, so the compiler can create the program. However, logic errors often are more subtle and usually do not inform the user exactly where in the program the error occurred. This appendix overviews both types of errors and details Visual Studio .NET's capabilities for detecting and correcting the these logic errors.

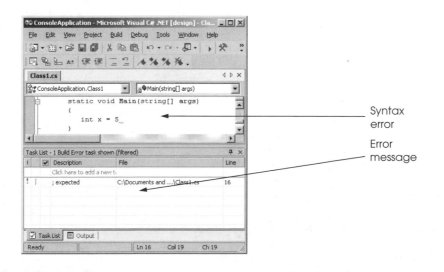

Fig. D.1   Syntax error.

Testing and Debugging Tip D.1

After fixing one error, you may observe that the number of overall errors perceived by the compiler is significantly reduced.

Testing and Debugging Tip D.2

When the compiler reports a syntax error on a particular line, check that line for the syntax error. If the error is not on that line, check the preceding few lines of code for the cause of the syntax error.

Debugging is the process of finding and correcting *logic errors* in applications. Logic errors are more subtle than syntax errors because a program that includes a logic error compiles successfully but does not run as expected. Logic errors often are difficult to debug, because the programmer cannot see the code as it executes. One strategy that novice programmers often use to debug programs is to display program data directly, using message boxes or **Console.WriteLine** statements. For example, the programmer might print the value of a variable when its value changes to determine whether the variable is assigned the correct value. This approach is cumbersome, because programmers must insert a line of code wherever they suspect there might be a problem. Furthermore, once the program has been debugged, the programmer then must remove the extraneous statements, which often can be difficult to distinguish from the original program code.

A *debugger* is software that allows a programmer to analyze program data and trace the flow of program execution while the application runs. A debugger provides capabilities that allow the programmer to suspend program execution, examine and modify variables, call methods without changing the program code and more. In this appendix, we introduce the Visual Studio .NET debugger and several of its debugging tools. [*Note*: A program must compile successfully before it can be used in the debugger.]

D.2 Breakpoints

Breakpoints are a simple but effective debugging tool. A breakpoint is a marker that a programmer places in a code listing. When a program reaches a breakpoint, execution pauses—this allows the programmer to examine the state of the program and ensure that it is working as expected. Figure D.2 is a program that outputs the value of ten factorial (10!),[1] but contains two logic errors—the first iteration of the loop multiplies **x** by **10** instead of multiplying **x** by **9**, and the result of the factorial calculation is multiplied by **0** (so the result is always **0**). We use this program to demonstrate Visual Studio .NET's debugging abilities—using its breakpoint capabilities as our first example.

```
1   // Fig. D.2: DebugExample.cs
2   // Sample program to debug.
3
4   using System;
5
```

Fig. D.2   Debug sample program. (Part 1 of 2.)

---

1. The factorial of **x** (**x**!) is defined as the product of all digits less than or equal to **x** but greater than zero. For example, 10! = 10 * 9 * 8 * 7 * 6 * 5 * 4 * 3 * 2 * 1.

```
6    namespace Debug
7    {
8       class DebugExample
9       {
10         static void Main( string[] args )
11         {
12            int x = 10;
13
14            Console.Write( "The value of " + x + " factorial is: " );
15
16            // loop to determine x factorial, contains logic error
17            for ( int i = x; i >= 0; i-- )
18               x *= i;
19
20            Console.Write( x );
21
22            Console.ReadLine(); // delay program exit
23
24         } // end main
25
26      } // end class DebugExample
27
28   } // end namespace Debug
```

```
The value of 10 factorial is: 0
```

Fig. D.2   Debug sample program. (Part 2 of 2.)

To set breakpoints in Visual Studio, click the gray area to the left of any line of code or right-click a line of code and select **Insert Breakpoint**. A solid red circle appears, indicating that the breakpoint has been set (Fig. D.3). The program execution is suspended when it reaches the line containing the breakpoint.

To enable breakpoints and other debugging features, we must compile the program using the debug configuration (Fig. D.4). Select **Debug** from the configuration toolbar if it is not already selected. Alternatively, select **Build > Configuration Manager** and change the **Active Solution Configuration** to **Debug**.

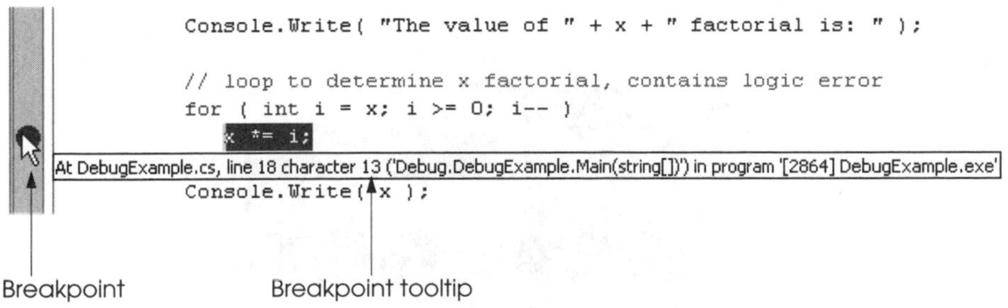

```
         Console.Write( "The value of " + x + " factorial is: " );

         // loop to determine x factorial, contains logic error
         for ( int i = x; i >= 0; i-- )
            x *= i;
   At DebugExample.cs, line 18 character 13 ('Debug.DebugExample.Main(string[])') in program '[2864] DebugExample.exe'
         Console.Write( x );
```

Breakpoint   Breakpoint tooltip

Fig. D.3   Setting a breakpoint.

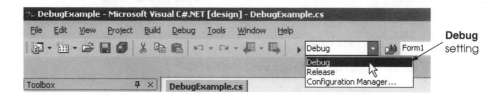

Fig. D.4   Debug configuration setting.

Selecting **Debug > Start** compiles the program and begins debugging. When debugging a console application, the console window appears (Fig. D.5), allowing program interaction (input and output). When the debugger reaches the breakpoint (line 18) program execution is suspended, and the IDE becomes the active window. Programmers may need to switch between the IDE and the console window while debugging programs.

Figure D.6 shows the IDE with program execution suspended at the breakpoint. The *yellow arrow* to the left of the statement

```
x *= i;
```

indicates the line at which execution is suspended and that the line contains the next statement to execute. Note that the title bar of the IDE displays **[break]**—this indicates that the IDE is in *break mode* (i.e., the debugger is running). Once the program reaches the breakpoint, a programmer can "hover" with the mouse on a variable (in this case **x** or **i**) in the source code to view the value of that variable in a tooltip as shown in Fig. D.6.

Testing and Debugging Tip D.3

Placing a breakpoint after a loop in a program allows the loop to complete without stopping before the breakpoint is reached.

D.3 Examining Data

Visual Studio .NET includes several debugging windows that allow programmers to examine variables and expressions. All the windows are accessible from the **Debug > Windows** submenu. Some windows are listed only when the IDE is in break mode (also called *debug mode)*. The **Watch** window, which is available only in break mode (Fig. D.7), allows programmers to examine the values of related groups of variables and expressions. Visual Studio .NET provides a total of four **Watch** windows.

Fig. D.5   Console application suspended for debugging.

Title bar displays **[break]**

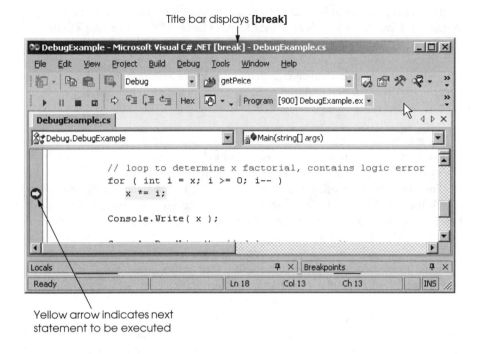

Yellow arrow indicates next
statement to be executed

Fig. D.6   Execution suspended at a breakpoint.

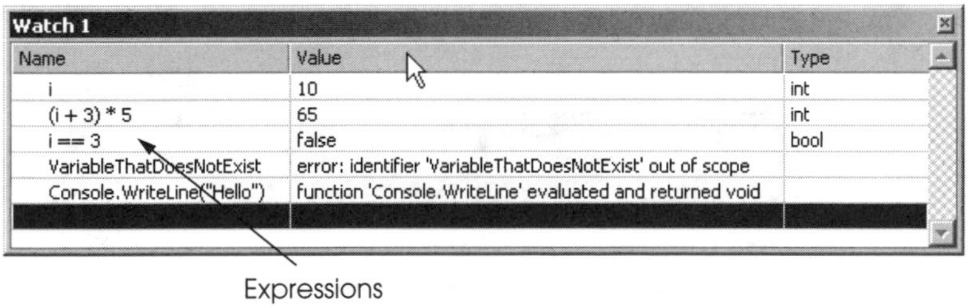

Expressions

Fig. D.7   **Watch** window.

Upon first opening, the **Watch** window will not contain any expressions to evaluate. To examine data, type an expression into the **Name** field. Most valid C# expressions can be entered in the **Name** field, including expressions that contain method calls. Consult the documentation under "**debugger, expressions**" for a full description of valid expressions.

Once an expression is entered, its type and value appear in the **Value** and **Type** fields. The first expression entered is the variable **i**, which has a value of **10** (line 12 assigns the value of **10** to variable **x**, and line 17 assigns the value of **x** to **i**). The **Watch** window also can evaluate more complex arithmetic expressions (e.g, **(i + 3) * 5**). Thus, the **Watch** window provides a convenient way to display various types of program data without modifying code.

By entering the variables and expressions that are relevant to a program's logic error, programmers can trace incorrect values to the source of the error and eliminate it. For example, to debug the program in Fig. D.2, we might enter the expression **i * x** in the **Watch** window. When we reach the breakpoint for the first time, the expression has a value **100** instead of **90**, which indicates a logic error in our program. This occurs because the loop at lines 17–18 started multiplying **x** by **10** as opposed to multiplying by **9**. We subtract **1** from the initial value that the **for** loop assigns to **i** (i.e., change **10** to **9**) to correct the error.

If a **Name** field in the **Watch** window contains a variable name, the variable's value can be modified for debugging purposes. To modify a variable's value, click its value in the **Value** field and enter a new value. Any modified value appears in red.

If an expression is invalid, an error appears in the **Value** field. For example, **Variable-ThatDoesNotExist** is not an identifier used in the program (fourth line in Fig. D.7). Therefore, Visual Studio .NET issues an error message in the **Value** field. To remove an expression, select it and press *Delete*.

Visual Studio also provides the *Locals*, *Autos* and *This* windows (Fig. D.8), which are similar to the **Watch** window, except the programmer does not specify their contents. The **Locals** window displays the name and current value for all the variables that have block scope in the method containing the current statement (indicated by the yellow arrow in Fig. D.6). The **Autos** window displays the variables and values of the current statement and the previous statement. Variables can be changed in either window by clicking the appropriate **Value** field and entering a new value. The **This** window displays data that has class scope for an object. If the program is inside a **static** method (such as method **Main** in a console application), the **This** window is empty.

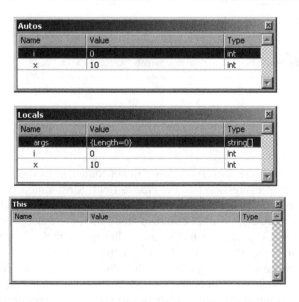

Fig. D.8   **Autos**, **Locals** and **This** windows.

A programmer can evaluate expressions line-by-line in the ***Immediate*** window (Fig. D.9). To evaluate an expression, a programmer types this expression into the window and presses *Enter*. For example, when a programmer enters `Console.WriteLine(i)` and presses *Enter*, the value of `i` is output to the console window. A developer also can use the assignment operator (`=`) to perform assignments in the **Immediate** window. Notice that the values for `i` and `x` in the **Locals** window contain these updated values.

Testing and Debugging Tip D.4

*Use the **Immediate** window to call a method one time. Placing a method call inside the **Watch** window calls that method every time the program breaks.*

D.4 Program Control

The Visual Studio .NET Debugger give programmers considerable control over the execution of a program. Using breakpoints and program-control commands provided by the debugger, programmers conveniently can analyze the execution of code at any point in a program. This is useful when a program contains multiple calls to methods that are known to execute properly. The **Debug** toolbar contains buttons that provide convenient access for controlling the debugging process (Fig. D.10). To display the **Debug** toolbar, select **View > Toolbars > Debug**.

The debug toolbar in Fig. D.10 controls debugger execution. The ***Restart*** button executes the program from the beginning, pausing at the beginning of the program to allow the programmer to set breakpoints before the program executes again. The ***Continue*** button resumes execution of a suspended program. The ***Stop Debugging*** button ends the debugging session, and the ***Break All*** button allows the programmer to suspend an executing program directly (i.e., without explicitly setting breakpoints). After execution suspends, the yellow arrow appears indicating the next statement to be executed.

Testing and Debugging Tip D.5

*When a program is executing, problems such as infinite loops usually can be interrupted by selecting **Debug > Break All** or by clicking the corresponding button on the toolbar.*

Clicking the ***Show Next Statement*** button places the cursor on the same line as the yellow arrow. This command is useful when a programmer needs to return to the current execution point after setting breakpoints in a program that contains many lines of code.

The ***Step Over*** button executes the next executable statement and advances the yellow arrow to the following line. If the next line of code contains a method call, the method is executed in its entirety as one step. This button allows the user to execute the program one line at a time without seeing the details of every method that is called. This is useful when a program contains multiple calls to methods that are known to execute properly. We discuss the **Step Into** and **Step Out** buttons in the next section.

The **Hex** button toggles the display format of data. If enabled, **Hex** displays data in hexadecimal (base 16) format, rather than displaying data in decimal (base 10) format. Experienced programmers often prefer to read values in hexadecimal format—especially large numbers because hexadecimal number representation is more concise and can be converted easily to binary (base 2) form. For more information about the hexadecimal and decimal number formats, see Appendix B, Number Systems.

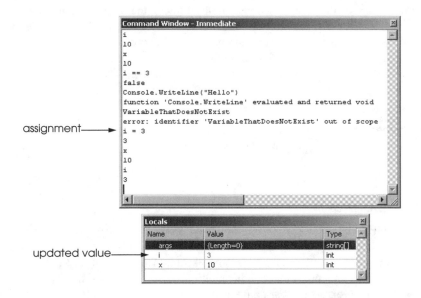

Fig. D.9 **Immediate** window.

The **Breakpoints** window displays all the breakpoints set for the program (Fig. D.11). A checkbox appears next to each breakpoint, indicating whether the breakpoint is *active* (checked) or *disabled* (unchecked). Lines with disabled breakpoints contain an unfilled red circle rather than a solid one (Fig. D.12). The debugger does not pause execution at disabled breakpoints.

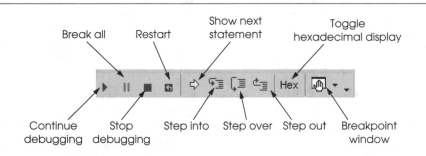

Fig. D.10 **Debug** toolbar icons.

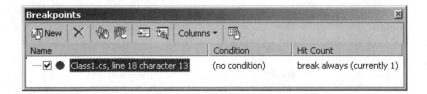

Fig. D.11 **Breakpoints** window.

```
// loop to determine x factorial, contains logic error
for ( int i = x; i >= 0; i-- )
    x *= i;

Console.Write( x );
```

Disabled breakpoint

Fig. D.12 Disabled breakpoint.

Testing and Debugging Tip D.6

Disabled breakpoints allow the programmer to maintain breakpoints in key locations in the program so they can be reactivated when needed. Disabled breakpoints are always visible.

In the **Breakpoints** window (Fig. D.11), the **Condition** field displays the condition that must be satisfied to suspend program execution at that breakpoint. The **Hit Count** field displays the number of times the debugger has stopped at each breakpoint. Double-clicking an item in the **Breakpoints** window moves the cursor to the line containing that breakpoint.

A programmer can add breakpoints to a program by clicking the **New** button in the **Breakpoints** window. This causes a **New Breakpoint** dialog to display (Fig. D.13). The **Function**, **File**, **Address** and **Data** tabs allow the programmer to suspend execution at either a method, a line in a particular file, an instruction in memory or when the value of a variable changes. The **Hit Count...** button (Fig. D.14) can be used to specify when the breakpoint should suspend the program (the default is to **always break**). A breakpoint can be set to suspend the program when the hit count reaches a specific number, when the hit count is a multiple of a number or is greater than or equal to a specific number.

The Visual Studio debugger also allows execution to suspend at a breakpoint depending on the value of an expression. Clicking the **Condition...** button opens the **Breakpoint Condition** dialog (Fig. D.15). The **Condition** checkbox indicates whether breakpoint conditions are enabled. The radio buttons determine how the expression in the text box is evaluated. The **is true** radio button pauses execution at the breakpoint whenever the expression is true. The **has changed** radio button causes program execution to suspend when it first encounters the breakpoint and again each time the expression differs from its previous value when the breakpoint is encountered. When the **New Breakpoint** dialog has been closed, the **Breakpoints** window displays the condition and hit count options for the new break point.

Suppose we set **x * i != 0** as the condition for the breakpoint in our loop, with the **has changed** option enabled. (We might choose to do this because the program produces an incorrect output of **0**). Program execution suspends when it first reaches the breakpoint and records that the expression has a value of **true**, because **x * i** is **100** (or **10** if we fixed the earlier logic error). We continue, and the loop decrements **i**. While **i** is between **10** and **1**, the condition's value never changes, and execution is not suspended at that breakpoint. When **i** is **0**, the expression **x * i != 0** is **false**, and execution is suspended. At this point, the programmer identifies the second logic error in our program—the final iteration of the **for** loop multiplies the result by **0**. To return the IDE to design mode, click the **Stop Debugging** button on the **Debug** toolbar.

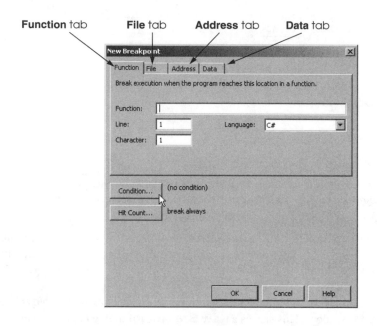

Function tab   File tab   Address tab   Data tab

Fig. D.13   **New Breakpoint** dialog.

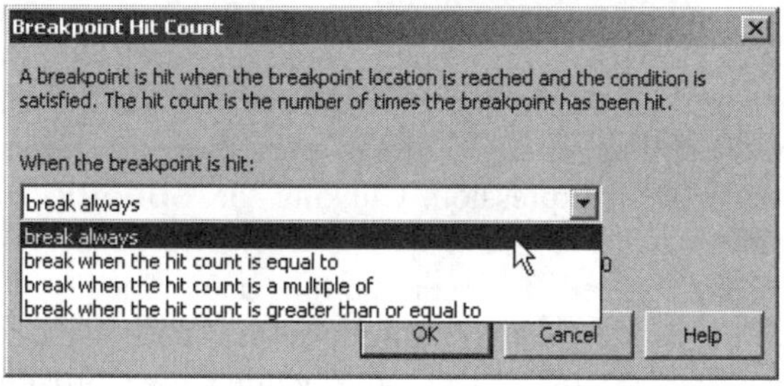

Fig. D.14   **Breakpoint Hit Count** dialog.

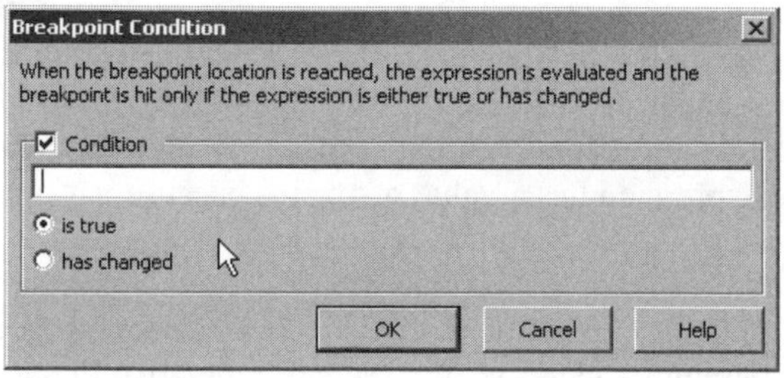

Fig. D.15   **Breakpoint Condition** dialog.

D.5 Additional Method Debugging Capabilities

In programs with many methods, it is often difficult to determine which methods may have been involved in incorrect calculations that resulted in a logic error. To simplify this process, the Visual Studio debugger includes tools for analyzing methods and method calls. We demonstrate some method-debugging tools in the following example (Fig. D.16).

The **Call Stack** window contains the program's *method call stack*, which allows the programmer to determine the exact sequence of calls that lead to the current method and to examine calling methods on the stack. This window allows the programmer to determine the flow of control in the program that resulted in the execution of the current method. For example, a breakpoint is inserted in **MyMethod**, the call stack in (Fig. D.17) indicates that the program called method **Main** first, followed by **MyMethod**.

```
1   // Fig. D.16: MethodDebugExample.cs
2   // Demonstrates debugging methods.
3
4   using System;
5
6   namespace Debug
7   {
8
9      // provides methods for demonstrating
10     // Visual Studio's debug tools
11     class MethodDebug
12     {
13        // entry point for application
14        static void Main( string[] args )
15        {
16           // display MyMethod return values
17           for ( int i = 0; i < 10; i++ )
18              Console.WriteLine( MyMethod( i ) );
19
20           Console.ReadLine();
21        } // end method Main
22
23        // perform calculation
24        static int MyMethod( int x )
25        {
26           return ( x * x ) - ( 3 * x ) + 7;
27        } // end method MyMethod
28
29        // method with logic error
30        static int BadMethod( int x )
31        {
32           return 1 / ( x - x );
33        } // end method BadMethod
34
35     } // end class MethodDebug
36
37  } // end namespace Debug
```

Fig. D.16 Debugging methods.

Most recently called method

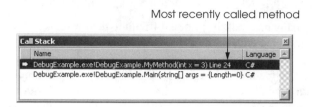

Fig. D.17   Call Stack window.

Double-clicking any line in the **Call Stack** window displays the next line to be executed in that method. This allows the programmer to determine how the result of each method will affect the calling method's execution. Visual Studio .NET highlights the line in green and displays the tooltip shown in Fig. D.18.

Visual Studio .NET also provides additional program-control buttons for debugging methods. The **Step Over** button executes one statement in a method, then pauses program execution at the following line. Using **Step Over**, if an evaluated statement invokes a method, the method is invoked, and execution stops at the next statement. Using *Step Into*, if a statement invokes a method, control transfers to the method for line-by-line. The *Step Out* button finishes executing the current method and returns control to the line that called the method.

Testing and Debugging Tip D.7

Use Step Out to finish a method that was stepped into accidentally.

Figure D.19 lists each program-control debug feature, its shortcut key and a description. Experienced programmers often prefer using these shortcut keys to access menu commands.

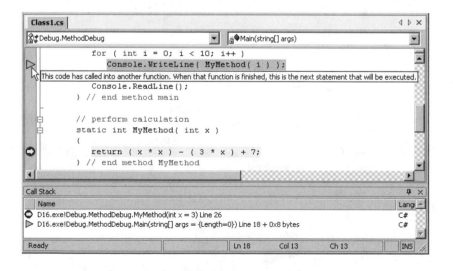

Fig. D.18   IDE displaying a method's calling point.

Control Button	Shortcut Key	Description
Continue	*F5*	Continues program execution. Execution continues until either a breakpoint is encountered or the program ends (through normal execution).
Stop Debugging	*Shift + F5*	Stops debugging and returns to Visual Studio design mode.
Step Over	*F10*	Advances to next statement, does not step into method calls.
Step Into	*F11*	Executes next statement. If the statement contains a method call, control transfers to the method for line-by-line debugging. If the statement does not contain a method call, **Step Into** behaves like **Step Over**.
Step Out	*Shift + F11*	Finishes executing the current method and suspends program execution in the calling method.

Fig. D.19 Debug program control features.

Programmers can use the **Immediate** window, discussed in Section D.3 for testing method arguments passed to a method (Fig. D.20). Testing the arguments helps determine if a method is functioning properly.

D.6 Additional Class Debugging Capabilities

In most sophisticated C# programs, a large portion of program data is contained in objects. For these purposes, Visual Studio includes class debugging features, which allow programmers to determine the current state of objects used in a program. We demonstrate some class debugging features using the code presented in Fig. D.21. To examine an instance of class **DebugEntry**, we place a breakpoint at line 43, as shown in Fig. D.22. [*Note*: A C# file may contain multiple classes, as is the case with this example.]

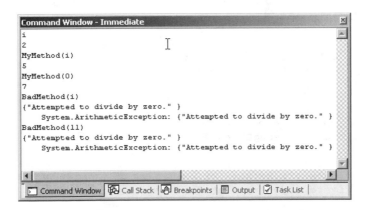

Fig. D.20 Using the **Immediate** window to debug methods.

```csharp
1  // Fig. D.21: DebugClass.cs
2  // Console application to demonstrate object debugging.
3
4  using System;
5
6  namespace ClassDebug
7  {
8
9     // creates array containing three different classes
10    public class DebugEntry
11    {
12       public int someInteger = 123;
13       private int[] integerArray = { 74, 101, 102, 102 };
14       private DebugClass debugClass;
15       private Random randomObject;
16       private object[] list = new object[ 3 ];
17
18       // constructor
19       public DebugEntry()
20       {
21          randomObject = new Random();
22          debugClass = new DebugClass( "Hello World",
23            new object() );
24
25          list[ 0 ] = integerArray;
26          list[ 1 ] = debugClass;
27          list[ 2 ] = randomObject;
28       }
29
30       // display values retrieved from three objects
31       public void DisplayValues()
32       {
33          Console.WriteLine( randomObject.Next() );
34          Console.WriteLine( debugClass.SomeString );
35          Console.WriteLine( integerArray[ 0 ] );
36       }
37
38       // main entry point for application
39       [STAThread]
40       public static void Main()
41       {
42          DebugEntry entry = new DebugEntry();
43          entry.DisplayValues();
44       }
45    } // end class DebugEntry
46
47    // demonstrates class debugging
48    public class DebugClass
49    {
50       // private variables
51       private string someString;
52       private object privateObject;
53
```

Fig. D.21   Object debugging example. (Part 1 of 2.)

```
54            // constructor
55            public DebugClass( string stringData,
56               object objectData )
57            {
58               someString = stringData;
59               privateObject = objectData;
60            }
61
62            // accessor property for someString
63            public string SomeString
64            {
65               get
66               {
67                  return someString;
68               }
69
70               set
71               {
72                  someString = value;
73               }
74            } // end property SomeString
75
76         } // end class DebugClass
77
78      } // end namespace ClassDebug
```

Fig. D.21   Object debugging example. (Part 2 of 2.)

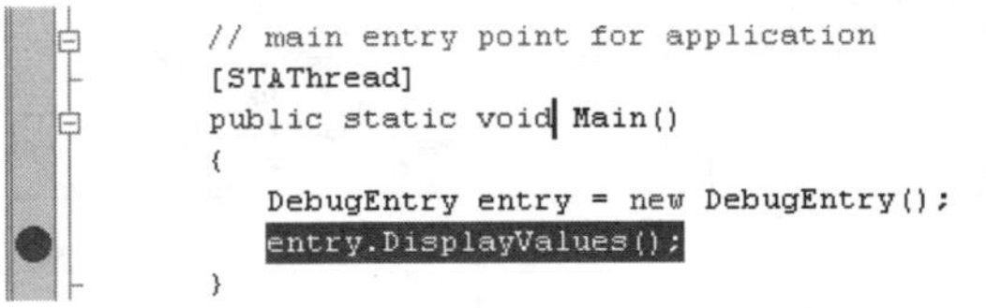

```
// main entry point for application
[STAThread]
public static void Main()
{
    DebugEntry entry = new DebugEntry();
    entry.DisplayValues();
}
```

Fig. D.22   Breakpoint location for class debugging.

To assist class debugging, Visual Studio .NET allows the programmer to expand and view all data members and properties of a class, including **private** members. In any of the three windows (i.e., **Watch**, **Locals**, **Autos** and **This**), a class that has data members is displayed with a plus (**+**) (Fig. D.23). When a programmer clicks the plus box, all the object's data members and their values display. If a member references an object, the object's data members also can be listed by clicking the object's plus box.

Many logic errors are the result of incorrect array calculations. To simplify the identification of such errors, the debugger includes the ability to display all the values in an array. Figure D.24 displays the contents of the **list** array. The object at index **0** is and **int** array, which is expanded to show its contents. Index **1** contains a **DebugClass** object—expanded to show the object's **private** data members, as well as a **public** property. Index **2** contains a **Random** object, defined in the Framework Class Library (FCL).

The Visual Studio debugger contains several other debugging windows, including **Threads**, **Modules**, **Memory**, **Disassembly** and **Registers**. These windows are used by experienced programmers to debug large, complex projects—consult the Visual Studio .NET documentation for more details on these features.

In this appendix, we demonstrated several techniques for debugging programs, methods and classes. The Visual Studio .NET debugger is a powerful tool that allows programmers to build more robust, fault-tolerant programs.

D.7 Summary

Debugging is the process of finding logic errors in applications. Syntax errors (or compilation errors) occur when program statements violate the grammatical rules of a programming language and are caught by the compiler. Logic errors occur when a program compiles successfully, but does not run as expected. Debuggers allow programmers to examine a program while it is executing.

A breakpoint is a marker set at a line of code. When a program reaches a breakpoint, execution is suspended. The programmer then can examine the state of the program and ensure that the program is working properly. To set breakpoints, click the gray area to the left of any line of code. Alternatively, right-click a line of code and select **Insert Breakpoint**. The **Breakpoints** window displays all the breakpoints currently set for a program. Disabled breakpoints allow the programmer to maintain breakpoints in key locations in the program so that they can be used again when needed.

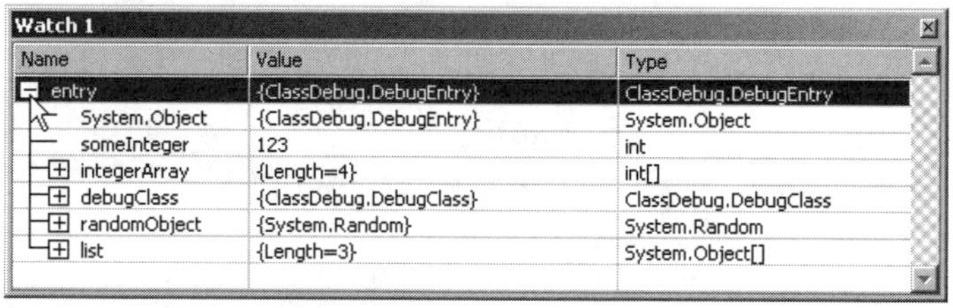

Fig. D.23 Expanded class in **Watch** window.

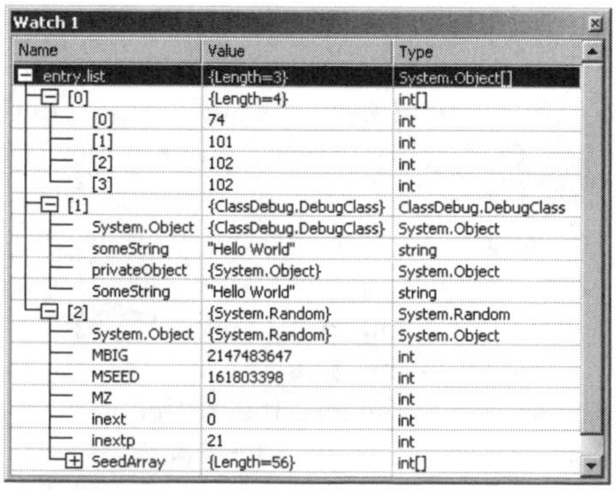

Fig. D.24 Expanded array in **Watch** window.

The **Watch** window allows the programmer to examine the values of variables and expressions. To examine data, type a valid C# expression, such as a variable name, into the **Name** field. Once the expression has been entered, its type and value appear in the **Type** and **Value** fields. Variables in the **Watch** window can be modified by the user for testing purposes. To modify a variable's value, click the **Value** field and enter a new value.

The **Locals** window displays the name and current value of all the local variables or objects in the current scope. The **Autos** window displays the variables and objects used in the previous statement and the current statement (indicated by the yellow arrow).

The **Immediate** window is useful for testing arguments passed to a method. This helps determine whether a method is functioning properly. To evaluate an expression in the **Immediate** window, simply type the expression into the window and press *Enter*.

The **Call Stack** window contains the program's method call stack, which allows the programmer to determine the exact sequence of calls that led to the current method and to examine calling methods on the stack.

The **Continue** button resumes execution of a suspended program. The **Stop Debugging** button ends the debugging session. The **Break All** button allows the programmer to place an executing program in break mode. The **Show Next Statement** button places the cursor on the same line as the yellow arrow that indicates the next statement to execute. The **Step Over** button executes the next executable line of code, advances the yellow arrow to the executable line that follows and, finally, pauses program execution. If the executed line of code contains a method call, the method is executed in its entirety as one step. The **Step Into** button executes the next statement. If the statement contains a method call, control transfers to the method for line-by-line debugging. If the statement does not contain a method call, **Step Into** behaves like **Step Over**. The **Step Out** button finishes executing the method and returns control to the line that called the method. The **Hex** button toggles the display format of data. If enabled, **Hex** displays data in a hexadecimal (base-16) form, rather than decimal (base-10) form.

Visual Studio .NET includes class debugging features that allow the programmer to determine the current state of any objects used in a program. To assist class debugging, Visual Studio .NET allows the programmer to expand and view all data members' variables and properties of an object, including those declared `private`.

ASCII Character Set

	0	1	2	3	4	5	6	7	8	9
0	nul	soh	stx	etx	eot	enq	ack	bel	bs	ht
1	nl	vt	ff	cr	so	si	dle	dc1	dc2	dc3
2	dc4	nak	syn	etb	can	em	sub	esc	fs	gs
3	rs	us	sp	!	"	#	$	%	&	`
4	(	)	*	+	,	-	.	/	0	1
5	2	3	4	5	6	7	8	9	:	;
6	<	=	>	?	@	A	B	C	D	E
7	F	G	H	I	J	K	L	M	N	O
8	P	Q	R	S	T	U	V	W	X	Y
9	Z	[	\	]	^	_	'	a	b	c
10	d	e	f	g	h	i	j	k	l	m
11	n	o	p	q	r	s	t	u	v	w
12	x	y	z	{			}	~	del		

Fig. E.1   ASCII character set.

The digits at the left of the table are the left digits of the decimal equivalent (0–127) of the character code, and the digits at the top of the table are the right digits of the character code. For example, the character code for "F" is 70, and the character code for "&" is 38.

Most readers of this book are interested in the ASCII character set used to represent English characters on many computers. The ASCII character set is a subset of the Unicode character set used by C# to represent characters from most of the world's languages. For more information on the Unicode character set, see Appendix F.

Unicode®

Objectives

- To become familiar with Unicode.
- To discuss the mission of the Unicode Consortium.
- To discuss the design basis of Unicode.
- To understand the three Unicode encoding forms:
  UTF-8, UTF-16 and UTF-32.
- To introduce characters and glyphs.
- To discuss the advantages and disadvantages of using
  Unicode.
- To provide a brief tour of the Unicode Consortium's
  Web site.

Outline

F.1 Introduction

The use of inconsistent character *encodings* (i.e., numeric values associated with characters) when developing global software products causes serious problems because computers process information using numbers. For example, the character "a" is converted to a numeric value so that a computer can manipulate that piece of data. Many countries and corporations have developed their own encoding systems that are incompatible with the encoding systems of other countries and corporations. For example, the Microsoft Windows operating system assigns the value 0xC0 to the character "A with a grave accent," while the Apple Macintosh operating system assigns that same value to an upside-down question mark. This results in the misrepresentation and possible corruption of data because the data is not processed as intended.

In the absence of a widely implemented universal character encoding standard, global software developers had to *localize* their products extensively before distribution. Localization includes the language translation and cultural adaptation of content. The process of localization usually includes significant modifications to the source code (such as the conversion of numeric values and the underlying assumptions made by programmers), which results in increased costs and delays releasing the software. For example, some English-speaking programmers might design global software products assuming that a single character can be represented by one byte. However, when those products are localized for Asian markets, the programmer's assumptions are no longer valid; thus, the majority, if not the entirety, of the code needs to be rewritten. Localization is necessary with each release of a version. By the time a software product is localized for a particular market, a newer version, which needs to be localized as well, may be ready for distribution. As a result, it is cumbersome and costly to produce and distribute global software products in a market where there is no universal character encoding standard.

In response to this situation, the *Unicode Standard*, an encoding standard that facilitates the production and distribution of software, was created. The Unicode Standard outlines a specification to produce consistent encoding of the world's characters and *symbols*. Software products that handle text encoded in the Unicode Standard need to be localized, but the localization process is simpler and more efficient because the numeric values need not be converted and the assumptions made by programmers about the character encoding are universal. The Unicode Standard is maintained by a nonprofit organization called the

Unicode Consortium, whose members include Apple, IBM, Microsoft, Oracle, Sun Microsystems, Sybase and many others.

When the Consortium envisioned and developed the Unicode Standard, they wanted an encoding system that was *universal*, *efficient*, *uniform* and *unambiguous*. A universal encoding system encompasses all commonly used characters. An efficient encoding system allows text files to be parsed easily. A uniform encoding system assigns fixed values to all characters. An unambiguous encoding system represents a given character in a consistent manner. These four terms are referred to as the Unicode Standard *design basis*.

F.2 Unicode Transformation Formats

Although Unicode incorporates the limited ASCII *character set* (i.e., a collection of characters), it encompasses a more comprehensive character set. In ASCII, each character is represented by a byte containing 0s and 1s. One byte is capable of storing the binary numbers from 0 to 255. Each character is assigned a number between 0 and 255; thus, ASCII-based systems can support only 256 characters, a tiny fraction of the world's characters. Unicode extends the ASCII character set by encoding the vast majority of the world's characters. The Unicode Standard encodes all of those characters in a uniform numerical space from 0 to 10FFFF hexadecimal. An implementation will express these numbers in one of several transformation formats, choosing the one that best fits the particular application at hand.

Three such formats are in use, called *UTF-8*, *UTF-16* and *UTF-32*, depending on the size of the units—in *bits*—being used. UTF-8, a variable width encoding form, requires one to four bytes to express each Unicode character. UTF-8 data consists of 8-bit bytes (sequences of one, two, three or four bytes depending on the character being encoded) and is well suited for ASCII-based systems when there is a predominance of one-byte characters (ASCII represents characters as one-byte). Currently, UTF-8 is widely implemented in UNIX systems and in databases. [*Note*: Currently, Internet Explorer 6.0 and Netscape Communicator 6 only support UTF-8, so document authors should use UTF-8 for encoding XML and XHTML documents.]

The variable width UTF-16 encoding form expresses Unicode characters in units of 16-bits (i.e., as two adjacent bytes, or a short integer in many machines). Most characters of Unicode are expressed in a single 16-bit unit. However, characters with values above FFFF hexadecimal are expressed with an ordered pair of 16-bit units called *surrogates*. Surrogates are 16-bit integers in the range D800 through DFFF, which are used solely for the purpose of "escaping" into higher numbered characters. Approximately one million characters can be expressed in this manner. Although a surrogate pair requires 32 bits to represent characters, it is space efficient to use these 16-bit units. Surrogates are rare characters in current implementations. Many string-handling implementations are written in terms of UTF-16. [*Note*: Details and sample code for UTF-16 handling are available on the Unicode Consortium Web site at **www.unicode.org**.]

Implementations that require significant use of rare characters or entire scripts encoded above FFFF hexadecimal should use UTF-32, a 32-bit, fixed-width encoding form that usually requires twice as much memory as UTF-16 encoded characters. The major advantage of the fixed-width UTF-32 encoding form is that it expresses all characters uniformly, so it is easy to handle in arrays.

There are few guidelines that state when to use a particular encoding form. The best encoding form to use depends on computer systems and business protocols, not on the data.

Typically, the UTF-8 encoding form should be used where computer systems and business protocols require data to be handled in 8-bit units, particularly in legacy systems being upgraded because it often simplifies changes to existing programs. For this reason, UTF-8 has become the encoding form of choice on the Internet. Likewise, UTF-16 is the encoding form of choice on Microsoft Windows applications. UTF-32 is likely to become more widely used in the future as more characters are encoded with values above FFFF hexadecimal. Also, UTF-32 requires less sophisticated handling than UTF-16 in the presence of surrogate pairs. Figure F.1 shows the different ways in which the three encoding forms handle character encoding.

F.3 Characters and Glyphs

The Unicode Standard consists of *characters*, written components (i.e., alphabetic letters, numerals, punctuation marks, accent marks, etc.) that can be represented by numeric values. Examples of characters include U+0041 LATIN CAPITAL LETTER A. In the first character representation, U+*yyyy* is a *code value*, in which U+ refers to Unicode code values, as opposed to other hexadecimal values. The *yyyy* represents a four-digit hexadecimal number of an encoded character. Code values are bit combinations that represent encoded characters. Characters are represented using *glyphs*, various shapes, fonts and sizes for displaying characters. There are no code values for glyphs in the Unicode Standard. Examples of glyphs are shown in Fig. F.2.

The Unicode Standard encompasses the alphabets, ideographs, syllabaries, punctuation marks, *diacritics*, mathematical operators, etc. that comprise the written languages and scripts of the world. A diacritic is a special mark added to a character to distinguish it from another letter or to indicate an accent (e.g., in Spanish, the tilde "~" above the character "n"). Currently, Unicode provides code values for 94,140 character representations, with more than 880,000 code values reserved for future expansion.

Character	UTF-8	UTF-16	UTF-32
LATIN CAPITAL LETTER A	0x41	0x0041	0x00000041
GREEK CAPITAL LETTER ALPHA	0xCD 0x91	0x0391	0x00000391
CJK UNIFIED IDEOGRAPH-4E95	0xE4 0xBA 0x95	0x4E95	0x00004E95
OLD ITALIC LETTER A	0xF0 0x80 0x83 0x80	0xDC00 0xDF00	0x00010300

Fig. F.1   Correlation between the three encoding forms.

Fig. F.2   Various glyphs of the character A.

F.4 Advantages and Disadvantages of Unicode

The Unicode Standard has several significant advantages that promote its use. One is the impact it has on the performance of the international economy. Unicode standardizes the characters for the world's writing systems to a uniform model that promotes transferring and sharing data. Programs developed using such a schema maintain their accuracy because each character has a single definition (i.e., *a* is always U+0061, % is always U+0025). This enables corporations to manage the high demands of international markets by processing different writing systems at the same time. Also, all characters can be managed in an identical manner, thus avoiding any confusion caused by different character code architectures. Moreover, managing data in a consistent manner eliminates data corruption, because data can be sorted, searched and manipulated using a consistent process.

Another advantage of the Unicode Standard is *portability* (i.e., the ability to execute software on disparate computers or with disparate operating systems). Most operating systems, databases, programming languages and Web browsers currently support, or are planning to support, Unicode. Additionally, Unicode includes more characters than any other character set in common use (although it does not yet include all of the world's characters).

A disadvantage of the Unicode Standard is the amount of memory required by UTF-16 and UTF-32. ASCII character sets are 8 bits in length, so they require less storage than the default 16-bit Unicode character set. However, the *double-byte character set (DBCS)* and the *multi-byte character set (MBCS)* that encode Asian characters (ideographs) require two to four bytes, respectively. In such instances, the UTF-16 or the UTF-32 encoding forms may be used with little hindrance on memory and performance.

F.5 Unicode Consortium's Web Site

If you would like to learn more about the Unicode Standard, visit **www.unicode.org**. This site provides a wealth of information about the Unicode Standard. Currently, the home page is organized into various sections: *New to Unicode*, *General Information*, *The Consortium*, *The Unicode Standard*, *Work in Progress* and *For Members*.

The *New to Unicode* section consists of two subsections: **What is Unicode?** and **How to Use this Site**. The first subsection provides a technical introduction to Unicode by describing design principles, character interpretations and assignments, text processing and Unicode conformance. This subsection is recommended reading for anyone new to Unicode. Also, this subsection provides a list of related links that provide the reader with additional information about Unicode. The **How to Use this Site** subsection contains information about using and navigating the site as well hyperlinks to additional resources.

The *General Information* section contains six subsections: **Where is my Character?**, **Display Problems?**, **Useful Resources**, **Enabled Products**, **Mail Lists** and **Conferences**. The main areas covered in this section include a link to the Unicode code charts (a complete listing of code values) assembled by the Unicode Consortium as well as a detailed outline on how to locate an encoded character in the code chart. Also, the section contains advice on how to configure different operating systems and Web browsers so that the Unicode characters can be viewed properly. Moreover, from this section, the user can navigate to other sites that provide information on various topics such as, fonts, linguistics and other standards such as the *Armenian Standards Page* and the *Chinese GB 18030 Encoding Standard*.

The Consortium section consists of five subsections: **Who we are**, **Our Members**, **How to Join**, **Press Info** and **Contact Us**. This section provides a list of the current Unicode Consortium members as well as information on how to become a member. Privileges for each member type—*full*, *associate*, *specialist* and *individual*—and the fees assessed to each member are listed here.

The Unicode Standard section consists of nine subsections: **Start Here**, **Latest Version**, **Technical Reports**, **Code Charts**, **Unicode Data**, **Updates & Errata**, **Unicode Policies**, **Glossary** and **Technical FAQ**. This section describes the updates applied to the latest version of the Unicode Standard, as well as categorizing all defined encoding. The user can learn how the latest version has been modified to encompass more features and capabilities. For instance, one enhancement of Version 3.2 is that it contains additional encoded characters. Also, if users are unfamiliar with vocabulary terms used by the Unicode Consortium, then they can navigate to the **Glossary** subsection.

The *Work in Progress* section consists of three subsections: **Calendar of Meetings**, **Proposed Characters** and **Submitting Proposals**. This section presents the user with a catalog of the recent characters included into the Unicode Standard scheme as well as those characters being considered for inclusion. If users determine that a character has been overlooked, then they can submit a written proposal for the inclusion of that character. The **Submitting Proposals** subsection contains strict guidelines that must be adhered to when submitting written proposals.

The *For Members* section consists of two subsections: **Member Resources** and **Working Documents**. These subsections are password protected; only consortium members can access these links.

F.6 Using Unicode

Visual Studio .NET uses Unicode UTF-16 encoding to represent all characters. Figure F.3 uses C# to display the text "Welcome to Unicode!" in eight different languages: English, French, German, Japanese, Portuguese, Russian, Spanish and Simplified Chinese. [*Note*: The Unicode Consortium's Web site contains a link to code charts that lists the 16-bit Unicode code values.]

```
1   // Fig F.3: Unicode.cs
2   // Using unicode encoding
3
4   using System;
5   using System.Drawing;
6   using System.Collections;
7   using System.ComponentModel;
8   using System.Windows.Forms;
9   using System.Data;
10
11  public class Unicode : System.Windows.Forms.Form
12  {
13      internal System.Windows.Forms.Label lblChinese;
14      internal System.Windows.Forms.Label lblSpanish;
15      internal System.Windows.Forms.Label lblRussian;
```

Fig. F.3   Unicode values for multiple languages. (Part 1 of 3.)

```
16        internal System.Windows.Forms.Label lblPortuguese;
17        internal System.Windows.Forms.Label lblJapanese;
18        internal System.Windows.Forms.Label lblGerman;
19        internal System.Windows.Forms.Label lblFrench;
20        internal System.Windows.Forms.Label lblEnglish;
21        private System.ComponentModel.Container components = null;
22
23        // Visual Studio .NET generated code
24
25        // main entry point for the application.
26        [STAThread]
27        static void Main()
28        {
29            Application.Run(new Unicode());
30        }
31
32        private void Unicode_Load(object sender, System.EventArgs e)
33        {
34            // English
35            char[] english = {'\u0057', '\u0065', '\u006C',
36                '\u0063', '\u006F', '\u006D', '\u0065', '\u0020',
37                '\u0074', '\u006F', '\u0020' };
38
39            lblEnglish.Text = new string(english) +
40                "Unicode" + '\u0021';
41
42            // French
43            char[] french = { '\u0042', '\u0069', '\u0065',
44                '\u006E', '\u0076', '\u0065', '\u006E', '\u0075',
45                '\u0065', '\u0020', '\u0061', '\u0075', '\u0020' };
46
47            lblFrench.Text = new string(french) +
48                "Unicode" + '\u0021';
49
50            // German
51            char[] german = {'\u0057', '\u0069', '\u006C',
52                '\u006B', '\u006F', '\u006D', '\u006D', '\u0065',
53                '\u006E', '\u0020', '\u007A', '\u0075', '\u0020'};
54
55            lblGerman.Text =  new string(german) +
56                "Unicode" + '\u0021';
57
58            // Japanese
59            char[] japanese = { '\u3078',  '\u3087', '\u3045',
60                '\u3053', '\u305D', '\u0021'};
61
62            lblJapanese.Text = "Unicode" + new string(japanese);
63
64            // Portuguese
65            char[] portuguese = {'\u0053', '\u0065', '\u006A',
66                '\u0061', '\u0020', '\u0062', '\u0065', '\u006D',
67                '\u0020', '\u0076', '\u0069', '\u006E', '\u0064',
68                '\u006F', '\u0020', '\u0061', '\u0020' };
```

Fig. F.3   Unicode values for multiple languages. (Part 2 of 3.)

```
69
70      lblPortuguese.Text = new string(portuguese) +
71         "Unicode" + '\u0021';
72
73      // Russian
74      char[] russian = {  '\u0414', '\u043E', '\u0431',
75         '\u0440', '\u043E', '\u0020', '\u043F', '\u043E',
76         '\u0436', '\u0430', '\u043B', '\u043E', '\u0432',
77         '\u0430', '\u0442', '\u044A', '\u0020', '\u0432',
78         '\u0020' };
79
80      lblRussian.Text = new string(russian) +
81         "Unicode" + '\u0021';
82
83      // Spanish
84      char[] spanish = {'\u0042', '\u0069', '\u0065',
85         '\u006E', '\u0076', '\u0065', '\u006E', '\u0069',
86         '\u0064', '\u006F', '\u0020', '\u0061', '\u0020' };
87
88      lblSpanish.Text = new string(spanish) +
89         "Unicode" + '\u0021';
90
91      // Simplified Chinese
92      char[] chinese = {'\u6B22', '\u8FCE', '\u4F7F',
93         '\u7528', '\u0020' };
94
95      lblChinese.Text = new string(chinese) +
96         "Unicode" + '\u0021';
97   }   // end method Unicode_Load
98 } // end class Unicode
```

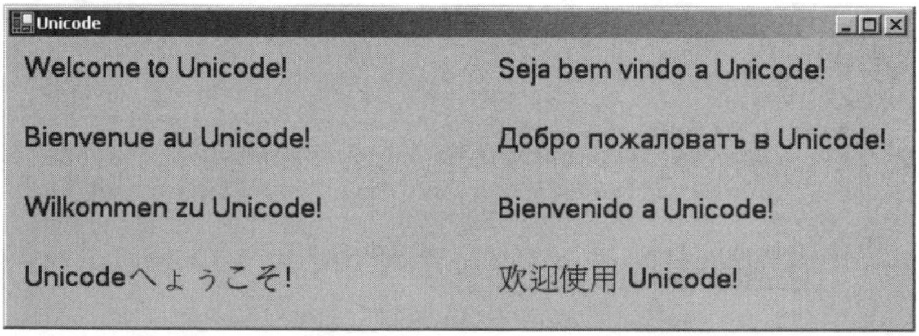

Fig. F.3   Unicode values for multiple languages. (Part 3 of 3.)

Lines 35–37 contain the hexadecimal codes for the English text. The **Code Charts** page on the Unicode Consortium Web site contains a document that lists the code values for the **Basic Latin** *block* (or category), which includes the English alphabet. The hexadecimal codes in lines 35–36 equate to "**Welcome** ". When using Unicode characters in C#, the format **\u**yyyy is used, where *yyyy* represents the hexadecimal Unicode encoding. For example, the letter "W" (in "Welcome") is denoted by **\u0057**. Line 36 contains the hexadecimal for the *space* character (**\u0020**). The unicode value for the word "**to** " is on line 37. Lines 39–40 create a new string from the character array and append the word "Unicode." "Unicode" is not encoded because it is a registered trademark and has no equivalent translation in most languages. Line 40 also contains the **\u0021** notation for the exclamation mark (!).

The remaining welcome messages (lines 43–96) contain the unicode values for the other seven languages. The code values used for the French, German, Portuguese and Spanish text are located in the **Basic Latin** block, the code values used for the Simplified Chinese text are located in the **CJK Unified Ideographs** block, the code values used for the Russian text are located in the **Cyrillic** block and the code values used for the Japanese text are located in the **Hiragana** block.

[*Note*: To render the Asian characters in a Windows application, you may need to install the proper language files on your computer. To do this in Windows 2000, open the **Regional Options** dialog from the **Control Panel** (**Start > Settings > Control Panel**). At the bottom of the **General** tab is a list of languages. Check the **Japanese** and the **Traditional Chinese** checkboxes and press **Apply**. Follow the directions of the install wizard to install the languages. For additional assistance, visit **www.unicode.org/help/display_problems.html**.]

F.7 Character Ranges

The Unicode Standard assigns code values, which range from **0000** (**Basic Latin**) to **E007F** (*Tags*), to the written characters of the world. Currently, there are code values for 94,140 characters. To simplify the search for a character and its associated code value, the Unicode Standard generally groups code values by *script* and function (i.e., Latin characters are grouped in a block, mathematical operators are grouped in another block, etc.). As a rule, a script is a single writing system that is used for multiple languages (e.g., the Latin script is used for English, French, Spanish, etc.) The **Code Charts** page on the Unicode Consortium Web site lists all the defined blocks and their respective code values. Figure F.4 lists some blocks (scripts) from the Web site and their range of code values.

Script	Range of Code Values
Arabic	U+0600–U+06FF
Basic Latin	U+0000–U+007F
Bengali (India)	U+0980–U+09FF
Cherokee (Native America)	U+13A0–U+13FF
CJK Unified Ideographs (East Asia)	U+4E00–U+9FAF
Cyrillic (Russia and Eastern Europe)	U+0400–U+04FF
Ethiopic	U+1200–U+137F
Greek	U+0370–U+03FF
Hangul Jamo (Korea)	U+1100–U+11FF
Hebrew	U+0590–U+05FF
Hiragana (Japan)	U+3040–U+309F

Fig. F.4   Some character ranges. (Part 1 of 2.)

Script	Range of Code Values
Khmer (Cambodia)	U+1780–U+17FF
Lao (Laos)	U+0E80–U+0EFF
Mongolian	U+1800–U+18AF
Myanmar	U+1000–U+109F
Ogham (Ireland)	U+1680–U+169F
Runic (Germany and Scandinavia)	U+16A0–U+16FF
Sinhala (Sri Lanka)	U+0D80–U+0DFF
Telugu (India)	U+0C00–U+0C7F
Thai	U+0E00–U+0E7F

Fig. F.4   Some character ranges. (Part 2 of 2.)

F.8 Summary

Before Unicode, software developers were plagued by the use of inconsistent character encoding (e.g., using numeric values for characters). Most countries and organizations had their own encoding systems, which were incompatible with each other. Without Unicode, localization of global software requires significant modifications to the source code, which results in increased cost and in delays in releasing the product.

The Unicode Consortium developed the Unicode Standard in response to the serious problems created by multiple character encodings and the use of those encodings. The Unicode Standard facilitates the production and distribution of localized software. It outlines a specification for the consistent encoding of the world's characters and symbols. Software products that handle text encoded in the Unicode Standard need to be localized, but the localization process is simpler and more efficient. The Unicode Standard is designed to be universal, efficient, uniform and unambiguous.

A universal encoding system encompasses all commonly used characters; an efficient encoding system parses text files easily; a uniform encoding system assigns fixed values to all characters; and an unambiguous encoding system represents the same character for any given value. Unicode extends the limited ASCII character set to include all the major characters of the world. Unicode makes use of three Unicode Transformation Formats (UTF)—UTF-8, UTF-16 and UTF-32—each of which may be appropriate for use in different contexts. UTF-8 data consists of 8-bit bytes (sequences of one, two, three or four bytes, depending on the character being encoded) and is well suited for ASCII-based systems when there is a predominance of one-byte characters. (ASCII represents characters with one-byte.) UTF-8 is a variable-width encoding form that is more compact for text involving mostly Latin characters and ASCII punctuation. UTF-16, the default encoding form of the Unicode Standard, is a variable-width encoding form that uses 16-bit code units instead of bytes. Most characters are represented by a single unit, but some characters require surrogate pairs. Surrogates are 16-bit integers in the range D800 through DFFF and are used solely for the purpose of "escaping" into higher numbered characters. Without surrogate pairs, the UTF-16 encoding form can encompass only 65,000 characters, but with the surrogate pairs, the number is expanded to include over a million characters. UTF-32 is a 32-bit, fixed-width encoding form whose major advantage is that it expresses all characters uniformly, so that they are easy to handle in arrays and other structures.

A character is any written component that can be represented by a numeric value. Characters are represented with glyphs, shapes, fonts and sizes. Code values are bit combinations that represent encoded characters. The Unicode notation for a code value is U+*yyyy*, in which U+ refers to the Unicode code values, as opposed to other hexadecimal values. The *yyyy* represents a four-digit hexadecimal number.

The Unicode Standard has become the default encoding system for XML and any language derived from XML, such as XHTML. The Visual Studio .NET IDE uses UTF-16 encoding to represent all characters. In using Unicode characters in C# code, the escape sequence \u*yyyy* is used, where *yyyy* represents the hexadecimal Unicode encoding.

Introduction to HyperText Markup Language 4: Part 1

Objectives

- To understand the key components of an HTML document.
- To be able to use basic HTML elements to create World Wide Web pages.
- To be able to add images to your Web pages.
- To understand how to create and use hyperlinks to traverse Web pages.
- To be able to create lists of information.

To read between the lines was easier than to follow the text.
Henry James

Mere colour, unspoiled by meaning, and annulled with definite form, can speak to the soul in a thousand different ways.
Oscar Wilde

High thoughts must have high language.
Aristophanes

I've gradually risen from lower-class background to lower-class foreground.
Marvin Cohen

Outline

G.1 Introduction

In this appendix we introduce the basics of creating Web pages in HTML. We write many simple Web pages. In Appendix H, Introduction to HyperText Markup Language 4: Part 2, we introduce more sophisticated HTML techniques, such as *tables*, which are particularly useful for structuring information from databases. In this appendix, we do not present any C# programming.

In this appendix, we introduce basic HTML *elements* and *attributes*. A key issue when using HTML is the separation of the *presentation of a document* (i.e., how the document is rendered on the screen by a browser) from the *structure of that document*. In this appendix and in Appendix H, we discuss this issue in depth.

G.2 Markup Languages

HTML is a *markup language*. It is used to format text and information. This "marking up" of information is different from the intent of traditional programming languages, which is to perform actions in a designated order.

In HTML, text is marked up with *elements*, delineated by *tags* that are keywords contained in pairs of angle brackets. For example, the HTML *element* itself, which indicates that we are writing a Web page to be rendered by a browser, begins with the start tag **`<html>`** and terminates with the end tag **`</html>`**. These elements format your page in a specified way. Over the course of the next two appendices, we introduce many of the commonly used tags and how to use them.

Good Programming Practice G.1

HTML tags are not case sensitive. However, keeping all the letters in one case improves program readability. Although the choice of case is up to you, we recommend that you write all of your code in lowercase. Writing in lowercase ensures greater compatibility with future markup languages that are designed to be written with only lowercase tags and elements.

Common Programming Error G.1

Forgetting to include end tags for elements that require them is a syntax error and can grossly affect the formatting and look of your page. Unlike conventional programming languages, a syntax error in HTML does not usually cause page display in browsers to fail completely.

G.3 Editing HTML

In this appendix we show how to write HTML in its *source-code form*. We create *HTML documents* using a text editor and store them in files with either the **.html** or **.htm** file name extension. A wide variety of text editors exist. We recommend that you initially use a text editor called Notepad, which is built into Windows. Notepad can be found inside the **Accessories** panel of your **Program** list, inside the **Start** menu. You can also download a free HTML source-code editor called HTML-Kit at **www.chami.com/html-kit**. Unix users can use popular text editors like *vi* or *emacs*.

Good Programming Practice G.2

*Assign names to your files that describe their functionality. This practice can help you identify documents faster. It also helps people who want to link to your page, by giving them an easier-to-remember name for the file. For example, if you are writing an HTML document that will display your products, you might want to call it **products.html**.*

As mentioned previously, errors in conventional programming languages like C, C++ and Visual Basic often prevent the program from running. Errors in HTML markup are usually not fatal. The browser will make its best effort at rendering the page, but will probably not display the page as you intended.

The file name of your *home page* (the first of your HTML pages that a user sees when browsing your Web site) should be **index.html**, because when a browser does not request a specific file in a directory, the normal default Web server response is to return **index.html** (this may be different for your server) if it exists in that directory. For example, if you direct your browser to **www.deitel.com**, the server actually sends the file **www.deitel.com/index.html** to your browser.

G.4 Common Elements

Throughout these HTML appendices, we will present both HTML source code and a sample screen capture of the rendering of that HTML in Internet Explorer. Figure G.1 shows an HTML file that displays one line of text.

Lines 1 and 2

```
<!DOCTYPE HTML PUBLIC "-//W3C//DTD HTML 4.01//EN"
            "http://www.w3.org/TR/html4/strict.dtd">
```

are required in every HTML document and are used to specify the *document type*. The document type specifies which version of HTML is used in the document and can be used with a validation tool, such as the W3C's **validator.w3.org**, to ensure an HTML document conforms to the HTML recommendation. In these examples we create HTML version 4.01 documents. All of the examples in these appendices have been validated through the Web site **validator.w3.org**.

The HTML document begins with the opening **<html>** tag (line 3) and ends with the closing **</html>** tag (line 17).

```
1   <!DOCTYPE HTML PUBLIC "-//W3C//DTD HTML 4.01//EN"
2           "http://www.w3.org/TR/html4/strict.dtd">
3   <html>
4
5   <!-- Fig. I.1: main.html -->
6   <!-- Our first Web page. -->
7
8   <head>
9       <title>C# How to Program - Welcome</title>
10  </head>
11
12  <body>
13
14      <p>Welcome to Our Web Site!</p>
15
16  </body>
17  </html>
```

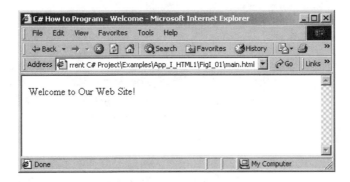

Fig. G.1   Basic HTML file.

Good Programming Practice G.3

Always include the **<html>...</html>** *tags in the beginning and end of your HTML document.*

Good Programming Practice G.4

Place comments throughout your code. Comments in HTML are placed inside the **<!--**... **-->** *tags. Comments help other programmers understand the code, assist in debugging and list other useful information that you do not want the browser to render. Comments also help you understand your own code, especially if you have not looked at it for a while.*

We see our first *comments* (i.e., text that documents or describes the HTML markup) on lines 5 and 6

```
<!-- Fig. I.1: main.html -->
<!-- Our first Web page. -->
```

Comments in HTML always begin with **<!--** and end with **-->**. The browser ignores any text and/or tags inside a comment. We place comments at the top of each HTML document giving the figure number, the file name and a brief description of the purpose of the example. In subsequent examples, we also include comments in the markup, especially when we introduce new features.

Every HTML document contains a *head* element, which generally contains information about the document, and a **body** element, which contains the page content. Information in the **head** element is not generally rendered in the display window, but may be made available to the user through other means. Lines 8–10

```
<head>
    <title>C# How to Program - Welcome</title>
</head>
```

show the **head** element section of our Web page. Including a *title* element is required for every HTML document. To include a title in your Web page, enclose your chosen title between the pair of tags *<title>...</title>* in the **head** element.

Good Programming Practice G.5

Use a consistent title-naming convention for all pages on your site. For example, if your site is called "Al's Web Site," then the title of your links page might best be "Al's Web Site - Links." This practice presents a clearer picture to those browsing your site.

The **title** element names your Web page. The title usually appears on the colored bar at the top of the browser window, and also will appear as the text identifying your page if a user adds your page to their list of **Favorites** or **Bookmarks**. The title is also used by search engines for cataloging purposes, so picking a meaningful title can help search engines direct a more focused group of people to your site.

Line 12

```
<body>
```

opens the *body* element. The body of an HTML document is the area where you place the content of your document. This includes text, images, links and forms. We discuss many elements that can be inserted in the **body** element later in this appendix. Remember to include the end **</body>** tag before the closing **</html>** tag.

Various elements enable you to place text in your HTML document. We see the *paragraph element* on line 14

```
<p>Welcome to Our Web Site!</p>
```

All text placed between the **<p>...</p>** tags forms one paragraph. Most Web browsers render paragraphs as set apart from all other material on the page by a line of vertical space both before and after the paragraph. The HTML in line 12 causes Internet Explorer to render the enclosed text as shown in Fig. G.1.

Our code example ends on lines 16 and 17 with

```
</body>
</html>
```

These two tags close the body and HTML sections of the document, respectively. As discussed earlier, the last tag in any HTML document should be **</html>**, which tells the browser that all HTML coding is complete. The closing **</body>** tag is placed before the **</html>** tag because the body section of the document is entirely enclosed by the HTML section. Therefore, the body section must be closed before the HTML section.

G.5 Headers

The six *headers* are used to delineate new sections and subsections of a page. Figure G.2 shows how these elements (**h1** through **h6**) are used. Note that the actual size of the text of each header element is selected by the browser and can vary significantly between browsers.

Good Programming Practice G.6

Adding comments to the right of short HTML lines is a clean-looking way to comment code.

```
1   <!DOCTYPE HTML PUBLIC "-//W3C//DTD HTML 4.01//EN"
2            "http://www.w3.org/TR/html4/strict.dtd">
3   <html>
4
5   <!-- Fig. I.2: header.html -->
6   <!-- HTML headers.          -->
7
8   <head>
9      <title>C# How to Program - Welcome</title>
10  </head>
11
12  <body>
13
14     <h1>Level 1 Header</h1>     <!-- Level 1 header -->
15     <h2>Level 2 header</h2>     <!-- Level 2 header -->
16     <h3>Level 3 header</h3>     <!-- Level 3 header -->
17     <h4>Level 4 header</h4>     <!-- Level 4 header -->
18     <h5>Level 5 header</h5>     <!-- Level 5 header -->
19     <h6>Level 6 header</h6>     <!-- Level 6 header -->
20
21  </body>
22  </html>
```

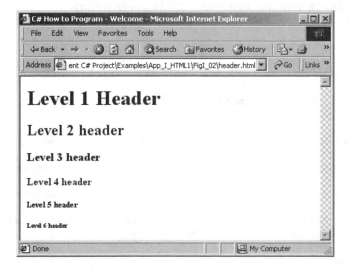

Fig. G.2   Header elements **h1** through **h6**.

Line 14

```
<h1>Level 1 Header</h1>
```

introduces the **h1** *header element*, with its start tag **<h1>** and its end tag **</h1>**. Any text to be displayed is placed between the two tags. All six header elements, **h1** through **h6**, follow the same pattern.

Good Programming Practice G.7

Putting a header at the top of every Web page helps those viewing your pages understand what the purpose of each page is.

G.6 Linking

The most important capability of HTML is its ability to create hyperlinks to other documents, making possible a worldwide network of linked documents and information. In HTML, both text and images can act as *anchors* to *link* to other pages on the Web. We introduce anchors and links in Fig. G.3.

The first link can be found on line 19

```
<p><a href = "http://www.yahoo.com">Yahoo</a></p>
```

```
1   <!DOCTYPE HTML PUBLIC "-//W3C//DTD HTML 4.01//EN"
2           "http://www.w3.org/TR/html4/strict.dtd">
3   <html>
4
5   <!-- Fig. I.3: links.html        -->
6   <!-- Introduction to hyperlinks. -->
7
8   <head>
9      <title>C# How to Program - Welcome</title>
10  </head>
11
12  <body>
13
14     <h1>Here are my favorite Internet Search Engines</h1>
15
16     <p><strong>Click on the Search Engine address to go to that
17        page.</strong></p>
18
19     <p><a href = "http://www.yahoo.com">Yahoo</a></p>
20
21     <p><a href = "http://www.altavista.com">AltaVista</a></p>
22
23     <p><a href = "http://www.askjeeves.com">Ask Jeeves</a></p>
24
25     <p><a href = "http://www.webcrawler.com">WebCrawler</a></p>
26
27  </body>
28  </html>
```

Fig. G.3   Linking to other Web pages. (Part 1 of 2.)

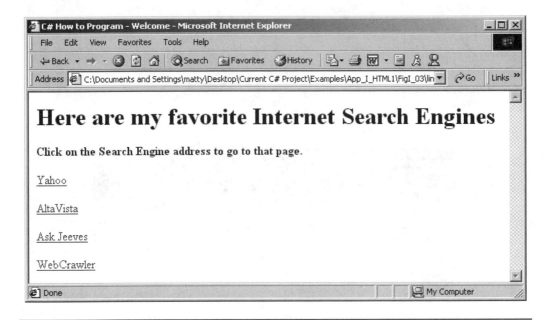

Fig. G.3   Linking to other Web pages. (Part 2 of 2.)

Links are inserted with the *a (anchor) element*. The anchor element is unlike the elements we have seen thus far in that it requires certain *attributes* (i.e., markup that provides information about the element) to specify the hyperlink. Attributes are placed inside an element's start tag and consist of a name and a value. The most important attribute for the **a** element is the location to which you would like the anchoring object to be linked. This location can be any resource on the Web, including pages, files and e-mail addresses. To specify the address to link to, add the **href** *attribute* to the anchor element as follows: **<a href = "***address***">**. In this case, the address we are linking to is **http://www.yahoo.com**. The hyperlink (line 19) makes the text **Yahoo** a link to the address specified in **href**.

Anchors can use **mailto** URLs to provide links to e-mail addresses. When someone selects this type of anchored link, most browsers launch the default e-mail program to initiate an e-mail message to the linked address. This type of anchor is demonstrated in Fig. G.4.

```
 1   <!DOCTYPE HTML PUBLIC "-//W3C//DTD HTML 4.01//EN"
 2               "http://www.w3.org/TR/html4/strict.dtd">
 3   <html>
 4
 5   <!-- Fig. I.4: contact.html   -->
 6   <!-- Adding email hyperlinks. -->
 7
 8   <head>
 9      <title>C# How to Program - Welcome</title>
10   </head>
11
```

Fig. G.4   Linking to an e-mail address. (Part 1 of 2.)

```
12   <body>
13
14      <p>My email address is <a href = "mailto:deitel@deitel.com">
15      deitel@deitel.com</a>. Click on the address and your browser
16      will open an email message and address it to me.</p>
17
18   </body>
19   </html>
```

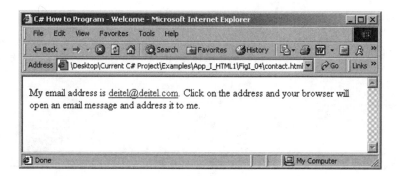

Fig. G.4   Linking to an e-mail address. (Part 2 of 2.)

We see an e-mail link on lines 14 and 15

```
<p>My email address is <a href = "mailto:deitel@deitel.com">
deitel@deitel.com</a>. Click on the address and your browser
```

The form of an e-mail anchor is **<a href = "mailto:**_emailaddress_**">...</a>**. It is important that this whole attribute, including the **mailto:**, be placed in quotation marks.

G.7 Images

We have thus far dealt exclusively with text. We now show how to incorporate images into Web pages (Fig. G.5).

```
1    <!DOCTYPE HTML PUBLIC "-//W3C//DTD HTML 4.01//EN"
2               "http://www.w3.org/TR/html4/strict.dtd">
3    <html>
4
5    <!-- Fig. I.5: picture.html    -->
6    <!-- Adding images with HTML. -->
7
8    <head>
9       <title>C# How to Program - Welcome</title>
10   </head>
11
```

Fig. G.5   Placing images in HTML files. (Courtesy of Prentice Hall, Inc.) (Part 1 of 2.)

```
12   <body>
13
14     <p><img src = "csphtp.jpg" height = "236" width = "181"
15        alt = "Demonstration of the alt attribute"></p>
16
17   </body>
18   </html>
```

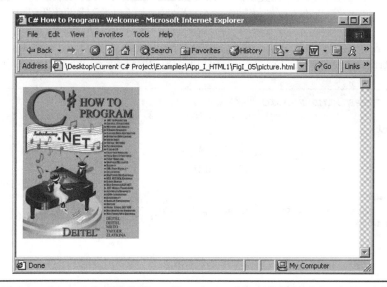

Fig. G.5   Placing images in HTML files. (Courtesy of Prentice Hall, Inc.) (Part 2 of 2.)

The image in this code example is inserted in lines 14 and 15:

```
<p><img src = "csphtp.jpg" height = "236" width = "181"
   alt = "Demonstration of the alt attribute"></p>
```

You specify the location of the image file in the **img** element. This is done by adding the **src = "**_location_**"** attribute. You can also specify the **height** and **width** of an image, measured in pixels. The term pixel stands for "picture element." Each pixel represents one dot of color on the screen. This image is 181 pixels wide and 236 pixels high.

Good Programming Practice G.8

*Always include the **height** and the **width** of an image inside the **img** tag. When the browser loads the HTML file, it will know immediately how much screen space to give the image and will therefore lay out the page properly, even before it downloads the image.*

Common Programming Error G.2

Entering new dimensions for an image that changes its inherent width-to-height ratio distorts the appearance of the image. For example, if your image is 200 pixels wide and 100 pixels high, you should always make sure that any new dimensions have a 2:1 width-to-height ratio.

The **alt** attribute is required for every **img** element. In Fig. G.5, the value of this attribute is

```
alt = "Demonstration of the alt attribute"
```

Attribute **alt** is provided for browsers that have images turned off or cannot view images (e.g., text-based browsers). The value of the **alt** attribute will appear on-screen in place of the image, giving the user an idea of what was in the image. The **alt** attribute is especially important for making Web pages *accessible* to users with disabilities, as discussed in Chapter 22, Accessibility.

Good Programming Practice G.9

Include a description of the purpose of every image, using the **alt** *attribute in the* **img** *tag.*

Now that we have discussed placing images on your Web page, we will show you how to transform images into anchors to provide links to other sites on the Internet (Fig. G.6).

```
1   <!DOCTYPE HTML PUBLIC "-//W3C//DTD HTML 4.01//EN"
2           "http://www.w3.org/TR/html4/strict.dtd">
3   <html>
4
5   <!-- Fig. I.6: nav.html          -->
6   <!-- Using images as link anchors. -->
7
8   <head>
9      <title>C# How to Program - Welcome</title>
10  </head>
11
12  <body>
13
14     <p>
15        <a href = "links.html">
16        <img src = "buttons/links.jpg" width = "65" height = "50"
17           alt = "Links Page"></a><br>
18
19        <a href = "list.html">
20        <img src = "buttons/list.jpg" width = "65" height = "50"
21           alt = "List Example Page"></a><br>
22
23        <a href = "contact.html">
24        <img src = "buttons/contact.jpg" width = "65" height = "50"
25           alt = "Contact Page"></a><br>
26
27        <a href = "header.html">
28        <img src = "buttons/header.jpg" width = "65" height = "50"
29           alt = "Header Page"></a><br>
30
31        <a href = "table.html">
32        <img src = "buttons/table.jpg" width = "65" height = "50"
33           alt = "Table Page"></a><br>
34
35        <a href = "form.html">
36        <img src = "buttons/form.jpg" width = "65" height = "50"
37           alt = "Feedback Form"></a><br>
38     </p>
39
```

Fig. G.6   Using images as link anchors. (Part 1 of 2.)

```
40   </body>
41   </html>
```

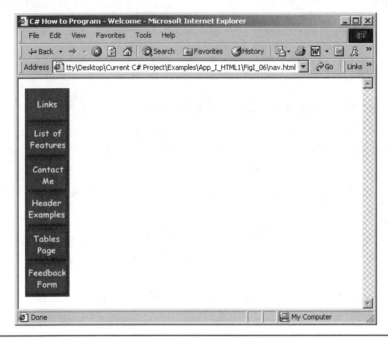

Fig. G.6   Using images as link anchors. (Part 2 of 2.)

We see an image hyperlink in lines 15–17

```
<a href = "links.html">
<img src = "buttons/links.jpg" width = "65" height = "50"
    alt = "Links Page"></a><br>
```

Here we use the **a** element and the **img** element. The anchor works the same way as when it surrounds text; the image becomes an active hyperlink to a location somewhere on the Internet, indicated by the **href** attribute inside the **<a>** tag. Remember to close the anchor element when you want the hyperlink to end.

If you direct your attention to the **src** attribute of the **img** element,

```
src = "buttons/links.jpg"
```

you will see that it is not in the same form as that of the image in the previous example. This is because the image we are using here, **about.jpg**, resides in a subdirectory called **buttons**, which is in the main directory for our site. We have done this so that we can keep all our button graphics in the same place, making them easier to find and edit.

You can always refer to files in different directories simply by putting the directory name in the correct format in the **src** attribute. If, for example, there was a directory inside the **buttons** directory called **images**, and we wanted to put a graphic from that directory onto our page, we would just have to make the source attribute reflect the location of the image: **src = "buttons/images/filename"**.

You can even insert an image from a different Web site into your site (after obtaining permission from the site's owner, of course). Just make the **src** attribute reflect the location and name of the image file.

On line 17

```
alt = "Links Page"></a><br>
```

we introduce the **br** *element*, which causes a *line break* to be rendered in most browsers.

G.8 Special Characters and More Line Breaks

In HTML, the old QWERTY typewriter setup no longer suffices for all our textual needs. HTML 4.01 has a provision for inserting special characters and symbols (Fig. G.7).

```
 1   <!DOCTYPE HTML PUBLIC "-//W3C//DTD HTML 4.01//EN"
 2              "http://www.w3.org/TR/html4/strict.dtd">
 3   <html>
 4
 5   <!-- Fig. I.7: contact.html        -->
 6   <!-- Inserting special characters. -->
 7
 8   <head>
 9      <title>C# How to Program - Welcome</title>
10   </head>
11
12   <body>
13
14      <!-- special characters are entered using the form &code; -->
15      <p>My email address is <a href = "mailto:deitel@deitel.com">
16      deitel@deitel.com</a>. Click on the address and your browser
17      will automatically open an email message and address it to my
18      address.</p>
19
20      <hr> <!-- inserts a horizontal rule -->
21
22      <p>All information on this site is <strong>&copy;</strong>
23      Deitel <strong>&amp;</strong> Associates, 2002.</p>
24
25      <!-- text can be struck out with a set of <del>...</del>  -->
26      <!-- tags, it can be set in subscript with <sub>...</sub>, -->
27      <!-- and it can be set into superscript with <sup...</sup> -->
28      <p><del>You may copy up to 3.14 x 10<sup>2</sup> characters
29      worth of information from this site.</del> Just make sure
30      you <sub>do not copy more information</sub> than is allowable.
31      </p>
32
33      <p>No permission is needed if you only need to use <strong>
34      &lt; &frac14;</strong> of the information presented here.</p>
35
36   </body>
37   </html>
```

Fig. G.7   Inserting special characters into HTML. (Part 1 of 2.)

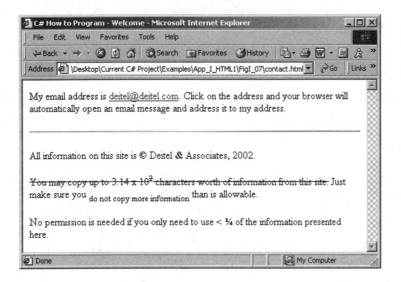

Fig. G.7   Inserting special characters into HTML. (Part 2 of 2.)

There are some *special characters* inserted into the text of lines 22 and 23:

```
<p>All information on this site is <strong>&copy;</strong>
Deitel <strong>&amp;</strong> Associates, 2002.</p>
```

All special characters are inserted in their code form. The format of the code is always **&***code***;**. An example of this is **&**, which inserts an ampersand. Codes are often abbreviated forms of the character (like **amp** for ampersand and **copy** for copyright) and can also be in the form of *hex codes*. (For example, the hex code for an ampersand is 38, so another method of inserting an ampersand is to use **&**.) Please refer to the chart in Appendix I for a listing of special characters and their respective codes.

In lines 28–31, we introduce three new styles.

```
<p><del>You may copy up to 3.14 x 10<sup>2</sup> characters
worth of information from this site.</del> Just make sure
you <sub>do not copy more information</sub> than is allow-
able.
</p>
```

You can indicate text that has been deleted from a document by including it in a ***del*** element. This could be used as an easy way to communicate revisions of an online document. Many browsers render the **del** element as strike-through text. To turn text into *superscript* (i.e., raised vertically to the top of the line and made smaller) or to turn text into *subscript* (the opposite of superscript, lowers text on a line and makes it smaller), use the ***sup*** or ***sub*** element, respectively.

Line 20

```
<hr> <!-- inserts a horizontal rule -->
```

inserts a horizontal rule, indicated by the **<hr>** tag. A horizontal rule is rendered by most browsers as a straight line going across the screen horizontally. The **hr** element also inserts a line break directly below it.

G.9 Unordered Lists

Figure G.8 demonstrates displaying text in an *unordered list*. Here, we reuse the HTML file from Fig. G.3, adding an unordered list to enhance the structure of the page. The *unordered list element* **ul** creates a list in which every line begins with a bullet mark in most Web browsers.

```
1   <!DOCTYPE HTML PUBLIC "-//W3C//DTD HTML 4.01//EN"
2              "http://www.w3.org/TR/html4/strict.dtd">
3   <html>
4
5   <!-- Fig. I.8: links.html                    -->
6   <!-- Unordered list containing hyperlinks. -->
7
8   <head>
9      <title>C# How to Program - Welcome</title>
10  </head>
11
12  <body>
13
14     <h1>Here are my favorite Internet Search Engines</h1>
15
16
17     <p><strong>Click on the Search Engine address to go to that
18        page.</strong></p>
19
20     <ul>
21        <li>
22           <a href = "http://www.yahoo.com">Yahoo</a>
23        </li>
24
25        <li>
26           <a href = "http://www.altavista.com">AltaVista</a>
27        </li>
28
29        <li>
30           <a href = "http://www.askjeeves.com">Ask Jeeves</a>
31        </li>
32
33        <li>
34           <a href = "http://www.webcrawler.com">WebCrawler</a>
35        </li>
36     </ul>
37
38  </body>
39  </html>
```

Fig. G.8   Unordered lists in HTML. (Part 1 of 2.)

Fig. G.8   Unordered lists in HTML. (Part 2 of 2.)

The first list item appears in lines 21–23

```
<li>
    <a href = "http://www.yahoo.com">Yahoo</a>
</li>
```

Each entry in an unordered list is a *li* (*list item*) element. Most Web browsers render these elements with a line break and a bullet mark at the beginning of the line.

G.10 Nested and Ordered Lists

Figure G.9 demonstrates *nested lists* (i.e., one list inside another list). This feature is useful for displaying information in outline form.

```
1    <!DOCTYPE HTML PUBLIC "-//W3C//DTD HTML 4.01//EN"
2              "http://www.w3.org/TR/html4/strict.dtd">
3    <html>
4
5    <!-- Fig. I.9: list.html               -->
6    <!-- Advanced Lists: nested and ordered. -->
7
8    <head>
9       <title>C# How to Program - Welcome</title>
10   </head>
11
12   <body>
13
14      <h1>The Best Features of the Internet</h1>
15
16      <ul>
17         <li>You can meet new people from countries around
18            the world.</li>
```

Fig. G.9   Nested and ordered lists in HTML. (Part 1 of 3.)

```
19          <li>You have access to new media as it becomes public:
20
21          <!-- this starts a nested list, which -->
22          <!-- uses a modified bullet. The list -->
23          <!-- ends when you close the <ul> tag -->
24          <ul>
25              <li>New games</li>
26              <li>New applications
27
28                  <!-- another nested list -->
29                  <ul>
30                      <li>For business</li>
31                      <li>For pleasure</li>
32                  </ul> <!-- this ends the double nested list -->
33              </li>
34
35              <li>Around the clock news</li>
36              <li>Search engines</li>
37              <li>Shopping</li>
38              <li>Programming
39
40                  <ul>
41                      <li>C#</li>
42                      <li>Java</li>
43                      <li>HTML</li>
44                      <li>Scripts</li>
45                      <li>New languages</li>
46                  </ul>
47
48              </li>
49
50          </ul> <!-- this ends the first level nested list -->
51      </li>
52
53      <li>Links</li>
54      <li>Keeping in touch with old friends</li>
55      <li>It is the technology of the future!</li>
56
57  </ul>     <!-- this ends the primary unordered list -->
58
59  <h1>My 3 Favorite <em>CEOs</em></h1>
60
61  <!-- ordered lists are constructed in the same way as   -->
62  <!-- unordered lists, except their starting tag is <ol> -->
63  <ol>
64      <li>Lawrence J. Ellison</li>
65      <li>Steve Jobs</li>
66      <li>Michael Dell</li>
67  </ol>
68
69  </body>
70  </html>
```

Fig. G.9   Nested and ordered lists in HTML. (Part 2 of 3.)

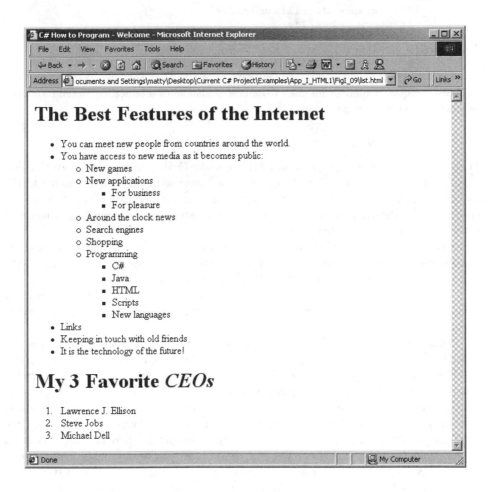

Fig. G.9   Nested and ordered lists in HTML. (Part 3 of 3.)

Our first nested list begins on line 24, and its first element is on 25.

```
<ul>
    <li>New games</li>
```

A nested list is created in the same way as the list in Fig. G.8, except that the nested list is itself contained in a list element. Most Web browsers render nested lists by indenting the list one level and changing the bullet type for the list elements.

 Good Programming Practice G.10

Indenting each level of a nested list in your code makes the code easier to edit and debug.

In Fig. G.9, lines 16–57 show a list with three levels of nesting. When nesting lists, be sure to insert the closing **</ul>** tags in the appropriate places. Lines 63–67

```
<ol>
   <li>Lawrence J. Ellison</li>
   <li>Steve Jobs</li>
   <li>Michael Dell</li>
</ol>
```

define an *ordered list* element with the tags **<ol>...</ol>**. Most browsers render ordered lists with a sequence number for each list element instead of a bullet. By default, ordered lists use decimal sequence numbers (1, 2, 3, ...).

G.11 Summary

HTML is not a procedural programming language like C, Fortran, Cobol or Pascal. It is a markup language which identifies the elements of a page so that a browser can render the page on the screen. HTML is used to format text and information. This "marking up" of information is different from the intent of traditional programming languages, which is to perform actions in a designated order.

In HTML, text is marked up with elements, delineated by tags that are keywords contained in pairs of angle brackets. HTML documents are created via text editors. All HTML documents stored in files require either the **.htm** or the **.html** file name extension. For most Web servers, the filename of a home page should be **index.html**. When a browser requests a directory, the default Web server response is to return **index.html** if it exists in that directory.

The document type specifies which version of HTML appears in the document and can be used with a validation tool, such as the W3C's **validator.w3.org**, to ensure that an HTML document conforms to the HTML specification. **<html>** tells the browser that everything contained between the opening **<html>** tag and the closing **</html>** tag is HTML. Every HTML file is separated into a header section and a body. Including a title is mandatory for every HTML document. Use the **<title>...</title>** tags to do so. They are placed inside the header. The **<body>** tag opens the **body** element. The body of an HTML document is the area where you place all content you would like browsers to display. Headers are a simple form of text formatting that typically increase text size, based on the header's "level" (**h1** through **h6**). Headers often used to delineate new sections and subsections of a page.

The most important capability of HTML is creating hyperlinks to documents on any server, to form a worldwide network of linked documents and information. Links are inserted with the **a** (anchor) element. To specify the address you would like to link to, add the **href** attribute to the anchor element, with the address as the value of **href**. Anchors can link to e-mail addresses. When someone clicks this type of anchored link, their default e-mail program initiates an e-mail message to the linked address.

You specify the location of an image file with the **src = "***location***"** attribute in the **<img>** tag. You can specify the **height** and **width** of an image, measured in pixels. The **alt** tag is provided for browsers that cannot view pictures or that have images turned off (e.g., text-based browsers). The value of the **alt** attribute will appear on the screen in place of the image, giving the user an idea of what was in the image.

HTML 4.01 has a provision for inserting special characters and symbols. All special characters are inserted in the format of the code, always **&***code***;**. An example of this is **&**, which inserts an ampersand. Codes are often abbreviated forms of the character (like **amp** for ampersand and **copy** for copyright) and also can be in the form of hex codes. (For example, the hex code for an ampersand is 38, so another method of inserting an ampersand is to use **&**.) The **del** element marks text as deleted, which is rendered with a strike-through by most browsers. To turn text into superscript or subscript, use the **sup** or **sub**element, respectively.

Most visual Web browsers place a bullet mark at the beginning of each element in an unordered list. All entries in an unordered list must be enclosed within **<ul>...</ul>** tags, which open and close the unordered list element. Each entry in an unordered list is contained in an **li** element. You then insert and format any text. Nested lists display information in outline form. A nested list is a list that is contained within an **li** element. Most visual Web browsers indent nested lists one level and change the type of bullet to reflect the nesting. An ordered list (**<ol>...</ol>**) is rendered by most browsers with a sequence number instead of a bullet at the beginning of each list element. By default, ordered lists use decimal sequence numbers (1, 2, 3, ...).

G.12 Internet and World Wide Web Resources

There are many resources available on the World Wide Web that go into more depth on the topics we cover. Visit the following sites for additional information on this appendix's topics:

www.w3.org
The *World Wide Web Consortium* (W3C) is the group that makes HTML recommendations. This Web site holds a variety of information about HTML—on both its history and its present status.

www.w3.org/TR/html401
The *HTML 4.01 Specification* contains all the nuances and fine points in HTML 4.01.

www.w3schools.com/html
The HTML School. This site contains a complete guide to HTML, starting with an introduction to the WWW and ending with advanced HTML features. The site also has a good reference for the features of HTML.

www2.utep.edu/~kross/tutorial
This University of Texas at El Paso site contains another guide to simple HTML programming. The site is helpful for beginners, because it focuses on teaching and gives specific examples.

www.w3scripts.com/html
This site, an offshoot of *W3Schools*, is a repository for examples of code exhibiting all of the features of HTML, from beginner to advanced level.

Introduction to HyperText Markup Language 4: Part 2

Objectives

- To be able to create tables with rows and columns of data.
- To be able to control the display and formatting of tables.
- To be able to create and use forms.
- To be able to create and use image maps to aid hyperlinking.
- To be able to make Web pages accessible to search engines.
- To be able to use the **frameset** element to create more interesting Web pages.

Yea, from the table of my memory
I'll wipe away all trivial fond records.
William Shakespeare

H.1 Introduction

In Appendix G, Introduction to HyperText Markup Language 4: Part 1, we discussed some basic HTML features. We built several complete Web pages featuring text, hyperlinks, images and such formatting tools as horizontal rules and line breaks.

In this appendix, we discuss more substantial HTML elements and features. We will see how to present information in *tables*. We discuss how to use forms to collect information from people browsing a site. We explain how to use *internal linking* and *image maps* to make pages more navigable. We also discuss how to use *frames* to make navigating Web sites easier. By the end of this appendix, you will be familiar with most commonly used HTML tags and features. You will then be able to create more complex Web sites. In this appendix, we do not present any C# programming.

H.2 Basic HTML Tables

HTML 4.0 *tables* are used to mark up tabular data, such as data stored in a database. The table in Fig. H.1 organizes data into rows and columns.

```
1   <!DOCTYPE HTML PUBLIC "-//W3C//DTD HTML 4.01//EN"
2            "http://www.w3.org/TR/html4/strict.dtd">
3   <html>
4
5   <!-- Fig. H.1: table.html -->
6   <!-- Basic table design.   -->
7
8   <head>
9      <title>C# How to Program - Tables</title>
10  </head>
```

Fig. H.1   HTML table. (Part 1 of 2.)

```
11
12   <body>
13
14      <h1>Table Example Page</h1>
15
16      <!-- the <table> tag opens a new table and lets you -->
17      <!-- put in design options and instructions         -->
18      <table border = "1" width = "40%">
19
20         <!-- use the <caption> tag to summarize the table's -->
21         <!-- contents (this helps the visually impaired)    -->
22         <caption>Here is a small sample table.</caption>
23
24         <!-- The <thead> is the first (non-scrolling)  -->
25         <!-- horizontal section. <th> inserts a header -->
26         <!--  cell and displays bold text              -->
27         <thead>
28            <tr><th>This is the head.</th></tr>
29         </thead>
30
31         <!-- All of your important content goes in the <tbody>. -->
32         <!-- Use this tag to format the entire section          -->
33         <!-- <td> inserts a data cell, with regular text        -->
34         <tbody>
35            <tr><td>This is the body.</td></tr>
36         </tbody>
37
38      </table>
39
40   </body>
41   </html>
```

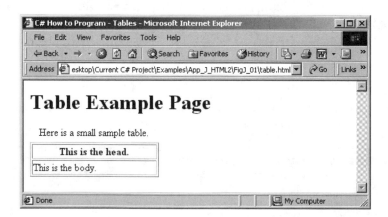

Fig. H.1   HTML table. (Part 2 of 2.)

All tags and text that apply to the table go inside the **<table>** element, which begins on line 18:

```
<table border = "1" width = "40%">
```

The **border** *attribute* lets you set the width of the table's border in pixels. If you want the border to be invisible, you can specify **border = "0"**. In the table shown in Fig. H.1, the value of the border attribute is set to **1**. The **width** attribute sets the width of the table as either a number of pixels or a percentage of the screen width.

Line 22

```
<caption>Here is a small sample table.</caption>
```

inserts a **caption** element into the table. The text inside the **caption** element is inserted directly above the table in most visual browsers. The caption text is also used to help *text-based browsers* interpret the table data.

Tables can be split into distinct horizontal and vertical sections. The first of these sections, the head area, appears in lines 27–29

```
<thead>
    <tr><th>This is the head.</th></tr>
</thead>
```

Put all header information (for example, the titles of the table and column headers) inside the **thead** element. The **tr**, or *table row element*, is used to create rows of table cells. All of the cells in a row belong in the **<tr>** element for that row.

The smallest unit of the table is the *data cell*. There are two types of data cells, one type—the **th** element—is located in the table header. The other type—the **td** element—is located in the table body. The code example in Fig. H.1 inserts a header cell, using the **th** element. Header cells, which are placed in the **<thead>** element, are suitable for column headings.

The second grouping section, the **tbody** element, appears in lines 34–36

```
<tbody>
    <tr><td>This is the body.</td></tr>
</tbody>
```

Like **thead**, the **tbody** element is used for formatting and grouping purposes. Although there is only one row and one cell (line 35) in the above example, most tables will use **tbody** to group the majority of their content in multiple rows and multiple cells.

Look-and-Feel Observation H.1

Use tables in your HTML pages to mark up tabular data.

Common Programming Error H.1

Forgetting to close any of the elements inside the **table** *element is an error and can distort the table format. Be sure to check that every element is opened and closed in its proper place to make sure that the table is structured as intended.*

H.3 Intermediate HTML Tables and Formatting

In the previous section and code example, we explored the structure of a basic table. In Fig. H.2, we extend our table example with more structural elements and attributes.

```
 1   <!DOCTYPE HTML PUBLIC "-//W3C//DTD HTML 4.01//EN"
 2             "http://www.w3.org/TR/html4/strict.dtd">
 3   <html>
 4
 5   <!-- Fig. H.2: table.html        -->
 6   <!-- Intermediate table design. -->
 7
 8   <head>
 9      <title>C# How to Program - Tables</title>
10   </head>
11
12   <body>
13
14      <h1>Table Example Page</h1>
15
16      <table border = "1">
17         <caption>Here is a more complex sample table.</caption>
18
19         <!-- <colgroup> and <col> are used to format     -->
20         <!-- entire columns at once. SPAN determines how -->
21         <!-- many columns the <col> tag effects.         -->
22         <colgroup>
23            <col align = "right">
24            <col span = "4">
25         </colgroup>
26
27         <thead>
28
29            <!-- rowspans and colspans combine the indicated -->
30            <!-- number of cells vertically or horizontally  -->
31            <tr>
32               <th rowspan = "2">
33                  <img src = "camel.gif" width = "205"
34                     height = "167" alt = "Picture of a camel">
35               </th>
36               <th colspan = "4" valign = "top">
37                  <h1>Camelid comparison</h1><br>
38                  <p>Approximate as of 8/99</p>
39               </th>
40            </tr>
41
42            <tr valign = "bottom">
43               <th># of Humps</th>
44               <th>Indigenous region</th>
45               <th>Spits?</th>
46               <th>Produces Wool?</th>
47            </tr>
48
49         </thead>
50
```

Fig. H.2   Complex HTML table. (Part 1 of 2.)

```
51          <tbody>
52
53             <tr>
54                <th>Camels (bactrian)</th>
55                <td>2</td>
56                <td>Africa/Asia</td>
57                <td rowspan = "2">Llama</td>
58                <td rowspan = "2">Llama</td>
59             </tr>
60
61             <tr>
62                <th>Llamas</th>
63                <td>1</td>
64                <td>Andes Mountains</td>
65             </tr>
66
67          </tbody>
68
69       </table>
70
71    </body>
72    </html>
```

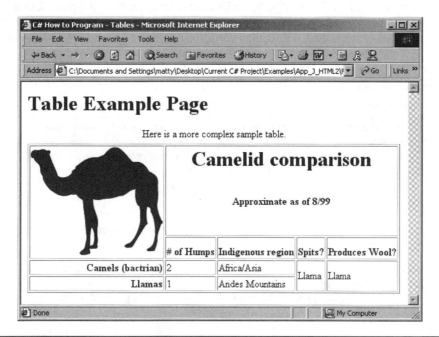

Fig. H.2   Complex HTML table. (Part 2 of 2.)

The table begins on line 16. The **colgroup** *element*, used for grouping columns, is shown on lines 22–25

```
<colgroup>
   <col align = "right">
```

```
    <col span = "4">
</colgroup>
```

The **colgroup** element can be used to group and format columns. Each **col** element in the **<colgroup>**...**</colgroup>** tags can format any number of columns (specified with the **span** attribute). Any formatting to be applied to a column or group of columns can be specified in both the **colgroup** and **col** tags. In this case, we align the text inside the leftmost column to the right. Another useful attribute to use here is **width**, which specifies the width of the column.

Most visual Web browsers automatically format data cells to fit the data they contain. However, it is possible to make some data cells larger than others. This effect is accomplished with the **rowspan** and **colspan** attributes, which can be placed inside any data cell element. The value of the attribute specifies the number of rows or columns to be occupied by the cell, respectively. For example, **rowspan = "2"** tells the browser that this data cell will span the area of two vertically adjacent cells. These cells will be joined vertically (and will thus span over two rows). An example of **colspan** appears in line 36,

```
    <th colspan = "4" valign = "top">
```

where the header cell is widened to span four cells.

We also see here an example of vertical alignment formatting. The **valign** attribute accepts the following values: **"top"**, **"middle"**, **"bottom"** and **"baseline"**. All cells in a row whose **valign** attribute is set to **"baseline"** will have the first text line occur on a common baseline. The default vertical alignment in all data and header cells is **valign = "middle"**.

The remaining code in Fig. H.2 demonstrates other uses of the **table** attributes and elements outlined above.

Common Programming Error H.2

*When using **colspan** and **rowspan** in table data cells, consider that the modified cells will cover the areas of other cells. Compensate for this in your code by reducing the number of cells in that row or column. If you do not, the formatting of your table will be distorted, and you could inadvertently create more columns and/or rows than you originally intended.*

H.4 Basic HTML Forms

HTML provides several mechanisms to collect information from people viewing your site; one is the *form* (Fig. H.3).

```
1   <!DOCTYPE HTML PUBLIC "-//W3C//DTD HTML 4.01//EN"
2               "http://www.w3.org/TR/html4/strict.dtd">
3   <html>
4
5   <!-- Fig. H.3: form.html    -->
6   <!-- Form design example 1. -->
7
8   <head>
9      <title>C# How to Program - Tables</title>
10  </head>
```

Fig. H.3   Simple form with hidden fields and a text box. (Part 1 of 2.)

```
11
12  <body>
13
14     <h1>Feedback Form</h1>
15
16     <p>Please fill out this form to help us improve our site.</p>
17
18     <!-- This tag starts the form, gives the method of sending -->
19     <!-- information and the location of form scripts.         -->
20     <!-- Hidden inputs give the server non-visual information  -->
21     <form method = "post" action = "/cgi-bin/formmail">
22
23     <p>
24        <input type = "hidden" name = "recipient"
25           value = "deitel@deitel.com">
26
27        <input type = "hidden" name = "subject"
28           value = "Feedback Form">
29
30        <input type = "hidden" name = "redirect"
31           value = "main.html">
32     </p>
33
34     <!-- <input type = "text"> inserts a text box -->
35     <p><label>Name:
36        <input name = "name" type = "text" size = "25">
37     </label></p>
38
39     <p>
40        <!-- input types "submit" and "reset" insert buttons -->
41        <!-- for submitting or clearing the form's contents  -->
42        <input type = "submit" value = "Submit Your Entries">
43        <input type = "reset" value = "Clear Your Entries">
44     </p>
45
46     </form>
47
48  </body>
49  </html>
```

Fig. H.3   Simple form with hidden fields and a text box. (Part 2 of 2.)

The form begins on line 21

```
<form method = "post" action = "/cgi-bin/formmail">
```

with the **form** element. The **method** attribute indicates the way the information gathered in the form will be sent to the *Web server* for processing. Use **method = "post"** in a form that causes changes to server data, for example when updating a database. The form data will be sent to the server as an *environment variable,* which scripts are able to access. The other possible value, **method = "get"**, should be used when your form does not cause any changes in server-side data, for example when making a database request. The form data from **method = "get"** is appended to the end of the URL (for example, **/cgi-bin/formmail?name=bob&order=5**). Also be aware that **method = "get"** is limited to standard characters and cannot submit any special characters.

A *Web server* is a machine that runs a software package like Microsoft's PWS (Personal Web Server), Microsoft's IIS (Internet Information Server) or Apache. Web servers handle browser requests. When a browser requests a page or file somewhere on a server, the server processes the request and returns an answer to the browser. In this example, the data from the form goes to a CGI (Common Gateway Interface) script, which is a means of interfacing an HTML page with a script (i.e., a program) written in Perl, C, Tcl or other languages. The script then handles the data fed to it by the server and typically returns some information for the user. The **action** attribute in the **form** tag is the URL for this script; in this case, it is a simple script that emails form data to an address. Most Internet Service Providers (ISPs) will have a script like this on their site, so you can ask your system administrator how to set up your HTML to use the script correctly.

For this particular script, there are several pieces of information (not seen by the user) needed in the form. Lines 24–31

```
<input type = "hidden" name = "recipient"
   value = "deitel@deitel.com">

<input type = "hidden" name = "subject"
   value = "Feedback Form">

<input type = "hidden" name = "redirect"
   value = "main.html">
```

specify this information using *hidden input elements.* The **input** element is common in forms and always requires the **type** attribute. Two other attributes are **name**, which provides a unique identifier for the **input** element, and **value**, which indicates the value that the **input** element sends to the server upon submission.

As shown above, hidden inputs always have the attribute **type = "hidden"**. The three hidden inputs shown are typical for this kind of CGI script: An email address to which the data will be sent, the subject line of the email and a URL to which the user is redirected after submitting the form.

Good Programming Practice H.1

*Place hidden **input** elements in the beginning of a form, right after the opening **<form>** tag. This makes these elements easier to find and identify.*

The usage of an **input** element is defined by the value of its **type** attribute. We introduce another of these options in lines 35–37:

```
<p><label>Name:
```

```
            <input name = "name" type = "text" size = "25">
            </label></p>
```

The input **type = "text"** inserts a one-line text box into the form (line 36). A good use of the textual input element is for names or other one-line pieces of information. The **label** element on lines 35–37 provide a description for the **input** element on line 36.

We also use the **size** attribute of the **input** element to specify the width of the text input, measured in characters. You can also set a maximum number of characters that the text input will accept using the **maxlength** attribute.

Good Programming Practice H.2

*When using **input** elements in forms, be sure to leave enough space with the **maxlength** attribute for users to input the pertinent information.*

Common Programming Error H.3

*Forgetting to include a **label** element for each form element is a design error. Without these labels, users will have no way of knowing what the function of individual form elements is.*

There are two types of **input** elements in lines 42–43

```
            <input type = "submit" value = "Submit Your Entries">
            <input type = "reset" value = "Clear Your Entries">
```

that should be inserted into every form. The **type = "submit"** input element allows the user to submit the data entered in the form to the server for processing. Most visual Web browsers place a button in the form that submits the data when clicked. The **value** attribute changes the text displayed on the button (the default value is **"submit"**). The input element **type = "reset"** allows a user to reset all form elements to the default values. This can help the user correct mistakes or simply start over. As with the **submit** input, the **value** attribute of the **reset input** element affects the text of the button on the screen, but does not affect its functionality.

Common Programming Error H.4

*Be sure to close your form code with the **</form>** tag. Neglecting to do so is an error and can affect the functionality of other forms on the same page.*

H.5 More Complex HTML Forms

We introduce additional form input options in Fig. H.4.

```
1   <!DOCTYPE HTML PUBLIC "-//W3C//DTD HTML 4.01//EN"
2            "http://www.w3.org/TR/html4/strict.dtd">
3   <html>
4
5   <!-- Fig. H.4: form.html    -->
6   <!-- Form design example 2. -->
7
8   <head>
9      <title>C# How to Program - Tables</title>
10  </head>
```

Fig. H.4   Form including textareas, password boxes and checkboxes. (Part 1 of 3.)

```
11
12    <body>
13
14       <h1>Feedback Form</h1>
15
16       <p>Please fill out this form to help us improve our site.</p>
17
18       <form method = "post" action = "/cgi-bin/formmail">
19
20          <p>
21             <input type = "hidden" name = "recipient"
22                value = "deitel@deitel.com">
23
24             <input type = "hidden" name = "subject"
25                value = "Feedback Form">
26
27             <input type = "hidden" name = "redirect"
28                value = "main.html">
29          </p>
30
31          <p><label>Name:
32             <input name = "name" type = "text" size = "25">
33          </label></p>
34
35          <!-- <textarea> creates a textbox of the size given -->
36          <p><label>Comments:
37             <textarea name = "comments" rows = "4" cols = "36">
38             </textarea>
39          </label></p>
40
41          <!-- <input type = "password"> inserts textbox whose -->
42          <!-- readout will be in *** not regular characters   -->
43          <p><label>Email Address:
44             <input name = "email" type = "password" size = "25">
45          </label></p>
46
47          <p>
48             <strong>Things you liked:</strong><br>
49
50             <label>Site design
51             <input name = "thingsliked" type = "checkbox"
52                value = "Design"></label>
53
54             <label>Links
55             <input name = "thingsliked" type = "checkbox"
56                value = "Links"></label>
57
58             <label>Ease of use
59             <input name = "thingsliked" type = "checkbox"
60                value = "Ease"></label>
61
62             <label>Images
```

Fig. H.4   Form including textareas, password boxes and checkboxes. (Part 2 of 3.)

```
63                 <input name = "thingsliked" type = "checkbox"
64                    value = "Images"></label>
65
66              <label>Source code
67              <input name = "thingsliked" type = "checkbox"
68                    value = "Code"></label>
69           </p>
70
71           <p>
72              <input type = "submit" value = "Submit Your Entries">
73              <input type = "reset" value = "Clear Your Entries">
74           </p>
75
76        </form>
77
78     </body>
79     </html>
```

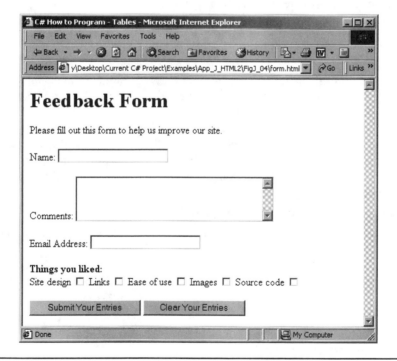

Fig. H.4   Form including textareas, password boxes and checkboxes. (Part 3 of 3.)

Lines 37–38

```
<textarea name = "comments" rows = "4" cols = "36">
</textarea>
```

introduce the **textarea** element. The **textarea** element inserts a text box into the form. You specify the size of the box with the ***rows*** *attribute*, which sets the number of rows that will appear in the **textarea**. With the ***cols*** *attribute*, you specify how wide the **textarea** should be. This **textarea** is four rows of characters tall and 36 characters wide. Any default text that you want to place inside the **textarea** should be contained in the **textarea** element.

The input *type = "password"* (line 44)

```
<input name = "email" type = "password" size = "25">
```

inserts a text box with the indicated size. The password input field provides a way for users to enter information that the user would not want others to be able to read on the screen. In visual browsers, the data the user types into a password input field is shown as asterisks. However, the actual value the user enters is sent to the server. Nonvisual browsers may render this type of input field differently.

Lines 50–68 introduce another type of form element, the checkbox. Every **input** element with **type = "checkbox"** creates a new checkbox item in the form. Checkboxes can be used individually or in groups. Each checkbox in a group should have the same **name** (in this case, **name = "thingsliked"**). This notifies the script handling the form that all of the checkboxes are related to one another.

Common Programming Error H.5

*When your form has several checkboxes with the same **name**, you must make sure that they have different **value**s, or else the script will have no way of distinguishing between them.*

Additional form elements are introduced in Fig. H.5. In this form example, we introduce two new types of input options. The first of these is the *radio button*, introduced in lines 80–97. Inserted into forms with the **input** attribute *type = "radio"*, radio buttons are similar in function and usage to checkboxes. Radio buttons are different in that only one element in the group may be selected at any time. All of the **name** attributes of a group of radio inputs must be the same and all of the **value** attributes different. Insert the attribute *checked* to indicate which radio button you would like selected initially. The **checked** attribute can also be applied to checkboxes.

Common Programming Error H.6

*When you are using a group of radio inputs in a form, forgetting to set the **name** values to the same name will let the user select all the radio buttons at the same time—an undesired result.*

```
1   <!DOCTYPE HTML PUBLIC "-//W3C//DTD HTML 4.01//EN"
2            "http://www.w3.org/TR/html4/strict.dtd">
3   <html>
4
5   <!-- Fig. H.5: form.html    -->
6   <!-- Form design example 3. -->
7
8   <head>
9      <title>C# How to Program - Tables</title>
10  </head>
11
12  <body>
13
14     <h1>Feedback Form</h1>
15
```

Fig. H.5   Form including radio buttons and pulldown lists. (Part 1 of 4.)

```
16      <p>Please fill out this form to help us improve our site.</p>
17
18      <form method = "post" action = "/cgi-bin/formmail">
19
20         <p>
21            <input type = "hidden" name = "recipient"
22               value = "deitel@deitel.com">
23
24            <input type = "hidden" name = "subject"
25               value = "Feedback Form">
26
27            <input type = "hidden" name = "redirect"
28               value = "main.html">
29         </p>
30
31         <p><label>Name:
32            <input name = "name" type = "text" size = "25">
33         </label></p>
34
35         <p><label>Comments:
36            <textarea name = "comments" rows = "4" cols = "36">
37               </textarea>
38         </label></p>
39
40         <p><label>Email Address:
41            <input name = "email" type = "password" size = "25">
42         </label></p>
43
44         <p>
45            <strong>Things you liked:</strong><br>
46
47            <label>Site design
48               <input name = "things" type = "checkbox"
49                  value = "Design">
50            </label>
51
52            <label>Links
53               <input name = "things" type = "checkbox"
54                  value = "Links">
55            </label>
56
57            <label>Ease of use
58               <input name = "things" type = "checkbox"
59                  value = "Ease">
60            </label>
61
62            <label>Images
63               <input name = "things" type = "checkbox"
64                  value = "Images">
65            </label>
66
67            <label>Source code
```

Fig. H.5   Form including radio buttons and pulldown lists. (Part 2 of 4.)

```
68                    <input name = "things" type = "checkbox"
69                        value = "Code">
70                </label>
71            </p>
72
73            <!-- <input type = "radio"> creates one radio button -->
74            <!-- radio buttons and checkboxes differ in that      -->
75            <!-- only one radio button in group can be selected   -->
76            <p>
77                <strong>How did you get to our site?:</strong><br>
78
79                <label>Search engine
80                    <input name = "how get to site" type = "radio"
81                        value = "search engine" checked></label>
82
83                <label>Links from another site
84                    <input name = "how get to site" type = "radio"
85                        value = "link"></label>
86
87                <label>Deitel.com Web site
88                    <input name = "how get to site" type = "radio"
89                        value = "deitel.com"></label>
90
91                <label>Reference in a book
92                    <input name = "how get to site" type = "radio"
93                        value = "book"></label>
94
95                <label>Other
96                    <input name = "how get to site" type = "radio"
97                        value = "other"></label>
98
99            </p>
100
101            <!-- <select> tags present drop down menus    -->
102            <!-- with choices indicated by <option> tags -->
103            <p>
104                <label>Rate our site:
105
106                <select name = "rating">
107                    <option selected>Amazing:-)</option>
108                    <option>10</option>
109                    <option>9</option>
110                    <option>8</option>
111                    <option>7</option>
112                    <option>6</option>
113                    <option>5</option>
114                    <option>4</option>
115                    <option>3</option>
116                    <option>2</option>
117                    <option>1</option>
118                    <option>The Pits:-(</option>
119                </select>
120
```

Fig. H.5   Form including radio buttons and pulldown lists. (Part 3 of 4.)

```
121            </label>
122        </p>
123
124        <p>
125            <input type = "submit" value = "Submit Your Entries">
126            <input type = "reset" value = "Clear Your Entries">
127        </p>
128
129    </form>
130
131 </body>
132 </html>
```

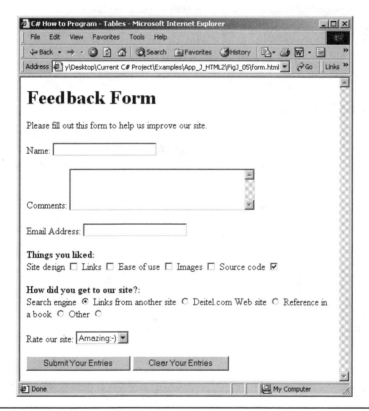

Fig. H.5   Form including radio buttons and pulldown lists. (Part 4 of 4.)

The last type of form input that we introduce here is the **select** element (lines 106–119). This will place a selectable list of items inside your form.

```
<select name = "rating">
    <option selected>Amazing:-)</option>
    <option>10</option>
    <option>9</option>
    <option>8</option>
    <option>7</option>
    <option>6</option>
```

```
<option>5</option>
<option>4</option>
<option>3</option>
<option>2</option>
<option>1</option>
<option>The Pits:-(</option>
</select>
```

This type of form input is created via a **select** element. Inside the opening **<select>** tag, be sure to include the **name** attribute.

To add an item to the list, add to the **select** element an *option* element containing the text to be displayed. The **selected** attribute, like the **checked** attribute for radio buttons and checkboxes, applies a default selection to your list.

The preceding code will generate a pull-down list of options in most visual browsers, as shown in Fig. H.5. You can change the number of list options visible at one time, using the *size* attribute of the **select** element. Use this attribute if you prefer an expanded version of the list to the one-line expandable list.

H.6 Internal Linking

In Appendix G, Introduction to HyperText Markup Language 4: Part 1, we discussed how to link one Web page to another with text and image anchors. Figure H.6 introduces *internal linking*, which lets you create named anchors for hyperlinks to particular parts of an HTML document.

```
1   <!DOCTYPE HTML PUBLIC "-//W3C//DTD HTML 4.01//EN"
2              "http://www.w3.org/TR/html4/strict.dtd">
3   <html>
4
5   <!-- Fig. H.6: links.html -->
6   <!-- Internal linking.     -->
7
8   <head>
9      <title>C# How to Program - Tables</title>
10  </head>
11
12  <body>
13
14     <!-- <a name = ".."></a> makes internal hyperlinks -->
15     <p>
16        <a name = "features"></a>
17     </p>
18
19     <h1>The Best Features of the Internet</h1>
20
21     <!-- internal link's address is "xx.html#linkname" -->
22     <p>
23        <a href = "#ceos">Go to <em>Favorite CEOs</em></a>
24     </p>
25
```

Fig. H.6   Using internal hyperlinks to make your pages more navigable. (Part 1 of 3.)

```
26    <ul>
27        <li>You can meet people from countries around the world.
28        </li>
29
30        <li>You have access to new media as it becomes public:
31
32            <ul>
33                <li>New games</li>
34                <li>New applications
35
36                    <ul>
37                        <li>For Business</li>
38                        <li>For Pleasure</li>
39                    </ul>
40
41                </li>
42
43                <li>Around the Clock news</li>
44                <li>Search Engines</li>
45                <li>Shopping</li>
46                <li>Programming
47
48                    <ul>
49                        <li>HTML</li>
50                        <li>Java</li>
51                        <li>Dynamic HTML</li>
52                        <li>Scripts</li>
53                        <li>New languages</li>
54                    </ul>
55
56                </li>
57            </ul>
58
59        </li>
60
61        <li>Links</li>
62        <li>Keeping In touch with old friends</li>
63        <li>It is the technology of the future!</li>
64    </ul>
65
66    <p><a name = "ceos"></a></p>
67
68    <h1>My 3 Favorite <em>CEOs</em></h1>
69
70    <p>
71        <a href = "#features">Go to <em>Favorite Features</em></a>
72    </p>
73
74    <ol>
75        <li>Lawrence J. Ellison</li>
76        <li>Steve Jobs</li>
77        <li>Michael Dell</li>
78    </ol>
```

Fig. H.6   Using internal hyperlinks to make your pages more navigable. (Part 2 of 3.)

```
79
80    </body>
81    </html>
```

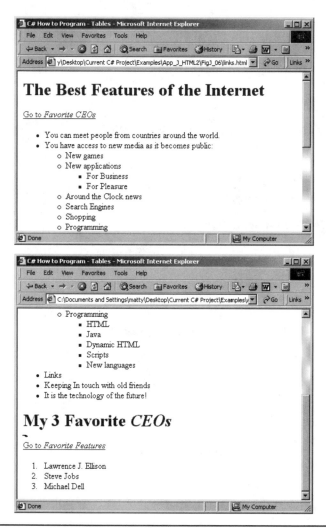

Fig. H.6   Using internal hyperlinks to make your pages more navigable. (Part 3 of 3.)

Lines 15–17

```
<p>
    <a name = "features"></a>
</p>
```

show a named anchor for an internal hyperlink. A named anchor is created via an **a** element with a **name** attribute. Line 15 creates an anchor named **features**. Because the name of the page is **list.html**, the URL of this anchor in the Web page is **list.html#features**. Line 71

```
<a href = "#features">Go to <em>Favorite Features</em></a>
```

shows a hyperlink with the anchor **features** as its target. Selecting this hyperlink in a visual browser would scroll the browser window to the **features** anchor (line 16). Examples of this occur in Fig. H.6, which shows two different screen captures from the same page, each at a different anchor. You can also link to an anchor in another page, using the URL of that location (using the format **href = "page.html#name"**).

Look-and-Feel Observation H.2

Internal hyperlinks are most useful in large HTML files with lots of information. You can link to various points on the page to save the user from having to scroll down and find a specific location.

H.7 Creating and Using Image Maps

We have seen that images can be used as links to other places on your site or elsewhere on the Internet. We now discuss how to create *image maps* (Fig. H.7), which allow you to designate certain sections of the image as *hotspots* and then use these hotspots as links.

All elements of an image map are contained inside the **<map>...</map>** tags. The required attribute for the **map** element is **name** (line 18):

```
<map name = "picture">
```

As we will see, this attribute is needed for referencing purposes. A hotspot on the image is designated with the **area** element. Every **area** element has the following attributes: **href** sets the target for the link on that spot, **shape** and **coords** set the characteristics of the area and **alt** functions just as it does in the **img** element.

```
1   <!DOCTYPE HTML PUBLIC "-//W3C//DTD HTML 4.01//EN"
2            "http://www.w3.org/TR/html4/strict.dtd">
3   <html>
4
5   <!-- Fig. H.7: picture.html         -->
6   <!-- Creating and using imape maps. -->
7
8   <head>
9      <title>C# How to Program - Tables</title>
10  </head>
11
12  <body>
13
14     <p>
15
16     <!-- <map> opens and names image map formatting -->
17     <!-- area and to be referenced later            -->
18     <map name = "picture">
19
20        <!-- "shape = rect" indicates rectangular -->
21        <!-- area, with coordinates of the        -->
22        <!-- upper-left and lower-right corners    -->
```

Fig. H.7   Picture with links anchored to an image map. (Part 1 of 2.)

```
23          <area href = "form.html" shape = "rect"
24             coords = "3, 122, 73, 143"
25             alt = "Go to the feedback form">
26
27          <area href = "contact.html" shape = "rect"
28             coords = "109, 123, 199, 142"
29             alt = "Go to the contact page">
30
31          <area href = "main.html" shape = "rect"
32             coords = "1, 2, 72, 17"
33             alt = "Go to the homepage">
34
35          <area href = "links.html" shape = "rect"
36             coords = "155, 0, 199, 18"
37             alt = "Go to the links page">
38
39          <!-- "shape = polygon" indicates area of -->
40          <!-- cusotmizable shape, with the        -->
41          <!-- coordinates of every vertex listed  -->
42          <area href = "mailto:deitel@deitel.com" shape = "poly"
43          coords = "28, 22, 24, 68, 46, 114, 84, 111, 99, 56, 86, 13"
44             alt = "Email the Deitels">
45
46          <!-- "shape = circle" indicates circular -->
47          <!-- area with center and radius listed  -->
48          <area href = "mailto:deitel@deitel.com" shape = "circle"
49             coords = "146, 66, 42" alt = "Email the Deitels">
50       </map>
51
52    <!-- <img src=... usemap = "#name"> says that     -->
53    <!-- indicated image map will be used with image -->
54    <img src = "deitel.gif" width = "200" height = "144"
55       alt = "Harvey and Paul Deitel" usemap = "#picture">
56    </p>
57
58 </body>
59 </html>
```

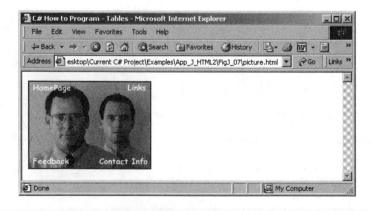

Fig. H.7   Picture with links anchored to an image map. (Part 2 of 2.)

The markup on lines 23–25

```
<area href = "form.html" shape = "rect"
    coords = "3, 122, 73, 143" alt = "Go to the feedback form">
```

causes a *rectangular hotspot* to be drawn around the *coordinates* given in the **coords** element. A coordinate pair consists of two numbers, which are the locations of the point on the *x* and *y* axes. The *x* axis extends horizontally from the upper-left corner, the *y* axis vertically. Every point on an image has a unique *x–y* coordinate. In the case of a rectangular hotspot, the required coordinates are those of the upper-left and lower-right corners of the rectangle. In this case, the upper-left corner of the rectangle is located at 3 on the *x* axis and 122 on the *y* axis, annotated as (*3, 122*). The lower-right corner of the rectangle is at (*73, 143*).

Another map area is in lines 42–44

```
<area href = "mailto:deitel@deitel.com" shape = "poly"
    coords = "28, 22, 24, 68, 46, 114, 84, 111, 99, 56, 86, 13
    alt = "Email the Deitels">
```

In this case, we use the value **poly** for the **shape** attribute. This creates a hotspot in the shape of a polygon, using the coordinates in the **coords** attribute. These coordinates represent each vertex, or corner, of the polygon. The browser will automatically connect these points with lines to form the area of the hotspot.

shape = "circle" is the last shape attribute that is commonly used in image maps. It creates a *circular hotspot*, and requires both the coordinates of the center of the circle and the radius of the circle, in pixels.

To use the image map with an **img** element, you must insert the **usemap = "#***name***"** attribute into the **img** element, where *name* is the value of the **name** attribute in the **map** element. Lines 54–55

```
<img src = "deitel.gif" width = "200" height= "144" alt =
    "Harvey and Paul Deitel" usemap = "#picture">
```

show how the image map **name = "picture"** is applied to the **img** element.

H.8 <meta> Tags

People use search engines to find interesting Web sites. Search engines usually catalog sites by following links from page to page and saving identification and classification information for each page visited. The main HTML element that search engines use to catalog pages is the **meta** tag (Fig. H.8).

A **meta** tag contains two attributes that should always be used. The first of these, **name**, identifies the type of **meta** tag you are including. The **content** attribute provides information the search engine will catalog about your site.

```
1  <!DOCTYPE HTML PUBLIC "-//W3C//DTD HTML 4.01//EN"
2              "http://www.w3.org/TR/html4/strict.dtd">
3  <html>
4
5  <!-- Fig. H.8: main.html        -->
6  <!-- <meta> and <!doctype> tags. -->
```

Fig. H.8   Using **meta** to provide keywords and a description. (Part 1 of 2.)

```
7
8   <head>
9      <!-- <meta> tags give search engines information -->
10     <!-- they need to catalog your site          -->
11     <meta name = "keywords" content = "Webpage, design, HTML,
12        tutorial, personal, help, index, form, contact, feedback,
13        list, links, frame, deitel">
14
15     <meta name = "description" content = "This Web site will help
16        you learn the basics of HTML and Webpage design through the
17        use of interactive examples and instruction.">
18
19     <title>C# How to Program - Tables</title>
20  </head>
21
22  <body>
23
24     <h1>Welcome to Our Web Site!</h1>
25
26     <p>
27        We have designed this site to teach about the wonders of
28        <em>HTML</em>. We have been using <em>HTML</em> since
29        version <strong>2.0</strong>, and we enjoy the features
30        that have been added recently. It seems only a short
31        time ago that we read our first <em>HTML</em> book.
32        Soon you will know about many of the great new
33        features of HTML 4.01.
34     </p>
35
36     <p>Have Fun With the Site!</p>
37
38  </body>
39  </html>
```

Fig. H.8   Using **meta** to provide keywords and a description. (Part 2 of 2.)

Lines 11–13 demonstrate the **meta** tag.

```
<meta name = "keywords" content = "Webpage, design, HTML,
   tutorial, personal, help, index, form, contact, feedback,
   list, links, frame, deitel">
```

The **content** of a **meta** tag with **name = "keywords"** provides search engines with a
list of words that describe key aspects of your site. These words are used to match with
searches—if someone searches for some of the terms in your **keywords meta** tag, they
have a better chance of being notified about your site in the search-engine output. Thus, including **meta** tags and their **content** information will draw more viewers to your site.

The *description* attribute value (lines 15–17)

```
<meta name = "description" content = "This Web site will help
   you learn the basics of HTML and Webpage design through the
   use of interactive examples and instruction.">
```

is quite similar to the **keywords** value. Instead of giving a list of words describing your page, the **content**s of the keywords **meta** element should be a readable 3-to-4-line description of your site, written in sentence form. This description is also used by search engines to catalog and display your site.

Software Engineering Observation H.1

meta *elements are not visible to users of the site and must be placed inside the header section of your HTML document.*

H.9 frameset Element

All of the Web pages we have designed so far have the ability to link to other pages but can display only one page at a time. Figure H.9 introduces *frames*, which can help you display more than one HTML file at a time. Frames, when used properly, can make your site more readable and usable for your users.

```
1   <!DOCTYPE HTML PUBLIC "-//W3C//DTD HTML 4.01 Frameset//EN"
2           "http://www.w3.org/TR/html4/frameset.dtd">
3   <html>
4
5   <!-- Fig. H.9: index.html -->
6   <!-- HTML Frames I.        -->
7
8   <head>
9      <meta name = "keywords" content = "Webpage, design, HTML,
10         tutorial, personal, help, index, form, contact, feedback,
11         list, links, frame, deitel">
12
13     <meta name = "description" content = "This Web site will help
14         you learn the basics of HTML and Webpage design through the
15         use of interactive examples and instruction.">
16
17     <title>C# How to Program - Tables</title>
18  </head>
19
20  <!-- the <frameset> tag gives dimensions of your frame -->
21  <frameset cols = "110,*">
22
23     <!-- the individual frame elements specify -->
24     <!-- which pages appear in given frames     -->
25     <frame name = "nav" src = "nav.html">
26     <frame name = "main" src = "main.html">
27
28     <noframes>
29        <p>
30           This page uses frames, but your browser
31              does not support them.
32        </p>
33
```

Fig. H.9   Web site using two frames—navigation and content. (Part 1 of 2.)

```
34              <p>
35                  Please, <a href = "nav.html">follow this link to
36                      browse our site without frames</a>.
37              </p>
38          </noframes>
39
40      </frameset>
41      </html>
```

Fig. H.9   Web site using two frames—navigation and content. (Part 2 of 2.)

On lines 1 and 2,

```
<!DOCTYPE HTML PUBLIC "-//W3C//DTD HTML 4.01 Frameset//EN"
            "http://www.w3.org/TR/html4/frameset.dtd">
```

we encounter a new document type. The document type specified here indicates that this HTML document uses frames. You should use this document type whenever you use frames in your HTML document.

The framed page begins with the opening **frameset** tag, on line 21

```
<frameset cols = "110,*">
```

This tag tells the browser that the page contains frames. The **cols** attribute of the opening **frameset** tag gives the layout of the frameset. The value of **cols** (or **rows**, if you will be writing a frameset with a horizontal layout) gives the width of each frame, either in pixels or as a percentage of the screen. In this case, the attribute **cols = "110,*"** tells the browser that there are two frames. The first one extends 110 pixels from the left edge of the screen, and the second frame fills the remainder of the screen (as indicated by the asterisk).

Now that we have defined the page layout, we have to specify what files will make up the frameset. We do this with the ***frame*** element in lines 25 and 26:

```
<frame name = "nav" src = "nav.html">
<frame name = "main" src = "main.html">
```

In each **frame** element, the **src** attribute gives the URL of the page that will be displayed in the frame. In the preceding example, the first frame (which covers 110 pixels on the left side of the **frameset**) will display the page **nav.html** and has the attribute **name = "nav"**. The second frame will display the page **main.html** and has the attribute **name = "main"**.

The purpose of a **name** attribute in the **frame** element is to identify the frame, enabling hyperlinks in a **frameset** to load in their intended target **frame**. For example,

```
<a href = "links.html" target = "main">
```

would load **links.html** in the frame whose **name** attribute is **"main"**.

A target in an anchor element can also be set to a number of preset values: **target="_blank"** loads the page in a new blank browser window, **target="_self"** loads the page into the same window as the anchor element, **target="_parent"** loads it in the parent **frameset** (i.e., the **frameset** which contains the current frame) and **target="_top"** loads the page into the full browser window (the page loads over the **frameset**).

In lines 28–38 of the code example in Fig. H.9, the **noframes** element displays HTML in those browsers that do not support frames.

Portability Tip H.1

*Not everyone uses a browser that supports frames. Use the **noframes** element inside the **frameset** to direct users to a nonframed version of your site.*

Look-and-Feel Observation H.3

Frames are capable of enhancing your page, but are often misused. Never use frames to accomplish what you could with other, simpler HTML formatting.

H.10 Nested **framesets**

You can use the **frameset** element to create more complex layouts in a framed Web site by nesting **frameset** areas as in Fig. H.10.

The first level of **frameset** tags is on lines 21 and 22

```
<frameset cols = "110,*">
    <frame name = "nav"src = "nav.html">
```

The **frameset** and **frame** elements here are constructed in the same manner as in Fig. H.9. We have one frame that extends over the first 110 pixels, starting at the left edge.

The second (nested) level of the **frameset** element covers only the remaining **frame** area that was not included in the primary **frameset**. Thus, any frames included in the second **frameset** will not include the leftmost 110 pixels of the screen. Lines 26–29 show the second level of **frameset** tags.

```
<frameset rows = "175,*">
   <frame name = "picture" src = "picture.html">
   <frame name = "main" src = "main.html">
</frameset>
```

In this **frameset** area, the first frame extends 175 pixels from the top of the screen, as indicated by the **rows = "175,*"**. Be sure to include the correct number of **frame** elements inside the second **frameset** area. Also, be sure to include a **noframes** element and to close both of the **frameset** areas at the end of the Web page.

```
1   <!DOCTYPE HTML PUBLIC "-//W3C//DTD HTML 4.01 Frameset//EN"
2            "http://www.w3.org/TR/html4/frameset.dtd">
3   <html>
4
5   <!-- Fig. H.10: index.html   -->
6   <!-- HTML frames II.          -->
7
8   <head>
9
10     <meta name = "keywords" content = "Webpage, design, HTML,
11        tutorial, personal, help, index, form, contact, feedback,
12        list, links, frame, deitel">
13
14     <meta name = "description" content = "This Web site will help
15        you learn the basics of HTML and Webpage design through
16        the use of interactive examples and instruction.">
17
18     <title>C# How to Program - Tables</title>
19   </head>
20
21   <frameset cols = "110,*">
22      <frame name = "nav" src = "nav.html">
23
24      <!-- nested framesets are used to change formatting -->
25      <!-- and spacing of frameset as whole                -->
26      <frameset rows = "175,*">
27         <frame name = "picture" src = "picture.html">
28         <frame name = "main" src = "main.html">
29      </frameset>
30
31      <noframes>
32         <p>
33            This page uses frames, but your browser does
34               not support them.
35         </p>
36
37         <p>
38            Please, <a href = "nav.html">follow this link
39               to browse our site without frames</a>.
```

Fig. H.10   Framed Web site with a nested frameset. (Part 1 of 2.)

```
40          </p>
41      </noframes>
42
43  </frameset>
44  </html>
```

Fig. H.10 Framed Web site with a nested frameset. (Part 2 of 2.)

Testing and Debugging Tip H.1

When using nested **frameset** *elements, indent every level of* **frame** *tag. This makes the page clearer and easier to debug.*

Look-and-Feel Observation H.4

Nested **frameset***s can help you create visually pleasing, easy-to-navigate Web sites.*

H.11 Summary

HTML tables organize data into rows and columns. All tags and text that apply to a table go inside the **<table>**...**</table>** tags. Tables can be split into distinct horizontal and vertical sections. Put all header information (such as table titles and column headers) inside the **<thead>**...**</thead>** tags. The **tr** (table row) element formats the cells of individual rows. All of the cells in a row belong within the **<tr>**...**</tr>** tags of that row. The smallest area of the table that we are able to format is the data cell. There are two types of data cells: those located in the header (**<th>**...**</th>**) and those located in the table body (**<td>**...**</td>**). Header cells, usually placed in the **<thead>** area, are suitable for titles and column headings. Like **thead**, **tbody** serves formatting and groups information. Most tables use **tbody** to mark up the majority of their content. **td** table data cells are left aligned by default. **th** cells are centered by default. Just as you can use the **thead** and

tbody elements to format groups of rows in a table, you can use the **colgroup** element to group and format columns. The **colgroup** element is used by setting in its opening tag the number of columns it affects and the formatting it imposes on that group of columns. Each **col** element contained inside the **<colgroup>**...**</colgroup>** tags can in turn format a specified number of columns.

HTML provides several mechanisms—including the **form**—to collect information from people viewing your site. Use **method = "post"** in a form that causes changes to server data—for example, when updating a database. The **form** data will be sent to the server as an environment variable, which scripts are able to access. The other possible value, **method = "get"**, should be used when your form does not cause any changes in server-side data—for example, when making a database request. The **form** data from **method = "get"** are appended to the end of the URL. The **action** attribute in the **form** tag is the path to a script that processes the **form** data. The input element is common in forms and always requires the **type** attribute. Two other attributes are **name**, which provides a unique identification for the **input**, and **value**, which indicates the value that the **input** element sends to the server upon submission. The input **type = "text"** inserts a one-line text bar into the form. The value of this **input** element and the information that the server sends to you from the **input** is the text that the user types into the text bar. The **type = "submit" input** element places a button in the form that, when clicked, submits data to the server. The **value** attribute of the **submit** input changes the text displayed on the button. The **type = "reset"** input element places a button on the form that, when clicked, will clear all entries the user has entered into the form. The **textarea** element inserts a box into the form. You specify the size of the box (which is scrollable) inside the opening **<textarea>** tag with the **rows** attribute and the **cols** attribute. Data entered in a **type = "password"** input appear on the screen as asterisks. The password is used to submit sensitive information that the user would not want others to be able to read. It is just the browser that displays asterisks—the real **form** data are still submitted to the server. Every **input** element with **type = "checkbox"** creates a new checkbox in the form. Checkboxes can be used individually or in groups. Each checkbox in a group should have the same **name**. Inserted into forms by means of the **input** attribute **type = "radio"**, radio buttons are different from checkboxes in that only one in the group may be selected at any time. All of the **name** attributes of a group of radio inputs must be the same and all of the **value** attributes different. The **select** element places a selectable list of items inside your form. To add an item to the list, insert an **option** element in the **<select>**...**</select>** area and type what you want the list item to display on the same line. You can change the number of list options visible at one time by including the **size = "***size***"** attribute inside the **<select>** tag. Use this attribute if you prefer an expanded version of the list to the one-line expandable list.

An image map allows you to designate certain sections of the image as hotspots and then use these hotspots as anchors for linking. All elements of an image map are contained inside the **<map>**...**</map>** tags. The required attribute for the **map** element is **name**. A hotspot on the image is designated with the **area** element. Every **<area>** tag has the following attributes: **href** sets the target for the link on that spot, and **shape** and **coords** set the characteristics of the area and **alt** function, just as they do in **<img>** tags. To use an image map with a graphic on your page, you must insert the **usemap = "#***name***"** attribute into the **img** element, where "name" is the value of the **name** attribute in the **map** element.

The main element that interacts with search engines is the **meta** element. **meta** tags contain two attributes that should always be used. The first of these, **name**, is an identification of the type of **meta** tag you are including. The **content** attribute gives the information the search engine will be cataloging. The **content** of a **meta** tag with **name = "keywords"** provides the search engines with a list of words that describe the key aspects of your site. By including **meta** tags and information on their content, you can give precise information about your site to search engines. This will help you draw a more focused audience to your site. The **description** value of the **name** attribute in the **meta** tag should be a three-to-four-line description of your site, written in sentence form. This description is used by the search engine to catalog and display your site. **meta** elements are not visible to users of the site and should be placed inside the header section of your HTML document.

The **frameset** tag informs the browser that the page contains frames. In each **frame** element, the **src** attribute gives the URL of the page that will be displayed in the specified frame. The purpose of a **name** attribute in the **frame** element is to give an identity to that specific frame, which enables hyperlinks in a **frameset** to load their intended **frame**. The **target** attribute in an anchor element is set to the **name** of the **frame** in which the new page should load. Not everyone viewing a page has a browser that can handle frames. You therefore need to include a **noframes** element inside of the **frameset**. You should include regular HTML tags and elements within the **<noframes>...</noframes>** tags. Use this area to direct the user to a nonframed version of the site. By nesting **frameset** elements, you can create more complex layouts.

H.12 Internet and World Wide Web Resources

There are many Web sites that cover the more advanced and difficult features of HTML.

www.geocities.com/SiliconValley/Orchard/5212
Adam's Advanced HTML Page is geared to those seeking to master the more advanced techniques of HTML. The site includes instructions for creating tables, frames and marquees and discusses other advanced topics.

www.w3scripts.com/html
This site, an offshoot of *W3Schools*, is a repository for examples exhibiting all of the features of HTML, from beginner to advanced.

www.blooberry.com/indexdot/html
Index Dot HTML, The Advance HTML Reference... is a site that has a great directory and a tree-based index of all HTML elements, plus more.

www.neiljohan.com/html/advancedhtml.htm
The *Advanced HTML Guide* gives insights into improving your site, using HTML in ways you might not have thought possible.

HTML
Special Characters

The table of Fig. I.1 shows many commonly used HTML special characters—called *character entity references* by the World Wide Web Consortium. For a complete list of character entity references, see the site

www.w3.org/TR/REC-html40/sgml/entities.html

Character	HTML/XHTML encoding	Character	HTML/XHTML encoding
non-breaking space	` `	ê	`&#234;`
§	`&#167;`	ì	`&#236;`
©	`&#169;`	í	`&#237;`
®	`&#174;`	î	`&#238;`
π	`&#188;`	ñ	`&#241;`
∫	`&#189;`	ò	`&#242;`
Ω	`&#190;`	ó	`&#243;`
à	`&#224;`	ô	`&#244;`
á	`&#225;`	õ	`&#245;`
â	`&#226;`	÷	`&#247;`
ã	`&#227;`	ù	`&#249;`
å	`&#229;`	ú	`&#250;`
ç	`&#231;`	û	`&#251;`
è	`&#232;`	•	`&#8226;`
é	`&#233;`	™	`&#8482;`

Fig. I.1   HTML special characters.

J

HTML Colors

Colors may be specified by using a standard name (such as **aqua**) or a hexadecimal RGB value (such as **#00FFFF** for **aqua**). Of the six hexadecimal digits in an RGB value, the first two represent the amount of red in the color, the middle two represent the amount of green in the color, and the last two represent the amount of blue in the color. For example, **black** is the absence of color and is defined by **#000000**, whereas **white** is the maximum amount of red, green and blue and is defined by **#FFFFFF**. Pure **red** is **#FF0000**, pure green (which is called **lime**) is **#00FF00** and pure **blue** is **#0000FF**. Note that **green** is defined as **#008000**. Figure J.1 contains the HTML standard color set. Figure J.2 contains the HTML extended color set.

Color name	Value	Color name	Value
aqua	#00FFFF	navy	#000080
black	#000000	olive	#808000
blue	#0000FF	purple	#800080
fuchsia	#FF00FF	red	#FF0000
gray	#808080	silver	#C0C0C0
green	#008000	teal	#008080
lime	#00FF00	yellow	#FFFF00
maroon	#800000	white	#FFFFFF

Fig. J.1 HTML standard colors and hexadecimal RGB values.

Color name	Value	Color name	Value
aliceblue	#F0F8FF	deeppink	#FF1493
antiquewhite	#FAEBD7	deepskyblue	#00BFFF
aquamarine	#7FFFD4	dimgray	#696969
azure	#F0FFFF	dodgerblue	#1E90FF
beige	#F5F5DC	firebrick	#B22222
bisque	#FFE4C4	floralwhite	#FFFAF0
blanchedalmond	#FFEBCD	forestgreen	#228B22
blueviolet	#8A2BE2	gainsboro	#DCDCDC
brown	#A52A2A	ghostwhite	#F8F8FF
burlywood	#DEB887	gold	#FFD700
cadetblue	#5F9EA0	goldenrod	#DAA520
chartreuse	#7FFF00	greenyellow	#ADFF2F
chocolate	#D2691E	honeydew	#F0FFF0
coral	#FF7F50	hotpink	#FF69B4
cornflowerblue	#6495ED	indianred	#CD5C5C
cornsilk	#FFF8DC	indigo	#4B0082
crimson	#DC1436	ivory	#FFFFF0
cyan	#00FFFF	khaki	#F0E68C
darkblue	#00008B	lavender	#E6E6FA
darkcyan	#008B8B	lavenderblush	#FFF0F5
darkgoldenrod	#B8860B	lawngreen	#7CFC00
darkgray	#A9A9A9	lemonchiffon	#FFFACD
darkgreen	#006400	lightblue	#ADD8E6
darkkhaki	#BDB76B	lightcoral	#F08080
darkmagenta	#8B008B	lightcyan	#E0FFFF
darkolivegreen	#556B2F	lightgoldenrodyellow	#FAFAD2
darkorange	#FF8C00	lightgreen	#90EE90
darkorchid	#9932CC	lightgrey	#D3D3D3
darkred	#8B0000	lightpink	#FFB6C1
darksalmon	#E9967A	lightsalmon	#FFA07A
darkseagreen	#8FBC8F	lightseagreen	#20B2AA
darkslateblue	#483D8B	lightskyblue	#87CEFA
darkslategray	#2F4F4F	lightslategray	#778899
darkturquoise	#00CED1	lightsteelblue	#B0C4DE
darkviolet	#9400D3	lightyellow	#FFFFE0

Fig. J.2   HTML extended colors and hexadecimal RGB values. (Part 1 of 2.)

Color name	Value	Color name	Value
limegreen	#32CD32	mediumblue	#0000CD
mediumpurple	#9370DB	mediumorchid	#BA55D3
mediumseagreen	#3CB371	plum	#DDA0DD
mediumslateblue	#7B68EE	powderblue	#B0E0E6
mediumspringgreen	#00FA9A	rosybrown	#BC8F8F
mediumturquoise	#48D1CC	royalblue	#4169E1
mediumvioletred	#C71585	saddlebrown	#8B4513
midnightblue	#191970	salmon	#FA8072
mintcream	#F5FFFA	sandybrown	#F4A460
mistyrose	#FFE4E1	seagreen	#2E8B57
moccasin	#FFE4B5	seashell	#FFF5EE
navajowhite	#FFDEAD	sienna	#A0522D
oldlace	#FDF5E6	skyblue	#87CEEB
olivedrab	#6B8E23	slateblue	#6A5ACD
orange	#FFA500	slategray	#708090
orangered	#FF4500	snow	#FFFAFA
orchid	#DA70D6	springgreen	#00FF7F
palegoldenrod	#EEE8AA	steelblue	#4682B4
palegreen	#98FB98	tan	#D2B48C
paleturquoise	#AFEEEE	thistle	#D8BFD8
palevioletred	#DB7093	tomato	#FF6347
papayawhip	#FFEFD5	turquoise	#40E0D0
peachpuff	#FFDAB9	violet	#EE82EE
peru	#CD853F	wheat	#F5DEB3
pink	#FFC0CB	whitesmoke	#F5F5F5
mediumaquamarine	#66CDAA	yellowgreen	#9ACD32

Fig. J.2   HTML extended colors and hexadecimal RGB values. (Part 2 of 2.)

Crystal Reports® for Visual Studio .NET

K.1 Introduction

All industries collect and maintain data relevant to their businesses. For example, manufacturing companies maintain information about inventories and production, retail shops record sales, health care organizations maintain patient records and publishers track book sales and inventories. However, just storing data is not enough: Managers must use these data to make informed business decisions. Information must be properly organized, easily accessible and shared among various individuals, departments and affiliates. This facilitates data analysis that can reveal business-critical information, such as sales trends or potential inventory shortages. To make this possible, developers have used reporting software—a key tool enabling the presentation of stored data sources.

Crystal Reports® was first released in 1992 as a Windows-based report writer, and Microsoft adopted Crystal Reports as the standard for Visual Basic in 1993.[1] Visual Studio .NET now integrates a special edition of Crystal Reports, further tying Crystal Reports to all .NET programming languages, including C#, and to Windows and Web development. This appendix presents the resources that *Crystal Decisions*, the company that produces Crystal Reports, offers on its Web site, and overviews Crystal Report's unique functionality and features in Visual Studio .NET.

K.2 Crystal Reports Web Site Resources

Crystal Decisions offers resources to developers working in Visual Studio .NET at their Web site, **www.crystaldecisions.com/net**. The site updates the changes in Visual Studio .NET versions in English, Simplified Chinese, Traditional Chinese, French, German, Italian, Japanese, Korean and Spanish. Crystal Decisions also provides technical support for Crystal Reports C# developers via e-mail or phone. The site offers walk-

---

1. "Company History," **<www.crystaldecisions.com/about/ourcompany/history.asp>**.

throughs, an online newsletter, a multimedia product demo, discussion groups, a developer's zone and an overview of Crystal Reports in Visual Studio .NET.

K.3 Crystal Reports and Visual Studio .NET

Developers working in Visual Studio .NET's integrated development environment (IDE) can create and integrate reports in their applications using Crystal Reports software. The Visual Studio .NET edition Crystal Reports provides powerful capabilities to developers. Features of Crystal Reports for Visual Studio .NET include an API (application programming interface) that allows developers to control how reports are cached on servers—setting timeouts, restrictions, etc. Developers can create reports in multiple languages, because Crystal Reports now fully supports Unicode data types. The reports that are created can be viewed in many file formats. A user can convert a report to Microsoft Word, Adobe's Portable Document Format (PDF), HyperText Markup Language (HTML) and others so that report information can be distributed easily and used in a wide variety of documentation. Figure K.1 displays a sample Crystal Report exported to a PDF document. Any Crystal Report created in Visual Studio .NET can become an embedded resource for use in Windows and Web applications and Web services. This section overviews the initial stages of creating reports as well as some more advanced capabilities.

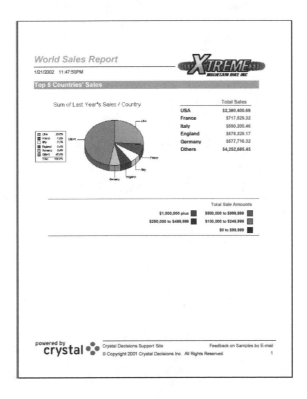

Fig. K.1   Crystal Report sample in PDF form. (Courtesy Crystal Decisions - **www.crystaldecisions.com**.)

To aid Visual Studio .NET developers design reports, Crystal Reports provides a *Report Expert*. Experts are similar to "templates" and "wizards"—they guide users through the creation of a variety of reports while handling the details of how the report is created, so the user need not be concerned with them. The available Experts create several types of reports, including standard, form-letter, form, cross-tab, subreport, mail label and drill-down reports (Fig. K.2). Figure K.3 illustrates the **Standard Report Expert** interface.

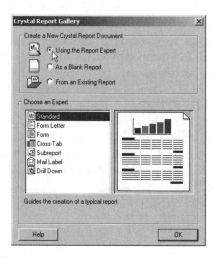

Fig. K.2   Report expert choices. (Courtesy Crystal Decisions - **www.crystaldecisions.com**.)

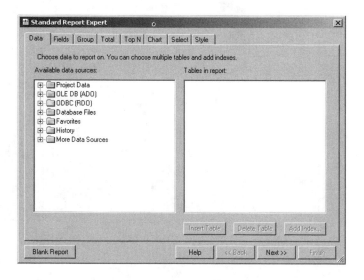

Fig. K.3   Expert formatting menu choices. (Courtesy Crystal Decisions - **www.crystaldecisions.com**.)

Crystal Reports for Visual Studio .NET is comprised of several components. Once a report is set up, either manually or by using an Expert, developers use the Crystal Reports Designer in Visual Studio .NET to modify, add and format objects and fields, as well as to format the report layout and manipulate the report design (Fig. K.4). The Designer then generates RPT files (**.rpt** is the file extension for a Crystal Report). These RPT files are processed by the Crystal Reports engine, which delivers the report output to one of two Crystal Report viewers—a Windows Forms viewer control or a Web Forms viewer control, depending on the type of application the developer specifies. The viewers then present the formatted information to the user.

Walkthroughs illustrating the new functionality are available on the Crystal Decisions Web site at **www.crystaldecisions.com/netzone**. The walkthroughs include integrating and viewing Web reports through Windows applications, creating interactive reports in Web applications, exposing Crystal Reports through Web services and reporting from ActiveX Data Objects (ADO) .NET data.[2] (For a detailed discussion of ADO .NET and other database tools, see Chapter 16, Database, SQL and ADO .NET.) This section overviews the functionality of some of the Web applications and Web services walkthroughs.

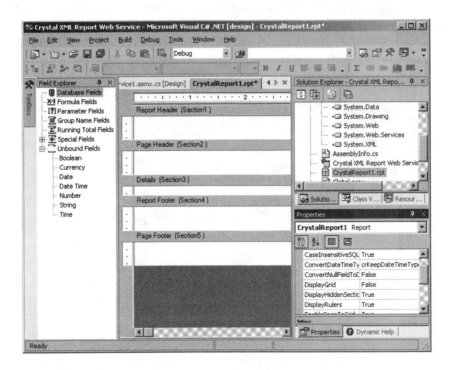

Fig. K.4   Crystal Reports designer interface. (Courtesy Crystal Decisions - **www.crystaldecisions.com**.)

2. The walkthroughs on the Crystal Decisions Web site were tested using C# in Visual Studio .NET, but a developer should be able to use the walkthroughs with any language supported by Visual Studio .NET.

K.3.1 Crystal Reports in Web Applications

Using Crystal Reports for Visual Studio .NET, a developer can integrate highly interactive Crystal Reports into a Web page. ASP .NET technology integrated into Visual Studio .NET enables interactivity by producing cross-platform, dynamic Web applications. We discuss these technologies in detail in Chapter 17, ASP .NET, Web Forms and Web Controls.

Web Forms consist of HTML files with embedded Web Controls and code-behind files that contain programming logic. Crystal Reports provides a Web Forms Report Viewer, which is a Web Form that hosts the report. When a client accesses such a Web Form, the event handler can update and format information in the report and send the report to the user.[3]

A walkthrough on the Crystal Decision's Web site instructs a programmer how to enable Web page interactivity and how to use ASP .NET and its controls. In the walkthrough, the user accesses information about countries by first entering a country name in the text box. When the user submits the information, the country name is passed to the Web forms viewer control and the report is updated—the Web forms page updates the report in HTML and sends it to the client browser.

K.3.2 Crystal Reports and Web Services

Any Crystal Report created in C# can be published as an "XML Report Web Service" using Crystal Reports for Visual Studio (Fig. K.5). A Web service provides methods that are accessible over the Internet to any application, independent of programming language or platform.

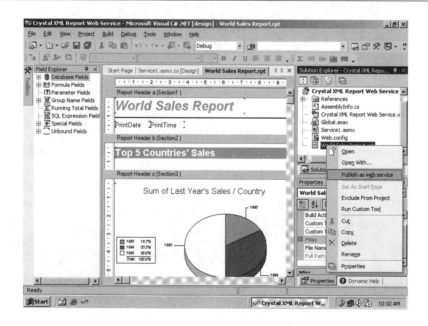

Fig. K.5   Crystal Report being published as Web service. (Courtesy Crystal Decisions - **www.crystaldecisions.com**.)

3. "Interactivity and Reports in Web Applications," *Crystal Reports for Visual Studio .NET.* **<www.crystaldecisions.com/netzone>**.

An XML Report Web service would be an excellent vehicle with which business partners could access specific report information. Crystal Decisions provides a walkthrough to overview the steps to familiarize the user with implementing a report as a Web service. (We discuss Web services in detail in Chapter 19, ASP .NET and Web Services.)

When a Crystal report is published as an XML Report Web service, Visual Studio .NET generates a DLL file that contains the report, and an XML file. Both files are published to a Web server so that a client can access the report. The XML-based Simple Object Access Protocol (SOAP) message passes the data to and from the Web service.

When a developer uses Visual Studio .NET to create and publish the Web service, the developer can bind the service either to a Windows or to a Web application to display the data returned from the Web service. The walkthrough details how to create and generate the Web service, bind the service to either a Windows or Web viewer and how to build the client application that will view the service.[4]

---

4. "Exposing Reports as Web Services," *Crystal Reports for Visual Studio .NET.* **<www.crystal-decidecisions.com/netzone>**.

Index

Symbols

! (logical NOT) 133, 135
!= is not equal to 65, 133
" (double quotation) 48, 51
"" 562
% (modulus operator) 60, 61, 62
%= (modulus assignment operator) 98
& (boolean logical AND) 133, 139
&& (logical AND) 133, 134
& 784
© 784
* SQL wildcard character 518
*/ end a multiline comment 45
*= (multiplication assignment operator) 98
+ operator 62, 432
++, preincrement/postincrement 98
+= (addition assignment operator) 97
--, predecrement/postdecrement 98, 99
. (dot operator) 54, 149, 246, 268
// single-line comment 45
/= (division assignment operator) 98
; (empty statement) 54, 81
; (statement terminator) 48
< is-less-than operator 65
<%@Page…%> directive 544
<= less than or equal 65, 133
<> angle brackets 559
= (assignment operator) 58, 97
-= (subtraction assignment operator) 98
== comparison operator 65, 423
> is-greater-than operator 65
>= is-greater-than-or-equal-to operator 65
? SQL wildcard character 519
?: (ternary conditional operator) 78, 100
[] (brackets) 198, 199, 209
\ ' escape sequence 52
**\ ** escape sequence 52
\n escape sequence 51, 52
\r escape sequence 52
\t escape sequence 52
\u$yyyy$ unicode format 767
^ (boolean logical exclusive OR) 133
_ (underscore) 46
{ (left brace) 47, 81
| (boolean logical inclusive OR) 133
|| (logical OR) 133, 134
} (right brace) 47, 81
, (comma) 121

A

A 12-element array 198
a element 778, 782
A portion of a **Shape** class hierarchy 297
A property of structure **Color** 460
abbreviating an assignment expression 97
Abort method of class **Thread** 410
AbortRetryIgnore member of **MessageBoxButtons** enumeration 120
Abs method of class **Math** 150
absolute positioning 553
absolute value 150
abstract data type (ADT) 12, 238
abstraction 293
AcceptButton property 365
AcceptSocket method of class **TcpListener** 597
AcceptsReturn property 376
access method 241
accessibility 638, 670, 672, 679, 683, 684, 686
accessibility aids in Visual Studio .NET 638, 639
Accessibility Wizard 672, 675, 679
Accessibility Wizard initialization option 673
Accessibility Wizard mouse cursor adjustment tool 675
AccessibilityDescription property of class **Control** 651
AccessibilityName property of class **Control** 651

The DEITEL™
Suite of Products...

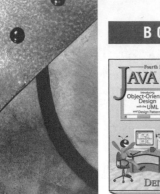

Java™ How to Program Fourth Edition

BOOK / CD-ROM

©2002, 1546 pp., paper
(0-13-034151-7)

The world's best-selling Java text is now even better! The Fourth Edition of *Java How to Program* includes a new focus on object-oriented design with the UML, design patterns, full-color program listings and figures and the most up-to-date Java coverage available.

Readers will discover key topics in Java programming, such as graphical user interface components, exception handling, multithreading, multimedia, files and streams, networking, data structures and more. In addition, a new chapter on design patterns explains frequently recurring architectural patterns—information that can help save designers considerable time when building large systems.

The highly detailed optional case study focuses on object-oriented design with the UML and presents fully implemented working Java code.

Updated throughout, the text includes new and revised discussions on topics such as Swing, graphics and socket- and packet-based networking. Three introductory chapters heavily emphasize problem solving and programming skills. The chapters on RMI, JDBC™, servlets and JavaBeans have been moved to *Advanced Java 2 Platform How to Program*, where they are now covered in much greater depth. (See *Advanced Java 2 Platform How to Program* below.)

Advanced Java™ 2 Platform How to Program

BOOK / CD-ROM

©2002, 1811 pp., paper
(0-13-089560-1)

Expanding on the world's best-selling Java textbook— *Java How to Program*— *Advanced Java 2 Platform How To Program* presents advanced Java topics for developing sophisticated, user-friendly GUIs; significant, scalable enterprise applications; wireless applications and distributed systems. Primarily based on Java 2 Enterprise Edition (J2EE), this textbook integrates technologies such as XML, JavaBeans, security, Java Database Connectivity (JDBC), JavaServer Pages (JSP), servlets, Remote Method Invocation (RMI), Enterprise JavaBeans™ (EJB) and design patterns into a production-quality system that allows developers to benefit from the leverage and platform independence Java 2 Enterprise Edition provides. The book also features the development of a complete, end-to-end e-business solution using advanced Java technologies. Additional topics include Swing, Java 2D and 3D, XML, design patterns, CORBA, Jini™, JavaSpaces™, Jiro™, Java Management Extensions (JMX) and Peer-to-Peer networking with an introduction to JXTA. This textbook also introduces the Java 2 Micro Edition (J2ME™) for building applications for handheld and wireless devices using MIDP and MIDlets. Wireless technologies covered include WAP, WML and i-mode.

C# How to Program

BOOK / CD-ROM

©2002, 1568 pp., paper
(0-13-062221-4)

An exciting new addition to the How to Program series, *C# How to Program* provides a comprehensive introduction to Microsoft's new object-oriented language. C# builds on the skills already mastered by countless C++ and Java programmers, enabling them to create powerful Web applications and components—ranging from XML-based Web services on Microsoft's .NET platform to middle-tier business objects and system-level applications. *C# How to Program* begins with a strong foundation in the introductory and intermediate programming principles students will need in industry. It then explores such essential topics as object-oriented programming and exception handling. Graphical user interfaces are extensively covered, giving readers the tools to build compelling and fully interactive programs. Internet technologies such as XML, ADO .NET and Web services are also covered as well as topics including regular expressions, multithreading, networking, databases, files and data structures.

Also coming soon in the Deitels' .NET Series:

- *Visual C++ .NET How to Program*

Visual Basic .NET How to Program
Second Edition

BOOK / CD-ROM

*©2002, 1400 pp., paper
(0-13-029363-6)*

Teach Visual Basic .NET
programming from the ground
up! This introduction of
Microsoft's .NET Framework marks the beginning
of major revisions to all of Microsoft's programming
languages. This book provides a comprehensive
introduction to the next version of Visual Basic—
Visual Basic .NET—featuring extensive updates
and increased functionality. *Visual Basic .NET How
to Program, Second Edition* covers introductory
programming techniques as well as more advanced
topics, featuring enhanced treatment of developing
Web-based applications. Other topics discussed
include an extensive treatment of XML and wireless
applications, databases, SQL and ADO .NET, Web
forms, Web services and ASP .NET.

Also coming soon in the Deitels' .NET Series:

• *Visual C++ .NET How to Program*

C How to Program
Third Edition

BOOK / CD-ROM

*©2001, 1253 pp., paper
(0-13-089572-5)*

Highly practical in approach,
the Third Edition of the
world's best-selling C text
introduces the fundamentals
of structured programming and software engineering
and gets up to speed quickly. This comprehensive
book not only covers the full C language, but also
reviews library functions and introduces object-based
and object-oriented programming in C++ and Java.
The Third Edition includes a new 346-page introduction
to Java 2 and the basics of GUIs, and the 298-page
introduction to C++ has been updated to be consistent
with the most current ANSI/ISO C++ standards. Plus,
icons throughout the book point out valuable programming
tips such as Common Programming Errors, Portability
Tips and Testing and Debugging Tips.

C++
How to Program
Fourth Edition

BOOK / CD-ROM

*©2003, 1400 pp., paper
(0-13-038474-7)*

The world's best selling C++
book is now even better!
Designed for beginning through
intermediate courses, this comprehensive, practical
introduction to C++ includes hundreds of hands-on exercises, plus roughly 250 complete programs written and
documented for easy learning. It also features exceptional
insight into good programming practices, maximizing
performance, avoiding errors, debugging and testing.
The Fourth Edition features a new code-highlighting
style that uses an alternate background color to focus
the reader on new code elements in a program. The
OOD/UML case study is upgraded to the latest UML
standard, and includes significant improvements to the
exception handling and operator overloading chapters.
It features enhanced treatment of strings and arrays as
objects using standard C++ classes, string and vector. It
also retains every key concept and technique ANSI C++
developers need to master, including control structures,
functions, arrays, pointers and strings, classes and data
abstraction, operator overloading, inheritance, virtual
functions, polymorphism, I/O, templates, exception
handling, file processing, data structures and more.
C++ How to Program Fourth Edition includes a detailed
introduction to Standard Template Library (STL) containers,
container adapters, algorithms and iterators.

Getting Started with Microsoft® Visual C++™ 6 with an Introduction to MFC

BOOK / CD-ROM

©2000, 163 pp., paper (0-13-016147-0)

Internet & World Wide Web How to Program, Second Edition

BOOK / CD-ROM

*©2002, 1428 pp., paper
(0-13-030897-8)*

The revision of this ground-
breaking book in the Deitels'
How to Program Series offers a thorough treatment of

programming concepts that yield visible or audible results in Web pages and Web-based applications. This book discusses effective Web-based design, server- and client-side scripting, multitier Web-based applications development, ActiveX® controls and electronic commerce essentials. This book offers an alternative to traditional programming courses using markup languages (such as XHTML, Dynamic HTML and XML) and scripting languages (such as JavaScript, VBScript, Perl/CGI, Python and PHP) to teach the fundamentals of programming "wrapped in the metaphor of the Web."

Updated material on **www.deitel.com** and **www.prenhall.com/deitel** provides additional resources for instructors who want to cover Microsoft® or non-Microsoft technologies. The Web site includes an extensive treatment of Netscape® 6 and alternate versions of the code from the Dynamic HTML chapters that will work with non-Microsoft environments as well.

Wireless Internet & Mobile Business How to Program

©2002, 1292 pp., paper
(0-13-062226-5)

While the rapid expansion of wireless technologies, such as cell phones, pagers and personal digital assistants (PDAs), offers many new opportunities for businesses and programmers, it also presents numerous challenges related to issues such as security and standardization. This book offers a thorough treatment of both the management and technical aspects of this growing area, including coverage of current practices and future trends. The first half explores the business issues surrounding wireless technology and mobile business, including an overview of existing and developing communication technologies and the application of business principles to wireless devices. It also discusses location-based services and location-identifying technologies, a topic that is revisited throughout the book. Wireless payment, security, legal and social issues, international communications and more are also discussed. The book then turns to programming for the wireless Internet, exploring topics such as WAP (including 2.0), WML, WMLScript, XML, XHTML™, wireless Java programming (J2ME)™, Web Clipping and more. Other topics covered include career resources, wireless marketing, accessibility, Palm™, PocketPC, Windows CE,

i-mode, Bluetooth, MIDP, MIDlets, ASP, Microsoft .NET Mobile Framework, BREW™, multimedia, Flash™ and VBScript.

Python How to Program

BOOK / CD-ROM

©2002, 1376 pp., paper
(0-13-092361-3)

This exciting new book provides a comprehensive introduction to Python— a powerful object-oriented programming language with clear syntax and the ability to bring together various technologies quickly and easily. This book covers introductory-programming techniques and more advanced topics such as graphical user interfaces, databases, wireless Internet programming, networking, security, process management, multithreading, XHTML, CSS, PSP and multimedia. Readers will learn principles that are applicable to both systems development and Web programming. The book features the consistent and applied pedagogy that the *How to Program Series* is known for, including the Deitels' signature LIVE-CODE™ Approach, with thousands of lines of code in hundreds of working programs; hundreds of valuable programming tips identified with icons throughout the text; an extensive set of exercises, projects and case studies; two-color four-way syntax coloring and much more.

e-Business & e-Commerce for Managers

©2001, 794 pp., cloth
(0-13-032364-0)

This comprehensive overview of building and managing e-businesses explores topics such as the decision to bring a business online, choosing a business model, accepting payments, marketing strategies and security, as well as many other important issues (such as career resources). The book features Web resources and online demonstrations that supplement the text and direct readers to additional materials. The book also includes an appendix that develops a complete Web-based shopping-cart application using HTML, JavaScript, VBScript, Active Server Pages, ADO, SQL, HTTP, XML and XSL. Plus, company-specific sections provide "real-world" examples of the concepts presented in the book.

XML How to Program

BOOK / CD-ROM

©2001, 934 pp., paper (0-13-028417-3)

This book is a comprehensive guide to programming in XML. It teaches how to use XML to create customized tags and includes chapters that address standard custom-markup languages for science and technology, multimedia, commerce and many other fields. Concise introductions to Java, JavaServer Pages, VBScript, Active Server Pages and Perl/CGI provide readers with the essentials of these programming languages and server-side development technologies to enable them to work effectively with XML. The book also covers cutting-edge topics such as XSL, DOM™ and SAX, plus a real-world e-commerce case study and a complete chapter on Web accessibility that addresses Voice XML. It includes tips such as Common Programming Errors, Software Engineering Observations, Portability Tips and Debugging Hints. Other topics covered include XHTML, CSS, DTD, schema, parsers, XPath, XLink, namespaces, XBase, XInclude, XPointer, XSLT, XSL Formatting Objects, JavaServer Pages, XForms, topic maps, X3D, MathML, OpenMath, CML, BML, CDF, RDF, SVG, Cocoon, WML, XBRL and BizTalk™ and SOAP™ Web resources.

Perl How to Program

BOOK / CD-ROM

©2001, 1057 pp., paper (0-13-028418-1)

This comprehensive guide to Perl programming emphasizes the use of the Common Gateway Interface (CGI) with Perl to create powerful, dynamic multi-tier Web-based client/server applications. The book begins with a clear and careful introduction to programming concepts at a level suitable for beginners, and proceeds through advanced topics such as references and complex data structures. Key Perl topics such as regular expressions and string manipulation are covered in detail. The authors address important and topical issues such as object-oriented programming, the Perl database interface (DBI), graphics and security. Also included is a treatment of XML, a bonus chapter introducing the Python programming language, supplemental material on career resources and a complete chapter on Web accessibility. The text includes tips such as Common Programming Errors, Software Engineering Observations, Portability Tips and Debugging Hints.

e-Business & e-Commerce How to Program

BOOK / CD-ROM

©2001, 1254 pp., paper (0-13-028419-X)

This innovative book explores programming technologies for developing Web-based e-business and e-commerce solutions, and covers e-business and e-commerce models and business issues. Readers learn a full range of options, from "build-your-own" to turnkey solutions. The book examines scores of the top e-businesses (examples include Amazon, eBay, Priceline, Travelocity, etc.), explaining the technical details of building successful e-business and e-commerce sites and their underlying business premises. Learn how to implement the dominant e-commerce models—shopping carts, auctions, name-your-own-price, comparison shopping and bots/ intelligent agents—by using markup languages (HTML, Dynamic HTML and XML), scripting languages (JavaScript, VBScript and Perl), server-side technologies (Active Server Pages and Perl/CGI) and database (SQL and ADO), security and online payment technologies. Updates are regularly posted to www.deitel.com and the book includes a CD-ROM with software tools, source code and live links.

Complete Training Courses

Each complete package includes the corresponding *How to Program Series* book and interactive multimedia CD-ROM Cyber Classroom. *Complete Training Courses* are perfect for anyone interested Web and e-commerce programming. They are affordable resources for college students and professionals learning programming for the first time or reinforcing their knowledge.

Each *Complete Training Course* is compatible with Windows 95, Windows 98, Windows NT and Windows 2000 and includes the following features:

Intuitive Browser-Based Interface

You'll love the *Complete Training Courses'* new browser-based interface, designed to be easy and accessible to anyone who's ever used a Web browser. Every *Complete Training Course* features the full text, illustrations and program listings of its corresponding *How to Program* book—all in full color—with full-text searching and hyperlinking.

Further Enhancements to the Deitels' Signature LIVE-CODE™ Approach

Every code sample from the main text can be found in the interactive, multimedia, CD-ROM-based *Cyber Classrooms* included in the *Complete Training Courses*. Syntax coloring of code is included for the *How to Program* books that are published in full color. Even the recent two-color and one-color books use effective multi-way syntax shading. The *Cyber Classroom* products always are in full color.

Audio Annotations

Hours of detailed, expert audio descriptions of thousands of lines of code help reinforce concepts.

Easily Executable Code

With one click of the mouse, you can execute the code or save it to your hard drive to manipulate using the programming environment of your choice. With selected *Complete Training Courses*, you can also load all of the code into a development environment such as Microsoft® Visual C++™, enabling you to modify and execute the programs with ease.

Abundant Self-Assessment Material

Practice exams test your understanding with hundreds of test questions and answers in addition to those found in the main text. Hundreds of self-review questions, all with answers, are drawn from the text; as are hundreds of programming exercises, half with answers.

www·phptr·com/phptrinteractive

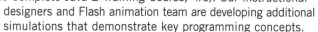

Future Publications

Here are some new titles we are considering for 2002/2003 release:

Computer Science Series: *Operating Systems 3/e, Data Structures in C++, Data Structures in Java, Theory and Principles of Database Systems.*

Database Series: *Oracle, SQL Server, MySQL.*

Internet and Web Programming Series: *Open Source Software Development: Apache, Linux, MySQL and PHP.*

Programming Series: *Flash™.*

.NET Programming Series: *ADO .NET with Visual Basic .NET, ASP .NET with Visual Basic .NET, ADO .NET with C#, ASP .NET with C#.*

Object Technology Series: *OOAD with the UML, Design Patterns, Java™ and XML.*

Advanced Java™ Series: *JDBC, Java 2 Enterprise Edition, Java Media Framework (JMF), Java Security and Java Cryptography (JCE), Java Servlets, Java2D and Java3D, JavaServer Pages™ (JSP), JINI and Java 2 Micro Edition™ (J2ME).*

DEITEL™ BUZZ ONLINE Newsletter

The Deitel and Associates, Inc. free opt-in newsletter includes:

- Updates and commentary on industry trends and developments
- Resources and links to articles from our published books and upcoming publications.
- Information on the Deitel publishing plans, including future publications and product-release schedules
- Support for instructors
- Resources for students
- Information on Deitel Corporate Training

To sign up for the Deitel™ Buzz Online newsletter, visit `www.deitel.com/newsletter/subscribe.html`.

E-Books

We are committed to providing our content in traditional print formats and in emerging electronic formats, such as e-books, to fulfill our customers' needs. Our R&D teams are currently exploring many leading-edge solutions.

Visit `www.deitel.com` and read the DEITEL™ BUZZ ONLINE for periodic updates.

Turn the page to find out more about Deitel & Associates!